# The Lives Of The Twelve Caesars

*by*

C. Suetonius Tranquillus

# The Lives Of The Twelve Caesars
## by C. Suetonius Tranquillus

Copyright © 2022

All Rights reserved.
No part of this publication may be reproduced, stored in a retrieval system, or transmitted in any form or by any means, electronic, mechanical, photocopying or Otherwise, without the written permission of the publisher.

The author/editor asserts the moral right to be identified as the author/editor of this work.

ISBN: 978-93-57271-09-7

Published by
## DOUBLE 9 BOOKS
2/13-B, Ansari Road
Daryaganj, New Delhi – 110002
info@double9books.com
www.double9books.com
Tel. 011-40042856

This book is under public domain

Printed in India.

# ABOUT THE AUTHOR

Gaius Suetonius Tranquillus, also known as Suetonius, was a Roman author who is best known for his biographies of the first 12 Caesars. Although being a biographer of others, Suetonius gives his readers relatively little information about his own life. Suetonius' actual birthdate is unknown, it is generally accepted that he was born between 69 and 75 CE. His birthplace (perhaps either Umbria or Hippo Regius in Numidia) and the year of his passing are also unknown. Since he was closely connected with the imperial court, he had access to otherwise private details, and he did not hold back when it came to disclosing some of Rome's most scandalous events. The writer's father, Suetonius Laetus, was a knight-a member of the equestrian class-and served as tribune of the 13th legion during the 69 CE civil war. He also commanded that unit at the Battle of Bedriacum in northern Italy. Suetonius' grandfather may have been a member of Caligula's court. In his later years, Suetonius served as the director of the imperial libraries and subsequently as Hadrian's private secretary. However, he was fired from this position, again for unclear reasons.

# CONTENTS

PREFACE ..................................................................................7
CAIUS JULIUS CASAR. ..........................................................10
D. OCTAVIUS CAESAR AUGUSTUS.......................................70
TIBERIUS NERO CAESAR.....................................................177
CAIUS CAESAR CALIGULA. .................................................229
TIBERIUS CLAUDIUS DRUSUS CAESAR. 465 ....................265
NERO CLAUDIUS CAESAR. ..................................................299
SERGIUS SULPICIUS GALBA. ...............................................354
A. SALVIUS OTHO.................................................................368
AULUS VITELLIUS. ...............................................................376
T. FLAVIUS VESPASIANUS AUGUSTUS. ............................388
TITUS FLAVIUS VESPASIANUS AUGUSTUS. .....................406
TITUS FLAVIUS DOMITIANUS. ...........................................417
LIVES OF EMINENT GRAMMARIANS.................................441
LIVES OF EMINENT RHETORICIANS. ................................455
LIVES OF THE POETS. ..........................................................461
THE LIFE OF TERENCE.........................................................461
THE LIFE OF JUVENAL. ........................................................466
THE LIFE OF PERSIUS. .........................................................468
THE LIFE OF HORACE. .........................................................471
THE LIFE OF PLINY. .............................................................475
FOOTNOTES ..........................................................................476
INDEX. ...................................................................................607

# PREFACE

C. Suetonius Tranquillus was the son of a Roman knight who commanded a legion, on the side of Otho, at the battle which decided the fate of the empire in favour of Vitellius. From incidental notices in the following History, we learn that he was born towards the close of the reign of Vespasian, who died in the year 79 of the Christian era. He lived till the time of Hadrian, under whose administration he filled the office of secretary; until, with several others, he was dismissed for presuming on familiarities with the empress Sabina, of which we have no further account than that they were unbecoming his position in the imperial court. How long he survived this disgrace, which appears to have befallen him in the year 121, we are not informed; but we find that the leisure afforded him by his retirement, was employed in the composition of numerous works, of which the only portions now extant are collected in the present volume.

Several of the younger Pliny's letters are addressed to Suetonius, with whom he lived in the closest friendship. They afford some brief, but generally pleasant, glimpses of his habits and career; and in a letter, in which Pliny makes application on behalf of his friend to the emperor Trajan, for a mark of favour, he speaks of him as "a most excellent, honourable, and learned man, whom he had the pleasure of entertaining under his own roof, and with whom the nearer he was brought into communion, the more he loved him." 1

The plan adopted by Suetonius in his Lives of the Twelve Caesars, led him to be more diffuse on their personal conduct and habits than on public events. He writes Memoirs rather than History. He neither dwells on the civil wars which sealed the fall of the Republic, nor on the military expeditions which extended the frontiers of the empire; nor does he attempt to develop the causes of the great political changes which marked the period of which he treats.

When we stop to gaze in a museum or gallery on the antique busts of the Caesars, we perhaps endeavour to trace in their sculptured physiognomy the characteristics of those princes, who, for good or evil, were in their times masters of the destinies of a large portion of the human race. The pages of Suetonius will amply gratify this natural curiosity. In them we find a series of individual portraits sketched to the life, with perfect truth and rigorous impartiality. La Harpe remarks of Suetonius, "He is scrupulously exact, and strictly methodical. He omits nothing which concerns the person whose life he is writing; he relates everything, but paints nothing. His work is, in some sense, a collection of anecdotes, but it is very curious to read and consult." 2

Combining as it does amusement and information, Suetonius's "Lives of the Caesars" was held in such estimation, that, so soon after the invention of printing as the year 1500, no fewer than eighteen editions had been published, and nearly one hundred have since been added to the number. Critics of the highest rank have devoted themselves to the task of correcting and commenting on the text, and the work has been translated into most European languages. Of the English translations, that of Dr. Alexander Thomson, published in 1796, has been made the basis of the present. He informs us in his Preface, that a version of Suetonius was with him only a secondary object, his principal design being to form a just estimate of Roman literature, and to elucidate the state of government, and the manners of the times; for which the work of Suetonius seemed a fitting vehicle. Dr. Thomson's remarks appended to each successive reign, are reprinted nearly verbatim in the present edition. His translation, however, was very diffuse, and retained most of the inaccuracies of that of Clarke, on which it was founded; considerable care therefore has been bestowed in correcting it, with the view of producing, as far as possible, a literal and faithful version.

To render the works of Suetonius, as far as they are extant, complete, his Lives of eminent Grammarians, Rhetoricians, and Poets, of which a translation has not before appeared in English, are added. These Lives abound with anecdote and curious information connected with learning and literary men during the period of which the author treats.

T. F.

# CAIUS JULIUS CASAR.

I. Julius Caesar, the Divine 3, lost his father 4 when he was in the sixteenth year of his age 5; and the year following, being nominated to the office of high-priest of Jupiter 6, he repudiated Cossutia, who was very wealthy, although her family belonged only to the equestrian order, and to whom he had been contracted when he was a mere boy. He then married (2) Cornelia, the daughter of Cinna, who was four times consul; and had by her, shortly afterwards, a daughter named Julia. Resisting all the efforts of the dictator Sylla to induce him to divorce Cornelia, he suffered the penalty of being stripped of his sacerdotal office, his wife's dowry, and his own patrimonial estates; and, being identified with the adverse faction 7, was compelled to withdraw from Rome. After changing his place of concealment nearly every night 8, although he was suffering from a quartan ague, and having effected his release by bribing the officers who had tracked his footsteps, he at length obtained a pardon through the intercession of the vestal virgins, and of Mamercus Aemilius and Aurelius Cotta, his near relatives. We are assured that when Sylla, having withstood for a while the entreaties of his own best friends, persons of distinguished rank, at last yielded to their importunity, he exclaimed—either by a divine impulse, or from a shrewd conjecture: "Your suit is granted, and you may take him among you; but know," he added, "that this man, for whose safety you are so extremely anxious, will, some day or other, be the ruin of the party of the nobles, in defence of which you are leagued with me; for in this one Caesar, you will find many a Marius."

II. His first campaign was served in Asia, on the staff of the praetor, M. Thermus; and being dispatched into Bithynia 9, to bring thence a fleet, he loitered so long at the court of Nicomedes, as to give occasion to reports of a criminal intercourse between him and that prince; which received additional credit from his hasty return to Bithynia, under the pretext of recovering a debt due to a freed-man, his client. The rest of his service was more favourable to his reputation; and (3) when Mitylene 10 was taken by storm, he was presented by Thermus with the civic crown. 11

III. He served also in Cilicia 12 , under Servilius Isauricus, but only for a short time; as upon receiving intelligence of Sylla's death, he returned with all speed to Rome, in expectation of what might follow from a fresh agitation set on foot by Marcus Lepidus. Distrusting, however, the abilities of this leader, and finding the times less favourable for the execution of this project than he had at first imagined, he abandoned all thoughts of joining Lepidus, although he received the most tempting offers.

IV. Soon after this civil discord was composed, he preferred a charge of extortion against Cornelius Dolabella, a man of consular dignity, who had obtained the honour of a triumph. On the acquittal of the accused, he resolved to retire to Rhodes 13 , with the view not only of avoiding the public odium (4) which he had incurred, but of prosecuting his studies with leisure and tranquillity, under Apollonius, the son of Molon, at that time the most celebrated master of rhetoric. While on his voyage thither, in the winter season, he was taken by pirates near the island of Pharmacusa 14 , and detained by them, burning with indignation, for nearly forty days; his only attendants being a physician and two chamberlains. For he had instantly dispatched his other servants and the friends who accompanied him, to raise money for his ransom 15 . Fifty talents having been paid down, he was landed on the coast, when, having collected some ships 16 , he lost no time in putting to sea in pursuit of the pirates, and having captured them, inflicted upon them the punishment with which he had often threatened them in jest. At that time Mithridates was ravaging the neighbouring districts, and on Caesar's arrival at Rhodes, that he might not appear to lie idle while danger threatened the allies of Rome, he passed over into Asia, and having collected some auxiliary forces, and driven the king's governor out of the province, retained in their allegiance the cities which were wavering, and ready to revolt.

V. Having been elected military tribune, the first honour he received from the suffrages of the people after his return to Rome, he zealously assisted those who took measures for restoring the tribunitian authority, which had been greatly diminished during the usurpation of Sylla. He likewise, by an act, which Plotius at his suggestion propounded to the people, obtained the recall of Lucius Cinna, his wife's brother, and others with him, who having been the adherents of Lepidus in the civil disturbances, had after that consul's death fled to Sertorius 17 ; which law he supported by a speech.

VI. During his quaestorship he pronounced funeral orations from the rostra, according to custom, in praise of his aunt (5) Julia, and his wife Cornelia. In the panegyric on his aunt, he gives the following account of her own and his father's genealogy, on both sides: "My aunt Julia derived her descent, by the mother, from a race of kings, and by her father, from the Immortal Gods. For the Marcii Reges 18 , her mother's family, deduce their pedigree from Ancus Marcius, and the Julii, her father's, from Venus; of which stock we are a branch. We therefore unite in our descent the sacred majesty of kings, the chiefest among men, and the divine majesty of Gods, to whom kings themselves are subject." To supply the place of Cornelia, he married Pompeia, the daughter of Quintus Pompeius, and grand-daughter of Lucius Sylla; but he afterwards divorced her, upon suspicion of her having been debauched by Publius Clodius. For so current was the report, that Clodius had found access to her disguised as a woman, during the celebration of a religious solemnity 19 , that the senate instituted an enquiry respecting the profanation of the sacred rites.

VII. Farther-Spain 20 fell to his lot as quaestor; when there, as he was going the circuit of the province, by commission from the praetor, for the administration of justice, and had reached Gades, seeing a statue of Alexander the Great in the temple of Hercules, he sighed deeply, as if weary of his sluggish life, for having performed no memorable actions at an age 21 at which Alexander had already conquered the world. He, therefore, immediately sued for his discharge, with the view of embracing the first opportunity, which might present itself in The City, of entering upon a more exalted career. In the stillness of the night following, he dreamt that he lay with his own mother; but his confusion was relieved, and his hopes were raised to the highest pitch, by the interpreters of his dream, who expounded it as an omen that he should possess universal empire; for (6) that the mother who in his sleep he had found submissive to his embraces, was no other than the earth, the common parent of all mankind.

VIII. Quitting therefore the province before the expiration of the usual term, he betook himself to the Latin colonies, which were then eagerly agitating the design of obtaining the freedom of Rome; and he would have stirred them up to some bold attempt, had not the consuls, to prevent any commotion, detained for some time the legions which had been raised for service in Cilicia. But this did not deter him from making, soon afterwards, a still greater effort within the precincts of the city itself.

IX. For, only a few days before he entered upon the aedileship, he incurred a suspicion of having engaged in a conspiracy with Marcus Crassus, a man of consular rank; to whom were joined Publius Sylla and Lucius Autronius, who, after they had been chosen consuls, were convicted of bribery. The plan of the conspirators was to fall upon the senate at the opening of the new year, and murder as many of them as should be thought necessary; upon which, Crassus was to assume the office of dictator, and appoint Caesar his master of the horse 22. When the commonwealth had been thus ordered according to their pleasure, the consulship was to have been restored to Sylla and Autronius. Mention is made of this plot by Tanusius Geminus 23 in his history, by Marcus Bibulus in his edicts 24, and by Curio, the father, in his orations 25. Cicero likewise seems to hint at this in a letter to Axius, where he says, that Caesar (7) had in his consulship secured to himself that arbitrary power 26 to which he had aspired when he was edile. Tanusius adds, that Crassus, from remorse or fear, did not appear upon the day appointed for the massacre of the senate; for which reason Caesar omitted to give the signal, which, according to the plan concerted between them, he was to have made. The agreement, Curio says, was that he should shake off the toga from his shoulder. We have the authority of the same Curio, and of M. Actorius Naso, for his having been likewise concerned in another conspiracy with young Cneius Piso; to whom, upon a suspicion of some mischief being meditated in the city, the province of Spain was decreed out of the regular course 27. It is said to have been agreed between them, that Piso should head a revolt in the provinces, whilst the other should attempt to stir up an insurrection at Rome, using as their instruments the Lambrani, and the tribes beyond the Po. But the execution of this design was frustrated in both quarters by the death of Piso.

X. In his aedileship, he not only embellished the Comitium, and the rest of the Forum 28, with the adjoining halls 29, but adorned the Capitol also, with temporary piazzas, constructed for the purpose of displaying some part of the superabundant collections (8) he had made for the amusement of the people 30. He entertained them with the hunting of wild beasts, and with games, both alone and in conjunction with his colleague. On this account, he obtained the whole credit of the expense to which they had jointly contributed; insomuch that his colleague, Marcus Bibulus, could not forbear remarking, that he was served in the manner of Pollux. For as the temple 31 erected in the Forum to the two brothers, went by the name of Castor alone, so his and Caesar's joint munificence was imputed to the latter only. To the other public spectacles exhibited to the people, Caesar added a fight of gladiators, but with fewer pairs of combatants than he had intended. For he had collected from all parts so great a company of them, that his enemies became alarmed; and a decree was made, restricting the number of gladiators which any one was allowed to retain at Rome.

XI. Having thus conciliated popular favour, he endeavoured, through his interest with some of the tribunes, to get Egypt assigned to him as a province, by an act of the people. The pretext alleged for the creation of this extraordinary government, was, that the Alexandrians had violently expelled their king 32, whom the senate had complimented with the title of an ally and friend of the Roman people. This was generally resented; but, notwithstanding, there was so much opposition from the faction of the nobles, that he could not carry his point. In order, therefore, to diminish their influence by every means in his power, he restored the trophies erected in honour of Caius Marius, on account of his victories over Jugurtha, the Cimbri, and the Teutoni, which had been demolished by Sylla; and when sitting in judgment upon murderers, he treated those as assassins, who, in the late proscription, had received money from the treasury, for bringing in the heads of Roman citizens, although they were expressly excepted in the Cornelian laws.

XII. He likewise suborned some one to prefer an impeachment (9) for treason against Caius Rabirius, by whose especial assistance the senate had, a few years before, put down Lucius Saturninus, the seditious tribune; and being drawn by lot a judge on the trial, he condemned him with so much animosity, that upon his appealing to the people, no circumstance availed him so much as the extraordinary bitterness of his judge.

XIII. Having renounced all hope of obtaining Egypt for his province, he stood candidate for the office of chief pontiff, to secure which, he had recourse to the most profuse bribery. Calculating, on this occasion, the enormous amount of the debts he had contracted, he is reported to have said to his mother, when she kissed him at his going out in the morning to the assembly of the people, "I will never return home unless I am elected pontiff." In effect, he left so far behind him two most powerful competitors, who were much his superiors both in age and rank, that he had more votes in their own tribes, than they both had in all the tribes together.

XIV. After he was chosen praetor, the conspiracy of Catiline was discovered; and while every other member of the senate voted for inflicting capital punishment on the accomplices in that crime 33 , he alone proposed that the delinquents should be distributed for safe custody among the towns of Italy, their property being confiscated. He even struck such terror into those who were advocates for greater severity, by representing to them what universal odium would be attached to their memories by the Roman people, that Decius Silanus, consul elect, did not hesitate to qualify his proposal, it not being very honourable to change it, by a lenient interpretation; as if it had been understood in a harsher sense than he intended, and Caesar would certainly have carried his point, having brought over to his side a great number of the senators, among whom was Cicero, the consul's brother, had not a speech by Marcus Cato infused new vigour into the resolutions of the senate. He persisted, however, in obstructing the measure, until a body of the Roman knights, who stood under arms as a guard, threatened him with instant death, if he continued his determined opposition. They even thrust at him with their drawn swords, so that those who sat next him moved away; (10) and a few friends, with no small difficulty, protected him, by throwing their arms round him, and covering him with their togas. At last, deterred by this violence, he not only gave way, but absented himself from the senate-house during the remainder of that year.

XV. Upon the first day of his praetorship, he summoned Quintus Catulus to render an account to the people respecting the repairs of the

Capitol 34 ; proposing a decree for transferring the office of curator to another person 35 . But being unable to withstand the strong opposition made by the aristocratical party, whom he perceived quitting, in great numbers, their attendance upon the new consuls 36 , and fully resolved to resist his proposal, he dropped the design.

XVI. He afterwards approved himself a most resolute supporter of Caecilius Metullus, tribune of the people, who, in spite of all opposition from his colleagues, had proposed some laws of a violent tendency 37 , until they were both dismissed from office by a vote of the senate. He ventured, notwithstanding, to retain his post and continue in the administration of justice; but finding that preparations were made to obstruct him by force of arms, he dismissed the lictors, threw off his gown, and betook himself privately to his own house, with the resolution of being quiet, in a time so unfavourable to his interests. He likewise pacified the mob, which two days afterwards flocked about him, and in a riotous manner made a voluntary tender of their assistance in the vindication of his (11) honour. This happening contrary to expectation, the senate, who met in haste, on account of the tumult, gave him their thanks by some of the leading members of the house, and sending for him, after high commendation of his conduct, cancelled their former vote, and restored him to his office.

XVII. But he soon got into fresh trouble, being named amongst the accomplices of Catiline, both before Novius Niger the quaestor, by Lucius Vettius the informer, and in the senate by Quintus Curius; to whom a reward had been voted, for having first discovered the designs of the conspirators. Curius affirmed that he had received his information from Catiline. Vettius even engaged to produce in evidence against him his own hand-writing, given to Catiline. Caesar, feeling that this treatment was not to be borne, appealed to Cicero himself, whether he had not voluntarily made a discovery to him of some particulars of the conspiracy; and so baulked Curius of his expected reward. He, therefore, obliged Vettius to give pledges for his behaviour, seized his goods, and after heavily fining him, and seeing him almost torn in pieces before the rostra, threw him into prison; to which he likewise sent Novius the quaestor, for having presumed to take an information against a magistrate of superior authority.

XVIII. At the expiration of his praetorship he obtained by lot the Farther-Spain 38 , and pacified his creditors, who were for detaining him, by finding sureties for his debts 39. Contrary, however, to both law and custom, he took his departure before the usual equipage and outfit were prepared. It is uncertain whether this precipitancy arose from the apprehension of an impeachment, with which he was threatened on the expiration of his former office, or from his anxiety to lose no time in relieving the allies, who implored him to come to their aid. He had no (12) sooner established tranquillity in the province, than, without waiting for the arrival of his successor, he returned to Rome, with equal haste, to sue for a triumph 40, and the consulship. The day of election, however, being already fixed by proclamation, he could not legally be admitted a candidate, unless he entered the city as a private person 41. On this emergency he solicited a suspension of the laws in his favour; but such an indulgence being strongly opposed, he found himself under the necessity of abandoning all thoughts of a triumph, lest he should be disappointed of the consulship.

XIX. Of the two other competitors for the consulship, Lucius Luceius and Marcus Bibulus, he joined with the former, upon condition that Luceius, being a man of less interest but greater affluence, should promise money to the electors, in their joint names. Upon which the party of the nobles, dreading how far he might carry matters in that high office, with a colleague disposed to concur in and second his measures, advised Bibulus to promise the voters as much as the other; and most of them contributed towards the expense, Cato himself admitting that bribery; under such circumstances, was for the public good 42. He was accordingly elected consul jointly with Bibulus. Actuated still by the same motives, the prevailing party took care to assign provinces of small importance to the new consuls, such as the care of the woods and roads. Caesar, incensed at this indignity, endeavoured by the most assiduous and flattering attentions to gain to his side Cneius Pompey, at that time dissatisfied with the senate for the backwardness they shewed to confirm his acts, after his victories over Mithridates. He likewise brought about a reconciliation between Pompey and Marcus Crassus, who had been at variance from (13) the time of their joint consulship, in which office they were continually clashing; and he entered into an agreement with both, that nothing should be transacted in the government, which was displeasing to any of the three.

XX. Having entered upon his office 43, he introduced a new regulation, that the daily acts both of the senate and people should be committed to writing, and published 44. He also revived an old custom, that an officer 45 should precede him, and his lictors follow him, on the alternate months when the fasces were not carried before him. Upon preferring a bill to the people for the division of some public lands, he was opposed by his colleague, whom he violently drove out of the forum. Next day the insulted consul made a complaint in the senate of this treatment; but such was the consternation, that no one having the courage to bring the matter forward or move a censure, which had been often done under outrages of less importance, he was so much dispirited, that until the expiration of his office he never stirred from home, and did nothing but issue edicts to obstruct his colleague's proceedings. From that time, therefore, Caesar had the sole management of public affairs; insomuch that some wags, when they signed any instrument as witnesses, did not add "in the consulship of Caesar and Bibulus," but, "of Julius and Caesar;" putting the same person down twice, under his name and surname. The following verses likewise were currently repeated on this occasion:

*Non Bibulo quidquam nuper, sed Caesare factum est;*
*Nam Bibulo fieri consule nil memini.*
*Nothing was done in Bibulus's year:*
*No; Caesar only then was consul here.*

(14) The land of Stellas, consecrated by our ancestors to the gods, with some other lands in Campania left subject to tribute, for the support of the expenses of the government, he divided, but not by lot, among upwards of twenty thousand freemen, who had each of them three or more children. He eased the publicans, upon their petition, of a third part of the sum which they had engaged to pay into the public treasury; and openly admonished them not to bid so extravagantly upon the next occasion. He made various profuse grants to meet the wishes of others, no one opposing him; or if any such attempt was made, it was soon suppressed. Marcus Cato, who interrupted him in his proceedings, he ordered to be dragged out of the senate-house by a lictor, and carried to prison. Lucius Lucullus, likewise, for opposing him with some warmth, he so terrified with the apprehension of being criminated, that, to deprecate the consul's resentment, he fell on his knees. And upon Cicero's lamenting in some

trial the miserable condition of the times, he the very same day, by nine o'clock, transferred his enemy, Publius Clodius, from a patrician to a plebeian family; a change which he had long solicited in vain 46. At last, effectually to intimidate all those of the opposite party, he by great rewards prevailed upon Vettius to declare, that he had been solicited by certain persons to assassinate Pompey; and when he was brought before the rostra to name those who had been concerted between them, after naming one or two to no purpose, not without great suspicion of subornation, Caesar, despairing of success in this rash stratagem, is supposed to have taken off his informer by poison.

XXI. About the same time he married Calpurnia, the daughter of Lucius Piso, who was to succeed him in the consulship, and gave his own daughter Julia to Cneius Pompey; rejecting Servilius Caepio, to whom she had been contracted, and by whose means chiefly he had but a little before baffled Bibulus. After this new alliance, he began, upon any debates in the senate, to ask Pompey's opinion first, whereas he used before to give that distinction to Marcus Crassus; and it was (15) the usual practice for the consul to observe throughout the year the method of consulting the senate which he had adopted on the calends (the first) of January.

XXII. Being, therefore, now supported by the interest of his father-in-law and son-in-law, of all the provinces he made choice of Gaul, as most likely to furnish him with matter and occasion for triumphs. At first indeed he received only Cisalpine-Gaul, with the addition of Illyricum, by a decree proposed by Vatinius to the people; but soon afterwards obtained from the senate Gallia-Comata 47 also, the senators being apprehensive, that if they should refuse it him, that province, also, would be granted him by the people. Elated now with his success, he could not refrain from boasting, a few days afterwards, in a full senate-house, that he had, in spite of his enemies, and to their great mortification, obtained all he desired, and that for the future he would make them, to their shame, submissive to his pleasure. One of the senators observing, sarcastically: "That will not be very easy for a woman 48 to do," he jocosely replied, "Semiramis formerly reigned in Assyria, and the Amazons possessed great part of Asia."

XXIII. When the term of his consulship had expired, upon a motion being made in the senate by Caius Memmius and Lucius Domitius, the praetors, respecting the transactions of the year past, he offered to refer himself to the house; but (16) they declining the business, after three days spent in vain altercation, he set out for his province. Immediately, however, his quaestor was charged with several misdemeanors, for the purpose of implicating Caesar himself. Indeed, an accusation was soon after preferred against him by Lucius Antistius, tribune of the people; but by making an appeal to the tribune's colleagues, he succeeded in having the prosecution suspended during his absence in the service of the state. To secure himself, therefore, for the time to come, he was particularly careful to secure the good-will of the magistrates at the annual elections, assisting none of the candidates with his interest, nor suffering any persons to be advanced to any office, who would not positively undertake to defend him in his absence for which purpose he made no scruple to require of some of them an oath, and even a written obligation.

XXIV. But when Lucius Domitius became a candidate for the consulship, and openly threatened that, upon his being elected consul, he would effect that which he could not accomplish when he was praetor, and divest him of the command of the armies, he sent for Crassus and Pompey to Lucca, a city in his province, and pressed them, for the purpose of disappointing Domitius, to sue again for the consulship, and to continue him in his command for five years longer; with both which requisitions they complied. Presumptuous now from his success, he added, at his own private charge, more legions to those which he had received from the republic; among the former of which was one levied in Transalpine Gaul, and called by a Gallic name, Alauda 49 , which he trained and armed in the Roman fashion, and afterwards conferred on it the freedom of the city. From this period he declined no occasion of war, however unjust and dangerous; attacking, without any provocation, as well the allies of Rome as the barbarous nations which were its enemies: insomuch, that the senate passed a decree for sending commissioners to examine into the condition of Gaul; and some members even proposed that he should be delivered up to the enemy. But so great had been the success of his enterprises, that he had the honour of obtaining more days 50 (17) of supplication, and those more frequently, than had ever before been decreed to any commander.

XXV. During nine years in which he held the government of the province, his achievements were as follows: he reduced all Gaul, bounded by the Pyrenean forest, the Alps, mount Gebenna, and the two rivers, the Rhine and the Rhone, and being about three thousand two hundred miles in compass, into the form of a province, excepting only the nations in alliance with the republic, and such as had merited his favour; imposing upon this new acquisition an annual tribute of forty millions of sesterces. He was the first of the Romans who, crossing the Rhine by a bridge, attacked the Germanic tribes inhabiting the country beyond that river, whom he defeated in several engagements. He also invaded the Britons, a people formerly unknown, and having vanquished them, exacted from them contributions and hostages. Amidst such a series of successes, he experienced thrice only any signal disaster; once in Britain, when his fleet was nearly wrecked in a storm; in Gaul, at Gergovia, where one of his legions was put to the rout; and in the territory of the Germans, his lieutenants Titurius and Aurunculeius were cut off by an ambuscade.

XXVI. During this period 51 he lost his mother 52, whose death was followed by that of his daughter 53, and, not long afterwards, of his granddaughter. Meanwhile, the republic being in consternation at the murder of Publius Clodius, and the senate passing a vote that only one consul, namely, Cneius Pompeius, should be chosen for the ensuing year, he prevailed with the tribunes of the people, who intended joining him in nomination with Pompey, to propose to the people a bill, enabling him, though absent, to become a candidate for his second consulship, when the term of his command should be near expiring, that he might not be obliged on that account to quit his province too soon, and before the conclusion of the war. Having attained this object, carrying his views still higher, and animated with the hopes of success, he omitted no (18) opportunity of gaining universal favour, by acts of liberality and kindness to individuals, both in public and private. With money raised from the spoils of the war, he began to construct a new forum, the ground-plot of which cost him above a hundred millions of sesterces 54. He promised the people a public entertainment of gladiators, and a feast in memory of his daughter, such as no one before him had ever given. The more to raise their expectations on this occasion, although he had agreed with victuallers of all denominations for his feast, he made yet farther preparations in private houses. He issued an order, that the most celebrated gladiators, if at any time during the combat they incurred the displeasure of the public, should be immediately carried off by force, and reserved for some future occasion. Young gladiators he trained up, not in the school, and by the masters, of defence, but in the houses of Roman knights, and even senators, skilled in the use of arms, earnestly requesting them, as appears from his letters, to undertake the discipline of those novitiates, and to give them the word during their exercises. He doubled the pay of the legions in perpetuity; allowing them likewise corn, when it was in plenty, without any restriction; and sometimes distributing to every soldier in his army a slave, and a portion of land.

XXVII. To maintain his alliance and good understanding with Pompey, he offered him in marriage his sister's grand-daughter Octavia, who had been married to Caius Marcellus; and requested for himself his daughter, lately contracted to Faustus Sylla. Every person about him, and a great part likewise of the senate, he secured by loans of money at low interest, or none at all; and to all others who came to wait upon him, either by invitation or of their own accord, he made liberal presents; not neglecting even the freed-men and slaves, who were favourites with their masters and patrons. He offered also singular and ready aid to all who were under prosecution, or in debt, and to prodigal youths; excluding from (19) his bounty those only who were so deeply plunged in guilt, poverty, or luxury, that it was impossible effectually to relieve them. These, he openly declared, could derive no benefit from any other means than a civil war.

XXVIII. He endeavoured with equal assiduity to engage in his interest princes and provinces in every part of the world; presenting some with thousands of captives, and sending to others the assistance of troops, at whatever time and place they desired, without any authority from either the senate or people of Rome. He likewise embellished with magnificent public buildings the most powerful cities not only of Italy, Gaul, and Spain, but of Greece and Asia; until all people being now astonished, and speculating on the obvious tendency of these proceedings, Claudius Marcellus, the consul, declaring first by proclamation, that he intended to propose a measure of the utmost importance to the state, made a motion in the senate that some person should be appointed to succeed Caesar in his province, before the term of his command was expired; because the war being brought to a conclusion, peace was restored, and the victorious army ought to be disbanded. He further moved, that Caesar being absent, his claims to be a candidate at the next election of consuls should not be admitted, as Pompey himself had afterwards abrogated that privilege by a decree of the people. The fact was, that Pompey, in his law relating to the choice of chief magistrates, had forgot to except Caesar, in the article in which he declared all such as were not present incapable of being candidates for any office; but soon afterwards, when the law was inscribed on brass, and deposited in the treasury, he corrected his mistake. Marcellus, not content with depriving Caesar of his provinces, and the privilege intended him by Pompey, likewise moved the senate, that the freedom of the city should be taken from those colonists whom, by the Vatinian law, he had settled at New Como 55 ; because it had been conferred upon them with ambitious views, and by a stretch of the laws.

(20) XXIX. Roused by these proceedings, and thinking, as he was often heard to say, that it would be a more difficult enterprise to reduce him, now that he was the chief man in the state, from the first rank of citizens to the second, than from the second to the lowest of all, Caesar made a vigorous opposition to the measure, partly by means of the tribunes, who interposed in his behalf, and partly through Servius Sulpicius, the other consul. The following year likewise, when Caius Marcellus, who succeeded his cousin Marcus in the consulship, pursued the same course, Caesar, by means of an immense bribe, engaged in his defence Aemilius Paulus, the other consul, and Caius Curio, the most violent of the tribunes. But finding the opposition obstinately bent against him, and that the consuls-elect were also of that party, he wrote a letter to the senate, requesting that they would not deprive him of the privilege kindly granted him by the people; or else that the other generals should resign the command of their armies as well as himself; fully persuaded, as it is thought, that he could more easily collect his veteran soldiers, whenever he pleased, than Pompey could his new-raised troops. At the same time, he made his adversaries an offer to disband eight of his legions and give up Transalpine-Gaul, upon condition that he might retain two legions, with the Cisalpine province, or but one legion with Illyricum, until he should be elected consul.

XXX. But as the senate declined to interpose in the business, and his enemies declared that they would enter into no compromise where the safety of the republic was at stake, he advanced into Hither-Gaul 56, and, having gone the circuit for the administration of justice, made a halt at Ravenna, resolved to have recourse to arms if the senate should proceed to extremity against the tribunes of the people who had espoused his cause. This was indeed his pretext for the civil war; but it is supposed that there were other motives for his conduct. Cneius Pompey used frequently to say, that he sought to throw every thing into confusion, because he was unable, with all his private wealth, to complete the works he had begun, and answer, at his return, the vast expectations which he had excited in the people. Others pretend that he was apprehensive of being (21) called to account for what he had done in his first consulship, contrary to the auspices, laws, and the protests of the tribunes; Marcus Cato having sometimes declared, and that, too, with an oath, that he would prefer an impeachment against him, as soon as he disbanded his army. A report likewise prevailed, that if he returned as a private person, he would, like Milo, have to plead his cause before the judges, surrounded by armed men. This conjecture is rendered highly probable by Asinius Pollio, who informs us that Caesar, upon viewing the vanquished and slaughtered enemy in the field of Pharsalia, expressed himself in these very words: "This was their intention: I, Caius Caesar, after all the great achievements I had performed, must have been condemned, had I not summoned the army to my aid!" Some think, that having contracted from long habit an extraordinary love of power, and having weighed his own and his enemies' strength, he embraced that occasion of usurping the supreme power; which indeed he had coveted from the time of his youth. This seems to have been the opinion entertained by Cicero, who tells us, in the third book of his Offices, that Caesar used to have frequently in his mouth two verses of Euripides, which he thus translates:

*Nam si violandum est jus, regnandi gratia*
*Violandum est: aliis rebus pietatem colas.*
*Be just, unless a kingdom tempts to break the laws,*
*For sovereign power alone can justify the cause.* 57.

XXXI. When intelligence, therefore, was received, that the interposition of the tribunes in his favour had been utterly rejected, and that they themselves had fled from the city, he immediately sent forward some cohorts, but privately, to prevent any suspicion of his design; and, to keep up appearances, attended at a public spectacle, examined the model of a fencing-school which he proposed to build, and, as usual, sat down to table with a numerous party of his friends. But after sun-set, mules being put to his carriage from a neighbouring mill, he set forward on his journey with all possible privacy, and a small retinue. The lights going out, he lost his way, and (22) wandered about a long time, until at length, by the help of a guide, whom he found towards day-break, he proceeded on foot through some narrow paths, and again reached the road. Coming up with his troops on the banks of the Rubicon, which was the boundary of his province 58, he halted for a while, and, revolving in his mind the importance of the step he was on the point of taking, he turned to those about him, and said: "We may still retreat; but if we pass this little bridge, nothing is left for us but to fight it out in arms."

XXXII. While he was thus hesitating, the following incident occurred. A person remarkable for his noble mien and graceful aspect, appeared close at hand, sitting and playing upon a pipe. When, not only the shepherds, but a number of soldiers also flocked from their posts to listen to him, and some trumpeters among them, he snatched a trumpet from one of them, ran to the river with it, and sounding the advance with a piercing blast, crossed to the other side. Upon this, Caesar exclaimed, "Let us go whither the omens of the Gods and the iniquity of our enemies call us. The die is now cast."

XXXIII. Accordingly, having marched his army over the river, he shewed them the tribunes of the people, who, upon their being driven from the city, had come to meet him; and, in the presence of that assembly, called upon the troops to pledge him their fidelity, with tears in his eyes, and his garment rent from his bosom. It has been supposed, that upon this occasion he promised to every soldier a knight's estate; but that opinion is founded on a mistake. For when, in his harangue to them, he frequently held out a finger of his left hand, and declared, that to recompense those who should support him in the defence of his honour, he would willingly part even with his ring; the soldiers at a distance, who could more easily see than hear him while he spoke, formed their conception of what he said, by the eye, not by the ear; and accordingly gave out, that he had promised to each of them the privilege (23) of wearing the gold ring, and an estate of four hundred thousand sesterces. 60

XXXIV. Of his subsequent proceedings I shall give a cursory detail, in the order in which they occurred 61. He took possession of Picenum, Umbria, and Etruria; and having obliged Lucius Domitius, who had been tumultuously nominated his successor, and held Corsinium with a garrison, to surrender, and dismissed him, he marched along the coast of the Upper Sea, to Brundusium, to which place the consuls and Pompey were fled with the intention of crossing the sea as soon as possible. After vain attempts, by all the obstacles he could oppose, to prevent their leaving the harbour, he turned his steps towards Rome, where he appealed to the senate on the present state of public affairs; and then set out for Spain, in which province Pompey had a numerous army, under the command of three lieutenants, Marcus Petreius, Lucius Afranius, and Marcus Varro; declaring amongst his friends, before he set forward, "That he was going against an army without a general, and should return thence against a general without an army." Though his progress was retarded both by the siege of Marseilles, which shut her gates against him, and a very great scarcity of corn, yet in a short time he bore down all before him.

XXXV. Thence he returned to Rome, and crossing the sea to Macedonia, blocked up Pompey during almost four months, within a line of ramparts of prodigious extent; and at last defeated him in the battle of Pharsalia. Pursuing him in his flight to Alexandria, where he was informed of his murder, he presently found himself also engaged, under all the disadvantages of time and place, in a very dangerous war, with king Ptolemy, who, he saw, had treacherous designs upon his life. It was winter, and he, within the walls of a well-provided and subtle enemy, was destitute of every thing, and wholly unprepared (24) for such a conflict. He succeeded, however, in his enterprise, and put the kingdom of Egypt into the hands of Cleopatra and her younger brother; being afraid to make it a province, lest, under an aspiring prefect, it might become the centre of revolt. From Alexandria he went into Syria, and thence to Pontus, induced by intelligence which he had received respecting Pharnaces. This prince, who was son of the great Mithridates, had seized the opportunity which the distraction of the times offered for making war upon his neighbours, and his insolence and fierceness had grown with his success. Caesar, however, within five days after entering his country, and four hours after coming in sight of him, overthrew him in one decisive battle. Upon which, he frequently remarked to those about him the good fortune of Pompey, who had obtained his military reputation, chiefly, by victory over so feeble an enemy. He afterwards defeated Scipio and Juba, who were rallying the remains of the party in Africa, and Pompey's sons in Spain.

XXXVI. During the whole course of the civil war, he never once suffered any defeat, except in the case of his lieutenants; of whom Caius Curio fell in Africa, Caius Antonius was made prisoner in Illyricum, Publius Dolabella lost a fleet in the same Illyricum, and Cneius Domitius Culvinus, an army in Pontus. In every encounter with the enemy where he himself commanded, he came off with complete success; nor was the issue ever doubtful, except on two occasions: once at Dyrrachium, when, being obliged to give ground, and Pompey not pursuing his advantage, he said that "Pompey knew not how to conquer;" the other instance occurred in his last battle in Spain, when, despairing of the event, he even had thoughts of killing himself.

XXXVII. For the victories obtained in the several wars, he triumphed five different times; after the defeat of Scipio: four times in one month, each triumph succeeding the former by an interval of a few days; and once again after the conquest of Pompey's sons. His first and most glorious triumph was for the victories he gained in Gaul; the next for that of Alexandria, the third for the reduction of Pontus, the fourth for his African victory, and the last for that in Spain; and (25) they all differed from each other in their varied pomp and pageantry. On the day of the Gallic triumph, as he was proceeding along the street called Velabrum, after narrowly escaping a fall from his chariot by the breaking of the axle-tree, he ascended the Capitol by torch-light, forty elephants 62 carrying torches on his right and left. Amongst the pageantry of the Pontic triumph, a tablet with this inscription was carried before him: I CAME, I SAW, I CONQUERED 63 ; not signifying, as other mottos on the like occasion, what was done, so much as the dispatch with which it was done.

XXXVIII. To every foot-soldier in his veteran legions, besides the two thousand sesterces paid him in the beginning of the civil war, he gave twenty thousand more, in the shape of prize-money. He likewise allotted them lands, but not in contiguity, that the former owners might not be entirely dispossessed. To the people of Rome, besides ten modii of corn, and as many pounds of oil, he gave three hundred sesterces a man, which he had formerly promised them, and a hundred more to each for the delay in fulfilling his engagement. He likewise remitted a year's rent due to the treasury, for such houses in Rome as did not pay above two thousand sesterces a year; and through the rest of Italy, for all such as did not exceed in yearly rent five hundred sesterces. To all this he added a public entertainment, and a distribution of meat, and, after his Spanish victory 64, two public dinners. For, considering the first he had given as too sparing, and unsuited to his profuse liberality, he, five days afterwards, added another, which was most plentiful.

XXXIX. The spectacles he exhibited to the people were of various kinds; namely, a combat of gladiators 65, and stage-plays in the several wards of the city, and in different languages; likewise Circensian games 66, wrestlers, and the representation of a sea-fight. In the conflict of gladiators presented in the Forum, Furius Leptinus, a man of praetorian family, entered the lists as a combatant, as did also Quintus Calpenus, formerly a senator, and a pleader of causes. The Pyrrhic dance was performed by some youths, who were sons to persons of the first distinction in Asia and Bithynia. In the plays, Decimus Laberius, who had been a Roman knight, acted in his own piece; and being presented on the spot with five hundred thousand sesterces, and a gold ring, he went from the stage, through the orchestra, and resumed his place in the seats (27) allotted for the equestrian order. In the Circensisn games; the circus being enlarged at each end, and a canal sunk round it, several of the young nobility drove chariots, drawn, some by four, and others by two horses, and likewise rode races on single horses. The Trojan game was acted by two distinct companies of boys, one differing from the other in age and rank. The hunting of wild beasts was presented for five days successively; and on the last day a battle was fought by five hundred foot, twenty elephants, and thirty horse on each side. To afford room for this engagement, the goals were removed, and in their space two camps were pitched, directly opposite to each other. Wrestlers likewise performed for three days successively, in a stadium provided for the purpose in the Campus Martius. A lake having been dug in the little Codeta 67, ships of the Tyrian and Egyptian fleets, containing two, three, and four banks of oars, with a number of men on board, afforded an animated representation of a sea-fight. To these various diversions there flocked such crowds of spectators from all parts, that most of the strangers were obliged to lodge in tents erected in the streets, or along the roads near the city. Several in the throng were squeezed to death, amongst whom were two senators.

XL. Turning afterwards his attention to the regulation of the commonwealth, he corrected the calendar 68, which had for (28) some time become extremely confused, through the unwarrantable liberty which the pontiffs had taken in the article of intercalation. To such a height had this abuse proceeded, that neither the festivals designed for the harvest fell in summer, nor those for the vintage in autumn. He accommodated the year to the course of the sun, ordaining that in future it should consist of three hundred and sixty-five days without any intercalary month; and that every fourth year an intercalary day should be inserted. That the year might thenceforth commence regularly with the calends, or first of January, he inserted two months between November and December; so that the year in which this regulation was made consisted of fifteen months, including the month of intercalation, which, according to the division of time then in use, happened that year.

XLI. He filled up the vacancies in the senate, by advancing several plebeians to the rank of patricians, and also increased the number of praetors, aediles, quaestors, and inferior magistrates; restoring, at the same time, such as had been degraded by the censors, or convicted of bribery at elections. The choice of magistrates he so divided with the people, that, excepting only the candidates for the consulship, they nominated one half of them, and he the other. The method which he practised in those cases was, to recommend such persons as he had pitched upon, by bills dispersed through the several tribes to this effect: "Caesar the dictator to such a tribe (naming it). I recommend to you (naming likewise the persons), that by the favour of your votes they may attain to the honours for which they sue." He likewise admitted to offices the sons of those who had been proscribed. The trial of causes he restricted to two orders of judges, the equestrian and senatorial; excluding the tribunes of the treasury who had before made a third class. The revised census of the people he ordered to be taken neither in the usual manner or place, but street by street, by the principal inhabitants of the several quarters of the city; and he reduced the number of those who received corn at the public cost, from three hundred and twenty, to a hundred and fifty, thousand. To prevent any tumults on account of the census, he ordered that the praetor should every year fill up by lot the vacancies occasioned by death, from those who were not enrolled for the receipt of corn.

(29) XLII. Eighty thousand citizens having been distributed into foreign colonies 69 , he enacted, in order to stop the drain on the population, that no freeman of the city above twenty, and under forty, years of age, who was not in the military service, should absent himself from Italy for more than three years at a time; that no senator's son should go abroad, unless in the retinue of some high officer; and as to those whose pursuit was tending flocks and herds, that no less than a third of the number of their shepherds free-born should be youths. He likewise made all those who practised physic in Rome, and all teachers of the liberal arts, free of the city, in order to fix them in it, and induce others to settle there. With respect to debts, he disappointed the expectation which was generally entertained, that they would be totally cancelled; and ordered that the debtors should satisfy their creditors, according to the valuation of their estates, at the rate at which they were purchased before the commencement of the civil war; deducting from the debt what had been paid for interest either in money or by bonds; by virtue of which provision about a fourth part of the debt was lost. He dissolved all the guilds, except such as were of ancient foundation. Crimes were punished with greater severity; and the rich being more easily induced to commit them because they were only liable to banishment, without the forfeiture of their property, he stripped murderers, as Cicero observes, of their whole estates, and other offenders of one half.

XLIII. He was extremely assiduous and strict in the administration of justice. He expelled from the senate such members as were convicted of bribery; and he dissolved the marriage of a man of pretorian rank, who had married a lady two days after her divorce from a former husband, although there was no suspicion that they had been guilty of any illicit connection. He imposed duties on the importation of foreign goods. The use of litters for travelling, purple robes, and jewels, he permitted only to persons of a certain age and station, and on particular days. He enforced a rigid execution of the sumptuary laws; placing officers about the markets, to seize upon all meats exposed to sale contrary to the rules, and bring them to him; sometimes sending his lictors and soldiers to (30) carry away such victuals as had escaped the notice of the officers, even when they were upon the table.

XLIV. His thoughts were now fully employed from day to day on a variety of great projects for the embellishment and improvement of the city, as well as for guarding and extending the bounds of the empire. In the first place, he meditated the construction of a temple to Mars, which should exceed in grandeur every thing of that kind in the world. For this purpose, he intended to fill up the lake on which he had entertained the people with the spectacle of a sea-fight. He also projected a most spacious theatre adjacent to the Tarpeian mount; and also proposed to reduce the civil law to a reasonable compass, and out of that immense and undigested mass of statutes to extract the best and most necessary parts into a few books; to make as large a collection as possible of works in the Greek and Latin languages, for the public use; the province of providing and putting them in proper order being assigned to Marcus Varro. He intended likewise to drain the Pomptine marshes, to cut a channel for the discharge of the waters of the lake Fucinus, to form a road from the Upper Sea through the ridge of the Appenine to the Tiber; to make a cut through the isthmus of Corinth, to reduce the Dacians, who had over-run Pontus and Thrace, within their proper limits, and then to make war upon the Parthians, through the Lesser Armenia, but not to risk a general engagement with them, until he had made some trial of their prowess in war. But in the midst of all his undertakings and projects, he was carried off by death; before I speak of which, it may not be improper to give an account of his person, dress, and manners; together with what relates to his pursuits, both civil and military.

XLV. It is said that he was tall, of a fair complexion, round limbed, rather full faced, with eyes black and piercing; and that he enjoyed excellent health, except towards the close of his life, when he was subject to sudden fainting-fits, and disturbance in his sleep. He was likewise twice seized with the falling sickness while engaged in active service. He was so nice in the care of his person, that he not only kept the hair of his head closely cut and had his face smoothly shaved, but (31) even caused the hair on other parts of the body to be plucked out by the roots, a practice for which some persons rallied him. His baldness gave him much uneasiness, having often found himself upon that account exposed to the jibes of his enemies. He therefore used to bring forward the hair from the crown of his head; and of all the honours conferred upon him by the senate and people, there was none which he either accepted or used with greater pleasure, than the right of wearing constantly a laurel crown. It is said that he was particular in his dress. For he used the Latus Clavus 70 with fringes about the wrists, and always had it girded about him, but rather loosely. This circumstance gave origin to the expression of Sylla, who often advised the nobles to beware of "the ill-girt boy."

XLVI. He first inhabited a small house in the Suburra 71, but after his advancement to the pontificate, he occupied a palace belonging to the state in the Via Sacra. Many writers say that he liked his residence to be elegant, and his entertainments sumptuous; and that he entirely took down a villa near the grove of Aricia, which he had built from the foundation and finished at a vast expense, because it did not exactly suit his taste, although he had at that time but slender means, and was in debt; and that he carried about in his expeditions tesselated and marble slabs for the floor of his tent.

XLVII. They likewise report that he invaded Britain in hopes of finding pearls 72, the size of which he would compare together, and ascertain the weight by poising them in his hand; that he would purchase, at any cost, gems, carved works, statues, and pictures, executed by the eminent masters of antiquity; and that he would give for young and handy slaves a price so extravagant, that he forbad its being entered in the diary of his expenses.

XLVIII. We are also told, that in the provinces he constantly maintained two tables, one for the officers of the army, and the gentry of the country, and the other for Romans of the highest rank, and provincials of the first distinction. He was so very exact in the management of his domestic affairs, both little and great, that he once threw a baker into prison, for serving him with a finer sort of bread than his guests; and put to death a freed-man, who was a particular favourite, for debauching the lady of a Roman knight, although no complaint had been made to him of the affair.

XLIX. The only stain upon his chastity was his having cohabited with Nicomedes; and that indeed stuck to him all the days of his life, and exposed him to much bitter raillery. I will not dwell upon those well-known verses of Calvus Licinius:

*Whate'er Bithynia and her lord possess'd,*
*Her lord who Caesar in his lust caress'd. 73_*

I pass over the speeches of Dolabella, and Curio, the father, in which the former calls him "the queen's rival, and the inner-side of the royal couch," and the latter, "the brothel of Nicomedes, and the Bithynian stew." I would likewise say nothing of the edicts of Bibulus, in which he proclaimed his colleague under the name of "the queen of Bithynia;" adding, that "he had formerly been in love with a king, but now coveted a kingdom." At which time, as Marcus Brutus relates, one Octavius, a man of a crazy brain, and therefore the more free in his raillery, after he had in a crowded assembly saluted Pompey by the title of king, addressed Caesar by that of queen. Caius Memmius likewise upbraided him with serving the king at table, among the rest of his catamites, in the presence of a large company, in which were some merchants from Rome, the names of whom he mentions. But Cicero was not content with writing in some of his letters, that he was conducted by the royal attendants into the king's bed-chamber, lay upon a bed of gold with a covering of purple, and that the youthful bloom of this scion of Venus had been tainted in Bithynia—but upon Caesar's pleading the cause of Nysa, the daughter of (32) Nicomedes before the senate, and recounting the king's kindnesses to him, replied, "Pray tell us no more of that; for it is well known what he gave you, and you gave him." To conclude, his soldiers in the Gallic triumph, amongst other verses, such as they jocularly sung on those occasions, following the general's chariot, recited these, which since that time have become extremely common:

*The Gauls to Caesar yield, Caesar to Nicomede,*
*Lo! Caesar triumphs for his glorious deed,*
*But Caesar's conqueror gains no victor's meed. 74_*

L. It is admitted by all that he was much addicted to women, as well as very expensive in his intrigues with them, and that he debauched many ladies of the highest quality; among whom were Posthumia, the wife of Servius Sulpicius; Lollia, the wife of Aulus

Gabinius; Tertulla, the wife of Marcus Crassus; and Mucia, the wife of Cneius Pompey. For it is certain that the Curios, both father and son, and many others, made it a reproach to Pompey, "That to gratify his ambition, he married the daughter of a man, upon whose account he had divorced his wife, after having had three children by her; and whom he used, with a deep sigh, to call Aegisthus." 75 But the mistress he most loved, was Servilia, the mother of Marcus Brutus, for whom he purchased, in his first consulship after the commencement of their intrigue, a pearl which cost him six millions of sesterces; and in the civil war, besides other presents, assigned to her, for a trifling consideration, some valuable farms when they were exposed to public auction. Many persons expressing their surprise at the lowness of the price, Cicero wittily remarked, "To let you know the real value of the purchase, between ourselves, Tertia was deducted:" for Servilia was supposed to have prostituted her daughter Tertia to Caesar. 76

(34) LI. That he had intrigues likewise with married women in the provinces, appears from this distich, which was as much repeated in the Gallic Triumph as the former: —

*Watch well your wives, ye cits, we bring a blade,*
*A bald-pate master of the wenching trade.*
*Thy gold was spent on many a Gallic w — -e;*
*Exhausted now, thou com'st to borrow more.* 77_

LII. In the number of his mistresses were also some queens; such as Eunoe, a Moor, the wife of Bogudes, to whom and her husband he made, as Naso reports, many large presents. But his greatest favourite was Cleopatra, with whom he often revelled all night until the dawn of day, and would have gone with her through Egypt in dalliance, as far as Aethiopia, in her luxurious yacht, had not the army refused to follow him. He afterwards invited her to Rome, whence he sent her back loaded with honours and presents, and gave her permission to call by his name a son, who, according to the testimony of some Greek historians, resembled Caesar both in person and gait. Mark Antony declared in the senate, that Caesar had acknowledged the child as his own; and that Caius Matias, Caius Oppius, and the rest of Caesar's friends knew it to be true. On which occasion, Oppius, as if it had been an imputation which he was called upon to refute, published a book to shew, "that the child which Cleopatra fathered upon Caesar, was not his." Helvius Cinna, tribune of the people, admitted to several persons the fact, that he had a bill ready drawn, which Caesar had ordered him to get enacted in his absence, allowing him, with the hope of leaving issue, to take any wife he chose, and as many of them as he pleased; and to leave no room for doubt of his infamous character for unnatural lewdness and adultery, Curio, the father, says, in one of his speeches, "He was every woman's man, and every man's woman."

LIII. It is acknowledged even by his enemies, that in regard to wine, he was abstemious. A remark is ascribed to Marcus Cato, "that Caesar was the only sober man amongst all those who were engaged in the design to subvert (35) the government." In the matter of diet, Caius Oppius informs us, "that he was so indifferent, that when a person in whose house he was entertained, had served him with stale, instead of fresh, oil 78 , and the rest of the company would not touch it, he alone ate very heartily of it, that he might not seem to tax the master of the house with rusticity or want of attention."

LIV. But his abstinence did not extend to pecuniary advantages, either in his military commands, or civil offices; for we have the testimony of some writers, that he took money from the proconsul, who was his predecessor in Spain, and from the Roman allies in that quarter, for the discharge of his debts; and plundered at the point of the sword some towns of the Lusitanians, notwithstanding they attempted no resistance, and opened their gates to him upon his arrival before them. In Gaul, he rifled the chapels and temples of the gods, which were filled with rich offerings, and demolished cities oftener for the sake of their spoil, than for any ill they had done. By this means gold became so plentiful with him, that he exchanged it through Italy and the provinces of the empire for three thousand sesterces the pound. In his first consulship he purloined from the Capitol three thousand pounds' weight of gold, and substituted for it the same quantity of gilt brass. He bartered likewise to foreign nations and princes, for gold, the titles of allies and kings; and squeezed out of Ptolemy alone near six thousand talents, in the name of himself and Pompey. He afterwards supported the expense of the civil wars, and of his triumphs and public spectacles, by the most flagrant rapine and sacrilege.

LV. In eloquence and warlike achievements, he equalled at least, if he did not surpass, the greatest of men. After his prosecution of

Dolabella, he was indisputably reckoned one of the most distinguished advocates. Cicero, in recounting to Brutus the famous orators, declares, "that he does not see that Caesar was inferior to any one of them;" and says, "that he (36) had an elegant, splendid, noble, and magnificent vein of eloquence." And in a letter to Cornelius Nepos, he writes of him in the following terms: "What! Of all the orators, who, during the whole course of their lives, have done nothing else, which can you prefer to him? Which of them is more pointed or terse in his periods, or employs more polished and elegant language?" In his youth, he seems to have chosen Strabo Caesar for his model; from whose oration in behalf of the Sardinians he has transcribed some passages literally into his Divination. In his delivery he is said to have had a shrill voice, and his action was animated, but not ungraceful. He has left behind him some speeches, among which are ranked a few that are not genuine, such as that on behalf of Quintus Metellus. These Augustus supposes, with reason, to be rather the production of blundering short-hand writers, who were not able to keep pace with him in the delivery, than publications of his own. For I find in some copies that the title is not "For Metellus," but "What he wrote to Metellus;" whereas the speech is delivered in the name of Caesar, vindicating Metellus and himself from the aspersions cast upon them by their common defamers. The speech addressed "To his soldiers in Spain," Augustus considers likewise as spurious. We meet with two under this title; one made, as is pretended, in the first battle, and the other in the last; at which time, Asinius Pollio says, he had not leisure to address the soldiers, on account of the suddenness of the enemy's attack.

LVI. He has likewise left Commentaries of his own actions both in the war in Gaul, and in the civil war with Pompey; for the author of the Alexandrian, African, and Spanish wars is not known with any certainty. Some think they are the production of Oppius, and some of Hirtius; the latter of whom composed the last book, which is imperfect, of the Gallic war. Of Caesar's Commentaries, Cicero, in his Brutus, speaks thus: "He wrote his Commentaries in a manner deserving of great approbation: they are plain, precise, and elegant, without any affectation of rhetorical ornament. In having thus prepared materials for others who might be inclined to write his history, he may perhaps have encouraged some silly creatures to enter upon such a work, who will needs be dressing up his actions in all the extravagance a (37) bombast; but he has discouraged wise men from ever attempting the subject." Hirtius delivers his opinion of these Commentaries in the following terms: "So great is the approbation with which they are universally perused, that, instead of rousing, he seems to have precluded, the efforts of any future historian. Yet, with respect to this work, we have more reason to admire him than others; for they only know how well and correctly he has written, but we know, likewise, how easily and quickly he did it." Pollio Asinius thinks that they were not drawn up with much care, or with a due regard to truth; for he insinuates that Caesar was too hasty of belief in regard to what was performed by others under his orders; and that, he has not given a very faithful account of his own acts, either by design, or through defect of memory; expressing at the same time an opinion that Caesar intended a new and more correct edition. He has left behind him likewise two books on Analogy, with the same number under the title of Anti-Cato, and a poem entitled The Itinerary. Of these books, he composed the first two in his passage over the Alps, as he was returning to the army after making his circuit in Hither-Gaul; the second work about the time of the battle of Munda; and the last during the four-and-twenty days he employed in his journey from Rome to Farther-Spain. There are extant some letters of his to the senate, written in a manner never practised by any before him; for they are distinguished into pages in the form of a memorandum book whereas the consuls and commanders till then, used constantly in their letters to continue the line quite across the sheet, without any folding or distinction of pages. There are extant likewise some letters from him to Cicero, and others to his friends, concerning his domestic affairs; in which, if there was occasion for secrecy, he wrote in cyphers; that is, he used the alphabet in such a manner, that not a single word could be made out. The way to decipher those epistles was to substitute the fourth for the first letter, as d for a, and so for the other letters respectively. Some things likewise pass under his name, said to have been written by him when a boy, or a very young man; as the Encomium of Hercules, a tragedy entitled Oedipus, and a collection of Apophthegms; all which Augustus forbad to be published, in a short and plain letter to Pompeius Macer, who was employed by him in the arrangement of his libraries.

(38) LVII. He was perfect in the use of arms, an accomplished rider, and able to endure fatigue beyond all belief. On a march, he used to go at the head of his troops, sometimes on horseback, but oftener on foot, with his head bare in all kinds of weather. He would travel post in a light carriage 79 without baggage, at the rate of a hundred miles a day; and if he was stopped by floods in the rivers, he swam across, or floated on skins inflated with wind, so that he often anticipated intelligence of his movements. 80

LVIII. In his expeditions, it is difficult to say whether his caution or his daring was most conspicuous. He never marched his army by roads which were exposed to ambuscades, without having previously examined the nature of the ground by his scouts. Nor did he cross over to Britain, before he had carefully examined, in person 81, the navigation, the harbours, and the most convenient point of landing in the island. When intelligence was brought to him of the siege of his camp in Germany, he made his way to his troops, through the enemy's stations, in a Gaulish dress. He crossed the sea from Brundisium and Dyrrachium, in the winter, through the midst of the enemy's fleets; and the troops, under orders to join him, being slow in their movements, notwithstanding repeated messages to hurry them, but to no purpose, he at last went privately, and alone, aboard a small vessel in the night time, with his head muffled up; nor did he make himself known, or suffer the master to put about, although the wind blew strong against them, until they were ready to sink.

LIX. He was never deterred from any enterprise, nor retarded in the prosecution of it, by superstition 82. When a victim, which he was about to offer in sacrifice, made its (39) escape, he did not therefore defer his expedition against Scipio and Juba. And happening to fall, upon stepping out of the ship, he gave a lucky turn to the omen, by exclaiming, "I hold thee fast, Africa." To chide the prophecies which were spread abroad, that the name of the Scipios was, by the decrees of fate, fortunate and invincible in that province, he retained in the camp a profligate wretch, of the family of the Cornelii, who, on account of his scandalous life, was surnamed Salutio.

LX. He not only fought pitched battles, but made sudden attacks when an opportunity offered; often at the end of a march, and sometimes during the most violent storms, when nobody could imagine he would stir. Nor was he ever backward in fighting, until towards the end of his life. He then was of opinion, that the oftener he had been crowned with success, the less he ought to expose himself to new hazards; and that nothing he could gain by a victory would compensate for what he might lose by a miscarriage. He never defeated the enemy without driving them from their camp; and giving them no time to rally their forces. When the issue of a battle was doubtful, he sent away all the horses, and his own first, that having no means of flight, they might be under the greater necessity of standing their ground.

LXI. He rode a very remarkable horse, with feet almost like those of a man, the hoofs being divided in such a manner as to have some resemblance to toes. This horse he had bred himself, and the soothsayers having interpreted these circumstances into an omen that its owner would be master of the world, he brought him up with particular care, and broke him in himself, as the horse would suffer no one else to mount him. A statue of this horse was afterwards erected by Caesar's order before the temple of Venus Genitrix.

LXII. He often rallied his troops, when they were giving way, by his personal efforts; stopping those who fled, keeping others in their ranks, and seizing them by their throat turned them towards the enemy; although numbers were so terrified, that an eagle-bearer 83, thus stopped, made a thrust at him with (40) the spear-head; and another, upon a similar occasion, left the standard in his hand.

LXIII. The following instances of his resolution are equally, and even more remarkable. After the battle of Pharsalia, having sent his troops before him into Asia, as he was passing the straits of the Hellespont in a ferry-boat, he met with Lucius Cassius, one of the opposite party, with ten ships of war; and so far from endeavouring to escape, he went alongside his ship, and calling upon him to surrender, Cassius humbly gave him his submission.

LXIV. At Alexandria, in the attack of a bridge, being forced by a sudden sally of the enemy into a boat, and several others hurrying in with him, he leaped into the sea, and saved himself by swimming to the next ship, which lay at the distance of two hundred paces; holding up his left hand out of the water, for fear of wetting some papers which he held in it; and pulling his general's cloak after him with his teeth, lest it should fall into the hands of the enemy.

LXV. He never valued a soldier for his moral conduct or his means, but for his courage only; and treated his troops with a mixture of severity and indulgence; for he did not always keep a strict hand over them, but only when the enemy was near. Then indeed he was so strict a disciplinarian, that he would give no notice of a march or a battle until the moment of action, in order that the troops might hold themselves in readiness for any sudden movement; and he would frequently draw them out of the camp without any necessity for it, especially in rainy weather, and upon holy-days. Sometimes, giving them orders not to lose sight of him, he would suddenly depart by day or by night, and lengthen the marches in order to tire them out, as they followed him at a distance.

LXVI. When at any time his troops were dispirited by reports of the great force of the enemy, he rallied their courage; not by denying the truth of what was said, or by diminishing the facts, but, on the contrary, by exaggerating every particular. (41) Accordingly, when his troops were in great alarm at the expected arrival of king Juba, he called them together, and said, "I have to inform you that in a very few days the king will be here, with ten legions, thirty thousand horse, a hundred thousand light-armed foot, and three hundred elephants. Let none of you, therefore, presume to make further enquiry, or indulge in conjectures, but take my word for what I tell you, which I have from undoubted intelligence; otherwise I shall put them aboard an old crazy vessel, and leave them exposed to the mercy of the winds, to be transported to some other country."

LXVII. He neither noticed all their transgressions, nor punished them according to strict rule. But for deserters and mutineers he made the most diligent enquiry, and their punishment was most severe: other delinquencies he would connive at. Sometimes, after a great battle ending in victory, he would grant them a relaxation from all kinds of duty, and leave them to revel at pleasure; being used to boast, "that his soldiers fought nothing the worse for being well oiled." In his speeches, he never addressed them by the title of "Soldiers," but by the kinder phrase of "Fellow-soldiers;" and kept them in such splendid order, that their arms were ornamented with silver and gold, not merely for parade, but to render the soldiers more resolute to save them in battle, and fearful of losing them. He loved his troops to such a degree, that when he heard of the defeat of those under Titurius, he neither cut his hair nor shaved his beard, until he had revenged it upon the enemy; by which means he engaged their devoted affection, and raised their valour to the highest pitch.

LXVIII. Upon his entering on the civil war, the centurions of every legion offered, each of them, to maintain a horseman at his own expense, and the whole army agreed to serve gratis, without either corn or pay; those amongst them who were rich, charging themselves with the maintenance of the poor. No one of them, during the whole course of the war, deserted to the enemy; and many of those who were made prisoners, though they were offered their lives, upon condition of bearing arms against him, refused to accept the terms. They endured want, and other hardships, not only (42) when they were besieged themselves, but when they besieged others, to such a degree, that Pompey, when blocked up in the neighbourhood of Dyrrachium, upon seeing a sort of bread made of an herb, which they lived upon, said, "I have to do with wild beasts," and ordered it immediately to be taken away; because, if his troops should see it, their spirit might be broken by perceiving the endurance and determined resolution of the enemy. With what bravery they fought, one instance affords sufficient proof; which is, that after an unsuccessful engagement at Dyrrachium, they called for punishment; insomuch that their general found it more necessary to comfort than to punish them. In other battles, in different quarters, they defeated with ease immense armies of the enemy, although they were much inferior to them in number. In short, one cohort of the sixth legion held out a fort against four legions belonging to Pompey, during several hours; being almost every one of them wounded by the vast number of arrows discharged against them, and of which there were found within the ramparts a hundred and thirty thousand. This is no way surprising, when we consider the conduct of some individuals amongst them; such as that of Cassius Scaeva, a centurion, or Caius Acilius, a common soldier, not to speak of others. Scaeva, after having an eye struck out, being run through the thigh and the shoulder, and having his shield pierced in an hundred and twenty places, maintained obstinately the guard of the gate of a fort, with the command of which he was intrusted. Acilius, in the seafight at Marseilles, having seized a ship of the enemy's with his right hand, and that being cut off, in imitation of that memorable instance of resolution in Cynaegirus amongst the Greeks, boarded the enemy's ship, bearing down all before him with the boss of his shield.

LXIX. They never once mutinied during all the ten years of the Gallic war, but were sometimes refractory in the course of the civil war. However, they always returned quickly to their duty, and that not through the indulgence, but in submission to the authority, of their general; for he never yielded to them when they were insubordinate, but constantly resisted their demands. He disbanded the whole ninth legion with ignominy at Placentia, although Pompey was still in arms, and would (43) not receive them again into his service, until they had not only made repeated and humble entreaties, but until the ringleaders in the mutiny were punished.

LXX. When the soldiers of the tenth legion at Rome demanded their discharge and rewards for their service, with violent threats and no small danger to the city, although the war was then raging in Africa, he did not hesitate, contrary to the advice of his friends, to meet the legion, and disband it. But addressing them by the title of "Quirites," instead of "Soldiers," he by this single word so thoroughly brought them round and changed their determination, that they immediately cried out, they were his "soldiers," and followed him to Africa, although he had refused their service. He nevertheless punished the most mutinous among them, with the loss of a third of their share in the plunder, and the land destined for them.

LXXI. In the service of his clients, while yet a young man, he evinced great zeal and fidelity. He defended the cause of a noble youth, Masintha, against king Hiempsal, so strenuously, that in a scuffle which took place upon the occasion, he seized by the beard the son of king Juba; and upon Masintha's being declared tributary to Hiempsal, while the friends of the adverse party were violently carrying him off, he immediately rescued him by force, kept him concealed in his house a long time, and when, at the expiration of his praetorship, he went to Spain, he took him away in his litter, in the midst of his lictors bearing the fasces, and others who had come to attend and take leave of him.

LXXII. He always treated his friends with such kindness and good-nature, that when Caius Oppius, in travelling with him through a forest, was suddenly taken ill, he resigned to him the only place there was to shelter them at night, and lay upon the ground in the open air. When he had placed himself at the head of affairs, he advanced some of his faithful adherents, though of mean extraction, to the highest offices; and when he was censured for this partiality, he openly said, "Had I been assisted by robbers and cut-throats in the defence of my honour, I should have made them the same recompense."

(44) LXXIII. The resentment he entertained against any one was never so implacable that he did not very willingly renounce it when opportunity offered. Although Caius Memmius had published some extremely virulent speeches against him, and he had answered him with equal acrimony, yet he afterwards assisted him with his vote and interest, when he stood candidate for the consulship. When C. Calvus, after publishing some scandalous epigrams upon him, endeavoured to effect a reconciliation by the intercession of friends, he wrote to him, of his own accord, the first letter. And when Valerius Catullus, who had, as he himself observed, fixed such a stain upon his character in his verses upon Mamurra as never could be obliterated, he begged his pardon, invited him to supper the same day; and continued to take up his lodging with his father occasionally, as he had been accustomed to do.

LXXIV. His temper was also naturally averse to severity in retaliation. After he had captured the pirates, by whom he had been taken, having sworn that he would crucify them, he did so indeed; but he first ordered their throats to be cut 84. He could never bear the thought of doing any harm to Cornelius Phagitas, who had dogged him in the night when he was sick and a fugitive, with the design of carrying him to Sylla, and from whose hands he had escaped with some difficulty by giving him a bribe. Philemon, his amanuensis, who had promised his enemies to poison him, he put to death without torture. When he was summoned as a witness against Publicus Clodius, his wife Pompeia's gallant, who was prosecuted for the profanation of religious ceremonies, he declared he knew nothing of the affair, although his mother Aurelia, and his sister Julia, gave the court an exact and full account of the circumstances. And being asked why then he had divorced his wife? "Because," he said, "my family should not only be free from guilt, but even from the suspicion of it."

LXXV. Both in his administration and his conduct towards the vanquished party in the civil war, he showed a wonderful moderation and clemency. For while Pompey declared that he would consider those as enemies who did not take arms in defence of the republic, he desired it to be understood, that he (45) should regard those who remained neuter as his friends. With regard to all those to whom he had, on Pompey's recommendation, given any command in the army, he left them at perfect liberty to go over to him, if they pleased. When some proposals were made at Ileria 85 for a surrender, which gave rise to a free communication between the two camps, and Afranius and Petreius, upon a sudden change of resolution, had put to the sword all Caesar's men who were found in the camp, he scorned to imitate the base treachery which they had practised against himself. On the field of Pharsalia, he called out to the soldiers "to spare their fellow-citizens," and afterwards gave permission to every man in his army to save an enemy. None of them, so far as appears, lost their lives but in battle, excepting only Afranius, Faustus, and young Lucius Caesar; and it is thought that even they were put to death without his consent. Afranius and Faustus had borne arms against him, after obtaining their pardon; and Lucius Caesar had not only in the most cruel manner destroyed with fire and sword his freed-men and slaves, but cut to pieces the wild beasts which he had prepared for the entertainment of the people. And finally, a little before his death, he permitted all whom he had not before pardoned, to return into Italy, and to bear offices both civil and military. He even replaced the statues of Sylla and Pompey, which had been thrown down by the populace. And after this, whatever was devised or uttered, he chose rather to check than to punish it. Accordingly, having detected certain conspiracies and nocturnal assemblies, he went no farther than to intimate by a proclamation that he knew of them; and as to those who indulged themselves in the liberty of reflecting severely upon him, he only warned them in a public speech not to persist in their offence. He bore with great moderation a virulent libel written against him by Aulus Caecinna, and the abusive lampoons of Pitholaus, most highly reflecting on his reputation.

LXXVI. His other words and actions, however, so far outweigh all his good qualities, that it is thought he abused his power, and was justly cut off. For he not only obtained excessive honours, such as the consulship every year, the dictatorship for life, and the censorship, but also the title of emperor 86, (46) and the surname of FATHER OF HIS COUNTRY 87, besides having his statue amongst the kings 88, and a lofty couch in the theatre. He even suffered some honours to be decreed to him, which were unbefitting the most exalted of mankind;

such as a gilded chair of state in the senate-house and on his tribunal, a consecrated chariot, and banners in the Circensian procession, temples, altars, statues among the gods, a bed of state in the temples, a priest, and a college of priests dedicated to himself, like those of Pan; and that one of the months should be called by his name. There were, indeed, no honours which he did not either assume himself, or grant to others, at his will and pleasure. In his third and fourth consulship, he used only the title of the office, being content with the power of dictator, which was conferred upon him with the consulship; and in both years he substituted other consuls in his room, during the three last months; so that in the intervals he held no assemblies of the people, for the election of magistrates, excepting only tribunes and ediles of the people; and appointed officers, under the name of praefects, instead of the praetors, to administer the affairs of the city during his absence. The office of consul having become vacant, by the sudden death of one of the consuls the day before the calends of January [the 1st Jan.], he conferred it on a person who requested it of him, for a few hours. Assuming the same licence, and regardless of the customs of his country, he appointed magistrates to hold their offices for terms of years. He granted the insignia of the consular dignity to ten persons of pretorian rank. He admitted into the senate some men who had been made free of the city, and even natives of Gaul, who were semi-barbarians. (47) He likewise appointed to the management of the mint, and the public revenue of the state, some servants of his own household; and entrusted the command of three legions, which he left at Alexandria, to an old catamite of his, the son of his freedman Rufinus.

LXXVII. He was guilty of the same extravagance in the language he publicly used, as Titus Ampius informs us; according to whom he said, "The republic is nothing but a name, without substance or reality. Sylla was an ignorant fellow to abdicate the dictatorship. Men ought to consider what is becoming when they talk with me, and look upon what I say as a law." To such a pitch of arrogance did he proceed, that when a soothsayer announced to him the unfavourable omen, that the entrails of a victim offered for sacrifice were without a heart, he said, "The entrails will be more favourable when I please; and it ought not to be regarded as a prodigy that a beast should be found wanting a heart."

LXXVIII. But what brought upon him the greatest odium, and was thought an unpardonable insult, was his receiving the whole body of the conscript fathers sitting, before the temple of Venus Genitrix, when they waited upon him with a number of decrees, conferring on him the highest dignities. Some say that, on his attempting to rise, he was held down by Cornelius Balbus; others, that he did not attempt to rise at all, but frowned on Caius Trebatius, who suggested to him that he should stand up to receive the senate. This behaviour appeared the more intolerable in him, because, when one of the tribunes of the people, Pontius Aquila, would not rise up to him, as he passed by the tribunes' seat during his triumph, he was so much offended, that he cried out, "Well then, you tribune, Aquila, oust me from the government." And for some days afterwards, he never promised a favour to any person, without this proviso, "if Pontus Aquila will give me leave."

LXXIX. To this extraordinary mark of contempt for the senate, he added another affront still more outrageous. For when, after the sacred rites of the Latin festival, he was returning home, amidst the immoderate and unusual acclamations (48) of the people, a man in the crowd put a laurel crown, encircled with a white fillet 89 , on one of his statues; upon which, the tribunes of the people, Epidius Marullus, and Caesetius Flavus, ordered the fillet to be removed from the crown, and the man to be taken to prison. Caesar, being much concerned either that the idea of royalty had been suggested to so little purpose, or, as was said, that he was thus deprived of the merit of refusing it, reprimanded the tribunes very severely, and dismissed them from their office. From that day forward, he was never able to wipe off the scandal of affecting the name of king, although he replied to the populace, when they saluted him by that title, "I am Caesar, and no king." And at the feast of the Lupercalia 90 , when the consul Antony placed a crown upon his head in the rostra several times, he as often put it away, and sent it to the Capitol for Jupiter, the Best and the Greatest. A report was very current, that he had a design of withdrawing to Alexandria or Ilium, whither he proposed to transfer the imperial power, to drain Italy by new levies, and to leave the government of the city to be administered by his friends. To this report it was added, that in the next meeting of the senate, Lucius Cotta, one of the fifteen 91 , would make a motion, that as there was in the Sibylline books a prophecy, that the Parthians would never be subdued but by a king, Caesar should have that title conferred upon him.

LXXX. For this reason the conspirators precipitated the execution of their design 92, that they might not be obliged to give their assent to the proposal. Instead, therefore, of caballing any longer separately, in small parties, they now united their counsels; the people themselves being dissatisfied with the present state of affairs, both privately and publicly (49) condemning the tyranny under which they lived, and calling on patriots to assert their cause against the usurper. Upon the admission of foreigners into the senate, a hand-bill was posted up in these words: "A good deed! let no one shew a new senator the way to the house." These verses were likewise currently repeated:

*The Gauls he dragged in triumph through the town,*
*Caesar has brought into the senate-house,*
*And changed their plaids 93 for the patrician gown.*
*Gallos Caesar in triumphum ducit: iidem in curiam*
*Galli braccas deposuerunt, latum clavum sumpserunt.*

When Quintus Maximus, who had been his deputy in the consulship for the last three months, entered the theatre, and the lictor, according to custom, bid the people take notice who was coming, they all cried out, "He is no consul." After the removal of Caesetius and Marullus from their office, they were found to have a great many votes at the next election of consuls. Some one wrote under the statue of Lucius Brutus, "Would you were now alive!" and under the statue of Caesar himself these lines:

*Because he drove from Rome the royal race,*
*Brutus was first made consul in their place.*
*This man, because he put the consuls down,*
*Has been rewarded with a royal crown.*
*Brutus, quia reges ejecit, consul primus factus est:*
*Hic, quia consules ejecit, rex postremo factus est.*

About sixty persons were engaged in the conspiracy against him, of whom Caius Cassius, and Marcus and Decimus Brutus were the chief. It was at first debated amongst them, whether they should attack him in the Campus Martius when he was taking the votes of the tribes, and some of them should throw him off the bridge, whilst others should be ready to stab him upon his fall; or else in the Via Sacra, or at the entrance of the theatre. But after public notice had been given by proclamation for the senate to assemble upon the ides of March [15th March], in the senate-house built by Pompey, they approved both of the time and place, as most fitting for their purpose.

LXXXI. Caesar had warning given him of his fate by indubitable (50) omens. A few months before, when the colonists settled at Capua, by virtue of the Julian law, were demolishing some old sepulchres, in building country-houses, and were the more eager at the work, because they discovered certain vessels of antique workmanship, a tablet of brass was found in a tomb, in which Capys, the founder of Capua, was said to have been buried, with an inscription in the Greek language to this effect "Whenever the bones of Capys come to be discovered, a descendant of Iulus will be slain by the hands of his kinsmen, and his death revenged by fearful disasters throughout Italy." Lest any person should regard this anecdote as a fabulous or silly invention, it was circulated upon the authority of Caius Balbus, an intimate friend of Caesar's. A few days likewise before his death, he was informed that the horses, which, upon his crossing the Rubicon, he had consecrated, and turned loose to graze without a keeper, abstained entirely from eating, and shed floods of tears. The soothsayer Spurinna, observing certain ominous appearances in a sacrifice which he was offering, advised him to beware of some danger, which threatened to befall him before the ides of March were past. The day before the ides, birds of various kinds from a neighbouring grove, pursuing a wren which flew into Pompey's senate-house 94, with a sprig of laurel in its beak, tore it in pieces. Also, in the night on which the day of his murder dawned, he dreamt at one time that he was soaring above the clouds, and, at another, that he had joined hands with Jupiter. His wife Calpurnia fancied in her sleep that the pediment of the house was falling down, and her husband stabbed on her bosom; immediately upon which the chamber doors flew open. On account of these omens, as well as his infirm health, he was in some doubt whether he should not remain at home, and defer to some other opportunity the business which he intended to propose to the senate; but Decimus Brutus advising him not to disappoint the senators, who were numerously assembled, and waited his coming, he was prevailed upon to go, and accordingly (51) set forward about the fifth hour. In his way, some person having thrust into his hand a paper, warning him against the plot, he mixed it with some other documents which he held in his left hand, intending to read it at leisure. Victim after victim was slain, without any favourable appearances in the entrails; but still, disregarding all omens, he entered the senate-house, laughing at Spurinna as a false prophet, because the ides of March were come, without any mischief having befallen him. To which the soothsayer replied, "They are come, indeed, but not past."

LXXXII. When he had taken his seat, the conspirators stood round him, under colour of paying their compliments; and immediately Tullius Cimber, who had engaged to commence the assault, advancing nearer than the rest, as if he had some favour to request, Caesar made signs that he should defer his petition to some other time. Tullius immediately seized him by the toga, on both shoulders; at which Caesar crying out, "Violence is meant!" one of the Cassii wounded him a little below the throat. Caesar seized him by the arm, and ran it through with his style 95 ; and endeavouring to rush forward was stopped by another wound. Finding himself now attacked on all hands with naked poniards, he wrapped the toga 96 about his head, and at the same moment drew the skirt round his legs with his left hand, that he might fall more decently with the lower part of his body covered. He was stabbed with three and twenty wounds, uttering a groan only, but no cry, at the first wound; although some authors relate, that when Marcus Brutus fell upon him, he exclaimed, "What! art thou, too, one of them? Thou, my son!" 97 The whole assembly instantly (52) dispersing, he lay for some time after he expired, until three of his slaves laid the body on a litter, and carried it home, with one arm hanging down over the side. Among so many wounds, there was none that was mortal, in the opinion of the surgeon Antistius, except the second, which he received in the breast. The conspirators meant to drag his body into the Tiber as soon as they had killed him; to confiscate his estate, and rescind all his enactments; but they were deterred by fear of Mark Antony, and Lepidus, Caesar's master of the horse, and abandoned their intentions.

LXXXIII. At the instance of Lucius Piso, his father-in-law, his will was opened and read in Mark Antony's house. He had made it on the ides [13th] of the preceding September, at his Lavican villa, and committed it to the custody of the chief of the Vestal Virgins. Quintus Tubero informs us, that in all the wills he had signed, from the time of his first consulship to the breaking out of the civil war, Cneius Pompey was appointed his heir, and that this had been publicly notified to the army. But in his last will, he named three heirs, the grandsons of his sisters; namely, Caius Octavius for three fourths of his estate, and Lucius Pinarius and Quintus Pedius for the remaining fourth. Other heirs [in remainder] were named at the close of the will, in which he also adopted Caius Octavius, who was to assume his name, into his family; and nominated most of those who were concerned in his death among the guardians of his son, if he should have any; as well as Decimus Brutus amongst his heirs of the second order. Be bequeathed to the Roman people his gardens near the Tiber, and three hundred sesterces each man.

LXXXIV. Notice of his funeral having been solemnly proclaimed, a pile was erected in the Campus Martius, near the tomb of his daughter Julia; and before the Rostra was placed a gilded tabernacle, on the model of the temple of Venus Genitrix; within which was an ivory bed, covered with purple and cloth of gold. At the head was a trophy, with the [bloodstained] robe in which he was slain. It being considered that the whole day would not suffice for carrying the funeral oblations in solemn procession before the corpse, directions were given for every one, without regard to order, to carry them from the city into the Campus Martius, by what way they pleased. To raise pity and indignation for his murder, in the plays acted at the funeral, a passage was sung from Pacuvius's tragedy, entitled, "The Trial for Arms:"

> *That ever I, unhappy man, should save*
> *Wretches, who thus have brought me to the grave!* 98_

And some lines also from Attilius's tragedy of "Electra," to the same effect. Instead of a funeral panegyric, the consul Antony ordered a herald to proclaim to the people the decree of the senate, in which they had bestowed upon him all honours, divine and human; with the oath by which they had engaged themselves for the defence of his person; and to these he added only a few words of his own. The magistrates and others who had formerly filled the highest offices, carried the bier from the Rostra into the Forum. While some proposed that the body should be burnt in the sanctuary of the temple of Jupiter

Capitolinus, and others in Pompey's senate-house; on a sudden, two men, with swords by their sides, and spears in their hands, set fire to the bier with lighted torches. The throng around immediately heaped upon it dry faggots, the tribunals and benches of the adjoining courts, and whatever else came to hand. Then the musicians and players stripped off the dresses they wore on the present occasion, taken from the wardrobe of his triumph at spectacles, rent them, and threw them into the flames. The legionaries, also, of his (54) veteran bands, cast in their armour, which they had put on in honour of his funeral. Most of the ladies did the same by their ornaments, with the bullae 99 , and mantles of their children. In this public mourning there joined a multitude of foreigners, expressing their sorrow according to the fashion of their respective countries; but especially the Jews 100 , who for several nights together frequented the spot where the body was burnt.

LXXXV. The populace ran from the funeral, with torches in their hands, to the houses of Brutus and Cassius, and were repelled with difficulty. Going in quest of Cornelius Cinna, who had in a speech, the day before, reflected severely upon Caesar, and mistaking for him Helvius Cinna, who happened to fall into their hands, they murdered the latter, and carried his head about the city on the point of a spear. They afterwards erected in the Forum a column of Numidian marble, formed of one stone nearly twenty feet high, and inscribed upon it these words, TO THE FATHER OF HIS COUNTRY. At this column they continued for a long time to offer sacrifices, make vows, and decide controversies, in which they swore by Caesar.

LXXXVI. Some of Caesar's friends entertained a suspicion, that he neither desired nor cared to live any longer, on account of his declining health; and for that reason slighted all the omens of religion, and the warnings of his friends. Others are of opinion, that thinking himself secure in the late decree of the senate, and their oaths, he dismissed his Spanish guards who attended him with drawn swords. Others again suppose, that he chose rather to face at once the dangers which threatened him on all sides, than to be for ever on the watch against them. Some tell us that he used to say, the commonwealth was more interested in the safety of his person than himself: for that he had for some time been satiated with power and glory; but that the commonwealth, if any thing should befall him, would have no rest, and, involved in another civil war, would be in a worse state than before.

(55) LXXXVII. This, however, was generally admitted, that his death was in many respects such as he would have chosen. For, upon reading the account delivered by Xenophon, how Cyrus in his last illness gave instructions respecting his funeral, Caesar deprecated a lingering death, and wished that his own might be sudden and speedy. And the day before he died, the conversation at supper, in the house of Marcus Lepidus, turning upon what was the most eligible way of dying, he gave his opinion in favour of a death that is sudden and unexpected.

LXXXVIII. He died in the fifty-sixth year of his age, and was ranked amongst the Gods, not only by a formal decree, but in the belief of the vulgar. For during the first games which Augustus, his heir, consecrated to his memory, a comet blazed for seven days together, rising always about eleven o'clock; and it was supposed to be the soul of Caesar, now received into heaven: for which reason, likewise, he is represented on his statue with a star on his brow. The senate-house in which he was slain, was ordered to be shut up 101, and a decree made that the ides of March should be called parricidal, and the senate should never more assemble on that day.

LXXXIX. Scarcely any of those who were accessary to his murder, survived him more than three years, or died a natural death 102. They were all condemned by the senate: some were taken off by one accident, some by another. Part of them perished at sea, others fell in battle; and some slew themselves with the same poniard with which they had stabbed Caesar 103.

(56) 104 The termination of the civil war between Caesar and Pompey forms a new epoch in the Roman History, at which a Republic, which had subsisted with unrivalled glory during a period of about four hundred and sixty years, relapsed into a state of despotism, whence it never more could emerge. So sudden a transition from prosperity to the ruin of public freedom, without the intervention of any foreign enemy, excites a reasonable conjecture, that the constitution in which it could take place, however vigorous in appearance, must have lost that soundness of political health which had enabled it to endure through so many ages. A short view of its preceding state, and of that

in which it was at the time of the revolution now mentioned, will best ascertain the foundation of such a conjecture.

Though the Romans, upon the expulsion of Tarquin, made an essential change in the political form of the state, they did not carry their detestation of regal authority so far as to abolish the religious institutions of Numa Pompilius, the second of their kings, according to which, the priesthood, with all the influence annexed to that order, was placed in the hands of the aristocracy. By this wise policy a restraint was put upon the fickleness and violence of the people in matters of government, and a decided superiority given to the Senate both in the deliberative and executive parts of administration. This advantage was afterwards indeed diminished by the creation of Tribunes of the people; a set of men whose ambition often embroiled the Republic in civil dissensions, and who at last abused their authority to such a degree, that they became instruments of aggrandizement to any leading men in the state who could purchase their friendship. In general, however, the majority of the Tribunes being actuated by views which comprehended the interests of the multitude, rather than those of individuals, they did not so much endanger the liberty, as they interrupted the tranquillity, of the public; and when the occasional commotions subsided, there remained no permanent ground for the establishment of personal usurpation.

In every government, an object of the last importance to the peace and welfare of society is the morals of the people; and in proportion as a community is enlarged by propagation, or the accession of a multitude of new members, a more strict attention is requisite to guard against that dissolution of manners to which a crowded and extensive capital has a natural tendency. Of this (57) the Romans became sensible in the growing state of the Republic. In the year of the City 312, two magistrates were first created for taking an account of the number of the people, and the value of their estates; and soon after, they were invested with the authority not only of inspecting the morals of individuals, but of inflicting public censure for any licentiousness of conduct, or violation of decency. Thus both the civil and religious institutions concurred to restrain the people within the bounds of good order and obedience to the laws; at the same time that the frugal life of the ancient Romans proved a strong security against those vices which operate most effectually towards sapping the foundations of a state.

But in the time of Julius Caesar the barriers of public liberty were become too weak to restrain the audacious efforts of ambitious and desperate men. The veneration for the constitution, usually a powerful check to treasonable designs, had been lately violated by the usurpations of Marius and Sylla. The salutary terrors of religion no longer predominated over the consciences of men. The shame of public censure was extinguished in general depravity. An eminent historian, who lived at that time, informs us, that venality universally prevailed amongst the Romans; and a writer who flourished soon after, observes, that luxury and dissipation had encumbered almost all so much with debt, that they beheld with a degree of complacency the prospect of civil war and confusion.

The extreme degree of profligacy at which the Romans were now arrived is in nothing more evident, than that this age gave birth to the most horrible conspiracy which occurs in the annals of humankind, viz. that of Catiline. This was not the project of a few desperate and abandoned individuals, but of a number of men of the most illustrious rank in the state; and it appears beyond doubt, that Julius Caesar was accessary to the design, which was no less than to extirpate the Senate, divide amongst themselves both the public and private treasures, and set Rome on fire. The causes which prompted to this tremendous project, it is generally admitted, were luxury, prodigality, irreligion, a total corruption of manners, and above all, as the immediate cause, the pressing necessity in which the conspirators were involved by their extreme dissipation.

The enormous debt in which Caesar himself was early involved, countenances an opinion that his anxiety to procure the province of Gaul proceeded chiefly from this cause. But during nine years in which he held that province, he acquired such riches as must have rendered him, without competition, the most opulent person in the state. If nothing more, therefore, than a (58) splendid establishment had been the object of his pursuit, he had attained to the summit of his wishes. But when we find him persevering in a plan of aggrandizement beyond this period of his fortunes, we can ascribe his conduct to no other motive than that of outrageous ambition. He projected the building of a new Forum at Rome, for the ground only of which he was to pay 800,000 pounds; he raised legions in Gaul at his own charges: he promised such entertainments to the people as had never been known at Rome from the foundation of the city. All these circumstances evince some latent design of procuring such a popularity as might give him an uncontrolled influence in the management of public affairs. Pompey, we are told, was wont to say, that Caesar not being able, with all his riches, to fulfil the promises which he had made, wished to throw everything into confusion. There may have been some foundation for this remark: but the opinion of Cicero is more probable, that Caesar's mind was seduced with the temptations of chimerical glory. It is observable that neither Cicero nor Pompey intimates any suspicion that Caesar was apprehensive of being impeached for his conduct, had he returned to Rome in a private station. Yet, that there was reason for such an apprehension, the positive declaration of L. Domitius leaves little room to doubt: especially when we consider the number of enemies that Caesar had in the Senate, and the coolness of his former friend Pompey ever after the death of Julia. The proposed impeachment was founded upon a notorious charge of prosecuting measures destructive of the interests of the commonwealth, and tending ultimately to an object incompatible with public freedom. Indeed, considering the extreme corruption which prevailed amongst the Romans at this time, it is more than probable that Caesar would have been acquitted of the charge, but at such an expense as must have stripped him of all his riches, and placed him again in a situation ready to attempt a disturbance of the public tranquillity. For it is said, that he purchased the friendship of Curio, at the commencement of the civil war, with a bribe little short of half a million sterling.

    Whatever Caesar's private motive may have been for taking arms against his country, he embarked in an enterprise of a nature the most dangerous: and had Pompey conducted himself in any degree suitable to the reputation which he had formerly acquired, the contest would in all probability have terminated in favour of public freedom. But by dilatory measures in the beginning, by imprudently withdrawing his army from Italy into a distant province, and by not pursuing the advantage he had gained by the vigorous repulse of Caesar's troops in their attack upon his camp, this commander lost every opportunity of extinguishing a war which was to determine the fate, and even the existence, of the Republic. It was accordingly determined on the plains of Pharsalia, where Caesar obtained a victory which was not more decisive than unexpected. He was now no longer amenable either to the tribunal of the Senate or the power of the laws, but triumphed at once over his enemies and the constitution of his country.

It is to the honour of Caesar, that when he had obtained the supreme power, he exercised it with a degree of moderation beyond what was generally expected by those who had fought on the side of the Republic. Of his private life either before or after this period, little is transmitted in history. Henceforth, however, he seems to have lived chiefly at Rome, near which he had a small villa, upon an eminence, commanding a beautiful prospect. His time was almost entirely occupied with public affairs, in the management of which, though he employed many agents, he appears to have had none in the character of actual minister. He was in general easy of access: but Cicero, in a letter to a friend, complains of having been treated with the indignity of waiting a considerable time amongst a crowd in an anti-chamber, before he could have an audience. The elevation of Caesar placed him not above discharging reciprocally the social duties in the intercourse of life. He returned the visits of those who waited upon him, and would sup at their houses. At table, and in the use of wine, he was habitually temperate. Upon the whole, he added nothing to his own happiness by all the dangers, the fatigues, and the perpetual anxiety which he had incurred in the pursuit of unlimited power. His health was greatly impaired: his former cheerfulness of temper, though not his magnanimity, appears to have forsaken him; and we behold in his fate a memorable example of illustrious talents rendered, by inordinate ambition, destructive to himself, and irretrievably pernicious to his country.

From beholding the ruin of the Roman Republic, after intestine divisions, and the distractions of civil war, it will afford some relief to take a view of the progress of literature, which flourished even during those calamities.

The commencement of literature in Rome is to be dated from the reduction of the Grecian States, when the conquerors imported into their own country the valuable productions of the Greek language, and the first essay of Roman genius was in dramatic composition. Livius Andronicus, who flourished about 240 years before the Christian aera, formed the Fescennine verses into a kind of regular drama, upon the model of the Greeks. He was followed some time after by Ennius, who, besides dramatic and other compositions, (60) wrote the annals of the Roman Republic in heroic verse. His style, like that of Andronicus, was rough and unpolished, in conformity to the language of those times; but for grandeur of sentiment and energy of expression, he was admired by the greatest poets in the subsequent ages. Other writers of distinguished reputation in the dramatic department were Naevius, Pacuvius, Plautus, Afranius, Caecilius, Terence, Accius, etc. Accius and Pacuvius are mentioned by Quintilian as writers of extraordinary merit. Of twenty-five comedies written by Plautus, the number transmitted to posterity is nineteen; and of a hundred and eight which Terence is said to have translated from Menander, there now remain only six. Excepting a few inconsiderable fragments, the writings of all the other authors have perished. The early period of Roman literature was distinguished for the introduction of satire by Lucilius, an author celebrated for writing with remarkable ease, but whose compositions, in the opinion of Horace, though Quintilian thinks otherwise, were debased with a mixture of feculency. Whatever may have been their merit, they also have perished, with the works of a number of orators, who adorned the advancing state of letters in the Roman Republic. It is observable, that during this whole period, of near two centuries and a half, there appeared not one historian of eminence sufficient to preserve his name from oblivion.

Julius Caesar himself is one of the most eminent writers of the age in which he lived. His commentaries on the Gallic and Civil Wars are written with a purity, precision, and perspicuity, which command approbation. They are elegant without affectation, and beautiful without ornament. Of the two books which he composed on Analogy, and those under the title of Anti-Cato, scarcely any fragment is preserved; but we may be assured of the justness of the observations on language, which were made by an author so much distinguished by the excellence of his own compositions. His poem entitled The Journey, which was probably an entertaining narrative, is likewise totally lost.

The most illustrious prose writer of this or any other age is M. Tullius Cicero; and as his life is copiously related in biographical works, it will be sufficient to mention his writings. From his earliest years, he applied himself with unremitting assiduity to the cultivation of literature, and, whilst he was yet a boy, wrote a poem, called Glaucus Pontius, which was extant in Plutarch's time. Amongst his juvenile productions was a translation into Latin verse, of Aratus on the Phaenomena of the Heavens; of which many fragments are still extant. He also published a poem of the heroic kind, in honour of his countryman C. Marius, who was born at Arpinum, the birth-place of Cicero. (61) This production was greatly admired by Atticus; and old Scaevola was so much pleased with it, that in an epigram written on the subject, he declares that it would live as long as the Roman name and learning subsisted. From a little specimen which remains of it, describing a memorable omen given to Marina from an oak at Arpinum, there is reason to believe that his poetical genius was scarcely inferior to his oratorical, had it been cultivated with equal industry. He published another poem called Limon, of which Donatus has preserved four lines in the life of Terence, in praise of the elegance and purity of that poet's style. He composed in the Greek language, and in the style and manner of Isocrates, a Commentary or Memoirs of the Transactions of his Consulship. This he sent to Atticus, with a desire, if he approved it, to publish it in Athens and the cities of Greece. He sent a copy of it likewise to Posidonius of Rhodes, and requested of him to undertake the same subject in a more elegant and masterly manner. But the latter returned for answer, that, instead of being encouraged to write by the perusal of his tract, he was quite deterred from attempting it.

Upon the plan of those Memoirs, he afterwards composed a Latin poem in three books, in which he carried down the history to the end of his exile, but did not publish it for several years, from motives of delicacy. The three books were severally inscribed to the three Muses; but of this work there now remain only a few fragments, scattered in different parts of his other writings. He published, about the same time, a collection of the principal speeches which he had made in his consulship, under the title of his Consular Orations. They consisted originally of twelve; but four are entirely lost, and some of the rest are imperfect. He now published also, in Latin verse, a translation of the

Prognostics of Aratus, of which work no more than two or three small fragments now remain. A few years after, he put the last hand to his Dialogues upon the Character and Idea of the perfect Orator. This admirable work remains entire; a monument both of the astonishing industry and transcendent abilities of its author. At his Cuman villa, he next began a Treatise on Politics, or on the best State of a City, and the Duties of a Citizen. He calls it a great and a laborious work, yet worthy of his pains, if he could succeed in it. This likewise was written in the form of a dialogue, in which the speakers were Scipio, Laelius, Philus, Manilius, and other great persons in the former times of the Republic. It was comprised in six books, and survived him for several ages, though it is now unfortunately lost. From the fragments which remain, it appears to have been a masterly production, in which all the important questions in politics and morality were discussed with elegance and accuracy.

(62) Amidst all the anxiety for the interests of the Republic, which occupied the thoughts of this celebrated personage, he yet found leisure to write several philosophical tracts, which still subsist, to the gratification of the literary world. He composed a treatise on the Nature of the Gods, in three books, containing a comprehensive view of religion, faith, oaths, ceremonies, etc. In elucidating this important subject, he not only delivers the opinions of all the philosophers who had written anything concerning it, but weighs and compares attentively all the arguments with each other; forming upon the whole such a rational and perfect system of natural religion, as never before was presented to the consideration of mankind, and approaching nearly to revelation. He now likewise composed in two books, a discourse on Divination, in which he discusses at large all the arguments that may be advanced for and against the actual existence of such a species of knowledge. Like the preceding works, it is written in the form of dialogue, and in which the chief speaker is Laelius. The same period gave birth to his treatise on Old Age, called Cato Major; and to that on Friendship, written also in dialogue, and in which the chief speaker is Laelius. This book, considered merely as an essay, is one of the most entertaining productions of ancient times; but, beheld as a picture drawn from life, exhibiting the real characters and sentiments of men of the first distinction for virtue and wisdom in the Roman Republic, it becomes doubly interesting to every reader

of observation and taste. Cicero now also wrote his discourse on Fate, which was the subject of a conversation with Hirtius, in his villa near Puteoli; and he executed about the same time a translation of Plato's celebrated Dialogue, called Timaeus, on the nature and origin of the universe. He was employing himself also on a history of his own times, or rather of his own conduct; full of free and severe reflections on those who had abused their power to the oppression of the Republic. Dion Cassius says, that he delivered this book sealed up to his son, with strict orders not to read or publish it till after his death; but from this time he never saw his son, and it is probable that he left the work unfinished. Afterwards, however, some copies of it were circulated; from which his commentator, Asconius, has quoted several particulars.

During a voyage which he undertook to Sicily, he wrote his treatise on Topics, or the Art of finding Arguments on any Question. This was an abstract from Aristotle's treatise on the same subject; and though he had neither Aristotle nor any other book to assist him, he drew it up from his memory, and finished it as he sailed along the coast of Calabria. The last (63) work composed by Cicero appears to have been his Offices, written for the use of his son, to whom it is addressed. This treatise contains a system of moral conduct, founded upon the noblest principles of human action, and recommended by arguments drawn from the purest sources of philosophy.

Such are the literary productions of this extraordinary man, whose comprehensive understanding enabled him to conduct with superior ability the most abstruse disquisitions into moral and metaphysical science. Born in an age posterior to Socrates and Plato, he could not anticipate the principles inculcated by those divine philosophers, but he is justly entitled to the praise, not only of having prosecuted with unerring judgment the steps which they trod before him, but of carrying his researches to greater extent into the most difficult regions of philosophy. This too he had the merit to perform, neither in the station of a private citizen, nor in the leisure of academic retirement, but in the bustle of public life, amidst the almost constant exertions of the bar, the employment of the magistrate, the duty of the senator, and the incessant cares of the statesman; through a period likewise chequered with domestic afflictions and fatal commotions in the

Republic. As a philosopher, his mind appears to have been clear, capacious, penetrating, and insatiable of knowledge. As a writer, he was endowed with every talent that could captivate either the judgment or taste. His researches were continually employed on subjects of the greatest utility to mankind, and those often such as extended beyond the narrow bounds of temporal existence. The being of a God, the immortality of the soul, a future state of rewards and punishments, and the eternal distinction of good and evil; these were in general the great objects of his philosophical enquiries, and he has placed them in a more convincing point of view than they ever were before exhibited to the pagan world. The variety and force of the arguments which he advances, the splendour of his diction, and the zeal with which he endeavours to excite the love and admiration of virtue, all conspire to place his character, as a philosophical writer, including likewise his incomparable eloquence, on the summit of human celebrity.

The form of dialogue, so much used by Cicero, he doubtless adopted in imitation of Plato, who probably took the hint of it from the colloquial method of instruction practised by Socrates. In the early stage of philosophical enquiry, this mode of composition was well adapted, if not to the discovery, at least to the confirmation of moral truth; especially as the practice was then not uncommon, for speculative men to converse together on important subjects, for mutual information. In treating of any subject respecting which the different sects of philosophers differed (64) from each other in point of sentiment, no kind of composition could be more happily suited than dialogue, as it gave alternately full scope to the arguments of the various disputants. It required, however, that the writer should exert his understanding with equal impartiality and acuteness on the different sides of the question; as otherwise he might betray a cause under the appearance of defending it. In all the dialogues of Cicero, he manages the arguments of the several disputants in a manner not only the most fair and interesting, but also such as leads to the most probable and rational conclusion.

After enumerating the various tracts composed and published by Cicero, we have now to mention his Letters, which, though not written for publication, deserve to be ranked among the most interesting remains of Roman literature. The number of such as are addressed to different correspondents is considerable, but those to Atticus alone, his confidential friend, amount to upwards of four hundred; among which are many of great length. They are all written in the genuine spirit of the most approved epistolary composition; uniting familiarity with elevation, and ease with elegance. They display in a beautiful light the author's character in the social relations of life; as a warm friend, a zealous patron, a tender husband, an affectionate brother, an indulgent father, and a kind master. Beholding them in a more extensive view, they exhibit an ardent love of liberty and the constitution of his country: they discover a mind strongly actuated with the principles of virtue and reason; and while they abound in sentiments the most judicious and philosophical, they are occasionally blended with the charms of wit, and agreeable effusions of pleasantry. What is likewise no small addition to their merit, they contain much interesting description of private life, with a variety of information relative to public transactions and characters of that age. It appears from Cicero's correspondence, that there was at that time such a number of illustrious Romans, as never before existed in any one period of the Republic. If ever, therefore, the authority of men the most respectable for virtue, rank, and abilities, could have availed to overawe the first attempts at a violation of public liberty, it must have been at this period; for the dignity of the Roman senate was now in the zenith of its splendour.

Cicero has been accused of excessive vanity, and of arrogating to himself an invidious superiority, from his extraordinary talents but whoever peruses his letters to Atticus, must readily acknowledge, that this imputation appears to be destitute of truth. In those excellent productions, though he adduces the strongest arguments for and against any object of consideration, that the (65) most penetrating understanding can suggest, weighs them with each other, and draws from them the most rational conclusions, he yet discovers such a diffidence in his own opinion, that he resigns himself implicitly to the judgment and direction of his friend; a modesty not very compatible with the disposition of the arrogant, who are commonly tenacious of their own opinion, particularly in what relates to any decision of the understanding.

It is difficult to say, whether Cicero appears in his letters more great or amiable: but that he was regarded by his contemporaries in both these lights, and that too in the highest degree, is sufficiently evident. We may thence infer, that the great poets in the subsequent age must have done violence to their own liberality and discernment, when, in compliment to Augustus, whose sensibility would have been wounded by the praises of Cicero, and even by the mention of his name, they have so industriously avoided the subject, as not to afford the most distant intimation that this immortal orator and philosopher had ever existed. Livy however, there is reason to think, did some justice to his memory: but it was not until the race of the Caesars had become extinct, that he received the free and unanimous applause of impartial posterity. Such was the admiration which Quintilian entertained of his writings, that he considered the circumstance or being delighted with them, as an indubitable proof of judgment and taste in literature. Ille se profecisse sciat, cui Cicero valde placebit. 105

In this period is likewise to be placed M. Terentius Varro, the celebrated Roman grammarian, and the Nestor of ancient learning. The first mention made of him is, that he was lieutenant to Pompey in his piratical wars, and obtained in that service a naval crown. In the civil wars he joined the side of the Republic, and was taken by Caesar; by whom he was likewise proscribed, but obtained a remission of the sentence. Of all the ancients, he has acquired the greatest fame for his extensive erudition; and we may add, that he displayed the same industry in communicating, as he had done in collecting it. His works originally amounted to no less than five hundred volumes, which have all perished, except a treatise De Lingua Latina, and one De Re Rustica. Of the former of these, which is addressed to Cicero, three books at the beginning are also lost. It appears from the introduction of the fourth book, that they all related to etymology. The first contained such observations as might be made against it; the second, such as might be made in its favour; and the third, observations upon it. He next proceeds to investigate the origin of (66) Latin words. In the fourth book, he traces those which relate to place; in the fifth, those connected with the idea of time; and in the sixth, the origin of both these classes, as they appear in the writings of the poets. The seventh book is employed on declension; in which the author enters upon a minute and extensive enquiry, comprehending a variety of acute and profound observations on the formation of Latin nouns, and their respective natural declinations from the nominative case. In the eighth, he examines the nature and limits of usage and analogy in language; and in the ninth and last book on the subject, takes a general view of what is the reverse of analogy, viz. anomaly. The precision and perspicuity which Varro displays in this work merit the highest encomiums, and justify the character given him in his own time, of being the most learned of the Latin grammarians. To the loss of the first three books, are to be added several chasms in the others; but fortunately they happen in such places as not to affect the coherency of the author's doctrine, though they interrupt the illustration of it. It is observable that this great grammarian makes use of quom for quum, heis for his, and generally queis for quibus. This practice having become rather obsolete at the time in which he wrote, we must impute his continuance of it to his opinion of its propriety, upon its established principles of grammar, and not to any prejudice of education, or an affectation of singularity. As Varro makes no mention of Caesar's treatise on Analogy, and had commenced author long before him, it is probable that Caesar's production was of a much later date; and thence we may infer, that those two writers differed from each other, at least with respect to some particulars on that subject.

This author's treatise De Re Rustica was undertaken at the desire of a friend, who, having purchased some lands, requested of Varro the favour of his instructions relative to farming, and the economy of a country life, in its various departments. Though Varro was at this time in his eightieth year, he writes with all the vivacity, though without the levity, of youth, and sets out with invoking, not the Muses, like Homer and Ennius, as he observes, but the twelve deities supposed to be chiefly concerned in the operations of agriculture. It appears from the account which he gives, that upwards of fifty Greek authors had treated of this subject in prose, besides Hesiod and Menecrates the Ephesian, who both wrote in verse; exclusive likewise of many Roman writers, and of Mago the Carthaginian, who wrote in the Punic language. Varro's work is divided into three books, the first of which treats of agriculture; the second, of rearing of cattle; and the third, of feeding animals for the use of the table. (67) In the last of these, we meet with a remarkable instance of the prevalence of habit and fashion over human sentiment, where the author delivers instructions relative to the best method of fattening rats.

We find from Quintilian, that Varro likewise composed satires in various kinds of verse. It is impossible to behold the numerous fragments of this venerable author without feeling the strongest regret for the loss of that vast collection of information which he had compiled, and of judicious observations which he had made on a variety of subjects, during a life of eighty-eight years, almost entirely devoted to literature. The remark of St. Augustine is well founded, That it is astonishing how Varro, who read such a number of books, could find time to compose so many volumes; and how he who composed so many volumes, could be at leisure to peruse such a variety of books, and to gain so much literary information.

Catullus is said to have been born at Verona, of respectable parents; his father and himself being in the habit of intimacy with Julius Caesar. He was brought to Rome by Mallius, to whom several of his epigrams are addressed. The gentleness of his manners, and his application to study, we are told, recommended him to general esteem; and he had the good fortune to obtain the patronage of Cicero. When he came to be known as a poet, all these circumstances would naturally contribute to increase his reputation for ingenuity; and accordingly we find his genius applauded by several of his contemporaries. It appears that his works are not transmitted entire to posterity; but there remain sufficient specimens by which we may be enabled to appreciate his poetical talents.

Quintilian, and Diomed the grammarian, have ranked Catullus amongst the iambic writers, while others have placed him amongst the lyric. He has properly a claim to each of these stations; but his versification being chiefly iambic, the former of the arrangements seems to be the most suitable. The principal merit of Catullus's Iambics consists in a simplicity of thought and expression. The thoughts, however, are often frivolous, and, what is yet more reprehensible, the author gives way to gross obscenity: in vindication of which, he produces the following couplet, declaring that a good poet ought to be chaste in his own person, but that his verses need not be so.

*Nam castum esse decet pium poetam*
*Ipsum: versiculos nihil necesse est.*

This sentiment has been frequently cited by those who were inclined to follow the example of Catullus; but if such a practice be in any case admissible, it is only where the poet personates (68) a profligate character; and the instances in which it is adopted by Catullus are not of that description. It had perhaps been a better apology, to have pleaded the manners of the times; for even Horace, who wrote only a few years after, has suffered his compositions to be occasionally debased by the same kind of blemish.

Much has been said of this poet's invective against Caesar, which produced no other effect than an invitation to sup at the dictator's house. It was indeed scarcely entitled to the honour of the smallest resentment. If any could be shewn, it must have been for the freedom used by the author, and not for any novelty in his lampoon. There are two poems on this subject, viz. the twenty-ninth and fifty-seventh, in each of which Caesar is joined with Mamurra, a Roman knight, who had acquired great riches in the Gallic war. For the honour of Catullus's gratitude, we should suppose that the latter is the one to which historians allude: but, as poetical compositions, they are equally unworthy of regard. The fifty seventh is nothing more than a broad repetition of the raillery, whether well or ill founded, with which Caesar was attacked on various occasions, and even in the senate, after his return from Bithynia. Caesar had been taunted with this subject for upwards of thirty years; and after so long a familiarity with reproach, his sensibility to the scandalous imputation must now have been much diminished, if not entirely extinguished. The other poem is partly in the same strain, but extended to greater length, by a mixture of common jocular ribaldry of the Roman soldiers, expressed nearly in the same terms which Caesar's legions, though strongly attached to his person, scrupled not to sport publicly in the streets of Rome, against their general, during the celebration of his triumph. In a word, it deserves to be regarded as an effusion of Saturnalian licentiousness, rather than of poetry. With respect to the Iambics of Catullus, we may observe in general, that the sarcasm is indebted for its force, not so much to ingenuity of sentiment, as to the indelicate nature of the subject, or coarseness of expression.

The descriptive poems of Catullus are superior to the others, and discover a lively imagination. Amongst the best of his productions, is a translation of the celebrated ode of Sappho:

*Ille mi par esse Deo videtur,*
*me, etc.*

This ode is executed both with spirit and elegance; it is, however, imperfect; and the last stanza seems to be spurious. Catullus's epigrams are entitled to little praise, with regard either to sentiment or point; and on the whole, his merit, as a poet, appears to have been magnified beyond its real extent. He is said to have died about the thirtieth year of his age.

(69) Lucretius is the author of a celebrated poem, in six books, De Rerum Natura; a subject which had been treated many ages before by Empedocles, a philosopher and poet of Agrigentum. Lucretius was a zealous partizan of Democritus, and the sect of Epicurus, whose principles concerning the eternity of matter, the materiality of the soul, and the non-existence of a future state of rewards and punishments, he affects to maintain with a certainty equal to that of mathematical demonstration. Strongly prepossessed with the hypothetical doctrines of his master, and ignorant of the physical system of the universe, he endeavours to deduce from the phenomena of the material world conclusions not only unsupported by legitimate theory, but repugnant to the principles of the highest authority in metaphysical disquisition. But while we condemn his speculative notions as degrading to human nature, and subversive of the most important interests of mankind, we must admit that he has prosecuted his visionary hypothesis with uncommon ingenuity. Abstracting from it the rhapsodical nature of this production, and its obscurity in some parts, it has great merit as a poem. The style is elevated, and the versification in general harmonious. By the mixture of obsolete words, it possesses an air of solemnity well adapted to abstruse researches; at the same time that by the frequent resolution of diphthongs, it instils into the Latin the sonorous and melodious powers of the Greek language.

While Lucretius was engaged in this work, he fell into a state of insanity, occasioned, as is supposed, by a philtre, or love-potion, given him by his wife Lucilia. The complaint, however, having lucid intervals, he employed them in the execution of his plan, and, soon after it was finished, laid violent hands upon himself, in the forty-third year of his age. This fatal termination of his life, which perhaps proceeded from insanity, was ascribed by his friends and admirers to his concern for the banishment of one Memmius, with whom he was intimately connected, and for the distracted state of the republic. It was, however, a catastrophe which the principles of Epicurus, equally erroneous and irreconcilable to resignation and fortitude, authorized in particular circumstances. Even Atticus, the celebrated correspondent of Cicero, a few years after this period, had recourse to the same desperate expedient, by refusing all sustenance, while he laboured under a lingering disease.

It is said that Cicero revised the poem of Lucretius after the death of the author, and this circumstance is urged by the abettors of atheism, as a proof that the principles contained in the work had the sanction of his authority. But no inference in favour of Lucretius's doctrine can justly be drawn from this circumstance. (70) Cicero, though already sufficiently acquainted with the principles of the Epicurean sect, might not be averse to the perusal of a production, which collected and enforced them in a nervous strain of poetry; especially as the work was likely to prove interesting to his friend Atticus, and would perhaps afford subject for some letters or conversation between them. It can have been only with reference to composition that the poem was submitted to Cicero's revisal: for had he been required to exercise his judgment upon its principles, he must undoubtedly have so much mutilated the work, as to destroy the coherency of the system. He might be gratified with the shew of elaborate research, and confident declamation, which it exhibited, but he must have utterly disapproved of the conclusions which the author endeavoured to establish. According to the best information, Lucretius died in the year from the building of Rome 701, when Pompey was the third time consul. Cicero lived several years beyond this period, and in the two last years of his life, he composed those valuable works which contain sentiments diametrically repugnant to the visionary system of Epicurus. The argument, therefore, drawn from Cicero's revisal, so far from confirming the principle of Lucretius, affords the strongest tacit declaration against their validity; because a period sufficient for mature consideration had elapsed, before Cicero published his own admirable system of philosophy. The poem of Lucretius, nevertheless, has been regarded as the bulwark of atheism—of atheism, which, while it impiously arrogates the support of reason, both reason and nature disclaim.

Many more writers flourished in this period, but their works have totally perished. Sallust was now engaged in historical productions; but as they were not yet completed, they will be noticed in the next division of the review.

# D. OCTAVIUS CAESAR AUGUSTUS.

**(71)**

I. That the family of the Octavii was of the first distinction in Velitrae 106, is rendered evident by many circumstances. For in the most frequented part of the town, there was, not long since, a street named the Octavian; and an altar was to be seen, consecrated to one Octavius, who being chosen general in a war with some neighbouring people, the enemy making a sudden attack, while he was sacrificing to Mars, he immediately snatched the entrails of the victim from off the fire, and offered them half raw upon the altar; after which, marching out to battle, he returned victorious. This incident gave rise to a law, by which it was enacted, that in all future times the entrails should be offered to Mars in the same manner; and the rest of the victim be carried to the Octavii.

II. This family, as well as several in Rome, was admitted into the senate by Tarquinius Priscus, and soon afterwards placed by Servius Tullius among the patricians; but in process of time it transferred itself to the plebeian order, and, after the lapse of a long interval, was restored by Julius Caesar to the rank of patricians. The first person of the family raised by the suffrages of the people to the magistracy, was Caius Rufus. He obtained the quaestorship, and had two sons, Cneius and Caius; from whom are descended the two branches of the Octavian family, which have had very different fortunes. For Cneius, and his descendants in uninterrupted succession, held all the highest offices of the state; whilst Caius and his posterity, whether from their circumstances or their choice, remained in the equestrian order until the father of Augustus. The great-grandfather of Augustus served as a military tribune in the second Punic war in Sicily, under the command of Aemilius Pappus. His grandfather contented himself with bearing the public offices of his own municipality, and grew old in the tranquil enjoyment of an ample patrimony. Such is the account given (72) by different authors. Augustus himself, however, tells us nothing more than that he was descended of an equestrian family, both ancient and rich, of which his father was the first who obtained the rank of senator. Mark Antony upbraidingly tells him that his great-grandfather was a freedman of the territory of Thurium 107, and a rope-maker, and his grandfather a usurer. This is all the information I have any where met with, respecting the ancestors of Augustus by the father's side.

III. His father Caius Octavius was, from his earliest years, a person both of opulence and distinction: for which reason I am surprised at those who say that he was a money-dealer 108, and was employed in scattering bribes, and canvassing for the candidates at elections, in the Campus Martius. For being bred up in all the affluence of a great estate, he attained with ease to honourable posts, and discharged the duties of them with much distinction. After his praetorship, he obtained by lot the province of Macedonia; in his way to which he cut off some banditti, the relics of the armies of Spartacus and Catiline, who had possessed themselves of the territory of Thurium; having received from the senate an extraordinary commission for that purpose. In his government of the province, he conducted himself with equal justice and resolution; for he defeated the Bessians and Thracians in a great battle, and treated the allies of the republic in such a manner, that there are extant letters from M. Tullius Cicero, in which he advises and exhorts his brother Quintus, who then held the proconsulship of Asia with no great reputation, to imitate the example of his neighbour Octavius, in gaining the affections of the allies of Rome.

IV. After quitting Macedonia, before he could declare himself a candidate for the consulship, he died suddenly, leaving behind him a daughter, the elder Octavia, by Ancharia; and another daughter, Octavia the younger, as well as Augustus, by Atia, who was the daughter of Marcus Atius Balbus, and Julia, sister to Caius Julius Caesar. Balbus was, by the father's (73) side, of a family who were natives of Aricia 109, and many of whom had been in the senate. By the mother's side he was nearly related to Pompey the Great; and after he had borne the office of praetor, was one of the twenty commissioners appointed by the Julian law to divide the land in Campania among the people. But Mark Antony, treating with contempt Augustus's descent even by the mother's side, says that his great grand-father was of African descent, and at one time kept a perfumer's shop, and at another, a bake-house, in Aricia. And Cassius of Parma, in a letter, taxes Augustus with being the son not only of a baker, but a usurer. These are his words: "Thou art a lump of thy mother's meal, which a money-changer of Nerulum taking from the newest bake-house of Aricia, kneaded into some shape, with his hands all discoloured by the fingering of money."

V. Augustus was born in the consulship of Marcus Tullius Cicero and Caius Antonius 110 , upon the ninth of the calends of October [the 23rd September], a little before sunrise, in the quarter of the Palatine Hill 111 , and the street called The Ox-Heads 112 , where now stands a chapel dedicated to him, and built a little after his death. For, as it is recorded in the proceedings of the senate, when Caius Laetorius, a young man of a patrician family, in pleading before the senators for a lighter sentence, upon his being convicted of adultery, alleged, besides his youth and quality, that he was the possessor, and as it were the guardian, of the ground which the Divine Augustus first touched upon his coming into the world; and entreated that (74) he might find favour, for the sake of that deity, who was in a peculiar manner his; an act of the senate was passed, for the consecration of that part of his house in which Augustus was born.

VI. His nursery is shewn to this day, in a villa belonging to the family, in the suburbs of Velitrae; being a very small place, and much like a pantry. An opinion prevails in the neighbourhood, that he was also born there. Into this place no person presumes to enter, unless upon necessity, and with great devotion, from a belief, for a long time prevalent, that such as rashly enter it are seized with great horror and consternation, which a short while since was confirmed by a remarkable incident. For when a new inhabitant of the house had, either by mere chance, or to try the truth of the report, taken up his lodging in that apartment, in the course of the night, a few hours afterwards, he was thrown out by some sudden violence, he knew not how, and was found in a state of stupefaction, with the coverlid of his bed, before the door of the chamber.

VII. While he was yet an infant, the surname of Thurinus was given him, in memory of the birth-place of his family, or because, soon after he was born, his father Octavius had been successful against the fugitive slaves, in the country near Thurium. That he was surnamed Thurinus, I can affirm upon good foundation, for when a boy, I had a small bronze statue of him, with that name upon it in iron letters, nearly effaced by age, which I presented to the emperor 113, by whom it is now revered amongst the other tutelary deities in his chamber. He is also often called Thurinus contemptuously, by Mark Antony in his letters; to which he makes only this reply: "I am surprised that my former name should be made a subject of reproach." He afterwards assumed the name of Caius Caesar, and then of Augustus; the former in compliance with the will of his great-uncle, and the latter upon a motion of Munatius Plancus in the senate. For when some proposed to confer upon him the name of Romulus, as being, in a manner, a second founder of the city, it was resolved that he should rather be called Augustus, a surname not only new, but of more dignity, because places devoted to religion, and those in which anything (75) is consecrated by augury, are denominated august, either from the word auctus, signifying augmentation, or ab avium gestu, gustuve, from the flight and feeding of birds; as appears from this verse of Ennius:

*When glorious Rome by august augury was built.* 114_

VIII. He lost his father when he was only four years of age; and, in his twelfth year, pronounced a funeral oration in praise of his grandmother Julia. Four years afterwards, having assumed the robe of manhood, he was honoured with several military rewards by Caesar in his African triumph, although he took no part in the war, on account of his youth. Upon his uncle's expedition to Spain against the sons of Pompey, he was followed by his nephew, although he was scarcely recovered from a dangerous sickness; and after being shipwrecked at sea, and travelling with very few attendants through roads that were infested with the enemy, he at last came up with him. This activity gave great satisfaction to his uncle, who soon conceived an increasing affection for him, on account of such indications of character. After the subjugation of Spain, while Caesar was meditating an expedition against the Dacians and Parthians, he was sent before him to Apollonia, where he applied himself to his studies; until receiving intelligence that his uncle was murdered, and that he was appointed his heir, he hesitated for some time whether he should call to his aid the legions stationed in the neighbourhood; but he abandoned the design as rash and premature. However, returning to Rome, he took possession of his inheritance, although his mother was apprehensive that such a measure might be attended with danger, and his step-father, Marcius Philippus, a man of consular rank, very earnestly dissuaded him from it. From this time, collecting together a strong military force, he first held the government in conjunction with Mark Antony and Marcus Lepidus, then with Antony only, for nearly twelve years, and at last in his own hands during a period of four and forty.

IX. Having thus given a very short summary of his life, I shall prosecute the several parts of it, not in order of time, but arranging his acts into distinct classes, for the sake of (76) perspicuity. He was engaged in five civil wars, namely those of Modena, Philippi, Perugia, Sicily, and Actium; the first and last of which were against Antony, and the second against Brutus and Cassius; the third against Lucius Antonius, the triumvir's brother, and the fourth against Sextus Pompeius, the son of Cneius Pompeius.

X. The motive which gave rise to all these wars was the opinion he entertained that both his honour and interest were concerned in revenging the murder of his uncle, and maintaining the state of affairs he had established. Immediately after his return from Apollonia, he formed the design of taking forcible and unexpected measures against Brutus and Cassius; but they having foreseen the danger and made their escape, he resolved to proceed against them by an appeal to the laws in their absence, and impeach them for the murder. In the mean time, those whose province it was to prepare the sports in honour of Caesar's last victory in the civil war, not daring to do it, he undertook it himself. And that he might carry into effect his other designs with greater authority, he declared himself a candidate in the room of a tribune of the people who happened to die at that time, although he was of a patrician family, and had not yet been in the senate. But the consul, Mark Antony, from whom he had expected the greatest assistance, opposing him in his suit, and even refusing to do him so much as common justice, unless gratified with a large bribe, he went over to the party of the nobles, to whom he perceived Sylla to be odious, chiefly for endeavouring to drive Decius Brutus, whom he besieged in the town of Modena, out of the province, which had been given him by Caesar, and confirmed to him by the senate. At the instigation of persons about him, he engaged some ruffians to murder his antagonist; but the plot being discovered, and dreading a similar attempt upon himself, he gained over Caesar's veteran soldiers, by distributing among them all the money he could collect. Being now commissioned by the senate to command the troops he had gathered, with the rank of praetor, and in conjunction with Hirtius and Pansa, who had accepted the consulship, to carry assistance to Decius Brutus, he put an end to the war by two battles in three months. Antony writes, that in the former of these he ran away, and two days afterwards made his appearance (77) without his general's cloak and his horse. In the last battle, however, it is certain that he performed the part not only of a general, but a soldier; for, in the heat of the battle; when the standard-bearer of his legion was severely wounded, he took the eagle upon his shoulders, and carried it a long time.

XI. In this war 115 , Hirtius being slain in battle, and Pansa dying a short time afterwards of a wound, a report was circulated that they both were killed through his means, in order that, when Antony fled, the republic having lost its consuls, he might have the victorious armies entirely at his own command. The death of Pansa was so fully believed to have been caused by undue means, that Glyco, his surgeon, was placed in custody, on a suspicion of having poisoned his wound. And to this, Aquilius Niger adds, that he killed Hirtius, the other consul, in the confusion of the battle, with his own hands.

XII. But upon intelligence that Antony, after his defeat, had been received by Marcus Lepidus, and that the rest of the generals and armies had all declared for the senate, he, without any hesitation, deserted from the party of the nobles; alleging as an excuse for his conduct, the actions and sayings of several amongst them; for some said, "he was a mere boy," and others threw out, "that he ought to be promoted to honours, and cut off," to avoid the making any suitable acknowledgment either to him or the veteran legions. And the more to testify his regret for having before attached himself to the other faction, he fined the Nursini in a large sum of money, which they were unable to pay, and then expelled them from the town, for having inscribed upon a monument, erected at the public charge to their countrymen who were slain in the battle of Modena, "That they fell in the cause of liberty."

XIII. Having entered into a confederacy with Antony and Lepidus, he brought the war at Philippi to an end in two battles, although he was at that time weak, and suffering from sickness 116 . In the first battle he was driven from his camp, (78) and with some difficulty made his escape to the wing of the army commanded by Antony. And now, intoxicated with success, he sent the head of Brutus 117 to be cast at the foot of Caesar's statue, and treated the most illustrious of the prisoners not only with cruelty, but with abusive language; insomuch that he is said to have answered one of them who humbly intreated that at least he might not remain unburied, "That will be in the power of the birds." Two others, father and son, who begged for their lives, he ordered to cast lots which of them should live, or settle it between themselves by the sword; and was a spectator of both their deaths: for the father offering his life to save his son, and being accordingly executed, the son likewise killed himself upon the spot. On this account, the rest of the prisoners, and amongst them Marcus Favonius, Cato's rival, being led up in fetters, after they had saluted Antony, the general, with much respect, reviled Octavius in the foulest language. After this victory, dividing between them the offices of the state, Mark Antony 118 undertook to restore order in the east, while Caesar conducted the veteran soldiers back to Italy, and settled them in colonies on the lands belonging to the municipalities. But he had the misfortune to please neither the soldiers nor the owners of the lands; one party complaining of the injustice done them, in being violently ejected from their possessions, and the other, that they were not rewarded according to their merit. 119

XIV. At this time he obliged Lucius Antony, who, presuming upon his own authority as consul, and his brother's power, was raising new commotions, to fly to Perugia, and forced him, by famine, to surrender at last, although not without having been exposed to great hazards, both before the war and during its continuance. For a common soldier having got into the seats of the equestrian order in the theatre, at the public spectacles, Caesar ordered him to be removed by an officer; and a rumour being thence spread by his enemies, that he had (79) put the man to death by torture, the soldiers flocked together so much enraged, that he narrowly escaped with his life. The only thing that saved him, was the sudden appearance of the man, safe and sound, no violence having been offered him. And whilst he was sacrificing under the walls of Perugia, he nearly fell into the hands of a body of gladiators, who sallied out of the town.

XV. After the taking of Perugia 120, he sentenced a great number of the prisoners to death, making only one reply to all who implored pardon, or endeavoured to excuse themselves, "You must die." Some authors write, that three hundred of the two orders, selected from the rest, were slaughtered, like victims, before an altar raised to Julius Caesar, upon the ides of March [15th April] 121. Nay, there are some who relate, that he entered upon the war with no other view, than that his secret enemies, and those whom fear more than affection kept quiet, might be detected, by declaring themselves, now they had an opportunity, with Lucius Antony at their head; and that having defeated them, and confiscated their estates, he might be enabled to fulfil his promises to the veteran soldiers.

XVI. He soon commenced the Sicilian war, but it was protracted by various delays during a long period 122; at one time for the purpose of repairing his fleets, which he lost twice by storm, even in the summer; at another, while patching up a peace, to which he was forced by the clamours of the people, in consequence of a famine occasioned by Pompey's cutting off the supply of corn by sea. But at last, having built a new fleet, and obtained twenty thousand manumitted slaves 123, who were given him for the oar, he formed the Julian harbour at Baiae, by letting the sea into the Lucrine and Avernian lakes; and having exercised his forces there during the whole winter, he defeated Pompey betwixt Mylae and Naulochus; although (80) just as the engagement commenced, he suddenly fell into such a profound sleep, that his friends were obliged to wake him to give the signal. This, I suppose, gave occasion for Antony's reproach: "You were not able to take a clear view of the fleet, when drawn up in line of battle, but lay stupidly upon your back, gazing at the sky; nor did you get up and let your men see you, until Marcus Agrippa had forced the enemies' ships to sheer off." Others imputed to him both a saying and an action which were indefensible; for, upon the loss of his fleets by storm, he is reported to have said: "I will conquer in spite of Neptune;" and at the next Circensian games, he would not suffer the statue of that God to be carried in procession as usual. Indeed he scarcely ever ran more or greater risks in any of his wars than in this. Having transported part of his army to Sicily, and being on his return for the rest, he was unexpectedly attacked by Demochares and Apollophanes, Pompey's admirals, from whom he escaped with great difficulty, and with one ship only. Likewise, as he was travelling on foot through the Locrian territory to Rhegium, seeing two of Pompey's vessels passing by that coast, and supposing them to be his own, he went down to the shore, and was very nearly taken prisoner. On this occasion, as he was making his escape by some bye-ways, a slave belonging to Aemilius Paulus, who accompanied him, owing him a grudge for the proscription of Paulus, the father of Aemilius, and thinking he had now an opportunity of revenging it, attempted to assassinate him. After the defeat of Pompey, one of his colleagues 124, Marcus Lepidus, whom he had summoned to his aid from Africa, affecting great superiority, because he was at the head of twenty legions, and claiming for himself the principal management of affairs in a threatening manner, he divested him of his command, but, upon his humble submission, granted him his life, but banished him for life to Circeii.

XVII. The alliance between him and Antony, which had always been precarious, often interrupted, and ill cemented by repeated reconciliations, he at last entirely dissolved. And to make it known to the world how far Antony had degenerated from patriotic feelings, he caused a will of his, which had been left at Rome, and in which he had nominated Cleopatra's children, amongst others, as his heirs, to be opened and read in an assembly of the people. Yet upon his being declared an enemy, he sent to him all his relations and friends, among whom were Caius Sosius and Titus Domitius, at that time consuls. He likewise spoke favourably in public of the people of Bologna, for joining in the association with the rest of Italy to support his cause, because they had, in former times, been under the protection of the family of the Antonii. And not long afterwards he defeated him in a naval engagement near Actium, which was prolonged to so late an hour, that, after the victory, he was obliged to sleep on board his ship. From Actium he went to the isle of Samoa to winter; but being alarmed with the accounts of a mutiny amongst the soldiers he had selected from the main body of his army sent to Brundisium after the victory, who insisted on their being rewarded for their service and discharged, he returned to Italy. In his passage thither, he encountered two violent storms, the first between the promontories of Peloponnesus and Aetolia, and the other about the Ceraunian mountains; in both which a part of his Liburnian squadron was sunk, the spars and rigging of his own ship carried away, and the rudder broken in pieces. He remained only twenty-seven days at Brundisium, until the demands of the soldiers were settled, and then went, by way of Asia and Syria, to Egypt, where laying siege to Alexandria, whither Antony had fled with Cleopatra, he made himself master of it in a short time. He drove Antony to kill himself, after he had used every effort to obtain conditions of peace, and he saw his corpse 126 . Cleopatra he anxiously wished to save for his triumph; and when she was supposed to have been bit to death by an asp, he sent for the Psylli 127 to (82) endeavour to suck out the poison. He allowed them to be buried together in the same grave, and ordered a mausoleum, begun by themselves, to be completed. The eldest of Antony's two sons by Fulvia he commanded to be taken by force from the statue of Julius Caesar, to which he had fled, after many fruitless supplications for his life, and put him to death. The same fate attended Caesario, Cleopatra's son by Caesar, as he pretended, who had fled for his life, but was retaken. The children which Antony had by Cleopatra he saved, and brought up and cherished in a manner suitable to their rank, just as if they had been his own relations.

XVIII. At this time he had a desire to see the sarcophagus and body of Alexander the Great, which, for that purpose, were taken out of the cell in which they rested 128 ; and after viewing them for some time, he paid honours to the memory of that prince, by offering a golden crown, and scattering flowers upon the body 129 . Being asked if he wished to see the tombs of the Ptolemies also; he replied, "I wish to see a king, not dead men." 130 He reduced Egypt into the form of a province and to render it more fertile, and more capable of supplying Rome with corn, he employed his army to scour the canals, into which the Nile, upon its rise, discharges itself; but which during a long series of years had become nearly choked up with mud. To perpetuate the glory of his victory at Actium, he built the city of Nicopolis on that part of the coast, and established games to be celebrated there every five years; enlarging likewise an old temple of Apollo, he ornamented with naval trophies 131 the spot on which he had pitched his camp, and consecrated it to Neptune and Mars.

(83) XIX. He afterwards 132 quashed several tumults and insurrections, as well as several conspiracies against his life, which were discovered, by the confession of accomplices, before they were

ripe for execution; and others subsequently. Such were those of the younger Lepidus, of Varro Muraena, and Fannius Caepio; then that of Marcus Egnatius, afterwards that of Plautius Rufus, and of Lucius Paulus, his grand-daughter's husband; and besides these, another of Lucius Audasius, an old feeble man, who was under prosecution for forgery; as also of Asinius Epicadus, a Parthinian mongrel 133, and at last that of Telephus, a lady's prompter 134; for he was in danger of his life from the plots and conspiracies of some of the lowest of the people against him. Audasius and Epicadus had formed the design of carrying off to the armies his daughter Julia, and his grandson Agrippa, from the islands in which they were confined. Telephus, wildly dreaming that the government was destined to him by the fates, proposed to fall both upon Octavius and the senate. Nay, once, a soldier's servant belonging to the army in Illyricum, having passed the porters unobserved, was found in the night-time standing before his chamber-door, armed with a hunting-dagger. Whether the person was really disordered in the head, or only counterfeited madness, is uncertain; for no confession was obtained from him by torture.

XX. He conducted in person only two foreign wars; the Dalmatian, whilst he was yet but a youth; and, after Antony's final defeat, the Cantabrian. He was wounded in the former of these wars; in one battle he received a contusion in the right knee from a stone—and in another, he was much hurt in (84) one leg and both arms, by the fall of a fridge 135. His other wars he carried on by his lieutenants; but occasionally visited the army, in some of the wars of Pannonia and Germany, or remained at no great distance, proceeding from Rome as far as Ravenna, Milan, or Aquileia.

XXI. He conquered, however, partly in person, and partly by his lieutenants, Cantabria 136, Aquitania and Pannonia 137, Dalmatia, with all Illyricum and Rhaetia 138, besides the two Alpine nations, the Vindelici and the Salassii 139. He also checked the incursions of the Dacians, by cutting off three of their generals with vast armies, and drove the Germans beyond the river Elbe; removing two other tribes who submitted, the Ubii and Sicambri, into Gaul, and settling them in the country bordering on the Rhine. Other nations also, which broke into revolt, he reduced to submission. But he never made war upon any nation without just and necessary cause; and was so far from being ambitious either to extend the empire, or advance his own military glory, that he obliged the chiefs of some barbarous tribes to swear in the temple of Mars the Avenger 140, that they would faithfully observe their engagements, and not violate the peace which they had implored. Of some he demanded a new description of hostages, their women, having found from experience that they cared little for their men when given as hostages; but he always afforded them the means of getting back their hostages whenever they wished it. Even those who engaged most frequently and with the greatest perfidy in their rebellion, he never punished more severely than by selling their captives, on the terms (85) of their not serving in any neighbouring country, nor being released from their slavery before the expiration of thirty years. By the character which he thus acquired, for virtue and moderation, he induced even the Indians and Scythians, nations before known to the Romans by report only, to solicit his friendship, and that of the Roman people, by ambassadors. The Parthians readily allowed his claim to Armenia; restoring at his demand, the standards which they had taken from Marcus Crassus and Mark Antony, and offering him hostages besides. Afterwards, when a contest arose between several pretenders to the crown of that kingdom, they refused to acknowledge any one who was not chosen by him.

XXII. The temple of Janus Quirinus, which had been shut twice only, from the era of the building of the city to his own time, he closed thrice in a much shorter period, having established universal peace both by sea and land. He twice entered the city with the honours of an Ovation 141, namely, after the war of Philippi, and again after that of Sicily. He had also three curule triumphs 142 for his several victories in (86) Dalmatia, at Actium, and Alexandria; each of which lasted three days.

XXIII. In all his wars, he never received any signal or ignominious defeat, except twice in Germany, under his lieutenants Lollius and Varus. The former indeed had in it more of dishonour than disaster; but that of Varus threatened the security of the empire itself; three legions, with the commander, his lieutenants, and all the auxiliaries, being cut off. Upon receiving intelligence of this disaster, he gave orders for keeping a strict watch over the city, to prevent any public disturbance, and prolonged the appointments of the prefects in the provinces, that the allies might be kept in order by experience of persons to whom they were used. He made a vow to celebrate the great games in honour of Jupiter, Optimus, Maximus, "if he would be pleased to restore the state to more prosperous circumstances." This had formerly been resorted to in the Cimbrian and Marsian wars. In short, we are informed that he was in such consternation at this event, that he let the hair of his head and beard grow for several months, and sometimes knocked his head against the door-posts, crying out, "O, Quintilius Varus! Give me back my legions!" And (87) ever after, he observed the anniversary of this calamity, as a day of sorrow and mourning.

XXIV. In military affairs he made many alterations, introducing some practices entirely new, and reviving others, which had become obsolete. He maintained the strictest discipline among the troops; and would not allow even his lieutenants the liberty to visit their wives, except reluctantly, and in the winter season only. A Roman knight having cut off the thumbs of his two young sons, to render them incapable of serving in the wars, he exposed both him and his estate to public sale. But upon observing the farmers of the revenue very greedy for the purchase, he assigned him to a freedman of his own, that he might send him into the country, and suffer him to retain his freedom. The tenth legion becoming mutinous, he disbanded it with ignominy; and did the same by some others which petulantly demanded their discharge; withholding from them the rewards usually bestowed on those who had served their stated time in the wars. The cohorts which yielded their ground in time of action, he decimated, and fed with barley. Centurions, as well as common sentinels, who deserted their posts when on guard, he punished with death. For other misdemeanors he inflicted upon them various kinds of disgrace; such as obliging them to stand all day before the praetorium, sometimes in their tunics only, and without their belts, sometimes to carry poles ten feet long, or sods of turf.

XXV. After the conclusion of the civil wars, he never, in any of his military harangues, or proclamations, addressed them by the title of "Fellow-soldiers," but as "Soldiers" only. Nor would he suffer them to be otherwise called by his sons or step-sons, when they were in command; judging the former epithet to convey the idea of a degree of condescension inconsistent with military discipline, the maintenance of order, and his own majesty, and that of his house.

Unless at Rome, in case of incendiary fires, or under the apprehension of public disturbances during a scarcity of provisions, he never employed in his army slaves who had been made freedmen, except upon two occasions; on one, for the security of the colonies bordering upon Illyricum, and on the other, to guard (88) the banks of the river Rhine. Although he obliged persons of fortune, both male and female, to give up their slaves, and they received their manumission at once, yet he kept them together under their own standard, unmixed with soldiers who were better born, and armed likewise after different fashion. Military rewards, such as trappings, collars, and other decorations of gold and silver, he distributed more readily than camp or mural crowns, which were reckoned more honourable than the former. These he bestowed sparingly, without partiality, and frequently even on common soldiers. He presented M. Agrippa, after the naval engagement in the Sicilian war, with a sea-green banner. Those who shared in the honours of a triumph, although they had attended him in his expeditions, and taken part in his victories, he judged it improper to distinguish by the usual rewards for service, because they had a right themselves to grant such rewards to whom they pleased. He thought nothing more derogatory to the character of an accomplished general than precipitancy and rashness; on which account he had frequently in his mouth those proverbs:

> *Speude bradeos,*
> *Hasten slowly,*

And

> *'Asphalaes gar est' ameinon, hae erasus strataelataes.*
> *The cautious captain's better than the bold.*

And "That is done fast enough, which is done well enough."

He was wont to say also, that "a battle or a war ought never to be undertaken, unless the prospect of gain overbalanced the fear of loss. For," said he, "men who pursue small advantages with no small hazard, resemble those who fish with a golden hook, the loss of which, if the line should happen to break, could never be compensated by all the fish they might take."

XXVI. He was advanced to public offices before the age at which he was legally qualified for them; and to some, also, of a new kind, and for life. He seized the consulship in the twentieth year of his age, quartering his legions in a threatening manner near the city, and sending deputies to demand it for him in the name of the army. When the senate demurred, (89) a centurion, named Cornelius, who was at the head of the chief deputation, throwing back his cloak, and shewing the hilt of his sword, had the presumption to say in the senate-house, "This will make him consul, if ye will not." His second consulship he filled nine years afterwards; his third, after the interval of only one year, and held the same office every year successively until the eleventh. From this period, although the consulship was frequently offered him, he always declined it, until, after a long interval, not less than seventeen years, he voluntarily stood for the twelfth, and two years after that, for a thirteenth; that he might successively introduce into the forum, on their entering public life, his two sons, Caius and Lucius, while he was invested with the highest office in the state. In his five consulships from the sixth to the eleventh, he continued in office throughout the year; but in the rest, during only nine, six, four, or three months, and in his second no more than a few hours. For having sat for a short time in the morning, upon the calends of January [1st January], in his curule chair 143, before the temple of Jupiter Capitolinus, he abdicated the office, and substituted another in his room. Nor did he enter upon them all at Rome, but upon the fourth in Asia, the fifth in the Isle of Samos, and the eighth and ninth at Tarragona. 144

XXVII. During ten years he acted as one of the triumvirate for settling the commonwealth, in which office he for some time opposed his colleagues in their design of a proscription; but after it was begun, he prosecuted it with more determined rigour than either of them. For whilst they were often prevailed upon, by the interest and intercession of friends, to shew mercy, he alone strongly insisted that no one should be spared, and even proscribed Caius Toranius 145, his guardian; who had (90) been formerly the colleague of his father Octavius in the aedileship. Junius Saturnius adds this farther account of him: that when, after the proscription was over, Marcus Lepidus made an apology in the senate for their past proceedings, and gave them hopes of a more mild administration for the future, because they had now sufficiently crushed their enemies; he, on the other hand, declared that the only limit he had fixed to the proscription was, that he should be free to act as he pleased. Afterwards, however, repenting of his severity, he advanced T. Vinius Philopoemen to the equestrian rank, for having concealed his patron at the time he was proscribed. In this same office he incurred great odium upon many accounts. For as he was one day making an harangue, observing among the soldiers Pinarius, a Roman knight, admit some private citizens, and engaged in taking notes, he ordered him to be stabbed before his eyes, as a busy-body and a spy upon him. He so terrified with his menaces Tedius Afer, the consul elect 146 , for having reflected upon some action of his, that he threw himself from a great height, and died on the spot. And when Quintus Gallius, the praetor, came to compliment him with a double tablet under his cloak, suspecting that it was a sword he had concealed, and yet not venturing to make a search, lest it should be found to be something else, he caused him to be dragged from his tribunal by centurions and soldiers, and tortured like a slave: and although he made no confession, ordered him to be put to death, after he had, with his own hands, plucked out his eyes. His own account of the matter, however, is, that Quintus Gallius sought a private conference with him, for the purpose of assassinating him; that he therefore put him in prison, but afterwards released him, and banished him the city; when he perished either in a storm at sea, or by falling into the hands of robbers.

He accepted of the tribunitian power for life, but more than once chose a colleague in that office for two lustra 147 successively. He also had the supervision of morality and observance of the laws, for life, but without the title of censor; yet he thrice (91) took a census of the people, the first and third time with a colleague, but the second by himself.

XXVIII. He twice entertained thoughts of restoring the republic 148 ; first, immediately after he had crushed Antony, remembering that he had often charged him with being the obstacle to its restoration. The second time, was in consequence of a long illness, when he sent for the magistrates and the senate to his own house, and delivered them a particular account of the state of the empire. But reflecting at the same time that it would be both hazardous to himself to return to the condition of a private person, and might be dangerous to the public to have the government placed again under the control of the people, he resolved to keep it in his own hands, whether with the better event or intention, is hard to say. His good intentions he often affirmed in private discourse, and also published an edict, in which it was declared in the following terms: "May it be permitted me to have the happiness of establishing the commonwealth on a safe and sound basis, and thus enjoy the reward of which I am ambitious, that of being celebrated for moulding it into the form best adapted to present circumstances; so that, on my leaving the world, I may carry with me the hope that the foundations which I have laid for its future government, will stand firm and stable."

XXIX. The city, which was not built in a manner suitable to the grandeur of the empire, and was liable to inundations of the Tiber 149 , as well as to fires, was so much improved under his administration, that he boasted, not without reason, that he "found it of brick, but left it of marble." 150 He also rendered (92) it secure for the time to come against such disasters, as far as could be effected by human foresight. A great number of public buildings were erected by him, the most considerable of which were a forum 151 , containing the temple of Mars the Avenger, the temple of Apollo on the Palatine hill, and the temple of Jupiter Tonans in the Capitol. The reason of his building a new forum was the vast increase in the population, and the number of causes to be tried in the courts, for which, the two already existing not affording sufficient space, it was thought necessary to have a third. It was therefore opened for public use before the temple of Mars was completely finished; and a law was passed, that causes should be tried, and judges chosen by lot, in that place. The temple of Mars was built in fulfilment of a vow made during the war of Philippi, undertaken by him to avenge his father's murder. He ordained that the senate should always assemble there when they met to deliberate respecting wars and triumphs; that thence should be despatched all those who were sent into the provinces in the command of armies; and that in it those who returned victorious from the wars, should lodge the trophies of their triumphs. He erected the temple of Apollo 152 in that part of his house on the Palatine hill which had been struck with lightning, and which, on that account, the soothsayers declared the God to have chosen. He added porticos to it, with a library of Latin and Greek authors 153 ; and when advanced in years, (93) used frequently there to hold the senate, and examine the rolls of the judges.

He dedicated the temple to Apollo Tonans 154, in acknowledgment of his escape from a great danger in his Cantabrian expedition; when, as he was travelling in the night, his litter was struck by lightning, which killed the slave who carried a torch before him. He likewise constructed some public buildings in the name of others; for instance, his grandsons, his wife, and sister. Thus he built the portico and basilica of Lucius and Caius, and the porticos of Livia and Octavia 155 , and the theatre of Marcellus 156 . He also often exhorted other persons of rank to embellish the city by new buildings, or repairing and improving the old, according to their means. In consequence of this recommendation, many were raised; such as the temple of Hercules and the Muses, by Marcius Philippus; a temple of Diana by Lucius Cornificius; the Court of Freedom by Asinius Pollio; a temple of Saturn by Munatius Plancus; a theatre by Cornelius Balbus 157 ; an amphitheatre by Statilius Taurus; and several other noble edifices by Marcus Agrippa. 158

(94) XXX. He divided the city into regions and districts, ordaining that the annual magistrates should take by lot the charge of the former; and that the latter should be superintended by wardens chosen out of the people of each neighbourhood. He appointed a nightly watch to be on their guard against accidents from fire; and, to prevent the frequent inundations, he widened and cleansed the bed of the Tiber, which had in the course of years been almost dammed up with rubbish, and the channel narrowed by the ruins of houses 159 . To render the approaches to the city more commodious, he took upon himself the charge of repairing the Flaminian way as far as Ariminum 160 , and distributed the repairs of the other roads amongst several persons who had obtained the honour of a triumph; to be defrayed out of the money arising from the spoils of war. Temples decayed by time, or destroyed by fire, he either repaired or rebuilt; and enriched them, as well as many others, with splendid offerings. On a single occasion, he deposited in the cell of the temple of Jupiter Capitolinus, sixteen thousand pounds of gold, with jewels and pearls to the amount of fifty millions of sesterces.

XXXI. The office of Pontifex Maximus, of which he could (95) not decently deprive Lepidus as long as he lived 161 , he assumed as soon as he was dead. He then caused all prophetical books, both in Latin and Greek, the authors of which were either unknown, or of no great authority, to be brought in; and the whole collection, amounting to upwards of two thousand volumes, he committed to the flames, preserving only the Sibylline oracles; but not even those without a strict examination, to ascertain which were genuine. This being done, he deposited them in two gilt coffers, under the pedestal of the statue of the Palatine Apollo. He restored the calendar, which had been corrected by Julius Caesar, but through negligence was again fallen into confusion 162, to its former regularity; and upon that occasion, called the month Sextilis 163, by his own name, August, rather than September, in which he was born; because in it he had obtained his first consulship, and all his most considerable victories 164. He increased the number, dignity, and revenues of the priests, and especially those of the Vestal Virgins. And when, upon the death of one of them, a new one was to be taken 165, and many persons made interest that their daughters' names might be omitted in the lists for election, he replied with an oath, "If either of my own grand-daughters were old enough, I would have proposed her."

He likewise revived some old religious customs, which had become obsolete; as the augury of public health 166, the office of high priest of Jupiter, the religious solemnity of the Lupercalia, with the Secular, and Compitalian games. He prohibited young boys from running in the Lupercalia; and in respect of the Secular games, issued an order, that no young persons of either sex should appear at any public diversions in the night-time, unless in the company of some elderly relation. He ordered the household gods to be decked twice a year with spring and summer flowers 167, in the Compitalian festival.

Next to the immortal gods, he paid the highest honours to the memory of those generals who had raised the Roman state from its low origin to the highest pitch of grandeur. He accordingly repaired or rebuilt the public edifices erected by them; preserving the former inscriptions, and placing statues of them all, with triumphal emblems, in both the porticos of his forum, issuing an edict on the occasion, in which he made the following declaration: "My design in so doing is, that the Roman people may require from me, and all succeeding princes, a conformity to those illustrious examples." He likewise removed the statue of Pompey from the senate-house, in which Caius Caesar had been killed, and placed it under a marble arch, fronting the palace attached to Pompey's theatre.

XXXII. He corrected many ill practices, which, to the detriment of the public, had either survived the licentious habits of the late civil wars, or else originated in the long peace. Bands of robbers showed themselves openly, completely armed, under colour of self-defence; and in different parts of the country, travellers, freemen and slaves without distinction, were forcibly carried off, and kept to work in the houses of correction 168 . Several associations were formed under the specious (97) name of a new college, which banded together for the perpetration of all kinds of villany. The banditti he quelled by establishing posts of soldiers in suitable stations for the purpose; the houses of correction were subjected to a strict superintendence; all associations, those only excepted which were of ancient standing, and recognised by the laws, were dissolved. He burnt all the notes of those who had been a long time in arrear with the treasury, as being the principal source of vexatious suits and prosecutions. Places in the city claimed by the public, where the right was doubtful, he adjudged to the actual possessors. He struck out of the list of criminals the names of those over whom prosecutions had been long impending, where nothing further was intended by the informers than to gratify their own malice, by seeing their enemies humiliated; laying it down as a rule, that if any one chose to renew a prosecution, he should incur the risk of the punishment which he sought to inflict. And that crimes might not escape punishment, nor business be neglected by delay, he ordered the courts to sit during the thirty days which were spent in celebrating honorary games. To the three classes of judges then existing, he added a fourth, consisting of persons of inferior order, who were called Ducenarii, and decided all litigations about trifling sums. He chose judges from the age of thirty years and upwards; that is five years younger than had been usual before. And a great many declining the office, he was with much difficulty prevailed upon to allow each class of judges a twelve-month's vacation in turn; and the courts to be shut during the months of November and December. 169

XXXIII. He was himself assiduous in his functions as a judge, and would sometimes prolong his sittings even into the night 170 : if he were indisposed, his litter was placed before (98) the tribunal, or he administered justice reclining on his couch at home; displaying always not only the greatest attention, but extreme lenity. To save a culprit, who evidently appeared guilty of parricide, from the extreme penalty of being sewn up in a sack, because none were punished in that manner but such as confessed the fact, he is said to have interrogated him thus: "Surely you did not kill your father, did you?" And when, in a trial of a cause about a forged will, all those who had signed it were liable to the penalty of the Cornelian law, he ordered that his colleagues on the tribunal should not only be furnished with the two tablets by which they decided, "guilty or not guilty," but with a third likewise, ignoring the offence of those who should appear to have given their signatures through any deception or mistake. All appeals in causes between inhabitants of Rome, he assigned every year to the praetor of the city; and where provincials were concerned, to men of consular rank, to one of whom the business of each province was referred.

XXXIV. Some laws he abrogated, and he made some new ones; such as the sumptuary law, that relating to adultery and the violation of chastity, the law against bribery in elections, and likewise that for the encouragement of marriage. Having been more severe in his reform of this law than the rest, he found the people utterly averse to submit to it, unless the penalties were abolished or mitigated, besides allowing an interval of three years after a wife's death, and increasing the premiums on marriage. The equestrian order clamoured loudly, at a spectacle in the theatre, for its total repeal; whereupon he sent for the children of Germanicus, and shewed them partly sitting upon his own lap, and partly on their father's; intimating by his looks and gestures, that they ought not to think it a grievance to follow the example of that young man. But finding that the force of the law was eluded, by marrying girls under the age of puberty, and by frequent change of wives, he limited the time for consummation after espousals, and imposed restrictions on divorce.

XXXV. By two separate scrutinies he reduced to their former number and splendour the senate, which had been swamped by a disorderly crowd; for they were now more than a (99) thousand, and some of them very mean persons, who, after Caesar's death, had been chosen by dint of interest and bribery, so that they had the nickname of Orcini among the people 171. The first of these scrutinies was left to themselves, each senator naming another; but the last was conducted by himself and Agrippa. On this occasion he is believed to have taken his seat as he presided, with a coat of mail under his tunic, and a sword by his side, and with ten of the stoutest men of senatorial rank, who were his friends, standing round his chair. Cordus Cremutius 172 relates that no senator was suffered to approach him, except singly, and after having his bosom searched [for secreted daggers]. Some he obliged to have the grace of declining the office; these he allowed to retain the privileges of wearing the distinguishing dress, occupying the seats at the solemn spectacles, and of feasting publicly, reserved to the senatorial order 173 . That those who were chosen and approved of, might perform their functions under more solemn obligations, and with less inconvenience, he ordered that every senator, before he took his seat in the house, should pay his devotions, with an offering of frankincense and wine, at the altar of that God in whose temple the senate then assembled 174 , and that their stated meetings should be only twice in the month, namely, on the calends and ides; and that in the months of September and October 175 , a certain number only, chosen by lot, such as the law required to give validity to a decree, should be required to attend. For himself, he resolved to choose every six (100) months a new council, with whom he might consult previously upon such affairs as he judged proper at any time to lay before the full senate. He also took the votes of the senators upon any subject of importance, not according to custom, nor in regular order, but as he pleased; that every one might hold himself ready to give his opinion, rather than a mere vote of assent.

XXXVI. He also made several other alterations in the management of public affairs, among which were these following: that the acts of the senate should not be published 176 ; that the magistrates should not be sent into the provinces immediately after the expiration of their office; that the proconsuls should have a certain sum assigned them out of the treasury for mules and tents, which used before to be contracted for by the government with private persons; that the management of the treasury should be transferred from the city-quaestors to the praetors, or those who had already served in the latter office; and that the decemviri should call together the court of One hundred, which had been formerly summoned by those who had filled the office of quaestor.

XXXVII. To augment the number of persons employed in the administration of the state, he devised several new offices; such as surveyors of the public buildings, of the roads, the aqueducts, and the bed of the Tiber; for the distribution of corn to the people; the praefecture of the city; a triumvirate for the election of the senators; and another for inspecting the several troops of the equestrian order, as often as it was necessary. He revived the office of censor 177, which had been long disused, and increased the number of praetors. He likewise required that whenever the consulship was conferred on him, he should have two colleagues instead of one; but his proposal (101) was rejected, all the senators declaring by acclamation that he abated his high majesty quite enough in not filling the office alone, and consenting to share it with another.

XXXVIII. He was unsparing in the reward of military merit, having granted to above thirty generals the honour of the greater triumph; besides which, he took care to have triamphal decorations voted by the senate for more than that number. That the sons of senators might become early acquainted with the administration of affairs, he permitted them, at the age when they took the garb of manhood 178, to assume also the distinction of the senatorian robe, with its broad border, and to be present at the debates in the senate-house. When they entered the military service, he not only gave them the rank of military tribunes in the legions, but likewise the command of the auxiliary horse. And that all might have an opportunity of acquiring military experience, he commonly joined two sons of senators in command of each troop of horse. He frequently reviewed the troops of the equestrian order, reviving the ancient custom of a cavalcade 179, which had been long laid aside. But he did not suffer any one to be obliged by an accuser to dismount while he passed in review, as had formerly been the practice. As for such as were infirm with age, or (102) any way deformed, he allowed them to send their horses before them, coming on foot to answer to their names, when the muster roll was called over soon afterwards. He permitted those who had attained the age of thirty-five years, and desired not to keep their horse any longer, to have the privilege of giving it up.

XXXIX. With the assistance of ten senators, he obliged each of the Roman knights to give an account of his life: in regard to those who fell under his displeasure, some were punished; others had a mark of infamy set against their names. The most part he only reprimanded, but not in the same terms. The mildest mode of reproof was by delivering them tablets 180, the contents of which, confined to themselves, they were to read on the spot. Some he disgraced for borrowing money at low interest, and letting it out again upon usurious profit.

XL. In the election of tribunes of the people, if there was not a sufficient number of senatorian candidates, he nominated others from the equestrian order; granting them the liberty, after the expiration of their office, to continue in whichsoever of the two orders they pleased. As most of the knights had been much reduced in their estates by the civil wars, and therefore durst not sit to see the public games in the theatre in the seats allotted to their order, for fear of the penalty provided by the law in that case, he enacted, that none were liable to it, who had themselves, or whose parents had ever, possessed a knight's estate. He took the census of the Roman people street by street: and that the people might not be too often taken from their business to receive the distribution of corn, it was his intention to deliver tickets three times a year for four months respectively; but at their request, he continued the former regulation, that they should receive their (103) share monthly. He revived the former law of elections, endeavouring, by various penalties, to suppress the practice of bribery. Upon the day of election, he distributed to the freemen of the Fabian and Scaptian tribes, in which he himself was enrolled, a thousand sesterces each, that they might look for nothing from any of the candidates. Considering it of extreme importance to preserve the Roman people pure, and untainted with a mixture of foreign or servile blood, he not only bestowed the freedom of the city with a sparing hand, but laid some restriction upon the practice of manumitting slaves. When Tiberius interceded with him for the freedom of Rome in behalf of a Greek client of his, he wrote to him for answer, "I shall not grant it, unless he comes himself, and satisfies me that he has just grounds for the application." And when Livia begged the freedom of the city for a tributary Gaul, he refused it, but offered to release him from payment of taxes, saying, "I shall sooner suffer some loss in my exchequer, than that the citizenship of Rome be rendered too common." Not content with interposing many obstacles to either the partial or complete emancipation of slaves, by quibbles respecting the number, condition and difference of those who were to be manumitted; he likewise enacted that none who had been put in chains or tortured, should ever obtain the freedom of the city in any degree. He endeavoured also to restore the old habit and dress of the

Romans; and upon seeing once, in an assembly of the people, a crowd in grey cloaks 181 , he exclaimed with indignation, "See there,

> *Romanos rerum dominos, gentemque togatem."* 182_
> Rome's conquering sons, lords of the wide-spread globe,
> Stalk proudly in the toga's graceful robe.

And he gave orders to the ediles not to permit, in future, any Roman to be present in the forum or circus unless they took off their short coats, and wore the toga.

(104) XLI. He displayed his munificence to all ranks of the people on various occasions. Moreover, upon his bringing the treasure belonging to the kings of Egypt into the city, in his Alexandrian triumph, he made money so plentiful, that interest fell, and the price of land rose considerably. And afterwards, as often as large sums of money came into his possession by means of confiscations, he would lend it free of interest, for a fixed term, to such as could give security for the double of what was borrowed. The estate necessary to qualify a senator, instead of eight hundred thousand sesterces, the former standard, he ordered, for the future, to be twelve hundred thousand; and to those who had not so much, he made good the deficiency. He often made donations to the people, but generally of different sums; sometimes four hundred, sometimes three hundred, or two hundred and fifty sesterces upon which occasions, he extended his bounty even to young boys, who before were not used to receive anything, until they arrived at eleven years of age. In a scarcity of corn, he would frequently let them have it at a very low price, or none at all; and doubled the number of the money tickets.

XLII. But to show that he was a prince who regarded more the good of his people than their applause, he reprimanded them very severely, upon their complaining of the scarcity and dearness of wine. "My son-in-law, Agrippa," he said, "has sufficiently provided for quenching your thirst, by the great plenty of water with which he has supplied the town." Upon their demanding a gift which he had promised them, he said, "I am a man of my word." But upon their importuning him for one which he had not promised, he issued a proclamation upbraiding them for their scandalous impudence; at the same time telling them, "I shall now give you nothing, whatever I may have intended to do." With the same strict firmness, when, upon a promise he had made of a donative, he found many slaves had been emancipated and enrolled amongst the citizens, he declared that no one should receive anything who was not included in the promise, and he gave the rest less than he had promised them, in order that the amount he had set apart might hold out. On one occasion, in a season of great scarcity, which it was difficult to remedy, he ordered out of the city the troops of slaves brought for sale, the gladiators (105) belonging to the masters of defence, and all foreigners, excepting physicians and the teachers of the liberal sciences. Part of the domestic slaves were likewise ordered to be dismissed. When, at last, plenty was restored, he writes thus "I was much inclined to abolish for ever the practice of allowing the people corn at the public expense, because they trust so much to it, that they are too lazy to till their lands; but I did not persevere in my design, as I felt sure that the practice would some time or other be revived by some one ambitious of popular favour." However, he so managed the affair ever afterwards, that as much account was taken of husbandmen and traders, as of the idle populace. 183

XLIII. In the number, variety, and magnificence of his public spectacles, he surpassed all former example. Four-and-twenty times, he says, he treated the people with games upon his own account, and three-and-twenty times for such magistrates as were either absent, or not able to afford the expense. The performances took place sometimes in the different streets of the city, and upon several stages, by players in all languages. The same he did not only in the forum and amphitheatre, but in the circus likewise, and in the septa 184 : and sometimes he exhibited only the hunting of wild beasts. He entertained the people with wrestlers in the Campus Martius, where wooden seats were erected for the purpose; and also with a naval fight, for which he excavated the ground near the Tiber, where there is now the grove of the Caesars. During these two entertainments he stationed guards in the city, lest, by robbers taking advantage of the small number of people left at home, it might be exposed to depredations. In the circus he exhibited chariot and foot races, and combats with wild beasts, in which the performers were often youths of the highest rank. His favourite spectacle was the Trojan game, acted by a select number of boys, in parties differing in age and station; thinking (106) that it was a practice both excellent in itself, and sanctioned by ancient usage, that the spirit of the young nobles should be displayed in such exercises. Caius Nonius Asprenas, who was lamed by a fall in this diversion, he presented with a gold collar, and allowed him and his posterity to bear the surname of Torquati. But soon afterwards he gave up the exhibition of this game, in consequence of a severe and bitter speech made in the senate by Asinius Pollio, the orator, in which he complained bitterly of the misfortune of Aeserninus, his grandson, who likewise broke his leg in the same diversion.

Sometimes he engaged Roman knights to act upon the stage, or to fight as gladiators; but only before the practice was prohibited by a decree of the senate. Thenceforth, the only exhibition he made of that kind, was that of a young man named Lucius, of a good family, who was not quite two feet in height, and weighed only seventeen pounds, but had a stentorian voice. In one of his public spectacles, he brought the hostages of the Parthians, the first ever sent to Rome from that nation, through the middle of the amphitheatre, and placed them in the second tier of seats above him. He used likewise, at times when there were no public entertainments, if any thing was brought to Rome which was uncommon, and might gratify curiosity, to expose it to public view, in any place whatever; as he did a rhinoceros in the Septa, a tiger upon a stage, and a snake fifty cubits lung in the Comitium. It happened in the Circensian games, which he performed in consequence of a vow, that he was taken ill, and obliged to attend the Thensae 185 , reclining on a litter. Another time, in the games celebrated for the opening of the theatre of Marcellus, the joints of his curule chair happening to give way, he fell on his back. And in the games exhibited by his (107) grandsons, when the people were in such consternation, by an alarm raised that the theatre was falling, that all his efforts to re-assure them and keep them quiet, failed, he moved from his place, and seated himself in that part of the theatre which was thought to be exposed to most danger.

XLIV. He corrected the confusion and disorder with which the spectators took their seats at the public games, after an affront which was offered to a senator at Puteoli, for whom, in a crowded theatre, no one would make room. He therefore procured a decree of the senate, that in all public spectacles of any sort, and in any place whatever, the first tier of benches should be left empty for the accommodation of senators. He would not even permit the ambassadors of free nations, nor of those which were allies of Rome, to sit in the orchestra; having found that some manumitted slaves had been sent under that character. He separated the soldiery from the rest of the people, and assigned to married plebeians their particular rows of seats. To the boys he assigned their own benches, and to their tutors the seats which were nearest it; ordering that none clothed in black should sit in the centre of the circle 186. Nor would he allow any women to witness the combats of gladiators, except from the upper part of the theatre, although they formerly used to take their places promiscuously with the rest of the spectators. To the vestal virgins he granted seats in the theatre, reserved for them only, opposite the praetor's bench. He excluded, however, the whole female sex from seeing the wrestlers: so that in the games which he exhibited upon his accession to the office of high-priest, he deferred producing a pair of combatants which the people called for, until the next morning; and intimated by proclamation, "his pleasure that no woman should appear in the theatre before five o'clock."

XLV. He generally viewed the Circensian games himself, from the upper rooms of the houses of his friends or freedmen; sometimes from the place appointed for the statues of the gods, and sitting in company with his wife and children. He (108) occasionally absented himself from the spectacles for several hours, and sometimes for whole days; but not without first making an apology, and appointing substitutes to preside in his stead. When present, he never attended to anything else either to avoid the reflections which he used to say were commonly made upon his father, Caesar, for perusing letters and memorials, and making rescripts during the spectacles; or from the real pleasure he took in attending those exhibitions; of which he made no secret, he often candidly owning it. This he manifested frequently by presenting honorary crowns and handsome rewards to the best performers, in the games exhibited by others; and he never was present at any performance of the Greeks, without rewarding the most deserving, according to their merit. He took particular pleasure in witnessing pugilistic contests, especially those of the Latins, not only between combatants who had been trained scientifically, whom he used often to match with the Greek champions; but even between mobs of the lower classes fighting in streets, and tilting at random, without any knowledge of the art. In short, he honoured with his patronage all sorts of people who contributed in any way to the success of the public entertainments. He not only maintained, but enlarged, the privileges of the wrestlers. He prohibited combats of gladiators where no quarter was given. He deprived the magistrates of the power of correcting the stage-players, which by an ancient law was allowed them at all times, and in all places; restricting their jurisdiction entirely to the time of performance and misdemeanours in the theatres. He would, however, admit, of no abatement, and exacted with the utmost rigour the greatest exertions of the wrestlers and gladiators in their several encounters. He went so far in restraining the licentiousness of stage-players, that upon discovering that Stephanio, a performer of the highest class, had a married woman with her hair cropped, and dressed in boy's clothes, to wait upon him at table, he ordered him to be whipped through all the three theatres, and then banished him. Hylas, an actor of pantomimes, upon a complaint against him by the praetor, he commanded to be scourged in the court of his own house, which, however, was open to the public. And Pylades he not only banished from the city, but from Italy also, for pointing with his finger at a spectator by whom he was hissed, and turning the eyes of the audience upon him.

(109) XLVI. Having thus regulated the city and its concerns, he augmented the population of Italy by planting in it no less than twenty-eight colonies 187 , and greatly improved it by public works, and a beneficial application of the revenues. In rights and privileges, he rendered it in a measure equal to the city itself, by inventing a new kind of suffrage, which the principal officers and magistrates of the colonies might take at home, and forward under seal to the city, against the time of the elections. To increase the number of persons of condition, and of children among the lower ranks, he granted the petitions of all those who requested the honour of doing military service on horseback as knights, provided their demands were seconded by the recommendation of the town in which they lived; and when he visited the several districts of Italy, he distributed a thousand sesterces a head to such of the lower class as presented him with sons or daughters.

XLVII. The more important provinces, which could not with ease or safety be entrusted to the government of annual magistrates, he reserved for his own administration: the rest he distributed by lot amongst the proconsuls: but sometimes he made exchanges, and frequently visited most of both kinds in person. Some cities in alliance with Rome, but which by their great licentiousness were hastening to ruin, he deprived of their independence. Others, which were much in debt, he relieved, and rebuilt such as had been destroyed by earthquakes. To those that could produce any instance of their having deserved well of the Roman people, he presented the freedom of Latium, or even that of the City. There is not, I believe, a province, except Africa and Sardinia, which he did not visit. After forcing Sextus Pompeius to take refuge in those provinces, he was indeed preparing to cross over from Sicily to them, but was prevented by continual and violent storms, and afterwards there was no occasion or call for such a voyage.

XLVIII. Kingdoms, of which he had made himself master by the right of conquest, a few only excepted, he either restored to their former possessors 188 , or conferred upon aliens. Between (110) kings of alliance with Rome, he encouraged most intimate union; being always ready to promote or favour any proposal of marriage or friendship amongst them; and, indeed, treated them all with the same consideration, as if they were members and parts of the empire. To such of them as were minors or lunatics he appointed guardians, until they arrived at age, or recovered their senses; and the sons of many of them he brought up and educated with his own.

XLIX. With respect to the army, he distributed the legions and auxiliary troops throughout the several provinces, he stationed a fleet at Misenum, and another at Ravenna, for the protection of the Upper and Lower Seas 189 . A certain number of the forces were selected, to occupy the posts in the city, and partly for his own body-guard; but he dismissed the Spanish guard, which he retained about him till the fall of Antony; and also the Germans, whom he had amongst his guards, until the defeat of Varus. Yet he never permitted a greater force than three cohorts in the city, and had no (pretorian) camps 190 . The rest he quartered in the neighbourhood of the nearest towns, in winter and summer camps. All the troops throughout the empire he reduced to one fixed model with regard to their pay and their pensions; determining these according to their rank in the army, the time they had served, and their private means; so that after their discharge, they might not be tempted by age or necessities to join the agitators for a revolution. For the purpose of providing a fund always ready to meet their pay and pensions, he instituted a military exchequer, and appropriated new taxes to that object. In order to obtain the earliest intelligence of what was passing in the provinces, he established posts, consisting at first of young men stationed at moderate distances along the military roads, and afterwards of regular couriers with fast vehicles; which appeared to him the most commodious, because the persons who were the bearers of dispatches, written on the spot, might then be questioned about the business, as occasion occurred.

L. In sealing letters-patent, rescripts, or epistles, he at first used the figure of a sphinx, afterwards the head of Alexander (111) the Great, and at last his own, engraved by the hand of Dioscorides; which practice was retained by the succeeding emperors. He was extremely precise in dating his letters, putting down exactly the time of the day or night at which they were dispatched.

LI. Of his clemency and moderation there are abundant and signal instances. For, not to enumerate how many and what persons of the adverse party he pardoned, received into favour, and suffered to rise to the highest eminence in the state; he thought it sufficient to punish Junius Novatus and Cassius Patavinus, who were both plebeians, one of them with a fine, and the other with an easy banishment; although the former had published, in the name of young Agrippa, a very scurrilous letter against him, and the other declared openly, at an entertainment where there was a great deal of company, "that he neither wanted inclination nor courage to stab him." In the trial of Aemilius Aelianus, of Cordova, when, among other charges exhibited against him, it was particularly insisted upon, that he used to calumniate Caesar, he turned round to the accuser, and said, with an air and tone of passion, "I wish you could make that appear; I shall let Aelianus know that I have a tongue too, and shall speak sharper of him than he ever did of me." Nor did he, either then or afterwards, make any farther inquiry into the affair. And when Tiberius, in a letter, complained of the affront with great earnestness, he returned him an answer in the following terms: "Do not, my dear Tiberius, give way to the ardour of youth in this affair; nor be so indignant that any person should speak ill of me. It is enough, for us, if we can prevent any one from really doing us mischief."

LII. Although he knew that it had been customary to decree temples in honour of the proconsuls, yet he would not permit them to be erected in any of the provinces, unless in the joint names of himself and Rome. Within the limits of the city, he positively refused any honour of that kind. He melted down all the silver statues which had been erected to him, and converted the whole into tripods, which he consecrated to the Palatine Apollo. And when the people importuned him to accept the dictatorship, he bent down on one knee, with his toga thrown over his shoulders, and his breast exposed to view, begging to be excused.

(112) LIII. He always abhorred the title of Lord 191, as ill-omened and offensive. And when, in a play, performed at the theatre, at which he was present, these words were introduced, "O just and gracious lord," and the whole company, with joyful acclamations, testified their approbation of them, as applied to him, he instantly put a stop to their indecent flattery, by waving his hand, and frowning sternly, and next day publicly declared his displeasure, in a proclamation. He never afterwards would suffer himself to be addressed in that manner, even by his own children or grand-children, either in jest or earnest and forbad them the use of all such complimentary expressions to one another. He rarely entered any city or town, or departed from it, except in the evening or the night, to avoid giving any person the trouble of complimenting him. During his consulships, he commonly walked the streets on foot; but at other times, rode in a close carriage. He admitted to court even plebeians, in common with people of the higher ranks; receiving the petitions of those who approached him with so much affability, that he once jocosely rebuked a man, by telling him, "You present your memorial with as much hesitation as if you were offering money to an elephant." On senate days, he used to pay his respects to the Conscript Fathers only in the house, addressing them each by name as they sat, without any prompter; and on his departure, he bade each of them farewell, while they retained their seats. In the same manner, he maintained with many of them a constant intercourse of mutual civilities, giving them his company upon occasions of any particular festivity in their families; until he became advanced in years, and was incommoded by the crowd at a wedding. Being informed that Gallus Terrinius, a senator, with whom he had only a slight acquaintance, had suddenly lost his sight, and

under that privation had resolved to starve himself to death, he paid him a visit, and by his consolatory admonitions diverted him from his purpose.

LIV. On his speaking in the senate, he has been told by (113) one of the members, "I did not understand you," and by another, "I would contradict you, could I do it with safety." And sometimes, upon his being so much offended at the heat with which the debates were conducted in the senate, as to quit the house in anger, some of the members have repeatedly exclaimed: "Surely, the senators ought to have liberty of speech on matters of government." Antistius Labeo, in the election of a new senate, when each, as he was named, chose another, nominated Marcus Lepidus, who had formerly been Augustus's enemy, and was then in banishment; and being asked by the latter, "Is there no other person more deserving?" he replied, "Every man has his own opinion." Nor was any one ever molested for his freedom of speech, although it was carried to the extent of insolence.

LV. Even when some infamous libels against him were dispersed in the senate-house, he was neither disturbed, nor did he give himself much trouble to refute them. He would not so much as order an enquiry to be made after the authors; but only proposed, that, for the future, those who published libels or lampoons, in a borrowed name, against any person, should be called to account.

LVI. Being provoked by some petulant jests, which were designed to render him odious, he answered them by a proclamation; and yet he prevented the senate from passing an act, to restrain the liberties which were taken with others in people's wills. Whenever he attended at the election of magistrates, he went round the tribes, with the candidates of his nomination, and begged the votes of the people in the usual manner. He likewise gave his own vote in his tribe, as one of the people. He suffered himself to be summoned as a witness upon trials, and not only to be questioned, but to be cross-examined, with the utmost patience. In building his Forum, he restricted himself in the site, not presuming to compel the owners of the neighbouring houses to give up their property. He never recommended his sons to the people, without adding these words, "If they deserve it." And upon the audience rising on their entering the theatre, while they were yet minors, and giving them applause in a standing position, he made it a matter of serious complaint.

(114) He was desirous that his friends should be great and powerful in the state, but have no exclusive privileges, or be exempt from the laws which governed others. When Asprenas Nonius, an intimate friend of his, was tried upon a charge of administering poison at the instance of Cassius Severus, he consulted the senate for their opinion what was his duty under the circumstances: "For," said he, "I am afraid, lest, if I should stand by him in the cause, I may be supposed to screen a guilty man; and if I do not, to desert and prejudge a friend." With the unanimous concurrence, therefore, of the senate, he took his seat amongst his advocates for several hours, but without giving him the benefit of speaking to character, as was usual. He likewise appeared for his clients; as on behalf of Scutarius, an old soldier of his, who brought an action for slander. He never relieved any one from prosecution but in a single instance, in the case of a man who had given information of the conspiracy of Muraena; and that he did only by prevailing upon the accuser, in open court, to drop his prosecution.

LVII. How much he was beloved for his worthy conduct in all these respects, it is easy to imagine. I say nothing of the decrees of the senate in his honour, which may seem to have resulted from compulsion or deference. The Roman knights voluntarily, and with one accord, always celebrated his birth for two days together; and all ranks of the people, yearly, in performance of a vow they had made, threw a piece of money into the Curtian lake 192 , as an offering for his welfare. They likewise, on the calends [first] of January, presented for his acceptance new-year's gifts in the Capitol, though he was not present with which donations he purchased some costly images of the Gods, which he erected in several streets of the city; as that of Apollo Sandaliarius, Jupiter Tragoedus 193 , and others. When his house on the Palatine hill was accidentally destroyed by fire, the veteran soldiers, the judges, the tribes, and even the people, individually, contributed, according to the ability of each, for rebuilding it; but he would (115) accept only of some small portion out of the several sums collected, and refused to take from any one person more than a single denarius 194 . Upon his return home from any of the provinces, they attended him not only with joyful acclamations, but with songs. It is also remarked, that as often as he entered the city, the infliction of punishment was suspended for the time.

LVIII. The whole body of the people, upon a sudden impulse, and with unanimous consent, offered him the title of FATHER OF HIS COUNTRY. It was announced to him first at Antium, by a deputation from the people, and upon his declining the honour, they repeated their offer on his return to Rome, in a full theatre, when they were crowned with laurel. The senate soon afterwards adopted the proposal, not in the way of acclamation or decree, but by commissioning M. Messala, in an unanimous vote, to compliment him with it in the following terms: "With hearty wishes for the happiness and prosperity of yourself and your family, Caesar Augustus, (for we think we thus most effectually pray for the lasting welfare of the state), the senate, in agreement with the Roman people, salute you by the title of FATHER OF YOUR COUNTRY." To this compliment Augustus replied, with tears in his eyes, in these words (for I give them exactly as I have done those of Messala): "Having now arrived at the summit of my wishes, O Conscript Fathers 195 , what else have I to beg of the Immortal (116) Gods, but the continuance of this your affection for me to the last moments of my life?"

LIX. To the physician Antonius Musa 196 , who had cured him of a dangerous illness, they erected a statue near that of Aesculapius, by a general subscription. Some heads of families ordered in their wills, that their heirs should lead victims to the Capitol, with a tablet carried before them, and pay their vows, "Because Augustus still survived." Some Italian cities appointed the day upon which he first visited them, to be thenceforth the beginning of their year. And most of the provinces, besides erecting temples and altars, instituted games, to be celebrated to his honour, in most towns, every five years.

LX. The kings, his friends and allies, built cities in their respective kingdoms, to which they gave the name of Caesarea; and all with one consent resolved to finish, at their common expense, the temple of Jupiter Olympius, at Athens, which had been begun long before, and consecrate it to his Genius. They frequently also left their kingdoms, laid aside the badges of royalty, and assuming the toga, attended and paid their respects to him daily, in the manner of clients to their patrons; not only at Rome, but when he was travelling through the provinces.

LXI. Having thus given an account of the manner in which he filled his public offices both civil and military, and his conduct in the government of the empire, both in peace and war; I shall now describe his private and domestic life, his habits at home and among his friends and dependents, and the fortune attending him in those scenes of retirement, from his youth to the day of his death. He lost his mother in his first consulship, and his sister Octavia, when he was in the fifty-fourth year of his age 197 . He behaved towards them both with the utmost kindness whilst living, and after their decease paid the highest honours to their memory.

(117) LXII. He was contracted when very young to the daughter of Publius Servilius Isauricus; but upon his reconciliation with Antony after their first rupture 198 , the armies on both sides insisting on a family alliance between them, he married Antony's step-daughter Claudia, the daughter of Fulvia by Publius Claudius, although at that time she was scarcely marriageable; and upon a difference arising with his mother-in-law Fulvia, he divorced her untouched, and a pure virgin. Soon afterwards he took to wife Scribonia, who had before been twice married to men of consular rank 199 , and was a mother by one of them. With her likewise he parted 200 , being quite tired out, as he himself writes, with the perverseness of her temper; and immediately took Livia Drusilla, though then pregnant, from her husband Tiberius Nero; and she had never any rival in his love and esteem.

LXIII. By Scribonia he had a daughter named Julia, but no children by Livia, although extremely desirous of issue. She, indeed, conceived once, but miscarried. He gave his daughter Julia in the first instance to Marcellus, his sister's son, who had just completed his minority; and, after his death, to Marcus Agrippa, having prevailed with his sister to yield her son-in-law to his wishes; for at that time Agrippa was married to one of the Marcellas, and had children by her. Agrippa dying also, he for a long time thought of several matches for Julia in even the equestrian order, and at last resolved upon selecting Tiberius for his step-son; and he obliged him to part with his wife at that time pregnant, and who had already brought him a child. Mark Antony writes, "That he first contracted Julia to his son, and afterwards to Cotiso, king of the Getae 201 , demanding at the same time the king's daughter in marriage for himself."

(118) LXIV. He had three grandsons by Agrippa and Julia, namely, Caius, Lucius, and Agrippa; and two grand-daughters, Julia and Agrippina. Julia he married to Lucius Paulus, the censor's son, and Agrippina to Germanicus, his sister's grandson. Caius and Lucius he adopted at home, by the ceremony of purchase 202 from their father, advanced them, while yet very young, to offices in the state, and when they were consuls-elect, sent them to visit the provinces and armies. In bringing up his daughter and grand-daughters, he accustomed them to domestic employments, and even spinning, and obliged them to speak and act every thing openly before the family, that it might be put down in the diary. He so strictly prohibited them from all converse with strangers, that he once wrote a letter to Lucius Vinicius, a handsome young man of a good family, in which he told him, "You have not behaved very modestly, in making a visit to my daughter at Baiae." He usually instructed his grandsons himself in reading, swimming, and other rudiments of knowledge; and he laboured nothing more than to perfect them in the imitation of his hand-writing. He never supped but he had them sitting at the foot of his couch; nor ever travelled but with them in a chariot before him, or riding beside him.

LXV. But in the midst of all his joy and hopes in his numerous and well-regulated family, his fortune failed him. The two Julias, his daughter and grand-daughter, abandoned themselves to such courses of lewdness and debauchery, that he banished them both. Caius and Lucius he lost within the space of eighteen months; the former dying in Lycia, and the latter at Marseilles. His third grandson Agrippa, with his step-son Tiberius, he adopted in the forum, by a law passed for the purpose by the Sections 203 ; but he soon afterwards discarded Agrippa for his coarse and unruly temper, and confined him at Surrentum. He bore the death of his relations with more patience than he did their disgrace; for he was not overwhelmed by the loss of Caius and Lucius; but in the case of his daughter, he stated the facts to the senate in a message read to them by (119) the quaestor, not having the heart to be present himself; indeed, he was so much ashamed of her infamous conduct, that for some time he avoided all company, and had thoughts of putting her to death. It is certain that when one Phoebe, a freed-woman and confidant of hers, hanged herself about the same time, he said, "I had rather be the father of Phoebe than of

Julia." In her banishment he would not allow her the use of wine, nor any luxury in dress; nor would he suffer her to be waited upon by any male servant, either freeman or slave, without his permission, and having received an exact account of his age, stature, complexion, and what marks or scars he had about him. At the end of five years he removed her from the island [where she was confined] to the continent 204 , and treated her with less severity, but could never be prevailed upon to recall her. When the Roman people interposed on her behalf several times with much importunity, all the reply he gave was: "I wish you had all such daughters and wives as she is." He likewise forbad a child, of which his grand-daughter Julia was delivered after sentence had passed against her, to be either owned as a relation, or brought up. Agrippa, who was equally intractable, and whose folly increased every day, he transported to an island  205 , and placed a guard of soldiers about him; procuring at the same time an act of the senate for his confinement there during life. Upon any mention of him and the two Julias, he would say, with a heavy sigh,

*Aith' ophelon agamos t' emenai, agonos t' apoletai.*
*Would I were wifeless, or had childless died! 206_*

nor did he usually call them by any other name than that of his "three imposthumes or cancers."

LXVI. He was cautious in forming friendships, but clung to them with great constancy; not only rewarding the virtues and merits of his friends according to their deserts, but bearing likewise with their faults and vices, provided that they were (120) of a venial kind. For amongst all his friends, we scarcely find any who fell into disgrace with him, except Salvidienus Rufus, whom he raised to the consulship, and Cornelius Gallus, whom he made prefect of Egypt; both of them men of the lowest extraction. One of these, being engaged in plotting a rebellion, he delivered over to the senate, for condemnation; and the other, on account of his ungrateful and malicious temper, he forbad his house, and his living in any of the provinces. When, however, Gallus, being denounced by his accusers, and sentenced by the senate, was driven to the desperate extremity of laying violent hands upon himself, he commended, indeed, the attachment to his person of those who manifested so much indignation, but he shed tears, and lamented his unhappy condition, "That I alone," said he, "cannot be allowed to resent the misconduct of my friends in such a way only as

I would wish." The rest of his friends of all orders flourished during their whole lives, both in power and wealth, in the highest ranks of their several orders, notwithstanding some occasional lapses. For, to say nothing of others, he sometimes complained that Agrippa was hasty, and Mecaenas a tattler; the former having thrown up all his employments and retired to Mitylene, on suspicion of some slight coolness, and from jealousy that Marcellus received greater marks of favour; and the latter having confidentially imparted to his wife Terentia the discovery of Muraena's conspiracy.

He likewise expected from his friends, at their deaths as well as during their lives, some proofs of their reciprocal attachment. For though he was far from coveting their property, and indeed would never accept of any legacy left him by a stranger, yet he pondered in a melancholy mood over their last words; not being able to conceal his chagrin, if in their wills they made but a slight, or no very honourable mention of him, nor his joy, on the other hand, if they expressed a grateful sense of his favours, and a hearty affection for him. And whatever legacies or shares of their property were left him by such as were parents, he used to restore to their children, either immediately, or if they were under age, upon the day of their assuming the manly dress, or of their marriage; with interest.

LXVII. As a patron and master, his behaviour in general was mild and conciliating; but when occasion required it, he (121) could be severe. He advanced many of his freedmen to posts of honour and great importance, as Licinus, Enceladus, and others; and when his slave, Cosmus, had reflected bitterly upon him, he resented the injury no further than by putting him in fetters. When his steward, Diomedes, left him to the mercy of a wild boar, which suddenly attacked them while they were walking together, he considered it rather a cowardice than a breach of duty; and turned an occurrence of no small hazard into a jest, because there was no knavery in his steward's conduct. He put to death Proculus, one of his most favourite freedmen, for maintaining a criminal commerce with other men's wives. He broke the legs of his secretary, Thallus, for taking a bribe of five hundred denarii to discover the contents of one of his letters. And the tutor and other attendants of his son Caius, having taken advantage of his sickness and death, to give loose to their insolence and rapacity in the province he governed, he caused heavy weights to be tied about their necks, and had them thrown into a river.

LXVIII. In his early youth various aspersions of an infamous character were heaped upon him. Sextus Pompey reproached him with being an effeminate fellow; and M. Antony, with earning his adoption from his uncle by prostitution. Lucius Antony, likewise Mark's brother, charges him with pollution by Caesar; and that, for a gratification of three hundred thousand sesterces, he had submitted to Aulus Hirtius in the same way, in Spain; adding, that he used to singe his legs with burnt nut-shells, to make the hair become softer 207. Nay, the whole concourse of the people, at some public diversions in the theatre, when the following sentence was recited, alluding to the Gallic priest of the mother of the gods 208, beating a drum 209,

*Videsne ut cinaedus orbem digito temperet?*
*See with his orb the wanton's finger play!*

applied the passage to him, with great applause.

(122) LXIX. That he was guilty of various acts of adultery, is not denied even by his friends; but they allege in excuse for it, that he engaged in those intrigues not from lewdness, but from policy, in order to discover more easily the designs of his enemies, through their wives. Mark Antony, besides the precipitate marriage of Livia, charges him with taking the wife of a man of consular rank from table, in the presence of her husband, into a bed-chamber, and bringing her again to the entertainment, with her ears very red, and her hair in great disorder: that he had divorced Scribonia, for resenting too freely the excessive influence which one of his mistresses had gained over him: that his friends were employed to pimp for him, and accordingly obliged both matrons and ripe virgins to strip, for a complete examination of their persons, in the same manner as if Thoranius, the dealer in slaves, had them under sale. And before they came to an open rupture, he writes to him in a familiar manner, thus: "Why are you changed towards me? Because I lie with a queen? She is my wife. Is this a new thing with me, or have I not done so for these nine years? And do you take freedoms with Drusilla only? May health and happiness so attend you, as when you read this letter, you are not in dalliance with Tertulla, Terentilla, Rufilla 210, or Salvia Titiscenia, or all of them. What matters it to you where, or upon whom, you spend your manly vigour?"

LXX. A private entertainment which he gave, commonly called the Supper of the Twelve Gods 211 , and at which the guests (123) were dressed in the habit of gods and goddesses, while he personated Apollo himself, afforded subject of much conversation, and was imputed to him not only by Antony in his letters, who likewise names all the parties concerned, but in the following well-known anonymous verses:

> *Cum primum istorum conduxit mensa choragum,*
> *Sexque deos vidit Mallia, sexque deas*
> *Impia dum Phoebi Caesar mendacia ludit,*
> *Dum nova divorum coenat adulteria:*
> *Omnia se a terris tunc numina declinarunt:*
> *Fugit et auratos Jupiter ipse thronos.*
> *When Mallia late beheld, in mingled train,*
> *Twelve mortals ape twelve deities in vain;*
> *Caesar assumed what was Apollo's due,*
> *And wine and lust inflamed the motley crew.*
> *At the foul sight the gods avert their eyes,*
> *And from his throne great Jove indignant flies.*

What rendered this supper more obnoxious to public censure, was that it happened at a time when there was a great scarcity, and almost a famine, in the city. The day after, there was a cry current among the people, "that the gods had eaten up all the corn; and that Caesar was indeed Apollo, but Apollo the Tormentor;" under which title that god was worshipped in some quarter of the city 212 . He was likewise charged with being excessively fond of fine furniture, and Corinthian vessels, as well as with being addicted to gaming. For, during the time of the proscription, the following line was written upon his statue:—

> *Pater argentarius, ego Corinthiarius;*
> *My father was a silversmith 213 , my dealings are in brass;*

because it was believed, that he had put some persons upon the list of the proscribed, only to obtain the Corinthian vessels in (124) their possession. And afterwards, in the Sicilian war, the following epigram was published:—

> *Postquam bis classe victus naves perdidit,*
> *Aliquando ut vincat, ludit assidue aleam.*

*Twice having lost a fleet in luckless fight,*
*To win at last, he games both day and night.*

LXXI. With respect to the charge or imputation of loathsome impurity before-mentioned, he very easily refuted it by the chastity of his life, at the very time when it was made, as well as ever afterwards. His conduct likewise gave the lie to that of luxurious extravagance in his furniture, when, upon the taking of Alexandria, he reserved for himself nothing of the royal treasures but a porcelain cup, and soon afterwards melted down all the vessels of gold, even such as were intended for common use. But his amorous propensities never left him, and, as he grew older, as is reported, he was in the habit of debauching young girls, who were procured for him, from all quarters, even by his own wife. To the observations on his gaming, he paid not the smallest regard; but played in public, but purely for his diversion, even when he was advanced in years; and not only in the month of December 214, but at other times, and upon all days, whether festivals or not. This evidently appears from a letter under his own hand, in which he says, "I supped, my dear Tiberius, with the same company. We had, besides, Vinicius, and Silvius the father. We gamed at supper like old fellows, both yesterday and today. And as any one threw upon the tali 215 aces or sixes, he put down for every talus a denarius; all which was gained by him who threw a Venus." 216 In another letter, he says: "We had, my dear Tiberius, a pleasant time of it during the festival of Minerva: for we played every day, and kept the gaming-board warm. Your brother uttered many exclamations at a desperate run of ill-fortune; but recovering by degrees, and unexpectedly, he in the end lost not much. I lost twenty thousand sesterces for my part; but then I was profusely (125) generous in my play, as I commonly am; for had I insisted upon the stakes which I declined, or kept what I gave away, I should have won about fifty thousand. But this I like better for it will raise my character for generosity to the skies." In a letter to his daughter, he writes thus: "I have sent you two hundred and fifty denarii, which I gave to every one of my guests; in case they were inclined at supper to divert themselves with the Tali, or at the game of Even-or-Odd."

LXXII. In other matters, it appears that he was moderate in his habits, and free from suspicion of any kind of vice. He lived at first near the Roman Forum, above the Ring-maker's Stairs, in a house which had once been occupied by Calvus the orator. He afterwards moved to the Palatine Hill, where he resided in a small house 217 belonging to Hortensius, no way remarkable either for size or ornament; the piazzas being but small, the pillars of Alban stone 218 , and the rooms without any thing of marble, or fine paving. He continued to use the same bed-chamber, both winter and summer, during forty years 219 : for though he was sensible that the city did not agree with his health in the winter, he nevertheless resided constantly in it during that season. If at any time he wished to be perfectly retired, and secure from interruption, he shut himself up in an apartment at the top of his house, which he called his Syracuse or Technophuon 220 , or he went to some villa belonging to his freedmen near the city. But when he was indisposed, he commonly took up his residence in the house of Mecaenas 221 . Of all the places of retirement from the city, he (126) chiefly frequented those upon the sea-coast, and the islands of Campania 222 , or the towns nearest the city, such as Lanuvium, Praeneste, and Tibur 223 , where he often used to sit for the administration of justice, in the porticos of the temple of Hercules. He had a particular aversion to large and sumptuous palaces; and some which had been raised at a vast expense by his grand-daughter, Julia, he levelled to the ground. Those of his own, which were far from being spacious, he adorned, not so much with statues and pictures, as with walks and groves, and things which were curious either for their antiquity or rarity; such as, at Capri, the huge limbs of sea-monsters and wild beasts, which some affect to call the bones of giants; and also the arms of ancient heroes.

LXXIII. His frugality in the furniture of his house appears even at this day, from some beds and tables still remaining, most of which are scarcely elegant enough for a private family. It is reported that he never lay upon a bed, but such as was low, and meanly furnished. He seldom wore any garment but what was made by the hands of his wife, sister, daughter, and grand-daughters. His togas 224 were neither scanty nor full; (127) and the clavus was neither remarkably broad or narrow. His shoes were a little higher than common, to make him appear taller than he was. He had always clothes and shoes, fit to appear in public, ready in his bed-chamber for any sudden occasion.

LXXIV. At his table, which was always plentiful and elegant, he constantly entertained company; but was very scrupulous in the choice of them, both as to rank and character. Valerius Messala informs us, that he never admitted any freedman to his table, except Menas, when rewarded with the privilege of citizenship, for betraying Pompey's fleet. He writes, himself, that he invited to his table a person in whose villa he lodged, and who had formerly been employed by him as a spy. He often came late to table, and withdrew early; so that the company began supper before his arrival, and continued at table after his departure. His entertainments consisted of three entries, or at most of only six. But if his fare was moderate, his courtesy was extreme. For those who were silent, or talked in whispers, he encouraged to join in the general conversation; and introduced buffoons and stage players, or even low performers from the circus, and very often itinerant humourists, to enliven the company.

LXXV. Festivals and holidays he usually celebrated very expensively, but sometimes only with merriment. In the Saturnalia, or at any other time when the fancy took him, he distributed to his company clothes, gold, and silver; sometimes coins of all sorts, even of the ancient kings of Rome and of foreign nations; sometimes nothing but towels, sponges, rakes, and tweezers, and other things of that kind, with tickets on them, which were enigmatical, and had a double meaning 225 . He used likewise to sell by lot among his guests articles of very unequal value, and pictures with their fronts reversed; and so, by the unknown quality of the lot, disappoint or gratify the expectation of the purchasers. This sort of traffic (128) went round the whole company, every one being obliged to buy something, and to run the chance of loss or gain wits the rest.

LXXVI. He ate sparingly (for I must not omit even this), and commonly used a plain diet. He was particularly fond of coarse bread, small fishes, new cheese made of cow's milk 226 , and green figs of the sort which bear fruit twice a year 227 . He did not wait for supper, but took food at any time, and in any place, when he had an appetite. The following passages relative to this subject, I have transcribed from his letters. "I ate a little bread and some small dates, in my carriage." Again. "In returning home from the palace in my litter, I ate an ounce of bread, and a few raisins." Again. "No Jew, my dear Tiberius, ever keeps such strict fast upon the Sabbath 228 , as I have to-day; for while in the bath, and after the first hour of the night, I only ate two biscuits, before I began to be rubbed with oil."

From this great indifference about his diet, he sometimes supped by himself, before his company began, or after they had finished, and would not touch a morsel at table with his guests.

LXXVII. He was by nature extremely sparing in the use of wine. Cornelius Nepos says, that he used to drink only three times at supper in the camp at Modena; and when he indulged himself the most, he never exceeded a pint; or if he did, his stomach rejected it. Of all wines, he gave the (129) preference to the Rhaetian 229, but scarcely ever drank any in the day-time. Instead of drinking, he used to take a piece of bread dipped in cold water, or a slice of cucumber, or some leaves of lettuce, or a green, sharp, juicy apple.

LXXVIII. After a slight repast at noon, he used to seek repose 230, dressed as he was, and with his shoes on, his feet covered, and his hand held before his eyes. After supper he commonly withdrew to his study, a small closet, where he sat late, until he had put down in his diary all or most of the remaining transactions of the day, which he had not before registered. He would then go to bed, but never slept above seven hours at most, and that not without interruption; for he would wake three or four times during that time. If he could not again fall asleep, as sometimes happened, he called for some one to read or tell stories to him, until he became drowsy, and then his sleep was usually protracted till after day-break. He never liked to lie awake in the dark, without somebody to sit by him. Very early rising was apt to disagree with him. On which account, if he was obliged to rise betimes, for any civil or religious functions, in order to guard as much as possible against the inconvenience resulting from it, he used to lodge in some apartment near the spot, belonging to any of his attendants. If at any time a fit of drowsiness seized him in passing along the streets, his litter was set down while he snatched a few moments' sleep.

LXXIX. In person he was handsome and graceful, through every period of his life. But he was negligent in his dress; and so careless about dressing his hair, that he usually had it done in great haste, by several barbers at a time. His beard he sometimes clipped, and sometimes shaved; and either read or wrote during the operation. His countenance, either when discoursing or silent, was so calm and serene, that a (130) Gaul of the first rank declared amongst his friends, that he was so softened by it, as to be restrained from throwing him down a precipice, in his passage over the Alps, when he had been admitted to approach him, under pretence of conferring with him. His eyes were bright and piercing; and he was willing it should be thought that there was something of a divine vigour in them. He was likewise not a little pleased to see people, upon his looking steadfastly at them, lower their countenances, as if the sun shone in their eyes. But in his old age, he saw very imperfectly with his left eye. His teeth were thin set, small and scaly, his hair a little curled, and inclining to a yellow colour. His eye-brows met; his ears were small, and he had an aquiline nose. His complexion was betwixt brown and fair; his stature but low; though Julius Marathus, his freedman, says he was five feet and nine inches in height. This, however, was so much concealed by the just proportion of his limbs, that it was only perceivable upon comparison with some taller person standing by him.

LXXX. He is said to have been born with many spots upon his breast and belly, answering to the figure, order, and number of the stars in the constellation of the Bear. He had besides several callosities resembling scars, occasioned by an itching in his body, and the constant and violent use of the strigil 231 in being rubbed. He had a weakness in his left hip, thigh, and leg, insomuch that he often halted on that side; but he received much benefit from the use of sand and reeds. He likewise sometimes found the fore-finger of his right hand so weak, that when it was benumbed and contracted with cold, to use it in writing, he was obliged to have recourse to a circular piece of horn. He had occasionally a complaint in the bladder; but upon voiding some stones in his urine, he was relieved from that pain.

LXXXI. During the whole course of his life, he suffered, at times, dangerous fits of sickness, especially after the conquest of Cantabria; when his liver being injured by a defluxion (131) upon it, he was reduced to such a condition, that he was obliged to undergo a desperate and doubtful method of cure: for warm applications having no effect, Antonius Musa 232 directed the use of those which were cold. He was likewise subject to fits of sickness at stated times every year; for about his birth-day 233 he was commonly a little indisposed. In the beginning of spring, he was attacked with an inflation of the midriff; and when the wind was southerly, with a cold in his head. By all these complaints, his constitution was so shattered, that he could not easily bear either heat or cold.

LXXXII. In winter, he was protected against the inclemency of the weather by a thick toga, four tunics, a shirt, a flannel stomacher, and swathings upon his legs and thighs 234 . In summer, he lay with the doors of his bedchamber open, and frequently in a piazza, refreshed by a bubbling fountain, and a person standing by to fan him. He could not bear even the winter's sun; and at home, never walked in the open air without a broad-brimmed hat on his head. He usually travelled in a litter, and by night: and so slow, that he was two days in going to Praeneste or Tibur. And if he could go to any place by sea, he preferred that mode of travelling. He carefully nourished his health against his many infirmities, avoiding chiefly the free use of the bath; but he was often rubbed with oil, and sweated in a stove; after which he was washed with tepid water, warmed either by a fire, or by being exposed to the heat of the sun. When, upon account of his nerves, he was obliged to have recourse to sea-water, or the waters of Albula 235 , he was contented with sitting over a wooden tub, which he called by a Spanish name (132) Dureta, and plunging his hands and feet in the water by turns.

LXXXIII. As soon as the civil wars were ended, he gave up riding and other military exercises in the Campus Martius, and took to playing at ball, or foot-ball; but soon afterwards used no other exercise than that of going abroad in his litter, or walking. Towards the end of his walk, he would run leaping, wrapped up in a short cloak or cape. For amusement he would sometimes angle, or play with dice, pebbles, or nuts, with little boys, collected from various countries, and particularly Moors and Syrians, for their beauty or amusing talk. But dwarfs, and such as were in any way deformed, he held in abhorrence, as lusus naturae (nature's abortions), and of evil omen.

LXXXIV. From early youth he devoted himself with great diligence and application to the study of eloquence, and the other liberal arts. In the war of Modena, notwithstanding the weighty affairs in which he was engaged, he is said to have read, written, and declaimed every day. He never addressed the senate, the people, or the army, but in a premeditated speech, though he did not want the talent of speaking extempore on the spur of the occasion. And lest his memory should fail him, as well as to prevent the loss of time in getting up his speeches, it was his general practice to recite them. In his intercourse with individuals, and even with his wife Livia, upon subjects of importance he wrote on his tablets all he wished to express, lest, if he spoke extempore, he should say more or less than was proper. He delivered himself in a sweet and peculiar tone, in which he was diligently instructed by a master of elocution. But when he had a cold, he sometimes employed a herald to deliver his speeches to the people.

LXXXV. He composed many tracts in prose on various subjects, some of which he read occasionally in the circle of his friends, as to an auditory. Among these was his "Rescript to Brutus respecting Cato." Most of the pages he read himself, although he was advanced in years, but becoming fatigued, he gave the rest to Tiberius to finish. He likewise read over to (133) his friends his "Exhortations to Philosophy," and the "History of his own Life," which he continued in thirteen books, as far as the Cantabrian war, but no farther. He likewise made some attempts at poetry. There is extant one book written by him in hexameter verse, of which both the subject and title is "Sicily." There is also a book of Epigrams, no larger than the last, which he composed almost entirely while he was in the bath. These are all his poetical compositions for though he begun a tragedy with great zest, becoming dissatisfied with the style, he obliterated the whole; and his friends saying to him, "What is your Ajax doing?" he answered, "My Ajax has met with a sponge." 236

LXXXVI. He cultivated a style which was neat and chaste, avoiding frivolous or harsh language, as well as obsolete words, which he calls disgusting. His chief object was to deliver his thoughts with all possible perspicuity. To attain this end, and that he might nowhere perplex, or retard the reader or hearer, he made no scruple to add prepositions to his verbs, or to repeat the same conjunction several times; which, when omitted, occasion some little obscurity, but give a grace to the style. Those who used affected language, or adopted obsolete words, he despised, as equally faulty, though in different ways. He sometimes indulged himself in jesting, particularly with his friend Mecaenas, whom he rallied upon all occasions for his fine phrases 237 , and bantered by imitating his way of talking. Nor did he spare Tiberius, who was fond of obsolete and far-fetched expressions. He charges Mark Antony with insanity, writing rather to make men stare, than to be understood; and by way of sarcasm upon his depraved and fickle taste in the choice of words, he writes to him thus: "And are you yet in doubt, whether Cimber Annius or Veranius Flaccus be more proper for your imitation? Whether you will adopt words which Sallustius Crispus has borrowed from the 'Origines' of Cato? Or do you think that the verbose empty bombast of Asiatic orators is fit to be transfused into (134) our language?" And in a letter where he commends the talent of his grand-daughter, Agrippina, he says, "But you must be particularly careful, both in writing and speaking, to avoid affectation."

LXXXVII. In ordinary conversation, he made use of several peculiar expressions, as appears from letters in his own hand-writing; in which, now and then, when he means to intimate that some persons would never pay their debts, he says, "They will pay at the Greek Calends." And when he advised patience in the present posture of affairs, he would say, "Let us be content with our Cato." To describe anything in haste, he said, "It was sooner done than asparagus is cooked." He constantly puts baceolus for stultus, pullejaceus for pullus, vacerrosus for cerritus, vapide se habere for male, and betizare for languere, which is commonly called lachanizare. Likewise simus for sumus, domos for domus in the genitive singular 238. With respect to the last two peculiarities, lest any person should imagine that they were only slips of his pen, and not customary with him, he never varies. I have likewise remarked this singularity in his hand-writing; he never divides his words, so as to carry the letters which cannot be inserted at the end of a line to the next, but puts them below the other, enclosed by a bracket.

LXXXVIII. He did not adhere strictly to orthography as laid down by the grammarians, but seems to have been of the opinion of those who think, that we ought to write as we speak; for as to his changing and omitting not only letters but whole syllables, it is a vulgar mistake. Nor should I have taken notice of it, but that it appears strange to me, that any person should have told us, that he sent a successor to a consular lieutenant of a province, as an ignorant, illiterate fellow, upon his observing that he had written ixi for ipsi. When he had occasion to write in cypher, he put b for a, c for b, and so forth; and instead of z, aa.

LXXXIX. He was no less fond of the Greek literature, in which he made considerable proficiency; having had Apollodorus (135) of Pergamus, for his master in rhetoric; whom, though much advanced in years, he took with him from The City, when he was himself very young, to Apollonia. Afterwards, being instructed in philology by Sephaerus, he received into his family Areus the philosopher, and his sons Dionysius and Nicanor; but he never could speak the Greek tongue readily, nor ever ventured to compose in it. For if there was occasion for him to deliver his sentiments in that language, he always expressed what he had to say in Latin, and gave it another to translate. He was evidently not unacquainted with the poetry of the Greeks, and had a great taste for the ancient comedy, which he often brought upon the stage, in his public spectacles. In reading the Greek and Latin authors, he paid particular attention to precepts and examples which might be useful in public or private life. Those he used to extract verbatim, and gave to his domestics, or send to the commanders of the armies, the governors of the provinces, or the magistrates of the city, when any of them seemed to stand in need of admonition. He likewise read whole books to the senate, and frequently made them known to the people by his edicts; such as the orations of Quintus Metellus "for the Encouragement of Marriage," and those of Rutilius "On the Style of Building;" 239 to shew the people that he was not the first who had promoted those objects, but that the ancients likewise had thought them worthy their attention. He patronised the men of genius of that age in every possible way. He would hear them read their works with a great deal of patience and good nature; and not only poetry 240 and history, but orations and dialogues. He was displeased, however, that anything should be written upon himself, except in a grave manner, and by men of the most eminent abilities: and he enjoined the praetors not to suffer his name to be made too common in the contests amongst orators and poets in the theatres.

XC. We have the following account of him respecting his (136) belief in omens and such like. He had so great a dread of thunder and lightning that he always carried about him a seal's skin, by way of preservation. And upon any apprehension of a violent storm, he would retire to some place of concealment in a vault under ground; having formerly been terrified by a flash of lightning, while travelling in the night, as we have already mentioned. 241

XCI. He neither slighted his own dreams nor those of other people relating to himself. At the battle of Philippi, although he had resolved not to stir out of his tent, on account of his being indisposed, yet, being warned by a dream of one of his friends, he changed his mind;

and well it was that he did so, for in the enemy's attack, his couch was pierced and cut to pieces, on the supposition of his being in it. He had many frivolous and frightful dreams during the spring; but in the other parts of the year, they were less frequent and more significative. Upon his frequently visiting a temple near the Capitol, which he had dedicated to Jupiter Tonans, he dreamt that Jupiter Capitolinus complained that his worshippers were taken from him, and that upon this he replied, he had only given him The Thunderer for his porter 242. He therefore immediately suspended little bells round the summit of the temple; because such commonly hung at the gates of great houses. In consequence of a dream, too, he always, on a certain day of the year, begged alms of the people, reaching out his hand to receive the dole which they offered him.

XCII. Some signs and omens he regarded as infallible. If in the morning his shoe was put on wrong, the left instead of the right, that boded some disaster. If when he commenced a long journey, by sea or land, there happened to fall a mizzling rain, he held it to be a good sign of a speedy and happy return. He was much affected likewise with any thing out of the common course of nature. A palm-tree 243 which (137) chanced to grow up between some stone's in the court of his house, he transplanted into a court where the images of the Household Gods were placed, and took all possible care to make it thrive in the island of Capri, some decayed branches of an old ilex, which hung drooping to the ground, recovered themselves upon his arrival; at which he was so delighted, that he made an exchange with the Republic 244 of Naples, of the island of Oenaria [Ischia], for that of Capri. He likewise observed certain days; as never to go from home the day after the Nundiae 245, nor to begin any serious business upon the nones 246; avoiding nothing else in it, as he writes to Tiberius, than its unlucky name.

XCIII. With regard to the religious ceremonies of foreign nations, he was a strict observer of those which had been established by ancient custom; but others he held in no esteem. For, having been initiated at Athens, and coming afterwards to hear a cause at Rome, relative to the privileges of the priests of the Attic Ceres, when some of the mysteries of their sacred rites were to be introduced in the pleadings, he dismissed those who sat upon the bench as judges with him, as well as the by-standers, and beard the argument upon those points himself. But, on the other hand, he not only declined, in his progress through Egypt, to go out of his way to pay a visit to Apis, but he likewise commended his grandson Caius (138) for not paying his devotions at Jerusalem in his passage through Judaea. 247

XCIV. Since we are upon this subject, it may not be improper to give an account of the omens, before and at his birth, as well as afterwards, which gave hopes of his future greatness, and the good fortune that constantly attended him. A part of the wall of Velletri having in former times been struck with thunder, the response of the soothsayers was, that a native of that town would some time or other arrive at supreme power; relying on which prediction, the Velletrians both then, and several times afterwards, made war upon the Roman people, to their own ruin. At last it appeared by the event, that the omen had portended the elevation of Augustus.

Julius Marathus informs us, that a few months before his birth, there happened at Rome a prodigy, by which was signified that Nature was in travail with a king for the Roman people; and that the senate, in alarm, came to the resolution that no child born that year should be brought up; but that those amongst them, whose wives were pregnant, to secure to themselves a chance of that dignity, took care that the decree of the senate should not be registered in the treasury.

I find in the theological books of Asclepiades the Mendesian 248, that Atia, upon attending at midnight a religious solemnity in honour of Apollo, when the rest of the matrons retired home, fell asleep on her couch in the temple, and that a serpent immediately crept to her, and soon after withdrew. She awaking upon it, purified herself, as usual after the embraces of her husband; and instantly there appeared upon her body a mark in the form of a serpent, which she never after could efface, and which obliged her, during the subsequent part of her life, to decline the use of the public baths. Augustus, it was added, was born in the tenth month after, and for that reason was thought to be the son of Apollo. The (139) same Atia, before her delivery, dreamed that her bowels stretched to the stars, and expanded through the whole circuit of heaven and earth. His father Octavius, likewise, dreamt that a sun-beam issued from his wife's womb.

Upon the day he was born, the senate being engaged in a debate on Catiline's conspiracy, and Octavius, in consequence of his wife's being in childbirth, coming late into the house, it is a well-known fact, that Publius Nigidius, upon hearing the occasion of his coming so late, and the hour of his wife's delivery, declared that the world had got a master. Afterwards, when Octavius, upon marching with his army through the deserts of Thrace, consulted the oracle in the grove of father Bacchus, with barbarous rites, concerning his son, he received from the priests an answer to the same purpose; because, when they poured wine upon the altar, there burst out so prodigious a flame, that it ascended above the roof of the temple, and reached up to the heavens; a circumstance which had never happened to any one but Alexander the Great, upon his sacrificing at the same altars. And next night he dreamt that he saw his son under a more than human appearance, with thunder and a sceptre, and the other insignia of Jupiter, Optimus, Maximus, having on his head a radiant crown, mounted upon a chariot decked with laurel, and drawn by six pair of milk-white horses.

Whilst he was yet an infant, as Caius Drusus relates, being laid in his cradle by his nurse, and in a low place, the next day he was not to be found, and after he had been sought for a long time, he was at last discovered upon a lofty tower, lying with his face towards the rising sun 249 . When he first began to speak, he ordered the frogs that happened to make a troublesome noise, upon an estate belonging to the family near the town, to be silent; and there goes a report that frogs never croaked there since that time. As he was dining in a grove at the fourth mile-stone on the Campanian road, an eagle suddenly snatched a piece of bread out of his hand, and, soaring to a prodigious height, after hovering, came down most unexpectedly, and returned it to him.

Quintus Catulus had a dream, for two nights successively after his dedication of the Capitol. The first night he dreamt (140) that Jupiter, out of several boys of the order of the nobility who were playing about his altar, selected one, into whose bosom he put the public seal of the commonwealth, which he held in his hand; but in his vision the next night, he saw in the bosom of Jupiter Capitolinus, the same boy; whom he ordered to be removed, but it was forbidden by the God, who declared that it must be brought up to become the guardian of the state. The next day, meeting Augustus, with whom till that hour he had not the least acquaintance, and looking at him with admiration, he said he was extremely like the boy he had seen in his dream. Some give a different account of Catulus's first dream, namely, that Jupiter, upon several noble lads requesting of him that they might have a guardian, had pointed to one amongst them, to whom they were to prefer their requests; and putting his fingers to the boy's mouth to kiss, he afterwards applied them to his own.

Marcus Cicero, as he was attending Caius Caesar to the Capitol, happened to be telling some of his friends a dream which he had the preceding night, in which he saw a comely youth, let down from heaven by a golden chain, who stood at the door of the Capitol, and had a whip put into his hands by Jupiter. And immediately upon sight of Augustus, who had been sent for by his uncle Caesar to the sacrifice, and was as yet perfectly unknown to most of the company, he affirmed that it was the very boy he had seen in his dream. When he assumed the manly toga, his senatorian tunic becoming loose in the seam on each side, fell at his feet. Some would have this to forbode, that the order, of which that was the badge of distinction, would some time or other be subject to him.

Julius Caesar, in cutting down a wood to make room for his camp near Munda 250 , happened to light upon a palm-tree, and ordered it to be preserved as an omen of victory. From the root of this tree there put out immediately a sucker, which, in a few days, grew to such a height as not only to equal, but overshadow it, and afford room for many nests of wild pigeons which built in it, though that species of bird particularly avoids a hard and rough leaf. It is likewise reported, that Caesar was chiefly influenced by this prodigy, to prefer his sister's grandson before all others for his successor.

(141) In his' retirement at Apollonia, he went with his friend Agrippa to visit Theogenes, the astrologer, in his gallery on the roof. Agrippa, who first consulted the fates, having great and almost incredible fortunes predicted of him, Augustus did not choose to make known his nativity, and persisted for some time in the refusal, from a mixture of shame and fear, lest his fortunes should be predicted as inferior to those of Agrippa. Being persuaded, however, after much importunity, to declare it, Theogenes started up from his seat, and paid him adoration. Not long afterwards, Augustus was so confident of the greatness of his destiny, that he published his horoscope, and struck a silver coin, bearing upon it the sign of Capricorn, under the influence of which he was born.

XCV. After the death of Caesar, upon his return from Apollonia, as he was entering the city, on a sudden, in a clear and bright sky, a circle resembling the rainbow surrounded the body of the sun; and, immediately afterwards, the tomb of Julia, Caesar's daughter, was struck by lightning. In his first consulship, whilst he was observing the auguries, twelve vultures presented themselves, as they had done to Romulus. And when he offered sacrifice, the livers of all the victims were folded inward in the lower part; a circumstance which was regarded by those present, who had skill in things of that nature, as an indubitable prognostic of great and wonderful fortune.

XCVI. He certainly had a presentiment of the issue of all his wars. When the troops of the Triumviri were collected about Bologna, an eagle, which sat upon his tent, and was attacked by two crows, beat them both, and struck them to the ground, in the view of the whole army; who thence inferred that discord would arise between the three colleagues, which would be attended with the like event: and it accordingly happened. At Philippi, he was assured of success by a Thessalian, upon the authority, as he pretended, of the Divine Caesar himself, who had appeared to him while he was travelling in a bye-road. At Perugia, the sacrifice not presenting any favourable intimations, but the contrary, he ordered fresh victims; the enemy, however, carrying off the sacred things in a sudden sally, it was agreed amongst the augurs, that all the (142) dangers and misfortunes which had threatened the sacrificer, would fall upon the heads of those who had got possession of the entrails. And, accordingly, so it happened. The day before the sea-fight near Sicily, as he was walking upon the shore, a fish leaped out of the sea, and laid itself at his feet. At Actium, while he was going down to his fleet to engage the enemy, he was met by an ass with a fellow driving it. The name of the man was Eutychus, and that of the animal, Nichon 251 . After the victory, he erected a brazen statue to each, in a temple built upon the spot where he had encamped.

XCVII. His death, of which I shall now speak, and his subsequent deification, were intimated by divers manifest prodigies. As he was finishing the census amidst a great crowd of people in the Campus Martius, an eagle hovered round him several times, and then directed its course to a neighbouring temple, where it settled upon the name of Agrippa, and at the first letter. Upon observing this, he ordered his colleague Tiberius to put up the vows, which it is usual to make on such occasions, for the succeeding Lustrum. For he declared he would not meddle with what it was probable he should never accomplish, though the tables were ready drawn for it. About the same time, the first letter of his name, in an inscription upon one of his statues, was struck out by lightning; which was interpreted as a presage that he would live only a hundred days longer, the letter C denoting that number; and that he would be placed amongst the Gods, as Aesar, which is the remaining part of the word Caesar, signifies, in the Tuscan language, a God 252 . Being, therefore, about dispatching Tiberius to Illyricum, and designing to go with him as far as Beneventum, but being detained by several persons who applied to him respecting causes they had depending, he cried out, (and it was afterwards regarded as an omen of his death), "Not all the business in the world, shall detain me at home one moment longer;" and setting out upon his journey, he went (143) as far as Astura 253 ; whence, contrary to his custom, he put to sea in the night-time, as there was a favourable wind.

XCVIII. His malady proceeded from diarrhoea; notwithstanding which, he went round the coast of Campania, and the adjacent islands, and spent four days in that of Capri; where he gave himself up entirely to repose and relaxation. Happening to sail by the bay of Puteoli, the passengers and mariners aboard a ship of Alexandria 254 , just then arrived, clad all in white, with chaplets upon their heads, and offering incense, loaded him with praises and joyful acclamations, crying out, "By you we live, by you we sail securely, by you enjoy our liberty and our fortunes." At which being greatly pleased, he distributed to each of those who attended him, forty gold pieces, requiring from them an assurance on oath, not to employ the sum given them in any other way, than the purchase of Alexandrian merchandize. And during several days afterwards, he distributed Togae 255 and Pallia, among other gifts, on condition that the Romans should use the Greek, and the Greeks the Roman dress and language. He likewise constantly attended to see the boys perform their exercises, according to an ancient custom still continued at Capri. He gave them likewise an entertainment in his presence, and not only permitted, but required from them the utmost freedom in jesting, and scrambling for fruit, victuals, and other things which he threw amongst them. In a word, he indulged himself in all the ways of amusement he could contrive.

He called an island near Capri, Apragopolis, "The City of the Do-littles," from the indolent life which several of his party led there. A favourite of his, one Masgabas 256, he used (144) to call Ktistaes. as if he had been the planter of the island. And observing from his room a great company of people with torches, assembled at the tomb of this Masgabas, who died the year before, he uttered very distinctly this verse, which he made extempore.

> *Ktistou de tumbo, eisoro pyroumenon.*
>
> Blazing with lights I see the founder's tomb.

Then turning to Thrasyllus, a companion of Tiberius, who reclined on the other side of the table, he asked him, who knew nothing about the matter, what poet he thought was the author of that verse; and on his hesitating to reply, he added another:

> *Oras phaessi Masgaban timomenon.*
>
> Honor'd with torches Masgabas you see;

and put the same question to him concerning that likewise. The latter replying, that, whoever might be the author, they were excellent verses 257, he set up a great laugh, and fell into an extraordinary vein of jesting upon it. Soon afterwards, passing over to Naples, although at that time greatly disordered in his bowels by the frequent returns of his disease, he sat out the exhibition of the gymnastic games which were performed in his honour every five years, and proceeded with Tiberius to the place intended. But on his return, his disorder increasing, he stopped at Nola, sent for Tiberius back again, and had a long discourse with him in private; after which, he gave no further attention to business of any importance.

XCIX. Upon the day of his death, he now and then enquired, if there was any disturbance in the town on his account; and calling for a mirror, he ordered his hair to be combed, and his shrunk cheeks to be adjusted. Then asking his friends who were admitted into the room, "Do ye think that I have acted my part on the stage of life well?" he immediately subjoined,

> *Ei de pan echei kalos, to paignio*
>
> *Dote kroton, kai pantes umeis meta charas ktupaesate.*
>
> If all be right, with joy your voices raise,

In loud applauses to the actor's praise.

(145) After which, having dismissed them all, whilst he was inquiring of some persons who were just arrived from Rome, concerning Drusus's daughter, who was in a bad state of health, he expired suddenly, amidst the kisses of Livia, and with these words: "Livia! live mindful of our union; and now, farewell!" dying a very easy death, and such as he himself had always wished for. For as often as he heard that any person had died quickly and without pain, he wished for himself and his friends the like euthanasian (an easy death), for that was the word he made use of. He betrayed but one symptom, before he breathed his last, of being delirious, which was this: he was all on a sudden much frightened, and complained that he was carried away by forty men. But this was rather a presage, than any delirium: for precisely that number of soldiers belonging to the pretorian cohort, carried out his corpse.

C. He expired in the same room in which his father Octavius had died, when the two Sextus's, Pompey and Apuleius, were consuls, upon the fourteenth of the calends of September [the 19th August], at the ninth hour of the day, being seventy-six years of age, wanting only thirty-five days 258 . His remains were carried by the magistrates of the municipal 259 towns and colonies, from Nola to Bovillae 260 , and in the nighttime, because of the season of the year. During the intervals, the body lay in some basilica, or great temple, of each town. At Bovillae it was met by the Equestrian Order, who carried it to the city, and deposited it in the vestibule of his own house. The senate proceeded with so much zeal in the arrangement of his funeral, and paying honour to his memory, that, amongst several other proposals, some were for having the funeral procession made through the triumphal gate, preceded by the image of Victory which is in the senate-house, and the children of highest rank and of both sexes singing the funeral (146) dirge. Others proposed, that on the day of the funeral, they should lay aside their gold rings, and wear rings of iron; and others, that his bones should be collected by the priests of the principal colleges. One likewise proposed to transfer the name of August to September, because he was born in the latter, but died in the former. Another moved, that the whole period of time, from his birth to his death, should be called the Augustan age, and be inserted in the calendar under that title. But at last it was judged proper to be moderate in the honours paid to his memory. Two funeral orations were pronounced in his praise, one before the temple of Julius, by Tiberius; and the other before the rostra, under the old shops, by Drusus, Tiberius's son. The body was then carried upon the shoulders of senators into the Campus Martius, and there burnt. A man of pretorian rank affirmed upon oath, that he saw his spirit ascend from the funeral pile to heaven. The most distinguished persons of the equestrian order, bare-footed, and with their tunics loose, gathered up his relics 261 , and deposited them in the mausoleum, which had been built in his sixth consulship between the Flaminian Way and the bank of the Tiber 262 ; at which time likewise he gave the groves and walks about it for the use of the people.

CI. He had made a will a year and four months before his death, upon the third of the nones of April [the 11th of April], in the consulship of Lucius Plancus, and Caius Silius. It consisted of two skins of parchment, written partly in his own hand, and partly by his freedmen Polybius and Hilarian; and had been committed to the custody of the Vestal Virgins, by whom it was now produced, with three codicils under seal, as well as the will: all these were opened and read in the senate. He appointed as his direct heirs, Tiberius for two (147) thirds of his estate, and Livia for the other third, both of whom he desired to assume his name. The heirs in remainder were Drusus, Tiberius's son, for one third, and Germanicus with his three sons for the residue. In the third place, failing them, were his relations, and several of his friends. He left in legacies to the Roman people forty millions of sesterces; to the tribes 263 three millions five hundred thousand; to the pretorian troops a thousand each man; to the city cohorts five hundred; and to the legions and soldiers three hundred each; which several sums he ordered to be paid immediately after his death, having taken due care that the money should be ready in his exchequer. For the rest he ordered different times of payment. In some of his bequests he went as far as twenty thousand sesterces, for the payment of which he allowed a twelvemonth; alleging for this procrastination the scantiness of his estate; and declaring that not more than a hundred and fifty millions of sesterces would come to his heirs: notwithstanding that during the twenty preceding years, he had received, in legacies from his friends, the sum of fourteen hundred millions; almost the whole of which, with his two paternal estates 264 , and others which had been left him, he had spent in the service of the state. He left orders that the two Julias, his daughter and grand-daughter, if anything happened to them, should not be buried in his tomb 265 . With regard to the three codicils before-mentioned, in one of them he gave orders about his funeral; another contained a summary of his acts, which he intended should be inscribed on brazen plates, and placed in front of his mausoleum; in the third he had drawn up a concise account of the state of the empire; the number of troops enrolled, what money there was in the treasury, the revenue, and arrears of taxes; to which were added the names of the freedmen and slaves from whom the several accounts might be taken.

\* \* \* \* \* \*

(148) OCTAVIUS CAESAR, afterwards Augustus, had now attained to the same position in the state which had formerly been occupied by Julius Caesar; and though he entered upon it by violence, he continued to enjoy it through life with almost uninterrupted tranquillity. By the long duration of the late civil war, with its concomitant train of public calamities, the minds of men were become less averse to the prospect of an absolute government; at the same time that the new emperor, naturally prudent and politic, had learned from the fate of Julius the art of preserving supreme power, without arrogating to himself any invidious mark of distinction. He affected to decline public honours, disclaimed every idea of personal superiority, and in all his behaviour displayed a degree of moderation which prognosticated the most happy effects, in restoring peace and prosperity to the harassed empire. The tenor of his future conduct was suitable to this auspicious commencement. While he endeavoured to conciliate the affections of the people by lending money to those who stood in need of it, at low interest, or without any at all, and by the exhibition of public shows, of which the Romans were remarkably fond; he was attentive to the preservation of a becoming dignity in the government, and to the correction of morals. The senate, which, in the time of Sylla, had increased to upwards of four hundred, and, during the civil war, to a thousand, members, by the admission of improper persons, he reduced to six hundred; and being invested with the ancient office of censor, which had for some time been disused, he exercised an arbitrary but legal authority over the conduct of every rank in the state; by which he could degrade senators and

knights, and inflict upon all citizens an ignominious sentence for any immoral or indecent behaviour. But nothing contributed more to render the new form of government acceptable to the people, than the frequent distribution of corn, and sometimes largesses, amongst the commonalty: for an occasional scarcity of provisions had always been the chief cause of discontents and tumults in the capital. To the interests of the army he likewise paid particular attention. It was by the assistance of the legions that he had risen to power; and they were the men who, in the last resort, if such an emergency should ever occur, could alone enable him to preserve it.

History relates, that after the overthrow of Antony, Augustus held a consultation with Agrippa and Mecaenas about restoring the republican form of government; when Agrippa gave his opinion in favour of that measure, and Mecaenas opposed it. (149) The object of this consultation, in respect to its future consequences on society, is perhaps the most important ever agitated in any cabinet, and required, for the mature discussion of it, the whole collective wisdom of the ablest men in the empire. But this was a resource which could scarcely be adopted, either with security to the public quiet, or with unbiassed judgment in the determination of the question. The bare agitation of such a point would have excited immediate and strong anxiety for its final result; while the friends of a republican government, who were still far more numerous than those of the other party, would have strained every nerve to procure a determination in their own favour; and the pretorian guards, the surest protection of Augustus, finding their situation rendered precarious by such an unexpected occurrence, would have readily listened to the secret propositions and intrigues of the republicans for securing their acquiescence to the decision on the popular side. If, when the subject came into debate, Augustus should be sincere in the declaration to abide by the resolution of the council, it is beyond all doubt, that the restoration of a republican government would have been voted by a great majority of the assembly. If, on the contrary, he should not be sincere, which is the more probable supposition, and should incur the suspicion of practising secretly with members for a decision according to his wish, he would have rendered himself obnoxious to the public odium, and given rise to discontents which might have endangered his future security.

But to submit this important question to the free and unbiassed decision of a numerous assembly, it is probable, neither suited the inclination of Augustus, nor perhaps, in his opinion, consisted with his personal safety. With a view to the attainment of unconstitutional power, he had formerly deserted the cause of the republic when its affairs were in a prosperous situation; and now, when his end was accomplished, there could be little ground to expect, that he should voluntarily relinquish the prize for which he had spilt the best blood of Rome, and contended for so many years. Ever since the final defeat of Antony in the battle of Actium, he had governed the Roman state with uncontrolled authority; and though there is in the nature of unlimited power an intoxicating quality, injurious both to public and private virtue, yet all history contradicts the supposition of its being endued with any which is unpalatable to the general taste of mankind.

There were two chief motives by which Augustus would naturally be influenced in a deliberation on this important subject; namely, the love of power, and the personal danger which (150) he might incur from relinquishing it. Either of these motives might have been a sufficient inducement for retaining his authority; but when they both concurred, as they seem to have done upon this occasion, their united force was irresistible. The argument, so far as relates to the love of power, rests upon a ground, concerning the solidity of which, little doubt can be entertained: but it may be proper to inquire, in a few words, into the foundation of that personal danger which he dreaded to incur, on returning to the station of a private citizen.

Augustus, as has been already observed, had formerly sided with the party which had attempted to restore public liberty after the death of Julius Caesar: but he afterwards abandoned the popular cause, and joined in the ambitious plans of Antony and Lepidus to usurp amongst themselves the entire dominion of the state. By this change of conduct, he turned his arms against the supporters of a form of government which he had virtually recognized as the legal constitution of Rome; and it involved a direct implication of treason against the sacred representatives of that government, the consuls, formally and duly elected. Upon such a charge he might be amenable to the capital laws of his country. This, however, was a danger which might be fully obviated, by procuring from the senate and people an act of oblivion, previously to his abdication of the supreme power; and this was a preliminary which doubtless they would have admitted and ratified with unanimous approbation. It therefore appears that he could be exposed to no inevitable danger on this account: but there was another quarter where his person was vulnerable, and where even the laws might not be sufficient to protect him against the efforts of private resentment. The bloody proscription of the Triumvirate no act of amnesty could ever erase from the minds of those who had been deprived by it of their nearest and dearest relations; and amidst the numerous connections of the illustrious men sacrificed on that horrible occasion, there might arise some desperate avenger, whose indelible resentment nothing less would satisfy than the blood of the surviving delinquent. Though Augustus, therefore, might not, like his great predecessor, be stabbed in the senate-house, he might perish by the sword or the poniard in a less conspicuous situation. After all, there seems to have been little danger from this quarter likewise for Sylla, who in the preceding age had been guilty of equal enormities, was permitted, on relinquishing the place of perpetual dictator, to end his days in quiet retirement; and the undisturbed security which Augustus ever afterwards enjoyed, affords sufficient proof, that all apprehension of danger to his person was merely chimerical.

(151) We have hitherto considered this grand consultation as it might be influenced by the passions or prejudices of the emperor: we shall now take a short view of the subject in the light in which it is connected with considerations of a political nature, and with public utility. The arguments handed down by history respecting this consultation are few, and imperfectly delivered; but they may be extended upon the general principles maintained on each side of the question.

For the restoration of the republican government, it might be contended, that from the expulsion of the kings to the dictatorship of Julius Caesar, through a period of upwards of four hundred and sixty years, the Roman state, with the exception only of a short interval, had flourished and increased with a degree of prosperity unexampled in the annals of humankind: that the republican form of government was not only best adapted to the improvement of national grandeur, but to the security of general freedom, the great object of all political association: that public virtue, by which alone nations could subsist in vigour, was cherished and protected by no mode of administration so much as by that which connected, in the strongest bonds of union, the private interests of individuals with those of the community: that the habits and prejudices of the Roman people were unalterably attached to the form of government established by so long a prescription, and they would never submit, for any length of time, to the rule of one person, without making every possible effort to recover their liberty: that though despotism, under a mild and wise prince, might in some respects be regarded as preferable to a constitution which was occasionally exposed to the inconvenience of faction and popular tumults, yet it was a dangerous experiment to abandon the government of the nation to the contingency of such a variety of characters as usually occurs in the succession of princes; and, upon the whole, that the interests of the people were more safely entrusted in the hands of annual magistrates elected by themselves, than in those of any individual whose power was permanent, and subject to no legal control.·

In favour of despotic government it might be urged, that though Rome had subsisted long and gloriously under a republican form of government, yet she had often experienced such violent shocks from popular tumults or the factions of the great, as had threatened her with imminent destruction: that a republican government was only accommodated to a people amongst whom the division of property gave to no class of citizens such a degree of pre-eminence as might prove dangerous to public freedom: that there was required in that form of political constitution, a simplicity (152) of life and strictness of manners which are never observed to accompany a high degree of public prosperity: that in respect of all these considerations, such a form of government was utterly incompatible with the present circumstances of the Romans that by the conquest of so many foreign nations, by the lucrative governments of provinces, the spoils of the enemy in war, and the rapine too often practised in time of peace, so great had been the aggrandizement of particular families in the preceding age, that though the form of the ancient constitution should still remain inviolate, the people would no longer live under a free republic, but an aristocratical usurpation, which was always productive of tyranny: that nothing could preserve the commonwealth from becoming a prey to some daring confederacy, but the firm and vigorous administration of one person, invested with the whole executive power of the state, unlimited and uncontrolled: in fine, that as Rome had been nursed to maturity by the government of six princes successively, so it was only by a similar form of political constitution that she could now be saved from aristocratical tyranny on one hand, or, on the other, from absolute anarchy.

On whichever side of the question the force of argument may be thought to preponderate, there is reason to believe that Augustus was guided in his resolution more by inclination and prejudice than by reason. It is related, however, that hesitating between the opposite opinions of his two counsellors, he had recourse to that of Virgil, who joined with Mecaenas in advising him to retain the imperial power, as being the form of government most suitable to the circumstances of the times.

It is proper in this place to give some account of the two ministers above-mentioned, Agrippa and Mecaenas, who composed the cabinet of Augustus at the settlement of his government, and seem to be the only persons employed by him in a ministerial capacity during his whole reign.

M. Vipsanius Agrippa was of obscure extraction, but rendered himself conspicuous by his military talents. He obtained a victory over Sextus Pompey; and in the battles of Philippi and Actium, where he displayed great valour, he contributed not a little to establish the subsequent power of Augustus. In his expeditions afterwards into Gaul and Germany, he performed many signal achievements, for which he refused the honours of a triumph. The expenses which others would have lavished on that frivolous spectacle, he applied to the more laudable purpose of embellishing Rome with magnificent buildings, one of which, the Pantheon, still remains. In consequence of a dispute with Marcellus, the nephew of Augustus, he retired to Mitylene, (153) whence, after an absence of two years, he was recalled by the emperor. He first married Pomponia, the daughter of the celebrated Atticus, and afterwards one of the Marcellas, the nieces of Augustus. While this lady, by whom he had children, was still living, the emperor prevailed upon his sister Octavia to resign to him her son-in-law, and gave him in marriage his own daughter Julia; so strong was the desire of Augustus to be united with him in the closest alliance. The high degree of favour in which he stood with the emperor was soon after evinced by a farther mark of esteem: for during a visit to the Roman provinces of Greece and Asia, in which Augustus was absent two years, he left the government of the empire to the care of Agrippa. While this minister enjoyed, and indeed seems to have merited, all the partiality of Augustus, he was likewise a favourite with the people. He died at Rome, in the sixty-first year of his age, universally lamented; and his remains were deposited in the tomb which Augustus had prepared for himself. Agrippa left by Julia three sons, Caius, Lucius, and Posthumus Agrippa, with two daughters, Agrippina and Julia.

    C. Cilnius Mecaenas was of Tuscan extraction, and derived his descent from the ancient kings of that country. Though in the highest degree of favour with Augustus, he never aspired beyond the rank of the equestrian order; and though he might have held the government of extensive provinces by deputies, he was content with enjoying the praefecture of the city and Italy; a situation, however, which must have been attended with extensive patronage. He was of a gay and social disposition. In principle he is said to have been of the Epicurean sect, and in his dress and manners to have bordered on effeminacy. With respect to his political talents, we can only speak from conjecture; but from his being the confidential minister of a prince of so much discernment as Augustus, during the infancy of a new form of government in an extensive empire, we may presume that he was endowed with no common abilities for that important station. The liberal patronage which he displayed towards men of genius and talents, will render his name for ever celebrated in the annals of learning. It is to be regretted that history has transmitted no particulars of this extraordinary personage, of whom all we know is derived chiefly from the writings of Virgil and Horace; but from the manner in which they address him, amidst the familiarity of their intercourse, there is the strongest reason to suppose, that he was not less amiable and respectable in private life, than illustrious in public situation. "O my glory!" is the emphatic expression employed by them both.

    (154) *O decus, O famae merito pars maxima nostrae.* Vir. Georg. ii.
    Light of my life, my glory, and my guide!
    *O et praesidium et dulce decus meum.* Hor. Ode I.
    My glory and my patron thou!

One would be inclined to think, that there was a nicety in the sense and application of the word decus, amongst the Romans, with which we are unacquainted, and that, in the passages now adduced, it was understood to refer to the honour of the emperor's patronage, obtained through the means of Mecaenas; otherwise, such language to the minister might have excited the jealousy of Augustus. But whatever foundation there may be for this conjecture, the compliment was compensated by the superior adulation which the poets appropriated to the emperor, whose deification is more than insinuated, in sublime intimations, by Virgil.

> *Tuque adeo quem mox quae sint habitura deorum*
> *Concilia, incertum est; urbisne invisere, Caesar,*
> *Terrarumque velis curam; et te maximus orbis*
> *Auctorem frugum, tempestatumque potentem*
> *Accipiat, cingens materna tempora myrto:*
> *An Deus immensi venias maris, ac tua nautae*
> *Numina sola colant: tibi serviat ultima Thule;*
> *Teque sibi generum Tethys emat omnibus undis. Geor. i. 1. 25, vi.*
>
> *Thou Caesar, chief where'er thy voice ordain*
> *To fix midst gods thy yet unchosen reign –*
> *Wilt thou o'er cities fix thy guardian sway,*
> *While earth and all her realms thy nod obey?*
> *The world's vast orb shall own thy genial power,*
> *Giver of fruits, fair sun, and favouring shower;*
> *Before thy altar grateful nations bow,*
> *And with maternal myrtle wreathe thy brow;*
> *O'er boundless ocean shall thy power prevail,*
> *Thee her sole lord the world of waters hail,*
> *Rule where the sea remotest Thule laves,*
> *While Tethys dowers thy bride with all her waves. Sotheby.*

Horace has elegantly adopted the same strain of compliment.

> *Te multa prece, te prosequitur mero*
> *Defuso pateris; et Laribus tuum*
> *Miscet numen, uti Graecia Castoris*
> *Et magni memor Herculis. Carm. IV. 5.*

> To thee he chants the sacred song,
> To thee the rich libation pours;
> Thee placed his household gods among,
> With solemn daily prayer adores
> So Castor and great Hercules of old,
> Were with her gods by grateful Greece enrolled.

(155) The panegyric bestowed upon Augustus by the great poets of that time, appears to have had a farther object than the mere gratification of vanity. It was the ambition of this emperor to reign in the hearts as well as over the persons of his subjects; and with this view he was desirous of endearing himself to their imagination. Both he and Mecaenas had a delicate sensibility to the beauties of poetical composition; and judging from their own feelings, they attached a high degree of influence to the charms of poetry. Impressed with these sentiments, it became an object of importance, in their opinion, to engage the Muses in the service of the imperial authority; on which account, we find Mecaenas tampering with Propertius, and we may presume, likewise with every other rising genius in poetry, to undertake an heroic poem, of which Augustus should be the hero. As the application to Propertius cannot have taken place until after Augustus had been amply celebrated by the superior abilities of Virgil and Horace, there seems to be some reason for ascribing Mecaenas's request to a political motive. Caius and Lucius, the emperor's grandsons by his daughter Julia, were still living, and both young. As one of them, doubtless, was intended to succeed to the government of the empire, prudence justified the adoption of every expedient that might tend to secure a quiet succession to the heir, upon the demise of Augustus. As a subsidiary resource, therefore, the expedient above mentioned was judged highly plausible; and the Roman cabinet indulged the idea of endeavouring to confirm imperial authority by the support of poetical renown. Lampoons against the government were not uncommon even in the time of Augustus; and elegant panegyric on the emperor served to counteract their influence upon the minds of the people. The idea was, perhaps, novel in the time of Augustus; but the history of later ages affords examples of its having been adopted, under different forms of government, with success.

The Roman empire, in the time of Augustus, had attained to a prodigious magnitude; and, in his testament, he recommended to his successors never to exceed the limits which he had prescribed to its extent. On the East it stretched to the Euphrates; on the South to the cataracts of the Nile, the deserts of Africa, and Mount Atlas; on the West to the Atlantic Ocean; and on the North to the Danube and the Rhine; including the best part of the then known world. The Romans, therefore, were not improperly called rerum domini 266 , and Rome, pulcherrima rerum 267 , maxima rerum 268 . Even the historians, Livy and Tacitus, (156) actuated likewise with admiration, bestow magnificent epithets on the capital of their country. The succeeding emperors, in conformity to the advice of Augustus, made few additions to the empire. Trajan, however, subdued Mesopotamia and Armenia, east of the Euphrates, with Dacia, north of the Danube; and after this period the Roman dominion was extended over Britain, as far as the Frith of Forth and the Clyde.

It would be an object of curiosity to ascertain the amount of the Roman revenue in the reign of Augustus; but such a problem, even with respect to contemporary nations, cannot be elucidated without access to the public registers of their governments; and in regard to an ancient monarchy, the investigation is impracticable. We can only be assured that the revenue must have been immense, which arose from the accumulated contribution of such a number of nations, that had supported their own civil establishments with great splendour, and many of which were celebrated for their extraordinary riches and commerce. The tribute paid by the Romans themselves, towards the support of the government, was very considerable during the latter ages of the republic, and it received an increase after the consulship of Hirtius and Pansa. The establishments, both civil and military, in the different provinces, were supported at their own expense; the emperor required but a small naval force, an arm which adds much to the public expenditure of maritime nations in modern times; and the state was burdened with no diplomatic charges. The vast treasure accruing from the various taxes centered in Rome, and the whole was at the disposal of the emperor, without any control. We may therefore justly conclude that, in the amount of taxes, customs, and every kind of financial resources, Augustus exceeded all sovereigns who had hitherto ever swayed the sceptre of imperial dominion; a noble acquisition, had it been judiciously employed by his successors, in promoting public happiness, with half the profusion in which it was lavished in disgracing human nature, and violating the rights of mankind.

The reign of Augustus is distinguished by the most extraordinary event recorded in history, either sacred or profane, the nativity of the Saviour of mankind; which has since introduced a new epoch into the chronology of all Christian nations. The commencement of the new aera being the most flourishing period of the Roman empire, a general view of the state of knowledge and taste at this period, may here not be improper.

Civilization was at this time extended farther over the world than it had ever been in any preceding period; but polytheism rather increased than diminished with the advancement of commercial intercourse between the nations of Europe, Asia, and Africa; and, though philosophy had been cultivated during several ages, at Athens, Cyrene, Rome, and other seats of learning, yet the morals of mankind were little improved by the diffusion of speculative knowledge. Socrates had laid an admirable foundation for the improvement of human nature, by the exertion of reason through the whole economy of life; but succeeding inquirers, forsaking the true path of ethic investigation, deviated into specious discussions, rather ingenious than useful; and some of them, by gratuitously adopting principles, which, so far from being supported by reason, were repugnant to its dictates, endeavoured to erect upon the basis of their respective doctrines a system peculiar to themselves. The doctrines of the Stoics and Epicureans were, in fact, pernicious to society; and those of the different academies, though more intimately connected with reason than the two former, were of a nature too abstract to have any immediate or useful influence on life and manners. General discussions of truth and probability, with magnificent declamations on the to kalon, and the summum bonum, constituted the chief objects of attention amongst those who cultivated moral science in the shades of academical retirement. Cicero endeavoured to bring back philosophy from speculation to practice, and clearly evinced the social duties to be founded in the unalterable dictates of virtue; but it was easier to demonstrate the truth of the principles which he maintained, than to enforce their observance, while the morals of mankind were little actuated by the exercise of reason alone.

The science chiefly cultivated at this period was rhetoric, which appears to have differed considerably from what now passes under the same name. The object of it was not so much justness of sentiment and propriety of expression, as the art of declaiming, or speaking copiously upon any subject. It is mentioned by Varro as the reverse of logic; and they are distinguished from each other by a simile, that the former resembles the palm of the hand expanded, and the latter, contracted into the fist. It is observable that logic, though a part of education in modern times, seems not to have been cultivated amongst the Romans. Perhaps they were apprehensive, lest a science which concentered the force of argument, might obstruct the cultivation of that which was meant to dilate it. Astronomy was long before known in the eastern nations; but there is reason to believe, from a passage in Virgil 269 , that it was little cultivated by the Romans; and it is certain, that in the reformation of the calendar, Julius Caesar was chiefly indebted to the scientific knowledge of (158) Sosigenes, a mathematician of Alexandria. The laws of the solar system were still but imperfectly known; the popular belief, that the sun moved round the earth, was universally maintained, and continued until the sixteenth century, when the contrary was proved by Copernicus. There existed many celebrated tracts on mathematics; and several of the mechanical powers, particularly that of the lever, were cultivated with success. The more necessary and useful rules of arithmetic were generally known. The use of the load-stone not being as yet discovered, navigation was conducted in the day-time by the sun, and in the night, by the observation of certain stars. Geography was cultivated during the present period by Strabo and Mela. In natural philosophy little progress was made; but a strong desire of its improvement was entertained, particularly by Virgil. Human anatomy being not yet introduced, physiology was imperfect. Chemistry, as a science, was utterly unknown. In medicine, the writings of Hippocrates, and other Greek physicians, were in general the standard of practice; but the Materia Medica contained few remedies of approved quality, and abounded with useless substances, as well as with many which stood upon no other foundation than the whimsical notions of those who first introduced them. Architecture flourished, through the elegant taste of

Vitruvius, and the patronage of the emperor. Painting, statuary, and music, were cultivated, but not with that degree of perfection which they had obtained in the Grecian states. The musical instruments of this period were the flute and the lyre, to which may be added the sistrum, lately imported from Egypt. But the chief glory of the period is its literature, of which we proceed to give some account.

At the head of the writers of this age, stands the emperor himself, with his minister Mecaenas; but the works of both have almost totally perished. It appears from the historian now translated, that Augustus was the author of several productions in prose, besides some in verse. He wrote Answers to Brutus in relation to Cato, Exhortations to Philosophy, and the History of his own Life, which he continued, in thirteen books, down to the war of Cantabria. A book of his, written in hexameter verse, under the title of Sicily, was extant in the time of Suetonius, as was likewise a book of Epigrams. He began a tragedy on the subject of Ajax, but, being dissatisfied with the composition, destroyed it. Whatever the merits of Augustus may have been as an author, of which no judgment can be formed, his attachment to learning and eminent writers affords a strong presumption that he was not destitute of taste. Mecaenas is said to have written two tragedies, Octavia and Prometheus; a History of (159) Animals; a Treatise on Precious Stones; a Journal of the Life of Augustus; and other productions. Curiosity is strongly interested to discover the literary talents of a man so much distinguished for the esteem and patronage of them in others; but while we regret the impossibility of such a development, we scarcely can suppose the proficiency to have been small, where the love and admiration were so great.

History was cultivated amongst the Romans during the present period, with uncommon success. This species of composition is calculated both for information and entertainment; but the chief design of it is to record all transactions relative to the public, for the purpose of enabling mankind to draw from past events a probable conjecture concerning the future; and, by knowing the steps which have led either to prosperity or misfortune, to ascertain the best means of promoting the former, and avoiding the latter of those objects. This useful kind of narrative was introduced about five hundred years before by Herodotus, who has thence received the appellation of the Father of History. His style, in conformity to the habits of thinking, and the simplicity of language, in an uncultivated age, is plain and unadorned; yet, by the happy modulation of the Ionic dialect, it gratified the ear, and afforded to the states of Greece a pleasing mixture of entertainment, enriched not only with various information, often indeed fabulous or unauthentic, but with the rudiments, indirectly interspersed, of political wisdom. This writer, after a long interval, was succeeded by Thucydides and Xenophon, the former of whom carried historical narrative to the highest degree of improvement it ever attained among the States of Greece. The plan of Thucydides seems to have continued to be the model of historical narrative to the writers of Rome; but the circumstances of the times, aided perhaps by the splendid exertion of genius in other departments of literature, suggested a new resource, which promised not only to animate, but embellish the future productions of the historic Muse. This innovation consisted in an attempt to penetrate the human heart, and explore in its innermost recesses the sentiments and secret motives which actuate the conduct of men. By connecting moral effects with their probable internal and external causes, it tended to establish a systematic consistency in the concatenation of transactions apparently anomalous, accidental, or totally independent of each other.

The author of this improvement in history was SALLUST, who likewise introduced the method of enlivening narrative with the occasional aid of rhetorical declamation, particularly in his account of the Catilinian conspiracy. The notorious (160) characters and motives of the principal persons concerned in that horrible plot, afforded the most favourable opportunity for exemplifying the former; while the latter, there is reason to infer from the facts which must have been at that time publicly known, were founded upon documents of unquestionable authority. Nay, it is probable that Sallust was present in the senate during the debate respecting the punishment of the Catilinian conspirators; his detail of which is agreeable to the characters of the several speakers: but in detracting, by invidious silence, or too faint representation, from the merits of Cicero on that important occasion, he exhibits a glaring instance of the partiality which too often debases the narratives of those who record the transactions of their own time. He had married Terentia, the divorced wife of Cicero; and there subsisted between the two husbands a kind of rivalship from that cause, to which was probably added some degree of animosity, on account of their difference in politics, during the late dictatorship of Julius Caesar, by whom Sallust was restored to the senate, whence he had been expelled for licentiousness, and was appointed governor of Numidia. Excepting the injustice with which Sallust treats Cicero, he is entitled to high commendation. In both his remaining works, the Conspiracy of Catiline, and the War of Jugurtha, there is a peculiar air of philosophical sentiment, which, joined to the elegant conciseness of style, and animated description of characters, gives to his writings a degree of interest, superior to that which is excited in any preceding work of the historical kind. In the occasional use of obsolete words, and in laboured exordiums to both his histories, he is liable to the charge of affectation; but it is an affectation of language which supports solemnity without exciting disgust; and of sentiment which not only exalts human nature, but animates to virtuous exertions. It seems to be the desire of Sallust to atone for the dissipation of his youth by a total change of conduct; and whoever peruses his exordiums with the attention which they deserve, must feel a strong persuasion of the justness of his remarks, if not the incentives of a resolution to be governed by his example. It seems to be certain, that from the first moment of his reformation, he incessantly practised the industry which he so warmly recommends. He composed a History of Rome, of which nothing remains but a few fragments. Sallust, during his administration of Numidia, is said to have exercised great oppression. On his return to Rome he built a magnificent house, and bought delightful gardens, the name of which, with his own, is to this day perpetuated on the spot which they formerly occupied. Sallust was born at Amiternum, in the country of the Sabines, and (161) received his education at Rome. He incurred great scandal by an amour with Fausta, the daughter of Sylla, and wife of Milo; who detecting the criminal intercourse, is said to have beat him with stripes, and extorted from him a large sum of money. He died, according to tradition, in the fifty-first year of his age.

CORNELIUS NEPOS was born at Hostilia, near the banks of the Po. Of his parentage we meet with no account; but from his respectable connections early in life, it is probable that he was of good extraction. Among his most intimate friends were Cicero and Atticus. Some authors relate that he composed three books of Chronicles, with a biographical account of all the most celebrated sovereigns, generals, and writers of antiquity.

The language of Cornelius Nepos is pure, his style perspicuous, and he holds a middle and agreeable course between diffuseness and brevity. He has not observed the same rule with respect to the treatment of every subject; for the account of some of the lives is so short, that we might suspect them to be mutilated, did they not contain evident marks of their being completed in miniature. The great extent of his plan induced him, as he informs us, to adopt this expedient. "Sed plura persequi, tum magnitudo voluminis prohibet, tum festinatio, ut ea explicem, quae exorsus sum." 270

Of his numerous biographical works, twenty-two lives only remain, which are all of Greeks, except two Carthaginians, Hamilcar and Hannibal; and two Romans, M. Porcius Cato and T. Pomponius Atticus. Of his own life, — of him who had written the lives of so many, no account is transmitted; but from the multiplicity of his productions, we may conclude that it was devoted to literature.

TITUS LIVIUS may be ranked among the most celebrated historians the world has ever produced. He composed a history of Rome from the foundation of the city, to the conclusion of the German war conducted by Drusus in the time of the emperor Augustus. This great work consisted, originally, of one hundred and forty books; of which there now remain only thirty-five, viz., the first decade, and the whole from book twenty-one to book forty-five, both inclusive. Of the other hundred and five books, nothing more has survived the ravages of time and barbarians than their general contents. In a perspicuous arrangement of his subject, in a full and circumstantial account of transactions, in the delineation of characters and other objects of description, to justness and aptitude of sentiment, and in an air of majesty (162) pervading the whole composition, this author may be regarded as one of the best models extant of historical narrative. His style is splendid without meretricious ornament, and copious without being redundant; a fluency to which Quintilian gives the expressive appellation of "lactea ubertas." Amongst the beauties which we admire in his writings, besides the animated speeches frequently interspersed, are those concise and peculiarly applicable eulogiums, with which he characterises every eminent person mentioned, at the close of their life. Of his industry in collating, and his judgment in deciding upon the preference due to, dissentient authorities, in matters of testimony, the work affords numberless proofs. Of the freedom and impartiality with which he treated even of the recent periods of history, there cannot be more convincing evidence, than that he was rallied by Augustus as a favourer of Pompey; and that, under the same emperor, he not only bestowed upon Cicero the tribute of warm approbation, but dared to ascribe, in an age when their names were obnoxious, even to Brutus and Cassius the virtues of consistency and patriotism. If in any thing the conduct of Livy violates our sentiments of historical dignity, it is the apparent complacency and reverence with which he every where mentions the popular belief in omens and prodigies; but this was the general superstition of the times; and totally to renounce the prejudices of superstitious education, is the last heroic sacrifice to philosophical scepticism. In general, however, the credulity of Livy appears to be rather affected than real; and his account of the exit of Romulus, in the following passage, may be adduced as an instance in confirmation of this remark.

"His immortalibus editis operibus, quum ad exercitum recensendum concionem in campo ad Caprae paludem haberet, subita coorta tempestate cum magno fragore tonitribusque tam denso regem operuit nimbo, ut conspectum ejus concioni abstulerit; nec deinde in terris Romulus fuit. Romana pubes, sedato tandem pavore, postquam ex tam turbido die serena, et tranquilla lux rediit, ubi vacuam sedem regiam vidit; etsi satis credebat Patribus, qui proximi steterant, sublimem raptum procella; tamen veluti orbitatis metu icta, maestum aliquamdiu silentium obtinuit. Deinde a paucis initio facto, Deum, Deo natum, regem parentemque urbis Romanae, salvere universi Romulum jubent; pacem precibus exposcunt, uti volens propitius suam semper sospitet progeniem. Fuisse credo tum quoque aliquos, qui discerptum regem Patrum manibus taciti arguerent; manavit enim haec quoque, et perobscura, fama. Illam alteram admiratio viri, et pavor praesens nobilitavit. Consilio etiam unius hominis addita rei dicitur fides; namque Proculus Julius sollicita civitate desiderio (163) regis, et infensa Patribus, gravis, ut traditur, quamvis magnae rei auctor, in concionem prodit. 'Romulus, inquit, Quirites, parens urbis hujus, prima hodierna luce coelo repente delapsus, se mihi obvium dedit; quam profusus horrore venerabundusque astitissem, petens precibus, ut contra intueri fas esset; Abi, nuncia, inquit,

Romanis, Coelestes ita velle, ut mea Roma caput orbis terrarum sit; proinde rem militarem colant; sciantque, et ita posteris tradant, nullas opes humanas armis Romanis resistere posse.' Haec, inquit, locutus, sublimis abiit. Mirum, quantum illi viro nuncianti haec fidei fuerit; quamque desiderium Romuli apud plebem exercitumque, facta fide immortalitatis, lenitum sit." 271

Scarcely any incident in ancient history savours more of the (164) marvellous than the account above delivered respecting the first Roman king; and amidst all the solemnity with which it is related, we may perceive that the historian was not the dupe of credulity. There is more implied than the author thought proper to avow, in the sentence, Fuisse credo, etc. In whatever light this anecdote be viewed, it is involved in perplexity. That Romulus affected a despotic power, is not only highly probable, from his aspiring disposition, but seems to be confirmed by his recent appointment of the Celeres, as a guard to his person. He might, therefore, naturally incur the odium of the patricians, whose importance was diminished, and their institution rendered abortive, by the increase of his power. But that they should choose the opportunity of a military review, for the purpose of removing the tyrant by a violent death, seems not very consistent with the dictates even of common prudence; and it is the more incredible, as the circumstance which favoured the execution of the plot is represented to have been entirely a fortuitous occurrence. The tempest which is said to have happened, is not easily reconcilable with our knowledge of that phenomenon. Such a cloud, or mist, as could have enveloped Romulus from the eyes of the assembly, is not a natural concomitant of a thunder-storm. There is some reason to suspect that both the noise and cloud, if they actually existed, were artificial; the former intended to divert the attention of the spectators, and the latter to conceal the transaction. The word fragor, a noise or crash, appears to be an unnecessary addition where thunder is expressed, though sometimes so used by the poets, and may therefore, perhaps, imply such a noise from some other cause. If Romulus was killed by any pointed or sharp-edged weapon, his blood might have been discovered on the spot; or, if by other means, still the body was equally an object for public observation. If the people suspected the patricians to be guilty of murder, why did they not endeavour to trace the fact by this evidence? And if the patricians were really innocent, why did they not urge the examination? But the body, without doubt, was secreted, to favour the imposture. The whole narrative is strongly marked with circumstances calculated to affect credulity with ideas of national importance; and, to countenance the design, there is evidently a chasm in the Roman history immediately preceding this transaction and intimately connected with it.

Livy was born at Patavium 272, and has been charged by Asinius Pollio and others with the provincial dialect of his country. The objections to his Pativinity, as it is called, relate chiefly to the (165) spelling of some words; in which, however, there seems to be nothing so peculiar, as either to occasion any obscurity or merit reprehension.

Livy and Sallust being the only two existing rivals in Roman history, it may not be improper to draw a short comparison between them, in respect of their principal qualities, as writers. With regard to language, there is less apparent affectation in Livy than in Sallust. The narrative of both is distinguished by an elevation of style: the elevation of Sallust seems to be often supported by the dignity of assumed virtue; that of Livy by a majestic air of historical, and sometimes national, importance. In delineating characters, Sallust infuses more expression, and Livy more fulness, into the features. In the speeches ascribed to particular persons, these writers are equally elegant and animated.

So great was the fame of Livy in his own life-time, that people came from the extremity of Spain and Gaul, for the purpose only of beholding so celebrated a historian, who was regarded, for his abilities, as a prodigy. This affords a strong proof, not only of the literary taste which then prevailed over the most extensive of the Roman provinces, but of the extraordinary pains with which so great a work must have been propagated, when the art of printing was unknown. In the fifteenth century, on the revival of learning in Europe, the name of this great writer recovered its ancient veneration; and Alphonso of Arragon, with a superstition characteristic of that age, requested of the people of Padua, where Livy was born, and is said to have been buried, to be favoured by them with the hand which had written so admirable a work.—

The celebrity of VIRGIL has proved the means of ascertaining his birth with more exactness than is common in the biographical memoirs of ancient writers. He was born at Andes, a village in the neighbourhood of Mantua, on the 15th of October, seventy years before the Christian aera. His parents were of moderate condition; but by their industry acquired some territorial possessions, which descended to their son. The first seven years of his life was spent at Cremona, whence he went to Mediolanum, now Milan, at that time the seat of the liberal arts, denominated, as we learn from Pliny the younger, Novae Athenae. From this place he afterwards moved to Naples, where he applied himself with great assiduity to Greek and Roman literature, particularly to the physical and mathematical sciences; for which he expressed a strong predilection in the second book of his Georgics.

> Me vero primum dulces ante omnia Musae,
> Quarum sacra fero ingenti perculsus amore,
> (166) Accipiant; coelique vias et sidera monstrent;
> Defectus Solis varios, Lunaeque labores:
> Unde tremor terris: qua vi maria alta tumescant
> Obicibus ruptis, rursusque in seipsa residant:
> Quid tantum Oceano properent se tingere soles
> Hiberni: vel quae tardis mora noctibus obstet.
> Geor. ii. 1. 591, etc.
>
> But most beloved, ye Muses, at whose fane,
> Led by pure zeal, I consecrate my strain,
> Me first accept! And to my search unfold,
> Heaven and her host in beauteous order rolled,
> The eclipse that dims the golden orb of day,
> And changeful labour of the lunar ray;
> Whence rocks the earth, by what vast force the main
> Now bursts its barriers, now subsides again;
> Why wintry suns in ocean swiftly fade,
> Or what delays night's slow-descending shade. Sotheby.

When, by a proscription of the Triumvirate, the lands of Cremona and Mantua were distributed amongst the veteran soldiers, Virgil had the good fortune to recover his possessions, through the favour of Asinius Pollio, the deputy of Augustus in those parts; to whom, as well as to the emperor, he has testified his gratitude in beautiful eclogues.

The first production of Virgil was his Bucolics, consisting of ten eclogues, written in imitation of the Idyllia or pastoral poems of Theocritus. It may be questioned whether any language which has its provincial dialects, but is brought to perfection, can ever be well adapted, in that state, to the use of pastoral poetry. There is such an apparent incongruity between the simple ideas of the rural swain and the polished language of the courtier, that it seems impossible to reconcile them together by the utmost art of composition. The Doric dialect of Theocritus, therefore, abstractedly from all consideration of simplicity of sentiment, must ever give to the Sicilian bard a pre-eminence in this species of poetry. The greater part of the Bucolics of Virgil may be regarded as poems of a peculiar nature, into which the author has happily transfused, in elegant versification, the native manners and ideas, without any mixture of the rusticity of pastoral life. With respect to the fourth eclogue, addressed to Pollio, it is avowedly of a nature superior to that of pastoral subjects:

*Sicelides Musae, paullo majora canamus.*
*Sicilian Muse, be ours a loftier strain.*

Virgil engaged in bucolic poetry at the request of Asinius Pollio, whom he highly esteemed, and for one of whose sons in particular, (167) with Cornelius Gallus, a poet likewise, he entertained the warmest affection. He has celebrated them all in these poems, which were begun, we are told, in the twenty-ninth year of his age, and completed in three years. They were held in so great esteem amongst the Romans, immediately after their publication, that it is said they were frequently recited upon the stage for the entertainment of the audience. Cicero, upon hearing some lines of them, perceived that they were written in no common strain of poetry, and desired that the whole eclogue might be recited: which being done, he exclaimed, "Magnae spes altera Romae." Another hope of mighty Rome! 273

Virgil's next work was the Georgics, the idea of which is taken from the Erga kai Hmerai, the Works and Days of Hesiod, the poet of Ascra. But between the productions of the two poets, there is no other similarity than that of their common subject. The precepts of Hesiod, in respect of agriculture, are delivered with all the simplicity of an unlettered cultivator of the fields, intermixed with plain moral reflections, natural and apposite; while those of Virgil, equally precise and important, are embellished with all the dignity of sublime versification. The work is addressed to Mecaenas, at whose request it appears to have been undertaken. It is divided into four books. The first treats of ploughing; the second, of planting; the third, of cattle, horses, sheep, goats, dogs, and of things which are hurtful to cattle; the fourth is employed on bees, their proper habitations, food, polity, the diseases to which they are liable, and the remedies of them, with the method of making honey, and a variety of other considerations connected with the subject. The Georgics (168) were written at Naples, and employed the author during a period of seven years. It is said that Virgil had concluded the Georgics with a laboured eulogium on his poetical friend Gallus; but the latter incurring about this time the displeasure of Augustus, he was induced to cancel it, and substitute the charming episode of Astaeus and Eurydice.

These beautiful poems, considered merely as didactic, have the justest claim to utility. In what relates to agriculture in particular, the precepts were judiciously adapted to the climate of Italy, and must have conveyed much valuable information to those who were desirous of cultivating that important art, which was held in great honour amongst the Romans. The same remark may be made, with greater latitude of application, in respect of the other subjects. But when we examine the Georgics as poetical compositions, when we attend to the elevated style in which they are written, the beauty of the similes, the emphatic sentiments interspersed, the elegance of diction, the animated strain of the whole, and the harmony of the versification, our admiration is excited, at beholding subjects, so common in their nature, embellished with the most magnificent decorations of poetry.

During four days which Augustus passed at Atella, to refresh himself from fatigue, in his return to Rome, after the battle of Actium, the Georgics, just then finished, were read to him by the author, who was occasionally relieved in the task by his friend Mecaenas. We may easily conceive the satisfaction enjoyed by the emperor, at finding that while he himself had been gathering laurels in the achievements of war, another glorious wreath was prepared by the Muses to adorn his temples; and that an intimation was given of his being afterwards celebrated in a work more congenial to the subject of heroic renown.

It is generally supposed that the Aeneid was written at the particular desire of Augustus, who was ambitious of having the Julian family represented as lineal descendants of the Trojan Aeneas.

In this celebrated poem, Virgil has happily united the characteristics of the Iliad and Odyssey, and blended them so judiciously together, that they mutually contribute to the general effect of the whole. By the esteem and sympathy excited for the filial piety and misfortunes of Aeneas at the catastrophe of Troy, the reader is strongly interested in his subsequent adventures; and every obstacle to the establishment of the Trojans in the promised land of Hesperia produces fresh sensations of increased admiration and attachment. The episodes, characters, and incidents, all concur to give beauty or grandeur to the poem. The picture of Troy in flames can never be sufficiently (169) admired! The incomparable portrait of Priam, in Homer, is admirably accommodated to a different situation, in the character of Anchises, in the Aeneid. The prophetic rage of the Cumaean Sibyl displays in the strongest colours the enthusiasm of the poet. For sentiment, passion, and interesting description, the episode of Dido is a master-piece in poetry. But Virgil is not more conspicuous for strength of description than propriety of sentiment; and wherever he takes a hint from the Grecian bard, he prosecutes the idea with a judgment peculiar to himself. It may be sufficient to mention one instance. In the sixth book of the Iliad, while the Greeks are making great slaughter amongst the Trojans, Hector, by the advice of Helenus, retires into the city, to desire that his mother would offer up prayers to the goddess Pallas, and vow to her a noble sacrifice, if she would drive Diomede from the walls of Troy. Immediately before his return to the field of battle, he has his last interview with Andromache, whom he meets with his infant son Astyanax, carried by a nurse. There occurs, upon this occasion, one of the most beautiful scenes in the Iliad, where Hector dandles the boy in his arms, and pours forth a prayer, that he may one day be superior in fame to his father. In the same manner, Aeneas, having armed himself for the decisive combat with Turnus, addresses his son Ascanius in a beautiful speech, which, while expressive of the strongest paternal affection, contains, instead of a prayer, a noble and emphatic admonition, suitable to a youth who had nearly attained the period of adult age. It is as follows:

> *Disce, puer, virtutem ex me, verumque laborem;*
> *Fortunam ex aliis; nunc te mea dextera bello*
> *Defensum dabit, et magna inter praemia ducet.*
> *Tu facito, mox cum matura adoleverit aetas,*

*Sis memor: et te animo repetentem exempla tuorum,*
*Et pater Aeneas, et avunculus excitet Hector. — Aeneid, xii.*
*My son! from my example learn the war*
*In camps to suffer, and in feuds to dare,*
*But happier chance than mine attend thy care!*
*This day my hand thy tender age shall shield,*
*And crown with honours of the conquered field:*
*Thou when thy riper years shall send thee forth*
*To toils of war, be mindful of my worth;*
*Assert thy birthright, and in arms be known,*
*For Hector's nephew and Aeneas' son.*

Virgil, though born to shine by his own intrinsic powers, certainly owed much of his excellence to the wonderful merits of Homer. His susceptible imagination, vivid and correct, was (170) impregnated by the Odyssey, and warmed with the fire of the Iliad. Rivalling, or rather on some occasions surpassing his glorious predecessor in the characters of heroes and of gods, he sustains their dignity with so uniform a lustre, that they seem indeed more than mortal.

Whether the Iliad or the Aeneid be the more perfect composition, is a question which has often been agitated, but perhaps will never be determined to general satisfaction. In comparing the genius of the two poets, however, allowance ought to be made for the difference of circumstances under which they composed their respective works. Homer wrote in an age when mankind had not as yet made any great progress in the exertion of either intellect or imagination, and he was therefore indebted for big resources to the vast capacity of his own mind. To this we must add, that he composed both his poems in a situation of life extremely unfavourable to the cultivation of poetry. Virgil, on the contrary, lived at a period when literature had attained to a high state of improvement. He had likewise not only the advantage of finding a model in the works of Homer, but of perusing the laws of epic poetry, which had been digested by Aristotle, and the various observations made on the writings of the Greek bard by critics of acuteness and taste; amongst the chief of whom was his friend Horace, who remarks that

*— — — quandoque bonus dormitat Homerus. — De Arte Poet.*

*E'en sometimes the good Homer naps.*

Virgil, besides, composed his poem in a state remote from indigence, where he was roused to exertion by the example of several contemporary poets; and what must have animated him beyond every other consideration, he wrote both at the desire, and under the patronage of the emperor and his minister Mecaenas. In what time Homer composed either of his poems, we know not; but the Aeneid, we are informed, was the employment of Virgil during eleven years. For some years, the repeated entreaties of Augustus could not extort from him the smallest specimen of the work; but at length, when considerably advanced in it, he condescended to recite three books—the second, the fourth, and the sixth—in the presence of the emperor and his sister Octavia, to gratify the latter of whom, in particular, the recital of the last book now mentioned, was intended. When the poet came to the words, Tu Marcellus eris, alluding to Octavia's son, a youth of great hopes, who had lately died, the mother fainted. After she had recovered from this fit, by the care of her attendants, she ordered ten sesterces to be given to Virgil for every line relating (171) to that subject; a gratuity which amounted to about two thousand pounds sterling.

In the composition of the Aeneid, Virgil scrupled not to introduce whole lines of Homer, and of the Latin poet Ennius; many of whose sentences he admired. In a few instances he has borrowed from Lucretius. He is said to have been at extraordinary pains in polishing his numbers; and when he was doubtful of any passage, he would read it to some of his friends, that he might have their opinion. On such occasions, it was usual with him to consult in particular his freedman and librarian Erotes, an old domestic, who, it is related, supplied extempore a deficiency in two lines, and was desired by his master to write them in the manuscript.

When this immortal work was completed, Virgil resolved on retiring into Greece and Asia for three years, that he might devote himself entirely to polishing it, and have leisure afterwards to pass the remainder of his life in the cultivation of philosophy. But meeting at Athens with Augustus, who was on his return from the East, he determined on accompanying the emperor back to Rome. Upon a visit to Megara, a town in the neighbourhood of Athens, he was seized with a languor, which increased during the ensuing voyage;

and he expired a few days after landing at Brundisium, on the 22nd of September, in the fifty-second year of his age. He desired that his body might be carried to Naples, where he had passed many happy years; and that the following distich, written in his last sickness, should be inscribed upon his tomb:

> Mantua me genuit: Calabri rapuere: tenet nunc
> Parthenope: cecini pascua, rura, duces. 274_

He was accordingly interred, by the order of Augustus, with great funeral pomp, within two miles of Naples, near the road to Puteoli, where his tomb still exists. Of his estate, which was very considerable by the liberality of his friends, he left the greater part to Valerius Proculus and his brother, a fourth to Augustus, a twelfth to Mecaenas, besides legacies to L. Varius and Plotius Tucca, who, in consequence of his own request, and the command of Augustus, revised and corrected the Aeneid after his death. Their instructions from the emperor were, to expunge whatever they thought improper, but upon no account to make any addition. This restriction is supposed to be the cause that many lines in the Aeneid are imperfect.

Virgil was of large stature, had a dark complexion, and his (172) features are said to have been such as expressed no uncommon abilities. He was subject to complaints of the stomach and throat, as well as to head-ache, and had frequent discharges of blood upwards: but from what part, we are not informed. He was very temperate both in food and wine. His modesty was so great, that at Naples they commonly gave him the name of Parthenias, "the modest man." On the subject of his modesty; the following anecdote is related.

Having written a distich, in which he compared Augustus to Jupiter, he placed it in the night-time over the gate of the emperor's palace. It was in these words:

> Nocte pluit tota, redeunt spectacula mane:
> Divisum imperium cum Jove Caesar habet.
> All night it rained, with morn the sports appear,
> Caesar and Jove between them rule the year.

By order of Augustus, an inquiry was made after the author; and Virgil not declaring himself, the verses were claimed by Bathyllus, a contemptible poet, but who was liberally rewarded on the occasion. Virgil, provoked at the falsehood of the impostor, again wrote the verses on some conspicuous part of the palace, and under them the following line:

> Hos ego versiculos feci, tulit alter honorem;
> I wrote the verse, another filched the praise;

with the beginning of another line in these words:

> Sic vos, non vobis,
> Not for yourselves, you — —

repeated four times. Augustus expressing a desire that the lines should be finished, and Bathyllus proving unequal to the task, Virgil at last filled up the blanks in this manner:

> Sic vos, non vobis, nidificatis, aves;
> Sic vos, non vobis, vellera fertis, oves;
> Sic vos, non vobis, mellificatis, apes;
> Sic vos, non vobis, fertis aratra, boves.
> Not for yourselves, ye birds, your nests ye build;
> Not for yourselves, ye sheep, your fleece ye yield;
> Not for yourselves, ye bees, your cells ye fill;
> Not for yourselves, ye beeves, ye plough and till.

The expedient immediately evinced him to be the author of the distich, and Bathyllus became the theme of public ridicule.

When at any time Virgil came to Rome, if the people, as was commonly the case, crowded to gaze upon him, or pointed at him with the finger in admiration, he blushed, and stole away (173) from them; frequently taking refuge in some shop. When he went to the theatre, the audience universally rose up at his entrance, as they did to Augustus, and received him with the loudest plaudits; a compliment which, however highly honourable, he would gladly have declined. When such was the just respect which they paid to the author of the Bucolics and Georgics, how would they have expressed their esteem, had they beheld him in the effulgence of epic renown! In the beautiful episode of the Elysian fields, in the Aeneid, where he dexterously introduced a glorious display of their country, he had touched the most elastic springs of Roman enthusiasm. The passion would have rebounded upon himself, and they would, in the heat of admiration, have idolized him.

HORACE was born at Venusia, on the tenth of December, in the consulship of L. Cotta and L. Torquatus. According to his own acknowledgment, his father was a freedman; by some it is said that he was a collector of the revenue, and by others, a fishmonger, or a dealer in salted meat. Whatever he was, he paid particular attention to the education of his son, for, after receiving instruction from the best masters in Rome, he sent him to Athens to study philosophy. From this place, Horace followed Brutus, in the quality of a military tribune, to the battle of Philippi, where, by his own confession, being seized with timidity, he abandoned the profession of a soldier, and returning to Rome, applied himself to the cultivation of poetry. In a short time he acquired the friendship of Virgil and Valerius, whom he mentions in his Satires, in terms of the most tender affection.

> *Postera lux oritur multo gratissima: namque*
> *Plotius et Varius Sinuessae, Virgiliusque,*
> *Occurrunt; animae, quales neque candidiores*
> *Terra tulit, neque queis me sit devinctior alter.*
> *O qui complexus, et gaudia quanta fuerunt!*
> *Nil ego contulerim jucundo sanus amico.* — Sat. I. 5.
> 
> *Next rising morn with double joy we greet,*
> *For Plotius, Varius, Virgil, here we meet:*
> *Pure spirits these; the world no purer knows,*
> *For none my heart with more affection glows:*
> *How oft did we embrace, our joys how great!*
> *For sure no blessing in the power of fate*
> *Can be compared, in sanity of mind,*
> *To friends of such companionable kind.* — Francis.

By the two friends above mentioned, he was recommended to the patronage not only of Mecaenas, but of Augustus, with whom he, as well as Virgil, lived on a footing of the greatest intimacy. Satisfied with the luxury which he enjoyed at the first tables in (174) Rome, he was so unambitious of any public employment, that when the emperor offered him the place of his secretary, he declined it. But as he lived in an elegant manner, having, besides his house in town, a cottage on his Sabine farm, and a villa at Tibur, near the falls of the Anio, he enjoyed, beyond all doubt. a handsome establishment, from the liberality of Augustus. He indulged himself in indolence and social pleasure, but was at the same time much devoted to reading; and enjoyed a tolerable good state of health, although often incommoded with a fluxion of rheum upon the eyes.

Horace, in the ardour of youth, and when his bosom beat high with the raptures of fancy, had, in the pursuit of Grecian literature, drunk largely, at the source, of the delicious springs of Castalia; and it seems to have been ever after his chief ambition, to transplant into the plains of Latium the palm of lyric poetry. Nor did he fail of success:

> *Exegi monumentum aere perennius. – Carm. iii. 30.*
> More durable than brass a monument I've raised.

In Greece, and other countries, the Ode appears to have been the most ancient, as well as the most popular species of literary production. Warm in expression, and short in extent, it concentrates in narrow bounds the fire of poetical transport: on which account, it has been generally employed to celebrate the fervours of piety, the raptures of love, the enthusiasm of praise; and to animate warriors to glorious exertions of valour:

> *Musa dedit fidibus Divos, puerosque Deorum,*
> *Et pugilem victorem, et equum certamine primnm,*
> *Et juvenum curas, et libera vina referre. – Hor. De Arte Poet.*
> The Muse to nobler subjects tunes her lyre;
> Gods, and the sons of Gods, her song inspire;
> Wrestler and steed, who gained the Olympic prize,
> Love's pleasing cares, and wine's unbounded joys. – Francis.
> *Misenum Aeoliden, quo non praestantior alter*
> *Aere ciere viros, Martemque accendere cnatu. 275_*
> Virgil, Aeneid, vi.
> . . . . . . . . . . .
> *Sed tum forte cava dum personat aequora concha*
> *Demens, et canto vocat in certamina Divos. – Ibid.*
> Misenus, son of Oeolus, renowned
> The warrior trumpet in the field to sound;
> With breathing brass to kindle fierce alarms,
> And rouse to dare their fate in honourable arms.

. . . . . . . . . . . .
(175) *Swollen with applause, and aiming still at more,*
*He now provokes the sea-gods from the shore.* – Dryden

There arose in this department, among the Greeks, nine eminent poets, viz. Alcaeus, Alcman, Anacreon, Bacchylides, Ibicus, Sappho, Stesichorus, Simonides, and Pindar. The greater number of this distinguished class are now known only by name. They seem all to have differed from one another, no less in the kind of measure which they chiefly or solely employed, than in the strength or softness, the beauty or grandeur, the animated rapidity or the graceful ease of their various compositions. Of the amorous effusions of the lyre, we yet have examples in the odes of Anacreon, and the incomparable ode of Sappho: the lyric strains which animated to battle, have sunk into oblivion; but the victors in the public games of Greece have their fame perpetuated in the admirable productions of Pindar.

Horace, by adopting, in the multiplicity of his subjects, almost all the various measures of the different Greek poets, and frequently combining different measures in the same composition, has compensated for the dialects of that tongue, so happily suited to poetry, and given to a language less distinguished for soft inflexions, all the tender and delicate modulations of the Eastern song. While he moves in the measures of the Greeks with an ease and gracefulness which rivals their own acknowledged excellence, he has enriched the fund of lyric harmony with a stanza peculiar to himself. In the artificial construction of the Ode, he may justly be regarded as the first of lyric poets. In beautiful imagery, he is inferior to none: in variety of sentiment and felicity of expression, superior to every existing competitor in Greek or Roman poetry. He is elegant without affectation; and what is more remarkable, in the midst of gaiety he is moral. We seldom meet in his Odes with the abrupt apostrophes of passionate excursion; but his transitions are conducted with ease, and every subject introduced with propriety.

The Carmen Seculare was written at the express desire of Augustus, for the celebration of the Secular Games, performed once in a hundred years, and which continued during three days and three nights, whilst all Rome resounded with the mingled effusions of choral addresses to gods and goddesses, and of festive joy. An occasion which so much interested the ambition of the poet, called into exertion the most vigorous efforts of his genius. More concise in mythological attributes than the hymns ascribed to Homer, this beautiful production, in variety and grandeur of invocation, and in pomp of numbers, surpasses all that Greece, (176) melodious but simple in the service of the altar, ever poured forth from her vocal groves in solemn adoration. By the force of native genius, the ancients elevated their heroes to a pitch of sublimity that excites admiration, but to soar beyond which they could derive no aid from mythology; and it was reserved for a bard, inspired with nobler sentiments than the Muses could supply, to sing the praises of that Being whose ineffable perfections transcend all human imagination. Of the praises of gods and heroes, there is not now extant a more beautiful composition, than the 12th Ode of the first book of Horace:

> Quem virum aut heroa lyra vel acri
> Tibia sumes celebrare, Clio?
> Quem Deum? cujus recinet jocosa
> Nomen imago,
> Aut in umbrosis Heliconis oris, etc.
> What man, what hero, on the tuneful lyre,
> Or sharp-toned flute, will Clio choose to raise,
> Deathless, to fame? What God? whose hallowed name
> The sportive image of the voice
> Shall in the shades of Helicon repeat, etc.

The Satires of Horace are far from being remarkable for poetical harmony, as he himself acknowledges. Indeed, according to the plan upon which several of them are written, it could scarcely be otherwise. They are frequently colloquial, sometimes interrogatory, the transitions quick, and the apostrophes abrupt. It was not his object in those compositions, to soothe the ear with the melody of polished numbers, but to rally the frailties of the heart, to convince the understanding by argument, and thence to put to shame both the vices and follies of mankind. Satire is a species of composition, of which the Greeks furnished no model; and the preceding Roman writers of this class, though they had much improved it from its original rudeness and licentiousness, had still not brought it to that degree of perfection which might answer the purpose of moral reform in a polished state of society. It received the most essential improvement from Horace, who has dexterously combined wit and argument, raillery and sarcasm, on the side of morality and virtue, of happiness and truth.

The Epistles of this author may be reckoned amongst the most valuable productions of antiquity. Except those of the second book, and one or two in the first, they are in general of the familiar kind; abounding in moral sentiments, and judicious observations on life and manners.

The poem De Arte Poetica comprises a system of criticism, in justness of principle and extent of application, correspondent to the various exertions of genius on subjects of invention and taste. (177) That in composing this excellent production, he availed himself of the most approved works of Grecian original, we may conclude from the advice which he there recommends:

— — — — — — *Vos exemplaria Graeca*

*Nocturna versate manu, versate diurna.*

Make the Greek authors your supreme delight;

Read them by day, and study them by night. — Francis.

In the writings of Horace there appears a fund of good sense, enlivened with pleasantry, and refined by philosophical reflection. He had cultivated his judgment with great application, and his taste was guided by intuitive perception of moral beauty, aptitude, and propriety. The few instances of indelicacy which occur in his compositions, we may ascribe rather to the manners of the times, than to any blameable propensity in the author. Horace died in the fifty-seventh year of his age, surviving his beloved Mecaenas only three weeks; a circumstance which, added to the declaration in an ode 276 to that personage, supposed to have been written in Mecaenas's last illness, has given rise to a conjecture, that Horace ended his days by a violent death, to accompany his friend. But it is more natural to conclude that he died of excessive grief, as, had he literally adhered to the affirmation contained in the ode, he would have followed his patron more closely. This seems to be confirmed by a fact immediately preceding his death; for though he declared Augustus heir to his whole estate, he was not able, on account of weakness, to put his signature to the will; a failure which it is probable that he would have taken care to obviate, had his death been premeditated. He was interred, at his own desire, near the tomb of Mecaenas. — —

OVID was born of an equestrian family, at Sulmo, a town of the Peligni, on the 21st of March, in the consulship of Hirtius and Pansa. His father intended him for the bar; and after passing him through the usual course of instruction at Rome, he was sent to Athens, the emporium of learning, to complete his education. On his return to Rome, in obedience to the desire of his father, he entered upon the offices of public life in the forum, and declaimed with great applause. But this was the effect of paternal authority, not of choice: for, from his earliest years, he discovered an extreme attachment to poetry; and no sooner was his father dead, than, renouncing the bar, he devoted himself entirely to the cultivation of that fascinating art, his propensity to which was invincible. His productions, all written either in heroic or pentameter verse, are numerous, and on various subjects. It will be sufficient to mention them briefly.

(178) The Heroides consist of twenty-one Epistles, all which, except three, are feigned to be written from celebrated women of antiquity, to their husbands or lovers, such as Penelope to Ulysses, Dido to Aeneas, Sappho to Phaon, etc. These compositions are nervous, animated and elegant: they discover a high degree of poetic enthusiasm, but blended with that lascivious turn of thought, which pervades all the amorous productions of this celebrated author.

The elegies on subjects of love, particularly the Ars Amandi, or Ars Amatoria, though not all uniform in versification, possess the same general character, of warmth of passion, and luscious description, as the epistles.

The Fasti were divided into twelve books, of which only the first six now remain. The design of them was to deliver an account of the Roman festivals in every month of the year, with a description of the rites and ceremonies, as well as the sacrifices on those occasions. It is to be regretted, that, on a subject so interesting, this valuable work should not have been transmitted entire: but in the part which remains, we are furnished with a beautiful description of the ceremonial transactions in the Roman calendar, from the first of January to the end of June. The versification, as in all the compositions of this author, is easy and harmonious.

The most popular production of this poet is his Metamorphoses, not less extraordinary for the nature of the subject, than for the admirable art with which the whole is conducted. The work is founded upon the traditions and theogony of the ancients, which consisted of various detached fables. Those Ovid has not only so happily arranged, that they form a coherent series of narratives, one rising out of another; but he describes the different changes with such an imposing plausibility, as to give a natural appearance to the most incredible fictions. This ingenious production, however perfect it may appear, we are told by himself, had not received his last corrections when he was ordered into banishment.

In the Ibis, the author imitates a poem of the same name, written by Callimachus. It is an invective against some person who publicly traduced his character at Rome, after his banishment. A strong sensibility, indignation, and implacable resentment, are conspicuous through the whole.

The Tristia were composed in his exile, in which, though his vivacity forsook him, he still retained a genius prolific in versification. In these poems, as well as in many epistles to different persons, he bewails his unhappy situation, and deprecates in the strongest terms the inexorable displeasure of Augustus.

Several other productions written by Ovid are now lost, and (179) amongst them a tragedy called Medea, of which Quintilian expresses a high opinion. Ovidii Medea videtur mihi ostendere quantum vir ille praestare potuerit, si ingenio suo temperare quam indulgere maluisset 277 . Lib. x. c. 1.

It is a peculiarity in the productions of this author, that, on whatever he employs his pen, he exhausts the subject; not with any prolixity that fatigues the attention, but by a quick succession of new ideas, equally brilliant and apposite, often expressed in antitheses. Void of obscenity in expression, but lascivious in sentiment, he may be said rather to stimulate immorally the natural passions, than to corrupt the imagination. No poet is more guided in versification by the nature of his subject than Ovid. In common narrative, his ideas are expressed with almost colloquial simplicity; but when his fancy glows with sentiment, or is animated by objects of grandeur, his style is proportionably elevated, and he rises to a pitch of sublimity.

No point in ancient history has excited more variety of conjectures than the banishment of Ovid; but after all the efforts of different writers to elucidate the subject, the cause of this extraordinary transaction remains involved in obscurity. It may therefore not be improper, in this place, to examine the foundation of the several conjectures which have been formed, and if they appear to be utterly imadmissible, to attempt a solution of the question upon principles more conformable to probability, and countenanced by historical evidence.

The ostensible reason assigned by Augustus for banishing Ovid, was his corrupting the Roman youth by lascivious publications; but it is evident, from various passages in the poet's productions after this period, that there was, besides, some secret reason, which would not admit of being divulged. He says in his Tristia, Lib. ii. 1—

*Perdiderent cum me duo crimina, carmen et errors.* 278_

It appears from another passage in the same work, that this inviolable arcanum was something which Ovid had seen, and, as he insinuates, through his own ignorance and mistake.

*Cur aliquid vidi? cur conscia lumina feci?*
*Cur imprudenti cognita culpa mihi est? – Ibid.*
\* \* \* \* \* \*

(180) *Inscia quod crimen viderunt lumina, plector:*
*Peccatumque oculos est habuisse meum.* 279_*De Trist. iii. 5.*

It seems, therefore, to be a fact sufficiently established, that Ovid had seen something of a very indecent nature, in which Augustus was concerned. What this was, is the question. Some authors, conceiving it to have been of a kind extremely atrocious, have gone so far as to suppose, that it must have been an act of criminality between Augustus and his own daughter Julia, who, notwithstanding the strict attention paid to her education by her father, became a woman of the most infamous character; suspected of incontinence during her marriage with Agrippa, and openly profligate after her union with her next husband, Tiberius. This supposition, however, rests entirely upon conjecture, and is not only discredited by its own improbability, but by a yet more forcible argument. It is certain that Julia was at this time in banishment for her scandalous life. She was about the same age with Tiberius, who was now forty seven, and they had not cohabited for many years. We know not exactly the year in which Augustus sent her into exile, but we may conclude with confidence, that it happened soon after her separation from Tiberius; whose own interest with the emperor, as well as that of his mother Livia, could not fail of being exerted, if any such application was necessary, towards removing from the capital a woman, who, by the notoriety of her prostitution, reflected disgrace upon all with whom she was connected, either by blood or alliance. But no application from Tiberius or his mother could be necessary, when we are assured that Augustus even presented to the senate a narrative respecting the infamous behaviour of his daughter, which was read by the quaestor. He was so much ashamed of her profligacy, that he for a long time declined all company, and had thoughts of putting her to death. She was banished to an island on the coast of Campania for five years; at the expiration of which period, she was removed to the continent, and the severity of her treatment a little mitigated; but though frequent applications were made in her behalf by the people, Augustus never could be prevailed upon to permit her return.

(181) Other writers have conjectured, that, instead of Julia, the daughter of Augustus, the person seen with him by Ovid may have been Julia his grand-daughter, who inherited the vicious disposition of her mother, and was on that account likewise banished by Augustus. The epoch of this lady's banishment it is impossible to ascertain; and therefore no argument can be drawn from that source to invalidate the present conjecture. But Augustus had shown the same solicitude for her being trained up in virtuous habits, as he had done in respect of her mother, though in both cases unsuccessfully; and this consideration, joined to the enormity of the supposed crime, and the great sensibility which Augustus had discovered with regard to the infamy of his daughter, seems sufficient to exonerate his memory from so odious a charge. Besides, is it possible that he could have sent her into banishment for the infamy of her prostitution, while (upon the supposition of incest) she was mistress of so important a secret, as that he himself had been more criminal with her than any other man in the empire?

Some writers, giving a wider scope to conjecture, have supposed the transaction to be of a nature still more detestable, and have even dragged Mecaenas, the minister, into a participation of the crime. Fortunately, however, for the reputation of the illustrious patron of polite learning, as well as for that of the emperor, this crude conjecture may be refuted upon the evidence of chronology. The commencement of Ovid's exile happened in the ninth year of the Christian aera, and the death of Mecaenas, eight years before that period. Between this and other calculations, we find a difference of three or four years; but allowing the utmost latitude of variation, there intervened, from the death of Mecaenas to the banishment of Ovid, a period of eleven years; an observation which fully invalidates the conjecture abovementioned.

Having now refuted, as it is presumed, the opinions of the different commentators on this subject, we shall proceed to offer a new conjecture, which seems to have a greater claim to probability than any that has hitherto been suggested.

Suetonius informs us, that Augustus, in the latter part of his life, contracted a vicious inclination for the enjoyment of young virgins, who were procured for him from all parts, not only with the connivance, but by the clandestine management of his consort Livia. It was therefore probably with one of those victims that he was discovered by Ovid. Augustus had for many years affected a decency of behaviour, and he would, therefore, naturally be not a little disconcerted at the unseasonable intrusion of the poet. That Ovid knew not of Augustus's being in the place, is beyond all doubt: and Augustus's consciousness (182) of this circumstance, together with the character of Ovid, would suggest an unfavourable suspicion of the motive which had brought the latter thither. Abstracted from the immorality of the emperor's own conduct, the incident might be regarded as ludicrous, and certainly was more fit to excite the shame than the indignation of Augustus. But the purpose of Ovid's visit appears, from his own acknowledgment, to have been not entirely free from blame, though of what nature we know not:

*Non equidem totam possum defendere culpam:*
*Sed partem nostri criminis error habet.*
De Trist. Lib. iii. Eleg. 5.
*I know I cannot wholly be defended,*
*Yet plead 'twas chance, no ill was then intended.* – Catlin.

Ovid was at this time turned of fifty, and though by a much younger man he would not have been regarded as any object of jealousy in love, yet by Augustus, now in his sixty-ninth year, he might be deemed a formidable rival. This passion, therefore, concurring with that which arose from the interruption or disappointment of gratification, inflamed the emperor's resentment, and he resolved on banishing to a distant country a man whom he considered as his rival, and whose presence, from what had happened, he never more could endure.

Augustus having determined on the banishment of Ovid, could find little difficulty in accommodating the ostensible to the secret and real cause of this resolution.

No argument to establish the date of publication, can be drawn from the order in which the various productions of Ovid are placed in the collection of his works: but reasoning from probability, we should suppose that the Ars Amandi was written during the period of his youth; and this seems to be confirmed by the following passage in the second book of the Fasti:

*Certe ego vos habui faciles in amore ministros;*
*Cum lusit numeris prima juventa suis.* 280_

That many years must have elapsed since its original publication, is evident from the subsequent lines in the second book of the Tristia:

*Nos quoque jam pridem scripto peccavimus uno.*
*Supplicium patitur non nova culpa novum.*
*Carminaque edideram, cum te delicta notantem*
*Praeterii toties jure quietus eques.*
*(183) Ergo, quae juveni mihi non nocitura putavi*
*Scripta parum prudens, nunc nocuere seni?* 281_

With what show, then, of justice, it may be asked, could Augustus now punish a fault, which, in his solemn capacity of censor, he had so long and repeatedly overlooked? The answer is obvious: in a production so popular as we may be assured the Ars Amandi was amongst the Roman youth, it must have passed through several editions in the course of some years: and one of those coinciding with the fatal discovery, afforded the emperor a specious pretext for the execution of his purpose. The severity exercised on this occasion, however, when the poet was suddenly driven into exile, unaccompanied even by the partner of his bed, who had been his companion for many years, was an act so inconsistent with the usual moderation of Augustus, that we cannot justly ascribe it to any other motive than personal resentment; especially as this arbitrary punishment of the author could answer no end of public utility, while the obnoxious production remained to affect, if it really ever did essentially affect, the morals of society. If the sensibility of Augustus could not thenceforth admit of any personal intercourse with Ovid, or even of his living within the limits of Italy, there would have been little danger from the example, in sending into honourable exile, with every indulgence which could alleviate so distressful a necessity, a man of respectable rank in the state, who was charged with no actual offence against the laws, and whose genius, with all its indiscretion, did immortal honour to his country. It may perhaps be urged, that, considering the predicament in which Augustus stood, he discovered a forbearance greater than might have been expected from an absolute prince, in sparing the life of Ovid. It will readily be granted, that Ovid, in the same circumstances, under any one of the four subsequent emperors, would have expiated the incident with his blood. Augustus, upon a late occasion, had shown himself equally sanguinary, for he put to death, by the hand of Varus, a poet of Parma, named Cassius, on account of his having written some satirical verses against him. By that recent example, therefore, and the power of pardoning which the emperor still retained, there was sufficient hold of the poet's secrecy respecting the fatal transaction, which, if divulged (184) to the world, Augustus would reprobate as a false and infamous libel, and punish the author accordingly. Ovid, on his part, was sensible, that, should he dare to violate the important but tacit injunction, the imperial vengeance would reach him even on the shores of the Euxine. It appears, however, from a passage in the Ibis, which can apply to no other than Augustus, that Ovid was not sent into banishment destitute of pecuniary provision:

*Di melius! quorum longe mihi maximus ille,*
*Qui nostras inopes noluit esse vias.*
*Huic igitur meritas grates, ubicumque licebit,*
*Pro tam mansueto pectore semper agam.*
*The gods defend! of whom he's far the chief,*
*Who lets me not, though banished, want relief.*
*For this his favour therefore whilst I live,*
*Where'er I am, deserved thanks I'll give.*

What sum the emperor bestowed, for the support of a banishment which he was resolved should be perpetual, it is impossible to ascertain; but he had formerly been liberal to Ovid, as well as to other poets.

If we might hazard a conjecture respecting the scene of the intrigue which occasioned the banishment of Ovid, we should place it in some recess in the emperor's gardens. His house, though called Palatium, the palace, as being built on the Palatine hill, and inhabited by the sovereign, was only a small mansion, which had formerly belonged to Hortensius, the orator. Adjoining to this place Augustus had built the temple of Apollo, which he endowed with a public library, and allotted for the use of poets, to recite their compositions to each other. Ovid was particularly intimate with Hyginus, one of Augustus's freedmen, who was librarian of the temple. He might therefore have been in the library, and spying from the window a young female secreting herself in the gardens, he had the curiosity to follow her.

The place of Ovid's banishment was Tomi 282 , now said to be Baba, a town of Bulgaria, towards the mouth of the Ister, where is a lake still called by the natives Ouvidouve Jesero, the lake of Ovid. In this retirement, and the Euxine Pontus, he passed the remainder of his life, a melancholy period of seven years. Notwithstanding the lascivious writings of Ovid, it does not appear that he was in his conduct a libertine. He was three times married: his first wife, who was of mean extraction, and (185) whom he had married when he was very young, he divorced; the second he dismissed on account of her immodest behaviour; and the third appears to have survived him. He had a number of respectable friends, and seems to have been much beloved by them.— —

TIBULLUS was descended of an equestrian family, and is said, but erroneously, as will afterwards appear, to have been born on the same day with Ovid. His amiable accomplishments procured him the friendship of Messala Corvinus, whom he accompanied in a military expedition to the island of Corcyra. But an indisposition with which he was seized, and a natural aversion to the toils of war, induced him to return to Rome, where he seems to have resigned himself to a life of indolence and pleasure, amidst which he devoted a part of his time to the composition of elegies. Elegiac poetry had been cultivated by several Greek writers, particularly Callimachus, Mimnermus, and Philetas; but, so far as we can find, had, until the present age, been unknown to the Romans in their own tongue. It consisted of a heroic and pentameter line alternately, and was not, like the elegy of the moderns, usually appropriated to the lamentation of the deceased, but employed chiefly in compositions relative to love or friendship, and might, indeed, be used upon almost any subject; though, from the limp in the pentameter line, it is not suitable to sublime subjects, which require a fulness of expression, and an expansion of sound. To this species of poetry Tibullus restricted his application, by which he cultivated that simplicity and tenderness, and agreeable ease of sentiment, which constitute the characteristic perfections of the elegiac muse.

In the description of rural scenes, the peaceful occupations of the field, the charms of domestic happiness, and the joys of reciprocal love, scarcely any poet surpasses Tibullus. His luxuriant imagination collects the most beautiful flowers of nature, and he displays them with all the delicate attraction of soft and harmonious numbers. With a dexterity peculiar to himself, in whatever subject he engages, he leads his readers imperceptibly through devious paths of pleasure, of which, at the outset of the poem, they could form no conception. He seems to have often written without any previous meditation or design. Several of his elegies may be said to have neither middle nor end: yet the transitions are so natural, and the gradations so easy, that though we wander through Elysian scenes of fancy, the most heterogeneous in their nature, we are sensible of no defect in the concatenation which has joined them together. It is, however, to be regretted that, in some instances, Tibullus betrays that licentiousness of manners which (186) formed too general a characteristic even of this refined age. His elegies addressed to Messala contain a beautiful amplification of sentiments founded in friendship and esteem, in which it is difficult to say, whether the virtues of the patron or the genius of the poet be more conspicuous.

Valerius Messala Corvinus, whom he celebrates, was descended of a very ancient family. In the civil wars which followed the death of Julius Caesar he joined the republican party, and made himself master of the camp of Octavius at Philippi; but he was afterwards reconciled to his opponent, and lived to an advanced age in favour and esteem with Augustus. He was distinguished not only by his military talents, but by his eloquence, integrity, and patriotism.

From the following passage in the writings of Tibullus, commentators have conjectured that he was deprived of his lands by the same proscription in which those of Virgil had been involved:

*Cui fuerant flavi ditantes ordine sulci*
*Horrea, faecundas ad deficientia messes,*
*Cuique pecus denso pascebant agmine colles,*
*Et domino satis, et nimium furique lupoque:*
*Nunc desiderium superest: nam cura novatur,*
*Cum memor anteactos semper dolor admovet annos.*
Lib. iv. El. 1.

But this seems not very probable, when we consider that Horace, several years after that period, represents him as opulent.

*Dii tibi divitias dederant, artemque fruendi.*
Epist. Lib. i. 4.
To thee the gods a fair estate
In bounty gave, with heart to know
How to enjoy what they bestow. — Francis.

We know not the age of Tibullus at the time of his death; but in an elegy written by Ovid upon that occasion, he is spoken of as a young man. Were it true, as is said by biographers, that he was born the same day with Ovid, we must indeed assign the event to an early period: for Ovid cannot have written the elegy after the forty-third year of his own life, and how long before is uncertain. In the tenth elegy of the fourth book, De Tristibus, he observes, that the fates had allowed little time for the cultivation of his friendship with Tibullus.

*Virgilium vidi tantum: nec avara Tibullo*
*Tempus amicitiae fata dedere meae.*
*Successor fuit hic tibi, Galle; Propertius illi:*
*Quartus ab his serie temporis ipse fui.*
*Utque ego majores, sic me coluere minores.*
(187) Virgil I only saw, and envious fate
Did soon my friend Tibullus hence translate.
He followed Gallus, and Propertius him,
And I myself was fourth in course of time. — Catlin.

As both Ovid and Tibullus lived at Rome, were both of the equestrian order, and of congenial dispositions, it is natural to suppose that their acquaintance commenced at an early period; and if, after all, it was of short duration, there would be no improbability in concluding, that Tibullus died at the age of some years under thirty. It is evident, however, that biographers have committed a mistake with regard to the birth of this poet; for in the passage above cited of the Tristia, Ovid mentions Tibullus as a writer, who, though his contemporary, was much older than himself. From this passage we should be justified in placing the death of Tibullus between the fortieth and fiftieth year of his age, and rather nearer to the latter period; for, otherwise, Horace would scarcely have mentioned him in the manner he does in one of his epistles.

> Albi, nostrorum sermonum candide judex,
> Quid nunc te dicam facere in regione Pedana?
> Scribere quod Cassi Parmensis opuscula vincat;
> An tacitum silvas inter reptare salubres,
> Curantem quicquid dignam sapiente bonoque est? – Epist. i. 4.

> Albius, in whom my satires find
> A critic, candid, just, and kind,
> Do you, while at your country seat,
> Some rhyming labours meditate,
> That shall in volumed bulk arise,
> And e'en from Cassius bear the prize;
> Or saunter through the silent wood,
> Musing on what befits the good. – Francis.

This supposition is in no degree inconsistent with the authority of Ovid, where he mentions him as a young man; for the Romans extended the period of youth to the fiftieth year. — —

PROPERTIUS was born at Mevania, a town of Umbria, seated at the confluence of the Tina and Clitumnus. This place was famous for its herds of white cattle, brought up there for sacrifice, and supposed to be impregnated with that colour by the waters of the river last mentioned.

> Hinc albi, Clitumne, greges, et maxima taurus
> Victima, saepe tuo perfusi fluorine sacro,
> Romanos ad templa Deum duxere triumphos. – Georg. ii.

> And where thy sacred streams, Clitumnus! flow,
> White herds, and stateliest bulls that oft have led

*Triumphant Rome, and on her altars bled.* — Sotheby.

(188) His father is said by some to have been a Roman knight, and they add, that he was one of those who, when L. Antony was starved out of Perasia, were, by the order of Octavius, led to the altar of Julius Caesar, and there slain. Nothing more is known with certainty, than that Propertius lost his father at an early age, and being deprived of a great part of his patrimony, betook himself to Rome, where his genius soon recommended him to public notice, and he obtained the patronage of Mecaenas. From his frequent introduction of historical and mythological subjects into his poems, he received the appellation of "the learned."

Of all the Latin elegiac poets, Propertius has the justest claim to purity of thought and expression. He often draws his imagery from reading, more than from the imagination, and abounds less in description than sentiment. For warmth of passion he is not conspicuous, and his tenderness is seldom marked with a great degree of sensibility; but, without rapture, he is animated, and, like Horace, in the midst of gaiety, he is moral. The stores with which learning supplies him diversify as well as illustrate his subject, while delicacy every where discovers a taste refined by the habit of reflection. His versification, in general, is elegant, but not uniformly harmonious.

Tibullus and Propertius have each written four books of Elegies; and it has been disputed which of them is superior in this department of poetry. Quintilian has given his suffrage in favour of Tibullus, who, so far as poetical merit alone is the object of consideration, seems entitled to the preference. — —

GALLUS was a Roman knight, distinguished not only for poetical, but military talents. Of his poetry we have only six elegies, written, in the person of an old man, on the subject of old age, but which, there is reason to think, were composed at an earlier part of the author's life. Except the fifth elegy, which is tainted with immodesty, the others, particularly the first, are highly beautiful, and may be placed in competition with any other productions of the elegiac kind. Gallus was, for some time, in great favour with Augustus, who appointed him governor of Egypt. It is said, however, that he not only oppressed the province by extortion, but entered into a conspiracy against his benefactor, for which he was banished. Unable to sustain such a reverse of fortune, he fell into despair, and laid violent hands on himself. This is the Gallus in honour of whom Virgil composed his tenth eclogue.

Such are the celebrated productions of the Augustan age, which have been happily preserved, for the delight and admiration of mankind, and will survive to the latest posterity. Many (189) more once existed, of various merit, and of different authors, which have left few or no memorials behind them, but have perished promiscuously amidst the indiscriminate ravages of time, of accidents, and of barbarians. Amongst the principal authors whose works are lost, are Varius and Valgius; the former of whom, besides a panegyric upon Augustus, composed some tragedies. According to Quintilian, his Thyestes was equal to any composition of the Greek tragic poets.

The great number of eminent writers, poets in particular, who adorned this age, has excited general admiration, and the phenomenon is usually ascribed to a fortuitous occurrence, which baffles all inquiry: but we shall endeavour to develop the various causes which seem to have produced this effect; and should the explanation appear satisfactory, it may favour an opinion, that under similar circumstances, if ever they should again be combined, a period of equal glory might arise in other ages and nations.

The Romans, whether from the influence of climate, or their mode of living, which in general was temperate, were endowed with a lively imagination, and, as we before observed, a spirit of enterprise. Upon the final termination of the Punic war, and the conquest of Greece, their ardour, which had hitherto been exercised in military achievements, was diverted into the channel of literature; and the civil commotions which followed, having now ceased, a fresh impulse was given to activity in the ambitious pursuit of the laurel, which was now only to be obtained by glorious exertions of intellect. The beautiful productions of Greece, operating strongly upon their minds, excited them to imitation; imitation, when roused amongst a number, produced emulation; and emulation cherished an extraordinary thirst of fame, which, in every exertion of the human mind, is the parent of excellence. This liberal contention was not a little promoted by the fashion introduced at Rome, for poets to recite their compositions in public; a practice which seems to have been carried even to a ridiculous excess.—Such was now the rage for poetical composition in the Roman capital, that Horace describes it in the following terms:

*Mutavit mentem populus levis, et calet uno*
*Scribendi studio: pueri patresque severi*
*Fronde comas vincti coenant, et carmina dictant.* – Epist. ii. 1.
\* \* \* \* \* \*

*Now the light people bend to other aims;*
*A lust of scribbling every breast inflames;*
*Our youth, our senators, with bays are crowned,*
*And rhymes eternal as our feasts go round.*
(190) *Scribimus indocti doctique poemata passim.* – Hor. Epeat. ii. 1.
*But every desperate blockhead dares to write,*
*Verse is the trade of every living wight.* – Francis.

The thirst of fame above mentioned, was a powerful incentive, and is avowed both by Virgil and Horace. The former, in the third book of his Georgics, announces a resolution of rendering himself celebrated, if possible.

– – – – *tentanda via est qua me quoque possim*
*Tollere humo, victorque virum volitare per ora.*
*I, too, will strive o'er earth my flight to raise,*
*And wing'd by victory, catch the gale of praise.* – Sotheby.

And Horace, in the conclusion of his first Ode, expresses himself in terms which indicate a similar purpose.

*Quad si me lyricis vatibis inseres,*
*Sublimi feriam sidera vertice.*
*But if you rank me with the choir,*
*Who tuned with art the Grecian lyre;*
*Swift to the noblest heights of fame,*
*Shall rise thy poet's deathless name.* – Francis.

Even Sallust, a historian, in his introduction to Catiline's Conspiracy, scruples not to insinuate the same kind of ambition. Quo mihi rectius videtur ingenii quam virium opibus gloriam quaerere; et quoniam vita ipsa, qua fruimur, brevis est, memoriam nostri quam maxume longam efficere. 283

Another circumstance of great importance, towards the production of such poetry as might live through every age, was the extreme attention which the great poets of this period displayed, both in the composition, and the polishing of their works. Virgil, when employed upon the Georgics, usually wrote in the morning, and applied much of the subsequent part of the day to correction and improvement. He compared himself to a bear, that licks her cub into form. If this was his regular practice in the Georgics, we may justly suppose that it was the same in the Aeneid. Yet, after all this labour, he intended to devote three years entirely to its farther amendment. Horace has gone so far in recommending careful correction, that he figuratively mentions nine years as an adequate period for that purpose. But whatever may be the time, there is no precept which he urges either oftener or more forcibly, than a due attention to this important subject.

(191) *Saepe stylum vertas, iterum quae digna legi sint*
*Scripturus. — Sat. i. x.*
Would you a reader's just esteem engage?
Correct with frequent care the blotted page. — *Francis.*
— — — — *Vos, O*
*Pompilius sanguis, carmen reprehendite, quod non*
*Multa dies et multa litura coercuit, atque*
*Perfectum decies non castigavit ad uuguem.*
*De. Art. Poet.*
Sons of Pompilius, with contempt receive,
Nor let the hardy poem hope to live,
Where time and full correction don't refine
The finished work, and polish every line. — *Francis.*

To the several causes above enumerated, as concurring to form the great superiority of the Augustan age, as respects the productions of literature, one more is to be subjoined, of a nature the most essential: the liberal and unparalleled encouragement given to distinguished talents by the emperor and his minister. This was a principle of the most powerful energy: it fanned the flame of genius, invigorated every exertion; and the poets who basked in the rays of imperial favour, and the animating patronage of Mecaenas, experienced a poetic enthusiasm which approached to real inspiration.

Having now finished the proposed explanation, relative to the celebrity of the Augustan age, we shall conclude with recapitulating in a few words the causes of this extraordinary occurrence.

The models, then, which the Romans derived from Grecian poetry, were the finest productions of human genius; their incentives to emulation were the strongest that could actuate the heart. With ardour, therefore, and industry in composing, and with unwearied patience in polishing their compositions, they attained to that glorious distinction in literature, which no succeeding age has ever rivalled.

# TIBERIUS NERO CAESAR.

(192)

I. The patrician family of the Claudii (for there was a plebeian family of the same name, no way inferior to the other either in power or dignity) came originally from Regilli, a town of the Sabines. They removed thence to Rome soon after the building of the city, with a great body of their dependants, under Titus Tatius, who reigned jointly with Romulus in the kingdom; or, perhaps, what is related upon better authority, under Atta Claudius, the head of the family, who was admitted by the senate into the patrician order six years after the expulsion of the Tarquins. They likewise received from the state, lands beyond the Anio for their followers, and a burying-place for themselves near the capitol 284 . After this period, in process of time, the family had the honour of twenty-eight consulships, five dictatorships, seven censorships, seven triumphs, and two ovations. Their descendants were distinguished by various praenomina and cognomina 285 , but rejected by common consent the praenomen of (193) Lucius, when, of the two races who bore it, one individual had been convicted of robbery, and another of murder. Amongst other cognomina, they assumed that of Nero, which in the Sabine language signifies strong and valiant.

II. It appears from record, that many of the Claudii have performed signal services to the state, as well as committed acts of delinquency. To mention the most remarkable only, Appius Caecus dissuaded the senate from agreeing to an alliance with Pyrrhus, as prejudicial to the republic 286 . Claudius Candex first passed the straits of Sicily with a fleet, and drove the Carthaginians out of the island 287 . Claudius Nero cut off Hasdrubal with a vast army upon his arrival in Italy from Spain, before he could form a junction with his brother Hannibal 288 . On the other hand, Claudius Appius Regillanus, one of the Decemvirs, made a violent attempt to have a free virgin, of whom he was enamoured, adjudged a slave; which caused the people to secede a second time from the senate 289 . Claudius Drusus erected a statue of himself wearing a crown at Appii Forum 290 , and endeavoured, by means of his dependants, to make himself master of Italy. Claudius Pulcher, when, off the coast of Sicily 291 , the pullets used for taking augury would not eat, in contempt of the omen threw them overboard, as if they should drink at least, if they would not eat; and then engaging the enemy, was routed. After his defeat, when he (194) was ordered by the senate to name a dictator, making a sort of jest of the public disaster, he named Glycias, his apparitor.

The women of this family, likewise, exhibited characters equally opposed to each other. For both the Claudias belonged to it; she, who, when the ship freighted with things sacred to the Idaean Mother of the Gods 292 , stuck fast in the shallows of the Tiber, got it off, by praying to the Goddess with a loud voice, "Follow me, if I am chaste;" and she also, who, contrary to the usual practice in the case of women, was brought to trial by the people for treason; because, when her litter was stopped by a great crowd in the streets, she openly exclaimed, "I wish my brother Pulcher was alive now, to lose another fleet, that Rome might be less thronged." Besides, it is well known, that all the Claudii, except Publius Claudius, who, to effect the banishment of Cicero, procured himself to be adopted by a plebeian 293 , and one younger than himself, were always of the patrician party, as well as great sticklers for the honour and power of that order; and so violent and obstinate in their opposition to the plebeians, that not one of them, even in the case of a trial for life by the people, would ever condescend to put on mourning, according to custom, or make any supplication to them for favour; and some of them in their contests, have even proceeded to lay hands on the tribunes of the people. A Vestal Virgin likewise of the family, when her brother was resolved to have the honour of a triumph contrary to the will of the people, mounted the chariot with him, and attended him into the Capitol, that it might not be lawful for any of the tribunes to interfere and forbid it. 294

III. From this family Tiberius Caesar is descended; indeed both by the father and mother's side; by the former from Tiberius Nero, and by the latter from Appius Pulcher, who were both sons of Appius Caecus. He likewise belonged to the family of the Livii, by the adoption of his mother's grandfather into it; which family, although plebeian, made a (195) distinguished figure, having had the honour of eight consulships, two censorships, three triumphs, one dictatorship, and the office of master of the horse; and was famous for eminent men, particularly, Salinator and the Drusi. Salinator, in his censorship 295, branded all the tribes, for their inconstancy in having made him consul a second time, as well as censor, although they had condemned him to a heavy fine after his first consulship. Drusus procured for himself and his posterity a new surname, by killing in single combat Drausus, the enemy's chief. He is likewise said to have recovered, when propraetor in the province of Gaul, the gold which was formerly given to the Senones, at the siege of the Capitol, and had not, as is reported, been forced from them by Camillus. His great-great-grandson, who, for his extraordinary services against the Gracchi, was styled the "Patron of the Senate," left a son, who, while plotting in a sedition of the same description, was treacherously murdered by the opposite party. 296

IV. But the father of Tiberius Caesar, being quaestor to Caius Caesar, and commander of his fleet in the war of Alexandria, contributed greatly to its success. He was therefore made one of the high-priests in the room of Publius Scipio 297; and was sent to settle some colonies in Gaul, and amongst the rest, those of Narbonne and Arles 298. After the assassination of Caesar, however, when the rest of the senators, for fear of public disturbances; were for having the affair buried in oblivion, he proposed a resolution for rewarding those who had killed the tyrant. Having filled the office of praetor 299, and at the end of the year a disturbance breaking out amongst the triumviri, he kept the badges of his office beyond the legal time; and following Lucius Antonius the consul, brother of the triumvir, to Perusia 300, though the rest submitted, yet he himself continued firm to the party, and escaped first to Praeneste, and then to Naples; whence, having in vain invited the slaves to liberty, he fled over to Sicily. But resenting (196) his not being immediately admitted into the presence of Sextus Pompey, and being also prohibited the use of the fasces, he went over into Achaia to Mark Antony; with whom, upon a reconciliation soon after brought about amongst the several contending parties, he returned to Rome; and, at the request of Augustus, gave up to him his wife Livia Drusilla, although she was then big with child, and had before borne him a son. He died not long after; leaving behind him two sons, Tiberius and Drusus Nero.

V. Some have imagined that Tiberius was born at Fundi, but there is only this trifling foundation for the conjecture, that his mother's grandmother was of Fundi, and that the image of Good Fortune was, by a decree of the senate, erected in a public place in that town. But according to the greatest number of writers, and those too of the best authority, he was born at Rome, in the Palatine quarter, upon the sixteenth of the calends of December [16th Nov.], when Marcus Aemilius Lepidus was second time consul, with Lucius Munatius Plancus 301, after the battle of Philippi; for so it is registered in the calendar, and the public acts. According to some, however, he was born the preceding year, in the consulship of Hirtius and Pansa; and others say, in the year following, during the consulship of Servilius Isauricus and Antony.

VI. His infancy and childhood were spent in the midst of danger and trouble; for he accompanied his parents everywhere in their flight, and twice at Naples nearly betrayed them by his crying, when they were privately hastening to a ship, as the enemy rushed into the town; once, when he was snatched from his nurse's breast, and again, from his mother's bosom, by some of the company, who on the sudden emergency wished to relieve the women of their burden. Being carried through Sicily and Achaia, and entrusted for some time to the care of the Lacedaemonians, who were under the protection of the Claudian family, upon his departure thence when travelling by night, he ran the hazard of his life, by a fire which, suddenly bursting out of a wood on all sides, surrounded the whole party so closely, that part of Livia's dress and hair was burnt. The presents which were made him (197) by Pompeia, sister to Sextus Pompey, in Sicily, namely, a cloak, with a clasp, and bullae of gold, are still in existence, and shewn at Baiae to this day. After his return to the city, being adopted by Marcus Gallius, a senator, in his will, he took possession of the estate; but soon afterwards declined the use of his name, because Gallius had been of the party opposed to Augustus. When only nine years of age, he pronounced a funeral oration in praise of his father upon the rostra; and afterwards, when he had nearly attained the age of manhood, he attended the chariot of Augustus, in his triumph for the victory at Actium, riding on the left-hand horse, whilst Marcellus,

Octavia's son, rode that on the right. He likewise presided at the games celebrated on account of that victory; and in the Trojan games intermixed with the Circensian, he commanded a troop of the biggest boys.

VII. After assuming the manly habit, he spent his youth, and the rest of his life until he succeeded to the government, in the following manner: he gave the people an entertainment of gladiators, in memory of his father, and another for his grandfather Drusus, at different times and in different places: the first in the forum, the second in the amphitheatre; some gladiators who had been honourably discharged, being induced to engage again, by a reward of a hundred thousand sesterces. He likewise exhibited public sports, at which he was not present himself. All these he performed with great magnificence, at the expense of his mother and father-in-law. He married Agrippina, the daughter of Marcus Agrippa, and grand-daughter of Caecilius Atticus, a Roman knight, the same person to whom Cicero has addressed so many epistles. After having by her his son Drusus, he was obliged to part with her 302 , though she retained his affection, and was again pregnant, to make way for marrying Augustus's daughter Julia. But this he did with extreme reluctance; for, besides having the warmest attachment to Agrippina, he was disgusted with the conduct of Julia, who had made indecent advances to him during the lifetime of her former husband; and that she was a woman of loose character, was the general opinion. At divorcing Agrippina he felt the deepest regret; and upon meeting her afterwards, (198) he looked after her with eyes so passionately expressive of affection, that care was taken she should never again come in his sight. At first, however, he lived quietly and happily with Julia; but a rupture soon ensued, which became so violent, that after the loss of their son, the pledge of their union, who was born at Aquileia and died in infancy 303 , he never would sleep with her more. He lost his brother Drusus in Germany, and brought his body to Rome, travelling all the way on foot before it.

VIII. When he first applied himself to civil affairs, he defended the several causes of king Archelaus, the Trallians, and the Thessalians, before Augustus, who sat as judge at the trials. He addressed the senate on behalf of the Laodiceans, the Thyatireans, and Chians, who had suffered greatly by an earthquake, and implored relief from

Rome. He prosecuted Fannius Caepio, who had been engaged in a conspiracy with Varro Muraena against Augustus, and procured sentence of condemnation against him. Amidst all this, he had besides to superintend two departments of the administration, that of supplying the city with corn, which was then very scarce, and that of clearing the houses of correction 304 throughout Italy, the masters of which had fallen under the odious suspicion of seizing and keeping confined, not only travellers, but those whom the fear of being obliged to serve in the army had driven to seek refuge in such places.

IX. He made his first campaign, as a military tribune, in the Cantabrian war 305 . Afterwards he led an army into the East 306 , where he restored the kingdom of Armenia to Tigranes; and seated on a tribunal, put a crown upon his head. He likewise recovered from the Parthians the standards which they had taken from Crassus. He next governed, for nearly a year, the province of Gallia Comata, which was then in great disorder, on account of the incursions of the barbarians, and the feuds of the chiefs. He afterwards commanded in the several wars against the Rhaetians, Vindelicians, Pannonians, and Germans. In the Rhaetian and Vindelician wars, he subdued the nations in the Alps; and in the Pannonian wars the Bruci, and (199) the Dalmatians. In the German war, he transplanted into Gaul forty thousand of the enemy who had submitted, and assigned them lands near the banks of the Rhine. For these actions, he entered the city with an ovation, but riding in a chariot, and is said by some to have been the first that ever was honoured with this distinction. He filled early the principal offices of state; and passed through the quaestorship 307 , praetorship 308 , and consulate 309 almost successively. After some interval, he was chosen consul a second time, and held the tribunitian authority during five years.

X. Surrounded by all this prosperity, in the prime of life and in excellent health, he suddenly formed the resolution of withdrawing to a greater distance from Rome 310 . It is uncertain whether this was the result of disgust for his wife, whom he neither durst accuse nor divorce, and the connection with whom became every day more intolerable; or to prevent that indifference towards him, which his constant residence in the city might produce; or in the hope of supporting and improving by absence his authority in the state, if the public should have occasion for his service. Some are of opinion, that as Augustus's sons were now grown up to years of maturity, he voluntarily relinquished the possession he had long enjoyed of the second place in the government, as Agrippa had done before him; who, when M. Marcellus was advanced to public offices, retired to Mitylene, that he might not seem to stand in the way of his promotion, or in any respect lessen him by his presence. The same reason likewise Tiberius gave afterwards for his retirement; but his pretext at this time was, that he was satiated with honours, and desirous of being relieved from the fatigue of business; requesting therefore that he might have leave to withdraw. And neither the earnest entreaties of his mother, nor the complaint of his father-in-law made even in the senate, that he was deserted by him, could prevail upon him to alter his resolution. Upon their persisting in the design of detaining him, he refused to take any sustenance for four days together. At last, having obtained permission, leaving his wife and son at Rome, he proceeded (200) to Ostia 311, without exchanging a word with those who attended him, and having embraced but very few persons at parting.

XI. From Ostia, journeying along the coast of Campania, he halted awhile on receiving intelligence of Augustus's being taken ill, but this giving rise to a rumour that he stayed with a view to something extraordinary, he sailed with the wind almost full against him, and arrived at Rhodes, having been struck with the pleasantness and healthiness of the island at the time of his landing therein his return from Armenia. Here contenting himself with a small house, and a villa not much larger, near the town, he led entirely a private life, taking his walks sometimes about the Gymnasia 312, without any lictor or other attendant, and returning the civilities of the Greeks with almost as much complaisance as if he had been upon a level with them. One morning, in settling the course of his daily excursion, he happened to say, that he should visit all the sick people in the town. This being not rightly understood by those about him, the sick were brought into a public portico, and ranged in order, according to their several distempers. Being extremely embarrassed by this unexpected occurrence, he was for some time irresolute how he should act; but at last he determined to go round them all, and make an apology for the mistake even to the meanest amongst them, and such as were entirely unknown to him. One instance only is mentioned, in which he appeared to exercise his tribunitian authority. Being a constant attendant upon the schools and lecture-rooms of the professors of the liberal arts, on occasion of a quarrel amongst the wrangling (201) sophists, in which he interposed to reconcile them, some person took the liberty to abuse him as an intruder, and partial in the affair. Upon this, withdrawing privately home, he suddenly returned attended by his officers, and summoning his accuser before his tribunal, by a public crier, ordered him to be taken to prison. Afterwards he received tidings that his wife Julia had been condemned for her lewdness and adultery, and that a bill of divorce had been sent to her in his name, by the authority of Augustus. Though he secretly rejoiced at this intelligence, he thought it incumbent upon him, in point of decency, to interpose in her behalf by frequent letters to Augustus, and to allow her to retain the presents which he had made her, notwithstanding the little regard she merited from him. When the period of his tribunitian authority expired 313, declaring at last that he had no other object in his retirement than to avoid all suspicion of rivalship with Caius and Lucius, he petitioned that, since he was now secure in that respect, as they were come to the age of manhood, and would easily maintain themselves in possession of the second place in the state, he might be permitted to visit his friends, whom he was very desirous of seeing. But his request was denied; and he was advised to lay aside all concern for his friends, whom he had been so eager to greet.

XII. He therefore continued at Rhodes much against his will, obtaining, with difficulty, through his mother, the title of Augustus's lieutenant, to cover his disgrace. He thenceforth lived, however, not only as a private person, but as one suspected and under apprehension, retiring into the interior of the country, and avoiding the visits of those who sailed that way, which were very frequent; for no one passed to take command of an army, or the government of a province, without touching at Rhodes. But there were fresh reasons for increased anxiety. For crossing over to Samos, on a visit to his step-son Caius, who had been appointed governor of the East, he found him prepossessed against him, by the insinuations of Marcus Lollius, his companion and director. He likewise fell under suspicion of sending by some centurions who had been promoted by himself, upon their return to the camp after a furlough, mysterious messages to several persons there, intended, apparently, to (202) tamper with them for a revolt. This jealousy respecting his designs being intimated to him by Augustus, he begged repeatedly that some person of any of the three Orders might be placed as a spy upon him in every thing he either said or did.

XIII. He laid aside likewise his usual exercises of riding and arms; and quitting the Roman habit, made use of the Pallium and Crepida 314 . In this condition he continued almost two years, becoming daily an object of increasing contempt and odium; insomuch that the people of Nismes pulled down all the images and statues of him in their town; and upon mention being made of him at table one of the company said to Caius, "I will sail over to Rhodes immediately, if you desire me, and bring you the head of the exile;" for that was the appellation now given him. Thus alarmed not only by apprehensions, but real danger, he renewed his solicitations for leave to return; and, seconded by the most urgent supplications of his mother, he at last obtained his request; to which an accident somewhat contributed. Augustus had resolved to determine nothing in the affair, but with the consent of his eldest son. The latter was at that time out of humour with Marcus Lollius, and therefore easily disposed to be favourable to his father-in-law. Caius thus acquiescing, he was recalled, but upon condition that he should take no concern whatever in the administration of affairs.

XIV. He returned to Rome after an absence of nearly eight years 315 , with great and confident hopes of his future elevation, which he had entertained from his youth, in consequence of various prodigies and predictions. For Livia, when pregnant with him, being anxious to discover, by different modes of divination, whether her offspring would be a son, amongst others, took an egg from a hen that was sitting, and kept it warm with her own hands, and those of her maids, by turns, until a fine cock-chicken, with a large comb, was hatched. Scribonius, the astrologer, predicted great things of him when he was a mere child. "He will come in time," said the prophet, "to be even a king, but without the usual badge of royal dignity;" the rule of the Caesars being as yet unknown. When he was (203) making his first expedition, and leading his army through Macedonia into Syria, the altars which had been formerly consecrated at Philippi by the victorious legions, blazed suddenly with spontaneous fires. Soon after, as he was marching to Illyricum, he stopped to consult the oracle of Geryon, near Padua; and having drawn a lot by which he was desired to throw golden tali into the fountain of Aponus 316 , for an answer to his inquiries, he did so, and the highest numbers came up. And those very tali are still to be seen at the bottom of the fountain. A few days before his leaving Rhodes, an eagle, a bird never before seen in that island, perched on the top of his house. And the day before he received intelligence of the permission granted him to return, as he was changing his dress, his tunic appeared to be all on fire. He then likewise had a remarkable proof of the skill of Thrasyllus, the astrologer, whom, for his proficiency in philosophical researches, he had taken into his family. For, upon sight of the ship which brought the intelligence, he said, good news was coming whereas every thing going wrong before, and quite contrary to his predictions, Tiberius had intended that very moment, when they were walking together, to throw him into the sea, as an impostor, and one to whom he had too hastily entrusted his secrets.

XV. Upon his return to Rome, having introduced his son Drusus into the forum, he immediately removed from Pompey's house, in the Carinae, to the gardens of Mecaenas, on the Esquiline 317 , and resigned himself entirely to his ease, performing only the common offices of civility in private life, without any preferment in the government. But Caius and Lucius being both carried off in the space of three years, he was adopted by Augustus, along with their brother Agrippa; being obliged in the first place to adopt Germanicus, his brother's son. After his adoption, he never more acted as master of a (204) family, nor exercised, in the smallest degree, the rights which he had lost by it. For he neither disposed of anything in the way of gift, nor manumitted a slave; nor so much as received any estate left him by will, nor any legacy, without reckoning it as a part of his peculium or property held under his father. From that day forward, nothing was omitted that might contribute to the advancement of his grandeur, and much more, when, upon Agrippa being discarded and banished, it was evident that the hope of succession rested upon him alone.

XVI. The tribunitian authority was again conferred upon him for five years 318 , and a commission given him to settle the affairs of Germany. The ambassadors of the Parthians, after having had an audience of Augustus, were ordered to apply to him likewise in his province. But on receiving intelligence of an insurrection in Illyricum 319 , he went over to superintend the management of that new war, which proved the most serious of all the foreign wars since the Carthaginian. This he conducted during three years, with fifteen legions and an equal number of auxiliary forces, under great difficulties, and an extreme scarcity of corn. And though he was several times recalled, he nevertheless persisted; fearing lest an enemy so powerful, and so near, should fall upon the army in their retreat. This resolution was attended with good success; for he at last reduced to complete subjection all Illyricum, lying between Italy and the kingdom of Noricum, Thrace, Macedonia, the river Danube, and the Adriatic gulf.

XVII. The glory he acquired by these successes received an increase from the conjuncture in which they happened. For almost about that very time 320 Quintilius Varus was cut off with three legions in Germany; and it was generally believed that the victorious Germans would have joined the Pannonians, had not the war of Illyricum been previously concluded. A triumph, therefore, besides many other great honours, was decreed him. Some proposed that the surname of "Pannonicus," others that of "Invincible," and others, of "O Pius," should be conferred on him; but Augustus interposed, engaging for him that he would be satisfied with that to which he would succeed at his death. He postponed his triumph, because (205) the state was at that time under great affliction for the disaster of Varus and his army. Nevertheless, he entered the city in a triumphal robe, crowned with laurel, and mounting a tribunal in the Septa, sat with Augustus between the two consuls, whilst the senate gave their attendance standing; whence, after he had saluted the people, he was attended by them in procession to the several temples.

XVIII. Next year he went again to Germany, where finding that the defeat of Varus was occasioned by the rashness and negligence of the commander, he thought proper to be guided in everything by the advice of a council of war; whereas, at other times, he used to follow the dictates of his own judgment, and considered himself alone as sufficiently qualified for the direction of affairs. He likewise used more cautions than usual. Having to pass the Rhine, he restricted the whole convoy within certain limits, and stationing himself on the bank of the river, would not suffer the waggons to cross the river, until he had searched them at the water-side, to see that they carried nothing but what was allowed or necessary. Beyond the Rhine, such was his way of living, that he took his meals sitting on the bare ground 321 , and often passed the night without a tent; and his regular orders for the day, as well as those upon sudden emergencies, he gave in writing, with this injunction, that in case of any doubt as to the meaning of them, they should apply to him for satisfaction, even at any hour of the night.

XIX. He maintained the strictest discipline amongst the troops; reviving many old customs relative to punishing and degrading offenders; setting a mark of disgrace even upon the commander of a legion, for sending a few soldiers with one of his freedmen across the river for the purpose of hunting. Though it was his desire to leave as little as possible in the power of fortune or accident, yet he always engaged the enemy with more confidence when, in his night-watches, the lamp failed and went out of itself; trusting, as he said, in an omen which had never failed him and his ancestors (206) in all their commands. But, in the midst of victory, he was very near being assassinated by some Bructerian, who mixing with those about him, and being discovered by his trepidation, was put to the torture, and confessed his intended crime.

XX. After two years, he returned from Germany to the city, and celebrated the triumph which he had deferred, attended by his lieutenants, for whom he had procured the honour of triumphal ornaments 322. Before he turned to ascend the Capitol, he alighted from his chariot, and knelt before his father, who sat by, to superintend the solemnity. Bato, the Pannonian chief, he sent to Ravenna, loaded with rich presents, in gratitude for his having suffered him and his army to retire from a position in which he had so enclosed them, that they were entirely at his mercy. He afterwards gave the people a dinner at a thousand tables, besides thirty sesterces to each man. He likewise dedicated the temple of Concord 323, and that of Castor and Pollux, which had been erected out of the spoils of the war, in his own and his brother's name.

XXI. A law having been not long after carried by the consuls 324 for his being appointed a colleague with Augustus in the administration of the provinces, and in taking the census, when that was finished he went into Illyricum 325. But being hastily recalled during his journey, he found Augustus alive indeed, but past all hopes of recovery, and was with him in private a whole day. I know, it is generally believed, that upon Tiberius's quitting the room, after their private conference, those who were in waiting overheard Augustus say, "Ah! unhappy Roman people, to be ground by the jaws of such a slow devourer!" Nor am I ignorant of its being reported by some, that Augustus so openly and undisguisedly condemned the sourness of his temper, that sometimes, upon his coming in, he would break off any jocular conversation in which he was engaged; and that he was only prevailed upon by the (207) importunity of his wife to adopt him; or actuated by the ambitious view of recommending his own memory from a comparison with such a successor. Yet I must hold to this opinion, that a prince so extremely circumspect and prudent as he was, did nothing rashly, especially in an affair of so great importance; but that, upon weighing the vices and virtues of Tiberius with each other, he judged the latter to preponderate; and this the rather since he swore publicly, in an assembly of the people, that "he adopted him for the public good." Besides, in several of his letters, he extols him as a consummate general, and the only security of the Roman people. Of such declarations I subjoin the following instances: "Farewell, my dear Tiberius, and may success attend you, whilst you are warring for me and the Muses 326 . Farewell, my most dear, and (as I hope to prosper) most gallant man, and accomplished general." Again. "The disposition of your summer quarters? In truth, my dear Tiberius, I do not think, that amidst so many difficulties, and with an army so little disposed for action, any one could have behaved more prudently than you have done. All those likewise who were with you, acknowledge that this verse is applicable to you:"

*Unus homo nobis vigilando restituit rem. 327_*
One man by vigilance restored the state.

"Whenever," he says, "anything happens that requires more than ordinary consideration, or I am out of humour upon any occasion, I still, by Hercules! long for my dear Tiberius; and those lines of Homer frequently occur to my thoughts:"

*Toutou d' espomenoio kai ek pyros aithomenoio*
*Ampho nostaesuimen, epei peri oide noaesai. 328_*
Bold from his prudence, I could ev'n aspire
To dare with him the burning rage of fire.

"When I hear and read that you are much impaired by the (208) continued fatigues you undergo, may the gods confound me if my whole frame does not tremble! So I beg you to spare yourself, lest, if we should hear of your being ill, the news prove fatal both to me and your mother, and the Roman people should be in peril for the safety of the empire. It matters nothing whether I be well or no, if you be not well. I pray heaven preserve you for us, and bless you with health both now and ever, if the gods have any regard for the Roman people."

XXII. He did not make the death of Augustus public, until he had taken off young Agrippa. He was slain by a tribune who commanded his guard, upon reading a written order for that purpose: respecting which order, it was then a doubt, whether Augustus left it in his last moments, to prevent any occasion of public disturbance after his decease, or Livia issued it, in the name of Augustus; and whether with the knowledge of Tiberius or not. When the tribune came to inform him that he had executed his command, he replied, "I commanded you no such thing, and you must answer for it to the senate;" avoiding, as it seems, the odium of the act for that time. And the affair was soon buried in silence.

XXIII. Having summoned the senate to meet by virtue of his tribunitian authority, and begun a mournful speech, he drew a deep sigh, as if unable to support himself under his affliction; and wishing that not his voice only, but his very breath of life, might fail him, gave his speech to his son Drusus to read. Augustus's will was then brought in, and read by a freedman; none of the witnesses to it being admitted, but such as were of the senatorian order, the rest owning their hand-writing without doors. The will began thus: "Since my ill-fortune has deprived me of my two sons, Caius and Lucius, let Tiberius Caesar be heir to two-thirds of my estate." These words countenanced the suspicion of those who were of opinion, that Tiberius was appointed successor more out of necessity than choice, since Augustus could not refrain from prefacing his will in that manner.

XXIV. Though he made no scruple to assume and exercise immediately the imperial authority, by giving orders that he (209) should be attended by the guards, who were the security and badge of the supreme power; yet he affected, by a most impudent piece of acting, to refuse it for a long time; one while sharply reprehending his friends who entreated him to accept it, as little knowing what a monster the government was; another while keeping in suspense the senate, when they implored him and threw themselves at his feet, by ambiguous answers, and a crafty kind of dissimulation; insomuch that some were out of patience, and one cried out, during the confusion, "Either let him accept it, or decline it at once;" and a second told him to his face, "Others are slow to perform what they promise, but you are slow to promise what you actually perform." At last, as if forced to it, and complaining of the miserable and burdensome service imposed upon him, he accepted the government; not, however, without giving hopes of his resigning it some time or other. The exact words he used were these: "Until the time shall come, when ye may think it reasonable to give some rest to my old age."

XXV. The cause of his long demur was fear of the dangers which threatened him on all hands; insomuch that he said, "I have got a wolf by the ears." For a slave of Agrippa's, Clemens by name, had drawn together a considerable force to revenge his master's death; Lucius Scribonius Libo, a senator of the first distinction, was secretly fomenting a rebellion; and the troops both in Illyricum and Germany were mutinous. Both armies insisted upon high demands, particularly that their pay should be made equal to that of the pretorian guards. The army in Germany absolutely refused to acknowledge a prince who was not their own choice; and urged, with all possible importunity, Germanicus 329 , who commanded them, to take the government on himself, though he obstinately refused it. It was Tiberius's apprehension from this quarter, which made him request the senate to assign him some part only in the administration, such as they should judge proper, since no man could be sufficient for the whole, without one or more to assist him. He pretended likewise to be in a bad state of health, that Germanicus might the more patiently wait in hopes of speedily succeeding him, or at least of being (210) admitted to be a colleague in the government. When the mutinies in the armies were suppressed, he got Clemens into his hands by stratagem. That he might not begin his reign by an act of severity, he did not call Libo to an account before the senate until his second year, being content, in the mean time, with taking proper precautions for his own security. For upon Libo's attending a sacrifice amongst the high-priests, instead of the usual knife, he ordered one of lead to be given him; and when he desired a private conference with him, he would not grant his request, but on condition that his son Drusus should be present; and as they walked together, he held him fast by the right hand, under the pretence of leaning upon him, until the conversation was over.

XXVI. When he was delivered from his apprehensions, his behaviour at first was unassuming, and he did not carry himself much above the level of a private person; and of the many and great honours offered him, he accepted but few, and such as were very moderate. His birth-day, which happened to fall at the time of the Plebeian Circensian games, he with difficulty suffered to be honoured with the addition of only a single chariot, drawn by two horses. He forbad temples, flamens, or priests to be appointed for him, as likewise the erection of any statues or effigies for him, without his permission; and this he granted only on condition that they should not be placed amongst the images of the gods, but only amongst the ornaments of houses. He also interposed to prevent the senate from swearing to maintain his acts; and the month of September from being called Tiberius, and October being named after Livia. The praenomen likewise of EMPEROR, with the cognomen of FATHER OF HIS COUNTRY, and a civic crown in the vestibule of his house, he would not accept. He never used the name of AUGUSTUS, although he inherited it, in any of his letters, excepting those addressed to kings and princes. Nor had he more than three consulships; one for a few days, another for three months, and a third, during his absence from the city, until the ides [fifteenth] of May.

XXVII. He had such an aversion to flattery, that he would never suffer any senator to approach his litter, as he passed the streets in it, either to pay him a civility, or upon business. (211) And when a man of consular rank, in begging his pardon for some offence he had given him, attempted to fall at his feet, he started from him in such haste, that he stumbled and fell. If any compliment was paid him, either in conversation or a set speech, he would not scruple to interrupt and reprimand the party, and alter what he had said. Being once called "lord," 330 by some person, he desired that he might no more be affronted in that manner. When another, to excite veneration, called his occupations "sacred," and a third had expressed himself thus: "By your authority I have waited upon the senate," he obliged them to change their phrases; in one of them adopting persuasion, instead of "authority," and in the other, laborious, instead of "sacred."

XXVIII. He remained unmoved at all the aspersions, scandalous reports, and lampoons, which were spread against him or his relations; declaring, "In a free state, both the tongue and the mind ought to be free." Upon the senate's desiring that some notice might be taken of those offences, and the persons charged with them, he replied, "We have not so much time upon our hands, that we ought to involve ourselves in more business. If you once make an opening 331 for such proceedings, you will soon have nothing else to do. All private quarrels will be brought before you under that pretence." There is also on record another sentence used by him in the senate, which is far from assuming: "If he speaks otherwise of me, I shall take care to behave in such a manner, as to be able to give a good account both of my words and actions; and if he persists, I shall hate him in my turn."

XXIX. These things were so much the more remarkable in him, because, in the respect he paid to individuals, or the whole body of the senate, he went beyond all bounds. Upon his differing with Quintus Haterius in the senate-house, "Pardon me, sir," he said, "I beseech you, if I shall, as a senator, speak my mind very freely in opposition to you." Afterwards, addressing the senate in general, he said: "Conscript Fathers, I have often said it both now and at other times, that a good (212) and useful prince, whom you have invested with so great and absolute power, ought to be a slave to the senate, to the whole body of the people, and often to individuals likewise: nor am I sorry that I have said it. I have always found you good, kind, and indulgent masters, and still find you so."

XXX. He likewise introduced a certain show of liberty, by preserving to the senate and magistrates their former majesty and power. All affairs, whether of great or small importance, public or private, were laid before the senate. Taxes and monopolies, the erecting or repairing edifices, levying and disbanding soldiers, the disposal of the legions and auxiliary forces in the provinces, the appointment of generals for the management of extraordinary wars, and the answers to letters from foreign princes, were all submitted to the senate. He compelled the commander of a troop of horse, who was accused of robbery attended with violence, to plead his cause before the senate. He never entered the senate-house but unattended; and being once brought thither in a litter, because he was indisposed, he dismissed his attendants at the door.

XXXI. When some decrees were made contrary to his opinion, he did not even make any complaint. And though he thought that no magistrates after their nomination should be allowed to absent themselves from the city, but reside in it constantly, to receive their honours in person, a praetor-elect obtained liberty to depart under the honorary title of a legate at large. Again, when he proposed to the senate, that the Trebians might have leave granted them to divert some money which had been left them by will for the purpose of building a new theatre, to that of making a road, he could not prevail to have the will of the testator set aside. And when, upon a division of the house, he went over to the minority, nobody followed him. All other things of a public nature were likewise transacted by the magistrates, and in the usual forms; the authority of the consuls remaining so great, that some ambassadors from Africa applied to them, and complained, that they could not have their business dispatched by Caesar, to whom they had been sent. And no wonder; since it was observed that he used to rise up as the consuls approached, and give them the way.

(213) XXXII. He reprimanded some persons of consular rank in command of armies, for not writing to the senate an account of their proceedings, and for consulting him about the distribution of military rewards; as if they themselves had not a right to bestow them as they judged proper. He commended a praetor, who, on entering office, revived an old custom of celebrating the memory of his ancestors, in a speech to the people. He attended the corpses of some persons of distinction to the funeral pile. He displayed the same moderation with regard to persons and things of inferior consideration. The magistrates of Rhodes, having dispatched to him a letter on public business, which was not subscribed, he sent for them, and without giving them so much as one harsh word, desired them to subscribe it, and so dismissed them. Diogenes, the grammarian, who used to hold public disquisitions, at Rhodes every sabbath-day, once refused him admittance upon his coming to hear him out of course, and sent him a message by a servant, postponing his admission until the next seventh day. Diogenes afterwards coming to Rome, and waiting at his door to be allowed to pay his respects to him, he sent him word to come again at the end of seven years. To some governors, who

advised him to load the provinces with taxes, he answered, "It is the part of a good shepherd to shear, not flay, his sheep."

XXXIII. He assumed the sovereignty 332 by slow degrees, and exercised it for a long time with great variety of conduct, though generally with a due regard to the public good. At first he only interposed to prevent ill management. Accordingly, he rescinded some decrees of the senate; and when the magistrates sat for the administration of justice, he frequently offered his service as assessor, either taking his place promiscuously amongst them, or seating himself in a corner of the tribunal. If a rumour prevailed, that any person under prosecution was likely to be acquitted by his interest, he would suddenly make his appearance, and from the floor of the court, (214) or the praetor's bench, remind the judges of the laws, and of their oaths, and the nature of the charge brought before them, he likewise took upon himself the correction of public morals, where they tended to decay, either through neglect, or evil custom.

XXXIV. He reduced the expense of the plays and public spectacles, by diminishing the allowances to actors, and curtailing the number of gladiators. He made grievous complaints to the senate, that the price of Corinthian vessels was become enormous, and that three mullets had been sold for thirty thousand sesterces: upon which he proposed that a new sumptuary law should be enacted; that the butchers and other dealers in viands should be subject to an assize, fixed by the senate yearly; and the aediles commissioned to restrain eating-houses and taverns, so far as not even to permit the sale of any kind of pastry. And to encourage frugality in the public by his own example, he would often, at his solemn feasts, have at his tables victuals which had been served up the day before, and were partly eaten, and half a boar, affirming, "It has all the same good bits that the whole had." He published an edict against the practice of people's kissing each other when they met; and would not allow new-year's gifts 333 to be presented after the calends [the first] of January was passed. He had been in the habit of returning these offerings four-fold, and making them with his own hand; but being annoyed by the continual interruption to which he was exposed during the whole month, by those who had not the opportunity of attending him on the festival, he returned none after that day.

XXXV. Married women guilty of adultery, though not prosecuted publicly, he authorised the nearest relations to punish by agreement among themselves, according to ancient custom. He discharged a Roman knight from the obligation of an oath he had taken, never to turn away his wife; and allowed him to divorce her, upon her being caught in criminal intercourse with her son-in-law. Women of ill-fame, divesting themselves of the rights and dignity of matrons, had now begun a practice of professing themselves prostitutes, to avoid (215) the punishment of the laws; and the most profligate young men of the senatorian and equestrian orders, to secure themselves against a decree of the senate, which prohibited their performing on the stage, or in the amphitheatre, voluntarily subjected themselves to an infamous sentence, by which they were degraded. All those he banished, that none for the future might evade by such artifices the intention and efficacy of the law. He stripped a senator of the broad stripes on his robe, upon information of his having removed to his gardens before the calends [the first] of July, in order that he might afterwards hire a house cheaper in the city. He likewise dismissed another from the office of quaestor, for repudiating, the day after he had been lucky in drawing his lot, a wife whom he had married only the day before.

XXXVI. He suppressed all foreign religions, and the Egyptian 334 and Jewish rites, obliging those who practised that kind of superstition, to burn their vestments, and all their sacred utensils. He distributed the Jewish youths, under the pretence of military service, among the provinces noted for an unhealthy climate; and dismissed from the city all the rest of that nation as well as those who were proselytes to that religion 335, under pain of slavery for life, unless they complied. He also expelled the astrologers; but upon their suing for pardon, and promising to renounce their profession, he revoked his decree.

XXXVII. But, above all things, he was careful to keep the (216) public peace against robbers, burglars, and those who were disaffected to the government. He therefore increased the number of military stations throughout Italy; and formed a camp at Rome for the pretorian cohorts, which, till then, had been quartered in the city. He suppressed with great severity all tumults of the people on their first breaking out; and took every precaution to prevent them.

Some persons having been killed in a quarrel which happened in the theatre, he banished the leaders of the parties, and the players about whom the disturbance had arisen; nor could all the entreaties of the people afterwards prevail upon him to recall them 336 . The people of Pollentia having refused to permit the removal of the corpse of a centurion of the first rank from the forum, until they had extorted from his heirs a sum of money for a public exhibition of gladiators, he detached a cohort from the city, and another from the kingdom of Cottius 337 '; who concealing the cause of their march, entered the town by different gates, with their arms suddenly displayed, and trumpets sounding; and having seized the greatest part of the people, and the magistrates, they were imprisoned for life. He abolished every where the privileges of all places of refuge. The Cyzicenians having committed an outrage upon some Romans, he deprived them of the liberty they had obtained for their good services in the Mithridatic war. Disturbances from foreign enemies he quelled by his lieutenants, without ever going against them in person; nor would he even employ his lieutenants, but with much reluctance, and when it was absolutely necessary. Princes who were ill-affected towards him, he kept in subjection, more by menaces and remonstrances, than by force of arms. Some whom he induced to come to him by fair words and promises, he never would permit to return home; as Maraboduus the German, Thrascypolis the (217) Thracian, and Archelaus the Cappadocian, whose kingdom he even reduced into the form of a province.

XXXVIII. He never set foot outside the gates of Rome, for two years together, from the time he assumed the supreme power; and after that period, went no farther from the city than to some of the neighbouring towns; his farthest excursion being to Antium 338 , and that but very seldom, and for a few days; though he often gave out that he would visit the provinces and armies, and made preparations for it almost every year, by taking up carriages, and ordering provisions for his retinue in the municipia and colonies. At last he suffered vows to be put up for his good journey and safe return, insomuch that he was called jocosely by the name of Callipides, who is famous in a Greek proverb, for being in a great hurry to go forward, but without ever advancing a cubit.

XXXIX. But after the loss of his two sons, of whom Germanicus died in Syria, and Drusus at Rome, he withdrew into Campania 339 ; at which time opinion and conversation were almost general, that he never would return, and would die soon. And both nearly turned out to be true. For indeed he never more came to Rome; and a few days after leaving it, when he was at a villa of his called the Cave, near Terracina 340 , during supper a great many huge stones fell from above, which killed several of the guests and attendants; but he almost hopelessly escaped.

XL. After he had gone round Campania, and dedicated the capitol at Capua, and a temple to Augustus at Nola 341 , which he made the pretext of his journey, he retired to Capri; being (218) greatly delighted with the island, because it was accessible only by a narrow beach, being on all sides surrounded with rugged cliffs, of a stupendous height, and by a deep sea. But immediately, the people of Rome being extremely clamorous for his return, on account of a disaster at Fidenae 342 , where upwards of twenty thousand persons had been killed by the fall of the amphitheatre, during a public spectacle of gladiators, he crossed over again to the continent, and gave all people free access to him; so much the more, because, at his departure from the city, he had caused it to be proclaimed that no one should address him, and had declined admitting any persons to his presence, on the journey.

XLI. Returning to the island, he so far abandoned all care of the government, that he never filled up the decuriae of the knights, never changed any military tribunes or prefects, or governors of provinces, and kept Spain and Syria for several years without any consular lieutenants. He likewise suffered Armenia to be seized by the Parthians, Moesia by the Dacians and Sarmatians, and Gaul to be ravaged by the Germans; to the great disgrace, and no less danger, of the empire.

XLII. But having now the advantage of privacy, and being remote from the observation of the people of Rome, he abandoned himself to all the vicious propensities which he had long but imperfectly concealed, and of which I shall here give a particular account from the beginning. While a young soldier in the camp, he was so remarkable for his excessive inclination to wine, that, for Tiberius, they called him Biberius; for Claudius, Caldius; and for Nero, Mero. And after he succeeded to the empire, and was invested with the office of reforming the morality of the people, he spent a whole night and two days together in feasting and drinking with Pomponius Flaccus and Lucius Piso; to one of whom he immediately gave the province of Syria, and to the other the prefecture of the city; declaring them, in his letters-patent, to be "very pleasant companions, and friends fit for all occasions." He made an appointment to sup with Sestius Gallus, a lewd and prodigal old fellow, who had been disgraced by Augustus, and reprimanded by himself but a few days before in the senate-house; upon condition that he should not recede in the least from his usual method of entertainment, and that they should be attended at table by naked girls. He preferred a very obscure candidate for the quaestorship, before the most noble competitors, only for taking off, in pledging him at table, an amphora of wine at a draught 343 . He presented Asellius Sabinus with two hundred thousand sesterces, for writing a dialogue, in the way of dispute, betwixt the truffle and the fig-pecker, the oyster and the thrush. He likewise instituted a new office to administer to his voluptuousness, to which he appointed Titus Caesonius Priscus, a Roman knight.

XLIII. In his retreat at Capri 344 , he also contrived an apartment containing couches, and adapted to the secret practice of abominable lewdness, where he entertained companies of girls and catamites, and assembled from all quarters inventors of unnatural copulations, whom he called Spintriae, who defiled one another in his presence, to inflame by the exhibition the languid appetite. He had several chambers set round with pictures and statues in the most lascivious attitudes, and furnished with the books of Elephantis, that none might want a pattern for the execution of any lewd project that was prescribed him. He likewise contrived recesses in woods and groves for the gratification of lust, where young persons of both sexes prostituted themselves in caves and hollow rocks, in the disguise of little Pans and Nymphs 345 . So that he was publicly and commonly called, by an abuse of the name of the island, Caprineus. 346

XLIV. But he was still more infamous, if possible, for an (220) abomination not fit to be mentioned or heard, much less credited. 347 ————————When a picture, painted by Parrhasius, in which the artist had represented Atalanta in the act of submitting to Meleager's lust in a most unnatural way, was bequeathed to him, with this proviso, that if the subject was offensive to him, he might receive in lieu of it a million of sesterces, he not only chose the picture, but hung it up in his bed-chamber. It is also reported that, during a sacrifice, he was so captivated with the form of a youth who held a censer, that, before the religious rites were well over, he took him aside and abused him; as also a brother of his who had been playing the flute; and soon afterwards broke the legs of both of them, for upbraiding one another with their shame.

XLV. How much he was guilty of a most foul intercourse with women even of the first quality 348 , appeared very plainly by the death of one Mallonia, who, being brought to his bed, but resolutely refusing to comply with his lust, he gave her up to the common informers. Even when she was upon her trial, he frequently called out to her, and asked her, "Do you repent?" until she, quitting the court, went home, and stabbed herself; openly upbraiding the vile old lecher for his gross obscenity 349 . Hence there was an allusion to him in a farce, which was acted at the next public sports, and was received with great applause, and became a common topic of ridicule 350 : that the old goat— — — —

XLVI. He was so niggardly and covetous, that he never allowed to his attendants, in his travels and expeditions, any salary, but their diet only. Once, indeed, he treated them liberally, at the instigation of his step-father, when, dividing them into three classes, according to their rank, he gave the (221) first six, the second four, and the third two, hundred thousand sesterces, which last class he called not friends, but Greeks.

XLVII. During the whole time of his government, he never erected any noble edifice; for the only things he did undertake, namely, building the temple of Augustus, and restoring Pompey's Theatre, he left at last, after many years, unfinished. Nor did he ever entertain the people with public spectacles; and he was seldom present at those which were given by others, lest any thing of that kind should be requested of him; especially after he was obliged to give freedom to the comedian Actius. Having relieved the poverty of a few senators, to avoid further demands, he declared that he should for the future assist none, but those who gave the senate full satisfaction as to the cause of their necessity. Upon this, most of the needy senators, from modesty and shame, declined troubling him. Amongst these was Hortalus, grandson to the celebrated orator Quintus Hortensius, who [marrying], by the persuasion of Augustus, had brought up four children upon a very small estate.

XLVIII. He displayed only two instances of public munificence. One was an offer to lend gratis, for three years, a hundred millions of sesterces to those who wanted to borrow; and the other, when, some large houses being burnt down upon Mount Caelius, he indemnified the owners. To the former of these he was compelled by the clamours of the people, in a great scarcity of money, when he had ratified a decree of the senate obliging all money-lenders to advance two-thirds of their capital on land, and the debtors to pay off at once the same proportion of their debts, and it was found insufficient to remedy the grievance. The other he did to alleviate in some degree the pressure of the times. But his benefaction to the sufferers by fire, he estimated at so high a rate, that he ordered the Caelian Hill to be called, in future, the Augustan. To the soldiery, after doubling the legacy left them by Augustus, he never gave any thing, except a thousand denarii a man to the pretorian guards, for not joining the party of Sejanus; and some presents to the legions in Syria, because they alone had not paid reverence to the effigies of Sejanus among their standards. He seldom gave discharges to the veteran soldiers, calculating (222) on their deaths from advanced age, and on what would be saved by thus getting rid of them, in the way of rewards or pensions. Nor did he ever relieve the provinces by any act of generosity, excepting Asia, where some cities had been destroyed by an earthquake.

XLIX. In the course of a very short time, he turned his mind to sheer robbery. It is certain that Cneius Lentulus, the augur, a man of vast estate, was so terrified and worried by his threats and importunities, that he was obliged to make him his heir; and that Lepida, a lady of a very noble family, was condemned by him, in order to gratify Quirinus, a man of consular rank, extremely rich, and childless, who had divorced her twenty years before, and now charged her with an old design to poison him. Several persons, likewise, of the first distinction in Gaul, Spain, Syria, and Greece, had their estates confiscated upon such despicably trifling and shameless pretences, that against some of them no other charge was preferred, than that they held large sums of ready money as part of their property. Old immunities, the rights of mining, and of levying tolls, were taken from several cities and private persons. And Vonones, king of the Parthians, who had been driven out of his dominions by his own subjects, and fled to Antioch with a vast treasure, claiming the protection of the Roman people, his allies, was treacherously robbed of all his money, and afterwards murdered.

L. He first manifested hatred towards his own relations in the case of his brother Drusus, betraying him by the production of a letter to himself, in which Drusus proposed that Augustus should be forced to restore the public liberty. In course of time, he shewed the same disposition with regard to the rest of his family. So far was he from performing any office of kindness or humanity to his wife, when she was banished, and, by her father's order, confined to one town, that he forbad her to stir out of the house, or converse with any men. He even wronged her of the dowry given her by her father, and of her yearly allowance, by a quibble of law, because Augustus had made no provision for them on her behalf in his will. Being harassed by his mother, Livia, who claimed an equal share in the government with him, he frequently avoided (223) seeing her, and all long and private conferences with her, lest it should be thought that he was governed by her counsels, which, notwithstanding, he sometimes sought, and was in the habit of adopting. He was much offended at the senate, when they proposed to add to his other titles that of the Son of Livia, as well as Augustus. He, therefore, would not suffer her to be called "the Mother of her Country," nor to receive any extraordinary public distinction. Nay, he frequently admonished her "not to meddle with weighty affairs, and such as did not suit her sex;" especially when he found her present at a fire which broke out near the Temple of Vesta 351 , and encouraging the people and soldiers to use their utmost exertions, as she had been used to do in the time of her husband.

LI. He afterwards proceeded to an open rupture with her, and, as is said, upon this occasion. She having frequently urged him to place among the judges a person who had been made free of the city, he refused her request, unless she would allow it to be inscribed on the roll, "That the appointment had been extorted from him by his mother." Enraged at this, Livia brought forth from her chapel some letters from Augustus to her, complaining of the sourness and insolence of Tiberius's temper, and these she read. So much was he offended at these letters having been kept so long, and now produced with so much bitterness against him, that some considered this incident as one of the causes of his going into seclusion, if not the principal reason for his so doing. In the (224) whole years she lived during his retirement, he saw her but once, and that for a few hours only. When she fell sick shortly afterwards, he was quite unconcerned about visiting her in her illness; and when she died, after promising to attend her funeral, he deferred his coming for several days, so that the corpse was in a state of decay and putrefaction before the interment; and he then forbad divine honours being paid to her, pretending that he acted according to her own directions. He likewise annulled her will, and in a short time ruined all her friends and acquaintance; not even sparing those to whom, on her death-bed, she had recommended the care of her funeral, but condemning one of them, a man of equestrian rank, to the treadmill. 352

LII. He entertained no paternal affection either for his own son Drusus, or his adopted son Germanicus. Offended at the vices of the former, who was of a loose disposition and led a dissolute life, he was not much affected at his death; but, almost immediately after the funeral, resumed his attention to business, and prevented the courts from being longer closed. The ambassadors from the people of Ilium coming rather late to offer their condolence, he said to them by way of banter, as if the affair had already faded from his memory, "And I heartily condole with you on the loss of your renowned countryman, Hector." He so much affected to depreciate Germanicus, that he spoke of his achievements as utterly insignificant, and railed at his most glorious victories as ruinous to the state; complaining of him also to the senate for going to Alexandria without his knowledge, upon occasion of a great and sudden famine at Rome. It was believed that he took care to have him dispatched by Cneius Piso, his lieutenant in Syria. This person was afterwards tried for the murder, and would, as was supposed, have produced his orders, had they not been contained in a private and confidential dispatch. The following words therefore were posted up in many places, and frequently shouted in the night: "Give us back our Germanicus." This suspicion was afterwards confirmed by the barbarous treatment of his wife and children.

(225) LIII. His daughter-in-law Agrippina, after the death of her husband, complaining upon some occasion with more than ordinary freedom, he took her by the hand, and addressed her in a Greek verse to this effect: "My dear child, do you think yourself injured, because

you are not empress?" Nor did he ever vouchsafe to speak to her again. Upon her refusing once at supper to taste some fruit which he presented to her, he declined inviting her to his table, pretending that she in effect charged him with a design to poison her; whereas the whole was a contrivance of his own. He was to offer the fruit, and she to be privately cautioned against eating what would infallibly cause her death. At last, having her accused of intending to flee for refuge to the statue of Augustus, or to the army, he banished her to the island of Pandataria 353 . Upon her reviling him for it, he caused a centurion to beat out one of her eyes; and when she resolved to starve herself to death, he ordered her mouth to be forced open, and meat to be crammed down her throat. But she persisting in her resolution, and dying soon afterwards, he persecuted her memory with the basest aspersions, and persuaded the senate to put her birth-day amongst the number of unlucky days in the calendar. He likewise took credit for not having caused her to be strangled and her body cast upon the Gemonian Steps, and suffered a decree of the senate to pass, thanking him for his clemency, and an offering of gold to be made to Jupiter Capitolinus on the occasion.

LIV. He had by Germanicus three grandsons, Nero, Drusus, and Caius; and by his son Drusus one, named Tiberius. Of these, after the loss of his sons, he commended Nero and Drusus, the two eldest sons of Germanicus, to the senate; and at their being solemnly introduced into the forum, distributed money among the people. But when he found that on entering upon the new year they were included in the public vows for his own welfare, he told the senate, "that such honours ought not to be conferred but upon those who had been proved, and were of more advanced years." By thus betraying his private feelings towards them, he exposed them to all sorts of accusations; and after practising many artifices to provoke (226) them to rail at and abuse him, that he might be furnished with a pretence to destroy them, he charged them with it in a letter to the senate; at the same time accusing them, in the bitterest terms, of the most scandalous vices. Upon their being declared enemies by the senate, he starved them to death; Nero in the island of Ponza, and Drusus in the vaults of the Palatium. It is thought by some, that Nero was driven to a voluntary death by the executioner's shewing him some halters and hooks, as if he had been sent to him by order of the senate. Drusus, it is said, was so rabid with hunger, that he attempted to eat the chaff with which his mattress was stuffed. The relics of both were so scattered, that it was with difficulty they were collected.

LV. Besides his old friends and intimate acquaintance, he required the assistance of twenty of the most eminent persons in the city, as counsellors in the administration of public affairs. Out of all this number, scarcely two or three escaped the fury of his savage disposition. All the rest he destroyed upon one pretence or another; and among them Aelius Sejanus, whose fall was attended with the ruin of many others. He had advanced this minister to the highest pitch of grandeur, not so much from any real regard for him, as that by his base and sinister contrivances he might ruin the children of Germanicus, and thereby secure the succession to his own grandson by Drusus.

LVI. He treated with no greater leniency the Greeks in his family, even those with whom he was most pleased. Having asked one Zeno, upon his using some far-fetched phrases, "What uncouth dialect is that?" he replied, "The Doric." For this answer he banished him to Cinara 354, suspecting that he taunted him with his former residence at Rhodes, where the Doric dialect is spoken. It being his custom to start questions at supper, arising out of what he had been reading in the day, and finding that Seleucus, the grammarian, used to inquire of his attendants what authors he was then studying, and so came prepared for his enquiries—he first turned him out of his family, and then drove him to the extremity of laying violent hands upon himself.

(227) LVII. His cruel and sullen temper appeared when he was still a boy; which Theodorus of Gadara 355, his master in rhetoric, first discovered, and expressed by a very apposite simile, calling him sometimes, when he chid him, "Mud mixed with blood." But his disposition shewed itself still more clearly on his attaining the imperial power, and even in the beginning of his administration, when he was endeavouring to gain the popular favour, by affecting moderation. Upon a funeral passing by, a wag called out to the dead man, "Tell Augustus, that the legacies he bequeathed to the people are not yet paid." The man being brought before him, he ordered that he should receive what was due to him, and then be led to execution, that he might deliver the message to his father himself. Not long afterwards, when one Pompey, a Roman knight, persisted in his opposition to

something he proposed in the senate, he threatened to put him in prison, and told him, "Of a Pompey I shall make a Pompeian of you;" by a bitter kind of pun playing upon the man's name, and the ill-fortune of his party.

LVIII. About the same time, when the praetor consulted him, whether it was his pleasure that the tribunals should take cognizance of accusations of treason, he replied, "The laws ought to be put in execution;" and he did put them in execution most severely. Some person had taken off the head of Augustus from one of his statues, and replaced it by another 356. The matter was brought before the senate, and because the case was not clear, the witnesses were put to the torture. The party accused being found guilty, and condemned, this kind of proceeding was carried so far, that it became capital for a man to beat his slave, or change his clothes, near the statue of Augustus; to carry his head stamped upon the coin, or cut in the stone of a ring, into a necessary house, or the stews; or to reflect upon anything that had been either said or done by him. In fine, a person was condemned to death, for suffering some honours to be decreed to him in the colony where he lived, upon the same day on which they had formerly been decreed to Augustus.

(228) LIX. He was besides guilty of many barbarous actions, under the pretence of strictness and reformation of manners, but more to gratify his own savage disposition. Some verses were published, which displayed the present calamities of his reign, and anticipated the future. 357

*Asper et immitis, breviter vis omnia dicam?*
*Dispeream si te mater amare potest.*
*Non es eques, quare? non sunt tibi millia centum?*
*Omnia si quaeras, et Rhodos exsilium est.*
*Aurea mutasti Saturni saecula, Caesar:*
*Incolumi nam te, ferrea semper erunt.*
*Fastidit vinum, quia jam sit it iste cruorem:*
*Tam bibit hunc avide, quam bibit ante merum.*
*Adspice felicem sibi, non tibi, Romule, Sullam:*
*Et Marium, si vis, adspice, sed reducem.*
*Nec non Antoni civilia bella moventis*

*Nec semel infectas adspice caeda manus.*
*Et dic, Roma perit: regnabit sanguine multo,*
*Ad regnum quisquis venit ab exsilio.*

Obdurate wretch! too fierce, too fell to move
The least kind yearnings of a mother's love!
No knight thou art, as having no estate;
Long suffered'st thou in Rhodes an exile's fate,
No more the happy Golden Age we see;
The Iron's come, and sure to last with thee.
Instead of wine he thirsted for before,
He wallows now in floods of human gore.
Reflect, ye Romans, on the dreadful times,
Made such by Marius, and by Sylla's crimes.
Reflect how Antony's ambitious rage
Twice scar'd with horror a distracted age,
And say, Alas! Rome's blood in streams will flow,
When banish'd miscreants rule this world below.

At first he would have it understood, that these satirical verses were drawn forth by the resentment of those who were impatient under the discipline of reformation, rather than that they spoke their real sentiments; and he would frequently say, "Let them hate me, so long as they do but approve my conduct." 358 At length, however, his behaviour showed that he was sensible they were too well founded.

(229) LX. A few days after his arrival at Capri, a fisherman coming up to him unexpectedly, when he was desirous of privacy, and presenting him with a large mullet, he ordered the man's face to be scrubbed with the fish; being terrified at the thought of his having been able to creep upon him from the back of the island, over such rugged and steep rocks. The man, while undergoing the punishment, expressing his joy that he had not likewise offered him a large crab which he had also taken, he ordered his face to be farther lacerated with its claws. He put to death one of the pretorian guards, for having stolen a peacock out of his orchard. In one of his journeys, his litter being obstructed by some bushes, he ordered the officer whose duty it was to ride on and examine the road, a centurion of the first cohorts, to be laid on his face upon the ground, and scourged almost to death.

LXI. Soon afterwards, he abandoned himself to every species of cruelty, never wanting occasions of one kind or another, to serve as a pretext. He first fell upon the friends and acquaintance of his mother, then those of his grandsons, and his daughter-in-law, and lastly those of Sejanus; after whose death he became cruel in the extreme. From this it appeared, that he had not been so much instigated by Sejanus, as supplied with occasions of gratifying his savage temper, when he wanted them. Though in a short memoir which he composed of his own life, he had the effrontery to write, "I have punished Sejanus, because I found him bent upon the destruction of the children of my son Germanicus," one of these he put to death, when he began to suspect Sejanus; and another, after he was taken off. It would be tedious to relate all the numerous instances of his cruelty: suffice it to give a few examples, in their different kinds. Not a day passed without the punishment of some person or other, not excepting holidays, or those appropriated to the worship of the gods. Some were tried even on New-Year's-Day. Of many who were condemned, their wives and children shared the same fate; and for those who were sentenced to death, the relations were forbid to put on mourning. Considerable rewards were voted for the prosecutors, and sometimes for the witnesses also. The information of any person, without exception, was taken; and all offences were capital, even speaking (230) a few words, though without any ill intention. A poet was charged with abusing Agamemnon; and a historian 359 , for calling Brutus and Cassius "the last of the Romans." The two authors were immediately called to account, and their writings suppressed; though they had been well received some years before, and read in the hearing of Augustus. Some, who were thrown into prison, were not only denied the solace of study, but debarred from all company and conversation. Many persons, when summoned to trial, stabbed themselves at home, to avoid the distress and ignominy of a public condemnation, which they were certain would ensue. Others took poison in the senate house. The wounds were bound up, and all who had not expired, were carried, half-dead, and panting for life, to prison. Those who were put to death, were thrown down the Gemonian stairs, and then dragged into the Tiber. In one day, twenty were treated in this manner; and amongst them women and boys. Because, according to an ancient custom, it was not lawful to strangle virgins, the young girls were first deflowered by the executioner, and afterwards strangled.

Those who were desirous to die, were forced to live. For he thought death so slight a punishment, that upon hearing that Carnulius, one of the accused, who was under prosecution, had killed himself, he exclaimed, "Carnulius has escaped me." In calling over his prisoners, when one of them requested the favour of a speedy death, he replied, "You are not yet restored to favour." A man of consular rank writes in his annals, that at table, where he himself was present with a large company, he was suddenly asked aloud by a dwarf who stood by amongst the buffoons, why Paconius, who was under a prosecution for treason, lived so long. Tiberius immediately reprimanded him for his pertness; but wrote to the senate a few days after, to proceed without delay to the punishment of Paconius.

LXII. Exasperated by information he received respecting the death of his son Drusus, he carried his cruelty still farther. He imagined that he had died of a disease occasioned (231) by his intemperance; but finding that he had been poisoned by the contrivance of his wife Livilla 360 and Sejanus, he spared no one from torture and death. He was so entirely occupied with the examination of this affair, for whole days together, that, upon being informed that the person in whose house he had lodged at Rhodes, and whom he had by a friendly letter invited to Rome, was arrived, he ordered him immediately to be put to the torture, as a party concerned in the enquiry. Upon finding his mistake, he commanded him to be put to death, that he might not publish the injury done him. The place of execution is still shown at Capri, where he ordered those who were condemned to die, after long and exquisite tortures, to be thrown, before his eyes, from a precipice into the sea. There a party of soldiers belonging to the fleet waited for them, and broke their bones with poles and oars, lest they should have any life left in them. Among various kinds of torture invented by him, one was, to induce people to drink a large quantity of wine, and then to tie up their members with harp-strings, thus tormenting them at once by the tightness of the ligature, and the stoppage of their urine. Had not death prevented him, and Thrasyllus, designedly, as some say, prevailed with him to defer some of his cruelties, in hopes of longer life, it is believed that he would have destroyed many more: and not have spared even the rest of his grandchildren: for he was jealous of Caius, and hated Tiberius as having been conceived in adultery. This conjecture is indeed highly probable; for he used often to say, "Happy Priam, who survived all his children!" 361

LXIII. Amidst these enormities, in how much fear and apprehension, as well as odium and detestation, he lived, is evident from many indications. He forbade the soothsayers to be consulted in private, and without some witnesses being present. He attempted to suppress the oracles in the neighbourhood of the city; but being terrified by the divine authority of the (232) Praenestine Lots 362 , he abandoned the design. For though they were sealed up in a box, and carried to home, yet they were not to be found in it, until it was returned to the temple. More than one person of consular rank, appointed governors of provinces, he never ventured to dismiss to their respective destinations, but kept them until several years after, when he nominated their successors, while they still remained present with him. In the meantime, they bore the title of their office; and he frequently gave them orders, which they took care to have executed by their deputies and assistants.

LXIV. He never removed his daughter-in-law, or grandsons 363 , after their condemnation, to any place, but in fetters and in a covered litter, with a guard to hinder all who met them on the road, and travellers, from stopping to gaze at them.

LXV. After Sejanus had plotted against him, though he saw that his birth-day was solemnly kept by the public, and divine honours paid to golden images of him in every quarter, yet it was with difficulty at last, and more by artifice than his imperial power, that he accomplished his death. In the first place, to remove him from about his person, under the pretext of doing him honour, he made him his colleague in his fifth consulship; which, although then absent from the city, he took upon him for that purpose, long after his preceding consulship. Then, having flattered him with the hope of an alliance by marriage with one of his own kindred, and the prospect of the tribunitian authority, he suddenly, while Sejanus little expected it, charged him with treason, in an abject and pitiful address to the senate; in which, among other things, he begged them "to send one of the consuls, to conduct himself, a poor solitary old man, with a guard of soldiers, into their presence." Still distrustful, however, and apprehensive of an insurrection, he ordered his grandson, Drusus, whom he still kept in confinement at Rome, to be set at liberty, and if occasion required, to head the troops. He had likewise ships in readiness to transport him to any of the legions to which he might consider it expedient to make his escape. Meanwhile, he was upon the (233) watch, from the summit of a lofty cliff, for the signals which he had ordered to be made if any thing occurred, lest the messengers should be tardy. Even when he had quite foiled the conspiracy of Sejanus, he was still haunted as much as ever with fears and apprehensions, insomuch that he never once stirred out of the Villa Jovis for nine months after.

LXVI. To the extreme anxiety of mind which he now experienced, he had the mortification to find superadded the most poignant reproaches from all quarters. Those who were condemned to die, heaped upon him the most opprobrious language in his presence, or by hand-bills scattered in the senators' seats in the theatre. These produced different effects: sometimes he wished, out of shame, to have all smothered and concealed; at other times he would disregard what was said, and publish it himself. To this accumulation of scandal and open sarcasm, there is to be subjoined a letter from Artabanus, king of the Parthians, in which he upbraids him with his parricides, murders, cowardice, and lewdness, and advises him to satisfy the furious rage of his own people, which he had so justly excited, by putting an end to his life without delay.

LXVII. At last, being quite weary of himself, he acknowledged his extreme misery, in a letter to the senate, which begun thus: "What to write to you, Conscript Fathers, or how to write, or what not to write at this time, may all the gods and goddesses pour upon my head a more terrible vengeance than that under which I feel myself daily sinking, if I can tell." Some are of opinion that he had a foreknowledge of those things, from his skill in the science of divination, and perceived long before what misery and infamy would at last come upon him; and that for this reason, at the beginning of his reign, he had absolutely refused the title of the "Father of his Country," and the proposal of the senate to swear to his acts; lest he should afterwards, to his greater shame, be found unequal to such extraordinary honours. This, indeed, may be justly inferred from the speeches which he made upon both those occasions; as when he says, "I shall ever be the same, and shall never change my conduct, so long as I retain my senses; but to avoid giving a bad precedent to posterity, the senate ought to beware of binding themselves to the acts of (234) any person whatever, who might by some accident or other be induced to alter them." And again: "If ye should at any time entertain a jealousy of my conduct, and my entire affection for you, which heaven prevent by putting a period to my days, rather than I should live to see such an alteration in your opinion of me, the title of Father will add no honour to me, but be a reproach to you, for your rashness in conferring it upon me, or inconstancy in altering your opinion of me."

LXVIII. In person he was large and robust; of a stature somewhat above the common size; broad in the shoulders and chest, and proportionable in the rest of his frame. He used his left hand more readily and with more force than his right; and his joints were so strong, that he could bore a fresh, sound apple through with his finger, and wound the head of a boy, or even a young man, with a fillip. He was of a fair complexion, and wore his hair so long behind, that it covered his neck, which was observed to be a mark of distinction affected by the family. He had a handsome face, but it was often full of pimples. His eyes, which were large, had a wonderful faculty of seeing in the night-time, and in the dark, for a short time only, and immediately after awaking from sleep; but they soon grew dim again. He walked with his neck stiff and upright: generally with a frowning countenance, being for the most part silent: when he spoke to those about him, it was very slowly, and usually accompanied with a slight gesticulation of his fingers. All which, being repulsive habits and signs of arrogance, were remarked by Augustus, who often endeavoured to excuse them to the senate and people, declaring that "they were natural defects, which proceeded from no viciousness of mind." He enjoyed a good state of health, without interruption, almost during the whole period of his rule; though, from the thirtieth year of his age, he treated it himself according to his own discretion, without any medical assistance.

LXIX. In regard to the gods, and matters of religion, he discovered much indifference; being greatly addicted to astrology, and fully persuaded that all things were governed by fate. Yet he was extremely afraid of lightning, and when the sky was in a disturbed state, always wore a laurel crown on his head; because it is supposed that the leaf of that tree is never touched by the lightning.

(235) LXX. He applied himself with great diligence to the liberal arts, both Greek and Latin. In his Latin style, he affected to imitate Messala Corvinus 364 , a venerable man, to whom he had paid much respect in his own early years. But he rendered his style obscure

by excessive affectation and abstruseness, so that he was thought to speak better extempore, than in a premeditated discourse. He composed likewise a lyric ode, under the title of "A Lamentation upon the death of Lucius Caesar;" and also some Greek poems, in imitation of Euphorion, Rhianus, and Parthenius 365 . These poets he greatly admired, and placed their works and statues in the public libraries, amongst the eminent authors of antiquity. On this account, most of the learned men of the time vied with each other in publishing observations upon them, which they addressed to him. His principal study, however, was the history of the fabulous ages, inquiring even into its trifling details in a ridiculous manner; for he used to try the grammarians, a class of men which, as I have already observed, he much affected, with such questions as these: "Who was Hecuba's mother? What name did Achilles assume among the virgins? What was it that the Sirens used to sing?" And the first day that he entered the senate-house, after the death of Augustus, as if he intended to pay respect at once to his father's memory and to the gods, he made an offering of frankincense and wine, but without any music, in imitation of Minos, upon the death of his son.

LXXI. Though he was ready and conversant with the Greek tongue, yet he did not use it everywhere; but chiefly he avoided it in the senate-house, insomuch that having occasion to employ the word monopolium (monopoly), he first begged pardon for being obliged to adopt a foreign word. And when, in a decree of the senate, the word emblaema (emblem) was read, he proposed to have it changed, and that a Latin word should be substituted in its room; or, if no proper one could be found, to express the thing by circumlocution. A soldier (236) who was examined as a witness upon a trial, in Greek 366 , he would not allow to reply, except in Latin.

LXXII. During the whole time of his seclusion at Capri, twice only he made an effort to visit Rome. Once he came in a galley as far as the gardens near the Naumachia, but placed guards along the banks of the Tiber, to keep off all who should offer to come to meet him. The second time he travelled on the Appian Way 367 , as far as the seventh milestone from the city, but he immediately returned, without entering it, having only taken a view of the walls at a distance. For what reason he did not disembark in his first excursion, is uncertain; but in the last, he was deterred from entering the city by a prodigy. He was in the habit of diverting himself with a snake, and upon going to feed it with his own hand, according to custom, he found it devoured by ants; from which he was advised to beware of the fury of the mob. On this account, returning in all haste to Campania, he fell ill at Astura 368 ; but recovering a little, went on to Circeii 369 . And to obviate any suspicion of his being in a bad state of health, he was not only present at the sports in the camp, but encountered, with javelins, a wild boar, which was let loose in the arena. Being immediately seized with a pain in the side, and catching cold upon his over-heating himself in the exercise, he relapsed into a worse condition than he was before. He held out, however, for some time; and sailing as far as Misenum 370 , omitted nothing (237) in his usual mode of life, not even in his entertainments, and other gratifications, partly from an ungovernable appetite, and partly to conceal his condition. For Charicles, a physician, having obtained leave of absence, on his rising from table, took his hand to kiss it; upon which Tiberius, supposing he did it to feel his pulse, desired him to stay and resume his place, and continued the entertainment longer than usual. Nor did he omit his usual custom of taking his station in the centre of the apartment, a lictor standing by him, while he took leave of each of the party by name.

LXXIII. Meanwhile, finding, upon looking over the acts of the senate, "that some person under prosecution had been discharged, without being brought to a hearing," for he had only written cursorily that they had been denounced by an informer; he complained in a great rage that he was treated with contempt, and resolved at all hazards to return to Capri; not daring to attempt any thing until he found himself in a place of security. But being detained by storms, and the increasing violence of his disorder, he died shortly afterwards, at a villa formerly belonging to Lucullus, in the seventy-eighth year of his age 371 , and the twenty-third of his reign, upon the seventeenth of the calends of April (16th March), in the consulship of Cneius Acerronius Proculus and Caius Pontius Niger. Some think that a slow-consuming poison was given him by Caius 372 . Others say that during the interval of the intermittent fever with which he happened to be seized, upon asking for food, it was denied him. Others report, that he was stifled by a pillow thrown upon him 373 , when, on his recovering from a swoon, he called for his ring, which had been taken from him in the fit. Seneca writes, "That finding himself dying, he took his signet ring off his finger, and held it a while, as if he would deliver it to somebody; but put it again upon his finger, and lay for some time, with his left hand clenched, and without stirring; when suddenly summoning his attendants, (238) and no one answering the call, he rose; but his strength failing him, he fell down at a short distance from his bed."

LXXIV. Upon his last birth-day, he had brought a full-sized statue of the Timenian Apollo from Syracuse, a work of exquisite art, intending to place it in the library of the new temple 374 ; but he dreamt that the god appeared to him in the night, and assured him "that his statue could not be erected by him." A few days before he died, the Pharos at Capri was thrown down by an earthquake. And at Misenum, some embers and live coals, which were brought in to warm his apartment, went out, and after being quite cold, burst out into a flame again towards evening, and continued burning very brightly for several hours.

LXXV. The people were so much elated at his death, that when they first heard the news, they ran up and down the city, some crying out, "Away with Tiberius to the Tiber;" others exclaiming, "May the earth, the common mother of mankind, and the infernal gods, allow him no abode in death, but amongst the wicked." Others threatened his body with the hook and the Gemonian stairs, their indignation at his former cruelty being increased by a recent atrocity. It had been provided by an act of the senate, that the execution of condemned criminals should always be deferred until the tenth day after the sentence. Now this fell on the very day when the news of Tiberius's death arrived, and in consequence of which the unhappy men implored a reprieve, for mercy's sake; but, as Caius had not yet arrived, and there was no one else to whom application could be made on their behalf, their guards, apprehensive of violating the law, strangled them, and threw them down the Gemonian stairs. This roused the people to a still greater abhorrence of the tyrant's memory, since his cruelty continued in use even after he was dead. As soon as his corpse was begun to be moved from Misenum, many cried out for its being carried to Atella 375 , and being half burnt there (239) in the amphitheatre. It was, however, brought to Rome, and burnt with the usual ceremony.

LXXVI. He had made about two years before, duplicates of his will, one written by his own hand, and the other by that of one of his freedmen; and both were witnessed by some persons of very mean rank. He appointed his two grandsons, Caius by Germanicus, and Tiberius by Drusus, joint heirs to his estate; and upon the death of one of them, the other was to inherit the whole. He gave likewise many legacies; amongst which were bequests to the Vestal Virgins, to all the soldiers, and each one of the people of Rome, and to the magistrates of the several quarters of the city.

\* \* \* \* \* \*

At the death of Augustus, there had elapsed so long a period from the overthrow of the republic by Julius Caesar, that few were now living who had been born under the ancient constitution of the Romans; and the mild and prosperous administration of Augustus, during forty-four years, had by this time reconciled the minds of the people to a despotic government. Tiberius, the adopted son of the former sovereign, was of mature age; and though he had hitherto lived, for the most part, abstracted from any concern with public affairs, yet, having been brought up in the family of Augustus, he was acquainted with his method of government, which, there was reason to expect, he would render the model of his own. Livia, too, his mother, and the relict of the late emperor, was still living, a woman venerable by years, who had long been familiar with the councils of Augustus, and from her high rank, as well as uncommon affability, possessed an extensive influence amongst all classes of the people.

Such were the circumstances in favour of Tiberius's succession at the demise of Augustus; but there were others of a tendency disadvantageous to his views. His temper was haughty and reserved: Augustus had often apologised for the ungraciousness of his manners. He was disobedient to his mother; and though he had not openly discovered any propensity to vice, he enjoyed none of those qualities which usually conciliate popularity. To these considerations it is to be added, that Postumus Agrippa, the grandson of Augustus by Julia, was living; and if consanguinity was to be the rule of succession, his right was indisputably preferable to that of an adopted son. Augustus had sent this youth into exile a few years before; but, towards the close (240) of his life, had expressed a design of recalling him, with the view, as was supposed, of appointing him his successor. The father of young Agrippa had been greatly beloved by the Romans; and the fate of his mother, Julia, though she was notorious for her profligacy, had ever been regarded by them with peculiar sympathy and tenderness. Many, therefore, attached to the son the partiality entertained for his parents; which was increased not only by a strong suspicion, but a general surmise, that his elder brothers, Caius and Lucius, had been violently taken off, to make way for the succession of Tiberius. That an obstruction was apprehended to Tiberius's succession from this quarter, is put beyond all doubt, when we find that the death of Augustus was industriously kept secret, until young Agrippa should be removed; who, it is generally agreed, was dispatched by an order from Livia and Tiberius conjointly, or at least from the former. Though, by this act, there remained no rival to Tiberius, yet the consciousness of his own want of pretensions to the Roman throne, seems to have still rendered him distrustful of the succession; and that he should have quietly obtained it, without the voice of the people, the real inclination of the senate, or the support of the army, can be imputed only to the influence of his mother, and his own dissimulation. Ardently solicitous to attain the object, yet affecting a total indifference; artfully prompting the senate to give him the charge of the government, at the time that he intimated an invincible reluctance to accept it; his absolutely declining it in perpetuity, but fixing no time for an abdication; his deceitful insinuation of bodily infirmities, with hints likewise of approaching old age, that he might allay in the senate all apprehensions of any great duration of his power, and repress in his adopted son, Germanicus, the emotions of ambition to displace him; form altogether a scene of the most insidious policy, inconsistency, and dissimulation.

    In this period died, in the eighty-sixth year of her age, Livia Drusilla, mother of the emperor, and the relict of Augustus, whom she survived fifteen years. She was the daughter of L. Drusus Calidianus and married Tiberius Claudius Nero, by whom she had two sons, Tiberius and Drusus. The conduct of this lady seems to justify the remark of Caligula, that "she was an Ulysses in a woman's dress." Octavius first saw her as she fled from the danger which threatened her husband, who had espoused the cause of Antony; and though she was then pregnant, he resolved to marry her; whether with her own inclination or not, is left by Tacitus undetermined. To pave the way for this union, he divorced his wife Scribonia, and with the approbation of the Augurs, which he could have no difficulty in obtaining, celebrated (241) his nuptials with Livia. There ensued from this marriage no issue, though much desired by both parties; but Livia retained, without interruption, an unbounded ascendancy over the emperor, whose confidence she abused, while the uxorious husband little suspected that he was cherishing in his bosom a viper who was to prove the destruction of his house. She appears to have entertained a predominant ambition of giving an heir to the Roman empire; and since it could not be done by any fruit of her marriage with Augustus, she resolved on accomplishing that end in the person of Tiberius, the eldest son by her former husband. The plan which she devised for this purpose, was to exterminate all the male offspring of Augustus by his daughter Julia, who was married to Agrippa; a stratagem which, when executed, would procure for Tiberius, through the means of adoption, the eventual succession to the empire. The cool yet sanguinary policy, and the patient perseverance of resolution, with which she prosecuted her design, have seldom been equalled. While the sons of Julia were yet young, and while there was still a possibility that she herself might have issue by Augustus, she suspended her project, in the hope, perhaps, that accident or disease might operate in its favour; but when the natural term of her constitution had put a period to her hopes of progeny, and when the grandsons of the emperor were risen to the years of manhood, and had been adopted by him, she began to carry into execution what she long had meditated. The first object devoted to destruction was C. Caesar Agrippa, the eldest of Augustus's grandsons. This promising youth was sent to Armenia, upon an expedition against the Persians; and Lollius, who had been his governor, either accompanied him thither from Rome, or met him in the East, where he had obtained some appointment. From the hand of this traitor, perhaps under the pretext of exercising the authority of a preceptor, but in reality instigated by Livia, the young prince received a fatal blow, of which he died some time after.

The manner of Caius's death seems to have been carefully kept from the knowledge of Augustus, who promoted Lollius to the consulship, and made him governor of a province; but, by his rapacity in this station, he afterwards incurred the emperor's displeasure. The true character of this person had escaped the keen discernment of Horace, as well as the sagacity of the emperor; for in two epistles addressed to Lollius, he mentions him as great and accomplished in the superlative degree; maxime Lolli, liberrime Lolli; so imposing had been the manners and address of this deceitful courtier.

Lucius, the second son of Julia, was banished into Campania, (242) for using, as it is said, so litious language against his grandfather. In the seventh year of his exile Augustus proposed to recall him; but Livia and Tiberius, dreading the consequences of his being restored to the emperor's favour, put in practice the expedient of having him immediately assassinated. Postumus Agrippa, the third son, incurred the displeasure of his grandfather in the same way as Lucius, and was confined at Surrentum, where he remained a prisoner until he was put to death by the order either of Livia alone, or in conjunction with Tiberius, as was before observed.

Such was the catastrophe, through the means of Livia, of all the grandsons of Augustus; and reason justifies the inference, that she who scruple not to lay violent hands upon those young men, had formerly practised every artifice that could operate towards rendering them obnoxious to the emperor. We may even ascribe to her dark intrigues the dissolute conduct of Julia for the woman who could secretly act as procuress to her own husband, would feel little restraint upon her mind against corrupting his daughter, when such an effect might contribute to answer the purpose which she had in view. But in the ingratitude of Tiberius, however undutiful and reprehensible in a son towards a parent, she at last experienced a just retribution for the crimes in which she had trained him to procure the succession to the empire. To the disgrace of her sex, she introduced amongst the Romans the horrible practice of domestic murder, little known before the times when the thirst or intoxication of unlimited power had vitiated the social affections; and she transmitted to succeeding ages a pernicious example, by which immoderate ambition might be gratified, at the expense of every moral obligation, as well as of humanity.

One of the first victims in the sanguinary reign of the present emperor, was Germanicus, the son of Drusus, Tiberius's own brother, and who had been adopted by his uncle himself. Under any sovereign, of a temper different from that of Tiberius, this amiable and meritorious prince would have been held in the highest esteem. At the death of his grandfather Augustus, he was employed in a war in Germany, where he greatly distinguished himself by his military achievements; and as soon as intelligence of that event arrived, the soldiers, by whom he was extremely beloved, unanimously saluted him emperor. Refusing, however, to accept this mark of their partiality, he persevered in allegiance to the government of his uncle, and prosecuted the war with success. Upon the conclusion of this expedition, he was sent, with the title of emperor in the East, to repress the seditions of the Armenians, in which he was equally successful. But the (243) fame which he acquired, served only to render him an object of jealousy to Tiberius, by whose order he was secretly poisoned at Daphne, near Antioch, in the thirty-fourth year of his age. The news of Germanicus's death was received at Rome with universal lamentation; and all ranks of the people entertained an opinion, that, had he survived Tiberius, he would have restored the freedom of the republic. The love and gratitude of the Romans decreed many honours to his memory. It was ordered, that his name should be sung in a solemn procession of the Salii; that crowns of oak, in allusion to his victories, should be placed upon curule chairs in the hall pertaining to the priests of Augustus; and that an effigy of him in ivory should be drawn upon a chariot, preceding the ceremonies of the Circensian games. Triumphal arches were erected, one at Rome, another on the banks of the Rhine, and a third upon Mount Amanus in Syria, with inscriptions of his achievements, and that he died for his services to the republic. 376

His obsequies were celebrated, not with the display of images and funeral pomp, but with the recital of his praises and the virtues which rendered him illustrious. From a resemblance in his personal accomplishments, his age, the manner of his death, and the vicinity of Daphne to Babylon, many compared his fate to that of Alexander the Great. He was celebrated for humanity and benevolence, as well as military talents, and amidst the toils of war, found leisure to cultivate the arts of literary genius. He composed two comedies in Greek, some epigrams, and a translation of Aratus into Latin verse. He married Agrippina, the daughter of M. Agrippa, by whom he had nine children. This lady, who had accompanied her husband into the east, carried his ashes to Italy, and accused his murderer, Piso; who, unable to bear up against the public odium incurred by that transaction, laid violent hands upon himself. Agrippina was now nearly in the same predicament with regard to Tiberius, that Ovid had formerly been in respect of Augustus. He was sensible, that when she accused Piso, she was not ignorant of the person by whom the perpetrator of the murder had been instigated; and her presence, therefore, seeming continually to reproach him with his guilt, he resolved to rid himself of a person become so obnoxious to his sight, and banished her to the island of Pandataria, where she died some time afterwards of famine.

But it was not sufficient to gratify this sanguinary tyrant, that he had, without any cause, cut off both Germanicus and his wife Agrippina: the distinguished merits and popularity of that prince were yet to be revenged upon his children; and accordingly he (244) set himself to invent a pretext for their destruction. After endeavouring in vain, by various artifices, to provoke the resentment of Nero and Drusus against him, he had recourse to false accusation, and not only charged them with seditious designs, to which their tender years were ill adapted, but with vices of a nature the most scandalous. By a sentence of the senate, which manifested the extreme servility of that assembly, he procured them both to be declared open enemies to their country. Nero he banished to the island of Pontia, where, like his unfortunate mother, he miserably perished by famine; and Drusus was doomed to the same fate, in the lower part of the Palatium, after suffering for nine days the violence of hunger, and having, as is related, devoured part of his bed. The remaining son, Caius, on account of his vicious disposition, he resolved to appoint his successor on the throne, that, after his own death, a comparison might be made in favour of his memory, when the Romans should be governed by a sovereign yet more vicious and more tyrannical, if possible, than himself.

Sejanus, the minister in the present reign, imitated with success, for some time, the hypocrisy of his master; and, had his ambitious temper, impatient of attaining its object, allowed him to wear the mask for a longer period, he might have gained the imperial diadem; in the pursuit of which he was overtaken by that fate which he merited still more by his cruelties than his perfidy to Tiberius. This man was a native of Volsinium in Tuscany, and the son of a Roman knight. He had first insinuated himself into the favour of Caius Caesar, the grandson of Augustus, after whose death he courted the friendship of Tiberius, and obtained in a short time his entire confidence, which he improved to the best advantage. The object which he next pursued, was to gain the attachment of the senate, and the officers of the army; besides whom, with a new kind of policy, he endeavoured to secure in his interest every lady of distinguished connections, by giving secretly to each of them a promise of marriage, as soon as he should arrive at the sovereignty. The chief obstacles in his way were the sons and grandsons of Tiberius; and these he soon sacrificed to his ambition, under various pretences. Drusus, the eldest of this progeny, having in a fit of passion struck the favourite, was destined by him to destruction. For this purpose, he had the presumption to seduce Livia, the wife of Drusus, to whom she had borne several children; and she consented to marry her adulterer upon the death of her husband, who was soon after poisoned, through the means of an eunuch named Lygdus, by order of her and Sejanus.

Drusus was the son of Tiberius by Vipsania, one of Agrippa's (245) daughters. He displayed great intrepidity during the war in the provinces of Illyricum and Pannonia, but appears to have been dissolute in his morals. Horace is said to have written the Ode in praise of Drusus at the desire of Augustus; and while the poet celebrates the military courage of the prince, he insinuates indirectly a salutary admonition to the cultivation of the civil virtues:

*Doctrina sed vim promovet insitam,*
*Rectique cultus pectora roborant:*
*Utcunque defecere mores,*
*Dedecorant bene nata culpae. – Ode iv. 4.*
*Yet sage instructions to refine the soul*
*And raise the genius, wondrous aid impart,*
*Conveying inward, as they purely roll,*
*Strength to the mind and vigour to the heart:*
*When morals fail, the stains of vice disgrace*
*The fairest honours of the noblest race. – Francis.*

Upon the death of Drusus, Sejanus openly avowed a desire of marrying the widowed princess; but Tiberius opposing this measure, and at the same time recommending Germanicus to the senate as his successor in the empire, the mind of Sejanus was more than ever inflamed by the united, and now furious, passions of love and ambition. He therefore urged his demand with increased importunity; but the emperor still refusing his consent, and things being not yet ripe for an immediate revolt, Sejanus thought nothing so favourable for the prosecution of his designs as the absence of Tiberius from the capital. With this view, under the pretence of relieving his master from the cares of government, he persuaded him to retire to a distance from Rome. The emperor, indolent and luxurious, approved of the proposal, and retired into Campania, leaving to his ambitious minister the whole direction of the empire. Had Sejanus now been governed by common prudence and moderation, he might have attained to the accomplishment of all his wishes; but a natural impetuosity of temper, and the intoxication of power, precipitated him into measures which soon effected his destruction. As if entirely emancipated from the control of a master, he publicly declared himself sovereign of the Roman empire, and that Tiberius, who had by this time retired to Capri, was only the dependent prince of that tributary island. He even went so far in degrading the emperor, as to have him introduced in a ridiculous light upon the stage. Advice of Sejanus's proceedings was soon carried to the emperor at Capri; his indignation was immediately excited; and with a confidence founded upon an authority exercised for several years, he sent orders for accusing Sejanus (246) before the senate. This mandate no sooner arrived, than the audacious minister was deserted by his adherents; he was in a short time after seized without resistance, and strangled in prison the same day.

Human nature recoils with horror at the cruelties of this execrable tyrant, who, having first imbrued his hands in the blood of his own relations, proceeded to exercise them upon the public with indiscriminate fury. Neither age nor sex afforded any exemption from his insatiable thirst for blood. Innocent children were condemned to death, and butchered in the presence of their parents; virgins, without any imputed guilt, were sacrificed to a similar destiny; but there being an ancient custom of not strangling females in that situation, they were first deflowered by the executioner, and afterwards strangled, as if an atrocious addition to cruelty could sanction the exercise of it. Fathers were constrained by violence to witness the death of their own children; and even the tears of a mother, at the execution of her child, were punished as a capital offence. Some extraordinary calamities, occasioned by accident, added to the horrors of the reign. A great number of houses on Mount Caelius were destroyed by fire; and by the fall of a temporary building at Fidenae, erected for the purpose of exhibiting public shows, about twenty thousand persons were either greatly hurt, or crushed to death in the rains.

By another fire which afterwards broke out, a part of the Circus was destroyed, with the numerous buildings on Mount Aventine. The only act of munificence displayed by Tiberius during his reign, was upon the occasion of those fires, when, to qualify the severity of his government, he indemnified the most considerable sufferers for the loss they had sustained.

Through the whole of his life, Tiberius seems to have conducted himself with a uniform repugnance to nature. Affable on a few occasions, but in general averse to society, he indulged, from his earliest years, a moroseness of disposition, which counterfeited the appearance of austere virtue; and in the decline of life, when it is common to reform from juvenile indiscretions, he launched forth into excesses, of a kind the most unnatural and most detestable. Considering the vicious passions which had ever brooded in his heart, it may seem surprising that he restrained himself within the bounds of decency during so many years after his accession; but though utterly destitute of reverence or affection for his mother, he still felt, during her life, a filial awe upon his mind: and after her death, he was actuated by a slavish fear of Sejanus, until at last political necessity absolved him likewise from this restraint. These checks being both removed, (247) he rioted without any control, either from sentiment or authority.

Pliny relates, that the art of making glass malleable was actually discovered under the reign of Tiberius, and that the shop and tools of the artist were destroyed, lest, by the establishment of this invention, gold and silver should lose their value. Dion adds, that the author of the discovery was put to death.

The gloom which darkened the Roman capital during this melancholy period, shed a baleful influence on the progress of science throughout the empire, and literature languished during the present reign, in the same proportion as it had flourished in the preceding. It is doubtful whether such a change might not have happened in some degree, even had the government of Tiberius been equally mild with that of his predecessor. The prodigious fame of the writers of the Augustan age, by repressing emulation, tended to a general diminution of the efforts of genius for some time; while the banishment of Ovid, it is probable, and the capital punishment of a subsequent poet, for censuring the character of Agamemnon, operated towards the farther discouragement of poetical exertions. There now existed no circumstance to counterbalance these disadvantages. Genius no longer found a patron either in the emperor or his minister; and the gates of the palace were shut against all who cultivated the elegant pursuits of the Muses. Panders, catamites, assassins, wretches stained with every crime, were the constant attendants, as the only fit companions, of the tyrant who now occupied the throne. We are informed, however, that even this emperor had a taste for the liberal arts, and that he composed a lyric poem upon the death of Lucius Caesar, with some Greek poems in imitation of Euphorion, Rhianus, and Parthenius. But none of these has been transmitted to posterity: and if we should form an opinion of them upon the principle of Catullus, that to be a good poet one ought to be a good man, there is little reason to regret that they have perished.

We meet with no poetical production in this reign; and of prose writers the number is inconsiderable, as will appear from the following account of them.— —

VELLEIUS PATERCULUS was born of an equestrian family in Campania, and served as a military tribune under Tiberius, in his expeditions in Gaul and Germany. He composed an Epitome of the History of Greece and Rome, with that of other nations of remote antiquity: but of this work there only remain fragments of the history of Greece and Rome, from the conquest of Perseus to the seventeenth year of the reign of Tiberius. It is written in two books, addressed to Marcus Vinicius, who had (248) the office of consul. Rapid in the narrative, and concise as well as elegant in style, this production exhibits a pleasing epitome of ancient transactions, enlivened occasionally with anecdotes, and an expressive description of characters. In treating of the family of Augustus, Paterculus is justly liable to the imputation of partiality, which he incurs still more in the latter period of his history, by the praise which is lavished on Tiberius and his minister Sejanus. He intimates a design of giving a more full account of the civil war which followed the death of Julius Caesar; but this, if he ever accomplished it, has not been transmitted to posterity.

Candid, but decided in his judgment of motives and actions, if we except his invectives against Pompey, he shows little propensity to censure; but in awarding praise, he is not equally parsimonious, and, on some occasions, risks the imputation of hyperbole. The grace, however, and the apparent sincerity with which it is bestowed, reconcile us to the compliment. This author concludes his history with a prayer for the prosperity of the Roman empire.— —

VALERIUS MAXIMUS was descended of a Patrician family; but we learn nothing more concerning him, than that for some time he followed a military life under Sextus Pompey. He afterwards betook himself to writing, and has left an account, in nine books, of the memorable apophthegms and actions of eminent persons; first of the Romans, and afterwards of foreign nations. The subjects are of various kinds, political, moral, and natural, ranged into distinct classes. His transitions from one subject to another are often performed with gracefulness; and where he offers any remarks, they generally show the author to be a man of judgment and observation. Valerius Maximus is chargeable with no affectation of style, but is sometimes deficient in that purity of language which might be expected in the age of Tiberius, to whom the work is addressed. What inducement the author had to this dedication, we know not; but as it is evident from a passage in the ninth book, that the compliment was paid after the death of Sejanus, and consequently in the most shameful period of Tiberius's reign, we cannot entertain any high opinion of the independent spirit of Valerius Maximus, who could submit to flatter a tyrant, in the zenith of infamy and detestation. But we cannot ascribe the cause to any delicate artifice, of conveying to Tiberius, indirectly, an admonition to reform his conduct. Such an expedient would have only provoked the severest resentment from his jealousy.— —

PHAEDRUS was a native of Thrace, and was brought to Rome as a slave. He had the good fortune to come into the service of Augustus, where, improving his talents by reading, he obtained (249) the favour of the emperor, and was made one of his freedmen. In the reign of Tiberius, he translated into Iambic verse the Fables of Aesop. They are divided into five books, and are not less conspicuous for precision and simplicity of thought, than for purity and elegance of style;

conveying moral sentiments with unaffected ease and impressive energy. Phaedrus underwent, for some time, a persecution from Sejanus, who, conscious of his own delinquency, suspected that he was obliquely satirised in the commendations bestowed on virtue by the poet. The work of Phaedrus is one of the latest which have been brought to light since the revival of learning. It remained in obscurity until two hundred years ago, when it was discovered in a library at Rheims.——

HYGINUS is said to have been a native of Alexandria, or, according to others, a Spaniard. He was, like Phaedrus, a freedman of Augustus; but, though industrious, he seems not to have improved himself so much as his companion, in the art of composition. He wrote, however, a mythological history, under the title of Fables, a work called Poeticon Astronomicon, with a treatise on agriculture, commentaries on Virgil, the lives of eminent men, and some other productions now lost. His remaining works are much mutilated, and, if genuine, afford an unfavourable specimen of his elegance and correctness as a writer.

CELSUS was a physician in the time of Tiberius, and has written eight books, De Medicina, in which he has collected and digested into order all that is valuable on the subject, in the Greek and Roman authors. The professors of Medicine were at that time divided into three sects, viz., the Dogmatists, Empirics, and Methodists; the first of whom deviated less than the others from the plan of Hippocrates; but they were in general irreconcilable to each other, in respect both of their opinions and practice. Celsus, with great judgment, has occasionally adopted particular doctrines from each of them; and whatever he admits into his system, he not only establishes by the most rational observations, but confirms by its practical utility. In justness of remark, in force of argument, in precision and perspicuity, as well as in elegance of expression, he deservedly occupies the most distinguished rank amongst the medical writers of antiquity. It appears that Celsus likewise wrote on agriculture, rhetoric, and military affairs; but of those several treatises no fragments now remain.

To the writers of this reign we must add APICIUS COELIUS, who has left a book De Re Coquinaria [of Cookery]. There were three Romans of the name of Apicius, all remarkable for their gluttony. The first lived in the time of the Republic, the last in that of Trajan, and the intermediate Apicius under the emperors Augustus and Tiberius. This man, as Seneca informs us, wasted on luxurious living, sexcenties sestertium, a sum equal to 484,375 pounds sterling. Upon examining the state of his affairs, he found that there remained no more of his estate than centies sestertium, 80,729l. 3s. 4d., which seeming to him too small to live upon, he ended his days by poison.

# CAIUS CAESAR CALIGULA.

(251)

I. Germanicus, the father of Caius Caesar, and son of Drusus and the younger Antonia, was, after his adoption by Tiberius, his uncle, preferred to the quaestorship 377 five years before he had attained the legal age, and immediately upon the expiration of that office, to the consulship 378 . Having been sent to the army in Germany, he restored order among the legions, who, upon the news of Augustus's death, obstinately refused to acknowledge Tiberius as emperor 379 , and offered to place him at the head of the state. In which affair it is difficult to say, whether his regard to filial duty, or the firmness of his resolution, was most conspicuous. Soon afterwards he defeated the enemy, and obtained the honours of a triumph. Being then made consul for the second time 380 , before he could enter upon his office he was obliged to set out suddenly for the east, where, after he had conquered the king of Armenia, and reduced Cappadocia into the form of a province, he died at Antioch, of a lingering distemper, in the thirty-fourth year of his age 381 , not without the suspicion of being poisoned. For besides the livid spots which appeared all over his body, and a foaming at the mouth; when his corpse was burnt, the heart was found entire among the bones; its nature being such, as it is supposed, that when tainted by poison, it is indestructible by fire. 382

II. It was a prevailing opinion, that he was taken off by the contrivance of Tiberius, and through the means of Cneius Piso. This person, who was about the same time prefect of Syria, and made no secret of his position being such, that (252) he must either offend the father or the son, loaded Germanicus, even during his sickness, with the most unbounded and scurrilous abuse, both by word and deed; for which, upon his return to Rome, he narrowly escaped being torn to pieces by the people, and was condemned to death by the senate.

III. It is generally agreed, that Germanicus possessed all the noblest endowments of body and mind in a higher degree than had ever before fallen to the lot of any man; a handsome person, extraordinary courage, great proficiency in eloquence and other branches of learning, both Greek and Roman; besides a singular humanity, and a behaviour so engaging, as to captivate the affections of all about him. The slenderness of his legs did not correspond with the symmetry and beauty of his person in other respects; but this defect was at length corrected by his habit of riding after meals. In battle, he often engaged and slew an enemy in single combat. He pleaded causes, even after he had the honour of a triumph. Among other fruits of his studies, he left behind him some Greek comedies. Both at home and abroad he always conducted himself in a manner the most unassuming. On entering any free and confederate town, he never would be attended by his lictors. Whenever he heard, in his travels, of the tombs of illustrious men, he made offerings over them to the infernal deities. He gave a common grave, under a mound of earth, to the scattered relics of the legionaries slain under Varus, and was the first to put his hand to the work of collecting and bringing them to the place of burial. He was so extremely mild and gentle to his enemies, whoever they were, or on what account soever they bore him enmity, that, although Piso rescinded his decrees, and for a long time severely harassed his dependents, he never showed the smallest resentment, until he found himself attacked by magical charms and imprecations; and even then the only steps he took was to renounce all friendship with him, according to ancient custom, and to exhort his servants to avenge his death, if any thing untoward should befall him.

IV. He reaped the fruit of his noble qualities in abundance, being so much esteemed and beloved by his friends, that Augustus (to say nothing of his other relations) being a long time in doubt, whether he should not appoint him his successor, at last ordered Tiberius to adopt him. He was so extremely popular, that many authors tell us, the crowds of those who went to meet him upon his coming to any place, or to attend him at his departure, were so prodigious, that he was sometimes in danger of his life; and that upon his return from Germany, after he had quelled the mutiny in the army there, all the cohorts of the pretorian guards marched out to meet him, notwithstanding the order that only two should go; and that all the people of Rome, both men and women, of every age, sex, and rank, flocked as far as the twentieth milestone to attend his entrance.

V. At the time of his death, however, and afterwards, they displayed still greater and stronger proofs of their extraordinary attachment to him. The day on which he died, stones were thrown at the temples, the altars of the gods demolished, the household gods, in some cases, thrown into the streets, and new-born infants exposed. It is even said that barbarous nations, both those engaged in intestine wars, and those in hostilities against us, all agreed to a cessation of arms, as if they had been mourning for some very near and common friend; that some petty kings shaved their beards and their wives' heads, in token of their extreme sorrow; and that the king of kings 383 forbore his exercise of hunting and feasting with his nobles, which, amongst the Parthians, is equivalent to a cessation of all business in a time of public mourning with us.

VI. At Rome, upon the first news of his sickness, the city was thrown into great consternation and grief, waiting impatiently for farther intelligence; when suddenly, in the evening, a report, without any certain author, was spread, that he was recovered; upon which the people flocked with torches (254) and victims to the Capitol, and were in such haste to pay the vows they had made for his recovery, that they almost broke open the doors. Tiberius was roused from out of his sleep with the noise of the people congratulating one another, and singing about the streets,

*Salva Roma, salva patria, salvus est Germanicus.*

*Rome is safe, our country safe, for our Germanicus is safe.*

But when certain intelligence of his death arrived, the mourning of the people could neither be assuaged by consolation, nor restrained by edicts, and it continued during the holidays in the month of December. The atrocities of the subsequent times contributed much to the glory of Germanicus, and the endearment of his memory; all people supposing, and with reason, that the fear and awe of him had laid a restraint upon the cruelty of Tiberius, which broke out soon afterwards.

VII. Germanicus married Agrippina, the daughter of Marcus Agrippa and Julia, by whom he had nine children, two of whom died in their infancy, and another a few years after; a sprightly boy, whose effigy, in the character of a Cupid, Livia set up in the temple of Venus in the Capitol. Augustus also placed another statue of him in his bedchamber, and used to kiss it as often as he entered the apartment. The rest survived their father; three daughters, Agrippina, Drusilla, and Livilla, who were born in three successive years; and as many sons, Nero, Drusus, and Caius Caesar. Nero and Drusus, at the accusation of Tiberius, were declared public enemies.

VIII. Caius Caesar was born on the day before the calends [31st August] of September, at the time his father and Caius Fonteius Capito were consuls 384. But where he was born, is rendered uncertain from the number of places which are said to have given him birth. Cneius Lentulus Gaetulicus 385 says that he was born at Tibur; Pliny the younger, in the country of the Treviri, at a village called Ambiatinus, above Confluentes 386; and he alleges, as a proof of it, that altars are there shown with this inscription: "For Agrippina's child-birth." Some verses which were published in his reign, intimate that he was born in the winter quarters of the legions,

*In castris natus, patriis nutritius in armis,*
*Jam designati principis omen erat.*
*Born in the camp, and train'd in every toil*
*Which taught his sire the haughtiest foes to foil;*
*Destin'd he seem'd by fate to raise his name,*
*And rule the empire with Augustan fame.*

I find in the public registers that he was born at Antium. Pliny charges Gaetulicus as guilty of an arrant forgery, merely to soothe the vanity of a conceited young prince, by giving him the lustre of being born in a city sacred to Hercules; and says that he advanced this false assertion with the more assurance, because, the year before the birth of Caius, Germanicus had a son of the same name born at Tibur; concerning whose amiable childhood and premature death I have already spoken 387. Dates clearly prove that Pliny is mistaken; for the writers of Augustus's history all agree, that Germanicus, at the expiration of his consulship, was sent into Gaul, after the birth of Caius. Nor will the inscription upon the altar serve to establish Pliny's opinion; because Agrippina was delivered of two daughters in that country, and any child-birth, without regard to sex, is called puerperium, as the ancients were used to call girls puerae, and boys puelli. There is also extant a letter written by Augustus, a few months before his death, to his granddaughter Agrippina, about the same Caius (for there was then no other child of hers living under that name). He writes as follows: "I gave orders yesterday for Talarius and Asellius to set out on their journey towards you, if the gods permit, with your child Caius, upon the fifteenth of the calends of June [18th May]. I also send with him a physician of mine, and I wrote to Germanicus that he may retain him if he pleases. Farewell, my dear Agrippina, and take what care you can to (256) come safe and well to your Germanicus." I imagine it is sufficiently evident that Caius could not be born at a place to which he was carried from The City when almost two years old. The same considerations must likewise invalidate the evidence of the verses, and the rather, because the author is unknown. The only authority, therefore, upon which we can depend in this matter, is that of the acts, and the public register; especially as he always preferred Antium to every other place of retirement, and entertained for it all that fondness which is commonly attached to one's native soil. It is said, too, that, upon his growing weary of the city, he designed to have transferred thither the seat of empire.

IX. It was to the jokes of the soldiers in the camp that he owed the name of Caligula 388, he having been brought up among them in the dress of a common soldier. How much his education amongst them recommended him to their favour and affection, was sufficiently apparent in the mutiny upon the death of Augustus, when the mere sight of him appeased their fury, though it had risen to a great height. For they persisted in it, until they observed that he was sent away to a neighbouring city 389, to secure him against all danger. Then, at last, they began to relent, and, stopping the chariot in which he was conveyed, earnestly deprecated the odium to which such a proceeding would expose them.

X. He likewise attended his father in his expedition to Syria. After his return, he lived first with his mother, and, when she was banished, with his great-grandmother, Livia Augusta, in praise of whom, after her decease, though then only a boy, he pronounced a funeral oration in the Rostra. He was then transferred to the family of his grandmother, Antonia, and afterwards, in the twentieth year of his age, being called by Tiberius to Capri, he in one and the same day assumed the manly habit, and shaved his beard, but without receiving any of the honours which had been paid to his brothers on a similar (257) occasion. While he remained in that island, many insidious artifices were practised, to extort from him complaints against Tiberius, but by his circumspection he avoided falling into the snare 390 . He affected to take no more notice of the ill-treatment of his relations, than if nothing had befallen them. With regard to his own sufferings, he seemed utterly insensible of them, and behaved with such obsequiousness to his grandfather 391 and all about him, that it was justly said of him, "There never was a better servant, nor a worse master."

XI. But he could not even then conceal his natural disposition to cruelty and lewdness. He delighted in witnessing the infliction of punishments, and frequented taverns and bawdy-houses in the night-time, disguised in a periwig and a long coat; and was passionately addicted to the theatrical arts of singing and dancing. All these levities Tiberius readily connived at, in hopes that they might perhaps correct the roughness of his temper, which the sagacious old man so well understood, that he often said, "That Caius was destined to be the ruin of himself and all mankind; and that he was rearing a hydra 392 for the people of Rome, and a Phaeton for all the world." 393

XII. Not long afterwards, he married Junia Claudilla, the daughter of Marcus Silanus, a man of the highest rank. Being then chosen augur in the room of his brother Drusus, before he could be inaugurated he was advanced to the pontificate, with no small commendation of his dutiful behaviour, and great capacity. The situation of the court likewise was at this time favourable to his fortunes, as it was now left destitute of support, Sejanus being suspected, and soon afterwards taken off; and he was by degrees flattered with the hope of succeeding Tiberius in the empire. In order more effectually to secure this object, upon Junia's dying in child-bed, he engaged in a criminal commerce with Ennia Naevia, the wife (258) of Macro, at that time prefect of the pretorian cohorts; promising to marry her if he became emperor, to which he bound himself, not only by an oath, but by a written obligation under his hand. Having by her means insinuated himself into Macro's favour, some are of opinion that he attempted to poison Tiberius, and ordered his ring to be taken from him, before the breath was out of his body; and that, because he seemed to hold it fast, he caused a pillow to be thrown upon him 394 , squeezing him by the throat, at the same time, with his own hand. One of his freedmen crying out at this horrid barbarity, he was immediately crucified. These circumstances are far from being improbable, as some authors relate that, afterwards, though he did not acknowledge his having a hand in the death of Tiberius, yet he frankly declared that he had formerly entertained such a design; and as a proof of his affection for his relations, he would frequently boast, "That, to revenge the death of his mother and brothers, he had entered the chamber of Tiberius, when he was asleep, with a poniard, but being seized with a fit of compassion, threw it away, and retired; and that Tiberius, though aware of his intention, durst not make any inquiries, or attempt revenge."

XIII. Having thus secured the imperial power, he fulfilled by his elevation the wish of the Roman people, I may venture to say, of all mankind; for he had long been the object of expectation and desire to the greater part of the provincials and soldiers, who had known him when a child; and to the whole people of Rome, from their affection for the memory of Germanicus, his father, and compassion for the family almost entirely destroyed. Upon his moving from Misenum, therefore, although he was in mourning, and following the corpse of Tiberius, he had to walk amidst altars, victims, and lighted torches, with prodigious crowds of people everywhere attending him, in transports of joy, and calling him, besides other auspicious names, by those of "their star," "their chick," "their pretty puppet," and "bantling."

XIV. Immediately on his entering the city, by the joint acclamations of the senate, and people, who broke into the senate-house, Tiberius's will was set aside, it having left his (259) other grandson 395 , then a minor, coheir with him, the whole government and administration of affairs was placed in his hands; so much to the joy and satisfaction of the public, that, in less than three months after, above a hundred and sixty thousand victims are said to have been offered in sacrifice. Upon his going, a few days afterwards, to the nearest islands on the coast of Campania 396 , vows were made for his safe return; every person emulously testifying their care and concern for his safety. And when he fell ill, the people hung about the Palatium all night long; some vowed, in public handbills, to risk their lives in the combats of the amphitheatre, and others to lay them down, for his recovery. To this extraordinary love entertained for him by his countrymen, was added an uncommon regard by foreign nations. Even Artabanus, king of the Parthians, who had always manifested hatred and contempt for Tiberius, solicited his friendship; came to hold a conference with his consular lieutenant, and passing the Euphrates, paid the highest honours to the eagles, the Roman standards, and the images of the Caesars. 397

XV. Caligula himself inflamed this devotion, by practising all the arts of popularity. After he had delivered, with floods of tears, a speech in praise of Tiberius, and buried him with the utmost pomp, he immediately hastened over to Pandataria and the Pontian islands 398 , to bring thence the ashes of his mother and brother; and, to testify the great regard he had for their memory, he performed the voyage in a very tempestuous season. He approached their remains with profound veneration, and deposited them in the urns with his own hands. Having brought them in grand solemnity to Ostia 399 , with an ensign flying in the stern of the galley, and thence up the Tiber to Rome, they were borne by persons of the first distinction in the equestrian order, on two biers, into the mausoleum 400 , (260) at noon-day. He appointed yearly offerings to be solemnly and publicly celebrated to their memory, besides Circensian games to that of his mother, and a chariot with her image to be included in the procession 401 . The month of September he called Germanicus, in honour of his father. By a single decree of the senate, he heaped upon his grandmother, Antonia, all the honours which had been ever conferred on the empress Livia. His uncle, Claudius, who till then continued in the equestrian order, he took for his colleague in the consulship. He adopted his brother, Tiberius 402 , on the day he took upon him the manly habit, and conferred upon him the title of "Prince of the Youths." As for his sisters, he ordered these words to be added to the oaths of allegiance to himself: "Nor will I hold myself or my own children more dear than I do Caius and his sisters:" 403 and commanded all resolutions proposed by the consuls in the senate to be prefaced thus: "May what we are going to do, prove fortunate and happy to Caius Caesar and his sisters." With the like popularity he restored all those who had been condemned and banished, and granted an act of indemnity against all impeachments and past offences. To relieve the informers and witnesses against his mother and brothers from all apprehension, he brought the records of their trials into the forum, and there burnt them, calling loudly on the gods to witness that he had not read or handled them. A memorial which was offered him relative to his own security, he would not receive, declaring, "that he had done nothing to make any one his enemy:" and said, at the same time, "he had no ears for informers."

XVI. The Spintriae, those panderers to unnatural lusts 404 , he banished from the city, being prevailed upon not to throw them (261) into the sea, as he had intended. The writings of Titus Labienus, Cordus Cremutius, and Cassius Severus, which had been suppressed by an act of the senate, he permitted to be drawn from obscurity, and universally read; observing, "that it would be for his own advantage to have the transactions of former times delivered to posterity." He published accounts of the proceedings of the government—a practice which had been introduced by Augustus, but discontinued by Tiberius 405 . He granted the magistrates a full and free jurisdiction, without any appeal to himself. He made a very strict and exact review of the Roman knights, but conducted it with moderation; publicly depriving of his horse every knight who lay under the stigma of any thing base and dishonourable; but passing over the names of those knights who were only guilty of venial faults, in calling over the list of the order. To lighten the labours of the judges, he added a fifth class to the former four. He attempted likewise to restore to the people their ancient right of voting in the choice of magistrates 406 . He paid very honourably, and without any dispute, the legacies left by Tiberius in his will, though it had been set aside; as likewise those left by the will of Livia Augusta, which Tiberius had annulled. He remitted the hundredth penny, due to the government in all auctions throughout Italy. He made up to many their losses sustained by fire; and when he restored their kingdoms to any princes, he likewise allowed them all the arrears of the taxes and revenues which had accrued in the interval; as in the case of Antiochus of Comagene, where the confiscation would have amounted to a hundred millions of sesterces. To prove to the world that he was ready to encourage good examples of every kind, he gave to a freed-woman eighty thousand sesterces, for not discovering a crime committed by her patron, though she had been put to exquisite torture for that purpose. For all these acts of beneficence, amongst other honours, a golden shield was decreed to him, which the colleges of priests were to carry annually, upon a fixed day, into the Capitol, with the senate attending, and the youth of the nobility, of both sexes, celebrating the praise of his virtues in (262) songs. It was likewise ordained, that the day on which he succeeded to the empire should be called Palilia, in token of the city's being at that time, as it were, new founded. 407

XVII. He held the consulship four times; the first 408, from the calends [the first] of July for two months: the second 409, from the calends of January for thirty days; the third 410, until the ides [the 13th] of January; and the fourth [411], until the seventh of the same ides [7th January]. Of these, the two last he held successively. The third he assumed by his sole authority at Lyons; not, as some are of opinion, from arrogance or neglect of rules; but because, at that distance, it was impossible for him to know that his colleague had died a little before the beginning of the new year. He twice distributed to the people a bounty of three hundred sesterces a man, and as often gave a splendid feast to the senate and the equestrian order, with their wives and children. In the latter, he presented to the men forensic garments, and to the women and children purple scarfs. To make a perpetual addition to the public joy for ever, he added to the Saturnalia 412 one day, which he called Juvenalis [the juvenile feast].

XVIII. He exhibited some combats of gladiators, either in the amphitheatre of Taurus 413, or in the Septa, with which he intermingled troops of the best pugilists from Campania and Africa. He did not always preside in person upon those occasions, but sometimes gave a commission to magistrates or friends to supply his place. He frequently entertained the people with stage-plays (263) of various kinds, and in several parts of the city, and sometimes by night, when he caused the whole city to be lighted. He likewise gave various things to be scrambled for among the people, and distributed to every man a basket of bread with other victuals. Upon this occasion, he sent his own share to a Roman knight, who was seated opposite to him, and was enjoying himself by eating heartily. To a senator, who was doing the same, he sent an appointment of praetor-extraordinary. He likewise exhibited a great number of Circensian games from morning until night; intermixed with the hunting of wild beasts from Africa, or the Trojan exhibition. Some of these games were celebrated with peculiar circumstances; the Circus being overspread with vermilion and chrysolite; and none drove in the chariot races who were not of the senatorian order. For some of these he suddenly gave the signal, when, upon his viewing from the Gelotiana 414 the preparations in the Circus, he was asked to do so by a few persons in the neighbouring galleries.

XIX. He invented besides a new kind of spectacle, such as had never been heard of before. For he made a bridge, of about three miles and a half in length, from Baiae to the mole of Puteoli 415 , collecting trading vessels from all quarters, mooring them in two rows by their anchors, and spreading earth upon them to form a viaduct, after the fashion of the Appian Way 416 . This bridge he crossed and recrossed for two days together; the first day mounted on a horse richly caparisoned, wearing on his head a crown of oak leaves, armed with a battle-axe, a Spanish buckler and a sword, and in a cloak made of cloth of gold; the day following, in the habit of a charioteer, standing in a chariot, drawn by two high-bred horses, having with him a young boy, Darius by name, one of the Parthian hostages, with a cohort of the pretorian guards attending him, and a (264) party of his friends in cars of Gaulish make 417 . Most people, I know, are of opinion, that this bridge was designed by Caius, in imitation of Xerxes, who, to the astonishment of the world, laid a bridge over the Hellespont, which is somewhat narrower than the distance betwixt Baiae and Puteoli. Others, however, thought that he did it to strike terror in Germany and Britain, which he was upon the point of invading, by the fame of some prodigious work. But for myself, when I was a boy, I heard my grandfather say 418 , that the reason assigned by some courtiers who were in habits of the greatest intimacy with him, was this; when Tiberius was in some anxiety about the nomination of a successor, and rather inclined to pitch upon his grandson, Thrasyllus the astrologer had assured him, "That Caius would no more be emperor, than he would ride on horseback across the gulf of Baiae."

XX. He likewise exhibited public diversions in Sicily, Grecian games at Syracuse, and Attic plays at Lyons in Gaul besides a contest for pre-eminence in the Grecian and Roman eloquence; in which we are told that such as were baffled bestowed rewards upon the best performers, and were obliged to compose speeches in their praise: but that those who performed the worst, were forced to blot out what they had written with a sponge or their tongue, unless they preferred to be beaten with a rod, or plunged over head and ears into the nearest river.

XXI. He completed the works which were left unfinished by Tiberius, namely, the temple of Augustus, and the theatre (265) of Pompey 419 . He began, likewise, the aqueduct from the neighbourhood of Tibur 420 , and an amphitheatre near the Septa 421 ; of which works, one was completed by his successor Claudius, and the other remained as he left it. The walls of Syracuse, which had fallen to decay by length of time, he repaired, as he likewise did the temples of the gods. He formed plans for rebuilding the palace of Polycrates at Samos, finishing the temple of the Didymaean Apollo at Miletus, and building a town on a ridge of the Alps; but, above all, for cutting through the isthmus in Achaia 422 ; and even sent a centurion of the first rank to measure out the work.

XXII. Thus far we have spoken of him as a prince. What remains to be said of him, bespeaks him rather a monster than a man. He assumed a variety of titles, such as "Dutiful," "The (266) Pious," "The Child of the Camp, the Father of the Armies," and "The Greatest and Best Caesar." Upon hearing some kings, who came to the city to pay him court, conversing together at supper, about their illustrious descent, he exclaimed,

*Eis koiranos eto, eis basileus.*

*Let there be but one prince, one king.*

He was strongly inclined to assume the diadem, and change the form of government, from imperial to regal; but being told that he far exceeded the grandeur of kings and princes, he began to arrogate to himself a divine majesty. He ordered all the images of the gods, which were famous either for their beauty, or the veneration paid them, among which was that of Jupiter Olympius, to be brought from Greece, that he might take the heads off, and put on his own. Having continued part of the Palatium as far as the Forum, and the temple of Castor and Pollux being converted into a kind of vestibule to his house, he often stationed himself between the twin brothers, and so presented himself to be worshipped by all votaries; some of whom saluted him by the name of Jupiter Latialis. He also instituted a temple and priests, with choicest victims, in honour of his own divinity. In his temple stood a statue of gold, the exact image of himself, which was daily dressed in garments corresponding with those he wore himself. The most opulent persons in the city offered themselves as candidates for the honour of being his priests, and purchased it successively at an immense price. The victims were flamingos, peacocks, bustards, guinea-fowls, turkey and pheasant hens, each sacrificed on their respective days. On nights when the moon was full, he was in the constant habit of inviting her to his embraces and his bed. In the daytime he talked in private to Jupiter Capitolinus; one while whispering to him, and another turning his ear to him: sometimes he spoke aloud, and in railing language. For he was overheard to threaten the god thus:

> Hae em' anaeir', hae ego se; 423_
> Raise thou me up, or I'll –

(267) until being at last prevailed upon by the entreaties of the god, as he said, to take up his abode with him, he built a bridge over the temple of the Deified Augustus, by which he joined the Palatium to the Capitol. Afterwards, that he might be still nearer, he laid the foundations of a new palace in the very court of the Capitol.

XXIII. He was unwilling to be thought or called the grandson of Agrippa, because of the obscurity of his birth; and he was offended if any one, either in prose or verse, ranked him amongst the Caesars. He said that his mother was the fruit of an incestuous commerce, maintained by Augustus with his daughter Julia. And not content with this vile reflection upon the memory of Augustus, he forbad his victories at Actium, and on the coast of Sicily, to be celebrated, as usual; affirming that they had been most pernicious and fatal to the Roman people. He called his grandmother Livia Augusta "Ulysses in a woman's dress," and had the indecency to reflect upon her in a letter to the senate, as of mean birth, and descended, by the mother's side, from a grandfather who was only one of the municipal magistrates of Fondi; whereas it is certain, from the public records, that Aufidius Lurco held high offices at Rome. His grandmother Antonia desiring a private conference with him, he refused to grant it, unless Macro, the prefect of the pretorian guards, were present. Indignities of this kind, and ill usage, were the cause of her death; but some think he also gave her poison. Nor did he pay the smallest respect to her memory after her death, but witnessed the burning from his private apartment. His brother Tiberius, who had no expectation of any violence, was suddenly dispatched by a military tribune sent by his order for that purpose. He forced Silanus, his father-in-law, to kill himself, by cutting his throat with a razor. The pretext he alleged for these murders was, that the latter had not followed him upon his putting to sea in stormy weather, but stayed behind with the view of seizing the city, if he should perish. The other, he said, smelt of an antidote, which he had taken to prevent his being poisoned by him; whereas Silanus was only afraid of being sea-sick, and the disagreeableness of a voyage; and Tiberius had merely taken a medicine for an habitual cough, (268) which was continually growing worse. As for his successor Claudius, he only saved him for a laughing-stock.

XXIV. He lived in the habit of incest with all his sisters; and at table, when much company was present, he placed each of them in turns below him, whilst his wife reclined above him. It is believed, that he deflowered one of them, Drusilla, before he had assumed the robe of manhood; and was even caught in her embraces by his grandmother Antonia, with whom they were educated together. When she was afterwards married to Cassius Longinus, a man of consular rank, he took her from him, and kept her constantly as if she were his lawful wife. In a fit of sickness, he by his will appointed her heiress both of his estate and the empire. After her death, he ordered a public mourning for her; during which it was capital for any person to laugh, use the bath, or sup with his parents, wife, or children. Being inconsolable under his affliction, he went hastily, and in the night-time, from the City; going through Campania to Syracuse, and then suddenly returned without shaving his beard, or trimming his hair. Nor did he ever afterwards, in matters of the greatest importance, not even in the assemblies of the people or before the soldiers, swear any otherwise, than "By the divinity of Drusilla." The rest of his sisters he did not treat with so much fondness or regard; but frequently prostituted them to his catamites. He therefore the more readily condemned them in the case of Aemilius Lepidus, as guilty of adultery, and privy to that conspiracy against him. Nor did he only divulge their own handwriting relative to the affair, which he procured by base and lewd means, but likewise consecrated to Mars the Avenger three swords which had been prepared to stab him, with an inscription, setting forth the occasion of their consecration.

XXV. Whether in the marriage of his wives, in repudiating them, or retaining them, he acted with greater infamy, it is difficult to say.

Being at the wedding of Caius Piso with Livia Orestilla, he ordered the bride to be carried to his own house, but within a few days divorced her, and two years after banished her; because it was thought, that upon her divorce she returned to the embraces of her former husband. (269) Some say, that being invited to the wedding-supper, he sent a messenger to Piso, who sat opposite to him, in these words: "Do not be too fond with my wife," and that he immediately carried her off. Next day he published a proclamation, importing, "That he had got a wife as Romulus and Augustus had done." 424 Lollia Paulina, who was married to a man of consular rank in command of an army, he suddenly called from the province where she was with her husband, upon mention being made that her grandmother was formerly very beautiful, and married her; but he soon afterwards parted with her, interdicting her from having ever afterwards any commerce with man. He loved with a most passionate and constant affection Caesonia, who was neither handsome nor young; and was besides the mother of three daughters by another man; but a wanton of unbounded lasciviousness. Her he would frequently exhibit to the soldiers, dressed in a military cloak, with shield and helmet, and riding by his side. To his friends he even showed her naked. After she had a child, he honoured her with the title of wife; in one and the same day, declaring himself her husband, and father of the child of which she was delivered. He named it Julia Drusilla, and carrying it round the temples of all the goddesses, laid it on the lap of Minerva; to whom he recommended the care of bringing up and instructing her. He considered her as his own child for no better reason than her savage temper, which was such even in her infancy, that she would attack with her nails the face and eyes of the children at play with her.

XXVI. It would be of little importance, as well as disgusting, to add to all this an account of the manner in which he treated his relations and friends; as Ptolemy, king Juba's son, his cousin (for he was the grandson of Mark Antony by his daughter Selene) 425 , and especially Macro himself, and Ennia likewise 426 , by whose assistance he had obtained the empire; all of whom, for their alliance and eminent services, he rewarded with violent deaths. Nor was he more mild or respectful in his behaviour towards the senate. Some who had borne the (270) highest offices in the government, he suffered to run by his litter in their togas for several miles together, and to attend him at supper, sometimes at the head of his couch, sometimes at his feet, with napkins. Others of them, after he had privately put them to death, he nevertheless continued to send for, as if they were still alive, and after a few days pretended that they had laid violent hands upon themselves. The consuls having forgotten to give public notice of his birth-day, he displaced them; and the republic was three days without any one in that high office. A quaestor who was said to be concerned in a conspiracy against him, he scourged severely, having first stripped off his clothes, and spread them under the feet of the soldiers employed in the work, that they might stand the more firm. The other orders likewise he treated with the same insolence and violence. Being disturbed by the noise of people taking their places at midnight in the circus, as they were to have free admission, he drove them all away with clubs. In this tumult, above twenty Roman knights were squeezed to death, with as many matrons, with a great crowd besides. When stage-plays were acted, to occasion disputes between the people and the knights, he distributed the money-tickets sooner than usual, that the seats assigned to the knights might be all occupied by the mob. In the spectacles of gladiators, sometimes, when the sun was violently hot, he would order the curtains, which covered the amphitheatre, to be drawn aside 427, and forbad any person to be let out; withdrawing at the same time the usual apparatus for the entertainment, and presenting wild beasts almost pined to death, the most sorry gladiators, decrepit with age, and fit only to work the machinery, and decent house-keepers, who were remarkable for some bodily infirmity. Sometimes shutting up the public granaries, he would oblige the people to starve for a while.

XXVII. He evinced the savage barbarity of his temper chiefly by the following indications. When flesh was only to be had at a high price for feeding his wild beasts reserved for the spectacles, he ordered that criminals should be given them (271) to be devoured; and upon inspecting them in a row, while he stood in the middle of the portico, without troubling himself to examine their cases he ordered them to be dragged away, from "bald-pate to bald-pate." 428 Of one person who had made a vow for his recovery to combat with a gladiator, he exacted its performance; nor would he allow him to desist until he came off conqueror, and after many entreaties. Another, who had vowed to give his life for the same cause, having shrunk from the sacrifice, he delivered, adorned as a victim, with garlands and fillets, to boys, who were to drive him through the streets, calling on him to fulfil his vow, until he was thrown headlong from the ramparts. After disfiguring many persons of honourable rank, by branding them in the face with hot irons, he condemned them to the mines, to work in repairing the high-ways, or to fight with wild beasts; or tying them by the neck and heels, in the manner of beasts carried to slaughter, would shut them up in cages, or saw them asunder. Nor were these severities merely inflicted for crimes of great enormity, but for making remarks on his public games, or for not having sworn by the Genius of the emperor. He compelled parents to be present at the execution of their sons; and to one who excused himself on account of indisposition, he sent his own litter. Another he invited to his table immediately after he had witnessed the spectacle, and coolly challenged him to jest and be merry. He ordered the overseer of the spectacles and wild beasts to be scourged in fetters, during several days successively, in his own presence, and did not put him to death until he was disgusted with the stench of his putrefied brain. He burned alive, in the centre of the arena of the amphitheatre, the writer of a farce, for some witty verse, which had a double meaning. A Roman knight, who had been exposed to the wild beasts, crying out that he was innocent, he called him back, and having had his tongue cut out, remanded him to the arena.

XXVIII. Asking a certain person, whom he recalled after a long exile, how he used to spend his time, he replied, with flattery, "I was always praying the gods for what has happened, that Tiberius might die, and you be emperor." Concluding, therefore, that those he had himself banished also (272) prayed for his death, he sent orders round the islands 429 to have them all put to death. Being very desirous to have a senator torn to pieces, he employed some persons to call him a public enemy, fall upon him as he entered the senate-house, stab him with their styles, and deliver him to the rest to tear asunder. Nor was he satisfied, until he saw the limbs and bowels of the man, after they had been dragged through the streets, piled up in a heap before him.

XXIX. He aggravated his barbarous actions by language equally outrageous. "There is nothing in my nature," said he, "that I commend or approve so much, as my adiatrepsia (inflexible rigour)." Upon his grandmother Antonia's giving him some advice, as if it was a small matter to pay no regard to it, he said to her, "Remember that all things are lawful for me." When about to murder his brother, whom he suspected of taking antidotes against poison, he said, "See then an antidote against Caesar!" And when he banished his sisters, he told them in a menacing tone, that he had not only islands at command, but likewise swords. One of pretorian rank having sent several times from Anticyra 430, whither he had gone for his health, to have his leave of absence prolonged, he ordered him to be put to death; adding these words "Bleeding is necessary for one that has taken hellebore so long, and found no benefit." It was his custom every tenth day to sign the lists of prisoners appointed for execution; and this he called "clearing his accounts." And having condemned several Gauls and Greeks at one time, he exclaimed in triumph, "I have conquered Gallograecia." 431

XXX. He generally prolonged the sufferings of his victims by causing them to be inflicted by slight and frequently repeated strokes; this being his well-known and constant order: (273) "Strike so that he may feel himself die." Having punished one person for another, by mistaking his name, he said, "he deserved it quite as much." He had frequently in his mouth these words of the tragedian,

*Oderint dum metuant.* 432

*I scorn their hatred, if they do but fear me.*

He would often inveigh against all the senators without exception, as clients of Sejanus, and informers against his mother and brothers, producing the memorials which he had pretended to burn, and excusing the cruelty of Tiberius as necessary, since it was impossible to question the veracity of such a number of accusers 433. He continually reproached the whole equestrian order, as devoting themselves to nothing but acting on the stage, and fighting as gladiators. Being incensed at the people's applauding a party at the Circensian games in opposition to him, he exclaimed, "I wish the Roman people had but one neck." 434 When Tetrinius, the highwayman, was denounced, he said his persecutors too were all Tetrinius's. Five Retiarii 435, in tunics, fighting in a company, yielded without a struggle to the same number of opponents; and being ordered to be slain, one of them taking up his lance again, killed all the conquerors. This he lamented in a proclamation as a most cruel butchery, and cursed all those who had borne the sight of it.

XXXI. He used also to complain aloud of the state of the times, because it was not rendered remarkable by any public (274) calamities; for, while the reign of Augustus had been made memorable to posterity by the disaster of Varus 436 , and that of Tiberius by the fall of the theatre at Fidenae 437 , his was likely to pass into oblivion, from an uninterrupted series of prosperity. And, at times, he wished for some terrible slaughter of his troops, a famine, a pestilence, conflagrations, or an earthquake.

XXXII. Even in the midst of his diversions, while gaming or feasting, this savage ferocity, both in his language and actions, never forsook him. Persons were often put to the torture in his presence, whilst he was dining or carousing. A soldier, who was an adept in the art of beheading, used at such times to take off the heads of prisoners, who were brought in for that purpose. At Puteoli, at the dedication of the bridge which he planned, as already mentioned 438 , he invited a number of people to come to him from the shore, and then suddenly, threw them headlong into the sea; thrusting down with poles and oars those who, to save themselves, had got hold of the rudders of the ships. At Rome, in a public feast, a slave having stolen some thin plates of silver with which the couches were inlaid, he delivered him immediately to an executioner, with orders to cut off his hands, and lead him round the guests, with them hanging from his neck before his breast, and a label, signifying the cause of his punishment. A gladiator who was practising with him, and voluntarily threw himself at his feet, he stabbed with a poniard, and then ran about with a palm branch in his hand, after the manner of those who are victorious in the games. When a victim was to be offered upon an altar, he, clad in the habit of the Popae 439 , and holding the axe aloft for a while, at last, instead of the animal, slaughtered an officer who attended to cut up the sacrifice. And at a sumptuous entertainment, he fell suddenly into a violent fit of laughter, and upon the consuls, who reclined next to him, respectfully asking him the occasion, "Nothing," replied he, "but that, upon a single nod of mine, you might both have your throats cut."

(275) XXXIII. Among many other jests, this was one: As he stood by the statue of Jupiter, he asked Apelles, the tragedian, which of them he thought was biggest? Upon his demurring about it, he lashed him most severely, now and then commending his voice, whilst he

entreated for mercy, as being well modulated even when he was venting his grief. As often as he kissed the neck of his wife or mistress, he would say, "So beautiful a throat must be cut whenever I please;" and now and then he would threaten to put his dear Caesonia to the torture, that he might discover why he loved her so passionately.

XXXIV. In his behaviour towards men of almost all ages, he discovered a degree of jealousy and malignity equal to that of his cruelty and pride. He so demolished and dispersed the statues of several illustrious persons, which had been removed by Augustus, for want of room, from the court of the Capitol into the Campus Martius, that it was impossible to set them up again with their inscriptions entire. And, for the future, he forbad any statue whatever to be erected without his knowledge and leave. He had thoughts too of suppressing Homer's poems: "For why," said he, "may not I do what Plato has done before me, who excluded him from his commonwealth?" 440 He was likewise very near banishing the writings and the busts of Virgil and Livy from all libraries; censuring one of them as "a man of no genius and very little learning;" and the other as "a verbose and careless historian." He often talked of the lawyers as if he intended to abolish their profession. "By Hercules!" he would say, "I shall put it out of their power to answer any questions in law, otherwise than by referring to me!"

XXXV. He took from the noblest persons in the city the ancient marks of distinction used by their families; as the collar from Torquatus 441 ; from Cincinnatus the curl of (276) hair 442 ; and from Cneius Pompey, the surname of Great, belonging to that ancient family. Ptolemy, mentioned before, whom he invited from his kingdom, and received with great honours, he suddenly put to death, for no other reason, but because he observed that upon entering the theatre, at a public exhibition, he attracted the eyes of all the spectators, by the splendour of his purple robe. As often as he met with handsome men, who had fine heads of hair, he would order the back of their heads to be shaved, to make them appear ridiculous. There was one Esius Proculus, the son of a centurion of the first rank, who, for his great stature and fine proportions, was called the Colossal. Him he ordered to be dragged from his seat in the arena, and matched with a gladiator in light armour, and afterwards with another completely armed; and upon his worsting them both, commanded him forthwith to be bound, to be led clothed in rags up and down the streets of the city, and, after being exhibited in that plight to the women, to be then butchered. There was no man of so abject or mean condition, whose excellency in any kind he did not envy. The Rex Nemorensis 443 having many years enjoyed the honour of the priesthood, he procured a still stronger antagonist to oppose him. One Porius, who fought in a chariot 444, having been victorious in an exhibition, and in his joy given freedom to a slave, was applauded so vehemently, that Caligula rose in such haste from his seat, that, treading upon the hem of his toga, he tumbled down the steps, full of indignation, (277) and crying out, "A people who are masters of the world, pay greater respect to a gladiator for a trifle, than to princes admitted amongst the gods, or to my own majesty here present amongst them."

XXXVI. He never had the least regard either to the chastity of his own person, or that of others. He is said to have been inflamed with an unnatural passion for Marcus Lepidus Mnester, an actor in pantomimes, and for certain hostages; and to have engaged with them in the practice of mutual pollution. Valerius Catullus, a young man of a consular family, bawled aloud in public that he had been exhausted by him in that abominable act. Besides his incest with his sisters, and his notorious passion for Pyrallis, the prostitute, there was hardly any lady of distinction with whom he did not make free. He used commonly to invite them with their husbands to supper, and as they passed by the couch on which he reclined at table, examine them very closely, like those who traffic in slaves; and if any one from modesty held down her face, he raised it up with his hand. Afterwards, as often as he was in the humour, he would quit the room, send for her he liked best, and in a short time return with marks of recent disorder about them. He would then commend or disparage her in the presence of the company, recounting the charms or defects of her person and behaviour in private. To some he sent a divorce in the name of their absent husbands, and ordered it to be registered in the public acts.

XXXVII. In the devices of his profuse expenditure, he surpassed all the prodigals that ever lived; inventing a new kind of bath, with strange dishes and suppers, washing in precious unguents, both warm and cold, drinking pearls of immense value dissolved in vinegar, and serving up for his guests loaves and other victuals modelled in gold; often saying, "that a man ought either to be a good economist or an emperor." Besides, he scattered money to a prodigious amount among the people, from the top of the Julian Basilica 445, during several days successively. He built two ships with ten banks of oars, after the Liburnian fashion, the poops of which blazed with jewels, and the sails were of various parti-colours. They were fitted up with ample baths, galleries, and saloons, and supplied with a great variety of vines and other fruit-trees. In these he would sail in the day-time along the coast of Campania, feasting (278) amidst dancing and concerts of music. In building his palaces and villas, there was nothing he desired to effect so much, in defiance of all reason, as what was considered impossible. Accordingly, moles were formed in the deep and adverse sea 446, rocks of the hardest stone cut away, plains raised to the height of mountains with a vast mass of earth, and the tops of mountains levelled by digging; and all these were to be executed with incredible speed, for the least remissness was a capital offence. Not to mention particulars, he spent enormous sums, and the whole treasures which had been amassed by Tiberius Caesar, amounting to two thousand seven hundred millions of sesterces, within less than a year.

XXXVIII. Having therefore quite exhausted these funds, and being in want of money, he had recourse to plundering the people, by every mode of false accusation, confiscation, and taxation, that could be invented. He declared that no one had any right to the freedom of Rome, although their ancestors had acquired it for themselves and their posterity, unless they were sons; for that none beyond that degree ought to be considered as posterity. When the grants of the Divine Julius and Augustus were produced to him, he only said, that he was very sorry they were obsolete and out of date. He also charged all those with making false returns, who, after the taking of the census, had by any means whatever increased their property. He annulled the wills of all who had been centurions of the first rank, as testimonies of their base ingratitude, if from the beginning of Tiberius's reign they had not left either that prince or himself their heir. He also set aside the wills of all others, if any person only pretended to say, that they designed at their death to leave Caesar their heir. The public becoming terrified at this proceeding, he was now appointed joint-heir with their friends, and in the case of parents with their children, by persons unknown to him. Those who lived any considerable time after making such a will, he said, were only making game of him;

and accordingly he sent many of them poisoned cakes. He used to try such causes himself; fixing previously the sum he proposed to raise during the sitting, and, after he had secured it, quitting the tribunal. Impatient of the least delay, he condemned by a single sentence forty (279) persons, against whom there were different charges; boasting to Caesonia when she awoke, "how much business he had dispatched while she was taking her mid-day sleep." He exposed to sale by auction, the remains of the apparatus used in the public spectacles; and exacted such biddings, and raised the prices so high, that some of the purchasers were ruined, and bled themselves to death. There is a well-known story told of Aponius Saturninus, who happening to fall asleep as he sat on a bench at the sale, Caius called out to the auctioneer, not to overlook the praetorian personage who nodded to him so often; and accordingly the salesman went on, pretending to take the nods for tokens of assent, until thirteen gladiators were knocked down to him at the sum of nine millions of sesterces 447, he being in total ignorance of what was doing.

XXXIX. Having also sold in Gaul all the clothes, furniture, slaves, and even freedmen belonging to his sisters, at prodigious prices, after their condemnation, he was so much delighted with his gains, that he sent to Rome for all the furniture of the old palace 448; pressing for its conveyance all the carriages let to hire in the city, with the horses and mules belonging to the bakers, so that they often wanted bread at Rome; and many who had suits at law in progress, lost their causes, because they could not make their appearance in due time according to their recognizances. In the sale of this furniture, every artifice of fraud and imposition was employed. Sometimes he would rail at the bidders for being niggardly, and ask them "if they were not ashamed to be richer than he was?" at another, he would affect to be sorry that the property of princes should be passing into the hands of private persons. He had found out that a rich provincial had given two hundred thousand sesterces to his chamberlains for an underhand invitation to his table, and he was much pleased to find that honour valued at so high a rate. The day following, as the same person was sitting at the sale, he sent him some bauble, for which he told him he must pay two hundred thousand sesterces, and "that he should sup with Caesar upon his own invitation."

(280) XL. He levied new taxes, and such as were never before known, at first by the publicans, but afterwards, because their profit was enormous, by centurions and tribunes of the pretorian guards; no description of property or persons being exempted from some kind of tax or other. For all eatables brought into the city, a certain excise was exacted: for all law-suits or trials in whatever court, the fortieth part of the sum in dispute; and such as were convicted of compromising litigations, were made liable to a penalty. Out of the daily wages of the porters, he received an eighth, and from the gains of common prostitutes, what they received for one favour granted. There was a clause in the law, that all bawds who kept women for prostitution or sale, should be liable to pay, and that marriage itself should not be exempted.

XLI. These taxes being imposed, but the act by which they were levied never submitted to public inspection, great grievances were experienced from the want of sufficient knowledge of the law. At length, on the urgent demands of the Roman people, he published the law, but it was written in a very small hand, and posted up in a corner, so that no one could make a copy of it. To leave no sort of gain untried, he opened brothels in the Palatium, with a number of cells, furnished suitably to the dignity of the place; in which married women and free-born youths were ready for the reception of visitors. He sent likewise his nomenclators about the forums and courts, to invite people of all ages, the old as well as the young, to his brothel, to come and satisfy their lusts; and he was ready to lend his customers money upon interest; clerks attending to take down their names in public, as persons who contributed to the emperor's revenue. Another method of raising money, which he thought not below his notice, was gaming; which, by the help of lying and perjury, he turned to considerable account. Leaving once the management of his play to his partner in the game, he stepped into the court, and observing two rich Roman knights passing by, he ordered them immediately to be seized, and their estates confiscated. Then returning, in great glee, he boasted that he had never made a better throw in his life.

XLII. After the birth of his daughter, complaining of his (281) poverty, and the burdens to which he was subjected, not only as an emperor, but a father, he made a general collection for her maintenance and fortune. He likewise gave public notice, that he would receive new-year's gifts on the calends of January following; and accordingly stood in the vestibule of his house, to clutch the presents which people of all ranks threw down before him by handfuls and lapfuls. At last, being seized with an invincible desire of feeling money, taking off his slippers, he repeatedly walked over great heaps of gold coin spread upon the spacious floor, and then laying himself down, rolled his whole body in gold over and over again.

XLIII. Only once in his life did he take an active part in military affairs, and then not from any set purpose, but during his journey to Mevania, to see the grove and river of Clitumnus 449 . Being recommended to recruit a body of Batavians, who attended him, he resolved upon an expedition into Germany. Immediately he drew together several legions, and auxiliary forces from all quarters, and made every where new levies with the utmost rigour. Collecting supplies of all kinds, such as never had been assembled upon the like occasion, he set forward on his march, and pursued it sometimes with so much haste and precipitation, that the pretorian cohorts were obliged, contrary to custom, to pack their standards on horses or mules, and so follow him. At other times, he would march so slow and luxuriously, that he was carried in a litter by eight men; ordering the roads to be swept by the people of the neighbouring towns, and sprinkled with water to lay the dust.

XLIV. On arriving at the camp, in order to show himself an active general, and severe disciplinarian, he cashiered the lieutenants who came up late with the auxiliary forces from different quarters. In reviewing the army, he deprived of their companies most of the centurions of the first rank, who had now served their legal time in the wars, and some whose time would have expired in a few days; alleging against them their age and infirmity; and railing at the covetous disposition (282) of the rest of them, he reduced the bounty due to those who had served out their time to the sum of six thousand sesterces. Though he only received the submission of Adminius, the son of Cunobeline, a British king, who being driven from his native country by his father, came over to him with a small body of troops 450 , yet, as if the whole island had been surrendered to him, he dispatched magnificent letters to Rome, ordering the bearers to proceed in their carriages directly up to the forum and the senate-house, and not to deliver the letters but to the consuls in the temple of Mars, and in the presence of a full assembly of the senators.

XLV. Soon after this, there being no hostilities, he ordered a few Germans of his guard to be carried over and placed in concealment on the other side of the Rhine, and word to be brought him after dinner, that an enemy was advancing with great impetuosity. This being accordingly done, he immediately threw himself, with his friends, and a party of the pretorian knights, into the adjoining wood, where lopping branches from the trees, and forming trophies of them, he returned by torch-light, upbraiding those who did not follow him, with timorousness and cowardice; but he presented the companions, and sharers of his victory with crowns of a new form, and under a new name, having the sun, moon, and stars represented on them, and which he called Exploratoriae. Again, some hostages were by his order taken from the school, and privately sent off; upon notice of which he immediately rose from table, pursued them with the cavalry, as if they had run away, and coming up with them, brought them back in fetters; proceeding to an extravagant pitch of ostentation likewise in this military comedy. Upon his again sitting down to table, it being reported to him that the troops were all reassembled, he ordered them to sit down as they were, in their armour, animating them in the words of that well-known verse of Virgil:

(283) *Durate, et vosmet rebus servate secundis.* — *Aen.* 1.

*Bear up, and save yourselves for better days.*

In the mean time, he reprimanded the senate and people of Rome in a very severe proclamation, "For revelling and frequenting the diversions of the circus and theatre, and enjoying themselves at their villas, whilst their emperor was fighting, and exposing himself to the greatest dangers."

XLVI. At last, as if resolved to make war in earnest, he drew up his army upon the shore of the ocean, with his balistae and other engines of war, and while no one could imagine what he intended to do, on a sudden commanded them to gather up the sea shells, and fill their helmets, and the folds of their dress with them, calling them "the spoils of the ocean due to the Capitol and the Palatium." As a monument of his success, he raised a lofty tower, upon which, as at Pharos 451 , he ordered lights to be burnt in the night-time, for the direction of ships at sea; and then promising the soldiers a donative of a hundred denarii 452 a man, as if he had surpassed the most eminent examples of generosity, "Go your ways," said he, "and be merry: go, ye are rich."

XLVII. In making preparations for his triumph, besides the prisoners and deserters from the barbarian armies, he picked out the men of greatest stature in all Gaul, such as he said were fittest to grace a triumph, with some of the chiefs, and reserved them to appear in the procession; obliging them not only to dye their hair yellow, and let it grow long, but to learn the German language, and assume the names commonly used in that country. He ordered likewise the gallies in which he had entered the ocean, to be conveyed to Rome a great part of the way by land, and wrote to his comptrollers in the city, "to make proper preparations for a triumph against (284) his arrival, at as small expense as possible; but on a scale such as had never been seen before, since they had full power over the property of every one."

XLVIII. Before he left the province, he formed a design of the most horrid cruelty—to massacre the legions which had mutinied upon the death of Augustus, for seizing and detaining by force his father, Germanicus, their commander, and himself, then an infant, in the camp. Though he was with great difficulty dissuaded from this rash attempt, yet neither the most urgent entreaties nor representations could prevent him from persisting in the design of decimating these legions. Accordingly, he ordered them to assemble unarmed, without so much as their swords; and then surrounded them with armed horse. But finding that many of them, suspecting that violence was intended, were making off, to arm in their own defence, he quitted the assembly as fast as he could, and immediately marched for Rome; bending now all his fury against the senate, whom he publicly threatened, to divert the general attention from the clamour excited by his disgraceful conduct. Amongst other pretexts of offence, he complained that he was defrauded of a triumph, which was justly his due, though he had just before forbidden, upon pain of death, any honour to be decreed him.

XLIX. In his march he was waited upon by deputies from the senatorian order, entreating him to hasten his return. He replied to them, "I will come, I will come, and this with me," striking at the same time the hilt of his sword. He issued likewise this proclamation: "I am coming, but for those only who wish for me, the equestrian order and the people; for I shall no longer treat the senate as their fellow-citizen or prince." He forbad any of the senators to come to meet him; and either abandoning or deferring his triumph, he entered the city in ovation on his birthday. Within four months from this period he was slain, after he had perpetrated enormous crimes, and while he was meditating the execution, if possible, of still greater. He had entertained a design of removing to Antium, and afterwards to Alexandria; having first cut off the flower of the equestrian and senatorian orders. This is placed beyond all question, by two books which were found in his cabinet (285) under different titles; one being called the sword, and the other, the dagger. They both contained private marks, and the names of those who were devoted to death. There was also found a large chest, filled with a variety of poisons which being afterwards thrown into the sea by order of Claudius, are said to have so infected the waters, that the fish were poisoned, and cast dead by the tide upon the neighbouring shores.

L. He was tall, of a pale complexion, ill-shaped, his neck and legs very slender, his eyes and temples hollow, his brows broad and knit, his hair thin, and the crown of the head bald. The other parts of his body were much covered with hair. On this account, it was reckoned a capital crime for any person to look down from above, as he was passing by, or so much as to name a goat. His countenance, which was naturally hideous and frightful, he purposely rendered more so, forming it before a mirror into the most horrible contortions. He was crazy both in body and mind, being subject, when a boy, to the falling sickness. When he arrived at the age of manhood, he endured fatigue tolerably well; but still, occasionally, he was liable to a faintness, during which he remained incapable of any effort. He was not insensible of the disorder of his mind, and sometimes had thoughts of retiring to clear his brain 453. It is believed that his wife Caesonia administered to him a love potion which threw him into a frenzy. What most of all disordered him, was want of sleep, for he seldom had more than three or four hours' rest in a night; and even then his sleep was not sound, but disturbed by strange dreams; fancying, among other things, that a form representing the ocean spoke to him. Being therefore often weary with lying awake so long, sometimes he sat up in his bed, at others, walked in the longest porticos about the house, and from time to time, invoked and looked out for the approach of day.

LI. To this crazy constitution of his mind may, I think, very justly be ascribed two faults which he had, of a nature directly repugnant one to the other, namely, an excessive confidence and the most abject timidity. For he, who affected so (286) much to despise the gods, was ready to shut his eyes, and wrap up his head in his cloak at the slightest storm of thunder and lightning; and if it was violent, he got up and hid himself under his bed. In his visit to Sicily, after ridiculing many strange objects which that country affords, he ran away suddenly in the night from Messini, terrified by the smoke and rumbling at the summit of Mount Aetna. And though in words he was very valiant against the barbarians, yet upon passing a narrow defile in Germany in his light car, surrounded by a strong body of his troops, some one happening to say, "There would be no small consternation amongst us, if an enemy were to appear," he immediately mounted his horse, and rode towards the bridges in great haste; but finding them blocked up with camp-followers and baggage-waggons, he was in such a hurry, that he caused himself to be carried in men's hands over the heads of the crowd. Soon afterwards, upon hearing that the Germans were again in rebellion, he prepared to quit Rome, and equipped a fleet; comforting himself with this consideration, that if the enemy should prove victorious, and possess themselves of the heights of the Alps, as the Cimbri 454 had done, or of the city, as the Senones 455 formerly did, he should still have in reserve the transmarine provinces 456. Hence it was, I suppose, that it occurred to his assassins, to invent the story intended to pacify the troops who mutinied at his death, that he had laid violent hands upon himself, in a fit of terror occasioned by the news brought him of the defeat of his army.

LII. In the fashion of his clothes, shoes, and all the rest of his dress, he did not wear what was either national, or properly civic, or peculiar to the male sex, or appropriate to mere mortals. He often appeared abroad in a short coat of stout cloth, richly embroidered and blazing with jewels, in a tunic with sleeves, and with bracelets upon his arms; sometimes all in silks and (287) habited like a woman; at other times in the crepidae or buskins; sometimes in the sort of shoes used by the light-armed soldiers, or in the sock used by women, and commonly with a golden beard fixed to his chin, holding in his hand a thunderbolt, a trident, or a caduceus, marks of distinction belonging to the gods only. Sometimes, too, he appeared in the habit of Venus.

He wore very commonly the triumphal ornaments, even before his expedition, and sometimes the breast-plate of Alexander the Great, taken out of his coffin. 457

LIII. With regard to the liberal sciences, he was little conversant in philology, but applied himself with assiduity to the study of eloquence, being indeed in point of enunciation tolerably elegant and ready; and in his perorations, when he was moved to anger, there was an abundant flow of words and periods. In speaking, his action was vehement, and his voice so strong, that he was heard at a great distance. When winding up an harangue, he threatened to draw "the sword of his lucubration," holding a loose and smooth style in such contempt, that he said Seneca, who was then much admired, "wrote only detached essays," and that "his language was nothing but sand without lime." He often wrote answers to the speeches of successful orators; and employed himself in composing accusations or vindications of eminent persons, who were impeached before the senate; and gave his vote for or against the party accused, according to his success in speaking, inviting the equestrian order, by proclamation, to hear him.

LIV. He also zealously applied himself to the practice of several other arts of different kinds, such as fencing, charioteering, singing, and dancing. In the first of these, he practised with the weapons used in war; and drove the chariot in circuses built in several places. He was so extremely fond of singing and dancing, that he could not refrain in the theatre from singing with the tragedians, and imitating the gestures of the actors, either by way of applause or correction. A night exhibition which he had ordered the day he was slain, was thought to be intended for no other reason, than to take the opportunity afforded by the licentiousness of the season, to make his first appearance upon the stage. Sometimes, also, (288) he danced in the night. Summoning once to the Palatium, in the second watch of the night 458 , three men of consular rank, who feared the words from the message, he placed them on the proscenium of the stage, and then suddenly came bursting out, with a loud noise of flutes and castanets 459 , dressed in a mantle and tunic reaching down to his heels. Having danced out a song, he retired. Yet he who had acquired such dexterity in other exercises, never learnt to swim.

LV. Those for whom he once conceived a regard, he favoured even to madness. He used to kiss Mnester, the pantomimic actor, publicly in the theatre; and if any person made the least noise while he was dancing, he would order him to be dragged from his seat, and scourged him with his own hand. A Roman knight once making some bustle, he sent him, by a centurion, an order to depart forthwith for Ostia 460, and carry a letter from him to king Ptolemy in Mauritania. The letter was comprised in these words: "Do neither good nor harm to the bearer." He made some gladiators captains of his German guards. He deprived the gladiators called Mirmillones of some of their arms. One Columbus coming off with victory in a combat, but being slightly wounded, he ordered some poison to be infused in the wound, which he thence called Columbinum. For thus it was certainly named with his own hand in a list of other poisons. He was so extravagantly fond of the party of charioteers whose colours were green 461, that he supped and lodged for some time constantly in the stable where their horses were kept. At a certain revel, he made a present of two millions of sesterces to one Cythicus, a driver of a chariot. The day before the Circensian games, he used to send his soldiers to enjoin silence in the (289) neighbourhood, that the repose of his horse Incitatus 462 might not be disturbed. For this favourite animal, besides a marble stable, an ivory manger, purple housings, and a jewelled frontlet, he appointed a house, with a retinue of slaves, and fine furniture, for the reception of such as were invited in the horse's name to sup with him. It is even said that he intended to make him consul.

LVI. In this frantic and savage career, numbers had formed designs for cutting him off; but one or two conspiracies being discovered, and others postponed for want of opportunity, at last two men concerted a plan together, and accomplished their purpose; not without the privity of some of the greatest favourites amongst his freedmen, and the prefects of the pretorian guards; because, having been named, though falsely, as concerned in one conspiracy against him, they perceived that they were suspected and become objects of his hatred. For he had immediately endeavoured to render them obnoxious to the soldiery, drawing his sword, and declaring, "That he would kill himself if they thought him worthy of death;" and ever after he was continually accusing them to one another, and setting them all mutually at variance. The conspirators having resolved to fall upon him as he returned at noon from the Palatine games, Cassius Chaerea, tribune of the pretorian guards, claimed the part of making the onset. This Chaerea was now an elderly man, and had been often reproached by Caius for effeminacy. When he came for the watchword, the latter would give "Priapus," or "Venus;" and if on any occasion he returned thanks, would offer him his hand to kiss, making with his fingers an obscene gesture.

LVII. His approaching fate was indicated by many prodigies. The statue of Jupiter at Olympia, which he had ordered to be taken down and brought to Rome, suddenly burst out into such a violent fit of laughter, that, the machines employed in the work giving way, the workmen took to their heels. When this accident happened, there came up a man named Cassius, who said that he was commanded in a dream to sacrifice a bull to Jupiter. The Capitol at Capua was (290) struck with lightning upon the ides of March [15th March] as was also, at Rome, the apartment of the chief porter of the Palatium. Some construed the latter into a presage that the master of the place was in danger from his own guards; and the other they regarded as a sign, that an illustrious person would be cut off, as had happened before on that day. Sylla, the astrologer, being, consulted by him respecting his nativity, assured him, "That death would unavoidably and speedily befall him." The oracle of Fortune at Antium likewise forewarned him of Cassius; on which account he had given orders for putting to death Cassius Longinus, at that time proconsul of Asia, not considering that Chaerea bore also that name. The day preceding his death he dreamt that he was standing in heaven near the throne of Jupiter, who giving him a push with the great toe of his right foot, he fell headlong upon the earth. Some things which happened the very day of his death, and only a little before it, were likewise considered as ominous presages of that event. Whilst he was at sacrifice, he was bespattered with the blood of a flamingo. And Mnester, the pantomimic actor, performed in a play, which the tragedian Neoptolemus had formerly acted at the games in which Philip, the king of Macedon, was slain. And in the piece called Laureolus, in which the principal actor, running out in a hurry, and falling, vomited blood, several of the inferior actors vying with each other to give the best specimen of their art, made the whole stage flow with blood. A spectacle had been purposed to be performed that night, in which the fables of the infernal regions were to be represented by Egyptians and Ethiopians.

LVIII. On the ninth of the calends of February [24th January], and about the seventh hour of the day, after hesitating whether he should rise to dinner, as his stomach was disordered by what he had eaten the day before, at last, by the advice of his friends, he came forth. In the vaulted passage through which he had to pass, were some boys of noble extraction, who had been brought from Asia to act upon the stage, waiting for him in a private corridor, and he stopped to see and speak to them; and had not the leader of the party said that he was suffering from cold, he would have gone back, and made them act immediately. Respecting what followed, (291) two different accounts are given. Some say, that, whilst he was speaking to the boys, Chaerea came behind him, and gave him a heavy blow on the neck with his sword, first crying out, "Take this:" that then a tribune, by name Cornelius Sabinus, another of the conspirators, ran him through the breast. Others say, that the crowd being kept at a distance by some centurions who were in the plot, Sabinus came, according to custom, for the word, and that Caius gave him "Jupiter," upon which Chaerea cried out, "Be it so!" and then, on his looking round, clove one of his jaws with a blow. As he lay on the ground, crying out that he was still alive 463 , the rest dispatched him with thirty wounds. For the word agreed upon among them all was, "Strike again." Some likewise ran their swords through his privy parts. Upon the first bustle, the litter bearers came running in with their poles to his assistance, and, immediately afterwards, his German body guards, who killed some of the assassins, and also some senators who had no concern in the affair.

LIX. He lived twenty-nine years, and reigned three years, ten months, and eight days. His body was carried privately into the Lamian Gardens 464 , where it was half burnt upon a pile hastily raised, and then had some earth carelessly thrown over it. It was afterwards disinterred by his sisters, on their return from banishment, burnt to ashes, and buried. Before this was done, it is well known that the keepers of the gardens were greatly disturbed by apparitions; and that not a night passed without some terrible alarm or other in the house where he was slain, until it was destroyed by fire. His wife Caesonia was killed with him, being stabbed by a centurion; and his daughter had her brains knocked out against a wall.

LX. Of the miserable condition of those times, any person (292) may easily form an estimate from the following circumstances. When his death was made public, it was not immediately credited. People entertained a suspicion that a report of his being killed had been contrived and spread by himself, with the view of discovering how they stood affected towards him. Nor had the conspirators fixed upon any one to succeed him. The senators were so unanimous in their resolution to assert the liberty of their country, that the consuls assembled them at first not in the usual place of meeting, because it was named after Julius Caesar, but in the Capitol. Some proposed to abolish the memory of the Caesars, and level their temples with the ground. It was particularly remarked on this occasion, that all the Caesars, who had the praenomen of Caius, died by the sword, from the Caius Caesar who was slain in the times of Cinna.

* * * * * *

Unfortunately, a great chasm in the Annals of Tacitus, at this period, precludes all information from that historian respecting the reign of Caligula; but from what he mentions towards the close of the preceding chapter, it is evident that Caligula was forward to seize the reins of government, upon the death of Tiberius, whom, though he rivalled him in his vices, he was far from imitating in his dissimulation. Amongst the people, the remembrance of Germanicus' virtues cherished for his family an attachment which was probably, increased by its misfortunes; and they were anxious to see revived in the son the popularity of the father. Considering, however, that Caligula's vicious disposition was already known, and that it had even been an inducement with Tiberius to procure his succession, in order that it might prove a foil to his own memory; it is surprising that no effort was made at this juncture to shake off the despotism which had been so intolerable in the last reign, and restore the ancient liberty of the republic. Since the commencement of the imperial dominion, there never had been any period so favourable for a counter-revolution as the present crisis. There existed now no Livia, to influence the minds of the senate and people in respect of the government; nor was there any other person allied to the family of Germanicus, whose countenance or intrigues could promote the views of Caligula. He himself was now only in the twenty-fifth year of his age, was totally inexperienced in the administration of public affairs, had never performed even the smallest service to his country, and was generally known to be of a character which (293) disgraced his illustrious descent. Yet, in spite of all these circumstances, such was the destiny of Rome, that his accession afforded joy to the soldiers, who had known him in his childhood, and to the populace in the capital, as well as the people in the provinces, who were flattered with the delusive expectation of receiving a prince who should adorn the throne with the amiable virtues of Germanicus.

It is difficult to say, whether weakness of understanding, or corruption of morals, were more conspicuous in the character of Caligula. He seems to have discovered from his earliest years an innate depravity of mind, which was undoubtedly much increased by defect of education. He had lost both his parents at an early period of life; and from Tiberius' own character, as well as his views in training the person who should succeed him on the throne, there is reason to think, that if any attention whatever was paid to the education of Caligula, it was directed to vitiate all his faculties and passions, rather than to correct and improve them. If such was really the object, it was indeed prosecuted with success.

The commencement, however, of his reign was such as by no means prognosticated its subsequent transition. The sudden change of his conduct, the astonishing mixture of imbecility and presumption, of moral turpitude and frantic extravagance, which he afterwards evinced; such as rolling himself over heaps of gold, his treatment of his horse Incitatus, and his design of making him consul, seem to justify a suspicion that his brain had actually been affected, either by the potion, said to have been given him by his wife Caesonia, or otherwise. Philtres, or love-potions, as they were called, were frequent in those times; and the people believed that they operated upon the mind by a mysterious and sympathetic power. It is, however, beyond a doubt, that their effects were produced entirely by the action of their physical qualities upon the organs of the body. They were usually made of the satyrion, which, according to Pliny, was a provocative. They were generally given by women to their husbands at bed-time; and it was necessary towards their successful operation, that the parties should sleep together. This circumstance explains the whole mystery. The philtres were nothing more than medicines of a stimulating quality, which, after exciting violent, but temporary effects, enfeebled the constitution, and occasioned nervous disorders, by which the mental faculties, as well as the corporeal, might be injured. That this was really the case with Caligula, seems probable, not only from the falling sickness, to which he was subject, but from the habitual wakefulness of which he complained.

(294) The profusion of this emperor, during his short reign of three years and ten months, is unexampled in history. In the midst of profound peace, without any extraordinary charges either civil or military, he expended, in less than one year, besides the current revenue of the empire, the sum of 21,796,875 pounds sterling, which had been left by Tiberius at his death. To supply the extravagance of future years, new and exorbitant taxes were imposed upon the people, and those too on the necessaries of life. There existed now amongst the Romans every motive that could excite a general indignation against the government; yet such was still the dread of imperial power, though vested in the hands of so weak and despicable a sovereign, that no insurrection was attempted, nor any extensive conspiracy formed; but the obnoxious emperor fell at last a sacrifice to a few centurions of his own guard.

This reign was of too short duration to afford any new productions in literature; but, had it been extended to a much longer period, the effects would probably have been the same. Polite learning never could flourish under an emperor who entertained a design of destroying the writings of Virgil and Livy. It is fortunate that these, and other valuable productions of antiquity, were too widely diffused over the world, and too carefully preserved, to be in danger of perishing through the frenzy of this capricious barbarian.

# TIBERIUS CLAUDIUS DRUSUS CAESAR. 465

**(295)**

I. Livia, having married Augustus when she was pregnant, was within three months afterwards delivered of Drusus, the father of Claudius Caesar, who had at first the praenomen of Decimus, but afterwards that of Nero; and it was suspected that he was begotten in adultery by his father-in-law. The following verse, however, was immediately in every one's mouth:

*Tois eutychousi kai primaena paidia.*

*Nine months for common births the fates decree;*

*But, for the great, reduce the term to three.*

This Drusus, during the time of his being quaestor and praetor, commanded in the Rhaetian and German wars, and was the first of all the Roman generals who navigated the Northern Ocean 466 . He made likewise some prodigious trenches beyond the Rhine 467 , which to this day are called by his name. He overthrew the enemy in several battles, and drove them far back into the depths of the desert. Nor did he desist from pursuing them, until an apparition, in the form of a barbarian woman, of more than human size, appeared to him, and, in the Latin tongue, forbad him to proceed any farther. For these achievements he had the honour of an ovation, and the triumphal ornaments. After his praetorship, he immediately entered on the office of consul, and returning again to Germany, died of disease, in the summer encampment, which thence obtained the name of "The Unlucky Camp." His corpse was carried to Rome by the principal persons of the several municipalities and colonies upon the road, being met and received by the recorders of each place, and buried in the Campus Martius. In honour of his (296) memory, the army erected a monument, round which the soldiers used, annually, upon a certain day, to march in solemn procession, and persons deputed from the several cities of Gaul performed religious rites. The senate likewise, among various other honours, decreed for him a triumphal arch of marble, with trophies, in the Appian Way, and gave the cognomen of Germanicus to him and his posterity. In him the civil and military virtues were equally displayed; for, besides his victories, he gained from the enemy the Spolia Opima 468 , and frequently marked out the German chiefs in the midst of their army, and encountered them in single combat, at the utmost hazard of his life. He likewise often declared that he would, some time or other, if possible, restore the ancient government. In this account, I suppose, some have ventured to affirm that Augustus was jealous of him, and recalled him; and because he made no haste to comply with the order, took him off by poison. This I mention, that I may not be guilty of any omission, more than because I think it either true or probable; since Augustus loved him so much when living, that he always, in his wills, made him joint-heir with his sons, as he once declared in the senate; and upon his decease, extolled him in a speech to the people, to that degree, that he prayed the gods "to make his Caesars like him, and to grant himself as honourable an exit out of this world as they had given him." And not satisfied with inscribing upon his tomb an epitaph in verse composed by himself, he wrote likewise the history of his life in prose. He had by the younger Antonia several children, but left behind him only three, namely, Germanicus, Livilla, and Claudius.

II. Claudius was born at Lyons, in the consulship of Julius Antonius, and Fabius Africanus, upon the first of August 469 , the very day upon which an altar was first dedicated there to Augustus. He was named Tiberius Claudius Drusus, but soon afterwards, (297) upon the adoption of his elder brother into the Julian family, he assumed the cognomen of Germanicus. He was left an infant by his father, and during almost the whole of his minority, and for some time after he attained the age of manhood, was afflicted with a variety of obstinate disorders, insomuch that his mind and body being greatly impaired, he was, even after his arrival at years of maturity, never thought sufficiently qualified for any public or private employment. He was, therefore, during a long time, and even after the expiration of his minority, under the direction of a pedagogue, who, he complains in a certain memoir, "was a barbarous wretch, and formerly superintendent of the mule-drivers, who was selected for his governor, on purpose to correct him severely on every trifling occasion." On account of this crazy constitution of body and mind, at the spectacle of gladiators, which he gave the people, jointly with his brother, in honour of his father's memory, he presided, muffled up in a pallium—a new fashion. When he assumed the manly habit, he was carried in a litter, at midnight, to the Capitol, without the usual ceremony.

III. He applied himself, however, from an early age, with great assiduity to the study of the liberal sciences, and frequently published specimens of his skill in each of them. But never, with all his endeavours, could he attain to any public post in the government, or afford any hope of arriving at distinction thereafter. His mother, Antonia, frequently called him "an abortion of a man, that had been only begun, but never finished, by nature." And when she would upbraid any one with dulness, she said, "He was a greater fool than her son, Claudius." His grandmother, Augusta, always treated him with the utmost contempt, very rarely spoke to him, and when she did admonish him upon any occasion, it was in writing, very briefly and severely, or by messengers. His sister, Livilla, upon hearing that he was about to be created emperor, openly and loudly expressed her indignation that the Roman people should experience a fate so severe and so much below their grandeur. To exhibit the opinion, both favourable and otherwise, entertained concerning him by Augustus, his great-uncle, I have here subjoined some extracts from the letters of that emperor.

IV. "I have had some conversation with Tiberius, according (298) to your desire, my dear Livia, as to what must be done with your grandson, Tiberius, at the games of Mars. We are both agreed in this, that, once for all, we ought to determine what course to take with him. For if he be really sound and, so to speak, quite right in his intellects 470 , why should we hesitate to promote him by the same steps and degrees we did his brother? But if we find him below par, and deficient both in body and mind, we must beware of giving occasion for him and ourselves to be laughed at by the world, which is ready enough to make such things the subject of mirth and derision. For we never shall be easy, if we are always to be debating upon every occasion of this kind, without settling, in the first instance, whether he be really capable of public offices or not. With regard to what you consult me about at the present moment, I am not against his superintending the feast of the priests, in the games of Mars, if he will suffer himself to be governed by his kinsman, Silanus's son, that he may do nothing to make the people stare and laugh at him. But I do not approve of his witnessing the Circensian games from the Pulvinar. He will be there exposed to view in the very front of the theatre. Nor do I like that he should go to the Alban Mount 471 , or be at Rome during the Latin festivals. For if he be capable of attending his brother to the mount, why is he not made prefect of the city? Thus, my dear Livia, you have my thoughts upon the matter. In my opinion, we ought to (299) settle this affair once for all, that we may not be always in suspense between hope and fear. You may, if you think proper, give your kinsman Antonia this part of my letter to read." In another letter, he writes as follows: "I shall invite the youth, Tiberius, every day during your absence, to supper, that he may not sup alone with his friends Sulpicius and Athenodorus. I wish the poor creature was more cautious and attentive in the choice of some one, whose manners, air, and gait might be proper for his imitation:

*Atuchei panu en tois spoudaiois lian.*

*In things of consequence he sadly fails.*

Where his mind does not run astray, he discovers a noble disposition." In a third letter, he says, "Let me die, my dear Livia, if I am not astonished, that the declamation of your grandson, Tiberius, should please me; for how he who talks so ill, should be able to declaim so clearly and properly, I cannot imagine." There is no doubt but Augustus, after this, came to a resolution upon the subject, and, accordingly, left him invested with no other honour than that of the Augural priesthood; naming him amongst the heirs of the third degree, who were but distantly allied to his family, for a sixth part of his estate only, with a legacy of no more than eight hundred thousand sesterces.

V. Upon his requesting some office in the state, Tiberius granted him the honorary appendages of the consulship, and when he pressed for a legitimate appointment, the emperor wrote word back, that "he sent him forty gold pieces for his expenses, during the festivals of the Saturnalia and Sigillaria." Upon this, laying aside all hope of advancement, he resigned himself entirely to an indolent life; living in great privacy, one while in his gardens, or a villa which he had near the city; another while in Campania, where he passed his time in the lowest society; by which means, besides his former character of a dull, heavy fellow, he acquired that of a drunkard and gamester.

VI. Notwithstanding this sort of life, much respect was shown him both in public and private. The equestrian (300) order twice made choice of him to intercede on their behalf; once to obtain from the consuls the favour of bearing on their shoulders the corpse of Augustus to Rome, and a second time to congratulate him upon the death of Sejanus. When he entered the theatre, they used to rise, and put off their cloaks. The senate likewise decreed, that he should be added to the number of the Augustal college of priests, who were chosen by lot; and soon afterwards, when his house was burnt down, that it should be rebuilt at the public charge; and that he should have the privilege of giving his vote amongst the men of consular rank. This decree was, however, repealed; Tiberius insisting to have him excused on account of his imbecility, and promising to make good his loss at his own expense. But at his death, he named him in his will, amongst his third heirs, for a third part of his estate; leaving him besides a legacy of two millions of sesterces, and expressly recommending him to the armies, the senate and people of Rome, amongst his other relations.

VII. At last, Caius 473 , his brother's son, upon his advancement to the empire, endeavouring to gain the affections of the public by all the arts of popularity, Claudius also was admitted to public offices, and held the consulship jointly with his nephew for two months. As he was entering the Forum for the first time with the fasces, an eagle which was flying that way; alighted upon his right shoulder. A second consulship was also allotted him, to commence at the expiration of the fourth year. He sometimes presided at the public spectacles, as the representative of Caius; being always, on those occasions, complimented with the acclamations of the people, wishing him all happiness, sometimes under the title of the emperor's uncle, and sometimes under that of Germanicus's brother.

VIII. Still he was subjected to many slights. If at any time he came in late to supper, he was obliged to walk round the room some time before he could get a place at table. When he indulged himself with sleep after eating, which was a common practice with him, the company used to throw olive-stones and dates at him. And the buffoons who attended would wake him, as if it were only in jest, with a cane or a whip. Sometimes they would put slippers upon his hands; as he lay snoring, that he might, upon awaking, rub his face with them.

IX. He was not only exposed to contempt, but sometimes likewise to considerable danger: first, in his consulship; for, having been too remiss in providing and erecting the statues of Caius's brothers, Nero and Drusus, he was very near being deprived of his office; and afterwards he was continually harassed with informations against him by one or other, sometimes even by his own domestics. When the conspiracy of Lepidus and Gaetulicus was discovered, being sent with some other deputies into Germany 474, to congratulate the emperor upon the occasion, he was in danger of his life; Caius being greatly enraged, and loudly complaining, that his uncle was sent to him, as if he was a boy who wanted a governor. Some even say, that he was thrown into a river, in his travelling dress. From this period, he voted in the senate always the last of the members of consular rank; being called upon after the rest, on purpose to disgrace him. A charge for the forgery of a will was also allowed to be prosecuted, though he had only signed it as a witness. At last, being obliged to pay eight millions of sesterces on entering upon a new office of priesthood, he was reduced to such straits in his private affairs, that in order to discharge his bond to the treasury, he was under the necessity of exposing to sale his whole estate, by an order of the prefects.

X. Having spent the greater part of his life under these and the like circumstances, he came at last to the empire in the fiftieth year of his age 475, by a very surprising turn of fortune. Being, as well as the rest, prevented from approaching Caius by the conspirators, who dispersed the crowd, under the pretext of his desiring to be private, he retired into an apartment called the Hermaeum 476; and soon afterwards, terrified by the report of Caius being slain, he crept into an adjoining balcony, where he hid himself behind the hangings of (302) the door. A common soldier, who happened to pass that way, spying his feet, and desirous to discover who he was, pulled him out; when immediately recognizing him, he threw himself in a great fright at his feet, and saluted him by the title of emperor. He then conducted him to his fellow-soldiers, who were all in a great rage, and irresolute what they should do. They put him into a litter, and as the slaves of the palace had all fled, took their turns in carrying him on their shoulders, and brought him into the camp, sad and trembling; the people who met him lamenting his situation, as if the poor innocent was being carried to execution. Being received within the ramparts 477 , he continued all night with the sentries on guard, recovered somewhat from his fright, but in no great hopes of the succession. For the consuls, with the senate and civic troops, had possessed themselves of the Forum and Capitol, with the determination to assert the public liberty; and he being sent for likewise, by a tribune of the people, to the senate-house, to give his advice upon the present juncture of affairs, returned answer, "I am under constraint, and cannot possibly come." The day afterwards, the senate being dilatory in their proceedings, and worn out by divisions amongst themselves, while the people who surrounded the senate-house shouted that they would have one master, naming Claudius, he suffered the soldiers assembled under arms to swear allegiance to him, promising them fifteen thousand sesterces a man; he being the first of the Caesars who purchased the submission of the soldiers with money. 478

XI. Having thus established himself in power, his first object was to abolish all remembrance of the two preceding days, in which a revolution in the state had been canvassed. Accordingly, he passed an act of perpetual oblivion and pardon for every thing said or done during that time; and this he faithfully observed, with the exception only of putting to death a few tribunes and centurions concerned in the conspiracy against Caius, both as an example, and because he understood that they had also planned his own death. He now turned (303) his thoughts towards paying respect to the memory of his relations. His most solemn and usual oath was, "By Augustus." He prevailed upon the senate to decree divine honours to his grandmother Livia, with a chariot in the Circensian procession drawn by elephants, as had been appointed for Augustus 479 ; and public offerings to the shades of his parents. Besides which, he instituted Circensian games for his father, to be celebrated every year, upon his birth-day, and, for his mother, a chariot to be drawn through the circus; with the title of Augusta, which had been refused by his grandmother 480 . To the memory of his brother 481 , to which, upon all occasions, he showed a great regard, he gave a Greek comedy, to be exhibited in the public diversions at Naples 482 , and awarded the crown for it, according to the sentence of the judges in that solemnity. Nor did he omit to make honourable and grateful mention of Mark Antony; declaring by a proclamation, "That he the more earnestly insisted upon the observation of his father Drusus's birth-day, because it was likewise that of his grandfather Antony." He completed the marble arch near Pompey's theatre, which had formerly been decreed by the senate in honour of Tiberius, but which had been neglected 483 . And though he cancelled all the acts of Caius, yet he forbad the day of his assassination, notwithstanding it was that of his own accession to the empire, to be reckoned amongst the festivals.

XII. But with regard to his own aggrandisement, he was sparing and modest, declining the title of emperor, and refusing all excessive honours. He celebrated the marriage of his daughter and the birth-day of a grandson with great privacy, at home. He recalled none of those who had been banished, without a decree of the senate: and requested of them permission for the prefect of the military tribunes and pretorian guards to attend him in the senate-house 484 ; and (304) also that they would be pleased to bestow upon his procurators judicial authority in the provinces 485 . He asked of the consuls likewise the privilege of holding fairs upon his private estate. He frequently assisted the magistrates in the trial of causes, as one of their assessors. And when they gave public spectacles, he would rise up with the rest of the spectators, and salute them both by words and gestures. When the tribunes of the people came to him while he was on the tribunal, he excused himself, because, on account of the crowd, he could not hear them unless they stood. In a short time, by this conduct, he wrought himself so much into the favour and affection of the public, that when, upon his going to Ostia, a report was spread in the city that he had been way-laid and slain, the people never ceased cursing the soldiers for traitors, and the senate as parricides, until one or two persons, and presently after several others, were brought by the magistrates upon the rostra, who assured them that he was alive, and not far from the city, on his way home.

XIII. Conspiracies, however, were formed against him, not only by individuals separately, but by a faction; and at last his government was disturbed with a civil war. A low fellow was found with a poniard about him, near his chamber, at midnight. Two men of the equestrian order were discovered waiting for him in the streets, armed with a tuck and a huntsman's dagger; one of them intending to attack him as he came out of the theatre, and the other as he was sacrificing in the temple of Mars. Gallus Asinius and Statilius Corvinus, grandsons of the two orators, Pollio and Messala 486 , formed a conspiracy against him, in which they engaged many of his freedmen and slaves. Furius Camillus Scribonianus, his lieutenant in Dalmatia, broke into rebellion, but was reduced in (305) the space of five days; the legions which he had seduced from their oath of fidelity relinquishing their purpose, upon an alarm occasioned by ill omens. For when orders were given them to march, to meet their new emperor, the eagles could not be decorated, nor the standards pulled out of the ground, whether it was by accident, or a divine interposition.

XIV. Besides his former consulship, he held the office afterwards four times; the first two successively 487 , but the following, after an interval of four years each 488 ; the last for six months, the others for two; and the third, upon his being chosen in the room of a consul who died; which had never been done by any of the emperors before him. Whether he was consul or out of office, he constantly attended the courts for the administration of justice, even upon such days as were solemnly observed as days of rejoicing in his family, or by his friends; and sometimes upon the public festivals of ancient institution. Nor did he always adhere strictly to the letter of the laws, but overruled the rigour or lenity of many of their enactments, according to his sentiments of justice and equity. For where persons lost their suits by insisting upon more than appeared to be their due, before the judges of private causes, he granted them the indulgence of a second trial. And with regard to such as were convicted of any great delinquency, he even exceeded the punishment appointed by law, and condemned them to be exposed to wild beasts. 489

XV. But in hearing and determining causes, he exhibited a strange inconsistency of temper, being at one time circumspect and sagacious, at another inconsiderate and rash, and sometimes frivolous, and like one out of his mind. In correcting the roll of judges, he struck off the name of one who, concealing the privilege his children gave him to be excused from serving, had answered to his name, as too eager for the office. Another who was summoned before him in a cause of his own, but alleged that the affair did not properly come under the (306) emperor's cognizance, but that of the ordinary judges, he ordered to plead the cause himself immediately before him, and show in a case of his own, how equitable a judge he would prove in that of other persons. A woman refusing to acknowledge her own son, and there being no clear proof on either side, he obliged her to confess the truth, by ordering her to marry the young man 490. He was much inclined to determine causes in favour of the parties who appeared, against those who did not, without inquiring whether their absence was occasioned by their own fault, or by real necessity. On proclamation of a man's being convicted of forgery, and that he ought to have his hand cut off, he insisted that an executioner should be immediately sent for, with a Spanish sword and a block. A person being prosecuted for falsely assuming the freedom of Rome, and a frivolous dispute arising between the advocates in the cause, whether he ought to make his appearance in the Roman or Grecian dress, to show his impartiality, he commanded him to change his clothes several times according to the character he assumed in the accusation or defence. An anecdote is related of him, and believed to be true, that, in a particular cause, he delivered his sentence in writing thus: "I am in favour of those who have spoken the truth." 491 By this he so much forfeited the good opinion of the world, that he was everywhere and openly despised. A person making an excuse for the non-appearance of a witness whom he had sent for from the provinces, declared it was impossible for him to appear, concealing the reason for some time: at last, after several interrogatories were put to him on the subject, he answered, "The man is dead;" to which Claudius replied, "I think that is a sufficient excuse." Another thanking him for suffering a person who was prosecuted to make his defence by counsel, added, "And yet it is no more than what is usual." I have likewise heard some old men say 492, that the advocates used to abuse his patience so grossly, that they would not only (307) call him back, as he was quitting the tribunal, but would seize him by the lap of his coat, and sometimes catch him by the heels, to make him stay. That such behaviour, however strange, is not incredible, will appear from this anecdote. Some obscure Greek, who was a litigant, had an altercation with him, in which he called out, "You are an old fool." 493 It is certain that a Roman knight, who was prosecuted by an impotent device of his enemies on a false charge of abominable obscenity with women, observing that common strumpets were summoned against him and allowed to give evidence, upbraided Claudius in very harsh and severe terms with his folly and cruelty, and threw his style, and some books which he had in his hands, in his face, with such violence as to wound him severely in the cheek.

XVI. He likewise assumed the censorship 494, which had been discontinued since the time that Paulus and Plancus had jointly held it. But this also he administered very unequally, and with a strange variety of humour and conduct. In his review of the knights, he passed over, without any mark of disgrace, a profligate young man, only because his father spoke of him in the highest terms; "for," said he, "his father is his proper censor." Another, who was infamous for debauching youths and for adultery, he only admonished "to indulge his youthful inclinations more sparingly, or at least more cautiously;" 495 adding, "why must I know what mistress you keep?" When, at the request of his friends, he had taken off a mark of infamy which he had set upon one knight's name, he said, "Let the blot, however, remain." He not only struck out of the list of judges, but likewise deprived of the freedom of Rome, an illustrious man of the highest provincial rank in Greece, only because he was ignorant of the Latin language. Nor in this review did he suffer any one to give an account of his conduct by an advocate, but obliged each man to speak for himself in the best way he could. He disgraced many, and some that little expected it, and for a reason entirely new, namely, for going out of Italy without his license; (308) and one likewise, for having in his province been the familiar companion of a king; observing, that, in former times, Rabirius Posthumus had been prosecuted for treason, although he only went after Ptolemy to Alexandria for the purpose of securing payment of a debt 496. Having tried to brand with disgrace several others, he, to his own greater shame, found them generally innocent, through the negligence of the persons employed to inquire into their characters; those whom he charged with living in celibacy, with want of children, or estate, proving themselves to be husbands, parents, and in affluent circumstances. One of the knights who was charged with stabbing himself, laid his bosom bare, to show that there was not the least mark of violence upon his body. The following incidents were remarkable in his censorship. He ordered a car, plated with silver, and of very sumptuous workmanship, which was exposed for sale in the Sigillaria 497, to be purchased, and broken in pieces before his eyes. He published twenty proclamations in one day, in one of which he advised the people, "Since the vintage was very plentiful, to have their casks well secured at the bung with pitch:" and in another, he told them, "that nothing would sooner cure the bite of a viper, than the sap of the yew-tree."

XVII. He undertook only one expedition, and that was of short duration. The triumphal ornaments decreed him by the senate, he considered as beneath the imperial dignity, and was therefore resolved to have the honour of a real triumph. For this purpose, he selected Britain, which had never been attempted by any one since Julius Caesar 498, and was then chafing (309) with rage, because the Romans would not give up some deserters. Accordingly, he set sail from Ostia, but was twice very near being wrecked by the boisterous wind called Circius 499, upon the coast of Liguria, and near the islands called Stoechades 500. Having marched by land from Marseilles to Gessoriacum 501, he thence passed over to Britain, and part of the island submitting to him, within a few days after his arrival, without battle or bloodshed, he returned to Rome in less than six months from the time of his departure, and triumphed in the most solemn manner 502; to witness which, he not only (310) gave leave to governors of provinces to come to Rome, but even to some of the exiles. Among the spoils taken from the enemy, he fixed upon the pediment of his house in the Palatium, a naval crown, in token of his having passed, and, as it were, conquered the Ocean, and had it suspended near the civic crown which was there before. Messalina, his wife, followed his chariot in a covered litter 503. Those who had attained the honour of triumphal ornaments in the same war, rode behind; the rest followed on foot, wearing the robe with the broad stripes. Crassus Frugi was mounted upon a horse richly caparisoned, in a robe embroidered with palm leaves, because this was the second time of his obtaining that honour.

XVIII. He paid particular attention to the care of the city, and to have it well supplied with provisions. A dreadful fire happening in the Aemiliana 504, which lasted some time, he passed two nights in the Diribitorium 505, and the soldiers and gladiators not being in sufficient numbers to extinguish it, he caused the magistrates to summon the people out of all the streets in the city, to their assistance. Placing bags of money before him, he encouraged them to do their utmost, declaring, that he would reward every one on the spot, according to their exertions.

XIX. During a scarcity of provisions, occasioned by bad crops for several successive years, he was stopped in the middle of the Forum by the mob, who so abused him, at the same time pelting him with fragments of bread, that he had some (311) difficulty in escaping into the palace by a back door. He therefore used all possible means to bring provisions to the city, even in the winter. He proposed to the merchants a sure profit, by indemnifying them against any loss that might befall them by storms at sea; and granted great privileges to those who built ships for that traffic. To a citizen of Rome he gave an exemption from the penalty of the Papia-Poppaean law 506 ; to one who had only the privilege of Latium, the freedom of the city; and to women the rights which by law belonged to those who had four children: which enactments are in force to this day.

XX. He completed some important public works, which, though not numerous, were very useful. The principal were an aqueduct, which had been begun by Caius; an emissary for the discharge of the waters of the Fucine lake 507 , and the harbour of Ostia; although he knew that Augustus had refused to comply with the repeated application of the Marsians for one of these; and that the other had been several times intended by Julius Caesar, but as often abandoned on account of the difficulty of its execution. He brought to the city the cool and plentiful springs of the Claudian water, one of which is called Caeruleus, and the other Curtius and Albudinus, as likewise the river of the New Anio, in a stone canal; and distributed them into many magnificent reservoirs. The canal from the Fucine lake was undertaken as much for the sake of profit, as for the honour of the enterprise; for there were parties who offered to drain it at their own expense, on condition of their having a grant of the land laid dry. With great difficulty he completed a canal three miles in length, partly by cutting through, and partly by tunnelling, a mountain; thirty thousand men being constantly employed in the work for eleven years 508 . He formed the harbour at Ostia, by carrying out circular piers on the right and on the left, with (312) a mole protecting, in deep water, the entrance of the port 509 . To secure the foundation of this mole, he sunk the vessel in which the great obelisk 510 had been brought from Egypt 511 ; and built upon piles a very lofty tower, in imitation of the Pharos at Alexandria, on which lights were burnt to direct mariners in the night.

XXI. He often distributed largesses of corn and money among the people, and entertained them with a great variety of public magnificent spectacles, not only such as were usual, and in the accustomed places, but some of new invention, and others revived from ancient models, and exhibited in places where nothing of the kind had been ever before attempted. In the games which he presented at the dedication of Pompey's theatre 512, which had been burnt down, and was rebuilt by him, he presided upon a tribunal erected for him in the orchestra; having first paid his devotions, in the temple above, and then coming down through the centre of the circle, while all the people kept their seats in profound silence 513. He likewise (313) exhibited the secular games 514, giving out that Augustus had anticipated the regular period; though he himself says in his history, "That they had been omitted before the age of Augustus, who had calculated the years with great exactness, and again brought them to their regular period." 515 The crier was therefore ridiculed, when he invited people in the usual form, "to games which no person had ever before seen, nor ever would again;" when many were still living who had already seen them; and some of the performers who had formerly acted in them, were now again brought upon the stage. He likewise frequently celebrated the Circensian games in the Vatican 516, sometimes exhibiting a hunt of wild beasts, after every five courses. He embellished the Circus Maximus with marble barriers, and gilded goals, which before were of common stone 517 and wood, and assigned proper places for the senators, who were used to sit promiscuously with the other spectators. Besides the chariot-races, he exhibited there the Trojan game, and wild beasts from Africa, which were encountered by a troop of pretorian knights, with their tribunes, and even the prefect at the head of them; besides Thessalian horse, who drive fierce bulls round the circus, leap upon their backs when they have exhausted their fury, and drag them by the horns to the ground. He gave exhibitions of gladiators in several places, and of various kinds; one yearly on the anniversary of his accession in the pretorian camp 518, but without any hunting, or the usual apparatus; another in the Septa as usual; and in the same place, another out of the common way, and of a few days' continuance only, which he called

Sportula; because when he was going to present it, he informed the people by proclamation, "that he invited them to a late supper, got up in haste, and without ceremony." Nor did he lend himself to any kind of public diversion with more freedom and hilarity; insomuch that he would hold out his left hand, and (314) joined by the common people, count upon his fingers aloud the gold pieces presented to those who came off conquerors. He would earnestly invite the company to be merry; sometimes calling them his "masters," with a mixture of insipid, far-fetched jests. Thus, when the people called for Palumbus 519 , he said, "He would give them one when he could catch it." The following was well-intended, and well-timed; having, amidst great applause, spared a gladiator, on the intercession of his four sons, he sent a billet immediately round the theatre, to remind the people, "how much it behoved them to get children, since they had before them an example how useful they had been in procuring favour and security for a gladiator." He likewise represented in the Campus Martius, the assault and sacking of a town, and the surrender of the British kings 520 , presiding in his general's cloak. Immediately before he drew off the waters from the Fucine lake, he exhibited upon it a naval fight. But the combatants on board the fleets crying out, "Health attend you, noble emperor! We, who are about to peril our lives, salute you;" and he replying, "Health attend you too," they all refused to fight, as if by that response he had meant to excuse them. Upon this, he hesitated for a time, whether he should not destroy them all with fire and sword. At last, leaping from his seat, and running along the shore of the lake with tottering steps, the result of his foul excesses, he, partly by fair words, and partly by threats, persuaded them to engage. This spectacle represented an engagement between the fleets of Sicily and Rhodes; consisting each of twelve ships of war, of three banks of oars. The signal for the encounter was given by a silver Triton, raised by machinery from the middle of the lake.

XXII. With regard to religious ceremonies, the administration of affairs both civil and military, and the condition of all orders of the people at home and abroad, some practices he corrected, others which had been laid aside he revived; and some regulations he introduced which were entirely new. In appointing new priests for the several colleges, he made no appointments without being sworn. When an earthquake (315) happened in the city, he never failed to summon the people together by the praetor, and appoint holidays for sacred rites. And upon the sight of any ominous bird in the City or Capitol, he issued an order for a supplication, the words of which, by virtue of his office of high priest, after an exhortation from the rostra, he recited in the presence of the people, who repeated them after him; all workmen and slaves being first ordered to withdraw.

XXIII. The courts of judicature, whose sittings had been formerly divided between the summer and winter months, he ordered, for the dispatch of business, to sit the whole year round. The jurisdiction in matters of trust, which used to be granted annually by special commission to certain magistrates, and in the city only, he made permanent, and extended to the provincial judges likewise. He altered a clause added by Tiberius to the Papia-Poppaean law 521 , which inferred that men of sixty years of age were incapable of begetting children. He ordered that, out of the ordinary course of proceeding, orphans might have guardians appointed them by the consuls; and that those who were banished from any province by the chief magistrate, should be debarred from coming into the City, or any part of Italy. He inflicted on certain persons a new sort of banishment, by forbidding them to depart further than three miles from Rome. When any affair of importance came before the senate, he used to sit between the two consuls upon the seats of the tribunes. He reserved to himself the power of granting license to travel out of Italy, which before had belonged to the senate.

XXIV. He likewise granted the consular ornaments to his Ducenarian procurators. From those who declined the senatorian dignity, he took away the equestrian. Although he had in the beginning of his reign declared, that he would admit no man into the senate who was not the great-grandson of a Roman citizen, yet he gave the "broad hem" to the son of a freedman, on condition that he should be adopted by a Roman knight. Being afraid, however, of incurring censure by such an act, he informed the public, that his ancestor Appius Caecus, the censor, had elected the sons of freedmen into (316) the senate; for he was ignorant, it seems, that in the times of Appius, and a long while afterwards, persons manumitted were not called freedmen, but only their sons who were free-born. Instead of the expense which the college of quaestors was obliged to incur in paving the high-ways, he ordered them to give the people an exhibition of gladiators; and relieving them of the provinces of Ostia and [Cisalpine] Gaul, he reinstated them in the charge of the treasury, which, since it was taken from them, had been managed by the praetors, or those who had formerly filled that office. He gave the triumphal ornaments to Silanus, who was betrothed to his daughter, though he was under age; and in other cases, he bestowed them on so many, and with so little reserve, that there is extant a letter unanimously addressed to him by all the legions, begging him "to grant his consular lieutenants the triumphal ornaments at the time of their appointment to commands, in order to prevent their seeking occasion to engage in unnecessary wars." He decreed to Aulus Plautius the honour of an ovation 522, going to meet him at his entering the city, and walking with him in the procession to the Capitol, and back, in which he took the left side, giving him the post of honour. He allowed Gabinius Secundus, upon his conquest of the Chauci, a German tribe, to assume the cognomen of Chaucius. 523

XXV. His military organization of the equestrian order was this. After having the command of a cohort, they were promoted to a wing of auxiliary horse, and subsequently received the commission of tribune of a legion. He raised a body of militia, who were called Supernumeraries, who, though they were a sort of soldiers, and kept in reserve, yet received pay. He procured an act of the senate to prohibit all soldiers from attending senators at their houses, in the way of respect and compliment. He confiscated the estates of all freedmen who presumed to take upon themselves the equestrian rank. Such of them as were ungrateful to their patrons, and were complained of by them, he reduced to their former condition of (317) slavery; and declared to their advocates, that he would always give judgment against the freedmen, in any suit at law which the masters might happen to have with them. Some persons having exposed their sick slaves, in a languishing condition, on the island of Aesculapius 524, because of the tediousness of their cure; he declared all who were so exposed perfectly free, never more to return, if they should recover, to their former servitude; and that if any one chose to kill at once, rather than expose, a slave, he should be liable for murder. He published a proclamation, forbidding all travellers to pass through the towns of Italy any otherwise than on foot, or in a litter or chair 525. He quartered a cohort of soldiers at Puteoli, and another at Ostia, to be in readiness against any accidents from fire. He prohibited foreigners from adopting Roman names, especially those which belonged to families 526 . Those who falsely pretended to the freedom of Rome, he beheaded on the Esquiline. He gave up to the senate the provinces of Achaia and Macedonia, which Tiberius had transferred to his own administration. He deprived the Lycians of their liberties, as a punishment for their fatal dissensions; but restored to the Rhodians their freedom, upon their repenting of their former misdemeanors. He exonerated for ever the people of Ilium from the payment of taxes, as being the founders of the Roman race; reciting upon the occasion a letter in Greek, (318) from the senate and people of Rome to king Seleucus 527 , on which they promised him their friendship and alliance, provided that he would grant their kinsmen the Iliensians immunity from all burdens.

He banished from Rome all the Jews, who were continually making disturbances at the instigation of one Chrestus 528 . He allowed the ambassadors of the Germans to sit at the public spectacles in the seats assigned to the senators, being induced to grant them favours by their frank and honourable conduct. For, having been seated in the rows of benches which were common to the people, on observing the Parthian and Armenian ambassadors sitting among the senators, they took upon themselves to cross over into the same seats, as being, they said, no way inferior to the others, in point either, of merit or rank. The religious rites of the Druids, solemnized with such horrid cruelties, which had only been forbidden the citizens of Rome during the reign of Augustus, he utterly abolished among the Gauls 529 . On the other hand, he attempted (319) to transfer the Eleusinian mysteries from Attica to Rome 530 . He likewise ordered the temple of Venus Erycina in Sicily, which was old and in a ruinous condition, to be repaired at the expense of the Roman people. He concluded treaties with foreign princes in the forum, with the sacrifice of a sow, and the form of words used by the heralds in former times. But in these and other things, and indeed the greater part of his administration, he was directed not so much by his own judgment, as by the influence of his wives and freedmen; for the most part acting in conformity to what their interests or fancies dictated.

XXVI. He was twice married at a very early age, first to Aemilia Lepida, the grand-daughter of Augustus, and afterwards to Livia

Medullina, who had the cognomen of Camilla, and was descended from the old dictator Camillus. The former he divorced while still a virgin, because her parents had incurred the displeasure of Augustus; and he lost the latter by sickness on the day fixed for their nuptials. He next married Plautia Urgulanilla, whose father had enjoyed the honour of a triumph; and soon afterwards, Aelia Paetina, the daughter of a man of consular rank. But he divorced them both; Paetina, upon some trifling causes of disgust; and Urgulanilla, for scandalous lewdness, and the suspicion of murder. After them he took in marriage Valeria Messalina, the daughter of Barbatus Messala, his cousin. But finding that, besides her other shameful debaucheries, she had even gone so far as to marry in his own absence Caius Silius, the settlement of her dower being formally signed, in the presence of the augurs, he put her to death. When summoning his pretorians to his presence, he made to them this declaration: "As I have been so unhappy in my unions, I am resolved to continue in future unmarried; and if I should not, I give you leave to stab me." He was, however, unable to persist in this resolution; for he began immediately to think of another wife; and even of taking back Paetina, whom he had formerly divorced: he thought also of Lollia Paulina, who had been married to Caius Caesar. But being ensnared by the arts of Agrippina, (320) the daughter of his brother Germanicus, who took advantage of the kisses and endearments which their near relationship admitted, to inflame his desires, he got some one to propose at the next meeting of the senate, that they should oblige the emperor to marry Agrippina, as a measure highly conducive to the public interest; and that in future liberty should be given for such marriages, which until that time had been considered incestuous. In less than twenty-four hours after this, he married her 531 . No person was found, however, to follow the example, excepting one freedman, and a centurion of the first rank, at the solemnization of whose nuptials both he and Agrippina attended.

XXVII. He had children by three of his wives: by Urgulanilla, Drusus and Claudia; by Paetina, Antonia; and by Messalina, Octavia, and also a son, whom at first he called Germanicus, but afterwards Britannicus. He lost Drusus at Pompeii, when he was very young; he being choked with a pear, which in his play he tossed into the air, and caught in his mouth. Only a few days before, he had betrothed him to one of Sejanus's daughters 532 ; and I am therefore surprised that some authors should say he lost his life by the treachery of Sejanus. Claudia, who was, in truth, the daughter of Boter his freedman, though she was born five months before his divorce, he ordered to be thrown naked at her mother's door. He married Antonia to Cneius Pompey the Great 533 , and afterwards to Faustus Sylla 534 , both youths of very noble parentage; Octavia to his step-son Nero 535 , after she had been contracted to Silanus. Britannicus was born upon the twentieth day of his reign, and in his second consulship. He often earnestly commended him to the soldiers, holding him in his arms before their ranks; and would likewise show him to the people in the theatre, setting him upon his lap, or holding him out whilst he was still very young; and was sure to receive their acclamations, and good wishes on his behalf. Of his (321) sons-in-law, he adopted Nero. He not only dismissed from his favour both Pompey and Silanus, but put them to death.

XXVIII. Amongst his freedmen, the greatest favourite was the eunuch Posides, whom, in his British triumph, he presented with the pointless spear, classing him among the military men. Next to him, if not equal, in favour was Felix 536 , whom he not only preferred to commands both of cohorts and troops, but to the government of the province of Judaea; and he became, in consequence of his elevation, the husband of three queens 537 . Another favourite was Harpocras, to whom he granted the privilege of being carried in a litter within the city, and of holding public spectacles for the entertainment of the people. In this class was likewise Polybius, who assisted him in his studies, and had often the honour of walking between the two consuls. But above all others, Narcissus, his secretary, and Pallas 538 , the comptroller of his accounts, were in high favour with him. He not only allowed them to receive, by decree of the senate, immense presents, but also to be decorated with the quaestorian and praetorian ensigns of honour. So much did he indulge them in amassing wealth, and plundering the public, that, upon his complaining, once, of the lowness of his exchequer, some one said, with great reason, that "It would be full enough, if those two freedmen of his would but take him into partnership with them."

XXIX. Being entirely governed by these freedmen, and, as I have already said, by his wives, he was a tool to others, rather than a prince. He distributed offices, or the command of armies, pardoned or punished, according as it suited their interests, (322) their passions, or their caprice; and for the most part, without knowing, or being sensible of what he did. Not to enter into minute details relative to the revocation of grants, the reversal of judicial decisions, obtaining his signature to fictitious appointments, or the bare-faced alteration of them after signing; he put to death Appius Silanus, the father of his son-in-law, and the two Julias, the daughters of Drusus and Germanicus, without any positive proof of the crimes with which they were charged, or so much as permitting them to make any defence. He also cut off Cneius Pompey, the husband of his eldest daughter; and Lucius Silanus, who was betrothed to the younger Pompey, was stabbed in the act of unnatural lewdness with a favourite paramour. Silanus was obliged to quit the office of praetor upon the fourth of the calends of January [29th Dec.], and to kill himself on new year's day 539 following, the very same on which Claudius and Agrippina were married. He condemned to death five and thirty senators, and above three hundred Roman knights, with so little attention to what he did, that when a centurion brought him word of the execution of a man of consular rank, who was one of the number, and told him that he had executed his order, he declared, "he had ordered no such thing, but that he approved of it;" because his freedmen, it seems, had said, that the soldiers did nothing more than their duty, in dispatching the emperor's enemies without waiting for a warrant. But it is beyond all belief, that he himself, at the marriage of Messalina with the adulterous Silius, should actually sign the writings relative to her dowry; induced, as it is pretended, by the design of diverting from himself and transferring upon another the danger which some omens seemed to threaten him.

XXX. Either standing or sitting, but especially when he lay asleep, he had a majestic and graceful appearance; for he was tall, but not slender. His grey looks became him well, and he had a full neck. But his knees were feeble, and failed him in walking, so that his gait was ungainly, both when he assumed state, and when he was taking diversion. He was outrageous in his laughter, and still more so in his wrath, for then he foamed at the mouth, and discharged from his nostrils. He also stammered in his speech, and had a tremulous motion (323) of the head at all times, but particularly when he was engaged in any business, however trifling.

XXXI. Though his health was very infirm during the former part of his life, yet, after he became emperor, he enjoyed a good state of health, except only that he was subject to a pain of the stomach. In a fit of this complaint, he said he had thoughts of killing himself.

XXXII. He gave entertainments as frequent as they were splendid, and generally when there was such ample room, that very often six hundred guests sat down together. At a feast he gave on the banks of the canal for draining the Fucine Lake, he narrowly escaped being drowned, the water at its discharge rushing out with such violence, that it overflowed the conduit. At supper he had always his own children, with those of several of the nobility, who, according to an ancient custom, sat at the feet of the couches. One of his guests having been suspected of purloining a golden cup, he invited him again the next day, but served him with a porcelain jug. It is said, too, that he intended to publish an edict, "allowing to all people the liberty of giving vent at table to any distension occasioned by flatulence," upon hearing of a person whose modesty, when under restraint, had nearly cost him his life.

XXXIII. He was always ready to eat and drink at any time or in any place. One day, as he was hearing causes in the Forum of Augustus, he smelt the dinner which was preparing for the Salii 540 , in the temple of Mars adjoining, whereupon he quitted (324) the tribunal, and went to partake of the feast with the priests.

He scarcely ever left the table until he had thoroughly crammed himself and drank to intoxication; and then he would immediately fall asleep, lying upon his back with his mouth open. While in this condition, a feather was put down his throat, to make him throw up the contents of his stomach. Upon composing himself to rest, his sleep was short, and he usually awoke before midnight; but he would sometimes sleep in the daytime, and that, even, when he was upon the tribunal; so that the advocates often found it difficult to wake him, though they raised their voices for that purpose. He set no bounds to his libidinous intercourse with women, but never betrayed any unnatural desires for the other sex. He was fond of gaming, and published a book upon the subject. He even used to play as he rode in his chariot, having the tables so fitted, that the game was not disturbed by the motion of the carriage.

XXXIV. His cruel and sanguinary disposition was exhibited upon great as well as trifling occasions. When any person was to be put to the torture, or criminal punished for parricide, he was impatient for the execution, and would have it performed in his own presence. When he was at Tibur, being desirous of seeing an example of the old way of putting malefactors to death, some were immediately bound to a stake for the purpose; but there being no executioner to be had at the place, he sent for one from Rome, and waited for his coming until night. In any exhibition of gladiators, presented either by himself or others, if any of the combatants chanced to fall, he ordered them to be butchered, especially the Retiarii, that he might see their faces in the agonies of death. Two gladiators happening to kill each other, he immediately ordered some little knives to be made of their swords for his own use. He took great pleasure in seeing men engage with wild beasts, and the combatants who appeared on the stage at noon. He would therefore come to the theatre by break of day, and at noon, dismissing the people to dinner, continued sitting himself; and besides those who were devoted to that sanguinary fate, he would match others with the beasts, upon slight or sudden occasions; as, for instance, the carpenters and their (326) assistants, and people of that sort, if a machine, or any piece of work in which they had been employed about the theatre did not answer the purpose for which it had been intended. To this desperate kind of encounter he forced one of his nomenclators, even encumbered as he was by wearing the toga.

XXXV. But the characteristics most predominant in him were fear and distrust. In the beginning of his reign, though he much affected a modest and humble appearance, as has been already observed, yet he durst not venture himself at an entertainment without being attended by a guard of spearmen, and made soldiers wait upon him at table instead of servants. He never visited a sick person, until the chamber had been first searched, and the bed and bedding thoroughly examined. At other times, all persons who came to pay their court to him were strictly searched by officers appointed for that purpose; nor was it until after a long time, and with much difficulty, that he was prevailed upon to excuse women, boys, and girls from such rude handling, or suffer their attendants or writing-masters to retain their cases for pens and styles. When Camillus formed his plot against him, not doubting but his timidity might be worked upon without a war, he wrote to him a scurrilous, petulant, and threatening letter, desiring him to resign the government, and betake himself to a life of privacy. Upon receiving this requisition, he had some thoughts of complying with it, and summoned together the principal men of the city, to consult with them on the subject.

XXXVI. Having heard some loose reports of conspiracies formed against him, he was so much alarmed, that he thought of immediately abdicating the government. And when, as I have before related, a man armed with a dagger was discovered near him while he was sacrificing, he instantly ordered the heralds to convoke the senate, and with tears and dismal exclamations, lamented that such was his condition, that he was safe no where; and for a long time afterwards he abstained from appearing in public. He smothered his ardent love for Messalina, not so much on account of her infamous conduct, as from apprehension of danger; believing that she aspired to share with Silius, her partner in adultery, the imperial dignity. (326) Upon this occasion he ran in a great fright, and a very shameful manner, to the camp, asking all the way he went, "if the empire were indeed safely his?"

XXXVII. No suspicion was too trifling, no person on whom it rested too contemptible, to throw him into a panic, and induce him to take precautions for his safety, and meditate revenge. A man engaged in a litigation before his tribunal, having saluted him, drew him aside, and told him he had dreamt that he saw him murdered; and shortly afterwards, when his adversary came to deliver his plea to the emperor, the plaintiff, pretending to have discovered the murderer, pointed to him as the man he had seen in his dream; whereupon, as if he had been taken in the act, he was hurried away to execution. We are informed, that Appius Silanus was got rid of in the same manner, by a contrivance betwixt Messalina and Narcissus, in which they had their several parts assigned them. Narcissus therefore burst into his lord's chamber before daylight, apparently in great fright, and told him that he had dreamt that Appius Silanus had murdered him. The empress, upon this, affecting great surprise, declared she had the like dream for several nights successively. Presently afterwards, word was brought, as it had been agreed on, that Appius was come, he having, indeed, received orders the preceding day to be there at that time; and, as if the truth of the dream was sufficiently confirmed by his appearance at that juncture, he was immediately ordered to be prosecuted and put to death. The day following, Claudius related the whole affair to the senate, and acknowledged his great obligation to his freedmen for watching over him even in his sleep.

XXXVIII. Sensible of his being subject to passion and resentment, he excused himself in both instances by a proclamation, assuring the public that "the former should be short and harmless, and the latter never without good cause." After severely reprimanding the people of Ostia for not sending some boats to meet him upon his entering the mouth of the Tiber, in terms which might expose them to the public resentment, he wrote to Rome that he had been treated as a private person; yet immediately afterwards he pardoned them, and that in a way which had the appearance of making them (327) satisfaction, or begging pardon for some injury he had done them. Some people who addressed him unseasonably in public, he pushed away with his own hand. He likewise banished a person who had been secretary to a quaestor, and even a senator who had filled the office of praetor, without a hearing, and although they were innocent; the former only because he had treated him with rudeness while he was in a private station, and the other, because in his aedileship he had fined some tenants of his, for selling cooked victuals contrary to law, and ordered his steward, who interfered, to be whipped. On this account, likewise, he took from the aediles the jurisdiction they had over cooks'-shops. He did not scruple to speak of his own absurdities, and declared in some short speeches which he published, that he had only feigned imbecility in the reign of Caius, because otherwise it would have been impossible for him to have escaped and arrived at the station he had then attained. He could not, however, gain credit for this assertion; for a short time afterwards, a book was published under the title of Moron anastasis, "The Resurrection of Fools," the design of which was to show "that nobody ever counterfeited folly."

XXXIX. Amongst other things, people admired in him his indifference and unconcern; or, to express it in Greek, his meteoria and ablepsia. Placing himself at table a little after Messalina's death, he enquired, "Why the empress did not come?" Many of those whom he had condemned to death, he ordered the day after to be invited to his table, and to game with him, and sent to reprimand them as sluggish fellows for not making greater haste. When he was meditating his incestuous marriage with Agrippina, he was perpetually calling her, "My daughter, my nursling, born and brought up upon my lap." And when he was going to adopt Nero, as if there was little cause for censure in his adopting a son-in-law, when he had a son of his own arrived at years of maturity; he continually gave out in public, "that no one had ever been admitted by adoption into the Claudian family."

XL. He frequently appeared so careless in what he said, and so inattentive to circumstances, that it was believed he never reflected who he himself was, or amongst whom, or at (328) what time, or in what place, he spoke. In a debate in the senate relative to the butchers and vintners, he cried out, "I ask you, who can live without a bit of meat?" And mentioned the great plenty of old taverns, from which he himself used formerly to have his wine. Among other reasons for his supporting a certain person who was candidate for the quaestorship, he gave this: "His father," said he, "once gave me, very seasonably, a draught of cold water when I was sick." Upon his bringing a woman as a witness in some cause before the senate, he said, "This woman was my mother's freedwoman and dresser, but she always considered me as her master; and this I say, because there are some still in my family that do not look upon me as such." The people of Ostia addressing him in open court with a petition, he flew into a rage at them, and said, "There is no reason why I should oblige you: if any one else is free to act as he pleases, surely I am." The following expressions he had in his mouth every day, and at all hours and seasons: "What! do you take me for a Theogonius?" 541 And in Greek lalei kai mae thingane, "Speak, but do not touch me;" besides many other familiar sentences, below the dignity of a private person, much more of an emperor, who was not deficient either in eloquence or learning, as having applied himself very closely to the liberal sciences.

XLI. By the encouragement of Titus Livius 542 , and with the assistance of Sulpicius Flavus, he attempted at an early age the composition of a history; and having called together a numerous auditory, to hear and give their judgment upon it, he read it over with much difficulty, and frequently interrupting himself. For after he had begun, a great laugh was raised amongst the company, by the breaking of several benches from the weight of a very fat man; and even when order was restored, he could not forbear bursting out into violent fits of laughter, at the remembrance of the accident. After he became emperor, likewise, he wrote several things (329) which he was careful to have recited to his friends by a reader. He commenced his history from the death of the dictator Caesar; but afterwards he took a later period, and began at the conclusion of the civil wars; because he found he could not speak with freedom, and a due regard to truth, concerning the former period, having been often taken to task both by his mother and grandmother. Of the earlier history he left only two books, but of the latter, one and forty. He compiled likewise the "History of his Own Life," in eight books, full of absurdities, but in no bad style; also, "A Defence of Cicero against the Books of Asinius Gallus," 543 which exhibited a considerable degree of learning. He besides invented three new letters, and added them to the former alphabet 544 , as highly necessary. He published a book to recommend them while he was yet only a private person; but on his elevation to imperial power he had little difficulty in introducing them into common use; and these letters are still extant in a variety of books, registers, and inscriptions upon buildings.

XLII. He applied himself with no less attention to the study of Grecian literature, asserting upon all occasions his love of that language, and its surpassing excellency. A stranger once holding a discourse both in Greek and Latin, he addressed him thus; "Since you are skilled in both our tongues." And recommending Achaia to the favour of the senate, he said, "I have a particular attachment to that province, on account of our common studies." In the senate he often made long replies to ambassadors in that language. On the tribunal he frequently quoted the verses of Homer. When at any time he had taken vengeance on an enemy or a conspirator, he scarcely ever gave to the tribune on guard, who, (330) according to custom, came for the word, any other than this.

*Andr' epamynastai, ote tis proteros chalepaenae.*
'Tis time to strike when wrong demands the blow.

To conclude; he wrote some histories likewise in Greek, namely, twenty books on Tuscan affairs, and eight on the Carthaginian; in consequence of which, another museum was founded at Alexandria, in addition to the old one, and called after his name; and it was ordered, that, upon certain days in every year, his Tuscan history should be read over in one of these, and his Carthaginian in the other, as in a school; each history being read through by persons who took it in turn.

XLIII. Towards the close of his life, he gave some manifest indications that he repented of his marriage with Agrippina, and his adoption of Nero. For some of his freedmen noticing with approbation his having condemned, the day before, a woman accused of adultery, he remarked, "It has been my misfortune to have wives who have been unfaithful to my bed; but they did not escape punishment." Often, when he happened to meet Britannicus, he would embrace him tenderly, and express a desire "that he might grow apace," and receive from him an account of all his actions: using the Greek phrase, "o trosas kai iasetai,—He who has wounded will also heal." And intending to give him the manly habit, while he was yet under age and a tender youth, because his stature would allow of it, he added, "I do so, that the Roman people may at last have a real Caesar." 545

XLIV. Soon afterwards he made his will, and had it signed by all the magistrates as witnesses. But he was prevented from proceeding further by Agrippina, accused by her own guilty conscience, as well as by informers, of a variety of crimes. It is agreed that he was taken off by poison; but where, and by whom administered, remains in uncertainty. Some authors say that it was given him as he was feasting with the priests in the Capitol, by the eunuch Halotus, his taster. Others say (331) by Agrippina, at his own table, in mushrooms, a dish of which he was very fond 546 . The accounts of what followed likewise differ. Some relate that he instantly became speechless, was racked with pain through the night, and died about day-break; others, that at first he fell into a sound sleep, and afterwards, his food rising, he threw up the whole; but had another dose given him; whether in water-gruel, under pretence of refreshment after his exhaustion, or in a clyster, as if designed to relieve his bowels, is likewise uncertain.

XLV. His death was kept secret until everything was settled relative to his successor. Accordingly, vows were made for his recovery, and comedians were called to amuse him, as it was pretended, by his own desire. He died upon the third of the ides of October [13th October], in the consulship of Asinius Marcellus and Acilius Aviola, in the sixty-fourth year of his age, and the fourteenth of his reign 547 . His funeral was celebrated with the customary imperial pomp, and he was ranked amongst the gods. This honour was taken from him by Nero, but restored by Vespasian.

XLVI. The chief presages of his death were, the appearance of a comet, his father Drusus's monument being struck by lightning, and the death of most of the magistrates of all ranks that year. It appears from several circumstances, that he was sensible of his approaching dissolution, and made no secret of it. For when he nominated the consuls, he appointed no one to fill the office beyond the month in which he died. At the last assembly of the senate in which he made his appearance, he earnestly exhorted his two sons to unity with each other, and with earnest entreaties commended to the fathers the care of their tender years. And in the last cause he heard from the tribunal, he repeatedly declared in open court, "That he was now arrived at the last stage of mortal existence;" whilst all who heard it shrunk at hearing these ominous words.

\* \* \* \* \* \*

The violent death of Caligula afforded the Romans a fresh opportunity to have asserted the liberty of their country; but the conspirators had concerted no plan, by which they should proceed upon the assassination of that tyrant; and the indecision of the senate, in a debate of two days, on so sudden an emergency, gave time to the caprice of the soldiers to interpose in the settlement of the government. By an accident the most fortuitous, a man devoid of all pretensions to personal merit, so weak in understanding as to be the common sport of the emperor's household, and an object of contempt even to his own kindred; this man, in the hour of military insolence, was nominated by the soldiers as successor to the Roman throne. Not yet in possession of the public treasury, which perhaps was exhausted, he could not immediately reward the services of his electors with a pecuniary gratification; but he promised them a largess of fifteen thousand sesterces a man, upwards of a hundred and forty pounds sterling; and as we meet with no account of any subsequent discontents in the army, we may justly conclude that the promise was soon after fulfilled. This transaction laid the foundation of that military despotism, which, through many succeeding ages, convulsed the Roman empire.

Besides the interposition of the soldiers upon this occasion, it appears that the populace of Rome were extremely clamorous for the government of a single person, and for that of Claudius in particular. This partiality for a monarchical government proceeded from two causes. The commonalty, from their obscure situation, were always the least exposed to oppression, under a tyrannical prince. They had likewise ever been remarkably fond of stage-plays and public shows, with which, as well as with scrambles, and donations of bread and other victuals, the preceding emperor had frequently gratified them. They had therefore less to fear, and more to hope, from the government of a single person than any other class of Roman citizens. With regard to the partiality for Claudius, it may be accounted for partly from the low habits of life to which he had been addicted, in consequence of which many of them were familiarly acquainted with him; and this circumstance likewise increased their hope of deriving some advantage from his accession. Exclusive of all these considerations, it is highly probable that the populace were instigated in favour of Claudius by the artifices of his freedmen, persons of mean extraction, by whom he was afterwards entirely governed, and who, upon such an occasion, would exert their utmost efforts to procure his appointment to the throne. From the debate in the senate having continued during (333) two days, it was evident that there was still a strong party for restoring the ancient form of government. That they were in the end overawed by the clamour of the multitude, is not surprising, when we consider that the senate was totally unprovided with resources of every kind for asserting the independence of the nation by arms; and the commonalty, who interrupted their deliberations, were the only people by whose assistance they ever could effect the restitution of public freedom. To this may be added, that the senate, by the total reduction of their political importance, ever since the overthrow of the republic, had lost both the influence and authority which they formerly enjoyed. The extreme cruelty, likewise, which had been exercised during the last two reigns, afforded a further motive for relinquishing all attempts in favour of liberty, as they might be severely revenged upon themselves by the subsequent emperor: and it was a degree of moderation in Claudius, which palliates the injustice of his cause, that he began his government with an act of amnesty respecting the public transactions which ensued upon the death of Caligula.

Claudius, at the time of his accession, was fifty years of age; and though he had hitherto lived apparently unambitious of public honours, accompanied with great ostentation, yet he was now seized with a desire to enjoy a triumph. As there existed no war, in which he might perform some military achievement, his vanity could only be gratified by invading a foreign country, where, contrary to the advice contained in the testament of Augustus, he might attempt to extend still further the limits of the empire. Either Britain, therefore, or some nation on the continent, at a great distance from the capital, became the object of such an enterprize; and the former was chosen, not only as more convenient, from its vicinity to the maritime province of Gaul, but on account of a remonstrance lately presented by the Britons to the court of Rome, respecting the protection afforded to some persons of that nation, who had fled thither to elude the laws of their country. Considering the state of Britain at that time, divided as it was into a number of principalities, amongst which there was no general confederacy for mutual defence, and where the alarm excited by the invasion of Julius Caesar, upwards of eighty years before, had long since been forgotten; a sudden attempt upon the island could not fail to be attended with success. Accordingly, an army was sent over, under the command of Aulus Plautius, an able general, who defeated the natives in several engagements, and penetrated a considerable way into the country. Preparations for the emperor's voyage now being made, Claudius set sail from Ostia, at the mouth of (334) the Tiber; but meeting with a violent storm in the Mediterranean, he landed at Marseilles, and proceeding thence to Boulogne in Picardy, passed over into Britain. In what part he debarked, is uncertain, but it seems to have been at some place on the south-east coast of the island. He immediately received the submission of several British states, the Cantii, Atrebates, Regni, and Trinobantes, who inhabited those parts; and returning to Rome, after an absence of six months, celebrated with great pomp the triumph, for which he had undertaken the expedition.

In the interior parts of Britain, the natives, under the command of Caractacus, maintained an obstinate resistance, and little progress was made by the Roman arms, until Ostorius Scapula was sent over to prosecute the war. He penetrated into the country of the Silures, a warlike tribe, who inhabited the banks of the Severn; and having defeated Caractacus in a great battle, made him prisoner, and sent him to Rome. The fame of the British prince had by this time spread over the provinces of Gaul and Italy; and upon his arrival in the Roman capital, the people flocked from all quarters to behold him. The ceremonial of his entrance was conducted with great solemnity. On a plain adjoining the Roman camp, the pretorian troops were drawn up in martial array: the emperor and his court took their station in front of the lines, and behind them was ranged the whole body of the people. The procession commenced with the different trophies which had been taken from the Britons during the progress of the war. Next followed the brothers of the vanquished prince, with his wife and daughter, in chains, expressing by their supplicating looks and gestures the fears with which they were actuated. But not so Caractacus himself. With a manly gait and an undaunted countenance, he marched up to the tribunal, where the emperor was seated, and addressed him in the following terms:

"If to my high birth and distinguished rank, I had added the virtues of moderation, Rome had beheld me rather as a friend than a captive; and you would not have rejected an alliance with a prince, descended from illustrious ancestors, and governing many nations. The reverse of my fortune to you is glorious, and to me humiliating. I had arms, and men, and horses; I possessed extraordinary riches; and can it be any wonder that I was unwilling to lose them? Because Rome aspires to universal dominion, must men therefore implicitly resign themselves to subjection? I opposed for a long time the progress of your arms, and had I acted otherwise, would either you have had the glory of conquest, or I of a brave resistance? I am now in your power: if you are determined to take revenge, my fate will soon be forgotten, and you will derive no honour from the transaction. Preserve my life, and I shall remain to the latest ages a monument of your clemency."

Immediately upon this speech, Claudius granted him his liberty, as he did likewise to the other royal captives. They all returned their thanks in a manner the most grateful to the emperor; and as soon as their chains were taken off, walking towards Agrippina, who sat upon a bench at a little distance, they repeated to her the same fervent declarations of gratitude and esteem.

History has preserved no account of Caractacus after this period; but it is probable, that he returned in a short time to his own country, where his former valour, and the magnanimity, which he had displayed at Rome, would continue to render him illustrious through life, even amidst the irretrievable ruin of his fortunes.

The most extraordinary character in the present reign was that of Valeria Messalina, the daughter of Valerius Messala Barbatus. She was married to Claudius, and had by him a son and a daughter. To cruelty in the prosecution of her purposes, she added the most abandoned incontinence. Not confining her licentiousness within the limits of the palace, where she committed the most shameful excesses, she prostituted her person in the common stews, and even in the public streets of the capital. As if her conduct was already not sufficiently scandalous, she obliged C. Silius, a man of consular rank, to divorce his wife, that she might procure his company entirely to herself. Not contented with this indulgence to her criminal passion, she next persuaded him to marry her; and during an excursion which the emperor made to Ostia, the ceremony of marriage was actually performed between them. The occasion was celebrated with a magnificent supper, to which she invited a large company; and lest the whole should be regarded as a frolic, not meant to be consummated, the adulterous parties ascended the nuptial couch in the presence of the astonished spectators. Great as was the facility of Claudius's temper in respect of her former behaviour, he could not overlook so flagrant a violation both of public decency and the laws of the country. Silius was condemned to death for the adultery which he had perpetrated with reluctance; and Messalina was ordered into the emperor's presence, to answer for her conduct. Terror now operating upon her mind in conjunction with remorse, she could not summon the resolution to support such an interview, but retired into the gardens of Lucullus, there to indulge at last the compunction which she felt for her crimes, and to meditate the entreaties by which she should endeavour to soothe the resentment (336) of her husband. In the extremity of her distress, she attempted to lay violent hands upon herself, but her courage was not equal to the emergency. Her mother, Lepida, who had not spoken with her for some years before, was present upon the occasion, and urged her to the act which alone could put a period to her infamy and wretchedness. Again she made an effort, but again her resolution abandoned her; when a tribune burst into the gardens, and plunging his sword into her body, she instantly expired. Thus perished a woman, the scandal of whose lewdness resounded throughout the empire, and of whom a great satirist, then living, has said, perhaps without a hyperbole,

*Et lassata viris, necdum satiata, recessit.* – Juvenal, Sat. VI.

It has been already observed, that Claudius was entirely governed by his freedmen; a class of retainers which enjoyed a great share of favour and confidence with their patrons in those times. They had before been the slaves of their masters, and had obtained their freedom as a reward for their faithful and attentive services. Of the esteem in which they were often held, we meet with an instance in Tiro, the freedman of Cicero, to whom that illustrious Roman addresses several epistles, written in the most familiar and affectionate strain of friendship. As it was common for them to be taught the more useful parts of education in the families of their masters, they were usually well qualified for the management of domestic concerns, and might even be competent to the superior departments of the state, especially in those times when negotiations and treaties with foreign princes seldom or never occurred; and in arbitrary governments, where public affairs were directed more by the will of the sovereign or his ministers, than by refined suggestions of policy.

From the character generally given of Claudius before his elevation to the throne, we should not readily imagine that he was endowed with any taste for literary composition; yet he seems to have exclusively enjoyed this distinction during his own reign, in which learning was at a low ebb. Besides history, Suetonius informs us that he wrote a Defence of Cicero against the Charges of Asinius Gallus. This appears to be the only tribute of esteem or approbation paid to the character of Cicero, from the time of Livy the historian, to the extinction of the race of the Caesars. Asinius Gallus was the son of Asinius Pollio, the orator. Marrying Vipsania after she had been divorced by Tiberius, he incurred the displeasure of that emperor, and died of famine, either voluntarily, or by order of the tyrant. He wrote a comparison between his father and Cicero, in which, with more filial partiality than justice, he gave the preference to the former.

# NERO CLAUDIUS CAESAR.

(337)

I. Two celebrated families, the Calvini and Aenobarbi, sprung from the race of the Domitii. The Aenobarbi derive both their extraction and their cognomen from one Lucius Domitius, of whom we have this tradition: —As he was returning out of the country to Rome, he was met by two young men of a most august appearance, who desired him to announce to the senate and people a victory, of which no certain intelligence had yet reached the city. To prove that they were more than mortals, they stroked his cheeks, and thus changed his hair, which was black, to a bright colour, resembling that of brass; which mark of distinction descended to his posterity, for they had generally red beards. This family had the honour of seven consulships 548, one triumph 549, and two censorships 550; and being admitted into the patrician order, they continued the use of the same cognomen, with no other praenomina 551 than those of Cneius and Lucius. These, however, they assumed with singular irregularity; three persons in succession sometimes adhering to one of them, and then they were changed alternately. For the first, second, and third of the Aenobarbi had the praenomen of Lucius, and again the three following, successively, that of Cneius, while those who came after were called, by turns, one, Lucius, and the other, Cneius. It appears to me proper to give a short account of several of the family, to show that Nero so far degenerated from the noble qualities of his ancestors, that he retained only their vices; as if those alone had been transmitted to him by his descent.

II. To begin, therefore, at a remote period, his great-grandfather's grandfather, Cneius Domitius, when he was tribune of the people, being offended with the high priests for electing another than himself in the room of his father, obtained the (338) transfer of the right of election from the colleges of the priests to the people. In his consulship

552, having conquered the Allobroges and the Arverni 553, he made a progress through the province, mounted upon an elephant, with a body of soldiers attending him, in a sort of triumphal pomp. Of this person the orator Licinius Crassus said, "It was no wonder he had a brazen beard, who had a face of iron, and a heart of lead." His son, during his praetorship 554, proposed that Cneius Caesar, upon the expiration of his consulship, should be called to account before the senate for his administration of that office, which was supposed to be contrary both to the omens and the laws. Afterwards, when he was consul himself 555, he tried to deprive Cneius of the command of the army, and having been, by intrigue and cabal, appointed his successor, he was made prisoner at Corsinium, in the beginning of the civil war. Being set at liberty, he went to Marseilles, which was then besieged; where having, by his presence, animated the people to hold out, he suddenly deserted them, and at last was slain in the battle of Pharsalia. He was a man of little constancy, and of a sullen temper. In despair of his fortunes, he had recourse to poison, but was so terrified at the thoughts of death, that, immediately repenting, he took a vomit to throw it up again, and gave freedom to his physician for having, with great prudence and wisdom, given him only a gentle dose of the poison. When Cneius Pompey was consulting with his friends in what manner he should conduct himself towards those who were neuter and took no part in the contest, he was the only one who proposed that they should be treated as enemies.

III. He left a son, who was, without doubt, the best of the family. By the Pedian law, he was condemned, although innocent, amongst others who were concerned in the death of Caesar 556. Upon this, he went over to Brutus and Cassius, his near relations; and, after their death, not only kept together the fleet, the command of which had been given him some time before, but even increased it. At last, when the party had everywhere been defeated, he voluntarily surrendered it to (339) Mark Antony; considering it as a piece of service for which the latter owed him no small obligations. Of all those who were condemned by the law above-mentioned, he was the only man who was restored to his country, and filled the highest offices. When the civil war again broke out, he was appointed lieutenant under the same Antony, and offered the chief command by those who were ashamed of Cleopatra; but not daring, on account of a sudden indisposition with which he was seized, either to accept or refuse it, he went over to Augustus 557, and died a few days after, not without an aspersion cast upon his memory. For Antony gave out, that he was induced to change sides by his impatience to be with his mistress, Servilia Nais. 558

IV. This Cneius had a son, named Domitius, who was afterwards well known as the nominal purchaser of the family property left by Augustus's will 559; and no less famous in his youth for his dexterity in chariot-driving, than he was afterwards for the triumphal ornaments which he obtained in the German war. But he was a man of great arrogance, prodigality, and cruelty. When he was aedile, he obliged Lucius Plancus, the censor, to give him the way; and in his praetorship, and consulship, he made Roman knights and married women act on the stage. He gave hunts of wild beasts, both in the Circus and in all the wards of the city; as also a show of gladiators; but with such barbarity, that Augustus, after privately reprimanding him, to no purpose, was obliged to restrain him by a public edict.

V. By the elder Antonia he had Nero's father, a man of execrable character in every part of his life. During his attendance upon Caius Caesar in the East, he killed a freedman of his own, for refusing to drink as much as he ordered him. Being dismissed for this from Caesar's society, he did not mend his habits; for, in a village upon the Appian road, he suddenly whipped his horses, and drove his chariot, on purpose, (340) over a poor boy, crushing him to pieces. At Rome, he struck out the eye of a Roman knight in the Forum, only for some free language in a dispute between them. He was likewise so fraudulent, that he not only cheated some silversmiths 560 of the price of goods he had bought of them, but, during his praetorship, defrauded the owners of chariots in the Circensian games of the prizes due to them for their victory. His sister, jeering him for the complaints made by the leaders of the several parties, he agreed to sanction a law, "That, for the future, the prizes should be immediately paid." A little before the death of Tiberius, he was prosecuted for treason, adulteries, and incest with his sister Lepida, but escaped in the timely change of affairs, and died of a dropsy, at Pyrgi 561; leaving behind him his son, Nero, whom he had by Agrippina, the daughter of Germanicus.

VI. Nero was born at Antium, nine months after the death of Tiberius 562, upon the eighteenth of the calends of January [15th

December], just as the sun rose, so that its beams touched him before they could well reach the earth. While many fearful conjectures, in respect to his future fortune, were formed by different persons, from the circumstances of his nativity, a saying of his father, Domitius, was regarded as an ill presage, who told his friends who were congratulating him upon the occasion, "That nothing but what was detestable, and pernicious to the public, could ever be produced of him and Agrippina." Another manifest prognostic of his future infelicity occurred upon his lustration day 563 . For Caius Caesar being requested by his sister to give the child what name he thought proper—looking at his uncle, Claudius, who (341) afterwards, when emperor, adopted Nero, he gave his: and this not seriously, but only in jest; Agrippina treating it with contempt, because Claudius at that time was a mere laughing-stock at the palace. He lost his father when he was three years old, being left heir to a third part of his estate; of which he never got possession, the whole being seized by his co-heir, Caius. His mother being soon after banished, he lived with his aunt Lepida, in a very necessitous condition, under the care of two tutors, a dancing-master and a barber. After Claudius came to the empire, he not only recovered his father's estate, but was enriched with the additional inheritance of that of his step-father, Crispus Passienus. Upon his mother's recall from banishment, he was advanced to such favour, through Nero's powerful interest with the emperor, that it was reported, assassins were employed by Messalina, Claudius's wife, to strangle him, as Britannicus's rival, whilst he was taking his noon-day repose. In addition to the story, it was said that they were frightened by a serpent, which crept from under his cushion, and ran away. The tale was occasioned by finding on his couch, near the pillow, the skin of a snake, which, by his mother's order, he wore for some time upon his right arm, inclosed in a bracelet of gold. This amulet, at last, he laid aside, from aversion to her memory; but he sought for it again, in vain, in the time of his extremity.

VII. When he was yet a mere boy, before he arrived at the age of puberty, during the celebration of the Circensian games 564 , he performed his part in the Trojan play with a degree of firmness which gained him great applause. In the eleventh year of his age, he was adopted by Claudius, and placed under the tuition of Annaeus Seneca 565 , who had been made a senator. It is said, that Seneca dreamt the night after, that he was giving a lesson to Caius Caesar 566 . Nero soon verified his dream, betraying the cruelty of his disposition in every way he could. For he attempted to persuade his father that his brother, Britannicus, was nothing but a changeling, because the latter had (342) saluted him, notwithstanding his adoption, by the name of Aenobarbus, as usual. When his aunt, Lepida, was brought to trial, he appeared in court as a witness against her, to gratify his mother, who persecuted the accused. On his introduction into the Forum, at the age of manhood, he gave a largess to the people and a donative to the soldiers: for the pretorian cohorts, he appointed a solemn procession under arms, and marched at the head of them with a shield in his hand; after which he went to return thanks to his father in the senate. Before Claudius, likewise, at the time he was consul, he made a speech for the Bolognese, in Latin, and for the Rhodians and people of Ilium, in Greek. He had the jurisdiction of praefect of the city, for the first time, during the Latin festival; during which the most celebrated advocates brought before him, not short and trifling causes, as is usual in that case, but trials of importance, notwithstanding they had instructions from Claudius himself to the contrary. Soon afterwards, he married Octavia, and exhibited the Circensian games, and hunting of wild beasts, in honour of Claudius.

VIII. He was seventeen years of age at the death of that prince 567 , and as soon as that event was made public, he went out to the cohort on guard between the hours of six and seven; for the omens were so disastrous, that no earlier time of the day was judged proper. On the steps before the palace gate, he was unanimously saluted by the soldiers as their emperor, and then carried in a litter to the camp; thence, after making a short speech to the troops, into the senate-house, where he continued until the evening; of all the immense honours which were heaped upon him, refusing none but the title of FATHER OF HIS COUNTRY, on account of his youth,

IX. He began his reign with an ostentation of dutiful regard to the memory of Claudius, whom he buried with the utmost pomp and magnificence, pronouncing the funeral oration himself, and then had him enrolled amongst the gods. He paid likewise the highest honours to the memory of his father Domitius. He left the management of affairs, both public and private, to his mother. The word which he gave the first day of his reign to the tribune on guard, was, "The (343)

Best of Mothers," and afterwards he frequently appeared with her in the streets of Rome in her litter. He settled a colony at Antium, in which he placed the veteran soldiers belonging to the guards; and obliged several of the richest centurions of the first rank to transfer their residence to that place; where he likewise made a noble harbour at a prodigious expense. 568

X. To establish still further his character, he declared, "that he designed to govern according to the model of Augustus;" and omitted no opportunity of showing his generosity, clemency, and complaisance. The more burthensome taxes he either entirely took off, or diminished. The rewards appointed for informers by the Papian law, he reduced to a fourth part, and distributed to the people four hundred sesterces a man. To the noblest of the senators who were much reduced in their circumstances, he granted annual allowances, in some cases as much as five hundred thousand sesterces; and to the pretorian cohorts a monthly allowance of corn gratis. When called upon to subscribe the sentence, according to custom, of a criminal condemned to die, "I wish," said he, "I had never learnt to read and write." He continually saluted people of the several orders by name, without a prompter. When the senate returned him their thanks for his good government, he replied to them, "It will be time enough to do so when I shall have deserved it." He admitted the common people to see him perform his exercises in the Campus Martius. He frequently declaimed in public, and recited verses of his own composing, not only at home, but in the theatre; so much to the joy of all the people, that public prayers were appointed to be put up to the gods upon that account; and the verses which had been publicly read, were, after being written in gold letters, consecrated to Jupiter Capitolinus.

(344) XI. He presented the people with a great number and variety of spectacles, as the Juvenal and Circensian games, stage-plays, and an exhibition of gladiators. In the Juvenal, he even admitted senators and aged matrons to perform parts. In the Circensian games, he assigned the equestrian order seats apart from the rest of the people, and had races performed by chariots drawn each by four camels. In the games which he instituted for the eternal duration of the empire, and therefore ordered to be called Maximi, many of the senatorian and equestrian order, of both sexes, performed. A distinguished Roman knight descended on the stage by a rope, mounted on an elephant.

A Roman play, likewise, composed by Afranius, was brought upon the stage. It was entitled, "The Fire;" and in it the performers were allowed to carry off, and to keep to themselves, the furniture of the house, which, as the plot of the play required, was burnt down in the theatre. Every day during the solemnity, many thousand articles of all descriptions were thrown amongst the people to scramble for; such as fowls of different kinds, tickets for corn, clothes, gold, silver, gems, pearls, pictures, slaves, beasts of burden, wild beasts that had been tamed; at last, ships, lots of houses, and lands, were offered as prizes in a lottery.

XII. These games he beheld from the front of the proscenium. In the show of gladiators, which he exhibited in a wooden amphitheatre, built within a year in the district of the Campus Martius 569 , he ordered that none should be slain, not even the condemned criminals employed in the combats. He secured four hundred senators, and six hundred Roman knights, amongst whom were some of unbroken fortunes and unblemished reputation, to act as gladiators. From the same orders, he engaged persons to encounter wild beasts, and for various other services in the theatre. He presented the public with the representation of a naval fight, upon sea-water, with huge fishes swimming in it; as also with the Pyrrhic dance, performed by certain youths, to each of whom, after the performance was over, he granted the freedom of Rome. During this diversion, a bull covered Pasiphae, concealed within a wooden statue of a cow, as many of the spectators believed. Icarus, upon his first attempt to fly, fell on the stage close to (345) the emperor's pavilion, and bespattered him with blood. For he very seldom presided in the games, but used to view them reclining on a couch, at first through some narrow apertures, but afterwards with the Podium 570 quite open. He was the first who instituted 571 , in imitation of the Greeks, a trial of skill in the three several exercises of music, wrestling, and horse-racing, to be performed at Rome every five years, and which he called Neronia. Upon the dedication of his bath 572 and gymnasium, he furnished the senate and the equestrian order with oil. He appointed as judges of the trial men of consular rank, chosen by lot, who sat with the praetors. At this time he went down into the orchestra amongst the senators, and received the crown for the best performance in Latin prose and verse, for which several persons of the greatest merit contended, but they unanimously yielded to him. The crown for the best performer on the harp, being likewise awarded to him by the judges, he devoutly saluted it, and ordered it to be carried to the statue of Augustus. In the gymnastic exercises, which he presented in the Septa, while they were preparing the great sacrifice of an ox, he shaved his beard for the first time 573, and putting it up in a casket of gold studded with pearls of great price, consecrated it to Jupiter Capitolinus. He invited the Vestal Virgins to see the (346) wrestlers perform, because, at Olympia, the priestesses of Ceres are allowed the privilege of witnessing that exhibition.

XIII. Amongst the spectacles presented by him, the solemn entrance of Tiridates 574 into the city deserves to be mentioned. This personage, who was king of Armenia, he invited to Rome by very liberal promises. But being prevented by unfavourable weather from showing him to the people upon the day fixed by proclamation, he took the first opportunity which occurred; several cohorts being drawn up under arms, about the temples in the forum, while he was seated on a curule chair on the rostra, in a triumphal dress, amidst the military standards and ensigns. Upon Tiridates advancing towards him, on a stage made shelving for the purpose, he permitted him to throw himself at his feet, but quickly raised him with his right hand, and kissed him. The emperor then, at the king's request, took the turban from his head, and replaced it by a crown, whilst a person of pretorian rank proclaimed in Latin the words in which the prince addressed the emperor as a suppliant. After this ceremony, the king was conducted to the theatre, where, after renewing his obeisance, Nero seated him on his right hand. Being then greeted by universal acclamation with the title of Emperor, and sending his laurel crown to the Capitol, Nero shut the temple of the two-faced Janus, as though there now existed no war throughout the Roman empire.

XIV. He filled the consulship four times 575 : the first for two months, the second and last for six, and the third for four; the two intermediate ones he held successively, but the others after an interval of some years between them.

XV. In the administration of justice, he scarcely ever gave his decision on the pleadings before the next day, and then in writing. His manner of hearing causes was not to allow any adjournment, but to dispatch them in order as they stood. When he withdrew to consult his assessors, he did not debate the matter openly with them; but silently and privately reading over their opinions, which they gave separately in writing, (347) he pronounced sentence from the tribunal according to his own view of the case, as if it was the opinion of the majority. For a long time he would not admit the sons of freedmen into the senate; and those who had been admitted by former princes, he excluded from all public offices. To supernumerary candidates he gave command in the legions, to comfort them under the delay of their hopes. The consulship he commonly conferred for six months; and one of the two consuls dying a little before the first of January, he substituted no one in his place; disliking what had been formerly done for Caninius Rebilus on such an occasion, who was consul for one day only. He allowed the triumphal honours only to those who were of quaestorian rank, and to some of the equestrian order; and bestowed them without regard to military service. And instead of the quaestors, whose office it properly was, he frequently ordered that the addresses, which he sent to the senate on certain occasions, should be read by the consuls.

XVI. He devised a new style of building in the city, ordering piazzas to be erected before all houses, both in the streets and detached, to give facilities from their terraces, in case of fire, for preventing it from spreading; and these he built at his own expense. He likewise designed to extend the city walls as far as Ostia, and bring the sea from thence by a canal into the old city. Many severe regulations and new orders were made in his time. A sumptuary law was enacted. Public suppers were limited to the Sportulae 576 ; and victualling-houses restrained from selling any dressed victuals, except pulse and herbs, whereas before they sold all kinds of meat. He likewise inflicted punishments on the Christians, a sort of people who held a new and impious 577 superstition.

(348) He forbad the revels of the charioteers, who had long assumed a licence to stroll about, and established for themselves a kind of prescriptive right to cheat and thieve, making a jest of it. The partisans of the rival theatrical performers were banished, as well as the actors themselves.

XVII. To prevent forgery, a method was then first invented, of having writings bored, run through three times with a thread, and then sealed. It was likewise provided that in wills, the two first pages, with only the testator's name upon them, should be presented blank to those who were to sign them as witnesses; and that no one who wrote a will for another, should insert any legacy for himself. It was likewise ordained that clients should pay their advocates a certain reasonable fee, but nothing for the court, which was to be gratuitous, the charges for it being paid out of the public treasury; that causes, the cognizance of which before belonged to the judges of the exchequer, should be transferred to the forum, and the ordinary tribunals; and that all appeals from the judges should be made to the senate.

XVIII. He never entertained the least ambition or hope of augmenting and extending the frontiers of the empire. On the contrary, he had thoughts of withdrawing the troops from Britain, and was only restrained from so doing by the fear of appearing to detract from the glory of his father 578 . All (349) that he did was to reduce the kingdom of Pontus, which was ceded to him by Polemon, and also the Alps 579 , upon the death of Cottius, into the form of a province.

XIX. Twice only he undertook any foreign expeditions, one to Alexandria, and the other to Achaia; but he abandoned the prosecution of the former on the very day fixed for his departure, by being deterred both by ill omens, and the hazard of the voyage. For while he was making the circuit of the temples, having seated himself in that of Vesta, when he attempted to rise, the skirt of his robe stuck fast; and he was instantly seized with such a dimness in his eyes, that he could not see a yard before him. In Achaia, he attempted to make a cut through the Isthmus 580 ; and, having made a speech encouraging his pretorians to set about the work, on a signal given by sound of trumpet, he first broke ground with a spade, and carried off a basket full of earth upon his shoulders. He made preparations for an expedition to the Pass of the Caspian mountains 581 ; forming a new legion out of his late levies in Italy, of men all six feet high, which he called the phalanx of Alexander the Great. These transactions, in part unexceptionable, and in part highly commendable, I have brought into one view, in order to separate them from the scandalous and criminal part of his conduct, of which I shall now give an account.

XX. Among the other liberal arts which he was taught in his youth, he was instructed in music; and immediately after (350) his advancement to the empire, he sent for Terpnus, a performer upon the harp 582, who flourished at that time with the highest reputation. Sitting with him for several days following, as he sang and played after supper, until late at night, he began by degrees to practise upon the instrument himself. Nor did he omit any of those expedients which artists in music adopt, for the preservation and improvement of their voices. He would lie upon his back with a sheet of lead upon his breast, clear his stomach and bowels by vomits and clysters, and forbear the eating of fruits, or food prejudicial to the voice. Encouraged by his proficiency, though his voice was naturally neither loud nor clear, he was desirous of appearing upon the stage, frequently repeating amongst his friends a Greek proverb to this effect: "that no one had any regard for music which they never heard." Accordingly, he made his first public appearance at Naples; and although the theatre quivered with the sudden shock of an earthquake, he did not desist, until he had finished the piece of music he had begun. He played and sung in the same place several times, and for several days together; taking only now and then a little respite to refresh his voice. Impatient of retirement, it was his custom to go from the bath to the theatre; and after dining in the orchestra, amidst a crowded assembly of the people, he promised them in Greek 583, "that after he had drank a little, he would give them a tune which would make their ears tingle." Being highly pleased with the songs that were sung in his praise by some Alexandrians belonging to the fleet just arrived at Naples 584, he sent for more of the like singers from Alexandria. At the same time, he chose young men of the equestrian order, and above five thousand robust young fellows from the common people, on purpose to learn various kinds of applause, called bombi, imbrices, and testae 585, which they were to practise in his favour, whenever he performed. They were (351) divided into several parties, and were remarkable for their fine heads of hair, and were extremely well dressed, with rings upon their left hands. The leaders of these bands had salaries of forty thousand sesterces allowed them.

XXI. At Rome also, being extremely proud of his singing, he ordered the games called Neronia to be celebrated before the time fixed for their return. All now becoming importunate to hear "his heavenly voice," he informed them, "that he would gratify those who desired it at the gardens." But the soldiers then on guard seconding the voice of the people, he promised to comply with their request immediately, and with all his heart. He instantly ordered his name to be entered upon the list of musicians who proposed to contend, and having thrown his lot into the urn among the rest, took his turn, and entered, attended by the prefects of the pretorian cohorts bearing his harp, and followed by the military tribunes, and several of his intimate friends. After he had taken his station, and made the usual prelude, he commanded Cluvius Rufus, a man of consular rank, to proclaim in the theatre, that he intended to sing the story of Niobe. This he accordingly did, and continued it until nearly ten o'clock, but deferred the disposal of the crown, and the remaining part of the solemnity, until the next year; that he might have more frequent opportunities of performing. But that being too long, he could not refrain from often appearing as a public performer during the interval. He made no scruple of exhibiting on the stage, even in the spectacles presented to the people by private persons, and was offered by one of the praetors, no less than a million of sesterces for his services. He likewise sang tragedies in a mask; the visors of the heroes and gods, as also of the heroines and goddesses, being formed into a resemblance of his own face, and that of any woman he was in love with. Amongst the rest, he sung "Canace in Labour,"  586  "Orestes the Murderer of his Mother," "Oedipus (352) Blinded," and "Hercules Mad." In the last tragedy, it is said that a young sentinel, posted at the entrance of the stage, seeing him in a prison dress and bound with fetters, as the fable of the play required, ran to his assistance.

XXII. He had from his childhood an extravagant passion for horses; and his constant talk was of the Circensian races, notwithstanding it was prohibited him. Lamenting once, among his fellow-pupils, the case of a charioteer of the green party, who was dragged round the circus at the tail of his chariot, and being reprimanded by his tutor for it, he pretended that he was talking of Hector. In the beginning of his reign, he used to amuse himself daily with chariots drawn by four horses, made of ivory, upon a table. He attended at all the lesser exhibitions in the circus, at first privately, but at last openly; so that nobody ever doubted of his presence on any particular day. Nor did he conceal his desire to have the number of the prizes doubled; so that the races being increased accordingly, the diversion continued until a late hour; the leaders of parties refusing now to bring out their companies for any time less than the whole day. Upon this, he took a fancy for driving the chariot himself, and that even publicly. Having made his first experiment in the gardens, amidst crowds of slaves and other rabble, he at length performed in the view of all the people, in the Circus Maximus, whilst one of his freedmen dropped the napkin in the place where the magistrates used to give the signal. Not satisfied with exhibiting various specimens of his skill in those arts at Rome, he went over to Achaia, as has been already said, principally for this purpose. The several cities, in which solemn trials of musical skill used to be publicly held, had resolved to send him the crowns belonging to those who bore away the prize. These he accepted so graciously, that he not only gave the deputies who brought them an immediate audience, but even invited them to his table. Being requested by some of them to sing at supper, and prodigiously applauded, he said, "the Greeks were the only people who has an ear for music, and were the only good judges of him and his attainments." Without delay he commenced his journey, and on his arrival at Cassiope 587 , (352) exhibited his first musical performance before the altar of Jupiter Cassius.

XXIII. He afterwards appeared at the celebration of all public games in Greece: for such as fell in different years, he brought within the compass of one, and some he ordered to be celebrated a second time in the same year. At Olympia, likewise, contrary to custom, he appointed a public performance in music: and that he might meet with no interruption in this employment, when he was informed by his freedman Helius, that affairs at Rome required his presence, he wrote to him in these words: "Though now all your hopes and wishes are for my speedy return, yet you ought rather to advise and hope that I may come back with a character worthy of Nero." During the time of his musical performance, nobody was allowed to stir out of the theatre upon any account, however necessary; insomuch, that it is said some women with child were delivered there. Many of the spectators being quite wearied with hearing and applauding him, because the town gates were shut, slipped privately over the walls; or counterfeiting themselves dead, were carried out for their funeral. With what extreme anxiety he engaged in these contests, with what keen desire to bear away the prize, and with how much awe of the judges, is scarcely to be believed. As if his adversaries had been on a level with himself, he would watch them narrowly, defame them privately, and sometimes, upon meeting them, rail at them in very scurrilous language; or bribe them, if they were better performers than himself. He always addressed the judges with the most profound reverence before he began, telling them, "he had done all things that were necessary, by way of preparation, but that the issue of the approaching trial was in the hand of fortune; and that they, as wise and skilful men, ought to exclude from their judgment things merely accidental." Upon their encouraging him to have a good heart, he went off with more assurance, but not entirely free from anxiety; interpreting the silence and modesty of some of them into sourness and ill-nature, and saying that he was suspicious of them.

XXIV. In these contests, he adhered so strictly to the rules, (354) that he never durst spit, nor wipe the sweat from his forehead in any other way than with his sleeve. Having, in the performance of a tragedy, dropped his sceptre, and not quickly recovering it, he was in a great fright, lest he should be set aside for the miscarriage, and could not regain his assurance, until an actor who stood by swore he was certain it had not been observed in the midst of the acclamations and exultations of the people. When the prize was adjudged to him, he always proclaimed it himself; and even entered the lists with the heralds. That no memory or the least monument might remain of any other victor in the sacred Grecian games, he ordered all their statues and pictures to be pulled down, dragged away with hooks, and thrown into the common sewers. He drove the chariot with various numbers of horses, and at the Olympic games with no fewer than ten; though, in a poem of his, he had reflected upon Mithridates for that innovation. Being thrown out of his chariot, he was again replaced, but could not retain his seat, and was obliged to give up, before he reached the goal, but was crowned notwithstanding. On his departure, he declared the whole province a free country, and conferred upon the judges in the several games the freedom of Rome, with large sums of money. All these favours he proclaimed himself with his own voice, from the middle of the Stadium, during the solemnity of the Isthmian games.

XXV. On his return from Greece, arriving at Naples, because he had commenced his career as a public performer in that city, he made his entrance in a chariot drawn by white horses through a breach in the city-wall, according to the practice of those who were victorious in the sacred Grecian games. In the same manner he entered Antium,

Alba, and Rome. He made his entry into the city riding in the same chariot in which Augustus had triumphed, in a purple tunic, and a cloak embroidered with golden stars, having on his head the crown won at Olympia, and in his right hand that which was given him at the Parthian games: the rest being carried in a procession before him, with inscriptions denoting the places where they had been won, from whom, and in what plays or musical performances; whilst a train followed him with loud acclamations, crying out, that "they (355) were the emperor's attendants, and the soldiers of his triumph." Having then caused an arch of the Circus Maximus 588 to be taken down, he passed through the breach, as also through the Velabrum 589 and the forum, to the Palatine hill and the temple of Apollo. Everywhere as he marched along, victims were slain, whilst the streets were strewed with saffron, and birds, chaplets, and sweetmeats scattered abroad. He suspended the sacred crowns in his chamber, about his beds, and caused statues of himself to be erected in the attire of a harper, and had his likeness stamped upon the coin in the same dress. After this period, he was so far from abating any thing of his application to music, that, for the preservation of his voice, he never addressed the soldiers but by messages, or with some person to deliver his speeches for him, when he thought fit to make his appearance amongst them. Nor did he ever do any thing either in jest or earnest, without a voice-master standing by him to caution him against overstraining his vocal organs, and to apply a handkerchief to his mouth when he did. He offered his friendship, or avowed (356) open enmity to many, according as they were lavish or sparing in giving him their applause.

XXVI. Petulancy, lewdness, luxury, avarice, and cruelty, he practised at first with reserve and in private, as if prompted to them only by the folly of youth; but, even then, the world was of opinion that they were the faults of his nature, and not of his age. After it was dark, he used to enter the taverns disguised in a cap or a wig, and ramble about the streets in sport, which was not void of mischief. He used to beat those he met coming home from supper; and, if they made any resistance, would wound them, and throw them into the common sewer. He broke open and robbed shops; establishing an auction at home for selling his booty. In the scuffles which took place on those occasions, he often ran the hazard of losing his eyes, and even his life; being beaten almost to death by a senator, for handling his wife indecently. After this adventure, he never again ventured abroad at that time of night, without some tribunes following him at a little distance. In the day-time he would be carried to the theatre incognito in a litter, placing himself upon the upper part of the proscenium, where he not only witnessed the quarrels which arose on account of the performances, but also encouraged them. When they came to blows, and stones and pieces of broken benches began to fly about, he threw them plentifully amongst the people, and once even broke a praetor's head.

XXVII. His vices gaining strength by degrees, he laid aside his jocular amusements, and all disguise; breaking out into enormous crimes, without the least attempt to conceal them. His revels were prolonged from mid-day to midnight, while he was frequently refreshed by warm baths, and, in the summer time, by such as were cooled with snow. He often supped in public, in the Naumachia, with the sluices shut, or in the Campus Martius, or the Circus Maximus, being waited upon at table by common prostitutes of the town, and Syrian strumpets and glee-girls. As often as he went down the Tiber to Ostia, or coasted through the gulf of Baiae, booths furnished as brothels and eating-houses, were erected along the shore and river banks; before which stood matrons, who, like bawds and hostesses, allured him to land. It was also his custom to invite (357) himself to supper with his friends; at one of which was expended no less than four millions of sesterces in chaplets, and at another something more in roses.

XXVIII. Besides the abuse of free-born lads, and the debauch of married women, he committed a rape upon Rubria, a Vestal Virgin. He was upon the point of marrying Acte 590 , his freedwoman, having suborned some men of consular rank to swear that she was of royal descent. He gelded the boy Sporus, and endeavoured to transform him into a woman. He even went so far as to marry him, with all the usual formalities of a marriage settlement, the rose-coloured nuptial veil, and a numerous company at the wedding. When the ceremony was over, he had him conducted like a bride to his own house, and treated him as his wife 591 . It was jocularly observed by some person, "that it would have been well for mankind, had such a wife fallen to the lot of his father Domitius." This Sporus he carried about with him in a litter round the solemn assemblies and fairs of Greece, and afterwards at Rome through the Sigillaria 592 , dressed in the rich attire of an empress; kissing him from time to time as they rode together. That he entertained an incestuous passion for his mother 593 , but was deterred by her enemies, for fear that this haughty and overbearing woman should, by her compliance, get him entirely into her power, and govern in every thing, was universally believed; especially after he had introduced amongst his concubines a strumpet, who was reported to have a strong resemblance to Agrippina 594 .————

XXIX. He prostituted his own chastity to such a degree, that (358) after he had defiled every part of his person with some unnatural pollution, he at last invented an extraordinary kind of diversion; which was, to be let out of a den in the arena, covered with the skin of a wild beast, and then assail with violence the private parts both of men and women, while they were bound to stakes. After he had vented his furious passion upon them, he finished the play in the embraces of his freedman Doryphorus 595 , to whom he was married in the same way that Sporus had been married to himself; imitating the cries and shrieks of young virgins, when they are ravished. I have been informed from numerous sources, that he firmly believed, no man in the world to be chaste, or any part of his person undefiled; but that most men concealed that vice, and were cunning enough to keep it secret. To those, therefore, who frankly owned their unnatural lewdness, he forgave all other crimes.

XXX. He thought there was no other use of riches and money than to squander them away profusely; regarding all those as sordid wretches who kept their expenses within due bounds; and extolling those as truly noble and generous souls, who lavished away and wasted all they possessed. He praised and admired his uncle Caius 596 , upon no account more, than for squandering in a short time the vast treasure left him by Tiberius. Accordingly, he was himself extravagant and profuse, beyond all bounds. He spent upon Tiridates eight hundred thousand sesterces a day, a sum almost incredible; and at his departure, presented him with upwards of a million 597 . He likewise bestowed upon Menecrates the harper, and Spicillus a gladiator, the estates and houses of men who had received the honour of a triumph. He enriched the usurer Cercopithecus Panerotes with estates both in town and country; and gave him a funeral, in pomp and magnificence little inferior to that of princes. He never wore the same garment twice. He (359) has been known to stake four hundred thousand sesterces on a throw of the dice. It was his custom to fish with a golden net, drawn by silken cords of purple and scarlet. It is said, that he never travelled with less than a thousand baggage-carts; the mules being all shod with silver, and the drivers dressed in scarlet jackets of the finest Canusian cloth 598 , with a numerous train of footmen, and troops of Mazacans 599 , with bracelets on their arms, and mounted upon horses in splendid trappings.

XXXI. In nothing was he more prodigal than in his buildings. He completed his palace by continuing it from the Palatine to the Esquiline hill, calling the building at first only "The Passage," but, after it was burnt down and rebuilt, "The Golden House." 600 Of its dimensions and furniture, it may be sufficient to say thus much: the porch was so high that there stood in it a colossal statue of himself a hundred and twenty feet in height; and the space included in it was so ample, that it had triple porticos a mile in length, and a lake like a sea, surrounded with buildings which had the appearance of a city. Within its area were corn fields, vineyards, pastures, and woods, containing a vast number of animals of various kinds, both wild and tame. In other parts it was entirely over-laid with gold, and adorned with jewels and mother of pearl. The supper rooms were vaulted, and compartments of the ceilings, inlaid with ivory, were made to revolve, and scatter flowers; while they contained pipes which (360) shed unguents upon the guests. The chief banqueting room was circular, and revolved perpetually, night and day, in imitation of the motion of the celestial bodies. The baths were supplied with water from the sea and the Albula. Upon the dedication of this magnificent house after it was finished, all he said in approval of it was, "that he had now a dwelling fit for a man." He commenced making a pond for the reception of all the hot streams from Baiae, which he designed to have continued from Misenum to the Avernian lake, in a conduit, enclosed in galleries; and also a canal from Avernum to Ostia, that ships might pass from one to the other, without a sea voyage. The length of the proposed canal was one hundred and sixty miles; and it was intended to be of breadth sufficient to permit ships with five banks of oars to pass each other. For the execution of these designs, he ordered all prisoners, in every part of the empire, to be brought to Italy; and that even those who were convicted of the most heinous crimes, in lieu of any other sentence, should be condemned to work at them. He was encouraged to all this wild and enormous profusion, not only by the great revenue of the empire, but by the sudden hopes given him of an immense hidden treasure, which queen Dido, upon her flight from Tyre, had brought with her to Africa. This, a Roman knight pretended to assure him, upon good grounds, was still hid there in some deep caverns, and might with a little labour be recovered.

XXXII. But being disappointed in his expectations of this resource, and reduced to such difficulties, for want of money, that he was obliged to defer paying his troops, and the rewards due to the veterans; he resolved upon supplying his necessities by means of false accusations and plunder. In the first place, he ordered, that if any freedman, without sufficient reason, bore the name of the family to which he belonged; the half, instead of three fourths, of his estate should be brought into the exchequer at his decease: also that the estates of all such persons as had not in their wills been mindful of their prince, should be confiscated; and that the lawyers who had drawn or dictated such wills, should be liable to a fine. He ordained likewise, that all words and actions, upon which any informer could ground a prosecution, should be deemed treason. He demanded an equivalent for the crowns which the cities of (361) Greece had at any time offered him in the solemn games. Having forbad any one to use the colours of amethyst and Tyrian purple, he privately sent a person to sell a few ounces of them upon the day of the Nundinae, and then shut up all the merchants' shops, on the pretext that his edict had been violated. It is said, that, as he was playing and singing in the theatre, observing a married lady dressed in the purple which he had prohibited, he pointed her out to his procurators; upon which she was immediately dragged out of her seat, and not only stripped of her clothes, but her property. He never nominated a person to any office without saying to him, "You know what I want; and let us take care that nobody has any thing he can call his own." At last he rifled many temples of the rich offerings with which they were stored, and melted down all the gold and silver statues, and amongst them those of the penates 601 , which Galba afterwards restored.

XXXIII. He began the practice of parricide and murder with Claudius himself; for although he was not the contriver of his death, he was privy to the plot. Nor did he make any secret of it; but used afterwards to commend, in a Greek proverb, mushrooms as food fit for the gods, because Claudius had been poisoned with them. He traduced his memory both by word and deed in the grossest manner; one while charging him with folly, another while with cruelty. For he used to say by way of jest, that he had ceased morari 602 amongst men, pronouncing the first syllable long; and treated as null many of his decrees and ordinances, as made by a doting old blockhead. He enclosed the place where his body was burnt with only a low wall of rough masonry. He attempted to poison (362) Britannicus, as much out of envy because he had a sweeter voice, as from apprehension of what might ensue from the respect which the people entertained for his father's memory. He employed for this purpose a woman named Locusta, who had been a witness against some persons guilty of like practices. But the poison she gave him, working more slowly than he expected, and only causing a purge, he sent for the woman, and beat her with his own hand, charging her with administering an antidote instead of poison; and upon her alleging in excuse, that she had given Britannicus but a gentle mixture in order to prevent suspicion, "Think you," said he, "that I am afraid of the Julian law;" and obliged her to prepare, in his own chamber and before his eyes, as quick and strong a dose as possible. This he tried upon a kid: but the animal lingering for five hours before it expired, he ordered her to go to work again; and when she had done, he gave the poison to a pig, which dying immediately, he commanded the potion to be brought into the eating-room and given to Britannicus, while he was at supper with him. The prince had no sooner tasted it than he sunk on the floor, Nero meanwhile, pretending to the guests, that it was only a fit of the falling sickness, to which, he said, he was subject. He buried him the following day, in a mean and hurried way, during violent storms of rain. He gave Locusta a pardon, and rewarded her with a great estate in land, placing some disciples with her, to be instructed in her trade.

XXXIV. His mother being used to make strict inquiry into what he said or did, and to reprimand him with the freedom of a parent, he was so much offended, that he endeavoured to expose her to public resentment, by frequently pretending a resolution to quit the government, and retire to Rhodes. Soon afterwards, he deprived her of all honour and power, took from her the guard of Roman and German soldiers, banished her from the palace and from his society, and persecuted her in every way he could contrive; employing persons to harass her when at Rome with law-suits, and to disturb her in her retirement from town with the most scurrilous and abusive language, following her about by land and sea. But being terrified with her menaces and violent spirit, he resolved upon her destruction, and thrice attempted it by poison. Finding, however, (363) that she had previously secured herself by antidotes, he contrived machinery, by which the floor over her bed-chamber might be made to fall upon her while she was asleep in the night. This design miscarrying likewise, through the little caution used by those who were in the secret, his next stratagem was to construct a ship which could be easily shivered, in hopes of destroying her either by drowning, or by the deck above her cabin crushing her in its fall. Accordingly, under colour of a pretended reconciliation, he wrote her an extremely affectionate letter, inviting her to Baiae, to celebrate with him the festival of Minerva. He had given private orders to the captains of the galleys which were to attend her, to shatter to pieces the ship in which she had come, by falling foul of it, but in such manner that it might appear to be done accidentally. He prolonged the entertainment, for the more convenient opportunity of executing the plot in the night; and at her return for Bauli 603 , instead of the old ship which had conveyed her to Baiae, he offered that which he had contrived for her destruction. He attended her to the vessel in a very cheerful mood, and, at parting with her, kissed her breasts; after which he sat up very late in the night, waiting with great anxiety to learn the issue of his project. But receiving information that every thing had fallen out contrary to his wish, and that she had saved herself by swimming,—not knowing what course to take, upon her freedman, Lucius Agerinus bringing word, with great joy, that she was safe and well, he privately dropped a poniard by him. He then commanded the freedman to be seized and put in chains, under pretence of his having been employed by his mother to assassinate him; at the same time ordering her to be put to death, and giving out, that, to avoid punishment for her intended crime, she had laid violent hands upon herself. Other circumstances, still more horrible, are related on good authority; as that he went to view her corpse, and handling her limbs, pointed out some blemishes, and commended other points; and that, growing thirsty during the survey, he called for drink. Yet he was never afterwards able to bear the stings of his own conscience for this atrocious act, although encouraged by the congratulatory addresses of the army, the senate, and people. He frequently affirmed that he was haunted by his mother's ghost, and persecuted with the whips (364) and burning torches of the Furies. Nay, he attempted by magical rites to bring up her ghost from below, and soften her rage against him. When he was in Greece, he durst not attend the celebration of the Eleusinian mysteries, at the initiation of which, impious and wicked persons are warned by the voice of the herald from approaching the rites 604. Besides the murder of his mother, he had been guilty of that of his aunt; for, being obliged to keep her bed in consequence of a complaint in her bowels, he paid her a visit, and she, being then advanced in years, stroking his downy chin, in the tenderness of affection, said to him: "May I but live to see the day when this is shaved for the first time 605, and I shall then die contented." He turned, however, to those about him, made a jest of it, saying, that he would have his beard immediately taken off, and ordered the physicians to give her more violent purgatives. He seized upon her estate before she had expired; suppressing her will, that he might enjoy the whole himself.

XXXV. He had, besides Octavia, two other wives: Poppaea Sabina, whose father had borne the office of quaestor, and who had been married before to a Roman knight: and, after her, Statilia Messalina, great-grand-daughter of Taurus 606 who was twice consul, and received the honour of a triumph. To obtain possession of her, he put to death her husband, Atticus Vestinus, who was then consul. He soon became disgusted with Octavia, and ceased from having any intercourse with her; and being censured by his friends for it, he replied, "She ought to be satisfied with having the rank and appendages of his wife." Soon afterwards, he made several attempts, but in vain, to strangle her, and then divorced her for barrenness. But the people, disapproving of the divorce, and making severe comments upon it, he also banished her 607. At last he (365) put her to death, upon a charge of adultery, so impudent and false, that, when all those who were put to the torture positively denied their knowledge of it, he suborned his pedagogue, Anicetus, to affirm, that he had secretly intrigued with and debauched her. He married Poppaea twelve days after the divorce of Octavia 608, and entertained a great affection for her; but, nevertheless, killed her with a kick which he gave her when she was big with child, and in bad health, only because she found fault with him for returning late from driving his chariot. He had by her a daughter, Claudia Augusta, who died an infant. There was no person at all connected with him who escaped his deadly and unjust cruelty. Under pretence of her being engaged in a plot against him, he put to death Antonia, Claudius's daughter, who refused to marry him after the death of Poppaea. In the same way, he destroyed all who were allied to him either by blood or marriage; amongst whom was young Aulus Plautinus. He first compelled him to submit to his unnatural lust, and then ordered him to be executed, crying out, "Let my mother bestow her kisses on my successor thus defiled;" pretending that he had been his mothers paramour, and by her encouraged to aspire to the empire. His step-son, Rufinus Crispinus, Poppaea's son, though a minor, he ordered to be drowned in the sea, while he was fishing, by his own slaves, because he was reported to act frequently amongst his play-fellows the part of a general or an emperor. He banished Tuscus, his nurse's son, for presuming, when he was procurator of Egypt, to wash in the baths which had been constructed in expectation of his own coming. Seneca, his preceptor, he forced to kill himself 609 , though, upon his desiring leave to retire, and offering to surrender his estate, he solemnly swore, "that there was no foundation for his suspicions, and that he would perish himself sooner than hurt him." Having promised Burrhus, the pretorian prefect, a remedy for a swelling in his throat, he sent him poison. Some old rich freedmen of Claudius, who had formerly not only promoted (366) his adoption, but were also instrumental to his advancement to the empire, and had been his governors, he took off by poison given them in their meat or drink.

XXXVI. Nor did he proceed with less cruelty against those who were not of his family. A blazing star, which is vulgarly supposed to portend destruction to kings and princes, appeared above the horizon several nights successively 610 . He felt great anxiety on account of this phenomenon, and being informed by one Babilus, an astrologer, that princes were used to expiate such omens by the sacrifice of illustrious persons,[1] and so avert the danger foreboded to their own persons, by bringing it on the heads of their chief men, he resolved on the destruction of the principal nobility in Rome. He was the more encouraged to this, because he had some plausible pretence for carrying it into execution, from the discovery of two conspiracies against him; the former and more dangerous of which was that formed by Piso 611 , and discovered at Rome; the other was that of Vinicius 612 , at Beneventum. The conspirators were brought to their trials loaded with triple fetters. Some ingenuously confessed the charge; others avowed that they thought the design against his life an act of favour for which he was obliged to them, as it was impossible in any other way than by death to relieve a person rendered infamous by crimes of the greatest enormity. The children of those who had been condemned, were banished the city, and afterwards either poisoned or starved to death. It is asserted that some of them, with their tutors, and the slaves who carried their satchels, were all poisoned together at one dinner; and others not suffered to seek their daily bread.

XXXVII. From this period he butchered, without distinction or quarter, all whom his caprice suggested as objects for his cruelty; and upon the most frivolous pretences. To mention only a few: Salvidienus Orfitus was accused of letting (367) out three taverns attached to his house in the Forum to some cities for the use of their deputies at Rome. The charge against Cassius Longinus, a lawyer who had lost his sight, was, that he kept amongst the busts of his ancestors that of Caius Cassius, who was concerned in the death of Julius Caesar. The only charge objected against Paetus Thrasea was, that he had a melancholy cast of features, and looked like a schoolmaster. He allowed but one hour to those whom he obliged to kill themselves; and, to prevent delay, he sent them physicians "to cure them immediately, if they lingered beyond that time;" for so he called bleeding them to death. There was at that time an Egyptian of a most voracious appetite, who would digest raw flesh, or any thing else that was given him. It was credibly reported, that the emperor was extremely desirous of furnishing him with living men to tear and devour. Being elated with his great success in the perpetration of crimes, he declared, "that no prince before himself ever knew the extent of his power." He threw out strong intimations that he would not even spare the senators who survived, but would entirely extirpate that order, and put the provinces and armies into the hands of the Roman knights and his own freedmen. It is certain that he never gave or vouchsafed to allow any one the customary kiss, either on entering or departing, or even returned a salute. And at the inauguration of a work, the cut through the Isthmus 613 , he, with a loud voice, amidst the assembled multitude, uttered a prayer, that "the undertaking might prove fortunate for himself and the Roman people," without taking the smallest notice of the senate.

XXXVIII. He spared, moreover, neither the people of Rome, nor the capital of his country. Somebody in conversation saying—

*Emou thanontos gaia michthaeto pyri*

*When I am dead let fire devour the world—*

"Nay," said he, "let it be while I am living" [emou xontos]. And he acted accordingly: for, pretending to be disgusted with the old buildings, and the narrow and winding streets, he set the city on fire so openly, that many of consular rank caught his own household servants on their property with tow, and (368) torches in their hands, but durst not meddle with them. There being near his Golden House some granaries, the site of which he exceedingly coveted, they were battered as if with machines of war, and set on fire, the walls being built of stone. During six days and seven nights this terrible devastation continued, the people being obliged to fly to the tombs and monuments for lodging and shelter. Meanwhile, a vast number of stately buildings, the houses of generals celebrated in former times, and even then still decorated with the spoils of war, were laid in ashes; as well as the temples of the gods, which had been vowed and dedicated by the kings of Rome, and afterwards in the Punic and Gallic wars: in short, everything that was remarkable and worthy to be seen which time had spared 614 . This fire he beheld from a tower in the house of Mecaenas, and "being greatly delighted," as he said, "with the beautiful effects of the conflagration," he sung a poem on the ruin of Troy, in the tragic dress he used on the stage. To turn this calamity to his own advantage by plunder and rapine, he promised to remove the bodies of those who had perished in the fire, and clear the rubbish at his own expense; suffering no one to meddle with the remains of their property. But he not only received, but exacted contributions on account of the loss, until he had exhausted the means both of the provinces and private persons.

XXXIX. To these terrible and shameful calamities brought upon the people by their prince, were added some proceeding from misfortune. Such were a pestilence, by which, within the space of one autumn, there died no less than thirty thousand persons, as appeared from the registers in the temple of Libitina; a great disaster in Britain

615, where two of the principal towns belonging to the Romans were plundered; and a (369) dreadful havoc made both amongst our troops and allies; a shameful discomfiture of the army of the East; where, in Armenia, the legions were obliged to pass under the yoke, and it was with great difficulty that Syria was retained. Amidst all these disasters, it was strange, and, indeed, particularly remarkable, that he bore nothing more patiently than the scurrilous language and railing abuse which was in every one's mouth; treating no class of persons with more gentleness, than those who assailed him with invective and lampoons. Many things of that kind were posted up about the city, or otherwise published, both in Greek and Latin: such as these,

> *Neron, Orestaes, Alkmaion, maetroktonai.*
> *Neonymphon 616_Neron, idian maeter apekteinen.*
> Orestes and Alcaeon – Nero too,
> The lustful Nero, worst of all the crew,
> Fresh from his bridal – their own mothers slew.
> *Quis neget Aeneae magna de stirpe Neronem?*
> *Sustulit hic matrem: sustulit 617_ille patrem.*
> Sprung from Aeneas, pious, wise and great,
> Who says that Nero is degenerate?
> Safe through the flames, one bore his sire; the other,
> To save himself, took off his loving mother.
> *Dum tendit citharam noster, dum cornua Parthus,*
> *Noster erit Paean, ille Ekataebeletaes.*
> His lyre to harmony our Nero strings;
> His arrows o'er the plain the Parthian wings:
> Ours call the tuneful Paean, – famed in war,
> The other Phoebus name, the god who shoots afar. 618_
> *Roma domus fiet: Vejos migrate, Quirites,*
> *Si non et Vejos occupat ista domus.*
> All Rome will be one house: to Veii fly,
> Should it not stretch to Veii, by and by. 619_

(370) But he neither made any inquiry after the authors, nor when information was laid before the senate against some of them, would he allow a severe sentence to be passed. Isidorus, the Cynic philosopher,

said to him aloud, as he was passing along the streets, "You sing the misfortunes of Nauplius well, but behave badly yourself." And Datus, a comic actor, when repeating these words in the piece, "Farewell, father! Farewell mother!" mimicked the gestures of persons drinking and swimming, significantly alluding to the deaths of Claudius and Agrippina: and on uttering the last clause,

*Orcus vobis ducit pedes;*
*You stand this moment on the brink of Orcus;*

he plainly intimated his application of it to the precarious position of the senate. Yet Nero only banished the player and philosopher from the city and Italy; either because he was insensible to shame, or from apprehension that if he discovered his vexation, still keener things might be said of him.

XL. The world, after tolerating such an emperor for little less than fourteen years, at length forsook him; the Gauls, headed by Julius Vindex, who at that time governed the province as pro-praetor, being the first to revolt. Nero had been formerly told by astrologers, that it would be his fortune to be at last deserted by all the world; and this occasioned that celebrated saying of his, "An artist can live in any country;" by which he meant to offer as an excuse for his practice of music, that it was not only his amusement as a prince, but might be his support when reduced to a private station. Yet some of the astrologers promised him, in his forlorn state, the rule of the East, and some in express words the kingdom of Jerusalem. But the greater part of them flattered him with assurances of his being restored to his former fortune. And being most inclined to believe the latter prediction, upon losing Britain and Armenia, he imagined he had run through all the misfortunes which the fates had decreed him. But when, upon consulting the oracle of Apollo at Delphi, he was advised to beware of the seventy-third year, as if he were not to die till then, never thinking of Galba's age, he conceived such hopes, not only of living to advanced years, but of constant and singular good fortune, that having lost some things of great value by shipwreck, he scrupled not to say amongst his friends, that (371) "the fishes would bring them back to him." At Naples he heard of the insurrection in Gaul, on the anniversary of the day on which he killed his mother, and bore it with so much unconcern, as to excite a suspicion that he was really glad of it, since he had now a fair opportunity of plundering those wealthy provinces by the right of war. Immediately going to the gymnasium, he witnessed the exercise of the wrestlers with the greatest delight. Being interrupted at supper with letters which brought yet worse news, he expressed no greater resentment, than only to threaten the rebels. For eight days together, he never attempted to answer any letters, nor give any orders, but buried the whole affair in profound silence.

XLI. Being roused at last by numerous proclamations of Vindex, treating him with reproaches and contempt, he in a letter to the senate exhorted them to avenge his wrongs and those of the republic; desiring them to excuse his not appearing in the senate-house, because he had got cold. But nothing so much galled him, as to find himself railed at as a pitiful harper, and, instead of Nero, styled Aenobarbus: which being his family name, since he was upbraided with it, he declared that he would resume it, and lay aside the name he had taken by adoption. Passing by the other accusations as wholly groundless, he earnestly refuted that of his want of skill in an art upon which he had bestowed so much pains, and in which he had arrived at such perfection; asking frequently those about him, "if they knew any one who was a more accomplished musician?" But being alarmed by messengers after messengers of ill news from Gaul, he returned in great consternation to Rome. On the road, his mind was somewhat relieved, by observing the frivolous omen of a Gaulish soldier defeated and dragged by the hair by a Roman knight, which was sculptured on a monument; so that he leaped for joy, and adored the heavens. Even then he made no appeal either to the senate or people, but calling together some of the leading men at his own house, he held a hasty consultation upon the present state of affairs, and then, during the remainder of the day, carried them about with him to view some musical instruments, of a new invention, which were played by water 620 (372) exhibiting all the parts, and discoursing upon the principles and difficulties of the contrivance; which, he told them, he intended to produce in the theatre, if Vindex would give him leave.

XLII. Soon afterwards, he received intelligence that Galba and the Spaniards had declared against him; upon which, he fainted, and losing his reason, lay a long time speechless, apparently dead. As soon as recovered from this state stupefaction he tore his clothes, and beat his head, crying out, "It is all over with me!" His nurse endeavouring to comfort him, and telling him that the like things had happened to other princes before him, he replied, "I am beyond all example wretched, for I have lost an empire whilst I am still living." He, nevertheless, abated nothing of his luxury and inattention to business. Nay, on the arrival of good news from the provinces, he, at a sumptuous entertainment, sung with an air of merriment, some jovial verses upon the leaders of the revolt, which were made public; and accompanied them with suitable gestures. Being carried privately to the theatre, he sent word to an actor who was applauded by the spectators, "that he had it all his own way, now that he himself did not appear on the stage."

XLIII. At the first breaking out of these troubles, it is believed that he had formed many designs of a monstrous nature, although conformable enough to his natural disposition. These were to send new governors and commanders to the provinces and the armies, and employ assassins to butcher all the former governors and commanders, as men unanimously engaged in a conspiracy against him; to massacre the exiles in every quarter, and all the Gaulish population in Rome; the former lest they should join the insurrection; the latter as privy to the designs of their countrymen, and ready to support (373) them; to abandon Gaul itself, to be wasted and plundered by his armies; to poison the whole senate at a feast; to fire the city, and then let loose the wild beasts upon the people, in order to impede their stopping the progress of the flames. But being deterred from the execution of these designs not so much by remorse of conscience, as by despair of being able to effect them, and judging an expedition into Gaul necessary, he removed the consuls from their office, before the time of its expiration was arrived; and in their room assumed the consulship himself without a colleague, as if the fates had decreed that Gaul should not be conquered, but by a consul. Upon assuming the fasces, after an entertainment at the palace, as he walked out of the room leaning on the arms of some of his friends, he declared, that as soon as he arrived in the province, he would make his appearance amongst the troops, unarmed, and do nothing but weep: and that, after he had brought the mutineers to repentance, he would, the next day, in the public rejoicings, sing songs of triumph, which he must now, without loss of time, apply himself to compose.

XLIV. In preparing for this expedition, his first care was to provide carriages for his musical instruments and machinery to be used upon the stage; to have the hair of the concubines he carried with him dressed in the fashion of men; and to supply them with battle-axes, and Amazonian bucklers. He summoned the city-tribes to enlist; but no qualified persons appearing, he ordered all masters to send a certain number of slaves, the best they had, not excepting their stewards and secretaries. He commanded the several orders of the people to bring in a fixed proportion of their estates, as they stood in the censor's books; all tenants of houses and mansions to pay one year's rent forthwith into the exchequer; and, with unheard-of strictness, would receive only new coin of the purest silver and the finest gold; insomuch that most people refused to pay, crying out unanimously that he ought to squeeze the informers, and oblige them to surrender their gains.

XLV. The general odium in which he was held received an increase by the great scarcity of corn, and an occurrence connected with it. For, as it happened just at that time, there arrived from Alexandria a ship, which was said to be freighted (374) with dust for the wrestlers belonging to the emperor  621 . This so much inflamed the public rage, that he was treated with the utmost abuse and scurrility. Upon the top of one of his statues was placed the figure of a chariot with a Greek inscription, that "Now indeed he had a race to run; let him be gone." A little bag was tied about another, with a ticket containing these words; "What could I do?" — "Truly thou hast merited the sack." 622  Some person likewise wrote on the pillars in the forum, "that he had even woke the cocks  623  with his singing." And many, in the night-time, pretending to find fault with their servants, frequently called for a Vindex. 624

XLVI. He was also terrified with manifest warnings, both old and new, arising from dreams, auspices, and omens. He had never been used to dream before the murder of his mother. After that event, he fancied in his sleep that he was steering a ship, and that the rudder was forced from him: that he was dragged by his wife Octavia into a prodigiously dark place; and was at one time covered over with a vast swarm of winged ants, and at another, surrounded by the national images which were set up near Pompey's theatre, and hindered from advancing farther; that a Spanish jennet he was fond of, had his hinder parts so changed, as to resemble those of an ape; and having his head only left unaltered, neighed very harmoniously. The doors of the mausoleum of Augustus flying open of themselves, there issued from it a voice, calling on him by name. The Lares being adorned with fresh garlands on the calends (the first) of January, fell down during the preparations for sacrificing to them. While he was taking (375) the omens, Sporus presented him with a ring, the stone of which had carved upon it the Rape of Proserpine. When a great multitude of the several orders was assembled, to attend at the solemnity of making vows to the gods, it was a long time before the keys of the Capitol could be found. And when, in a speech of his to the senate against Vindex, these words were read, "that the miscreants should be punished and soon make the end they merited," they all cried out, "You will do it, Augustus." It was likewise remarked, that the last tragic piece which he sung, was Oedipus in Exile, and that he fell as he was repeating this verse:

*Thanein m' anoge syngamos, maetaer, pataer.*

*Wife, mother, father, force me to my end.*

XLVII. Meanwhile, on the arrival of the news, that the rest of the armies had declared against him, he tore to pieces the letters which were delivered to him at dinner, overthrew the table, and dashed with violence against the ground two favourite cups, which he called Homer's, because some of that poet's verses were cut upon them. Then taking from Locusta a dose of poison, which he put up in a golden box, he went into the Servilian gardens, and thence dispatching a trusty freedman to Ostia, with orders to make ready a fleet, he endeavoured to prevail with some tribunes and centurions of the pretorian guards to attend him in his flight; but part of them showing no great inclination to comply, others absolutely refusing, and one of them crying out aloud,

*Usque adeone mori miserum est?*

*Say, is it then so sad a thing to die?* 625_

he was in great perplexity whether he should submit himself to Galba, or apply to the Parthians for protection, or else appear before the people dressed in mourning, and, upon the rostra, in the most piteous manner, beg pardon for his past misdemeanors, and, if he could not prevail, request of them to grant him at least the government of Egypt. A speech to this purpose was afterwards found in his writing-case. But it is conjectured that he durst not venture upon this project, for fear of being torn to pieces, before he could get to the Forum. Deferring, therefore, his resolution until the next (376) day, he awoke about midnight, and finding the guards withdrawn, he leaped out of bed, and sent round for his friends. But none of them vouchsafing any message in reply, he went with a few attendants to their houses. The doors being every where shut, and no one giving him any answer, he returned to his bed-chamber; whence those who had the charge of it had all now eloped; some having gone one way, and some another, carrying off with them his bedding and box of poison. He then endeavoured to find Spicillus, the gladiator, or some one to kill him; but not being able to procure any one, "What!" said he, "have I then neither friend nor foe?" and immediately ran out, as if he would throw himself into the Tiber.

XLVIII. But this furious impulse subsiding, he wished for some place of privacy, where he might collect his thoughts; and his freedman Phaon offering him his country-house, between the Salarian 626 and Nomentan 627 roads, about four miles from the city, he mounted a horse, barefoot as he was, and in his tunic, only slipping over it an old soiled cloak; with his head muffled up, and an handkerchief before his face, and four persons only to attend him, of whom Sporus was one. He was suddenly struck with horror by an earthquake, and by a flash of lightning which darted full in his face, and heard from the neighbouring camp 628 the shouts of the soldiers, wishing his destruction, and prosperity to Galba. He also heard a traveller they met on the road, say, "They are (377) in pursuit of Nero:" and another ask, "Is there any news in the city about Nero?" Uncovering his face when his horse was started by the scent of a carcase which lay in the road, he was recognized and saluted by an old soldier who had been discharged from the guards. When they came to the lane which turned up to the house, they quitted their horses, and with much difficulty he wound among bushes, and briars, and along a track through a bed of rushes, over which they spread their cloaks for him to walk on. Having reached a wall at the back of the villa, Phaon advised him to hide himself awhile in a sand-pit; when he replied, "I will not go under-ground alive." Staying there some little time, while preparations were made for bringing him privately into the villa, he took up some water out of a neighbouring tank in his hand, to drink, saying, "This is Nero's distilled water." 629 Then his cloak having been torn by the brambles, he pulled out the thorns which stuck in it. At last, being admitted, creeping upon his hands and knees, through a hole made for him in the wall, he lay down in the first closet he came to, upon a miserable pallet, with an old coverlet thrown over it; and being both hungry and thirsty, though he refused some coarse bread that was brought him, he drank a little warm water.

XLIX. All who surrounded him now pressing him to save himself from the indignities which were ready to befall him, he ordered a pit to be sunk before his eyes, of the size of his body, and the bottom to be covered with pieces of marble put together, if any could be found about the house; and water and wood 630 , to be got ready for immediate use about his corpse; weeping at every thing that was done, and frequently saying, "What an artist is now about to perish!" Meanwhile, letters being brought in by a servant belonging to Phaon, he snatched them out of his hand, and there read, "That he had been declared an enemy by the senate, and that search was making for him, that he might be punished according to the ancient custom of the Romans." He then inquired what kind of punishment that was; and being told, that the (378) practice was to strip the criminal naked, and scourge him to death, while his neck was fastened within a forked stake, he was so terrified that he took up two daggers which he had brought with him, and after feeling the points of both, put them up again, saying, "The fatal hour is not yet come." One while, he begged of Sporus to begin to wail and lament; another while, he entreated that one of them would set him an example by killing himself; and then again, he condemned his own want of resolution in these words: "I yet live to my shame and disgrace: this is not becoming for Nero: it is not becoming. Thou oughtest in such circumstances to have a good heart: Come, then: courage, man!" 631 The horsemen who had received orders to bring him away alive, were now approaching the house. As soon as he heard them coming, he uttered with a trembling voice the following verse,

> Hippon m' okupodon amphi ktupos ouata ballei; 632_
> The noise of swift-heel'd steeds assails my ears;

he drove a dagger into his throat, being assisted in the act by Epaphroditus, his secretary. A centurion bursting in just as he was half-dead, and applying his cloak to the wound, pretending that he was come to his assistance, he made no other reply but this, "'Tis too late;" and "Is this your loyalty?" Immediately after pronouncing these words, he expired, with his eyes fixed and starting out of his head, to the terror of all who beheld him. He had requested of his attendants, as the most essential favour, that they would let no one have his head, but that by all means his body might be burnt entire. And this, Icelus, Galba's freedman, granted. He had but a little before been discharged from the prison into which he had been thrown, when the disturbances first broke out.

L. The expenses of his funeral amounted to two hundred thousand sesterces; the bed upon which his body was carried to the pile and burnt, being covered with the white robes, interwoven with gold, which he had worn upon the calends of January preceding. His nurses, Ecloge and Alexandra, with his concubine Acte, deposited his remains in the tomb belonging (379) to the family of the Domitii, which stands upon the top of the Hill of the Gardens 633 , and is to be seen from the Campus Martius. In that monument, a coffin of porphyry, with an altar of marble of Luna over it, is enclosed by a wall built of stone brought from Thasos. 634

LI. In stature he was a little below the common height; his skin was foul and spotted; his hair inclined to yellow; his features were agreeable, rather than handsome; his eyes grey and dull, his neck was thick, his belly prominent, his legs very slender, his constitution sound. For, though excessively luxurious in his mode of living, he had, in the course of fourteen years, only three fits of sickness; which were so slight, that he neither forbore the use of wine, nor made any alteration in his usual diet. In his dress, and the care of his person, he was so careless, that he had his hair cut in rings, one above another; and when in Achaia, he let it grow long behind; and he generally appeared in public in the loose dress which he used at table, with a handkerchief about his neck, and without either a girdle or shoes.

LII. He was instructed, when a boy, in the rudiments of almost all the liberal sciences; but his mother diverted him from the study of philosophy, as unsuited to one destined to be an emperor; and his preceptor, Seneca, discouraged him from reading the ancient orators, that he might longer secure his devotion to himself. Therefore, having a turn for poetry, (380) he composed verses both with pleasure and ease; nor did he, as some think, publish those of other writers as his own. Several little pocket-books and loose sheets have cone into my possession, which contain some well-known verses in his own hand, and written in such a manner, that it was very evident, from the blotting and interlining, that they had not been transcribed from a copy, nor dictated by another, but were written by the composer of them.

LIII. He had likewise great taste for drawing and painting, as well as for moulding statues in plaster. But, above all things, he most eagerly coveted popularity, being the rival of every man who obtained the applause of the people for any thing he did. It was the general belief, that, after the crowns he won by his performances on the stage, he would the next lustrum have taken his place among the wrestlers at the Olympic games. For he was continually practising that art; nor did he witness the gymnastic games in any part of Greece otherwise than sitting upon the ground in the stadium, as the umpires do. And if a pair of wrestlers happened to break the bounds, he would with his own hands drag them back into the centre of the circle. Because he was thought to equal Apollo in music, and the sun in chariot-driving, he resolved also to imitate the achievements of Hercules. And they say that a lion was got ready for him to kill, either with a club, or with a close hug, in view of the people in the amphitheatre; which he was to perform naked.

LIV. Towards the end of his life, he publicly vowed, that if his power in the state was securely re-established, he would, in the spectacles which he intended to exhibit in honour of his success, include a performance upon organs 635 , as well as upon flutes and bagpipes, and, on the last day of the games, would act in the play, and take the part of Turnus, as we find it in Virgil. And there are some who say, that he put to death the player Paris as a dangerous rival.

LV. He had an insatiable desire to immortalize his name, and acquire a reputation which should last through all succeeding ages; but it was capriciously directed. He therefore (381) took from several things and places their former appellations, and gave them new names derived from his own. He called the month of April, Neroneus, and designed changing the name of Rome into that of Neropolis.

LVI. He held all religious rites in contempt, except those of the Syrian Goddess 636 ; but at last he paid her so little reverence, that he made water upon her; being now engaged in another superstition, in which only he obstinately persisted. For having received from some obscure plebeian a little image of a girl, as a preservative against plots, and discovering a conspiracy immediately after, he constantly worshipped his imaginary protectress as the greatest amongst the gods, offering to her three sacrifices daily. He was also desirous to have it supposed that he had, by revelations from this deity, a knowledge of future events. A few months before he died, he attended a sacrifice, according to the Etruscan rites, but the omens were not favourable.

LVII. He died in the thirty-second year of his age 637, upon the same day on which he had formerly put Octavia to death; and the public joy was so great upon the occasion, that the common people ran about the city with caps upon their heads. Some, however, were not wanting, who for a long time decked his tomb with spring and summer flowers. Sometimes they placed his image upon the rostra, dressed in robes of state; at another, they published proclamations in his name, as if he were still alive, and would shortly return to Rome, and take vengeance on all his enemies. Vologesus, king of the Parthians, when he sent ambassadors to the senate to renew his alliance with the Roman people, earnestly requested that due honour should be paid to the memory of Nero; and, to conclude, when, twenty years afterwards, at which time I was a young man 638, some person of obscure birth gave himself out for Nero, that name secured him so favourable a reception (382) from the Parthians, that he was very zealously supported, and it was with much difficulty that they were prevailed upon to give him up.

\* \* \* \* \* \* \*

Though no law had ever passed for regulating the transmission of the imperial power, yet the design of conveying it by lineal descent was implied in the practice of adoption. By the rule of hereditary succession, Britannicus, the son of Claudius, was the natural heir to the throne; but he was supplanted by the artifices of his stepmother, who had the address to procure it for her own son, Nero. From the time of Augustus it had been the custom of each of the new sovereigns to commence his reign in such a manner as tended to acquire popularity, however much they all afterwards degenerated from those specious beginnings. Whether this proceeded entirely from policy, or that nature was not yet vitiated by the intoxication of uncontrolled power, is uncertain; but such were the excesses into which they afterwards plunged, that we can scarcely exempt any of them, except, perhaps, Claudius, from the imputation of great original depravity. The vicious temper of Tiberius was known to his own mother, Livia; that of Caligula had been obvious to those about him from his infancy; Claudius seems to have had naturally a stronger tendency to weakness than to vice; but the inherent wickedness of Nero was discovered at an early period by his preceptor, Seneca. Yet even this emperor commenced his reign in a manner which procured him approbation. Of all the Roman emperors who had hitherto reigned, he seems to have been most corrupted by profligate favourites, who flattered his follies and vices, to promote their own aggrandisement. In the number of these was Tigellinus, who met at last with the fate which he had so amply merited.

The several reigns from the death of Augustus present us with uncommon scenes of cruelty and horror; but it was reserved for that of Nero to exhibit to the world the atrocious act of an emperor deliberately procuring the death of his mother.

Julia Agrippina was the daughter of Germanicus, and married Domitius Aenobarbus, by whom she had Nero. At the death of Messalina she was a widow; and Claudius, her uncle, entertaining a design of entering again into the married state, she aspired to an incestuous alliance with him, in competition with Lollia Paulina, a woman of beauty and intrigue, who had been married to C. Caesar. The two rivals were strongly supported by their (383) respective parties; but Agrippina, by her superior interest with the emperor's favourites, and the familiarity to which her near relation gave her a claim, obtained the preference; and the portentous nuptials of the emperor and his niece were publicly solemnized in the palace. Whether she was prompted to this flagrant indecency by personal ambition alone, or by the desire of procuring the succession to the empire for her son, is uncertain; but there remains no doubt of her having removed Claudius by poison, with a view to the object now mentioned. Besides Claudius, she projected the death of L. Silanus, and she accomplished that of his brother, Junius Silanus, by means likewise of poison. She appears to have been richly endowed with the gifts of nature, but in her disposition intriguing, violent, imperious, and ready to sacrifice every principle of virtue, in the pursuit of supreme power or sensual gratification. As she resembled Livia in the ambition of a mother, and the means by which she indulged it, so she more than equalled her in the ingratitude of an unnatural son and a parricide. She is said to have left behind her some memoirs, of which Tacitus availed himself in the composition of his Annals.

In this reign, the conquest of the Britons still continued to be the principal object of military enterprise, and Suetonius Paulinus was invested with the command of the Roman army employed in the reduction of that people. The island of Mona, now Anglesey, being the chief seat of the Druids, he resolved to commence his operations with attacking a place which was the centre of superstition, and to which the vanquished Britons retreated as the last asylum of liberty. The inhabitants endeavoured, both by force of arms and the terrors of religion, to obstruct his landing on this sacred island. The women and Druids assembled promiscuously with the soldiers upon the shore, where running about in wild disorder, with flaming torches in their hands, and pouring forth the most hideous exclamations, they struck the Romans with consternation. But Suetonius animating his troops, they boldly attacked the inhabitants, routed them in the field, and burned the Druids in the same fires which had been prepared by those priests for the catastrophe of the invaders, destroying at the same time all the consecrated groves and altars in the island. Suetonius having thus triumphed over the religion of the Britons, flattered himself with the hopes of soon effecting the reduction of the people. But they, encouraged by his absence, had taken arms, and under the conduct of Boadicea, queen of the Iceni, who had been treated in the most ignominious manner by the Roman tribunes, had already driven the hateful invaders from their several settlements. Suetonius hastened to (384) the protection of London, which was by this time a flourishing Roman colony; but he found upon his arrival, that any attempt to preserve it would be attended with the utmost danger to the army. London therefore was reduced to ashes; and the Romans, and all strangers, to the number of seventy thousand, were put to the sword without distinction, the Britons seeming determined to convince the enemy that they would acquiesce in no other terms than a total evacuation of the island. This massacre, however, was revenged by Suetonius in a decisive engagement, where eighty thousand of the Britons are said to have been killed; after which, Boadicea, to avoid falling into the hands of the insolent conquerors, put a period to her own life by means of poison. It being judged unadvisable that Suetonius should any longer conduct the war against a people whom he had exasperated by his severity, he was recalled, and Petronius Turpilianus appointed in his room. The command was afterwards given successively to Trebellius Maximus and Vettius Bolanus; but the plan pursued by these generals was only to retain, by a conciliatory administration, the parts of the island which had already submitted to the Roman arms.

During these transactions in Britain, Nero himself was exhibiting, in Rome or some of the provinces, such scenes of extravagance as almost exceed credibility. In one place, entering the lists amongst the competitors in a chariot race; in another, contending for victory with the common musicians on the stage; revelling in open day in the company of the most abandoned prostitutes and the vilest of men; in the night, committing depredations on the peaceful inhabitants of the capital; polluting with detestable lust, or drenching with human blood, the streets, the palace, and the habitations of private families; and, to crown his enormities, setting fire to Rome, while he sung with delight in beholding the dreadful conflagration. In vain would history be ransacked for a parallel to this emperor, who united the most shameful vices to the most extravagant vanity, the most abject meanness to the strongest but most preposterous ambition; and the whole of whose life was one continued scene of lewdness, sensuality, rapine, cruelty, and folly. It is emphatically observed by Tacitus, "that Nero, after the murder of many illustrious personages, manifested a desire of extirpating virtue itself."

Among the excesses of Nero's reign, are to be mentioned the horrible cruelties exercised against the Christians in various parts of the empire, in which inhuman transactions the natural barbarity of the emperor was inflamed by the prejudices and interested policy of the pagan priesthood.

(385) The tyrant scrupled not to charge them with the act of burning Rome; and he satiated his fury against them by such outrages as are unexampled in history. They were covered with the skins of wild beasts, and torn by dogs; were crucified, and set on fire, that they might serve for lights in the night-time. Nero offered his gardens for this spectacle, and exhibited the games of the Circus by this dreadful illumination. Sometimes they were covered with wax and other

combustible materials, after which a sharp stake was put under their chin, to make them stand upright, and they were burnt alive, to give light to the spectators.

In the person of Nero, it is observed by Suetonius, the race of the Caesars became extinct; a race rendered illustrious by the first and second emperors, but which their successors no less disgraced. The despotism of Julius Caesar, though haughty and imperious, was liberal and humane: that of Augustus, if we exclude a few instances of vindictive severity towards individuals, was mild and conciliating; but the reigns of Tiberius, Caligula, and Nero (for we except Claudius from part of the censure), while discriminated from each other by some peculiar circumstances, exhibited the most flagrant acts of licentiousness and perverted authority. The most abominable lust, the most extravagant luxury, the most shameful rapaciousness, and the most inhuman cruelty, constitute the general characteristics of those capricious and detestable tyrants. Repeated experience now clearly refuted the opinion of Augustus, that he had introduced amongst the Romans the best form of government: but while we make this observation, it is proper to remark, that, had he even restored the republic, there is reason to believe that the nation would again have been soon distracted with internal divisions, and a perpetual succession of civil wars. The manners of the people were become too dissolute to be restrained by the authority of elective and temporary magistrates; and the Romans were hastening to that fatal period when general and great corruption, with its attendant debility, would render them an easy prey to any foreign invaders.

But the odious government of the emperors was not the only grievance under which the people laboured in those disastrous times: patrician avarice concurred with imperial rapacity to increase the sufferings of the nation. The senators, even during the commonwealth, had become openly corrupt in the dispensation of public justice; and under the government of the emperors pernicious abuse was practised to a yet greater extent. That class being now, equally with other Roman citizens, dependent on the sovereign power, their sentiments of duty and (386) honour were degraded by the loss of their former dignity; and being likewise deprived of the lucrative governments of provinces, to which they had annually succeeded by an elective rotation in the times of the republic, they endeavoured to compensate the reduction of their emoluments by an unbounded venality in the judicial decisions of the forum. Every source of national happiness and prosperity was by this means destroyed. The possession of property became precarious; industry, in all its branches, was effectually discouraged, and the amor patriae, which had formerly been the animating principle of the nation, was almost universally extinguished.

It is a circumstance corresponding to the general singularity of the present reign, that, of the few writers who flourished in it, and whose works have been transmitted to posterity, two ended their days by the order of the emperor, and the third, from indignation at his conduct. These unfortunate victims were Seneca, Petronius Arbiter, and Lucan.

SENECA was born about six years before the Christian aera, and gave early indication of uncommon talents. His father, who had come from Corduba to Rome, was a man of letters, particularly fond of declamation, in which he instructed his son, and placed him, for the acquisition of philosophy, under the most celebrated stoics of that age. Young Seneca, imbibing the precepts of the Pythagorean doctrine, religiously abstained from eating the flesh of animals, until Tiberius having threatened to punish some Jews and Egyptians, who abstained from certain meats, he was persuaded by his father to renounce the Pythagorean practice. Seneca displayed the talents of an eloquent speaker; but dreading the jealousy of Caligula, who aspired to the same excellence, he thought proper to abandon that pursuit, and apply himself towards suing for the honours and offices of the state. He accordingly obtained the place of quaestor, in which office incurring the imputation of a scandalous amour with Julia Livia, he removed from Rome, and was banished by the emperor Claudius to Corsica.

Upon the marriage of Claudius with Agrippina, Seneca was recalled from his exile, in which he had remained near eight years, and was appointed to superintend the education of Nero, now destined to become the successor to the throne. In the character of preceptor he appears to have acquitted himself with ability and credit; though he has been charged by his enemies with having initiated his pupil in those detestable vices which disgraced the reign of Nero. Could he have indeed been guilty of such immoral conduct, it is probable that he would not so easily have (387) forfeited the favour of that emperor;

and it is more reasonable to suppose, that his disapprobation of Nero's conduct was the real cause of that odium which soon after proved fatal to him. By the enemies whom distinguished merit and virtue never fail to excite at a profligate court, Seneca was accused of having maintained a criminal correspondence with Agrippina in the life-time of Claudius; but the chief author of this calumny was Suilius, who had been banished from Rome at the instance of Seneca. He was likewise charged with having amassed exorbitant riches, with having built magnificent houses, and formed beautiful gardens, during the four years in which he had acted as preceptor to Nero. This charge he considered as a prelude to his destruction; which to avoid, if possible, he requested of the emperor to accept of the riches and possessions which he had acquired in his situation at court, and to permit him to withdraw himself into a life of studious retirement. Nero, dissembling his secret intentions, refused this request; and Seneca, that he might obviate all cause of suspicion or offence, kept himself at home for some time, under the pretext of indisposition.

Upon the breaking out of the conspiracy of Piso, in which some of the principal senators were concerned, Natalis, the discoverer of the plot, mentioned Seneca's name, as an accessory. There is, however, no satisfactory evidence that Seneca had any knowledge of the plot. Piso, according to the declaration of Natalis, had complained that he never saw Seneca; and the latter had observed, in answer, that it was not conducive to their common interest to see each other often. Seneca likewise pleaded indisposition, and said that his own life depended upon the safety of Piso's person. Nero, however, glad of such an occasion of sacrificing the philosopher to his secret jealousy, sent him an order to destroy himself. When the messenger arrived with this mandate, Seneca was sitting at table, with his wife Paulina and two of his friends. He heard the message not only with philosophical firmness, but even with symptoms of joy, and observed, that such an honour might long have been expected from a man who had assassinated all his friends, and even murdered his own mother. The only request which he made, was, that he might be permitted to dispose of his possessions as he pleased; but this was refused him. Immediately turning himself to his friends, who were weeping at his melancholy fate, he said to them, that, since he could not leave them what he considered as his own property, he should leave at least his own life for an example; an innocence of conduct which they might imitate, and by which they might acquire immortal fame. He remonstrated with composure against their unavailing tears and (388) lamentations, and asked them, whether they had not learnt better to sustain the shocks of fortune, and the violence of tyranny?

The emotions of his wife he endeavoured to allay with philosophical consolation; and when she expressed a resolution to die with him, he said, that he was glad to find his example imitated with so much fortitude. The veins of both were opened at the same time; but Nero's command extending only to Seneca, the life of Paulina was preserved; and, according to some authors, she was not displeased at being prevented from carrying her precipitate resolution into effect. Seneca's veins bleeding but slowly, an opportunity was offered him of displaying in his last moments a philosophical magnanimity similar to that of Socrates; and it appears that his conversation during this solemn period was maintained with dignified composure. To accelerate his lingering fate, he drank a dose of poison; but this producing no effect, he ordered his attendants to carry him into a warm bath, for the purpose of rendering the haemorrhage from his veins more copious. This expedient proving likewise ineffectual, and the soldiers who witnessed the execution of the emperor's order being clamorous for its accomplishment, he was removed into a stove, and suffocated by the steam. He underwent his fate on the 12th of April, in the sixty-fifth year of the Christian aera, and the fifty-third year of his age. His body was burnt, and his ashes deposited in a private manner, according to his will, which had been made during the period when he was in the highest degree of favour with Nero.

The writings of Seneca are numerous, and on various subjects. His first composition, addressed to Novacus, is on Anger, and continued through three books. After giving a lively description of this passion, the author discusses a variety of questions concerning it: he argues strongly against its utility, in contradiction to the peripatetics, and recommends its restraint, by many just and excellent considerations. This treatise may be regarded, in its general outlines, as a philosophical amplification of the passage in Horace:—

*Ira furor brevis est: animum rege; qui, nisi paret,*
*Imperat: hunc fraenis, hunc tu compesce catena.*
Epist. I. ii.

*Anger's a fitful madness: rein thy mind,*
*Subdue the tyrant, and in fetters bind,*
*Or be thyself the slave.*

The next treatise is on Consolation, addressed to his mother, Helvia, and was written during his exile. He there informs his mother that he bears his banishment with fortitude, and advises her to do the same. He observes, that, in respect to himself, (389) change of place, poverty, ignominy, and contempt, are not real evils; that there may be two reasons for her anxiety on his account; first, that, by his absence, she is deprived of his protection; and in the next place, of the satisfaction arising from his company; on both which heads he suggests a variety of pertinent observations. Prefixed to this treatise, are some epigrams written on the banishment of Seneca, but whether or not by himself, is uncertain.

Immediately subsequent to the preceding, is another treatise on Consolation, addressed to one of Claudius's freedmen, named Polybius, perhaps after the learned historian. In this tract, which is in several parts mutilated, the author endeavours to console Polybius for the loss of a brother who had lately died. The sentiments and admonitions are well suggested for the purpose; but they are intermixed with such fulsome encomiums on the imperial domestic, as degrade the dignity of the author, and can be ascribed to no other motive than that of endeavouring to procure a recall from his exile, through the interest of Polybius.

A fourth treatise on Consolation is addressed to Marcia, a respectable and opulent lady, the daughter of Cremutius Cordus, by whose death she was deeply affected. The author, besides many consolatory arguments, proposes for her imitation a number of examples, by attending to which she may be enabled to overcome a passion that is founded only in too great sensibility of mind. The subject is ingeniously prosecuted, not without the occasional mixture of some delicate flattery, suitable to the character of the correspondent.

These consolatory addresses are followed by a treatise on Providence, which evinces the author to have entertained the most just and philosophical sentiments on that subject. He infers the necessary existence of a Providence from the regularity and constancy observed in the government of the universe but his chief object is to show, why, upon the principle that a Providence exists, good men should be liable to evils. The enquiry is conducted with a variety of just observations, and great force of argument; by which the author vindicates the goodness and wisdom of the Almighty, in a strain of sentiment corresponding to the most approved suggestions of natural religion.

The next treatise, which is on Tranquillity of Mind, appears to have been written soon after his return from exile. There is a confusion in the arrangement of this tract; but it contains a variety of just observations, and may be regarded as a valuable production.

(390) Then follows a discourse on the Constancy of a Wise Man. This has by some been considered as a part of the preceding treatise; but they are evidently distinct. It is one of the author's best productions, in regard both of sentiment and composition, and contains a fund of moral observations, suited to fortify the mind under the oppression of accidental calamities.

We next meet with a tract on Clemency, in two books, addressed to Nero. This appears to have been written in the beginning of the reign of Nero, on whom the author bestows some high encomiums, which, at that time, seem not to have been destitute of foundation. The discourse abounds with just observation, applicable to all ranks of men; and, if properly attended to by that infatuated emperor, might have prevented the perpetration of those acts of cruelty, which, with his other extravagancies, have rendered his name odious to posterity.

The discourse which succeeds is on the Shortness of Life, addressed to Paulinus. In this excellent treatise the author endeavours to show, that the complaint of the shortness of life is not founded in truth: that it is men who make life short, either by passing it in indolence, or otherwise improperly. He inveighs against indolence, luxury, and every unprofitable avocation; observing, that the best use of time is to apply it to the study of wisdom, by which life may be rendered sufficiently long.

Next follows a discourse on a Happy Life, addressed to Gallio. Seneca seems to have intended this as a vindication of himself, against those who calumniated him on account of his riches and manner of living. He maintained that a life can only be rendered happy by its conformity to the dictates of virtue, but that such a life is perfectly compatible with the possession of riches, where they happen to accrue. The author pleads his own cause with great ability, as well as justness of argument. His vindication is in many parts highly beautiful, and accompanied with admirable sentiments respecting the moral obligations to a virtuous life. The conclusion of this discourse bears no similarity, in point of composition, to the preceding parts, and is evidently spurious.

The preceding discourse is followed by one upon the Retirement of a Wise Man. The beginning of this tract is wanting; but in the sequel the author discusses a question which was much agitated amongst the Stoics and Epicureans, viz., whether a wise man ought to concern himself with the affairs of the public. Both these sects of philosophers maintained that a life of retirement was most suitable to a wise man, but they differed with respect to the circumstances in which it might be proper to deviate from this conduct; one party considering the deviation (391) as prudent, when there existed a just motive for such conduct, and the other, when there was no forcible reason against it. Seneca regards both these opinions as founded upon principles inadequate to the advancement both of public and private happiness, which ought ever to be the ultimate object of moral speculation.

The last of the author's discourses, addressed to Aebucius, is on Benefits, and continued through seven books. He begins with lamenting the frequency of ingratitude amongst mankind, a vice which he severely censures. After some preliminary considerations respecting the nature of benefits, he proceeds to show in what manner, and on whom, they ought to be conferred. The greater part of these books is employed on the solution of abstract questions relative to benefits, in the manner of Chrysippus; where the author states explicitly the arguments on both sides, and from the full consideration of them, deduces rational conclusions.

The Epistles of Seneca consist of one hundred and twenty-four, all on moral subjects. His Natural Questions extend through seven books, in which he has collected the hypotheses of Aristotle and other ancient writers. These are followed by a whimsical effusion on the death of Caligula. The remainder of his works comprises seven Persuasive Discourses, five books of Controversies, and ten books containing Extracts of Declamations.

From the multiplicity of Seneca's productions, it is evident, that, notwithstanding the luxurious life he is said to have led, he was greatly devoted to literature, a propensity which, it is probable, was confirmed by his banishment during almost eight years in the island of Corsica, where he was in a great degree secluded from every other resource of amusement to a cultivated mind. But with whatever splendour Seneca's domestic economy may have been supported, it seems highly improbable that he indulged himself in luxurious enjoyment to any vicious excess. His situation at the Roman court, being honourable and important, could not fail of being likewise advantageous, not only from the imperial profusion common at that time, but from many contingent emoluments which his extensive interest and patronage would naturally afford him. He was born of a respectable rank, lived in habits of familiar intercourse with persons of the first distinction, and if, in the course of his attendance upon Nero, he had acquired a large fortune, no blame could justly attach to his conduct in maintaining an elegant hospitality. The imputation of luxury was thrown upon him from two quarters, viz, by the dissolute companions of Nero, to whom the mention of such an example served as an apology for their own extreme dissipation; (392) and by those who envied him for the affluence and dignity which he had acquired. The charge, however, is supported only by vague assertion, and is discredited by every consideration which ought to have weight in determining the reality of human characters. It seems totally inconsistent with his habits of literary industry, with the virtuous sentiments which he every where strenuously maintains, and the esteem with which he was regarded by a numerous acquaintance, as a philosopher and a moralist.

The writings of Seneca have been traduced almost equally with his manner of living, though in both he has a claim to indulgence, from the fashion of the times. He is more studious of minute embellishments in style than the writers of the Augustan age; and the didactic strain, in which he mostly prosecutes his subjects, has a tendency to render him sententious; but the expression of his thoughts is neither enfeebled by decoration, nor involved in obscurity by conciseness. He is not more rich in artificial ornament than in moral admonition. Seneca has been charged with depreciating former writers, to render himself more conspicuous; a charge which, so far as appears from his writings, is founded rather in negative than positive testimony. He has not endeavoured to establish his fame by any affectation of singularity in doctrine; and while he passes over in silence the names of illustrious authors, he avails himself with judgment of the most valuable stores with which they had enriched philosophy. On the whole, he is an author whose principles may be adopted not only with safety, but great advantage; and his writings merit a degree of consideration, superior to what they have hitherto ever enjoyed in the literary world.

Seneca, besides his prose works, was the author of some tragedies. The Medea, the Troas, and the Hippolytus, are ascribed to him. His father is said to have written the Hercules Furens, Thyestes, Agamemnon, and Hercules Oetaeus. The three remaining tragedies, the Thebais, Oedipus, and Octavia, usually published in the same collection with the seven preceding, are supposed to be the productions of other authors, but of whom, is uncertain. These several pieces are written in a neat style; the plots and characters are conducted with an attention to probability and nature: but none of them is so forcible, in point of tragical distress, as to excite in the reader any great degree of emotion.— —

PETRONIUS was a Roman knight, and apparently of considerable fortune. In his youth he seems to have given great application to polite literature, in which he acquired a justness of taste, as well as an elegance of composition. Early initiated in the gaieties of fashionable life, he contracted a habit of voluptuousness which rendered him an accommodating companion to the dissipated and the luxurious. The court of Claudius, entirely governed for some time by Messalina, was then the residence of pleasure; and here Petronius failed not of making a conspicuous appearance. More delicate, however, than sensual, he rather joined in the dissipation, than indulged in the vices of the palace. To interrupt a course of life too uniform to afford him perpetual satisfaction, he accepted of the proconsulship of Bithynia, and went to that province, where he discharged the duties of his office with great credit. Upon his return to Rome, Nero, who had succeeded Claudius, made him consul, in recompense of his services. This new dignity, by giving him frequent and easy access to the emperor, created an intimacy between them, which was increased to friendship and esteem on the side of Nero, by the elegant entertainments often given him by Petronius. In a short time, this gay voluptuary became so much a favourite at court, that nothing was agreeable but what was approved by Petronius and the authority which he acquired, by being umpire in whatever related to the economy of gay dissipation, procured him the title of Arbiter elegantiarum. Things continued in this state whilst the emperor kept within the bounds of moderation; and Petronius acted as intendant of his pleasures, ordering him shows, games, comedies, music, feats, and all that could contribute to make the hours of relaxation pass agreeably; seasoning, at the same time, the innocent delights which he procured for the emperor with every possible charm, to prevent him from seeking after such as might prove pernicious both to morals and the republic. Nero, however, giving way to his own disposition, which was naturally vicious, at length changed his conduct, not only in regard to the government of the empire, but of himself and listening to other counsels than those of Petronius, gave the entire reins to his passions, which afterwards plunged him in ruin. The emperor's new favourite was Tigellinus, a man of the most profligate morals, who omitted nothing that could gratify the inordinate appetites of his prince, at the expense of all decency and virtue. During this period, Petronius gave vent to his indignation, in the satire transmitted under his name by the title of Satyricon. But his total retirement from court did not secure him from the artifices of Tigellinus, who laboured with all his power to destroy the man whom he had industriously supplanted in the emperor's favour. With this view he insinuated to Nero, that Petronius was too intimately connected with Scevinus not to be engaged in Piso's conspiracy; and, to support his calumny, caused the emperor to be present at the examination (394) of one of Petronius's slaves, whom he had secretly suborned to swear against his master. After this transaction, to deprive Petronius of all means of justifying himself, they threw into prison the greatest part of his domestics. Nero embraced with joy the opportunity of removing a man, to whom he knew the present manners of the court were utterly obnoxious, and he soon after issued orders for arresting Petronius. As it required, however, some time to deliberate whether they should put a person of his consideration to death, without more evident proofs of the charges preferred against him, such was his disgust at living in the power of so detestable and capricious a tyrant, that he resolved to die. For this purpose, making choice of the same expedient which had been adopted by Seneca, he caused his veins to be opened, but he closed them again, for a little time, that he might enjoy the conversation of his friends, who came to see him in his last moments. He desired them, it is said, to entertain him, not with discourses on the immortality of the soul, or the consolation of philosophy, but with agreeable tales and poetic gallantries. Disdaining to imitate the servility of those who, dying by the orders of Nero, yet made him their heir, and filled their wills with encomiums on the tyrant and his favourites, he broke to pieces a goblet of precious stones, out of which he had commonly drank, that Nero, who he knew would seize upon it after his death, might not have the pleasure of using it. As the only present suitable to such a prince, he sent him, under a sealed cover, his Satyricon, written purposely against him; and then broke his signet, that it might not, after his death, become the means of accusation against the person in whose custody it should be found.

The Satyricon of Petronius is one of the most curious productions in the Latin language. Novel in its nature, and without any parallel in the works of antiquity, some have imagined it to be a spurious composition, fabricated about the time of the revival of learning in Europe. This conjecture, however, is not more destitute of support, than repugnant to the most circumstantial evidence in favour of its authenticity. Others, admitting the work to be a production of the age of Nero, have questioned the design with which it was written, and have consequently imputed to the author a most immoral intention. Some of the scenes, incidents, and characters, are of so extraordinary a nature, that the description of them, without a particular application, must have been regarded as extremely whimsical, and the work, notwithstanding its ingenuity, has been doomed to perpetual oblivion: but history justifies the belief, that in the court of Nero, the extravagancies mentioned by Petronius were realized (395) to a degree which authenticates the representation given of them. The inimitable character of Trimalchio, which exhibits a person sunk in the most debauched effeminacy, was drawn for Nero; and we are assured, that there were formerly medals of that emperor, with these words, C. Nero August. Imp., and on the reverse, Trimalchio. The various characters are well discriminated, and supported with admirable propriety. Never was such licentiousness of description united to such delicacy of colouring. The force of the satire consists not in poignancy of sentiment, but in the ridicule which arises from the whimsical, but characteristic and faithful exhibition of the objects introduced. That Nero was struck with the justness of the representation, is evident from the displeasure which he showed, at finding Petronius so well acquainted with his infamous excesses. After levelling his suspicion on all who could possibly have betrayed him, he at last fixed on a senator's wife, named Silia, who bore a part in his revels, and was an intimate friend of Petronius upon which she was immediately sent into banishment. Amongst the miscellaneous materials in this work, are some pieces of poetry, written in an elegant taste. A poem on the civil war between Caesar and Pompey, is beautiful and animated.

Though the Muses appear to have been mostly in a quiescent state from the time of Augustus, we find from Petronius Arbiter, who exhibits the manners of the capital during the reign of Nero, that poetry still continued to be a favourite pursuit amongst the Romans, and one to which, indeed, they seem to have had a national propensity.

– – – – *Ecce inter pocula quaerunt*
*Romulidae saturi, quid dia poemata narrent.* – Persius, Sat. i. 30.
– – *Nay, more! Our nobles, gorged, and swilled with wine,*
*Call o'er the banquet for a lay divine!* – Gifford.

It was cultivated as a kind of fashionable exercise, in short and desultory attempts, in which the chief ambition was to produce verses extempore. They were publicly recited by their authors with great ostentation; and a favourable verdict from an audience, however partial, and frequently obtained either by intrigue or bribery, was construed by those frivolous pretenders into a real adjudication of poetical fame.

The custom of publicly reciting poetical compositions, with the view of obtaining the opinion of the hearers concerning them, and for which purpose Augustus had built the Temple of Apollo, was well calculated for the improvement of taste and judgment, as well as the excitement of emulation; but, conducted as it now was, it led to a general degradation of poetry. Barbarism in (396) language, and a corruption of taste, were the natural consequences of this practice, while the judgment of the multitude was either blind or venal, and while public approbation sanctioned the crudities of hasty composition. There arose, however, in this period, some candidates for the bays, who carried their efforts beyond the narrow limits which custom and inadequate genius prescribed to the poetical exertions of their contemporaries. Amongst these were Lucan and Persius.———

LUCAN was the son of Annaeus Mela, the brother of Seneca, the philosopher. He was born at Corduba, the original residence of the family, but came early to Rome, where his promising talents, and the patronage of his uncle, recommended him to the favour of Nero; by whom he was raised to the dignity of an augur and quaestor before he had attained the usual age. Prompted by the desire of displaying his political abilities, he had the imprudence to engage in a competition with his imperial patron. The subject chosen by Nero was the tragical fate of Niobe; and that of Lucan was Orpheus. The ease with which the latter obtained the victory in the contest, excited the jealousy of the emperor, who resolved upon depressing his rising genius. With this view, he exposed him daily to the mortification of fresh insults, until at last the poet's resentment was so much provoked, that he entered into the conspiracy of Piso for cutting off the tyrant. The plot being discovered, there remained for the unfortunate Lucan no hope of pardon: and choosing the same mode of death which was employed by his uncle, he had his veins opened, while he sat in a warm bath, and expired in pronouncing with great emphasis the following lines in his Pharsalia:—

> *Scinditur avulsus; nec sicut vulnere sanguis*
> *Emicuit lentus: ruptis cadit undique venis;*
> *Discursusque animae diversa in membra meantis*
> *Interceptus aquis, nullius, vita perempti*
> *Est tanta dimissa via.* — *Lib. iii. 638.*
>
> — — *Asunder flies the man.*
> *No single wound the gaping rupture seems,*
> *Where trickling crimson flows in tender streams;*
> *But from an opening horrible and wide*
> *A thousand vessels pour the bursting tide;*
> *At once the winding channel's course was broke,*
> *Where wandering life her mazy journey took.* — *Rowe.*

Some authors have said that he betrayed pusillanimity at the hour of death; and that, to save himself from punishment, he (397) accused his mother of being involved in the conspiracy. This circumstance, however, is not mentioned by other writers, who relate, on the contrary, that he died with philosophical fortitude. He was then only in the twenty-sixth year of his age.

Lucan had scarcely reached the age of puberty when he wrote a poem on the contest between Hector and Achilles. He also composed in his youth a poem on the burning of Rome; but his only surviving work is the Pharsalia, written on the civil war between Caesar and Pompey. This poem, consisting of ten books, is unfinished, and its character has been more depreciated than that of any other production of antiquity. In the plan of the poem, the author prosecutes the different events in the civil war, beginning his narrative at the passage of the Rubicon by Caesar. He invokes not the muses, nor engages any gods in the dispute; but endeavours to support an epic dignity by vigour of sentiment, and splendour of description. The horrors of civil war, and the importance of a contest which was to determine the fate of Rome and the empire of the world, are displayed with variety of colouring, and great energy of expression. In the description of scenes, and the recital of heroic actions, the author discovers a strong and lively imagination; while, in those parts of the work which are addressed either to the understanding or the passions, he is bold, figurative, and animated. Indulging too much in amplification, he is apt to tire with prolixity; but in all his excursions he is ardent, elevated, impressive, and often brilliant. His versification has not the smoothness which we admire in the compositions of Virgil, and his language is often involved in the intricacies of technical construction: but with all his defects, his beauties are numerous; and he discovers a greater degree of merit than is commonly found in the productions of a poet of twenty-six years of age, at which time he died. — —

PERSIUS was born at Volaterrae, of an equestrian family, about the beginning of the Christian aera. His father dying when he was six years old, he was left to the care of his mother, for whom and for his sisters he expresses the warmest affection. At the age of twelve he came to Rome, where, after attending a course of grammar and rhetoric under the respective masters of those branches of education, he placed himself under the tuition of Annaeus Cornutus, a celebrated stoic philosopher of that time. There subsisted between him and this preceptor so great a friendship, that at his death, which happened in the twenty-ninth year of his age, he bequeathed to Cornutus a handsome sum of money, and his library. The latter, however, accepting only the books, left the money to Persius's sisters.

Priscian, Quintilian, and other ancient writers, spear of Persius's satires as consisting of a book without any division. They have since, however, been generally divided into six different satires, but by some only into five. The subjects of these compositions are, the vanity of the poets in his time; the backwardness of youth to the cultivation of moral science; ignorance and temerity in political administration, chiefly in allusion to the government of Nero: the fifth satire is employed in evincing that the wise man also is free; in discussing which point, the author adopts the observations used by Horace on the same subject. The last satire of Persius is directed against avarice. In the fifth, we meet with a beautiful address to Cornutus, whom the author celebrates for his amiable virtues, and peculiar talents for teaching. The following lines, at the same time that they show how diligently the preceptor and his pupil were employed through the whole day in the cultivation of moral science, afford a more agreeable picture of domestic comfort and philosophical conviviality, than might be expected in the family of a rigid stoic:

*Tecum etenim longos memini consumere soles,*
*Et tecum primas epulis decerpere noctes.*
*Unum opus, et requiem pariter disponimus ambo:*
*Atque verecunda laxamus feria mensa.* – Sat. v.
Can I forget how many a summer's day,
Spent in your converse, stole, unmarked, away?
Or how, while listening with increased delight,
I snatched from feasts the earlier hours of night? – Gifford.

The satires of Persius are written in a free, expostulatory, and argumentative manner; possessing the same justness of sentiment as those of Horace, but exerted in the way of derision, and not with the admirable raillery of that facetious author. They are regarded by many as obscure; but this imputation arises more from unacquaintance with the characters and manners to which the author alludes, than from any peculiarity either in his language or composition. His versification is harmonious; and we have only to remark, in addition to similar examples in other Latin writers, that, though Persius is acknowledged to have been both virtuous and modest, there are in the fourth satire a few passages which cannot decently admit of being translated. Such was the freedom of the Romans, in the use of some expressions, which just refinement has now exploded.—

Another poet, in this period, was FABRICIUS VEIENTO, who wrote a severe satire against the priests of his time; as also one (399) against the senators, for corruption in their judicial capacity. Nothing remains of either of those productions; but, for the latter, the author was banished by Nero.

There now likewise flourished a lyric poet, CAESIUS BASSUS, to whom Persius has addressed his sixth satire. He is said to have been, next to Horace, the best lyric poet among the Romans; but of his various compositions, only a few inconsiderable fragments are preserved.

To the two poets now mentioned must be added POMPONIUS SECUNDUS, a man of distinguished rank in the army, and who obtained the honour of a triumph for a victory over a tribe of barbarians in Germany. He wrote several tragedies, which in the judgment of Quintilian, were beautiful compositions.

# SERGIUS SULPICIUS GALBA.

(400)

I. The race of the Caesars became extinct in Nero; an event prognosticated by various signs, two of which were particularly significant. Formerly, when Livia, after her marriage with Augustus, was making a visit to her villa at Veii 639, an eagle flying by, let drop upon her lap a hen, with a sprig of laurel in her mouth, just as she had seized it. Livia gave orders to have the hen taken care of, and the sprig of laurel set; and the hen reared such a numerous brood of chickens, that the villa, to this day, is called the Villa of the Hens 640. The laurel groves flourished so much, that the Caesars procured thence the boughs and crowns they bore at their triumphs. It was also their constant custom to plant others on the same spot, immediately after a triumph; and it was observed that, a little before the death of each prince, the tree which had been set by him died away. But in the last year of Nero, the whole plantation of laurels perished to the very roots, and the hens all died. About the same time, the temple of the Caesars 641 being struck with lightning, the heads of all the statues in it fell off at once; and Augustus's sceptre was dashed from his hands.

II. Nero was succeeded by Galba 642, who was not in the remotest degree allied to the family of the Caesars, but, without doubt, of very noble extraction, being descended from a great and ancient family; for he always used to put amongst his other titles, upon the bases of his statues, his being great-grandson to Q. Catulus Capitolinus. And when he came to (401) be emperor, he set up the images of his ancestors in the hall 643 of the palace; according to the inscriptions on which, he carried up his pedigree on the father's side to Jupiter; and by the mother's to Pasiphae, the wife of Minos.

III. To give even a short account of the whole family, would be tedious. I shall, therefore, only slightly notice that branch of it from which he was descended. Why, or whence, the first of the Sulpicii who had the cognomen of Galba, was so called, is uncertain. Some are of opinion, that it was because he set fire to a city in Spain, after he had a long time attacked it to no purpose, with torches dipped in the gum called Galbanum: others said he was so named, because, in a lingering disease, he made use of it as a remedy, wrapped up in wool: others, on account of his being prodigiously corpulent, such a one being called, in the language of the Gauls, Galba; or, on the contrary, because he was of a slender habit of body, like those insects which breed in a sort of oak, and are called Galbae. Sergius Galba, a person of consular rank 644, and the most eloquent man of his time, gave a lustre to the family. History relates, that, when he was pro-praetor of Spain, he perfidiously put to the sword thirty thousand Lusitanians, and by that means gave occasion to the war of Viriatus 645. His grandson being incensed against Julius Caesar, whose lieutenant he had been in Gaul, because he was through him disappointed of the consulship 646, joined with Cassius and Brutus in the conspiracy against him, for which he was condemned by the Pedian law. From him were descended the grandfather and father of the emperor Galba. The grandfather was more celebrated for his application to study, than (402) for any figure he made in the government. For he rose no higher than the praetorship, but published a large and not uninteresting history. His father attained to the consulship 647: he was a short man and hump-backed, but a tolerable orator, and an industrious pleader. He was twice married: the first of his wives was Mummia Achaica, daughter of Catulus, and great-grand-daughter of Lucius Mummius, who sacked Corinth 648; and the other, Livia Ocellina, a very rich and beautiful woman, by whom it is supposed he was courted for the nobleness of his descent. They say, that she was farther encouraged to persevere in her advances, by an incident which evinced the great ingenuousness of his disposition. Upon her pressing her suit, he took an opportunity, when they were alone, of stripping off his toga, and showing her the deformity of his person, that he might not be thought to impose upon her. He had by Achaica two sons, Caius and Sergius. The elder of these, Caius 649, having very much reduced his estate, retired from town, and being prohibited by Tiberius from standing for a pro-consulship in his year, put an end to his own life.

IV. The emperor Sergius Galba was born in the consulship of M. Valerius Messala, and Cn. Lentulus, upon the ninth of the calends of January [24th December] [650], in a villa standing upon a hill, near Terracina, on the left-hand side of the road to Fundi 651 . Being adopted by his step-mother 652 , he assumed the name of Livius, with the cognomen of Ocella, and changed his praenomen; for he afterwards used that of Lucius, instead of Sergius, until he arrived at the imperial dignity. It is well known, that when he came once, amongst other boys of his own age, to pay his respects to Augustus, the latter, pinching his cheek, said to him, "And thou, child, too, wilt taste our imperial dignity." Tiberius, likewise, being told that he would come to be emperor, but at an advanced age, exclaimed, "Let him live, then, since that does not concern me!" When his grandfather was offering sacrifice to (403) avert some ill omen from lightning, the entrails of the victim were snatched out of his hand by an eagle, and carried off into an oak-tree loaded with acorns. Upon this, the soothsayers said, that the family would come to be masters of the empire, but not until many years had elapsed: at which he, smiling, said, "Ay, when a mule comes to bear a foal." When Galba first declared against Nero, nothing gave him so much confidence of success, as a mule's happening at that time to have a foal. And whilst all others were shocked at the occurrence, as a most inauspicious prodigy, he alone regarded it as a most fortunate omen, calling to mind the sacrifice and saying of his grandfather. When he took upon him the manly habit, he dreamt that the goddess Fortune said to him, "I stand before your door weary; and unless I am speedily admitted, I shall fall into the hands of the first who comes to seize me." On his awaking, when the door of the house was opened, he found a brazen statue of the goddess, above a cubit long, close to the threshold, which he carried with slim to Tusculum, where he used to pass the summer season; and having consecrated it in an apartment of his house, he ever after worshipped it with a monthly sacrifice, and an anniversary vigil. Though but a very young man, he kept up an ancient but obsolete custom, and now nowhere observed, except in his own family, which was, to have his freedmen and slaves appear in a body before him twice a day, morning and evening, to offer him their salutations.

V. Amongst other liberal studies, he applied himself to the law. He married Lepida 653 , by whom he had two sons; but the mother and children all dying, he continued a widower; nor could he be prevailed upon to marry again, not even Agrippina herself, at that time left a widow by the death of Domitius, who had employed all her blandishments to allure him to her embraces, while he was a married man; insomuch that Lepida's mother, when in company with several married women, rebuked her for it, and even went so far as to cuff her. Most of all, he courted the empress Livia 654, by whose favour, while she was living, he made a considerable figure, and narrowly missed being enriched by the will which she left at her death; in which she distinguished him from the rest of the (404) legatees, by a legacy of fifty millions of sesterces. But because the sum was expressed in figures, and not in words at length, it was reduced by her heir, Tiberius, to five hundred thousand: and even this he never received. 655

VI. Filling the great offices before the age required for it by law, during his praetorship, at the celebration of games in honour of the goddess Flora, he presented the new spectacle of elephants walking upon ropes. He was then governor of the province of Aquitania for near a year, and soon afterwards took the consulship in the usual course, and held it for six months 656. It so happened that he succeeded L. Domitius, the father of Nero, and was succeeded by Salvius Otho, father to the emperor of that name; so that his holding it between the sons of these two men, looked like a presage of his future advancement to the empire. Being appointed by Caius Caesar to supersede Gaetulicus in his command, the day after his joining the legions, he put a stop to their plaudits in a public spectacle, by issuing an order, "That they should keep their hands under their cloaks." Immediately upon which, the following verse became very common in the camp:

*Disce, miles, militare: Galba est, non Gaetulicus.*

*Learn, soldier, now in arms to use your hands,*

*'Tis Galba, not Gaetulicus, commands.*

With equal strictness, he would allow of no petitions for leave of absence from the camp. He hardened the soldiers, both old and young, by constant exercise; and having quickly reduced within their own limits the barbarians who had made inroads into Gaul, upon Caius's coming into Germany, he so far recommended himself and his army to that emperor's approbation, that, amongst the innumerable troops drawn from all the provinces of the empire, none met with higher commendation, or greater rewards from him. He likewise distinguished himself by heading an escort, with a shield in his hand 658 , and running at the side of the emperor's chariot twenty miles together.

VII. Upon the news of Caius's death, though many earnestly pressed him to lay hold of that opportunity of seizing the empire, he chose rather to be quiet. On this account, he was in great favour with Claudius, and being received into the number of his friends, stood so high in his good opinion, that the expedition to Britain 659 was for some time suspended, because he was suddenly seized with a slight indisposition. He governed Africa, as pro-consul, for two years; being chosen out of the regular course to restore order in the province, which was in great disorder from civil dissensions, and the alarms of the barbarians. His administration was distinguished by great strictness and equity, even in matters of small importance. A soldier upon some expedition being charged with selling, in a great scarcity of corn, a bushel of wheat, which was all he had left, for a hundred denarii, he forbad him to be relieved by any body, when he came to be in want himself; and accordingly he died of famine. When sitting in judgment, a cause being brought before him about some beast of burden, the ownership of which was claimed by two persons; the evidence being slight on both sides, and it being difficult to come at the truth, he ordered the beast to be led to a pond at which he had used to be watered, with his head muffled up, and the covering being there removed, that he should be the property of the person whom he followed of his own accord, after drinking.

VIII. For his achievements, both at this time in Africa, and formerly in Germany, he received the triumphal ornaments, and three sacerdotal appointments, one among The Fifteen, another in the college of Titius, and a third amongst the Augustals; and from that time to the middle of Nero's reign, he lived for the most part in retirement. He never went abroad (405) so much as to take the air, without a carriage attending him, in which there was a million of sesterces in gold, ready at hand; until at last, at the time he was living in the town of Fundi, the province of Hispania Tarraconensis was offered him. After his arrival in the province, whilst he was sacrificing in a temple, a boy who attended with a censer, became all on a sudden grey-headed.

This incident was regarded by some as a token of an approaching revolution in the government, and that an old man would succeed a young one: that is, that he would succeed Nero. And not long after, a thunderbolt falling into a lake in Cantabria 660, twelve axes were found in it; a manifest sign of the supreme power.

IX. He governed the province during eight years, his administration being of an uncertain and capricious character. At first he was active, vigorous, and indeed excessively severe, in the punishment of offenders. For, a money-dealer having committed some fraud in the way of his business, he cut off his hands, and nailed them to his counter. Another, who had poisoned an orphan, to whom he was guardian, and next heir to the estate, he crucified. On this delinquent imploring the protection of the law, and crying out that he was a Roman citizen, he affected to afford him some alleviation, and to mitigate his punishment, by a mark of honour, ordered a cross, higher than usual, and painted white, to be erected for him. But by degrees he gave himself up to a life of indolence and inactivity, from the fear of giving Nero any occasion of jealousy, and because, as he used to say, "Nobody was obliged to render an account of their leisure hours." He was holding a court of justice on the circuit at New Carthage 661, when he received intelligence of the insurrection in Gaul 662; and while the lieutenant of Aquitania was soliciting his assistance, letters were brought from Vindex, requesting him "to assert the rights of mankind, and put himself at their head to relieve them from the tyranny of Nero." Without any long demur, he accepted the invitation, from a mixture of fear and hope. For he had discovered that private orders had been sent by Nero to his procurators in the province to get (407) him dispatched; and he was encouraged to the enterprise, as well by several auspices and omens, as by the prophecy of a young woman of good, family. The more so, because the priest of Jupiter at Clunia 663, admonished by a dream, had discovered in the recesses of the temple some verses similar to those in which she had delivered her prophecy. These had also been uttered by a girl under divine inspiration, about two hundred years before. The import of the verses was, "That in time, Spain should give the world a lord and master."

X. Taking his seat on the tribunal, therefore, as if there was no other business than the manumitting of slaves, he had the effigies of a number of persons who had been condemned and put to death by Nero, set up before him, whilst a noble youth stood by, who had been banished, and whom he had purposely sent for from one of the neighbouring Balearic isles; and lamenting the condition of the times, and being thereupon unanimously saluted by the title of Emperor, he publicly declared himself "only the lieutenant of the senate and people of Rome." Then shutting the courts, he levied legions and auxiliary troops among the provincials, besides his veteran army consisting of one legion, two wings of horse, and three cohorts. Out of the military leaders most distinguished for age and prudence, he formed a kind of senate, with whom to advise upon all matters of importance, as often as occasion should require. He likewise chose several young men of the equestrian order, who were to be allowed the privilege of wearing the gold ring, and, being called "The Reserve," should mount guard before his bed-chamber, instead of the legionary soldiers. He likewise issued proclamations throughout the provinces of the empire, exhorting all to rise in arms unanimously, and aid the common cause, by all the ways and means in their power. About the same time, in fortifying a town, which he had pitched upon for a military post, a ring was found, of antique workmanship, in the stone of which was engraved the goddess Victory with a trophy. Presently after, a ship of Alexandria arrived at Dertosa 664, loaded with arms, without any person to steer it, or so much as a single sailor or passenger (408) on board. From this incident, nobody entertained the least doubt but the war upon which they were entering was just and honourable, and favoured likewise by the gods; when all on a sudden the whole design was exposed to failure. One of the two wings of horse, repenting of the violation of their oath to Nero, attempted to desert him upon his approach to the camp, and were with some difficulty kept in their duty. And some slaves who had been presented to him by a freedman of Nero's, on purpose to murder him, had like to have killed him as he went through a narrow passage to the bath. Being overheard to encourage one another not to lose the opportunity, they were called to an account concerning it; and recourse being had to the torture, a confession was extorted from them.

XI. These dangers were followed by the death of Vindex, at which being extremely discouraged, as if fortune had quite forsaken him, he had thoughts of putting an end to his own life; but receiving advice by his messengers from Rome that Nero was slain, and that all had taken an oath to him as emperor, he laid aside the title of lieutenant, and took upon him that of Caesar. Putting himself upon his march in his general's cloak, and a dagger hanging from his neck before his breast, he did not resume the use of the toga, until Nymphidius Sabinus, prefect of the pretorian guards at Rome, with the two lieutenants, Fonteius Capito in Germany, and Claudius Macer in Africa, who opposed his advancement, were all put down.

XII. Rumours of his cruelty and avarice had reached the city before his arrival; such as that he had punished some cities of Spain and Gaul, for not joining him readily, by the imposition of heavy taxes, and some by levelling their walls; and had put to death the governors and procurators with their wives and children: likewise that a golden crown, of fifteen pounds weight, taken out of the temple of Jupiter, with which he was presented by the people of Tarracona, he had melted down, and had exacted from them three ounces which were wanting in the weight. This report of him was confirmed and increased, as soon as he entered the town. For some seamen who had been taken from the fleet, and enlisted (409) among the troops by Nero, he obliged to return to their former condition; but they refusing to comply, and obstinately clinging to the more honourable service under their eagles and standards, he not only dispersed them by a body of horse, but likewise decimated them. He also disbanded a cohort of Germans, which had been formed by the preceding emperors, for their body-guard, and upon many occasions found very faithful; and sent them back into their own country, without giving them any gratuity, pretending that they were more inclined to favour the advancement of Cneius Dolabella, near whose gardens they encamped, than his own. The following ridiculous stories were also related of him; but whether with or without foundation, I know not; such as, that when a more sumptuous entertainment than usual was served up, he fetched a deep groan: that when one of the stewards presented him with an account of his expenses, he reached him a dish of legumes from his table as a reward for his care and diligence; and when Canus, the piper, had played much to his satisfaction, he presented him, with his own hand, five denarii taken out of his pocket.

XIII. His arrival, therefore, in town was not very agreeable to the people; and this appeared at the next public spectacle. For when the actors in a farce began a well-known song,

> *Venit, io, Simus 665 a villa:*
> Lo! Clodpate from his village comes;

all the spectators, with one voice, went on with the rest, repeating and acting the first verse several times over.

XIV. He possessed himself of the imperial power with more favour and authority than he administered it, although he gave many proofs of his being an excellent prince: but these were not so grateful to the people, as his misconduct was offensive. He was governed by three favourites, who, because they lived in the palace, and were constantly about him, obtained the name of his pedagogues. These were Titus Vinius, who had been his lieutenant in Spain, a man of insatiable (410) avarice; Cornelius Laco, who, from an assessor to the prince, was advanced to be prefect of the pretorian guards, a person of intolerable arrogance, as well as indolence; and his freedman Icelus, dignified a little before with the privilege of wearing the gold ring, and the use of the cognomen Martianus, who became a candidate for the highest honour within the reach of any person of the equestrian order 666. He resigned himself so implicitly into the power of those three favourites, who governed in every thing according to the capricious impulse of their vices and tempers, and his authority was so much abused by them, that the tenor of his conduct was not very consistent with itself. At one time, he was more rigorous and frugal, at another, more lavish and negligent, than became a prince who had been chosen by the people, and was so far advanced in years. He condemned some men of the first rank in the senatorian and equestrian orders, upon a very slight suspicion, and without trial. He rarely granted the freedom of the city to any one; and the privilege belonging to such as had three children, only to one or two; and that with great difficulty, and only for a limited time. When the judges petitioned to have a sixth decury added to their number, he not only denied them, but abolished the vacation which had been granted them by Claudius for the winter, and the beginning of the year.

XV. It was thought that he likewise intended to reduce the offices held by senators and men of the equestrian order, to a term of two years' continuance; and to bestow them only on those who were unwilling to accept them, and had refused them. All the grants of Nero he recalled, saving only the tenth part of them. For this purpose he gave a commission to fifty Roman knights; with orders, that if players or wrestlers had sold what had been formerly given them, it should be exacted from the purchasers, since the others, having, no doubt, spent the money, were not in a condition to pay. But on the other hand, he suffered his attendants and freedmen to sell or give away the revenue of the state, or immunities from taxes, and to punish the innocent, or pardon criminals, at pleasure. Nay, when the Roman people were very clamorous for the punishment of Halotus and Tigellinus, two of the (411) most mischievous amongst all the emissaries of Nero, he protected them, and even bestowed on Halotus one of the best procurations in his disposal. And as to Tigellinus, he even reprimanded the people for their cruelty by a proclamation.

XVI. By this conduct, he incurred the hatred of all orders of the people, but especially of the soldiery. For their commanders having promised them in his name a donative larger than usual, upon their taking the oath to him before his arrival at Rome; he refused to make it good, frequently bragging, "that it was his custom to choose his soldiers, not buy them." Thus the troops became exasperated against him in all quarters. The pretorian guards he alarmed with apprehensions of danger and unworthy treatment; disbanding many of them occasionally as disaffected to his government, and favourers of Nymphidius. But most of all, the army in Upper Germany was incensed against him, as being defrauded of the rewards due to them for the service they had rendered in the insurrection of the Gauls under Vindex. They were, therefore, the first who ventured to break into open mutiny, refusing upon the calends [the 1st] of January, to take any oath of allegiance, except to the senate; and they immediately dispatched deputies to the pretorian troops, to let them know, "they did not like the emperor who had been set up in Spain," and to desire that "they would make choice of another, who might meet with the approbation of all the armies."

XVII. Upon receiving intelligence of this, imagining that he was slighted not so much on account of his age, as for having no children, he immediately singled out of a company of young persons of rank, who came to pay their compliments to him, Piso Frugi Licinianus, a youth of noble descent and great talents, for whom he had before contracted such a regard, that he had appointed him in his will the heir both of his estate and name. Him he now styled his son, and taking him to the camp, adopted him in the presence of the assembled troops, but without making any mention of a donative. This circumstance afforded the better opportunity to Marcus Salvius Otho of accomplishing his object, six days after the adoption.

XVIII. Many remarkable prodigies had happened from the (412) very beginning of his reign, which forewarned him of his approaching fate. In every town through which he passed in his way from Spain to Rome, victims were slain on the right and left of the roads; and one of these, which was a bull, being maddened with the stroke of the axe, broke the rope with which it was tied, and running straight against his chariot, with his fore-feet elevated, bespattered him with blood. Likewise, as he was alighting, one of the guard, being pushed forward by the crowd, had very nearly wounded him with his lance. And upon his entering the city and, afterwards, the palace, he was welcomed with an earthquake, and a noise like the bellowing of cattle. These signs of ill-fortune were followed by some that were still more apparently such. Out of all his treasures he had selected a necklace of pearls and jewels, to adorn his statue of Fortune at Tusculum. But it suddenly occurring to him that it deserved a more august place, he consecrated it to the Capitoline Venus; and next night, he dreamt that Fortune appeared to him, complaining that she had been defrauded of the present intended her, and threatening to resume what she had given him. Terrified at this denunciation, at break of day he sent forward some persons to Tusculum, to make preparations for a sacrifice which might avert the displeasure of the goddess; and when he himself arrived at the place, he found nothing but some hot embers upon the altar, and an old man in black standing by, holding a little incense in a glass, and some wine in an earthern pot. It was remarked, too, that whilst he was sacrificing upon the calends of January, the chaplet fell from his head, and upon his consulting the pullets for omens, they flew away. Farther, upon the day of his adopting Piso, when he was to harangue the soldiers, the seat which he used upon those occasions, through the neglect of his attendants, was not placed, according to custom, upon his tribunal; and in the senate-house, his curule chair was set with the back forward.

XIX. The day before he was slain, as he was sacrificing in the morning, the augur warned him from time to time to be upon his guard, for that he was in danger from assassins, and that they were near at hand. Soon after, he was informed, that Otho was in possession of the pretorian camp. And though most of his friends advised him to repair thither immediately, (413) in hopes that he might quell the tumult by his authority and presence, he resolved to do nothing more than keep close within the palace, and secure himself by guards of the legionary soldiers, who were quartered in different parts about the city. He put on a linen coat of mail, however, remarking at the same time, that it would avail him little against the points of so many swords. But being tempted out by false reports, which the conspirators had purposely spread to induce him to venture abroad—some few of those about him too hastily assuring him that the tumult had ceased, the mutineers were apprehended, and the rest coming to congratulate him, resolved to continue firm in their obedience—he went forward to meet them with so much confidence, that upon a soldier's boasting that he had killed Otho, he asked him, "By what authority?" and proceeded as far as the Forum. There the knights, appointed to dispatch him, making their way through the crowd of citizens, upon seeing him at a distance, halted a while; after which, galloping up to him, now abandoned by all his attendants, they put him to death.

XX. Some authors relate, that upon their first approach he cried out, "What do you mean, fellow-soldiers? I am yours, and you are mine," and promised them a donative: but the generality of writers relate, that he offered his throat to them, saying, "Do your work, and strike, since you are resolved upon it." It is remarkable, that not one of those who were at hand, ever made any attempt to assist the emperor; and all who were sent for, disregarded the summons, except a troop of Germans. They, in consideration of his late kindness in showing them particular attention during a sickness which prevailed in the camp, flew to his aid, but came too late; for, being not well acquainted with the town, they had taken a circuitous route. He was slain near the Curtian Lake 667, and there left, until a common soldier returning from the receipt of his allowance of corn, throwing down the load which he carried, cut off his head. There being upon it no hair, by which he might hold it, he hid it in the bosom of his dress; but afterwards thrusting his thumb into the mouth, he carried it in that manner to Otho, who gave it to the drudges and slaves who attended the soldiers; and they, fixing it upon the (414) point of a spear, carried it in derision round the camp, crying out as they went along, "You take your fill of joy in your old age." They were irritated to this pitch of rude banter, by a report spread a few days before, that, upon some one's commending his person as still florid and vigorous, he replied,

*Eti moi menos empedoi estin. 668*
*My strength, as yet, has suffered no decay.*

A freedman of Petrobius's, who himself had belonged to Nero's family, purchased the head from them at the price of a hundred gold pieces, and threw it into the place where, by Galba's order, his patron had been put to death. At last, after some time, his steward Argius buried it, with the rest of his body, in his own gardens near the Aurelian Way.

XXI. In person he was of a good size, bald before, with blue eyes, and an aquiline nose; and his hands and feet were so distorted with the gout, that he could neither wear a shoe, nor turn over the leaves of a book, or so much as hold it. He had likewise an excrescence in his right side, which hung down to that degree, that it was with difficulty kept up by a bandage.

XXII. He is reported to have been a great eater, and usually took his breakfast in the winter-time before day. At supper, he fed very heartily, giving the fragments which were left, by handfuls, to be distributed amongst the attendants. In his lust, he was more inclined to the male sex, and such of them too as were old. It is said of him, that in Spain, when Icelus, an old catamite of his, brought him the news of Nero's death, he not only kissed him lovingly before company, but begged of him to remove all impediments, and then took him aside into a private apartment.

XXIII. He perished in the seventy-third year of his age, and the seventh month of his reign 669. The senate, as soon as they could with safety, ordered a statue to be erected for him upon the naval column, in that part of the Forum where he (415) was slain. But Vespasian cancelled the decree, upon a suspicion that he had sent assassins from Spain into Judaea to murder him.

\* \* \* \* \* \*

GALBA was, for a private man, the most wealthy of any who had ever aspired to the imperial dignity. He valued himself upon his being descended from the family of the Servii, but still more upon his relation to Quintus Catulus Capitolinus, celebrated for integrity and virtue. He was likewise distantly related to Livia, the wife of Augustus; by whose interest he was preferred from the station which he held in the palace, to the dignity of consul; and who left him a great legacy at her death. His parsimonious way of living, and his aversion to all superfluity or excess, were construed into avarice as soon as he became emperor; whence Plutarch observes, that the pride which he took in his temperance and economy was unseasonable. While he endeavoured to reform the profusion in the public expenditure, which prevailed in the reign of Nero, he ran into the opposite extreme; and it is objected to him by some historians, that he maintained not the imperial dignity in a degree consistent even with decency. He was not sufficiently attentive either to his own security or the tranquillity of the state, when he refused to pay the soldiers the donative which he had promised them. This breach of faith seems to be the only act in his life that affects his integrity; and it contributed more to his ruin than even the odium which he incurred by the open venality and rapaciousness of his favourites, particularly Vinius.

# A. SALVIUS OTHO.

**(416)**

I. The ancestors of Otho were originally of the town of Ferentum, of an ancient and honourable family, and, indeed, one of the most considerable in Etruria. His grandfather, M. Salvius Otho (whose father was a Roman knight, but his mother of mean extraction, for it is not certain whether she was free-born), by the favour of Livia Augusta, in whose house he had his education, was made a senator, but never rose higher than the praetorship. His father, Lucius Otho, was by the mother's side nobly descended, allied to several great families, and so dearly beloved by Tiberius, and so much resembled him in his features, that most people believed Tiberius was his father. He behaved with great strictness and severity, not only in the city offices, but in the pro-consulship of Africa, and some extraordinary commands in the army. He had the courage to punish with death some soldiers in Illyricum, who, in the disturbance attempted by Camillus, upon changing their minds, had put their generals to the sword, as promoters of that insurrection against Claudius. He ordered the execution to take place in the front of the camp 670 , and under his own eyes; though he knew they had been advanced to higher ranks in the army by Claudius, on that very account. By this action he acquired fame, but lessened his favour at court; which, however, he soon recovered, by discovering to Claudius a design upon his life, carried on by a Roman knight 671 , and which he had learnt from some of his slaves. For the senate ordered a statue of him to be erected in the palace; an honour which had been conferred but upon very few before him. And Claudius advanced him to the dignity of a patrician, commending him, at the same time, in the highest terms, and concluding with these words: "A man, than whom I don't so (417) much as wish to have children that should be better." He had two sons by a very noble woman, Albia Terentia, namely; Lucius

Titianus, and a younger called Marcus, who had the same cognomen as himself. He had also a daughter, whom he contracted to Drusus, Germanicus's son, before she was of marriageable age.

II. The emperor Otho was born upon the fourth of the calends of May [28th April], in the consulship of Camillus Aruntius and Domitius Aenobarbus 672. He was from his earliest youth so riotous and wild, that he was often severely scourged by his father. He was said to run about in the night-time, and seize upon any one he met, who was either drunk or too feeble to make resistance, and toss him in a blanket 673. After his father's death, to make his court the more effectually to a freedwoman about the palace, who was in great favour, he pretended to be in love with her, though she was old, and almost decrepit. Having by her means got into Nero's good graces, he soon became one of the principal favourites, by the congeniality of his disposition to that of the emperor or, as some say, by the reciprocal practice of mutual pollution. He had so great a sway at court, that when a man of consular rank was condemned for bribery, having tampered with him for a large sum of money, to procure his pardon; before he had quite effected it, he scrupled not to introduce him into the senate, to return his thanks.

III. Having, by means of this woman, insinuated himself into all the emperor's secrets, he, upon the day designed for the murder of his mother, entertained them both at a very splendid feast, to prevent suspicion. Poppaea Sabina, for whom Nero entertained such a violent passion that he had taken her from her husband 674 and entrusted her to him, he received, and went through the form of marrying her. And not satisfied with obtaining her favours, he loved her so extravagantly, that he could not with patience bear Nero for his rival. It is certainly believed that he not only refused admittance to those who were sent by Nero to fetch her, but that, on one (418) occasion, he shut him out, and kept him standing before the door, mixing prayers and menaces in vain, and demanding back again what was entrusted to his keeping. His pretended marriage, therefore, being dissolved, he was sent lieutenant into Lusitania. This treatment of him was thought sufficiently severe, because harsher proceedings might have brought the whole farce to light, which, notwithstanding, at last came out, and was published to the world in the following distich:—

*Cur Otho mentitus sit, quaeritis, exul honore?*

> *Uxoris moechus caeperat esse suae.*
>
> You ask why Otho's banish'd? Know, the cause
> Comes not within the verge of vulgar laws.
> Against all rules of fashionable life,
> The rogue had dared to sleep with his own wife.

He governed the province in quality of quaestor for ten years, with singular moderation and justice.

IV. As soon as an opportunity of revenge offered, he readily joined in Galba's enterprises, and at the same time conceived hopes of obtaining the imperial dignity for himself. To this he was much encouraged by the state of the times, but still more by the assurances given him by Seleucus, the astrologer, who, having formerly told him that he would certainly out-live Nero, came to him at that juncture unexpectedly, promising him again that he should succeed to the empire, and that in a very short time. He, therefore, let slip no opportunity of making his court to every one about him by all manner of civilities. As often as he entertained Galba at supper, he distributed to every man of the cohort which attended the emperor on guard, a gold piece; endeavouring likewise to oblige the rest of the soldiers in one way or another. Being chosen an arbitrator by one who had a dispute with his neighbour about a piece of land, he bought it, and gave it him; so that now almost every body thought and said, that he was the only man worthy of succeeding to the empire.

V. He entertained hopes of being adopted by Galba, and expected it every day. But finding himself disappointed, by Piso's being preferred before him, he turned his thoughts to obtaining his purpose by the use of violence; and to this he was instigated, as well by the greatness of his debts, as by resentment (419) at Galba's conduct towards him. For he did not conceal his conviction, "that he could not stand his ground unless he became emperor, and that it signified nothing whether he fell by the hands of his enemies in the field, or of his creditors in the Forum." He had a few days before squeezed out of one of the emperor's slaves a million of sesterces for procuring him a stewardship; and this was the whole fund he had for carrying on so great an enterprise. At first the design was entrusted to only five of the guard, but afterwards to ten others, each of the five naming two. They had every one ten thousand sesterces paid down, and were promised fifty thousand more. By these, others were drawn in, but not many; from a confident assurance, that when the matter came to the crisis, they should have enough to join them.

VI. His first intention was, immediately after the departure of Piso, to seize the camp, and fall upon Galba, whilst he was at supper in the palace; but he was restrained by a regard for the cohort at that time on duty, lest he should bring too great an odium upon it; because it happened that the same cohort was on guard before, both when Caius was slain, and Nero deserted. For some time afterwards, he was restrained also by scruples about the omens, and by the advice of Seleucus. Upon the day fixed at last for the enterprise, having given his accomplices notice to wait for him in the Forum near the temple of Saturn, at the gilded mile-stone 675 , he went in the morning to pay his respects to Galba; and being received with a kiss as usual, he attended him at sacrifice, and heard the predictions of the augur 676 . A freedman of his, then bringing (420) him word that the architects were come, which was the signal agreed upon, he withdrew, as if it were with a design to view a house upon sale, and went out by a back-door of the palace to the place appointed. Some say he pretended to be seized with an ague fit, and ordered those about him to make that excuse for him, if he was inquired after. Being then quickly concealed in a woman's litter, he made the best of his way for the camp. But the bearers growing tired, he got out, and began to run. His shoe becoming loose, he stopped again, but being immediately raised by his attendants upon their shoulders, and unanimously saluted by the title of EMPEROR, he came amidst auspicious acclamations and drawn swords into the Principia 677 in the camp; all who met him joining in the cavalcade, as if they had been privy to the design. Upon this, sending some soldiers to dispatch Galba and Piso, he said nothing else in his address to the soldiery, to secure their affections, than these few words: "I shall be content with whatever ye think fit to leave me."

VII. Towards the close of the day, he entered the senate, and after he had made a short speech to them, pretending that he had been seized in the streets, and compelled by violence to assume the imperial authority, which he designed to exercise in conjunction with them, he retired to the palace. Besides other compliments which he received from those who flocked about him to congratulate and flatter him, he was called Nero by the mob, and manifested no intention of declining that cognomen. Nay, some authors relate, that he used it in his official acts, and the first letters he sent to the (421) governors of provinces. He suffered all his images and statues to be replaced, and restored his procurators and freedmen to their former posts. And the first writing which he signed as emperor, was a promise of fifty millions of sesterces to finish the Golden-house 678. He is said to have been greatly frightened that night in his sleep, and to have groaned heavily; and being found, by those who came running in to see what the matter was, lying upon the floor before his bed, he endeavoured by every kind of atonement to appease the ghost of Galba, by which he had found himself violently tumbled out of bed. The next day, as he was taking the omens, a great storm arising, and sustaining a grievous fall, he muttered to himself from time to time:

*Ti gar moi kai makrois aulois; 679*

*What business have I the loud trumpets to sound!*

VIII. About the same time, the armies in Germany took an oath to Vitellius as emperor. Upon receiving this intelligence, he advised the senate to send thither deputies, to inform them, that a prince had been already chosen; and to persuade them to peace and a good understanding. By letters and messages, however, he offered Vitellius to make him his colleague in the empire, and his son-in-law. But a war being now unavoidable, and the generals and troops sent forward by Vitellius, advancing, he had a proof of the attachment and fidelity of the pretorian guards, which had nearly proved fatal to the senatorian order. It had been judged proper that some arms should be given out of the stores, and conveyed to the fleet by the marine troops. While they were employed in fetching these from the camp in the night, some of the guards suspecting treachery, excited a tumult; and suddenly the whole body, without any of their officers at their head, ran to the palace, demanding that the entire senate should be put to the sword; and having repulsed some of the (422) tribunes who endeavoured to stop them, and slain others, they broke, all bloody as they were, into the banquetting room, inquiring for the emperor; nor would they quit the place until they had seen him. He now entered upon his expedition against Vitellius with great alacrity, but too much precipitation, and without any regard to the ominous circumstances which attended it. For the Ancilia 680 had been taken out of the temple of Mars, for the usual procession, but were not yet replaced; during which interval it had of old been looked upon as very unfortunate to engage in any enterprise. He likewise set forward upon the day when the worshippers of the Mother of the gods 681 begin their lamentations and wailing. Besides these, other unlucky omens attended him. For, in a victim offered to Father Dis 682, he found the signs such as upon all other occasions are regarded as favourable; whereas, in that sacrifice, the contrary intimations are judged the most propitious. At his first setting forward, he was stopped by inundations of the Tiber; and at twenty miles' distance from the city, found the road blocked up by the fall of houses.

IX. Though it was the general opinion that it would be proper to protract the war, as the enemy were distressed by (423) famine and the straitness of their quarters, yet he resolved with equal rashness to force them to an engagement as soon as possible; whether from impatience of prolonged anxiety, and in the hope of bringing matters to an issue before the arrival of Vitellius, or because he could not resist the ardour of the troops, who were all clamorous for battle. He was not, however, present at any of those which ensued, but stayed behind at Brixellum 683. He had the advantage in three slight engagements, near the Alps, about Placentia, and a place called Castor's 684; but was, by a fraudulent stratagem of the enemy, defeated in the last and greatest battle, at Bedriacum 685. For, some hopes of a conference being given, and the soldiers being drawn up to hear the conditions of peace declared, very unexpectedly, and amidst their mutual salutations, they were obliged to stand to their arms. Immediately upon this he determined to put an end to his life, more, as many think, and not without reason, out of shame, at persisting in a struggle for the empire to the hazard of the public interest and so many lives, than from despair, or distrust of his troops. For he had still in reserve, and in full force, those whom he had kept about him for a second trial of his fortune, and others were coming up from Dalmatia, Pannonia, and Moesia; nor were the troops lately defeated so far discouraged as not to be ready, even of themselves, to run all risks in order to wipe off their recent disgrace.

X. My father, Suetonius Lenis 686, was in this battle, being at (424) that time an angusticlavian tribune in the thirteenth legion. He used frequently to say, that Otho, before his advancement to the empire, had such an abhorrence of civil war, that once, upon hearing an account given at table of the death of Cassius and Brutus, he fell into a trembling, and that he never would have interfered with Galba, but that he was confident of succeeding in his enterprise without a war. Moreover, that he was then encouraged to despise life by the example of a common soldier, who bringing news of the defeat of the army, and finding that he met with no credit, but was railed at for a liar and a coward, as if he had run away from the field of battle, fell upon his sword at the emperor's feet; upon the sight of which, my father said that Otho cried out, "that he would expose to no farther danger such brave men, who had deserved so well at his hands." Advising therefore his brother, his brother's son, and the rest of his friends, to provide for their security in the best manner they could, after he had embraced and kissed them, he sent them away; and then withdrawing into a private room by himself, he wrote a letter of consolation to his sister, containing two sheets. He likewise sent another to Messalina, Nero's widow, whom he had intended to marry, committing to her the care of his relics and memory. He then burnt all the letters which he had by him, to prevent the danger and mischief that might otherwise befall the writers from the conqueror. What ready money he had, he distributed among his domestics.

XI. And now being prepared, and just upon the point of dispatching himself, he was induced to suspend the execution of his purpose by a great tumult which had broken out in the camp. Finding that some of the soldiers who were making off had been seized and detained as deserters, "Let us add," said he, "this night to our life." These were his very words.

He then gave orders that no violence should be offered to any one; and keeping his chamber-door open until late at night, he allowed all who pleased the liberty to come and see him. At last, after quenching his thirst with a draught of cold water, he took up two poniards, and having examined the points of both, put one of them under his pillow, and shutting his chamber-door, slept very soundly, until, awaking about break of day, he stabbed himself under the left pap. Some persons bursting into the room upon his first groan, he at one time covered, and at another exposed his wound to the view of the bystanders, and thus life soon ebbed away. His funeral was hastily performed, according to his own order, in the thirty-eighth year of his age, and ninety-fifth day of his reign. 687

XII. The person and appearance of Otho no way corresponded to the great spirit he displayed on this occasion; for he is said to have been of low stature, splay-footed, and bandy-legged. He was, however, effeminately nice in the care of his person: the hair on his body he plucked out by the roots; and because he was somewhat bald, he wore a kind of peruke, so exactly fitted to his head, that nobody could have known it for such. He used to shave every day, and rub his face with soaked bread; the use of which he began when the down first appeared upon his chin, to prevent his having any beard. It is said likewise that he celebrated publicly the sacred rites of Isis 688, clad in a linen garment, such as is used by the worshippers of that goddess. These circumstances, I imagine, caused the world to wonder the more that his death was so little in character with his life. Many of the soldiers who were present, kissing and bedewing with their tears his hands and feet as he lay dead, and celebrating him as "a most gallant man, and an incomparable emperor," immediately put an end to their own lives upon the spot, not far from his funeral pile.

(426) Many of those likewise who were at a distance, upon hearing the news of his death, in the anguish of their hearts, began fighting amongst themselves, until they dispatched one another. To conclude: the generality of mankind, though they hated him whilst living, yet highly extolled him after his death; insomuch that it was the common talk and opinion, "that Galba had been driven to destruction by his rival, not so much for the sake of reigning himself, as of restoring Rome to its ancient liberty."

\* \* \* \* \* \*

It is remarkable, in the fortune of this emperor, that he owed both his elevation and catastrophe to the inextricable embarrassments in which he was involved; first, in respect of pecuniary circumstances, and next, of political. He was not, so far as we can learn, a follower of any of the sects of philosophers which justified, and even recommended suicide, in particular cases: yet he perpetrated that act with extraordinary coolness and resolution; and, what is no less remarkable, from the motive, as he avowed, of public expediency only. It was observed of him, for many years after his death, that "none ever died like Otho."

# AULUS VITELLIUS.

**(427)**

I. Very different accounts are given of the origin of the Vitellian family. Some describe it as ancient and noble, others as recent and obscure, nay, extremely mean. I am inclined to think, that these several representations have been made by the flatterers and detractors of Vitellius, after he became emperor, unless the fortunes of the family varied before. There is extant a memoir addressed by Quintus Eulogius to Quintus Vitellius, quaestor to the Divine Augustus, in which it is said, that the Vitellii were descended from Faunus, king of the aborigines, and Vitellia 689, who was worshipped in many places as a goddess, and that they reigned formerly over the whole of Latium: that all who were left of the family removed out of the country of the Sabines to Rome, and were enrolled among the patricians: that some monuments of the family continued a long time; as the Vitellian Way, reaching from the Janiculum to the sea, and likewise a colony of that name, which, at a very remote period of time, they desired leave from the government to defend against the Aequicolae 690, with a force raised by their own family only: also that, in the time of the war with the Samnites, some of the Vitellii who went with the troops levied for the security of Apulia, settled at Nuceria 691, and their descendants, a long time afterwards, returned again to Rome, and were admitted (428) into the patrician order. On the other hand, the generality of writers say that the founder of the family was a freedman. Cassius Severus 692 and some others relate that he was likewise a cobbler, whose son having made a considerable fortune by agencies and dealings in confiscated property, begot, by a common strumpet, daughter of one Antiochus, a baker, a child, who afterwards became a Roman knight. Of these different accounts the reader is left to take his choice.

II. It is certain, however, that Publius Vitellius, of Nuceria, whether of an ancient family, or of low extraction, was a Roman knight, and a procurator to Augustus. He left behind him four sons, all men of very high station, who had the same cognomen, but the different praenomina of Aulus, Quintus, Publius, and Lucius. Aulus died in the enjoyment of the consulship 693, which office he bore jointly with Domitius, the father of Nero Caesar. He was elegant to excess in his manner of living, and notorious for the vast expense of his entertainments. Quintus was deprived of his rank of senator, when, upon a motion made by Tiberius, a resolution passed to purge the senate of those who were in any respect not duly qualified for that honour. Publius, an intimate friend and companion of Germanicus, prosecuted his enemy and murderer, Cneius Piso, and procured sentence against him. After he had been made proctor, being arrested among the accomplices of Sejanus, and delivered into the hands of his brother to be confined in his house, he opened a vein with a penknife, intending to bleed himself to death. He suffered, however, the wound to be bound up and cured, not so much from repenting the resolution he had formed, as to comply with the importunity of his relations. He died afterwards a natural death during his confinement. Lucius, after his consulship 694, was made governor of Syria 695, and by his politic management not only brought Artabanus, king of the Parthians, to give him an interview, but to worship the standards of the Roman legions. He afterwards filled two ordinary consulships 696, and also the censorship 697 jointly with the emperor Claudius. Whilst that (429) prince was absent upon his expedition into Britain 698, the care of the empire was committed to him, being a man of great integrity and industry. But he lessened his character not a little, by his passionate fondness for an abandoned freedwoman, with whose spittle, mixed with honey, he used to anoint his throat and jaws, by way of remedy for some complaint, not privately nor seldom, but daily and publicly. Being extravagantly prone to flattery, it was he who gave rise to the worship of Caius Caesar as a god, when, upon his return from Syria, he would not presume to accost him any otherwise than with his head covered, turning himself round, and then prostrating himself upon the earth. And to leave no artifice untried to secure the favour of Claudius, who was entirely governed by his wives and freedmen, he requested as the greatest favour from Messalina, that she would be pleased to let him take off her shoes; which, when he had done, he took her right shoe, and wore it constantly betwixt his toga and his tunic, and from time to time covered it with kisses. He likewise worshipped golden images of Narcissus and Pallas among his household gods. It was he, too, who, when Claudius exhibited the secular games, in his compliments to him upon that occasion, used this expression, "May you often do the same."

III. He died of palsy, the day after his seizure with it, leaving behind him two sons, whom he had by a most excellent and respectable wife, Sextilia. He had lived to see them both consuls, the same year and during the whole year also; the younger succeeding the elder for the last six months 699 . The senate honoured him after his decease with a funeral at the public expense, and with a statue in the Rostra, which had this inscription upon the base: "One who was steadfast in his loyalty to his prince." The emperor Aulus Vitellius, the son of this Lucius, was born upon the eighth of the calends of October [24th September], or, as some say, upon the seventh of the ides of September [7th September], in the consulship of Drusus Caesar and Norbanus Flaccus 700 . His parents were so (430) terrified with the predictions of astrologers upon the calculation of his nativity, that his father used his utmost endeavours to prevent his being sent governor into any of the provinces, whilst he was alive. His mother, upon his being sent to the legions 701 , and also upon his being proclaimed emperor, immediately lamented him as utterly ruined. He spent his youth amongst the catamites of Tiberius at Capri, was himself constantly stigmatized with the name of Spintria 702 , and was supposed to have been the occasion of his father's advancement, by consenting to gratify the emperor's unnatural lust.

IV. In the subsequent part of his life, being still most scandalously vicious, he rose to great favour at court; being upon a very intimate footing with Caius [Caligula], because of his fondness for chariot-driving, and with Claudius for his love of gaming. But he was in a still higher degree acceptable to Nero, as well on the same accounts, as for a particular service which he rendered him. When Nero presided in the games instituted by himself, though he was extremely desirous to perform amongst the harpers, yet his modesty would not permit him, notwithstanding the people entreated much for it. Upon his quitting the theatre, Vitellius fetched him back again, pretending to represent the determined wishes of the people, and so afforded him the opportunity of yielding to their in treaties.

V. By the favour of these three princes, he was not only advanced to the great offices of state, but to the highest dignities of the sacred order; after which he held the proconsulship of Africa, and had the superintendence of the public works, in which appointment his conduct, and, consequently, his reputation, were very different. For he governed the province with singular integrity during two years, in the latter of which he acted as deputy to his brother, who succeeded him. But in his office in the city, he was said to pillage the temples of their gifts and ornaments, and to have exchanged brass and tin for gold and silver. 703

VI. He took to wife Petronia, the daughter of a man of consular rank, and had by her a son named Petronius, who was blind of an eye. The mother being willing to appoint this youth her heir, upon condition that he should be released from his father's authority, the latter discharged him accordingly; but shortly after, as was believed, murdered him, charging him with a design upon his life, and pretending that he had, from consciousness of his guilt, drank the poison he had prepared for his father. Soon afterwards, he married Galeria Fundana, the daughter of a man of pretorian rank, and had by her both sons and daughters. Among the former was one who had such a stammering in his speech, that he was little better than if he had been dumb.

VII. He was sent by Galba into Lower Germany 704 , contrary to his expectation. It is supposed that he was assisted in procuring this appointment by the interest of Titus Junius, a man of great influence at that time; whose friendship he had long before gained by favouring the same set of charioteers with him in the Circensian games. But Galba openly declared that none were less to be feared than those who only cared for their bellies, and that even his enormous appetite must be satisfied with the plenty of that province; so that it is evident he was selected for that government more out of contempt than kindness. It is certain, that when he was to set out, he had not money for the expenses of his journey; he being at that time so much straitened in his circumstances, that he was obliged to put his wife and children, whom he left at Rome, into a poor lodging which he hired for them, in order that he might let his own house for the remainder of the year;

and he pawned a pearl taken from his mother's ear-ring, to defray his expenses on the road. A crowd of creditors who were waiting to stop him, and amongst them the people of Sineussa and Formia, whose taxes he had converted to his own use, he eluded, by alarming them with the apprehension of false accusation. He had, however, sued a certain freedman, who was clamorous in demanding a debt of him, under pretence that he had kicked him; which action he would not withdraw, until he had wrung from the freedman fifty thousand sesterces. Upon his arrival in the province, the army, (432) which was disaffected to Galba, and ripe for insurrection, received him with open arms, as if he had been sent them from heaven. It was no small recommendation to their favour, that he was the son of a man who had been thrice consul, was in the prime of life, and of an easy, prodigal disposition. This opinion, which had been long entertained of him, Vitellius confirmed by some late practices; having kissed all the common soldiers whom he met with upon the road, and been excessively complaisant in the inns and stables to the muleteers and travellers; asking them in a morning, if they had got their breakfasts, and letting them see, by belching, that he had eaten his.

    VIII. After he had reached the camp, he denied no man any thing he asked for, and pardoned all who lay under sentence for disgraceful conduct or disorderly habits. Before a month, therefore, had passed, without regard to the day or season, he was hurried by the soldiers out of his bed-chamber, although it was evening, and he in an undress, and unanimously saluted by the title of EMPEROR 705 . He was then carried round the most considerable towns in the neighbourhood, with the sword of the Divine Julius in his hand; which had been taken by some person out of the temple of Mars, and presented to him when he was first saluted. Nor did he return to the pretorium, until his dining-room was in flames from the chimney's taking fire. Upon this accident, all being in consternation, and considering it as an unlucky omen, he cried out, "Courage, boys! it shines brightly upon us." And this was all he said to the soldiers. The army of the Upper Province likewise, which had before declared against Galba for the senate, joining in the proceedings, he very eagerly accepted the cognomen of Germanicus, offered him by the unanimous consent of both armies, but deferred assuming that of Augustus, and refused for ever that of Caesar.

IX. Intelligence of Galba's death arriving soon after, when he had settled his affairs in Germany he divided his troops into two bodies, intending to send one of them before him against Otho, and to follow with the other himself. The army he sent forward had a lucky omen; for, suddenly, an eagle cams flying up to them on the right, and having hovered (433) round the standards, flew gently before them on their road. But, on the other hand, when he began his own march, all the equestrian statues, which were erected for him in several places, fell suddenly down with their legs broken; and the laurel crown, which he had put on as emblematical of auspicious fortune, fell off his head into a river. Soon afterwards, at Vienne 706 , as he was upon the tribunal administering justice, a cock perched upon his shoulder, and afterwards upon his head. The issue corresponded to these omens; for he was not able to keep the empire which had been secured for him by his lieutenants.

X. He heard of the victory at Bedriacum 707 , and the death of Otho, whilst he was yet in Gaul, and without the least hesitation, by a single proclamation, disbanded all the pretorian cohorts, as having, by their repeated treasons, set a dangerous example to the rest of the army; commanding them to deliver up their arms to his tribunes. A hundred and twenty of them, under whose hands he had found petitions presented to Otho, for rewards of their service in the murder of Galba, he besides ordered to be sought out and punished. So far his conduct deserved approbation, and was such as to afford hope of his becoming an excellent prince, had he not managed his other affairs in a way more corresponding with his own disposition, and his former manner of life, than to the imperial dignity. For, having begun his march, he rode through every city in his route in a triumphal procession; and sailed down the rivers in ships, fitted out with the greatest elegance, and decorated with various kinds of crowns, amidst the most extravagant entertainments. Such was the want of discipline, and the licentiousness both in his family and army, that, not satisfied with the provision every where made for them at the public expense, they committed every kind of robbery and insult upon the inhabitants, setting slaves at liberty as they pleased; and if any dared to make resistance, they dealt blows and abuse, frequently wounds, and sometimes slaughter amongst them. When he reached the plains on which the battles (434) were fought 708 , some of those around him being offended at the smell of the carcases which lay rotting upon the ground, he had the audacity to encourage them by a most detestable remark, "That a dead enemy smelt not amiss, especially if he were a fellow-citizen." To qualify, however, the offensiveness of the stench, he quaffed in public a goblet of wine, and with equal vanity and insolence distributed a large quantity of it among his troops. On his observing a stone with an inscription upon it to the memory of Otho, he said, "It was a mausoleum good enough for such a prince." He also sent the poniard, with which Otho killed himself, to the colony of Agrippina 709 , to be dedicated to Mars. Upon the Appenine hills he celebrated a Bacchanalian feast.

XI. At last he entered the City with trumpets sounding, in his general's cloak, and girded with his sword, amidst a display of standards and banners; his attendants being all in the military habit, and the arms of the soldiers unsheathed. Acting more and more in open violation of all laws, both divine and human, he assumed the office of Pontifex Maximus, upon the day of the defeat at the Allia 710 ; ordered the magistrates to be elected for ten years of office; and made himself consul for life. To put it out of all doubt what model he intended to follow in his government of the empire, he made his offerings to the shade of Nero in the midst of the Campus Martius, and with a full assembly of the public priests attending him. And at a solemn entertainment, he desired a harper who pleased the company much, to sing something in praise of Domitius; and upon his beginning some songs of Nero's, he started up in presence of the whole assembly, and could not refrain from applauding him, by clapping his hands.

XII. After such a commencement of his career, he conducted (435) his affairs, during the greater part of his reign, entirely by the advice and direction of the vilest amongst the players and charioteers, and especially his freedman Asiaticus. This fellow had, when young, been engaged with him in a course of mutual and unnatural pollution, but, being at last quite tired of the occupation, ran away. His master, some time after, caught him at Puteoli, selling a liquor called Posca 711 , and put him in chains, but soon released him, and retained him in his former capacity. Growing weary, however, of his rough and stubborn temper, he sold him to a strolling fencing-master; after which, when the fellow was to have been brought up to play his part at the conclusion of an entertainment of gladiators, he suddenly carried him off, and at length, upon his being advanced to the government of a province, gave him his freedom. The first day of his reign, he presented him with the gold rings at supper, though in the morning, when all about him requested that favour in his behalf, he expressed the utmost abhorrence of putting so great a stain upon the equestrian order.

XIII. He was chiefly addicted to the vices of luxury and cruelty. He always made three meals a day, sometimes four: breakfast, dinner, and supper, and a drunken revel after all. This load of victuals he could well enough bear, from a custom to which he had enured himself, of frequently vomiting. For these several meals he would make different appointments at the houses of his friends on the same day. None ever entertained him at less expense than four hundred thousand sesterces 712 . The most famous was a set entertainment given him by his brother, at which, it is said, there were served up no less than two thousand choice fishes, and seven thousand birds. Yet even this supper he himself outdid, at a feast which he gave upon the first use of a dish which had been made for him, and which, for its extraordinary size, he called "The Shield of Minerva." In this dish there were tossed up together the livers of char-fish, the brains of pheasants and peacocks, with the tongues of flamingos, and the entrails of lampreys, which had been brought in ships of war as far as (436) from the Carpathian Sea, and the Spanish Straits. He was not only a man of an insatiable appetite, but would gratify it likewise at unseasonable times, and with any garbage that came in his way; so that, at a sacrifice, he would snatch from the fire flesh and cakes, and eat them upon the spot. When he travelled, he did the same at the inns upon the road, whether the meat was fresh dressed and hot, or what had been left the day before, and was half-eaten.

XIV. He delighted in the infliction of punishments, and even those which were capital, without any distinction of persons or occasions. Several noblemen, his school-fellows and companions, invited by him to court, he treated with such flattering caresses, as seemed to indicate an affection short only of admitting them to share the honours of the imperial dignity; yet he put them all to death by some base means or other. To one he gave poison with his own hand, in a cup of cold water which he called for in a fever. He scarcely spared one of all the usurers, notaries, and publicans, who had ever demanded a debt of him at Rome, or any toll or custom upon the road. One of these, while in the very act of saluting him, he ordered for execution, but immediately sent for him back; upon which all about him applauding his clemency, he commanded him to be slain in his own presence, saying, "I have a mind to feed my eyes." Two sons who interceded for their father, he ordered to be executed with him. A Roman knight, upon his being dragged away for execution, and crying out to him, "You are my heir," he desired to produce his will: and finding that he had made his freedman joint heir with him, he commanded that both he and the freedman should have their throats cut. He put to death some of the common people for cursing aloud the blue party in the Circensian games; supposing it to be done in contempt of himself, and the expectation of a revolution in the government. There were no persons he was more severe against than jugglers and astrologers; and as soon as any one of them was informed against, he put him to death without the formality of a trial. He was enraged against them, because, after his proclamation by which he commanded all astrologers to quit home, and Italy also, before the calends [the first] of October, a bill was immediately posted about the city, with the following words:—"TAKE NOTICE: 713 The Chaldaeans also decree that Vitellius Germanicus shall be no more, by the day of the said calends." He was even suspected of being accessary to his mother's death, by forbidding sustenance to be given her when she was unwell; a German witch 714, whom he held to be oracular, having told him, "That he would long reign in security if he survived his mother." But others say, that being quite weary of the state of affairs, and apprehensive of the future, she obtained without difficulty a dose of poison from her son.

XV. In the eighth month of his reign, the troops both in Moesia and Pannonia revolted from him; as did likewise, of the armies beyond sea, those in Judaea and Syria, some of which swore allegiance to Vespasian as emperor in his own presence, and others in his absence. In order, therefore, to secure the favour and affection of the people, Vitellius lavished on all around whatever he had it in his power to bestow, both publicly and privately, in the most extravagant manner. He also levied soldiers in the city, and promised all who enlisted as volunteers, not only their discharge after the victory was gained, but all the rewards due to veterans who had served their full time in the wars. The enemy now pressing forward both by sea and land, on one hand he opposed against them his brother with a fleet, the new levies, and a body of gladiators, and in another quarter the troops and generals who were engaged at Bedriacum. But being beaten or betrayed in every direction, he agreed with Flavius Sabinus, Vespasian's brother, to abdicate, on condition of having his life spared, and a hundred millions of sesterces granted him; and he immediately, upon the palace-steps, publicly declared to a large body of soldiers there assembled, "that he resigned the government, which he had accepted reluctantly;" but they all remonstrating against it, he deferred the conclusion of the treaty. Next day, early in the morning, he came down to the Forum in a very mean habit, and with many tears repeated the (438) declaration from a writing which he held in his hand; but the soldiers and people again interposing, and encouraging him not to give way, but to rely on their zealous support, he recovered his courage, and forced Sabinus, with the rest of the Flavian party, who now thought themselves secure, to retreat into the Capitol, where he destroyed them all by setting fire to the temple of Jupiter, whilst he beheld the contest and the fire from Tiberius's house 715, where he was feasting. Not long after, repenting of what he had done, and throwing the blame of it upon others, he called a meeting, and swore "that nothing was dearer to him than the public peace;" which oath he also obliged the rest to take. Then drawing a dagger from his side, he presented it first to the consul, and, upon his refusing it, to the magistrates, and then to every one of the senators; but none of them being willing to accept it, he went away, as if he meant to lay it up in the temple of Concord; but some crying out to him, "You are Concord," he came back again, and said that he would not only keep his weapon, but for the future use the cognomen of Concord.

XVI. He advised the senate to send deputies, accompanied by the Vestal Virgins, to desire peace, or, at least, time for consultation. The day after, while he was waiting for an answer, he received intelligence by a scout, that the enemy was advancing. Immediately, therefore, throwing himself into a small litter, borne by hand, with only two attendants, a baker and a cook, he privately withdrew to his father's house, on the Aventine hill, intending to escape thence into Campania. But a groundless report being circulated, that the enemy was willing to come to terms, he suffered himself to be carried back to the palace. Finding, however, nobody there, and those who were with him stealing away, he girded round his waist a belt full of gold pieces, and then ran into the porter's lodge, tying the dog before the door, and piling up against it the bed and bedding.

XVII. By this time the forerunners of the enemy's army had broken into the palace, and meeting with nobody, searched, as was natural, every corner. Being dragged by them out of his cell, and asked "who he was?" (for they did not recognize him), "and if he knew where Vitellius was?" he deceived them by a falsehood. But at last being discovered, he begged hard to be detained in custody, even were it in a prison; pretending to have something to say which concerned Vespasian's security. Nevertheless, he was dragged half-naked into the Forum, with his hands tied behind him, a rope about his neck, and his clothes torn, amidst the most contemptuous abuse, both by word and deed, along the Via Sacra; his head being held back by the hair, in the manner of condemned criminals, and the point of a sword put under his chin, that he might hold up his face to public view; some of the mob, meanwhile, pelting him with dung and mud, whilst others called him "an incendiary and glutton." They also upbraided him with the defects of his person, for he was monstrously tall, and had a face usually very red with hard-drinking, a large belly, and one thigh weak, occasioned by a chariot running against him, as he was attending upon Caius 716 , while he was driving. At length, upon the Scalae Gemoniae, he was tormented and put to death in lingering tortures, and then dragged by a hook into the Tiber.

XVIII. He perished with his brother and son 717 , in the fifty-seventh year of his age 718 , and verified the prediction of those who, from the omen which happened to him at Vienne, as before related 719 , foretold that he would be made prisoner by some man of Gaul. For he was seized by Antoninus Primus, a general of the adverse party, who was born at Toulouse, and, when a boy, had the cognomen of Becco 720 , which signifies a cock's beak.

\* \* \* \* \* \*

(440) After the extinction of the race of the Caesars, the possession of the imperial power became extremely precarious; and great influence in the army was the means which now invariably led to the throne. The soldiers having arrogated to themselves the right

of nomination, they either unanimously elected one and the same person, or different parties supporting the interests of their respective favourites, there arose between them a contention, which was usually determined by an appeal to arms, and followed by the assassination of the unsuccessful competitor. Vitellius, by being a parasite of all the emperors from Tiberius to Nero inclusively, had risen to a high military rank, by which, with a spirit of enterprise, and large promises to the soldiery, it was not difficult to snatch the reins of government, while they were yet fluctuating in the hands of Otho. His ambition prompted to the attempt, and his boldness was crowned with success. In the service of the four preceding emperors, Vitellius had imbibed the principal vices of them all: but what chiefly distinguished him was extreme voraciousness, which, though he usually pampered it with enormous luxury, could yet be gratified by the vilest and most offensive garbage. The pusillanimity discovered by this emperor at his death, forms a striking contrast to the heroic behaviour of Otho.

# T. FLAVIUS VESPASIANUS AUGUSTUS.

**(441)**

I. The empire, which had been long thrown into a disturbed and unsetted state, by the rebellion and violent death of its three last rulers, was at length restored to peace and security by the Flavian family, whose descent was indeed obscure, and which boasted no ancestral honours; but the public had no cause to regret its elevation; though it is acknowledged that Domitian met with the just reward of his avarice and cruelty. Titus Flavius Petro, a townsman of Reate 721, whether a centurion or an evocatus 722 of Pompey's party in the civil war, is uncertain, fled out of the battle of Pharsalia and went home; where, having at last obtained his pardon and discharge, he became a collector of the money raised by public sales in the way of auction. His son, surnamed Sabinus, was never engaged in the military service, though some say he was a centurion of the first order, and others, that whilst he held that rank, he was discharged on account of his bad state of health: this Sabinus, I say, was a publican, and received the tax of the fortieth penny in Asia. And there were remaining, at the time of the advancement of the family, several statues, which had been erected to him by the cities of that province, with this inscription: "To the honest Tax-farmer." 723 He afterwards turned usurer amongst the Helvetii, and there died, leaving behind him his wife, Vespasia Pella, and two sons by her; the elder of whom, Sabinus, came to be prefect of the city, and the younger, Vespasian, to be emperor. Polla, descended of a good family, at Nursia 724, had for her father Vespasius Pollio, thrice appointed (442) military tribune, and at last prefect of the camp; and her brother was a senator of praetorian dignity. There is to this day, about six miles from Nursia, on the road to Spoletum, a place on the summit of a hill, called Vespasiae, where are several monuments of the Vespasii, a sufficient proof of the splendour and antiquity of the family. I will not deny that some have pretended to say, that Petro's father was a native of Gallia Transpadana 725, whose employment was to hire workpeople who used to emigrate every year from the country of the Umbria into that of the Sabines, to assist them in their husbandry 726; but who settled at last in the town of Reate, and there married. But of this I have not been able to discover the least proof, upon the strictest inquiry.

II. Vespasian was born in the country of the Sabines, beyond Reate, in a little country-seat called Phalacrine, upon the fifth of the calends of December [27th November], in the evening, in the consulship of Quintus Sulpicius Camerinus and Caius Poppaeus Sabinus, five years before the death of Augustus 727; and was educated under the care of Tertulla, his grandmother by the father's side, upon an estate belonging to the family, at Cosa 728. After his advancement to the empire, he used frequently to visit the place where he had spent his infancy; and the villa was continued in the same condition, that he might see every thing about him just as he had been used to do. And he had so great a regard for the memory of his grandmother, that, upon solemn occasions and festival days, he constantly drank out of a silver cup which she had been accustomed to use. After assuming the manly habit, he had a long time a distaste for the senatorian toga, though his brother had obtained it; nor could he be persuaded by any one but his mother to sue for that badge of honour. She at length drove him to it, more by taunts and reproaches, than by her entreaties (443) and authority, calling him now and then, by way of reproach, his brother's footman. He served as military tribune in Thrace. When made quaestor, the province of Crete and Cyrene fell to him by lot. He was candidate for the aedileship, and soon after for the praetorship, but met with a repulse in the former case; though at last, with much difficulty, he came in sixth on the poll-books. But the office of praetor he carried upon his first canvass, standing amongst the highest at the poll. Being incensed against the senate, and desirous to gain, by all possible means, the good graces of Caius 729, he obtained leave to exhibit extraordinary 730 games for the emperor's victory in Germany, and advised them to increase the punishment of the conspirators against his life, by exposing their corpses unburied. He likewise gave him thanks in that august assembly for the honour of being admitted to his table.

III. Meanwhile, he married Flavia Domitilla, who had formerly been the mistress of Statilius Capella, a Roman knight of Sabrata in Africa, who [Domitilla] enjoyed Latin rights; and was soon after declared fully and freely a citizen of Rome, on a trial before the court of Recovery, brought by her father Flavius Liberalis, a native of Ferentum, but no more than secretary to a quaestor. By her he had the following children: Titus, Domitian, and Domitilla. He outlived his wife and daughter, and lost them both before he became emperor. After the death of his wife, he renewed his union 731 with his former concubine Caenis, the freedwoman of Antonia, and also her amanuensis, and treated her, even after he was emperor, almost as if she had been his lawful wife. 732

(444) IV. In the reign of Claudius, by the interest of Narcissus, he was sent to Germany, in command of a legion; whence being removed into Britain, he engaged the enemy in thirty several battles. He reduced under subjection to the Romans two very powerful tribes, and above twenty great towns, with the Isle of Wight, which lies close to the coast of Britain; partly under the command of Aulus Plautius, the consular lieutenant, and partly under Claudius himself 733. For this success he received the triumphal ornaments, and in a short time after two priesthoods, besides the consulship, which he held during the two last months of the year 734. The interval between that and his proconsulship he spent in leisure and retirement, for fear of Agrippina, who still held great sway over her son, and hated all the friends of Narcissus, who was then dead. Afterwards he got by lot the province of Africa, which he governed with great reputation, excepting that once, in an insurrection at Adrumetum, he was pelted with turnips. It is certain that he returned thence nothing richer; for his credit was so low, that he was obliged to mortgage his whole property to his brother, and was reduced to the necessity of dealing in mules, for the support of his rank; for which reason he was commonly called "the Muleteer." He is said likewise to have been convicted of extorting from a young man of fashion two hundred thousand sesterces for procuring him the broad-stripe, contrary to the wishes of his father, and was severely reprimanded for it. While in attendance upon Nero in Achaia, he frequently withdrew from the theatre while Nero was singing, and went to sleep if he remained, which gave so much (445) offence, that he was not only excluded from his society, but debarred

the liberty of saluting him in public. Upon this, he retired to a small out-of-the-way town, where he lay skulking in constant fear of his life, until a province, with an army, was offered him.

A firm persuasion had long prevailed through all the East 735, that it was fated for the empire of the world, at that time, to devolve on some who should go forth from Judaea. This prediction referred to a Roman emperor, as the event shewed; but the Jews, applying it to themselves, broke out into rebellion, and having defeated and slain their governor 736, routed the lieutenant of Syria 737, a man of consular rank, who was advancing to his assistance, and took an eagle, the standard, of one of his legions. As the suppression of this revolt appeared to require a stronger force and an active general, who might be safely trusted in an affair of so much importance, Vespasian was chosen in preference to all others, both for his known activity, and on account of the obscurity of his origin and name, being a person of whom (446) there could be not the least jealousy. Two legions, therefore, eight squadrons of horse, and ten cohorts, being added to the former troops in Judaea, and, taking with him his eldest son as lieutenant, as soon as he arrived in his province, he turned the eyes of the neighbouring provinces upon him, by reforming immediately the discipline of the camp, and engaging the enemy once or twice with such resolution, that, in the attack of a castle 738, he had his knee hurt by the stroke of a stone, and received several arrows in his shield.

V. After the deaths of Nero and Galba, whilst Otho and Vitellius were contending for the sovereignty, he entertained hopes of obtaining the empire, with the prospect of which he had long before flattered himself, from the following omens. Upon an estate belonging to the Flavian family, in the neighbourhood of Rome, there was an old oak, sacred to Mars, which, at the three several deliveries of Vespasia, put out each time a new branch; evident intimations of the future fortune of each child. The first was but a slender one, which quickly withered away; and accordingly, the girl that was born did not live long. The second became vigorous, which portended great good fortune; but the third grew like a tree. His father, Sabinus, encouraged by these omens, which were confirmed by the augurs, told his mother, "that her grandson would be emperor of Rome;" at which she laughed heartily, wondering, she said, "that her son should be in his dotage whilst she continued still in full possession of her faculties."

Afterwards in his aedileship, when Caius Caesar, being enraged at his not taking care to have the streets kept clean, ordered the soldiers to fill the bosom of his gown with dirt, some persons at that time construed it into a sign that the government, being trampled under foot and deserted in some civil commotion, would fall under his protection, and as it were into his lap. Once, while he was at dinner, a strange dog, that wandered about the streets, brought a man's hand 739 , and laid it under the table. And another time, while he was at supper, a plough-ox throwing the yoke off his neck, broke into the room, and after he had frightened away all the attendants, (447) on a sudden, as if he was tired, fell down at his feet, as he lay still upon his couch, and hung down his neck. A cypress-tree likewise, in a field belonging to the family, was torn up by the roots, and laid flat upon the ground, when there was no violent wind; but next day it rose again fresher and stronger than before.

He dreamt in Achaia that the good fortune of himself and his family would begin when Nero had a tooth drawn; and it happened that the day after, a surgeon coming into the hall, showed him a tooth which he had just extracted from Nero. In Judaea, upon his consulting the oracle of the divinity at Carmel 740 , the answer was so encouraging as to assure him of success in anything he projected, however great or important it might be. And when Josephus 741 , one of the noble prisoners, was put in chains, he confidently affirmed that he should be released in a very short time by the same Vespasian, but he would be emperor first 742 . Some omens were likewise mentioned in the news from Rome, and among others, that Nero, towards the close of his days, was commanded in a dream to carry Jupiter's sacred chariot out of the sanctuary where it stood, to Vespasian's house, and conduct it thence into the circus. Also not long afterwards, as Galba was going to the election, in which he was created consul for the second time, a statue of the Divine Julius 743 turned towards the east. And in the field of Bedriacum 744 , before the battle began, two eagles engaged in the sight of the army; and one of them being beaten, a third came from the east, and drove away the conqueror.

(448) VI. He made, however, no attempt upon the sovereignty, though his friends were very ready to support him, and even pressed him to the enterprise, until he was encouraged to it by the fortuitous aid of persons unknown to him and at a distance. Two thousand men,

drawn out of three legions in the Moesian army, had been sent to the assistance of Otho. While they were upon their march, news came that he had been defeated, and had put an end to his life; notwithstanding which they continued their march as far as Aquileia, pretending that they gave no credit to the report. There, tempted by the opportunity which the disorder of the times afforded them, they ravaged and plundered the country at discretion; until at length, fearing to be called to an account on their return, and punished for it, they resolved upon choosing and creating an emperor. "For they were no ways inferior," they said, "to the army which made Galba emperor, nor to the pretorian troops which had set up Otho, nor the army in Germany, to whom Vitellius owed his elevation." The names of all the consular lieutenants, therefore, being taken into consideration, and one objecting to one, and another to another, for various reasons; at last some of the third legion, which a little before Nero's death had been removed out of Syria into Moesia, extolled Vespasian in high terms; and all the rest assenting, his name was immediately inscribed on their standards. The design was nevertheless quashed for a time, the troops being brought to submit to Vitellius a little longer.

However, the fact becoming known, Tiberius Alexander, governor of Egypt, first obliged the legions under his command to swear obedience to Vespasian as their emperor, on the calends [the 1st] of July, which was observed ever after as the day of his accession to the empire; and upon the fifth of the ides of the same month [the 28th July], the army in Judaea, where he then was, also swore allegiance to him. What contributed greatly to forward the affair, was a copy of a letter, whether real or counterfeit, which was circulated, and said to have been written by Otho before his decease to Vespasian, recommending to him in the most urgent terms to avenge his death, and entreating him to come to the aid of the commonwealth; as well as a report which was circulated, that Vitellius, after his success against Otho, proposed to change the winter quarters of the legions, and remove those in Germany to a less (449) hazardous station and a warmer climate. Moreover, amongst the governors of provinces, Licinius Mucianus dropping the grudge arising from a jealousy of which he had hitherto made no secret, promised to join him with the Syrian army, and, among the allied kings, Volugesus, king of the Parthians, offered him a reinforcement of forty thousand archers.

VII. Having, therefore, entered on a civil war, and sent forward his generals and forces into Italy, he himself, in the meantime, passed over to Alexandria, to obtain possession of the key of Egypt 745. Here having entered alone, without attendants, the temple of Serapis, to take the auspices respecting the establishment of his power, and having done his utmost to propitiate the deity, upon turning round, [his freedman] Basilides 746 appeared before him, and seemed to offer him the sacred leaves, chaplets, and cakes, according to the usage of the place, although no one had admitted him, and he had long laboured under a muscular debility, which would hardly have allowed him to walk into the temple; besides which, it was certain that at the very time he was far away. Immediately after this, arrived letters with intelligence that Vitellius's troops had been defeated at Cremona, and he himself slain at Rome. Vespasian, the new emperor, having been raised unexpectedly from a low estate, wanted something which might clothe him with divine majesty and authority. This, likewise, was now added. A poor man who was blind, and another who was lame, came both together before him, when he was seated on the tribunal, imploring him to heal them 747, and saying that they were admonished (450) in a dream by the god Serapis to seek his aid, who assured them that he would restore sight to the one by anointing his eyes with his spittle, and give strength to the leg of the other, if he vouchsafed but to touch it with his heel. At first he could scarcely believe that the thing would any how succeed, and therefore hesitated to venture on making the experiment. At length, however, by the advice of his friends, he made the attempt publicly, in the presence of the assembled multitudes, and it was crowned with success in both cases 748. About the same time, at Tegea in Arcadia, by the direction (451) of some soothsayers, several vessels of ancient workmanship were dug out of a consecrated place, on which there was an effigy resembling Vespasian.

VIII. Returning now to Rome, under these auspices, and with a great reputation, after enjoying a triumph for victories over the Jews, he added eight consulships 749 to his former one. He likewise assumed the censorship, and made it his principal concern, during the whole of his government, first to restore order in the state, which had been almost ruined, and was in a tottering condition, and then to improve it. The soldiers, one part of them emboldened by victory, and the other smarting with the disgrace of their defeat, had abandoned themselves to every species of licentiousness and insolence. Nay, the provinces, too, and free cities, and some kingdoms in alliance with Rome, were all in a disturbed state. He, therefore, disbanded many of Vitellius's soldiers, and punished others; and so far was he from granting any extraordinary favours to the sharers of his success, that it was late before he paid the gratuities due to them by law. That he might let slip no opportunity of reforming the discipline of the army, upon a young man's coming much perfumed to return him thanks (452) for having appointed him to command a squadron of horse, he turned away his head in disgust, and, giving him this sharp reprimand, "I had rather you had smelt of garlic," revoked his commission. When the men belonging to the fleet, who travelled by turns from Ostia and Puteoli to Rome, petitioned for an addition to their pay, under the name of shoe-money, thinking that it would answer little purpose to send them away without a reply, he ordered them for the future to run barefooted; and so they have done ever since. He deprived of their liberties, Achaia, Lycia, Rhodes, Byzantium, and Samos; and reduced them into the form of provinces; Thrace, also, and Cilicia, as well as Comagene, which until that time had been under the government of kings. He stationed some legions in Cappadocia on account of the frequent inroads of the barbarians, and, instead of a Roman knight, appointed as governor of it a man of consular rank. The ruins of houses which had been burnt down long before, being a great desight to the city, he gave leave to any one who would, to take possession of the void ground and build upon it, if the proprietors should hesitate to perform the work themselves. He resolved upon rebuilding the Capitol, and was the foremost to put his hand to clearing the ground of the rubbish, and removed some of it upon his own shoulder. And he undertook, likewise, to restore the three thousand tables of brass which had been destroyed in the fire which consumed the Capitol; searching in all quarters for copies of those curious and ancient records, in which were contained the decrees of the senate, almost from the building of the city, as well as the acts of the people, relative to alliances, treaties, and privileges granted to any person.

IX. He likewise erected several new public buildings, namely, the temple of Peace 750 near the Forum, that of Claudius on the

(453) Coelian mount, which had been begun by Agrippina, but almost entirely demolished by Nero 751 ; and an amphitheatre 752 in the middle of the city, upon finding that Augustus had projected such a work. He purified the senatorian and equestrian orders, which had been much reduced by the havoc made amongst them at several times, and was fallen into disrepute by neglect. Having expelled the most unworthy, he chose in their room the most honourable persons in Italy and the provinces. And to let it be known that those two orders differed not so much in privileges as in dignity, he declared publicly, when some altercation passed between a senator and a Roman knight, "that senators ought not to be treated with scurrilous language, unless they were the aggressors, and then it was fair and lawful to return it."

X. The business of the courts had prodigiously accumulated, partly from old law-suits which, on account of the interruption that had been given to the course of justice, still remained undecided, and partly from the accession of new suits arising out of the disorder of the times. He, therefore, chose commissioners by lot to provide for the restitution of what had been seized by violence during the war, and others with extraordinary jurisdiction to decide causes belonging to the centumviri, and reduce them to as small a number as possible, for the dispatch of which, otherwise, the lives of the litigants could scarcely allow sufficient time.

XI. Lust and luxury, from the licence which had long prevailed, had also grown to an enormous height. He, therefore, obtained a decree of the senate, that a woman who formed an union with the slave of another person, should be considered (454) a bondwoman herself; and that usurers should not be allowed to take proceedings at law for the recovery of money lent to young men whilst they lived in their father's family, not even after their fathers were dead.

XII. In other affairs, from the beginning to the end of his government, he conducted himself with great moderation and clemency. He was so far from dissembling the obscurity of his extraction, that he frequently made mention of it himself. When some affected to trace his pedigree to the founders of Reate, and a companion of Hercules 753 , whose monument is still to be seen on the Salarian road, he laughed at them for it. And he was so little fond of external and adventitious ornaments, that, on the day of his triumph 754 , being quite tired of the length and tediousness of the procession, he could not forbear saying, "he was rightly served, for having in his old age been so silly as to desire a triumph; as if it was either due to his ancestors, or had ever been expected by himself." Nor would he for a long time accept of the tribunitian authority, or the title of Father of his Country. And in regard to the custom of searching those who came to salute him, he dropped it even in the time of the civil war.

XIII. He bore with great mildness the freedom used by his friends, the satirical allusions of advocates, and the petulance of philosophers. Licinius Mucianus, who had been guilty of notorious acts of lewdness, but, presuming upon his great services, treated him very rudely, he reproved only in private; and when complaining of his conduct to a common friend of theirs, he concluded with these words, "However, I am a man." Salvius Liberalis, in pleading the cause of a rich man under prosecution, presuming to say, "What is it to Caesar, if Hipparchus possesses a hundred millions of sesterces?" he commended him for it. Demetrius, the Cynic philosopher 755, (455) who had been sentenced to banishment, meeting him on the road, and refusing to rise up or salute him, nay, snarling at him in scurrilous language, he only called him a cur.

XIV. He was little disposed to keep up the memory of affronts or quarrels, nor did he harbour any resentment on account of them. He made a very splendid marriage for the daughter of his enemy Vitellius, and gave her, besides, a suitable fortune and equipage. Being in a great consternation after he was forbidden the court in the time of Nero, and asking those about him, what he should do? or, whither he should go? one of those whose office it was to introduce people to the emperor, thrusting him out, bid him go to Morbonia 756. But when this same person came afterwards to beg his pardon, he only vented his resentment in nearly the same words. He was so far from being influenced by suspicion or fear to seek the destruction of any one, that, when his friends advised him to beware of Metius Pomposianus, because it was commonly believed, on his nativity being cast, that he was destined by fate to the empire, he made him consul, promising for him, that he would not forget the benefit conferred.

XV. It will scarcely be found, that so much as one innocent person suffered in his reign, unless in his absence, and without his knowledge, or, at least, contrary to his inclination, and when he was imposed upon. Although Helvidius Priscus 757 was the only man who presumed to salute him on his return from Syria by his private name of Vespasian, and, when he came to be praetor, omitted any mark of honour to him, or even any mention of him in his edicts, yet he was not angry, until Helvidius proceeded to inveigh against him with the most scurrilous language. (456) Though he did indeed banish him, and afterwards ordered him to be put to death, yet he would gladly have saved him notwithstanding, and accordingly dispatched messengers to fetch back the executioners; and he would have saved him, had he not been deceived by a false account brought, that he had already perished. He never rejoiced at the death of any man; nay he would shed tears, and sigh, at the just punishment of the guilty.

XVI. The only thing deservedly blameable in his character was his love of money. For not satisfied with reviving the imposts which had been repealed in the time of Galba, he imposed new and onerous taxes, augmented the tribute of the provinces, and doubled that of some of them. He likewise openly engaged in a traffic, which is discreditable 758 even to a private individual, buying great quantities of goods, for the purpose of retailing them again to advantage. Nay, he made no scruple of selling the great offices of the state to candidates, and pardons to persons under prosecution, whether they were innocent or guilty. It is believed, that he advanced all the most rapacious amongst the procurators to higher offices, with the view of squeezing them after they had acquired great wealth. He was commonly said, "to have used them as sponges," because it was his practice, as we may say, to wet them when dry, and squeeze them when wet. It is said that he was naturally extremely covetous, and was upbraided with it by an old herdsman of his, who, upon the emperor's refusing to enfranchise him gratis, which on his advancement he humbly petitioned for, cried out, "That the fox changed his hair, but not his nature." On the other hand, some are of opinion, that he was urged to his rapacious proceedings by necessity, and the extreme poverty of the treasury and exchequer, of which he took public notice in the beginning of his reign; declaring that "no less than four hundred thousand millions of sesterces were wanting to carry on the government." This is the more likely to be true, because he applied to the best purposes what he procured by bad means.

XVII. His liberality, however, to all ranks of people, was excessive. He made up to several senators the estate required (457) by law to qualify them for that dignity; relieving likewise such men of consular rank as were poor, with a yearly allowance of five hundred thousand sesterces 759 ; and rebuilt, in a better manner than before, several cities in different parts of the empire, which had been damaged by earthquakes or fires.

XVIII. He was a great encourager of learning and the liberal arts. He first granted to the Latin and Greek professors of rhetoric the yearly stipend of a hundred thousand sesterces 760 each out of the exchequer. He also bought the freedom of superior poets and artists 761 , and gave a noble gratuity to the restorer of the Coan of Venus 762 , and to another artist who repaired the Colossus 763 . Some one offering to convey some immense columns into the Capitol at a small expense by a mechanical contrivance, he rewarded him very handsomely for his invention, but would not accept his service, saying, "Suffer me to find maintenance for the poor people." 764

XIX. In the games celebrated when the stage-scenery of (458) the theatre of Marcellus 765 was repaired, he restored the old musical entertainments. He gave Apollinaris, the tragedian, four hundred thousand sesterces, and to Terpinus and Diodorus, the harpers, two hundred thousand; to some a hundred thousand; and the least he gave to any of the performers was forty thousand, besides many golden crowns. He entertained company constantly at his table, and often in great state and very sumptuously, in order to promote trade. As in the Saturnalia he made presents to the men which they were to carry away with them, so did he to the women upon the calends of March 766 ; notwithstanding which, he could not wipe off the disrepute of his former stinginess. The Alexandrians called him constantly Cybiosactes; a name which had been given to one of their kings who was sordidly avaricious. Nay, at his funeral, Favo, the principal mimic, personating him, and imitating, as actors do, both his manner of speaking and his gestures, asked aloud of the procurators, "how much his funeral and the procession would cost?" And being answered "ten millions of sesterces," he cried out, "give him but a hundred thousand sesterces, and they might throw his body into the Tiber, if they would."

XX. He was broad-set, strong-limbed, and his features gave the idea of a man in the act of straining himself. In consequence, one of the city wits, upon the emperor's desiring him "to say something droll respecting himself," facetiously answered, "I will, when you have done relieving your bowels." 767 He enjoyed a good state of health, though he used no other means to preserve it, than repeated friction, as much (459) as he could bear, on his neck and other parts of his body, in the tennis-court attached to the baths, besides fasting one day in every month.

XXI. His method of life was commonly this. After he became emperor, he used to rise very early, often before daybreak. Having read over his letters, and the briefs of all the departments of the government offices; he admitted his friends; and while they were paying him their compliments, he would put on his own shoes, and dress himself with his own hands. Then, after the dispatch of such business as was brought before him, he rode out, and afterwards retired to repose, lying on his couch with one of his mistresses, of whom he kept several after the death of Caenis 768. Coming out of his private apartments, he passed to the bath, and then entered the supper-room. They say that he was never more good-humoured and indulgent than at that time: and therefore his attendants always seized that opportunity, when they had any favour to ask.

XXII. At supper, and, indeed, at other times, he was extremely free and jocose. For he had humour, but of a low kind, and he would sometimes use indecent language, such as is addressed to young girls about to be married. Yet there are some things related of him not void of ingenious pleasantry; amongst which are the following. Being once reminded by Mestrius Florus, that plaustra was a more proper expression than plostra, he next day saluted him by the name of Flaurus 769. A certain lady pretending to be desperately enamoured of him, he was prevailed upon to admit her to his bed; and after he had gratified her desires, he gave her 770 four hundred (460) thousand sesterces. When his steward desired to know how he would have the sum entered in his accounts, he replied, "For Vespasian's being seduced."

XXIII. He used Greek verses very wittily; speaking of a tall man, who had enormous parts:

*Makxi bibas, kradon dolichoskion enchos;*

*Still shaking, as he strode, his vast long spear.*

And of Cerylus, a freedman, who being very rich, had begun to pass himself off as free-born, to elude the exchequer at his decease, and assumed the name of Laches, he said:

— — *O Lachaes, Lachaes,*
*Epan apothanaes, authis ex archaes esae Kaerylos.*
*Ah, Laches, Laches! when thou art no more,*
*Thou'lt Cerylus be called, just as before.*

He chiefly affected wit upon his own shameful means of raising money, in order to wipe off the odium by some joke, and turn it into ridicule. One of his ministers, who was much in his favour, requesting of him a stewardship for some person, under pretence of his being his brother, he deferred granting him his petition, and in the meantime sent for the candidate, and having squeezed out of him as much money as he had agreed to give to his friend at court, he appointed him immediately to the office. The minister soon after renewing his application, "You must," said he, "find another brother; for the one you adopted is in truth mine."

Suspecting once, during a journey, that his mule-driver had alighted to shoe his mules, only in order to have an opportunity for allowing a person they met, who was engaged in a law-suit, to speak to him, he asked him, "how much he got for shoeing his mules?" and insisted on having a share of the profit. When his son Titus blamed him for even laying a tax upon urine, he applied to his nose a piece of the money he received in the first instalment, and asked him, "if it stunk?" And he replying no, "And yet," said he, "it is derived from urine."

Some deputies having come to acquaint him that a large statue, which would cost a vast sum, was ordered to be erected for him at the public expense, he told them to pay it down immediately, (461) holding out the hollow of his hand, and saying, "there was a base ready for the statue." Not even when he was under the immediate apprehension and peril of death, could he forbear jesting. For when, among other prodigies, the mausoleum of the Caesars suddenly flew open, and a blazing star appeared in the heavens; one of the prodigies, he said, concerned Julia Calvina, who was of the family of Augustus 771 ; and the other, the king of the Parthians, who wore his hair long.

And when his distemper first seized him, "I suppose," said he, "I shall soon be a god." 772

XXIV. In his ninth consulship, being seized, while in Campania, with a slight indisposition, and immediately returning to the city, he soon afterwards went thence to Cutiliae 773, and his estates in the country about Reate, where he used constantly to spend the summer. Here, though his disorder much increased, and he injured his bowels by too free use of the cold waters, he nevertheless attended to the dispatch of business, and even gave audience to ambassadors in bed. At last, being taken ill of a diarrhoea, to such a degree that he was ready to faint, he cried out, "An emperor ought to die standing upright." In endeavouring to rise, he died in the hands of those who were helping him up, upon the eighth of the calends of July [24th June] 774, being sixty-nine years, one month, and seven days old.

XXV. All are agreed that he had such confidence in the calculations on his own nativity and that of his sons, that, after several conspiracies against him, he told the senate, that either his sons would succeed him, or nobody. It is said likewise, that he once saw in a dream a balance in the middle of the porch of the Palatine house exactly poised; in one (462) scale of which stood Claudius and Nero, in the other, himself and his sons. The event corresponded to the symbol; for the reigns of the two parties were precisely of the same duration. 775

\* \* \* \* \* \*

Neither consanguinity nor adoption, as formerly, but great influence in the army having now become the road to the imperial throne, no person could claim a better title to that elevation than Titus Flavius Vespasian. He had not only served with great reputation in the wars both in Britain and Judaea, but seemed as yet untainted with any vice which could pervert his conduct in the civil administration of the empire. It appears, however, that he was prompted more by the persuasion of friends, than by his own ambition, to prosecute the attainment of the imperial dignity. To render this enterprise more successful, recourse was had to a new and peculiar artifice, which, while well accommodated to the superstitious credulity of the Romans, impressed them with an idea, that Vespasian's destiny to the throne was confirmed by supernatural indications. But, after his elevation, we hear no more of his miraculous achievements.

The prosecution of the war in Britain, which had been suspended for some years, was resumed by Vespasian; and he sent thither Petilius Cerealis, who by his bravery extended the limits of the Roman province. Under Julius Frontinus, successor to that general, the invaders continued to make farther progress in the reduction of the island: but the commander who finally established the dominion of the Romans in Britain, was Julius Agricola, not less distinguished for his military achievements, than for his prudent regard to the civil administration of the country. He began his operations with the conquest of North Wales, whence passing over into the island of Anglesey, which had revolted since the time of Suetonius Paulinus, he again reduced it to subjection. Then proceeding northwards with his victorious army, he defeated the Britons in every engagement, took possession of all the territories in the southern parts of the island, and driving before him all who refused to submit to the Roman arms, penetrated even into the forests and mountains of Caledonia. He defeated the natives under Galgacus, their leader, in a decisive battle; and fixing a line of garrisons between the friths of Clyde and Forth, he secured the Roman province from the incursions of the people who occupied the parts of the island (463) beyond that boundary. Wherever he established the Roman power, he introduced laws and civilization amongst the inhabitants, and employed every means of conciliating their affection, as well as of securing their obedience.

The war in Judaea, which had been commenced under the former reign, was continued in that of Vespasian; but he left the siege of Jerusalem to be conducted by his son Titus, who displayed great valour and military talents in the prosecution of the enterprise. After an obstinate defence by the Jews, that city, so much celebrated in the sacred writings, was finally demolished, and the glorious temple itself, the admiration of the world, reduced to ashes; contrary, however, to the will of Titus, who exerted his utmost efforts to extinguish the flames.

The manners of the Romans had now attained to an enormous pitch of depravity, through the unbounded licentiousness of the tines; and, to the honour of Vespasian, he discovered great zeal in his endeavours to effect a national reformation. Vigilant, active, and persevering, he was indefatigable in the management of public affairs, and rose in the winter before day-break, to give audience to his officers of state. But if we give credit to the whimsical imposition of a tax upon urine, we cannot entertain any high opinion, either of his talents as a financier, or of the resources of the Roman empire. By his encouragement of science, he displayed a liberality, of which there occurs no example under all the preceding emperors, since the time of Augustus. Pliny the elder was now in the height of reputation, as well as in great favour with Vespasian; and it was probably owing not a little to the advice of that minister, that the emperor showed himself so much the patron of literary men. A writer mentioned frequently by Pliny, and who lived in this reign, was Licinius Mucianus, a Roman knight: he treated of the history and geography of the eastern countries. Juvenal, who had begun his Satires several years before, continued to inveigh against the flagrant vices of the times; but the only author whose writings we have to notice in the present reign, is a poet of a different class.

C. VALERIUS FLACCUS wrote a poem in eight books, on the Expedition of the Argonauts; a subject which, next to the wars of Thebes and Troy, was in ancient times the most celebrated. Of the life of this author, biographers have transmitted no particulars; but we may place his birth in the reign of Tiberius, before all the writers who flourished in the Augustan age were extinct. He enjoyed the rays of the setting sun which had illumined that glorious period, and he discovers the efforts of an ambition to recall its meridian splendour. As the poem was left (464) incomplete by the death of the author, we can only judge imperfectly of the conduct and general consistency of the fable: but the most difficult part having been executed, without any room for the censure of candid criticism, we may presume that the sequel would have been finished with an equal claim to indulgence, if not to applause. The traditional anecdotes relative to the Argonautic expedition are introduced with propriety, and embellished with the graces of poetical fiction. In describing scenes of tenderness, this author is happily pathetic, and in the heat of combat, proportionably animated. His similes present the imagination with beautiful imagery, and not only illustrate, but give additional force to the subject. We find in Flaccus a few expressions not countenanced by the authority of the most celebrated Latin writers. His language, however, in general, is pure; but his words are perhaps not always the best that might have been chosen. The versification is elevated, though not uniformly harmonious; and there pervades the whole poem an epic dignity, which renders it superior to the production ascribed to Orpheus, or to that of Apollonius, on the same subject.

# TITUS FLAVIUS VESPASIANUS AUGUSTUS.

**(465)**

I. Titus, who had the same cognomen with his father, was the darling and delight of mankind; so much did the natural genius, address, or good fortune he possessed tend to conciliate the favour of all. This was, indeed, extremely difficult, after he became emperor, as before that time, and even during the reign of his father, he lay under public odium and censure. He was born upon the third of the calends of January, [30th Dec.] in the year remarkable for the death of Caius [776], near the Septizonium 777, in a mean house, and a very small and dark room, which still exists, and is shown to the curious.

II. He was educated in the palace with Britannicus, and instructed in the same branches of learning, and under the same masters. During this time, they say, that a physiognomist being introduced by Narcissus, the freedman of Claudius, to examine the features of Britannicus 778, positively affirmed that he would never become emperor, but that Titus, who stood by, would. They were so familiar, that Titus being next him at table, is thought to have tasted of the fatal potion which put an end to Britannicus's life, and to have contracted from it a distemper which hung about him a long time. In remembrance of all these circumstances, he afterwards erected a golden statue of him in the Palatium, and dedicated to him an equestrian statue of ivory; attending it in the Circensian procession, in which it is still carried to this day.

(466) III. While yet a boy, he was remarkable for his noble endowments both of body and mind; and as he advanced in years, they became still more conspicuous. He had a fine person, combining an equal mixture of majesty and grace; was very strong, though not tall, and somewhat corpulent. Gifted with an excellent memory, and

a capacity for all the arts of peace and war; he was a perfect master of the use of arms and riding; very ready in the Latin and Greek tongues, both in verse and prose; and such was the facility he possessed in both, that he would harangue and versify extempore. Nor was he unacquainted with music, but could both sing and play upon the harp sweetly and scientifically. I have likewise been informed by many persons, that he was remarkably quick in writing short-hand, would in merriment and jest engage with his secretaries in the imitation of any hand-writing he saw, and often say, "that he was admirably qualified for forgery."

IV. He filled with distinction the rank of a military tribune both in Germany and Britain, in which he conducted himself with the utmost activity, and no less modesty and reputation; as appears evident from the great number of statues, with honourable inscriptions, erected to him in various parts of both those provinces. After serving in the wars, he frequented the courts of law, but with less assiduity than applause. About the same time, he married Arricidia, the daughter of Tertullus, who was only a knight, but had formerly been prefect of the pretorian guards. After her decease, he married Marcia Furnilla, of a very noble family, but afterwards divorced her, taking from her the daughter he had by her. Upon the expiration of his quaestorship, he was raised to the rank of commander of a legion 779 , and took the two strong cities of Tarichaea and Gamala, in Judaea; and having his horse killed under him in a battle, he mounted another, whose rider he had encountered and slain.

V. Soon afterwards, when Galba came to be emperor, he was sent to congratulate him, and turned the eyes of all people upon himself, wherever he came; it being the general opinion amongst them, that the emperor had sent for him with a design to adopt him for his son. But finding all things again in confusion, he turned back upon the road; and going to consult (467) the oracle of Venus at Paphos about his voyage, he received assurances of obtaining the empire for himself. These hopes were speedily strengthened, and being left to finish the reduction of Judaea, in the final assault of Jerusalem, he slew seven of its defenders, with the like number of arrows, and took it upon his daughter's birth-day 780 . So great was the joy and attachment of the soldiers, that, in their congratulations, they unanimously saluted him by the title of Emperor 781 ; and, upon his quitting the province soon afterwards, would needs have detained him, earnestly begging him, and that not without threats, "either to stay, or take them all with him." This occurrence gave rise to the suspicion of his being engaged in a design to rebel against his father, and claim for himself the government of the East; and the suspicion increased, when, on his way to Alexandria, he wore a diadem at the consecration of the ox Apis at Memphis; and, though he did it only in compliance with an ancient religious usage of the country, yet there was some who put a bad construction upon it. Making, therefore, what haste he could into Italy, he arrived first at Rhegium, and sailing thence in a merchant ship to Puteoli, went to Rome with all possible expedition. Presenting himself unexpectedly to his father, he said, by way of contradicting the strange reports raised concerning him, "I am come, father, I am come."

VI. From that time he constantly acted as colleague with his father, and, indeed, as regent of the empire. He triumphed 782 (468) with his father, bore jointly with him the office of censor 783 , and was, besides, his colleague not only in the tribunitian authority 784 , but in seven consulships 785 . Taking upon himself the care and inspection of all offices, he dictated letters, wrote proclamations in his father's name, and pronounced his speeches in the senate in place of the quaestor. He likewise assumed the command of the pretorian guards, although no one but a Roman knight had ever before been their prefect. In this he conducted himself with great haughtiness and violence, taking off without scruple or delay all those he had most reason to suspect, after he had secretly sent his emissaries into the theatres and camp, to demand, as if by general consent, that the suspected persons should be delivered up to punishment. Among these, he invited to supper A. Caecina, a man of consular rank, whom he ordered to be stabbed at his departure, immediately after he had gone out of the room. To this act, indeed, he was provoked by an imminent danger; for he had discovered a writing under the hand of Caecina, containing an account of a plot hatched among the soldiers. By these acts, though he provided for his future security, yet for the present he so much incurred the hatred of the people, that scarcely ever any one came to the empire with a more odious character, or more universally disliked.

VII. Besides his cruelty, he lay under the suspicion of giving (469) way to habits of luxury, as he often prolonged his revels till midnight with the most riotous of his acquaintance. Nor was he unsuspected of lewdness, on account of the swarms of catamites and eunuchs about him, and his well-known attachment to queen Berenice 786 , who received from him, as it is reported, a promise of marriage. He was supposed, besides, to be of a rapacious disposition; for it is certain, that, in causes which came before his father, he used to offer his interest for sale, and take bribes. In short, people publicly expressed an unfavourable opinion of him, and said he would prove another Nero. This prejudice, however, turned out in the end to his advantage, and enhanced his praises to the highest pitch when he was found to possess no vicious propensities, but, on the contrary, the noblest virtues. His entertainments were agreeable rather than extravagant; and he surrounded himself with such excellent friends, that the succeeding princes adopted them as most serviceable to themselves and the state. He immediately sent away Berenice from the city, much against both their inclinations. Some of his old eunuchs, though such accomplished dancers, that they bore an uncontrollable sway upon the stage, he was so far from treating with any extraordinary kindness, that he would not so much as witness their performances in the crowded theatre. He violated no private right; (470) and if ever man refrained from injustice, he did; nay, he would not accept of the allowable and customary offerings. Yet, in munificence, he was inferior to none of the princes before him. Having dedicated his amphitheatre 787 , and built some warm baths 788 close by it with great expedition, he entertained the people with most magnificent spectacles. He likewise exhibited a naval fight in the old Naumachia, besides a combat of gladiators; and in one day brought into the theatre five thousand wild beasts of all kinds. 789

(471) VIII. He was by nature extremely benevolent; for whereas all the emperors after Tiberius, according to the example he had set them, would not admit the grants made by former princes to be valid, unless they received their own sanction, he confirmed them all by one general edict, without waiting for any applications respecting them. Of all who petitioned for any favour, he sent none away without hopes. And when his ministers represented to him that he promised more than he could perform, he replied, "No one ought to

go away downcast from an audience with his prince." Once at supper, reflecting that he had done nothing for any that day, he broke out into that memorable and justly-admired saying, "My friends, I have lost a day." 790 More particularly, he treated the people on all occasions with so much courtesy, that, on his presenting them with a show of gladiators, he declared, "He should manage it, not according to his own fancy, but that of the spectators," and did accordingly. He denied them nothing, and very frankly encouraged them to ask what they pleased. Espousing the cause of the Thracian party among the gladiators, he frequently joined in the popular demonstrations in their favour, but without compromising his dignity or doing injustice. To omit no opportunity of acquiring popularity, he sometimes made use himself of the baths he had erected, without excluding the common people. There happened in his reign some dreadful accidents; an eruption of Mount Vesuvius 791, in Campania, and a fire in Rome, which continued during three days and three nights 792; besides a plague, such as was scarcely ever known before. Amidst these many great disasters, he not only manifested the concern (472) which might be expected from a prince but even the affection of a father, for his people; one while comforting them by his proclamations, and another while relieving them to the utmost of his power. He chose by lot, from amongst the men of consular rank, commissioners for repairing the losses in Campania. The estates of those who had perished by the eruption of Vesuvius, and who had left no heirs, he applied to the repair of the ruined cities. With regard to the public buildings destroyed by fire in the City, he declared that nobody should be a loser but himself. Accordingly, he applied all the ornaments of his palaces to the decoration of the temples, and purposes of public utility, and appointed several men of the equestrian order to superintend the work. For the relief of the people during the plague, he employed, in the way of sacrifice and medicine, all means both human and divine. Amongst the calamities of the times, were informers and their agents; a tribe of miscreants who had grown up under the licence of former reigns. These he frequently ordered to be scourged or beaten with sticks in the Forum, and then, after he had obliged them to pass through the amphitheatre as a public spectacle, commanded them to be sold for slaves, or else banished them to some rocky islands. And to discourage such practices for the future, amongst other things, he prohibited actions to be successively brought under different laws for the same cause, or the state of affairs of deceased persons to be inquired into after a certain number of years.

IX. Having declared that he accepted the office of Pontifex Maximus for the purpose of preserving his hands undefiled, he faithfully adhered to his promise. For after that time he was neither directly nor indirectly concerned in the death of any person, though he sometimes was justly irritated. He swore "that he would perish himself, rather than prove the destruction of any man." Two men of patrician rank being convicted of aspiring to the empire, he only advised them to desist, saying, "that the sovereign power was disposed of by fate," and promised them, that if there was any thing else they desired of him, he would grant it. He also immediately sent messengers to the mother of one of them, who was at a great distance, and in deep anxiety about her son, to assure her of his safety. Nay, he not only invited them to sup with (473) him, but next day, at a show of gladiators, purposely placed them close by him; and handed to them the arms of the combatants for his inspection. It is said likewise, that having had their nativities cast, he assured them, "that a great calamity was impending on both of them, but from another hand, and not from his." Though his brother was continually plotting against him, almost openly stirring up the armies to rebellion, and contriving to get away, yet he could not endure to put him to death, or to banish him from his presence; nor did he treat him with less respect than before. But from his first accession to the empire, he constantly declared him his partner in it, and that he should be his successor; begging of him sometimes in private, with tears in his eyes, "to return the affection he had for him."

X. Amidst all these favourable circumstances, he was cut off by an untimely death, more to the loss of mankind than himself. At the close of the public spectacles, he wept bitterly in the presence of the people, and then retired into the Sabine country 793 , rather melancholy, because a victim had made its escape while he was sacrificing, and loud thunder had been heard while the atmosphere was serene. At the first resting-place on the road, he was seized with a fever, and being carried forward in a litter, they say that he drew back the curtains, and looked up to heaven, complaining heavily, "that his life was taken from him, though he had done nothing to deserve it; for there was no action of his that he had occasion to repent of, but one." What that was, he neither disclosed himself, nor is it easy for us to conjecture. Some imagine that he alluded to the connection which he had formerly had with his brother's wife. But Domitia solemnly denied it on oath; which she would never have done, had there been any truth in the report; nay, she would certainly have gloried in it, as she was forward enough to boast of all her scandalous intrigues.

XI. He died in the same villa where his father had died (474) before him, upon the Ides of September [the 13th of September]; two years, two months, and twenty days after he had succeeded his father; and in the one-and-fortieth year of his age 794. As soon as the news of his death was published, all people mourned for him, as for the loss of some near relative. The senate assembled in haste, before they could be summoned by proclamation, and locking the doors of their house at first, but afterwards opening them, gave him such thanks, and heaped upon him such praises, now he was dead, as they never had done whilst he was alive and present amongst them.

\* \* \* \* \* \*

TITUS FLAVIUS VESPASIAN, the younger, was the first prince who succeeded to the empire by hereditary right; and having constantly acted, after his return from Judaea, as colleague with his father in the administration, he seemed to be as well qualified by experience as he was by abilities, for conducting the affairs of the empire. But with respect to his natural disposition, and moral behaviour, the expectations entertained by the public were not equally flattering. He was immoderately addicted to luxury; he had betrayed a strong inclination to cruelty; and he lived in the habitual practice of lewdness, no less unnatural than intemperate. But, with a degree of virtuous resolution unexampled in history, he had no sooner taken into his hands the entire reins of government, than he renounced every vicious attachment. Instead of wallowing in luxury, as before, he became a model of temperance; instead of cruelty, he displayed the strongest proofs of humanity and benevolence; and in the room of lewdness, he exhibited a transition to the most unblemished chastity and virtue. In a word, so sudden and great a change was never known in the character of mortal; and he had the peculiar glory to receive the appellation of "the darling and delight of mankind."

Under a prince of such a disposition, the government of the empire could not but be conducted with the strictest regard to the public welfare. The reform, which was begun in the late reign, he prosecuted with the most ardent application; and, had he lived for a longer time, it is probable that his authority and example would have produced the most beneficial effects upon the manners of the Romans.

During the reign of this emperor, in the seventy-ninth year of (475) the Christian era, happened the first eruption of Mount Vesuvius, which has ever since been celebrated for its volcano. Before this time, Vesuvius is spoken of, by ancient writers, as being covered with orchards and vineyards, and of which the middle was dry and barren. The eruption was accompanied by an earthquake, which destroyed several cities of Campania, particularly Pompeii and Herculaneum; while the lava, pouring down the mountain in torrents, overwhelmed, in various directions, the adjacent plains. The burning ashes were carried not only over the neighbouring country, but as far as the shores of Egypt, Libya, and even Syria. Amongst those to whom this dreadful eruption proved fatal, was Pliny, the celebrated naturalist, whose curiosity to examine the phenomenon led him so far within the verge of danger, that he could not afterwards escape.

PLINY, surnamed the Elder, was born at Verona, of a noble family. He distinguished himself early by his military achievements in the German war, received the dignity of an Augur, at Rome, and was afterwards appointed governor of Spain. In every public character, he acquitted himself with great reputation, and enjoyed the esteem of the several emperors under whom he lived. The assiduity with which he applied himself to the collection of information, either curious or useful, surpasses all example. From an early hour in the morning, until late at night, he was almost constantly employed in discharging the duties of his public station, in reading or hearing books read by his amanuensis, and in extracting from them whatever seemed worthy of notice. Even during his meals, and while travelling in his carriage upon business, he prosecuted with unremitting zeal and diligence his taste for enquiry and compilation. No man ever displayed so strong a persuasion of the value of time, or availed himself so industriously of it. He considered every moment as lost which was not employed in literary pursuits. The books which he wrote, in consequence of this indefatigable exertion, were, according to the account transmitted by his nephew, Pliny the younger, numerous, and on various subjects. The catalogue of them is as follows: a book on Equestrian Archery, which discovered much skill in the art; the Life of Q. Pomponius Secundus; twenty books of the Wars of Germany; a complete treatise on the Education of an Orator, in six volumes; eight books of Doubtful Discourses, written in the latter part of the reign of Nero, when every kind of moral discussion was attended with danger; with a hundred and sixty volumes of remarks on the writings of the various authors which he had perused. For the last-mentioned production only, and before it was brought near to its accomplishment, we are told, that he (476) was offered by Largius Licinius four hundred thousand sesterces, amounting to upwards of three thousand two hundred pounds sterling; an enormous sum for the copyright of a book before the invention of printing! But the only surviving work of this voluminous author is his Natural History, in thirty-seven books, compiled from the various writers who had treated of that extensive and interesting subject.

If we estimate this great work either by the authenticity of the information which it contains, or its utility in promoting the advancement of arts and sciences, we should not consider it as an object of any extraordinary encomiums; but when we view it as a literary monument, which displays the whole knowledge of the ancients, relative to Natural History, collected during a period of about seven hundred years, from the time of Thales the Milesian, it has a just claim to the attention of every speculative enquirer. It is not surprising, that the progress of the human mind, which, in moral science, after the first dawn of enquiry, was rapid both amongst the Greeks and Romans, should be slow in the improvement of such branches of knowledge as depended entirely on observation and facts, which were peculiarly difficult of attainment. Natural knowledge can only be brought to perfection by the prosecution of enquiries in different climates, and by a communication of discoveries amongst those by whom it is cultivated. But neither could enquiries be prosecuted, nor discoveries communicated, with success, while the greater part of the world was involved in barbarism, while navigation was slow and limited, and the art of printing unknown. The consideration of these circumstances will afford sufficient apology for the imperfect state in which natural science existed amongst the ancients. But we proceed to give an abstract of their extent, as they appear in the compilation of Pliny.

This work is divided into thirty-seven books; the first of which contains the Preface, addressed to the emperor Vespasian, probably the father, to whom the author pays high compliments. The second book treats of the world, the elements, and the stars. In respect to the world, or rather the universe, the author's opinion is the same with that of several ancient philosophers, that it is a Deity, uncreated, infinite, and eternal. Their notions, however, as might be expected, on a subject so incomprehensible, are vague, confused, and imperfect. In a subsequent chapter of the same book, where the nature of the Deity is more particularly considered, the author's conceptions of infinite power are so inadequate, that, by way of consolation for the limited powers of man, he observes that there are many things even beyond the power of the Supreme Being; such, for instance, as the annihilation of his own existence; to which the author adds, the power (477) of rendering mortals eternal, and of raising the dead. It deserves to be remarked, that, though a future state of rewards and punishments was maintained by the most eminent among the ancient philosophers, the resurrection of the body was a doctrine with which they were wholly unacquainted.

The author next treats of the planets, and the periods of their respective revolutions; of the stars, comets, winds, thunder, lightning, and other natural phenomena, concerning all which he delivers the hypothetical notions maintained by the ancients, and mentions a variety of extraordinary incidents which had occurred in different parts of the world. The third book contains a general system of geography, which is continued through the fourth, fifth, and sixth books. The seventh treats of conception, and the generation of the human species, with a number of miscellaneous observations, unconnected with the general subject. The eighth treats of quadrupeds; the ninth, of aquatic animals; the tenth, of birds; the eleventh, of insects and reptiles; the twelfth, of trees; the thirteenth, of ointments, and of trees which grow near the sea-coast; the fourteenth, of vines; the fifteenth, of fruit-trees; the sixteenth, of forest-trees; the seventeenth, of the cultivation of trees; the eighteenth, of agriculture; the nineteenth, of the nature of lint, hemp, and similar productions; the twentieth, of the medicinal qualities of vegetables cultivated in gardens; the twenty-first, of flowers; the twenty-second, of the properties of herbs; the twenty-third, of the medicines yielded by cultivated trees; the twenty-fourth, of medicines derived from forest-trees; the twenty-fifth, of the properties of wild herbs, and the origin of their use; the twenty-sixth, of other remedies for diseases, and of some new diseases; the twenty-seventh, of different kinds of herbs; the twenty-eighth, twenty-ninth, and thirtieth, of medicines procured from animals; the thirty-first and thirty-second, of medicines obtained from aquatic animals, with some extraordinary facts relative to the subject; the thirty-third, of the nature of metals; the thirty-fourth, of brass, iron, lead, and tin; the thirty-fifth, of pictures, and observations relative to painting; the thirty-sixth, of the nature of stones and marbles; the thirty-seventh, of the origin of gems. To the contents of each book, the author subjoins a list of the writers from whom his observations have been collected.

Of Pliny's talents as a writer, it might be deemed presumptuous to form a decided opinion from his Natural History, which is avowedly a compilation from various authors, and executed with greater regard to the matter of the work, than to the elegance of composition. Making allowance, however, for a degree of credulity, common to the human mind in the early stage of physical (478) researches, he is far from being deficient in the essential qualifications of a writer of Natural History. His descriptions appear to be accurate, his observations precise, his narrative is in general perspicuous, and he often illustrates his subject by a vivacity of thought, as well as by a happy turn of expression. It has been equally his endeavour to give novelty to stale disquisitions, and authority to new observations. He has both removed the rust, and dispelled the obscurity, which enveloped the doctrines of many ancient naturalists; but, with all his care and industry, he has exploded fewer errors, and sanctioned a greater number of doubtful opinions, than was consistent with the exercise of unprejudiced and severe investigation.

Pliny was fifty-six years of age at the time of his death; the manner of which is accurately related by his nephew, the elegant Pliny the Younger, in a letter to Tacitus, who entertained a design of writing the life of the naturalist.

# TITUS FLAVIUS DOMITIANUS.

(479)

I. Domitian was born upon the ninth of the calends of November [24th October] [795], when his father was consul elect, (being to enter upon his office the month following,) in the sixth region of the city, at the Pomegranate 796 , in the house which he afterwards converted into a temple of the Flavian family. He is said to have spent the time of his youth in so much want and infamy, that he had not one piece of plate belonging to him; and it is well known, that Clodius Pollio, a man of pretorian rank, against whom there is a poem of Nero's extant, entitled Luscio, kept a note in his hand-writing, which he sometimes produced, in which Domitian made an assignation with him for the foulest purposes. Some, likewise, have said, that he prostituted himself to Nerva, who succeeded him. In the war with Vitellius, he fled into the Capitol with his uncle Sabinus, and a part of the troops they had in the city 797 . But the enemy breaking in, and the temple being set on fire, he hid himself all night with the sacristan; and next morning, assuming the disguise of a worshipper of Isis, and mixing with the priests of that idle superstition, he got over the Tiber 798 , with only one attendant, to the house of a woman who was the mother of one of his school-fellows, and lurked there so close, that, though the enemy, who were at his heels, searched very strictly after him, they could not discover him. At last, after the success of his party, appearing in public, and being unanimously saluted by the title of Caesar, he assumed the office of praetor of the City, with consular authority, but in fact had nothing but the name; for the jurisdiction he transferred to his next colleague. He used, however, his absolute (480) power so licentiously, that even then he plainly discovered what sort of prince he was likely to prove. Not to go into details, after he had made free with the wives of many men of distinction, he took Domitia Longina from her husband, Aelias Lamia, and married her; and in one day disposed of above twenty offices in the city and the provinces; upon which Vespasian said several times, "he wondered he did not send him a successor too."

II. He likewise designed an expedition into Gaul and Germany 799, without the least necessity for it, and contrary to the advice of all his father's friends; and this he did only with the view of equalling his brother in military achievements and glory. But for this he was severely reprimanded, and that he might the more effectually be reminded of his age and position, was made to live with his father, and his litter had to follow his father's and brother's carriage, as often as they went abroad; but he attended them in their triumph for the conquest of Judaea 800, mounted on a white horse. Of the six consulships which he held, only one was ordinary; and that he obtained by the cession and interest of his brother. He greatly affected a modest behaviour, and, above all, a taste for poetry; insomuch, that he rehearsed his performances in public, though it was an art he had formerly little cultivated, and which he afterwards despised and abandoned. Devoted, however, as he was at this time to poetical pursuits, yet when Vologesus, king of the Parthians, desired succours against the Alani, with one of Vespasian's sons to command them, he laboured hard to procure for himself that appointment. But the scheme proving abortive, he endeavoured by presents and promises to engage other kings of the East to make a similar request. After his father's death, he was for some time in doubt, whether he should not offer the soldiers a donative double to that of his brother, and made no scruple of saying frequently, "that he had been left his partner in the empire, but that his father's will had been fraudulently set aside." From that time forward, he was constantly engaged in plots against his brother, both publicly and privately; until, falling dangerously ill, he ordered all his attendants to (481) leave him, under pretence of his being dead, before he really was so; and, at his decease, paid him no other honour than that of enrolling him amongst the gods; and he often, both in speeches and edicts, carped at his memory by sneers and insinuations.

III. In the beginning of his reign, he used to spend daily an hour by himself in private, during which time he did nothing else but catch flies, and stick them through the body with a sharp pin. When some one therefore inquired, "whether any one was with the emperor," it was significantly answered by Vibius Crispus, "Not so much as a fly." Soon after his advancement, his wife Domitia, by whom he had a son in his second consulship, and whom the year following he complimented with the title of Augusta, being desperately in love with Paris, the actor, he put her away; but within a short time afterwards, being unable to bear the separation, he took her again, under pretence of complying with the people's importunity. During some time, there was in his administration a strange mixture of virtue and vice, until at last his virtues themselves degenerated into vices; being, as we may reasonably conjecture concerning his character, inclined to avarice through want, and to cruelty through fear.

IV. He frequently entertained the people with most magnificent and costly shows, not only in the amphitheatre, but the circus; where, besides the usual races with chariots drawn by two or four horses a-breast, he exhibited the representation of an engagement between both horse and foot, and a sea-fight in the amphitheatre. The people were also entertained with the chase of wild beasts and the combat of gladiators, even in the night-time, by torch-light. Nor did men only fight in these spectacles, but women also. He constantly attended at the games given by the quaestors, which had been disused for some time, but were revived by him; and upon those occasions, always gave the people the liberty of demanding two pair of gladiators out of his own school, who appeared last in court uniforms. Whenever he attended the shows of gladiators, there stood at his feet a little boy dressed in scarlet, with a prodigiously small head, with whom he used to talk very much, and sometimes seriously. We are assured, that he was (482) overheard asking him, "if he knew for what reason he had in the late appointment, made Metius Rufus governor of Egypt?" He presented the people with naval fights, performed by fleets almost as numerous as those usually employed in real engagements; making a vast lake near the Tiber 801 , and building seats round it. And he witnessed them himself during a very heavy rain. He likewise celebrated the Secular games 802 , reckoning not from the year in which they had been exhibited by Claudius, but from the time of Augustus's celebration of them. In these, upon the day of the Circensian sports, in order to have a hundred races performed, he reduced each course from seven rounds to five. He likewise instituted, in honour of Jupiter Capitolinus, a solemn contest in music to be performed every five years; besides horse-racing and gymnastic exercises, with more prizes than are at present allowed. There was also a public performance in elocution, both Greek and Latin and besides the musicians who sung to the harp, there were others who played concerted pieces or solos, without vocal accompaniment. Young girls also ran races in the Stadium, at which he presided in his sandals, dressed in a purple robe, made after the Grecian fashion, and wearing upon his head a golden crown bearing the effigies of Jupiter, Juno, and Minerva; with the flamen of Jupiter, and the college of priests sitting by his side in the same dress; excepting only that their crowns had also his own image on them. He celebrated also upon the Alban mount every year the festival of Minerva, for whom he had appointed a college of priests, out of which were chosen by lot persons to preside as governors over the college; who were obliged to entertain the people with extraordinary chases of wild-beasts, and stage-plays, besides contests for prizes in oratory and poetry. He thrice bestowed upon the people a largess of three hundred sesterces each man; and, at a public show of gladiators, a very plentiful feast. At the festival of the Seven Hills 803 , he distributed large hampers of provisions (483) to the senatorian and equestrian orders, and small baskets to the common people, and encouraged them to eat by setting them the example. The day after, he scattered among the people a variety of cakes and other delicacies to be scrambled for; and on the greater part of them falling amidst the seats of the crowd, he ordered five hundred tickets to be thrown into each range of benches belonging to the senatorian and equestrian orders.

V. He rebuilt many noble edifices which had been destroyed by fire, and amongst them the Capitol, which had been burnt down a second time 804 ; but all the inscriptions were in his own name, without the least mention of the original founders. He likewise erected a new temple in the Capitol to Jupiter Custos, and a forum, which is now called Nerva's 805 , as also the temple of the Flavian family 806 , a stadium 807 , an odeum 808 , and a naumachia 809 ; out of the stone dug from which, the sides of the Circus Maximus, which had been burnt down, were rebuilt.

VI. He undertook several expeditions, some from choice, and some from necessity. That against the Catti 810 was unprovoked, but that against the Sarmatians was necessary; an entire legion, with its commander, having been cut off by them. He sent two expeditions against the Dacians; the first upon the defeat of Oppius Sabinus, a man of consular rank; and (484) the other, upon that of Cornelius Fuscus, prefect of the pretorian cohorts, to whom he had entrusted the conduct of that war. After several battles with the Catti and Daci, he celebrated a double triumph. But for his successes against the Sarmatians, he only bore in procession the laurel crown to Jupiter Capitolinus. The civil war, begun by Lucius Antonius, governor of Upper Germany, he quelled, without being obliged to be personally present at it, with remarkable good fortune. For, at the very moment of joining battle, the Rhine suddenly thawing, the troops of the barbarians which were ready to join L. Antonius, were prevented from crossing the river. Of this victory he had notice by some presages, before the messengers who brought the news of it arrived. For upon the very day the battle was fought, a splendid eagle spread its wings round his statue at Rome, making most joyful cries. And shortly after, a rumour became common, that Antonius was slain; nay, many positively affirmed, that they saw his head brought to the city.

VII. He made many innovations in common practices. He abolished the Sportula 811 , and revived the old practice of regular suppers. To the four former parties in the Circensian games, he added two new, who were gold and scarlet. He prohibited the players from acting in the theatre, but permitted them the practice of their art in private houses. He forbad the castration of males; and reduced the price of the eunuchs who were still left in the hands of the dealers in slaves. On the occasion of a great abundance of wine, accompanied by a scarcity of corn, supposing that the tillage of the ground was neglected for the sake of attending too much to the cultivation of vineyards, he published a proclamation forbidding the planting of any new vines in Italy, and ordering the vines in the provinces to be cut down, nowhere permitting more than one half of them to remain 812 . But he did not persist in the execution of this project. Some of the greatest offices he conferred upon his freedmen and soldiers. He forbad two legions to be quartered in the same camp, and more than a thousand sesterces to be deposited by any soldier with the standards; because it was thought that Lucius Antonius had been encouraged in his late project by the large sum deposited in the military chest by the two legions which he had in the same winter-quarters. He made an addition to the soldiers' pay, of three gold pieces a year.

VIII. In the administration of justice he was diligent and assiduous; and frequently sat in the Forum out of course, to cancel the judgments of the court of The One Hundred, which had been procured through favour, or interest. He occasionally cautioned the judges of the court of recovery to beware of being too ready to admit claims for freedom brought before them. He set a mark of infamy upon judges who were convicted of taking bribes, as well as upon their assessors. He likewise instigated the tribunes of the people to prosecute a corrupt aedile for extortion, and to desire the senate to appoint judges for his trial. He likewise took such effectual care in punishing magistrates of the city, and governors of provinces, guilty of malversation, that they never were at any time more moderate or more just. Most of these, since his reign, we have seen prosecuted for crimes of various kinds. Having taken upon himself the reformation of the public manners, he restrained the licence of the populace in sitting promiscuously with the knights in the theatre. Scandalous libels, published to defame persons of rank, of either sex, he suppressed, and inflicted upon their authors a mark of infamy. He expelled a man of quaestorian rank from the senate, for practising mimicry and dancing. He debarred infamous women the use of litters; as also the right of receiving legacies, or inheriting estates. He struck out of the list of judges a Roman knight for taking again his wife whom he had divorced and prosecuted for adultery. He condemned several men of the senatorian and equestrian orders, upon the Scantinian law  813 . The lewdness of the Vestal Virgins, which had been overlooked by his father and brother, he punished severely, but in different ways; viz. offences committed before his reign, with death, and those since its commencement, according to ancient custom. For to the two sisters called Ocellatae, he gave liberty to choose the mode of death which they preferred, and banished (486) their paramours. But Cornelia, the president of the Vestals, who had formerly been acquitted upon a charge of incontinence, being a long time after again prosecuted and condemned, he ordered to be buried alive; and her gallants to be whipped to death with rods in the Comitium; excepting only a man of praetorian rank, to whom, because he confessed the fact, while the case was dubious, and it was not established against him, though the witnesses had been put to the torture, he granted the favour of banishment. And to preserve pure and undefiled the reverence due to the gods, he ordered the soldiers to demolish a tomb, which one of his freedmen had erected for his son out of the stones designed for the temple of Jupiter Capitolinus, and to sink in the sea the bones and relics buried in it.

IX. Upon his first succeeding to power, he felt such an abhorrence for the shedding of blood, that, before his father's arrival in Rome, calling to mind the verse of Virgil,

*Impia quam caesis gens est epulata juvencis, 814*
*Ere impious man, restrain'd from blood in vain,*
*Began to feast on flesh of bullocks slain,*

he designed to have published a proclamation, "to forbid the sacrifice of oxen." Before his accession to the imperial authority, and during some time afterwards, he scarcely ever gave the least grounds for being suspected of covetousness or avarice; but, on the contrary, he often afforded proofs, not only of his justice, but his liberality. To all about him he was generous even to profusion, and recommended nothing more earnestly to them than to avoid doing anything mean. He would not accept the property left him by those who had children. He also set aside a legacy bequeathed by the will of Ruscus Caepio, who had ordered "his heir to make a present yearly to each of the senators upon their first assembling." He exonerated all those who had been under prosecution from the treasury for above five years before; and would not suffer suits to be renewed, unless it was done within a year, and on condition, that the prosecutor should be banished, if he could not make good his cause. The secretaries of the quaestors having engaged in trade, according to custom, but contrary to (487) the Clodian law 815 , he pardoned them for what was past. Such portions of land as had been left when it was divided amongst the veteran soldiers, he granted to the ancient possessors, as belonging to then by prescription. He put a stop to false prosecutions in the exchequer, by severely punishing the prosecutors; and this saying of his was much taken notice of "that a prince who does not punish informers, encourages them."

X. But he did not long persevere in this course of clemency and justice, although he sooner fell into cruelty than into avarice. He put to death a scholar of Paris, the pantomimic 816 , though a minor, and then sick, only because, both in person and the practice of his art, he resembled his master; as he did likewise Hermogenes of Tarsus for some oblique reflections in his History; crucifying, besides, the scribes

who had copied the work. One who was master of a band of gladiators, happening to say, "that a Thrax was a match for a Marmillo 817, but not so for the exhibitor of the games", he ordered him to be dragged from the benches into the arena, and exposed to the dogs, with this label upon him, "A Parmularian 818 guilty of talking impiously." He put to death many senators, and amongst them several men of consular rank. In this number were, Civica Cerealis, when he was proconsul in Africa, Salvidienus Orfitus, and Acilius Glabrio in exile, under the pretence of their planning to revolt against him. The rest he punished upon very trivial occasions; as Aelius Lamia for some jocular expressions, which were of old date, and perfectly harmless; because, upon his commending his voice after he had taken his wife from him 819, he replied, "Alas! I hold my tongue." And when Titus advised him to take another wife, he answered him thus: "What! have you a mind to marry?" Salvius Cocceianus was condemned to death for keeping the birth-day of his uncle Otho, the emperor: Metius Pomposianus, because he was commonly reported to have an imperial nativity 820, and to carry about with (488) him a map of the world upon vellum, with the speeches of kings and generals extracted out of Titus Livius; and for giving his slaves the names of Mago and Hannibal; Sallustius Lucullus, lieutenant in Britain, for suffering some lances of a new invention to be called "Lucullean;" and Junius Rusticus, for publishing a treatise in praise of Paetus Thrasea and Helvidius Priscus, and calling them both "most upright men." Upon this occasion, he likewise banished all the philosophers from the city and Italy. He put to death the younger Helvidius, for writing a farce, in which, under the character of Paris and Oenone, he reflected upon his having divorced his wife; and also Flavius Sabinus, one of his cousins, because, upon his being chosen at the consular election to that office, the public crier had, by a blunder, proclaimed him to the people not consul, but emperor. Becoming still more savage after his success in the civil war, he employed the utmost industry to discover those of the adverse party who absconded: many of them he racked with a new-invented torture, inserting fire through their private parts; and from some he cut off their hands. It is certain, that only two of any note were pardoned, a tribune who wore the narrow stripe, and a centurion; who, to clear themselves from the charge of being concerned in any rebellious project, proved themselves to have been guilty of prostitution, and consequently incapable of exercising any influence either over the general or the soldiers.

XI. His cruelties were not only excessive, but subtle and unexpected. The day before he crucified a collector of his rents, he sent for him into his bed-chamber, made him sit down upon the bed by him, and sent him away well pleased, and, so far as could be inferred from his treatment, in a state of perfect security; having vouchsafed him the favour of a plate of meat from his own table. When he was on the point of condemning to death Aretinus Clemens, a man of consular rank, and one of his friends and emissaries, he retained him about his person in the same or greater favour than ever; until at last, as they were riding together in the same litter, upon seeing the man who had informed against him, he said, "Are you willing that we should hear this base slave tomorrow?" Contemptuously abusing the patience of men, he never pronounced a severe sentence without prefacing it (489) with words which gave hopes of mercy; so that, at last, there was not a more certain token of a fatal conclusion, than a mild commencement. He brought before the senate some persona accused of treason, declaring, "that he should prove that day how dear he was to the senate;" and so influenced them, that they condemned the accused to be punished according to the ancient usage 821 . Then, as if alarmed at the extreme severity of their punishment, to lessen the odiousness of the proceeding, he interposed in these words; for it is not foreign to the purpose to give them precisely as they were delivered: "Permit me, Conscript Fathers, so far to prevail upon your affection for me, however extraordinary the request may seem, as to grant the condemned criminals the favour of dying in the manner they choose. For by so doing, ye will spare your own eyes, and the world will understand that I interceded with the senate on their behalf."

XII. Having exhausted the exchequer by the expense of his buildings and public spectacles, with the augmentation of pay lately granted to the troops, he made an attempt at the reduction of the army, in order to lessen the military charges. But reflecting, that he should, by this measure, expose himself to the insults of the barbarians, while it would not suffice to extricate him from his embarrassments, he had recourse to plundering his subjects by every mode of exaction. The estates of the living and the dead were sequestered upon any accusation, by whomsoever preferred. The unsupported allegation of any one person, relative to a word or action construed to affect the dignity of the emperor, was sufficient. Inheritances, to which he had not the slightest pretension, were confiscated, if there was found so much as one person to say, he had heard from the deceased when living, "that he had made the emperor his heir." Besides the exactions from others, the poll-tax on the Jews was levied with extreme rigour, both on those who lived after the manner of Jews in the city, without publicly professing themselves to be such 822 , and on those who, by (490) concealing their origin, avoided paying the tribute imposed upon that people. I remember, when I was a youth, to have been present 823 , when an old man, ninety years of age, had his person exposed to view in a very crowded court, in order that, on inspection, the procurator might satisfy himself whether he was circumcised. 824

From his earliest years Domitian was any thing but courteous, of a forward, assuming disposition, and extravagant both in his words and actions. When Caenis, his father's concubine, upon her return from Istria, offered him a kiss, as she had been used to do, he presented her his hand to kiss. Being indignant, that his brother's son-in-law should be waited on by servants dressed in white 825 , he exclaimed,

*ouk agathon polykoiraniae.* 826_
*Too many princes are not good.*

XIII. After he became emperor, he had the assurance to boast in the senate, "that he had bestowed the empire on his father and brother, and they had restored it to him." And upon taking his wife again, after the divorce, he declared by proclamation, "that he had recalled her to his pulvinar." 827 He was not a little pleased too, at hearing the acclamations of the people in the amphitheatre on a day of festival, "All happiness to our lord and lady." But when, during the celebration of the Capitoline trial of skill, the whole concourse of people entreated him with one voice to restore Palfurius Sura to his place in the senate, from which he had been long before expelled—he having then carried away the prize of eloquence from all the orators who had contended for it,—he did not vouchsafe to give them any answer, but only commanded silence to be proclaimed by the voice of the crier. With equal arrogance, when he dictated the form of a letter to be used by his procurators, he began it thus: "Our lord and god commands so and so;" whence it became a rule that no one should (491) style him otherwise either in writing or speaking. He suffered no statues to be erected for him in the Capitol, unless they were of gold and silver, and of a certain weight. He erected so many magnificent gates and arches, surmounted by representations of chariots drawn by four horses, and other triumphal ornaments, in different quarters of the city, that a wag inscribed on one of the arches the Greek word Axkei, "It is enough." 828 He filled the office of consul seventeen times, which no one had ever done before him, and for the seven middle occasions in successive years; but in scarcely any of them had he more than the title; for he never continued in office beyond the calends of May [the 1st May], and for the most part only till the ides of January [13th January]. After his two triumphs, when he assumed the cognomen of Germanicus, he called the months of September and October, Germanicus and Domitian, after his own names, because he commenced his reign in the one, and was born in the other.

XIV. Becoming by these means universally feared and odious, he was at last taken off by a conspiracy of his friends and favourite freedmen, in concert with his wife 829 . He had long entertained a suspicion of the year and day when he should die, and even of the very hour and manner of his death; all which he had learned from the Chaldaeans, when he was a very young man. His father once at supper laughed at him for refusing to eat some mushrooms, saying, that if he knew his fate, he would rather be afraid of the sword. Being, therefore, in perpetual apprehension and anxiety, he was keenly alive to the slightest suspicions, insomuch that he is thought to have withdrawn the edict ordering the destruction of the vines, chiefly because the copies of it which were dispersed had the following lines written upon them:

> Kaen me phagaes epi rizanomos epi kartophoraeso,
> Osson epispeisai Kaisari thuomeno. 830_
> Gnaw thou my root, yet shall my juice suffice
> To pour on Caesar's head in sacrifice.

(492) It was from the same principle of fear, that he refused a new honour, devised and offered him by the senate, though he was greedy of all such compliments. It was this: "that as often as he held the consulship, Roman knights, chosen by lot, should walk before him, clad in the Trabea, with lances in their hands, amongst his lictors and apparitors." As the time of the danger which he apprehended drew near, he became daily more and more disturbed in mind; insomuch

that he lined the walls of the porticos in which he used to walk, with the stone called Phengites 831 , by the reflection of which he could see every object behind him. He seldom gave an audience to persons in custody, unless in private, being alone, and he himself holding their chains in his hand. To convince his domestics that the life of a master was not to be attempted upon any pretext, however plausible, he condemned to death Epaphroditus his secretary, because it was believed that he had assisted Nero, in his extremity, to kill himself.

XV. His last victim was Flavius Clemens 832 , his cousin-german, a man below contempt for his want of energy, whose sons, then of very tender age, he had avowedly destined for his successors, and, discarding their former names, had ordered one to be called Vespasian, and the other Domitian. Nevertheless, he suddenly put him to death upon some very slight suspicion 833 , almost before he was well out of his consulship. By this violent act he very much hastened his own destruction. During eight months together there was so much lightning at Rome, and such accounts of the phaenomenon were brought from other parts, that at last he cried out, "Let him now strike whom he will." The Capitol was struck by lightning, as well as the temple of the Flavian family, with the Palatine-house, and his own bed-chamber. The tablet also, inscribed upon the base of his triumphal statue was carried away by the violence of the storm, and fell upon a neighbouring (493) monument. The tree which just before the advancement of Vespasian had been prostrated, and rose again 834 , suddenly fell to the ground. The goddess Fortune of Praeneste, to whom it was his custom on new year's day to commend the empire for the ensuing year, and who had always given him a favourable reply, at last returned him a melancholy answer, not without mention of blood. He dreamt that Minerva, whom he worshipped even to a superstitious excess, was withdrawing from her sanctuary, declaring she could protect him no longer, because she was disarmed by Jupiter. Nothing, however, so much affected him as an answer given by Ascletario, the astrologer, and his subsequent fate. This person had been informed against, and did not deny his having predicted some future events, of which, from the principles of his art, he confessed he had a foreknowledge. Domitian asked him, what end he thought he should come to himself? To which replying, "I shall in a short time be torn to pieces by dogs," he ordered him immediately to be slain, and, in order to demonstrate the vanity of his art, to be carefully buried. But during the preparations for executing this order, it happened that the funeral pile was blown down by a sudden storm, and the body, half-burnt, was torn to pieces by dogs; which being observed by Latinus, the comic actor, as he chanced to pass that way, he told it, amongst the other news of the day, to the emperor at supper.

XVI. The day before his death, he ordered some dates 835, served up at table, to be kept till the next day, adding, "If I have the luck to use them." And turning to those who were nearest him, he said, "To-morrow the moon in Aquarius will be bloody instead of watery, and an event will happen, which will be much talked of all the world over." About midnight, he was so terrified that he leaped out of bed. That morning he tried and passed sentence on a soothsayer sent from Germany, who being consulted about the lightning that had lately (494) happened, predicted from it a change of government. The blood running down his face as he scratched an ulcerous tumour on his forehead, he said, "Would this were all that is to befall me!" Then, upon his asking the time of the day, instead of five o'clock, which was the hour he dreaded, they purposely told him it was six. Overjoyed at this information; as if all danger were now passed, and hastening to the bath, Parthenius, his chamberlain, stopped him, by saying that there was a person come to wait upon him about a matter of great importance, which would admit of no delay. Upon this, ordering all persons to withdraw, he retired into his chamber, and was there slain.

XVII. Concerning the contrivance and mode of his death, the common account is this. The conspirators being in some doubt when and where they should attack him, whether while he was in the bath, or at supper, Stephanus, a steward of Domitilla's 836, then under prosecution for defrauding his mistress, offered them his advice and assistance; and wrapping up his left arm, as if it was hurt, in wool and bandages for some days, to prevent suspicion, at the hour appointed, he secreted a dagger in them. Pretending then to make a discovery of a conspiracy, and being for that reason admitted, he presented to the emperor a memorial, and while he was reading it in great astonishment, stabbed him in the groin. But Domitian, though wounded, making resistance, Clodianus, one of his guards, Maximus, a freedman of Parthenius's, Saturius, his principal chamberlain, with some gladiators, fell upon him, and stabbed him in seven places. A boy who had the charge of the Lares in his bed-chamber, and was then in attendance as usual, gave these further particulars: that he was ordered by Domitian, upon receiving his first wound, to reach him a dagger which lay under his pillow, and call in his domestics; but that he found nothing at the head of the bed, excepting the hilt of a (495) poniard, and that all the doors were fastened: that the emperor in the mean time got hold of Stephanus, and throwing him upon the ground, struggled a long time with him; one while endeavouring to wrench the dagger from him, another while, though his fingers were miserably mangled, to tear out his eyes. He was slain upon the fourteenth of the calends of October [18th Sept.], in the forty-fifth year of his age, and the fifteenth of his reign 837. His corpse was carried out upon a common bier by the public bearers, and buried by his nurse Phyllis, at his suburban villa on the Latin Way. But she afterwards privately conveyed his remains to the temple of the Flavian family 838, and mingled them with the ashes of Julia, the daughter of Titus, whom she had also nursed.

XVIII. He was tall in stature, his face modest, and very ruddy; he had large eyes, but was dim-sighted; naturally graceful in his person, particularly in his youth, excepting only that his toes were bent somewhat inward, he was at last disfigured by baldness, corpulence, and the slenderness of his legs, which were reduced by a long illness. He was so sensible how much the modesty of his countenance recommended him, that he once made this boast to the senate, "Thus far you have approved both of my disposition and my countenance." His baldness so much annoyed him, that he considered it an affront to himself, if any other person was reproached with it, either in jest or in earnest; though in a small tract he published, addressed to a friend, "concerning the preservation of the hair," he uses for their mutual consolation the words following:

*Ouch oraas oios kago kalos te megas te;*
*Seest thou my graceful mien, my stately form?*

"and yet the fate of my hair awaits me; however, I bear with fortitude this loss of my hair while I am still young. Remember that nothing is more fascinating than beauty, but nothing of shorter duration."

XIX. He so shrunk from undergoing fatigue, that he scarcely ever walked through the city on foot. In his (496) expeditions and on a march, he seldom rode on horse-back; but was generally carried in a litter. He had no inclination for the exercise of arms, but was very expert in the use of the bow. Many persons have seen him often kill a hundred wild animals, of various kinds, at his Alban retreat, and fix his arrows in their heads with such dexterity, that he could, in two shots, plant them, like a pair of horns, in each. He would sometimes direct his arrows against the hand of a boy standing at a distance, and expanded as a mark, with such precision, that they all passed between the boy's fingers, without hurting him.

XX. In the beginning of his reign, he gave up the study of the liberal sciences, though he took care to restore, at a vast expense, the libraries which had been burnt down; collecting manuscripts from all parts, and sending scribes to Alexandria 839, either to copy or correct them. Yet he never gave himself the trouble of reading history or poetry, or of employing his pen even for his private purposes. He perused nothing but the Commentaries and Acts of Tiberius Caesar. His letters, speeches, and edicts, were all drawn up for him by others; though he could converse with elegance, and sometimes expressed himself in memorable sentiments. "I could wish," said he once, "that I was but as handsome as Metius fancies himself to be." And of the head of some one whose hair was partly reddish, and partly grey, he said, "that it was snow sprinkled with mead."

XXI. "The lot of princes," he remarked, "was very miserable, for no one believed them when they discovered a conspiracy, until they were murdered." When he had leisure, he amused himself with dice, even on days that were not festivals, and in the morning. He went to the bath early, and made a plentiful dinner, insomuch that he seldom ate more at supper than a Matian apple 840, to which he added a (497) draught of wine, out of a small flask. He gave frequent and splendid entertainments, but they were soon over, for he never prolonged them after sun-set, and indulged in no revel after. For, till bed-time, he did nothing else but walk by himself in private.

XXII. He was insatiable in his lusts, calling frequent commerce with women, as if it was a sort of exercise, klinopalaen, bed-wrestling; and it was reported that he plucked the hair from his concubines, and swam about in company with the lowest prostitutes. His brother's daughter 841 was offered him in marriage when she was a virgin; but being at that time enamoured of Domitia, he obstinately refused her. Yet not long afterwards, when she was given to another, he was ready enough to debauch her, and that even while Titus was living. But after she had lost both her father and her husband, he loved her most passionately, and without disguise; insomuch that he was the occasion of her death, by obliging her to procure a miscarriage when she was with child by him.

XXIII. The people shewed little concern at his death, but the soldiers were roused by it to great indignation, and immediately endeavoured to have him ranked among the gods. They were also ready to revenge his loss, if there had been any to take the lead. However, they soon after effected it, by resolutely demanding the punishment of all those who had been concerned in his assassination. On the other hand, the senate was so overjoyed, that they met in all haste, and in a full assembly reviled his memory in the most bitter terms; ordering ladders to be brought in, and his shields and images to be pulled down before their eyes, and dashed in pieces upon the floor of the senate-house passing at the same time a decree to obliterate his titles every where, and abolish all memory of him. A few months before he was slain, a raven on the Capitol uttered these words: "All will be well." Some person gave the following interpretation of this prodigy:

> (498) *Nuper Tarpeio quae sedit culmine cornix.*
> *"Est bene," non potuit dicere; dixit, "Erit."*
> Late croaked a raven from Tarpeia's height,
> "All is not yet, but shall be, right."

They say likewise that Domitian dreamed that a golden hump grew out of the back of his neck, which he considered as a certain sign of happy days for the empire after him. Such an auspicious change indeed shortly afterwards took place, through the justice and moderation of the succeeding emperors.

\* \* \* \* \* \*

If we view Domitian in the different lights in which he is represented, during his lifetime and after his decease, his character and conduct discover a greater diversity than is commonly observed in the objects of historical detail. But as posthumous character is always the most just, its decisive verdict affords the surest criterion by which this variegated emperor must be estimated by impartial posterity.

According to this rule, it is beyond a doubt that his vices were more predominant than his virtues: and when we follow him into his closet, for some time after his accession, when he was thirty years of age, the frivolity of his daily employment, in the killing of flies, exhibits an instance of dissipation, which surpasses all that has been recorded of his imperial predecessors. The encouragement, however, which the first Vespasian had shown to literature, continued to operate during the present reign; and we behold the first fruits of its auspicious influence in the valuable treatise of QUINTILIAN.

Of the life of this celebrated writer, little is known upon any authority that has a title to much credit. We learn, however, that he was the son of a lawyer in the service of some of the preceding emperors, and was born in Rome, though in what consulship, or under what emperor, it is impossible to determine. He married a woman of a noble family, by whom he had two sons. The mother died in the flower of her age, and the sons, at the distance of some time from each other, when their father was advanced in years. The precise time of Quintilian's own death is equally inauthenticated with that of his birth; nor can we rely upon an author of suspicious veracity, who says that he passed the latter part of his life in a state of indigence which was alleviated by the liberality of his pupil, Pliny the Younger. Quintilian opened a school of rhetoric at Rome, where he not only discharged that labourious employment with great applause, (499) during more than twenty years, but pleaded at the bar, and was the first who obtained a salary from the state, for executing the office of a public teacher. He was also appointed by Domitian preceptor to the two young princes who were intended to succeed him on the throne.

After his retirement from the situation of a teacher, Quintilian devoted his attention to the study of literature, and composed a treatise on the Causes of the Corruption of Eloquence. At the earnest solicitation of his friends, he was afterwards induced to undertake his Institutiones Oratoriae, the most elaborate system of oratory extant in any language. This work is divided into twelve books, in which the author treats with great precision of the qualities of a perfect orator; explaining not only the fundamental principles of eloquence, as connected with the constitution of the human mind, but pointing out, both by argument and observation, the most successful method of exercising that admirable art, for the accomplishment of its purpose.

So minutely, and upon so extensive a plan, has he prosecuted the subject, that he delineates the education suitable to a perfect orator, from the stage of infancy in the cradle, to the consummation of rhetorical fame, in the pursuits of the bar, or those, in general, of any public assembly. It is sufficient to say, that in the execution of this elaborate work, Quintilian has called to the assistance of his own acute and comprehensive understanding, the profound penetration of Aristotle, the exquisite graces of Cicero; all the stores of observation, experience, and practice; and in a word, the whole accumulated exertions of ancient genius on the subject of oratory.

It may justly be regarded as an extraordinary circumstance in the progress of scientific improvement, that the endowments of a perfect orator were never fully exhibited to the world, until it had become dangerous to exercise them for the important purposes for which they were originally cultivated. And it is no less remarkable, that, under all the violence and caprice of imperial despotism which the Romans had now experienced, their sensibility to the enjoyment of poetical compositions remained still unabated; as if it served to console the nation for the irretrievable loss of public liberty. From this source of entertainment, they reaped more pleasure during the present reign, than they had done since the time of Augustus. The poets of this period were Juvenal, Statius, and Martial.

JUVENAL was born at Aquinum, but in what year is uncertain; though, from some circumstances, it seems to have been in the reign of Augustus. Some say that he was the son of a freedman, (500) while others, without specifying the condition of his father, relate only that he was brought up by a freedman. He came at an early age to Rome, where he declaimed for many years, and, pleaded causes in the forum with great applause; but at last he betook himself to the writing of satires, in which he acquired great fame. One of the first, and the most constant object of is satire, was the pantomime Paris, the great favourite of the emperor Nero, and afterwards of Domitian. During the reign of the former of these emperors, no resentment was shown towards the poet; but he experienced not the same impunity after the accession of the latter; when, to remove him from the capital, he was sent as governor to the frontiers of Egypt, but in reality, into an honourable exile. According to some authors, he died of chagrin in that province: but this is not authenticated, and seems to be a mistake:

for in some of Martial's epigrams, which appear to have been written after the death of Domitian, Juvenal is spoken of as residing at Rome. It is said that he lived to upwards of eighty years of age.

The remaining compositions of this author are sixteen satires, all written against the dissipation and enormous vices which prevailed at Rome in his time. The various objects of animadversion are painted in the strongest colours, and placed in the most conspicuous points of view. Giving loose reins to just and moral indignation, Juvenal is every where animated, vehement, petulant, and incessantly acrimonious. Disdaining the more lenient modes of correction, or despairing of their success, he neither adopts the raillery of Horace, nor the derision of Persius, but prosecutes vice and folly with all the severity of sentiment, passion, and expression. He sometimes exhibits a mixture of humour with his invectives; but it is a humour which partakes more of virulent rage than of pleasantry; broad, hostile, but coarse, and rivalling in indelicacy the profligate manners which it assails. The satires of Juvenal abound in philosophical apophthegms; and, where they are not sullied by obscene description, are supported with a uniform air of virtuous elevation. Amidst all the intemperance of sarcasm, his numbers are harmonious. Had his zeal permitted him to direct the current of his impetuous genius into the channel of ridicule, and endeavour to put to shame the vices and follies of those licentious times, as much as he perhaps exasperated conviction rather than excited contrition, he would have carried satire to the highest possible pitch, both of literary excellence and moral utility. With every abatement of attainable perfection, we hesitate not to place him at the head of this arduous department of poetry.

Of STATIUS no farther particulars are preserved than that he (501) was born at Naples; that his father's name was Statius of Epirus, and his mother's Agelina, and that he died about the end of the first century of the Christian era. Some have conjectured that he maintained himself by writing for the stage, but of this there is no sufficient evidence; and if ever he composed dramatic productions, they have perished. The works of Statius now extant, are two poems, viz. the Thebais and the Achilleis, besides a collection, named Silvae.

The Thebais consists of twelve books, and the subject of it is the Theban war, which happened 1236 years before the Christian era, in consequence of a dispute between Eteocles and Polynices, the sons of Oedipus and Jocasta. These brothers had entered into an agreement with each other to reign alternately for a year at a time; and Eteocles being the elder, got first possession of the throne. This prince refusing to abdicate at the expiration of the year, Polynices fled to Argos, where marrying Argia, the daughter of Adrastus, king of that country, he procured the assistance of his father-in-law, to enforce the engagement stipulated with his brother Eteocles. The Argives marched under the command of seven able generals, who were to attack separately the seven gates of Thebes. After much blood had been spilt without any effect, it was at last agreed between the two parties, that the brothers should determine the dispute by single combat. In the desperate engagement which ensued, they both fell; and being burnt together upon the funeral pile, it is said that their ashes separated, as if actuated by the implacable resentment which they had borne to each other.

If we except the Aeneid, this is the only Latin production extant which is epic in its form; and it likewise approaches nearest in merit to that celebrated poem, which Statius appears to have been ambitious of emulating. In unity and greatness of action, the Thebais corresponds to the laws of the Epopea; but the fable may be regarded as defective in some particulars, which, however, arise more from the nature of the subject, than from any fault of the poet. The distinction of the hero is not sufficiently prominent; and the poem possesses not those circumstances which are requisite towards interesting the reader's affections in the issue of the contest. To this it may be added, that the unnatural complexion of the incestuous progeny diffuses a kind of gloom which obscures the splendour of thought, and restrains the sympathetic indulgence of fancy to some of the boldest excursions of the poet. For grandeur, however, and animation of sentiment and description, as well as for harmony of numbers, the Thebais is eminently conspicuous, and deserves to be held in a much higher degree of estimation than it has (502) generally obtained. In the contrivance of some of the episodes, and frequently in the modes of expression, Statius keeps an attentive eye to the style of Virgil. It is said that he was twelve years employed in the composition of this poem; and we have his own authority for affirming, that he polished it with all the care and assiduity practised by the poets in the Augustan age:

*Quippe, te fido monitore, nostra*

*Thebais, multa cruciata lima,*
*Tentat audaci fide Mantuanae*
*Gaudia famae.* – Silvae, lib. iv. 7.

For, taught by you, with steadfast care
I trim my "Song of Thebes," and dare
With generous rivalry to share
The glories of the Mantuan bard.

The Achilleis relates to the same hero who is celebrated by Homer in the Iliad; but it is the previous history of Achilles, not his conduct in the Trojan war, which forms the subject of the poem of Statius. While the young hero is under the care of the Centaur Chiron, Thetis makes a visit to the preceptor's sequestered habitation, where, to save her son from the fate which, it was predicted, would befall him at Troy, if he should go to the siege of that place, she orders him to be dressed in the disguise of a girl, and sent to live in the family of Lycomedes, king of Scyros. But as Troy could not be taken without the aid of Achilles, Ulysses, accompanied by Diomede, is deputed by the Greeks to go to Scyros, and bring him thence to the Grecian camp. The artifice by which the sagacious ambassador detected Achilles amongst his female companions, was by placing before them various articles of merchandise, amongst which was some armour. Achilles no sooner perceived the latter, than he eagerly seized a sword and shield, and manifesting the strongest emotions of heroic enthusiasm, discovered his sex. After an affectionate parting with Lycomedes' daughter, Deidamia, whom he left pregnant of a son, he set sail with the Grecian chiefs, and, during the voyage, gives them an account of the manner of his education with Chiron.

This poem consists of two books, in heroic measure, and is written with taste and fancy. Commentators are of opinion, that the Achilleis was left incomplete by the death of the author; but this is extremely improbable, from various circumstances, and appears to be founded only upon the word Hactenus, in the conclusion of the poem:

(503) *Hactenus annorum, comites, elementa meorum*
*Et memini, et meminisse juvat: scit caetera mater.*
Thus far, companions dear, with mindful joy I've told
My youthful deeds; the rest my mother can unfold.

That any consequential reference was intended by hactenus, seems to me plainly contradicted by the words which immediately follow, scit caetera mater. Statius could not propose the giving any further account of Achilles's life, because a general narrative of it had been given in the first book. The voyage from Scyros to the Trojan coast, conducted with the celerity which suited the purpose of the poet, admitted of no incidents which required description or recital: and after the voyagers had reached the Grecian camp, it is reasonable to suppose, that the action of the Iliad immediately commenced. But that Statius had no design of extending the plan of the Achilleis beyond this period, is expressly declared in the exordium of the poem:

*Magnanimum Aeaciden, formidatamque Tonanti*
*Progeniem, et patrio vetitam succedere coelo,*
*Diva, refer; quanquam acta viri multum inclyta cantu*
*Maeonio; sed plura vacant. Nos ire per omnem*
*(Sic amor est) heroa velis, Scyroque latentem*
*Dulichia proferre tuba: nec in Hectore tracto*
*Sistere, sed tota juvenem deducere Troja.*
Aid me, O goddess! while I sing of him,
Who shook the Thunderer's throne, and, for his crime,
Was doomed to lose his birthright in the skies;
The great Aeacides. Maeonian strains
Have made his mighty deeds their glorious theme;
Still much remains: be mine the pleasing task
To trace the future hero's young career,
Not dragging Hector at his chariot wheels,
But while disguised in Scyros yet he lurked,
Till trumpet-stirred, he sprung to manly arms,
And sage Ulysses led him to the Trojan coast.

The Silvae is a collection of poems almost entirely in heroic verse, divided into five books, and for the most part written extempore. Statius himself affirms, in his Dedication to Stella, that the production of none of them employed him more than two days; yet many of them consist of between one hundred and two hundred hexameter lines. We meet with one of two hundred and sixteen lines; one, of two hundred and thirty-four; one, of two hundred and sixty-two; and one of two hundred and seventy-seven; a rapidity of composition approaching to what Horace mentions of the poet Lucilius. It is no small encomium to observe, that, considered as extemporaneous productions, (504) the meanest in the collection is far from meriting censure, either in point of sentiment or expression; and many of them contain passages which command our applause.

The poet MARTIAL, surnamed likewise Coquus, was born at Bilbilis, in Spain, of obscure parents. At the age of twenty-one, he came to Rome, where he lived during five-and-thirty years under the emperors Galba, Otho, Vitellius, the two Vespasians, Domitian, Nerva, and the beginning of the reign of Trajan. He was the panegyrist of several of those emperors, by whom he was liberally rewarded, raised to the Equestrian order, and promoted by Domitian to the tribuneship; but being treated with coldness and neglect by Trajan, he returned to his native country, and, a few years after, ended his days, at the age of seventy-five.

He had lived at Rome in great splendour and affluence, as well as in high esteem for his poetical talents; but upon his return to Bilbilis, it is said that he experienced a great reverse of fortune, and was chiefly indebted for his support to the gratuitous benefactions of Pliny the Younger, whom he had extolled in some epigrams.

The poems of Martial consist of fourteen books, all written in the epigrammatic form, to which species of composition, introduced by the Greeks, he had a peculiar propensity. Amidst such a multitude of verses, on a variety of subjects, often composed extempore, and many of them, probably, in the moments of fashionable dissipation, it is not surprising that we find a large number unworthy the genius of the author. Delicacy, and even decency, is often violated in the productions of Martial. Grasping at every thought which afforded even the shadow of ingenuity, he gave unlimited scope to the exercise of an active and fruitful imagination. In respect to composition, he is likewise liable to censure. At one time he wearies, and at another tantalises the reader, with the prolixity or ambiguity of his preambles. His prelusive sentiments are sometimes far-fetched, and converge not with a natural declination into the focus of epigram. In dispensing praise and censure, he often seems to be governed more by prejudice or policy, than by justice and truth; and he is more constantly attentive to the production of wit, than to the improvement of morality.

But while we remark the blemishes and imperfections of this poet, we must acknowledge his extraordinary merits. In composition he is, in general, elegant and correct; and where the subject is capable of connection with sentiment, his inventive ingenuity never fails to extract from it the essence of delight and surprise. His fancy is prolific of beautiful images, and his (505) judgment expert in arranging them to the greatest advantage. He bestows panegyric with inimitable grace, and satirises with equal dexterity. In a fund of Attic salt, he surpasses every other writer; and though he seems to have at command all the varied stores of gall, he is not destitute of candour. With almost every kind of versification he appears to be familiar; and notwithstanding a facility of temper, too accommodating, perhaps, on many occasions, to the licentiousness of the times, we may venture from strong indications to pronounce, that, as a moralist, his principles were virtuous. It is observed of this author, by Pliny the Younger, that, though his compositions might, perhaps, not obtain immortality, he wrote as if they would. [Aeterna, quae scripsit, non erunt fortasse: ille tamen scripsit tanquam futura.] The character which Martial gives of his epigrams, is just and comprehensive:

*Sunt bona, sunt quaedam mediocria, sunt mala plura,*
*Quae legis: hic aliter non fit, Avite, liber.*
*Some are good, some indifferent, and some again still worse;*
*Such, Avitus, you will find is a common case with verse.*

THE END OF THE TWELVE CAESARS

# LIVES OF EMINENT GRAMMARIANS

(506)

I. The science of grammar 842 was in ancient times far from being in vogue at Rome; indeed, it was of little use in a rude state of society, when the people were engaged in constant wars, and had not much time to bestow on the cultivation of the liberal arts 843. At the outset, its pretensions were very slender, for the earliest men of learning, who were both poets and orators, may be considered as half-Greek: I speak of Livius 844 and Ennius 845, who are acknowledged to have taught both languages as well at Rome as in foreign parts 846. But they (507) only translated from the Greek, and if they composed anything of their own in Latin, it was only from what they had before read. For although there are those who say that this Ennius published two books, one on "Letters and Syllables," and the other on "Metres," Lucius Cotta has satisfactorily proved that they are not the works of the poet Ennius, but of another writer of the same name, to whom also the treatise on the "Rules of Augury" is attributed.

II. Crates of Mallos 847, then, was, in our opinion, the first who introduced the study of grammar at Rome. He was cotemporary with Aristarchus 848, and having been sent by king Attalus as envoy to the senate in the interval between the second and third Punic wars 849, soon after the death of Ennius 850, he had the misfortune to fall into an open sewer in the Palatine quarter of the city, and broke his leg. After which, during the whole period of his embassy and convalescence, he gave frequent lectures, taking much pains to instruct his hearers, and he has left us an example well worthy of imitation. It was so far followed, that poems hitherto little known, the works either of deceased friends or other approved writers, were brought to light, and being read and commented on, were explained to others. Thus, Caius Octavius Lampadio edited the Punic War of Naevius 851, which having been written in one volume without any break in the manuscript, he divided into seven books. After that, Quintus Vargonteius undertook the Annals of Ennius, which he read on certain fixed days to crowded audiences. So Laelius Archelaus, and Vectius Philocomus, read and commented on the Satires of their friend Lucilius 852, which Lenaeus Pompeius, a freedman, tells us he studied under Archelaus; and Valerius Cato, under Philocomus. Two others also taught and promoted (508) grammar in various branches, namely, Lucius Aelius Lanuvinus, the son-in-law of Quintus Aelius, and Servius Claudius, both of whom were Roman knights, and men who rendered great services both to learning and the republic.

III. Lucius Aelius had a double cognomen, for he was called Praeconius, because his father was a herald; Stilo, because he was in the habit of composing orations for most of the speakers of highest rank; indeed, he was so strong a partisan of the nobles, that he accompanied Quintus Metellus Numidicus 853 in his exile. Servius 854 having clandestinely obtained his father-in-law's book before it was published, was disowned for the fraud, which he took so much to heart, that, overwhelmed with shame and distress, he retired from Rome; and being seized with a fit of the gout, in his impatience, he applied a poisonous ointment to his feet, which half-killed him, so that his lower limbs mortified while he was still alive. After this, more attention was paid to the science of letters, and it grew in public estimation, insomuch, that men of the highest rank did not hesitate in undertaking to write something on the subject; and it is related that sometimes there were no less than twenty celebrated scholars in Rome. So high was the value, and so great were the rewards, of grammarians, that Lutatius Daphnides, jocularly called "Pan's herd" 855 by Lenaeus Melissus, was purchased by Quintus Catullus for two hundred thousand sesterces, and shortly afterwards made a freedman; and that Lucius Apuleius, who was taken into the pay of Epicius Calvinus, a wealthy Roman knight, at the annual salary of ten thousand crowns, had many scholars. Grammar also penetrated into the provinces, and some of the most eminent amongst the learned taught it in foreign parts, particularly in Gallia Togata. In the number of these, we may reckon Octavius (509) Teucer, Siscennius Jacchus, and Oppius Cares 856, who persisted in teaching to a most advanced period of his life, at a time when he was not only unable to walk, but his sight failed.

IV. The appellation of grammarian was borrowed from the Greeks; but at first, the Latins called such persons literati. Cornelius Nepos, also, in his book, where he draws a distinction between a literate and a philologist, says that in common phrase, those are properly called literati who are skilled in speaking or writing with care or accuracy, and those more especially deserve the name who translated the poets, and were called grammarians by the Greeks. It appears that they were named literators by Messala Corvinus, in one of his letters, when he says, "that it does not refer to Furius Bibaculus, nor even to Sigida, nor to Cato, the literator," 857 meaning, doubtless, that Valerius Cato was both a poet and an eminent grammarian. Some there are who draw a distinction between a literati and a literator, as the Greeks do between a grammarian and a grammatist, applying the former term to men of real erudition, the latter to those whose pretensions to learning are moderate; and this opinion Orbilius supports by examples. For he says that in old times, when a company of slaves was offered for sale by any person, it was not customary, without good reason, to describe either of them in the catalogue as a literati, but only as a literator, meaning that he was not a proficient in letters, but had a smattering of knowledge.

The early grammarians taught rhetoric also, and we have many of their treatises which include both sciences; whence it arose, I think, that in later times, although the two professions had then become distinct, the old custom was retained, or the grammarians introduced into their teaching some of the elements required for public speaking, such as the problem, the periphrasis, the choice of words, description of character, and the like; in order that they might not transfer (510) their pupils to the rhetoricians no better than ill-taught boys. But I perceive that these lessons are now given up in some cases, on account of the want of application, or the tender years, of the scholar, for I do not believe that it arises from any dislike in the master. I recollect that when I was a boy it was the custom of one of these, whose name was Princeps, to take alternate days for declaiming and disputing; and sometimes he would lecture in the morning, and declaim in the afternoon, when he had his pulpit removed. I heard, also, that even within the memories of our own fathers, some of the pupils of the grammarians passed directly from the schools to the courts, and at once took a high place in the ranks of the most distinguished advocates. The professors at that time were, indeed, men of great eminence, of some of whom I may be able to give an account in the following chapters.

V. SAEVIUS 858 NICANOR first acquired fame and reputation by his teaching: and, besides, he made commentaries, the greater part of which, however, are said to have been borrowed. He also wrote a satire, in which he informs us that he was a freedman, and had a double cognomen, in the following verses;

Saevius Nicanor Marci libertus negabit,
Saevius Posthumius idem, sed Marcus, docebit.
What Saevius Nicanor, the freedman of Marcus, will deny,
The same Saevius, called also Posthumius Marcus, will assert.

It is reported, that in consequence of some infamy attached to his character, he retired to Sardinia, and there ended his days.

VI. AURELIUS OPILIUS 859, the freedman of some Epicurean, first taught philosophy, then rhetoric, and last of all, grammar. (511) Having closed his school, he followed Rutilius Rufus, when he was banished to Asia, and there the two friends grew old together. He also wrote several volumes on a variety of learned topics, nine books of which he distinguished by the number and names of the nine Muses; as he says, not without reason, they being the patrons of authors and poets. I observe that its title is given in several indexes by a single letter, but he uses two in the heading of a book called Pinax.

VII. MARCUS ANTONIUS GNIPHO 860, a free-born native of Gaul, was exposed in his infancy, and afterwards received his freedom from his foster-father; and, as some say, was educated at Alexandria, where Dionysius Scytobrachion 861 was his fellow pupil. This, however, I am not very ready to believe, as the times at which they flourished scarcely agree. He is said to have been a man of great genius, of singular memory, well read in Greek as well as Latin, and of a most obliging and agreeable temper, who never haggled about remuneration, but generally left it to the liberality of his scholars. He first taught in the house of Julius Caesar 862, when the latter was yet but a boy, and, afterwards, in his own private house. He gave instruction in rhetoric also, teaching the rules of eloquence every day, but declaiming only on festivals. It is said that some very celebrated men frequented his school, —and, among others, Marcus Cicero, during the time he held the praetorship 863 . He wrote a number of works, although he did not live beyond his fiftieth year; but Atteius, the philologist 864 , says, that he left only two volumes, "De Latino Sermone;" and, that the other works ascribed to him, were composed by his disciples, and were not his, although his name is sometimes to be found in them.

VIII. M. POMPILIUS ANDRONICUS, a native of Syria, while he professed to be a grammarian, was considered an idle follower of the Epicurean sect, and little qualified to be a master (512) of a school. Finding, therefore, that, at Rome, not only Antonius Gnipho, but even other teachers of less note were preferred to him, he retired to Cumae, where he lived at his ease; and, though he wrote several books, he was so needy, and reduced to such straits, as to be compelled to sell that excellent little work of his, "The Index to the Annals," for sixteen thousand sesterces. Orbilius has informed us, that he redeemed this work from the oblivion into which it had fallen, and took care to have it published with the author's name.

IX. ORBILIUS PUPILLUS, of Beneventum, being left an orphan, by the death of his parents, who both fell a sacrifice to the plots of their enemies on the same day, acted, at first, as apparitor to the magistrates. He then joined the troops in Macedonia, when he was first decorated with the plumed helmet 865 , and, afterwards, promoted to serve on horseback. Having completed his military service, he resumed his studies, which he had pursued with no small diligence from his youth upwards; and, having been a professor for a long period in his own country, at last, during the consulship of Cicero, made his way to Rome, where he taught with more reputation than profit. For in one of his works he says, that "he was then very old, and lived in a garret." He also published a book with the title of Perialogos; containing complaints of the injurious treatment to which professors submitted, without seeking redress at the hands of parents. His sour temper betrayed itself, not only in his disputes with the sophists opposed to him, whom he lashed on every occasion, but also towards his scholars, as Horace tells us, who calls him "a flogger;" 866 and Domitius Marsus 867 , who says of him:

> Si quos Orbilius ferula scuticaque cecidit.
> If those Orbilius with rod or ferule thrashed.

(513) And not even men of rank escaped his sarcasms; for, before he became noticed, happening to be examined as a witness in a crowded court, Varro, the advocate on the other side, put the question to him, "What he did and by what profession he gained his livelihood?" He replied, "That he lived by removing hunchbacks from the sunshine into the shade," alluding to Muraena's deformity. He lived till he was near a hundred years old; but he had long lost his memory, as the verse of Bibaculus informs us:

*Orbilius ubinam est, literarum oblivio?*
Where is Orbilius now, that wreck of learning lost?

His statue is shown in the Capitol at Beneventum. It stands on the left hand, and is sculptured in marble 868, representing him in a sitting posture, wearing the pallium, with two writing-cases in his hand. He left a son, named also Orbilius, who, like his father, was a professor of grammar.

X. ATTEIUS, THE PHILOLOGIST, a freedman, was born at Athens. Of him, Capito Atteius 869, the well-known jurisconsult, says that he was a rhetorician among the grammarians, and a grammarian among the rhetoricians. Asinius Pollio 870, in the book in which he finds fault with the writings of Sallust for his great affectation of obsolete words, speaks thus: "In this work his chief assistant was a certain Atteius, a man of rank, a splendid Latin grammarian, the aider and preceptor of those who studied the practice of declamation; in short, one who claimed for himself the cognomen of Philologus." Writing to Lucius Hermas, he says, "that he had made great proficiency in Greek literature, and some in Latin; that he had been a hearer of Antonius Gnipho, and his Hermas 871, and afterwards began to teach others. Moreover, that he had for pupils many illustrious youths, among whom were the two (514) brothers, Appius and Pulcher Claudius; and that he even accompanied them to their province." He appears to have assumed the name of Philologus, because, like Eratosthenes 872, who first adopted that cognomen, he was in high repute for his rich and varied stores of learning; which, indeed, is evident from his commentaries, though but few of them are extant. Another letter, however, to the same Hermas, shews that they were very numerous: "Remember," it says, "to recommend generally our Extracts, which we have collected, as you know, of all kinds, into eight hundred books." He afterwards formed an intimate acquaintance with Caius

Sallustius, and, on his death, with Asinius Pollio; and when they undertook to write a history, he supplied the one with short annals of all Roman affairs, from which he could select at pleasure; and the other, with rules on the art of composition. I am, therefore, surprised that Asinius Pollio should have supposed that he was in the habit of collecting old words and figures of speech for Sallust, when he must have known that his own advice was, that none but well known, and common and appropriate expressions should be made use of; and that, above all things, the obscurity of the style of Sallust, and his bold freedom in translations, should be avoided.

XI. VALERIUS CATO was, as some have informed us, the freedman of one Bursenus, a native of Gaul. He himself tells us, in his little work called "Indignatio," that he was born free, and being left an orphan, was exposed to be easily stripped of his patrimony during the licence of Sylla's administrations. He had a great number of distinguished pupils, and was highly esteemed as a preceptor suited to those who had a poetical turn, as appears from these short lines:

*Cato grammaticus, Latina Siren,*
*Qui solus legit ac facit poetas.*
*Cato, the Latin Siren, grammar taught and verse,*
*To form the poet skilled, and poetry rehearse.*

Besides his Treatise on Grammar, he composed some poems, (515) of which, his Lydia and Diana are most admired. Ticida mentions his "Lydia."

*Lydia, doctorum maxima cura liber.*
*"Lydia," a work to men of learning dear.*

Cinna 873 thus notices the "Diana."

*Secula permaneat nostri Diana Catonis.*
*Immortal be our Cato's song of Dian.*

He lived to extreme old age, but in the lowest state of penury, and almost in actual want; having retired to a small cottage when he gave up his Tusculan villa to his creditors; as Bibaculus tells us:

*Si quis forte mei domum Catonis,*
*Depictas minio assulas, et illos*
*Custodis vidit hortulos Priapi,*
*Miratur, quibus ille disciplinis,*

*Tantam sit sapientiam assecutus,*
*Quam tres cauliculi et selibra farris;*
*Racemi duo, tegula sub una,*
*Ad summam prope nutriant senectam.*

"If, perchance, any one has seen the house of my Cato, with marble slabs of the richest hues, and his gardens worthy of having Priapus 874 for their guardian, he may well wonder by what philosophy he has gained so much wisdom, that a daily allowance of three coleworts, half-a-pound of meal, and two bunches of grapes, under a narrow roof, should serve for his subsistence to extreme old age."

And he says in another place:
*Catonis modo, Galle, Tusculanum*
*Tota creditor urbe venditabat.*
*Mirati sumus unicum magistrum,*
*Summum grammaticum, optimum poëtam,*
*Omnes solvere posse quaestiones,*
*Unum difficile expedire nomen.*
*En cor Zenodoti, en jecur Cratetis!*

"We lately saw, my Gallus, Cato's Tusculan villa exposed to public sale by his creditors; and wondered that such an unrivalled master of (516) the schools, most eminent grammarian, and accomplished poet, could solve all propositions and yet found one question too difficult for him to settle,—how to pay his debts. We find in him the genius of Zenodotus 875, the wisdom of Crates." 876

XII. CORNELIUS EPICADIUS, a freedman of Lucius Cornelius Sylla, the dictator, was his apparitor in the Augural priesthood, and much beloved by his son Faustus; so that he was proud to call himself the freedman of both. He completed the last book of Sylla's Commentaries, which his patron had left unfinished. 877

XIII. LABERIUS HIERA was bought by his master out of a slave-dealer's cage, and obtained his freedom on account of his devotion to learning. It is reported that his disinterestedness was such, that he gave gratuitous instruction to the children of those who were proscribed in the time of Sylla.

XIV. CURTIUS NICIA was the intimate friend of Cneius Pompeius and Caius Memmius; but having carried notes from Memmius to

Pompey's wife 878, when she was debauched by Memmius, Pompey was indignant, and forbad him his house. He was also on familiar terms with Marcus Cicero, who thus speaks of him in his epistle to Dolabella 879 : "I have more need of receiving letters from you, than you have of desiring them from me. For there is nothing going on at Rome in which I think you would take any interest, except, perhaps, that you may like to know that I am appointed umpire between our friends Nicias and Vidius. The one, it appears, alleges in two short verses that Nicias owes him (517) money; the other, like an Aristarchus, cavils at them. I, like an old critic, am to decide whether they are Nicias's or spurious."

Again, in a letter to Atticus 880, he says: "As to what you write about Nicias, nothing could give me greater pleasure than to have him with me, if I was in a position to enjoy his society; but my province is to me a place of retirement and solitude. Sicca easily reconciled himself to this state of things, and, therefore, I would prefer having him. Besides, you are well aware of the feebleness, and the nice and luxurious habits, of our friend Nicias. Why should I be the means of making him uncomfortable, when he can afford me no pleasure? At the same time, I value his goodwill."

XV. LENAEUS was a freedman of Pompey the Great, and attended him in most of his expeditions. On the death of his patron and his sons, he supported himself by teaching in a school which he opened near the temple of Tellus, in the Carium, in the quarter of the city where the house of the Pompeys stood 881. Such was his regard for his patron's memory, that when Sallust described him as having a brazen face, and a shameless mind, he lashed the historian in a most bitter satire 882, as "a bull's-pizzle, a gormandizer, a braggart, and a tippler, a man whose life and writings were equally monstrous;" besides charging him with being "a most unskilful plagiarist, who borrowed the language of Cato and other old writers." It is related, that, in his youth, having escaped from slavery by the contrivance of some of his friends, he took refuge in his own country; and, that after he had applied himself to the liberal arts, he brought the price of his freedom to his former master, who, however, struck by his talents and learning, gave him manumission gratuitously.

XVI. QUINTUS CAECILIUS, an Epirot by descent, but born at Tusculum, was a freedman of Atticus Satrius, a Roman (518) knight, to whom Cicero addressed his Epistles 883. He became the tutor of his patron's daughter 884, who was contracted to Marcus Agrippa, but being suspected of an illicit intercourse with her, and sent away on that account, he betook himself to Cornelius Gallus, and lived with him on terms of the greatest intimacy, which, indeed, was imputed to Gallus as one of his heaviest offences, by Augustus. Then, after the condemnation and death of Gallus 885, he opened a school, but had few pupils, and those very young, nor any belonging to the higher orders, excepting the children of those he could not refuse to admit. He was the first, it is said, who held disputations in Latin, and who began to lecture on Virgil and the other modern poets; which the verse of Domitius Marcus 886 points out.

*Epirota tenellorum nutricula vatum.*

The Epirot who,
With tender care, our unfledged poets nursed.

XVII. VERRIUS FLACCUS 887, a freedman, distinguished himself by a new mode of teaching; for it was his practice to exercise the wits of his scholars, by encouraging emulation among them; not only proposing the subjects on which they were to write, but offering rewards for those who were successful in the contest. These consisted of some ancient, handsome, or rare book. Being, in consequence, selected by Augustus, as preceptor to his grandsons, he transferred his entire school to the Palatium, but with the understanding that he should admit no fresh scholars. The hall in Catiline's house, (519) which had then been added to the palace, was assigned him for his school, with a yearly allowance of one hundred thousand sesterces. He died of old age, in the reign of Tiberius. There is a statue of him at Praeneste, in the semi-circle at the lower side of the forum, where he had set up calendars arranged by himself, and inscribed on slabs of marble.

XVIII. LUCIUS CRASSITIUS, a native of Tarentum, and in rank a freedman, had the cognomen of Pasides, which he afterwards changed for Pansa. His first employment was connected with the stage, and his business was to assist the writers of farces. After that, he took to giving lessons in a gallery attached to a house, until his commentary on "The Smyrna" 888 so brought him into notice, that the following lines were written on him:

*Uni Crassitio se credere Smyrna probavit.*

*Desinite indocti, conjugio hanc petere.*
*Soli Crassitio se dixit nubere velle:*
*Intima cui soli nota sua exstiterint.*

*Crassitius only counts on Smyrna's love,*
*Fruitless the wooings of the unlettered prove;*
*Crassitius she receives with loving arms,*
*For he alone unveiled her hidden charms.*

However, after having taught many scholars, some of whom were of high rank, and amongst others, Julius Antonius, the triumvir's son, so that he might be even compared with Verrius Flaccus; he suddenly closed his school, and joined the sect of Quintus Septimius, the philosopher.

XIX. SCRIBONIUS APHRODISIUS, the slave and disciple of Orbilius, who was afterwards redeemed and presented with his freedom by Scribonia 889, the daughter of Libo who had been the wife of Augustus, taught in the time of Verrius; whose books on Orthography he also revised, not without some severe remarks on his pursuits and conduct.

XX. C. JULIUS HYGINUS, a freedman of Augustus, was a native of Spain, (although some say he was born at Alexandria,) (520) and that when that city was taken, Caesar brought him, then a boy, to Rome. He closely and carefully imitated Cornelius Alexander 890, a Greek grammarian, who, for his antiquarian knowledge, was called by many Polyhistor, and by some History. He had the charge of the Palatine library, but that did not prevent him from having many scholars; and he was one of the most intimate friends of the poet Ovid, and of Caius Licinius, the historian, a man of consular rank 891, who has related that Hyginus died very poor, and was supported by his liberality as long as he lived. Julius Modestus 892, who was a freedman of Hyginus, followed the footsteps of his patron in his studies and learning.

XXI. CAIUS MELISSUS 893, a native of Spoletum, was free-born, but having been exposed by his parents in consequence of quarrels between them, he received a good education from his foster-father, by whose care and industry he was brought up, and was made a present of to Mecaenas, as a grammarian. Finding himself valued and treated as a friend, he preferred to continue in his state of servitude, although he was claimed by his mother, choosing rather his present condition than that which his real origin entitled him to. In consequence, his freedom was speedily given him, and he even became a favourite with Augustus. By his appointment he was made curator of the library in the portico of Octavia 894 ; and, as he himself informs us, undertook to compose, when he was a sexagenarian, his books of "Witticisms," which are now called "The Book of Jests." Of these he accomplished one hundred and fifty, to which he afterwards added several more. He (521) also composed a new kind of story about those who wore the toga, and called it "Trabeat." 895

XXII. MARCUS POMPONIUS MARCELLUS, a very severe critic of the Latin tongue, who sometimes pleaded causes, in a certain address on the plaintiff's behalf, persisted in charging his adversary with making a solecism, until Cassius Severus appealed to the judges to grant an adjournment until his client should produce another grammarian, as he was not prepared to enter into a controversy respecting a solecism, instead of defending his client's rights. On another occasion, when he had found fault with some expression in a speech made by Tiberius, Atteius Capito 896 affirmed, "that if it was not Latin, at least it would be so in time to come;" "Capito is wrong," cried Marcellus; "it is certainly in your power, Caesar, to confer the freedom of the city on whom you please, but you cannot make words for us." Asinius Gallus 897 tells us that he was formerly a pugilist, in the following epigram.

> Qui caput ad laevam deicit, glossemata nobis
> Praecipit; os nullum, vel potius pugilis.
> Who ducked his head, to shun another's fist,
> Though he expound old saws, – yet, well I wist,
> With pummelled nose and face, he's but a pugilist.

XXIII. REMMIUS PALAEMON 898, of Vicentia 899, the offspring of a bond-woman, acquired the rudiments of learning, first as the companion of a weaver's, and then of his master's, son, at school. Being afterwards made free, he taught at Rome, where he stood highest in the rank of the grammarians; but he was so infamous for every sort of vice, that Tiberius and his successor Claudius publicly denounced him as an improper person to have the education of boys and young men entrusted to him. Still, his powers of narrative and agreeable style of speaking made him very popular; besides which, he had the gift of making extempore verses. He also wrote a great many in (522) various and uncommon metres. His insolence was such, that he called Marcus Varro "a hog;" and bragged that "letters were born and would perish with him;" and that "his name was not introduced inadvertently in the Bucolics 900, as Virgil divined that a Palaemon would some day be the judge of all poets and poems." He also boasted, that having once fallen into the hands of robbers, they spared him on account of the celebrity his name had acquired.

He was so luxurious, that he took the bath many times in a day; nor did his means suffice for his extravagance, although his school brought him in forty thousand sesterces yearly, and he received not much less from his private estate, which he managed with great care. He also kept a broker's shop for the sale of old clothes; and it is well known that a vine 901, he planted himself, yielded three hundred and fifty bottles of wine. But the greatest of all his vices was his unbridled licentiousness in his commerce with women, which he carried to the utmost pitch of foul indecency 902. They tell a droll story of some one who met him in a crowd, and upon his offering to kiss him, could not escape the salute, "Master," said he, "do you want to mouth every one you meet with in a hurry?"

XXIV. MARCUS VALERIUS PROBUS, of Berytus 903, after long aspiring to the rank of centurion, being at last tired of waiting, devoted himself to study. He had met with some old authors at a bookseller's shop in the provinces, where the memory of ancient times still lingers, and is not quite forgotten, as it is at Rome. Being anxious carefully to reperuse these, and afterwards to make acquaintance with other works of the same kind, he found himself an object of contempt, and was laughed (523) at for his lectures, instead of their gaining him fame or profit. Still, however, he persisted in his purpose, and employed himself in correcting, illustrating, and adding notes to many works which he had collected, his labours being confined to the province of a grammarian, and nothing more. He had, properly speaking, no scholars, but some few followers. For he never taught in such a way as to maintain the character of a master; but was in the habit of admitting one or two, perhaps at most three or four, disciples in the afternoon; and while he lay at ease and chatted freely on ordinary topics, he occasionally read some book to them, but that did not often happen. He published a few slight treatises on some subtle questions, besides which, he left a large collection of observations on the language of the ancients.

# LIVES OF EMINENT RHETORICIANS.

(524)

I. Rhetoric, also, as well as Grammar, was not introduced amongst us till a late period, and with still more difficulty, inasmuch as we find that, at times, the practice of it was even prohibited. In order to leave no doubt of this, I will subjoin an ancient decree of the senate, as well as an edict of the censors:—"In the consulship of Caius Fannius Strabo, and Marcus Palerius Messala 904 : the praetor Marcus Pomponius moved the senate, that an act be passed respecting Philosophers and Rhetoricians. In this matter, they have decreed as follows: 'It shall be lawful for M. Pomponius, the praetor, to take such measures, and make such provisions, as the good of the Republic, and the duty of his office, require, that no Philosophers or Rhetoricians be suffered at Rome.'"

After some interval, the censor Cnaeus Domitius Aenobarbus and Lucius Licinius Crassus issued the following edict upon the same subject: "It is reported to us that certain persons have instituted a new kind of discipline; that our youth resort to their schools; that they have assumed the title of Latin Rhetoricians; and that young men waste their time there for whole days together. Our ancestors have ordained what instruction it is fitting their children should receive, and what schools they should attend. These novelties, contrary to the customs and instructions of our ancestors, we neither approve, nor do they appear to us good. Wherefore it appears to be our duty that we should notify our judgment both to those who keep such schools, and those who are in the practice of frequenting them, that they meet our disapprobation."

However, by slow degrees, rhetoric manifested itself to be a (525) useful and honourable study, and many persons devoted themselves to it, both as a means of defence and of acquiring reputation. Cicero declaimed in Greek until his praetorship, but afterwards, as he grew older, in Latin also; and even in the consulship of Hirtius and Pansa 905, whom he calls "his great and noble disciples." Some historians state that Cneius Pompey resumed the practice of declaiming even during the civil war, in order to be better prepared to argue against Caius Curio, a young man of great talents, to whom the defence of Caesar was entrusted. They say, likewise, that it was not forgotten by Mark Antony, nor by Augustus, even during the war of Modena. Nero also declaimed 906 even after he became emperor, in the first year of his reign, which he had done before in public but twice. Many speeches of orators were also published. In consequence, public favour was so much attracted to the study of rhetoric, that a vast number of professors and learned men devoted themselves to it; and it flourished to such a degree, that some of them raised themselves by it to the rank of senators and the highest offices.

But the same mode of teaching was not adopted by all, nor, indeed, did individuals always confine themselves to the same system, but each varied his plan of teaching according to circumstances. For they were accustomed, in stating their argument with the utmost clearness, to use figures and apologies, to put cases, as circumstances required, and to relate facts, sometimes briefly and succinctly, and, at other times, more at large and with greater feeling. Nor did they omit, on occasion, to resort to translations from the Greek, and to expatiate in the praise, or to launch their censures on the faults, of illustrious men. They also dealt with matters connected with every-day life, pointing out such as are useful and necessary, and such as are hurtful and needless. They had occasion often to support the authority of fabulous accounts, and to detract from that of historical narratives, which sort the Greeks call "Propositions," "Refutations" and "Corroboration," until by a gradual process they have exhausted these topics, and arrive at the gist of the argument.

Among the ancients, subjects of controversy were drawn either from history, as indeed some are even now, or from (526) actual facts, of recent occurrence. It was, therefore, the custom to state them precisely, with details of the names of places. We certainly so find them collected and published, and it may be well to give one or two of them literally, by way of example:

"A company of young men from the city, having made an excursion to Ostia in the summer season, and going down to the beach, fell in with some fishermen who were casting their nets in the sea. Having bargained with them for the haul, whatever it might turn out to be, for a certain sum, they paid down the money. They waited a long time while the nets were being drawn, and when at last they were dragged on shore, there was no fish in them, but some gold sewn up in a basket. The buyers claim the haul as theirs, the fishermen assert that it belongs to them."

Again: "Some dealers having to land from a ship at Brundusium a cargo of slaves, among which there was a handsome boy of great value, they, in order to deceive the collectors of the customs, smuggled him ashore in the dress of a freeborn youth, with the bullum 907 hung about his neck. The fraud easily escaped detection. They proceed to Rome; the affair becomes the subject of judicial inquiry; it is alleged that the boy was entitled to his freedom, because his master had voluntarily treated him as free."

Formerly, they called these by a Greek term, syntaxeis, but of late "controversies;" but they may be either fictitious cases, or those which come under trial in the courts. Of the eminent professors of this science, of whom any memorials are extant, it would not be easy to find many others than those of whom I shall now proceed to give an account.

II. LUCIUS PLOTIUS GALLUS. Of him Marcus Tullius Cicero thus writes to Marcus Titinnius 908 : "I remember well that when we were boys, one Lucius Plotius first began to teach Latin; and as great numbers flocked to his school, so that all who were most devoted to study were eager to take lessons from him, it was a great trouble to me that I too was not allowed to do so. I was prevented, however, by the decided opinion (527) of men of the greatest learning, who considered that it was best to cultivate the genius by the study of Greek." This same Gallus, for he lived to a great age, was pointed at by M. Caelius, in a speech which he was forced to make in his own cause, as having supplied his accuser, Atracinus 909 , with materials for his charge. Suppressing his name, he says that such a rhetorician was like barley bread 910 compared to a wheaten loaf,—windy, chaffy, and coarse.

III. LUCIUS OCTACILIUS PILITUS is said to have been a slave, and, according to the old custom, chained to the door like a watch-dog 911 ; until, having been presented with his freedom for his genius and devotion to learning, he drew up for his patron the act of accusation in a cause he was prosecuting. After that, becoming a professor of rhetoric, he gave instructions to Cneius Pompey the Great, and composed an account of his actions, as well as of those of his father, being the first freedman, according to the opinion of Cornelius Nepos 912 , who ventured to write history, which before his time had not been done by any one who was not of the highest ranks in society.

IV. About this time, EPIDIUS 913 having fallen into disgrace for bringing a false accusation, opened a school of instruction, in which he taught, among others, Mark Antony and Augustus. On one occasion Caius Canutius jeered them for presuming to belong to the party of the consul Isauricus 914 in his administration of the republic; upon which he replied, that he would rather be the disciple of Isauricus, than of Epidius, the false accuser. This Epidius claimed to be descended from Epidius Nuncio, who, as (528) ancient traditions assert, fell into the fountain of the river Sarnus 915 when the streams were overflown, and not being afterwards found, was reckoned among the number of the gods.

V. SEXTUS CLODIUS, a native of Sicily, a professor both of Greek and Latin eloquence, had bad eyes and a facetious tongue. It was a saying of his, that he lost a pair of eyes from his intimacy with Mark Antony, the triumvir 916 . Of his wife, Fulvia, when there was a swelling in one of her cheeks, he said that "she tempted the point of his style;" 917 nor did Antony think any the worse of him for the joke, but quite enjoyed it; and soon afterwards, when Antony was consul 918 , he even made him a large grant of land, which Cicero charges him with in his Philippics 919 . "You patronize," he said, "a master of the schools for the sake of his buffoonery, and make a rhetorician one of your pot-companions; allowing him to cut his jokes on any one he pleased; a witty man, no doubt, but it was an easy matter to say smart things of such as you and your companions. But listen, Conscript Fathers, while I tell you what reward was given to this rhetorician, and let the wounds of the republic be laid bare to view. You assigned two thousand acres of the Leontine territory 920 to Sextus Clodius, the rhetorician, and not content with that, exonerated the estate from all taxes. Hear this, and learn from the extravagance of the grant, how little wisdom is displayed in your acts."

VI. CAIUS ALBUTIUS SILUS, of Novara 921, while, in the execution (529) of the office of edile in his native place, he was sitting for the administration of justice, was dragged by the feet from the tribunal by some persons against whom he was pronouncing a decree. In great indignation at this usage, he made straight for the gate of the town, and proceeded to Rome. There he was admitted to fellowship, and lodged, with Plancus the orator 922, whose practice it was, before he made a speech in public, to set up some one to take the contrary side in the argument. The office was undertaken by Albutius with such success, that he silenced Plancus, who did not venture to put himself in competition with him. This bringing him into notice, he collected an audience of his own, and it was his custom to open the question proposed for debate, sitting; but as he warmed with the subject, he stood up, and made his peroration in that posture. His declamations were of different kinds; sometimes brilliant and polished, at others, that they might not be thought to savour too much of the schools, he curtailed them of all ornament, and used only familiar phrases. He also pleaded causes, but rarely, being employed in such as were of the highest importance, and in every case undertaking the peroration only.

In the end, he gave up practising in the forum, partly from shame, partly from fear. For, in a certain trial before the court of the One Hundred 923, having lashed the defendant as a man void of natural affection for his parents, he called upon him by a bold figure of speech, "to swear by the ashes of his father and mother which lay unburied;" his adversary taking him up for the suggestion, and the judges frowning upon it, he lost his cause, and was much blamed. At another time, on a trial for murder at Milan, before Lucius Piso, the proconsul, having to defend the culprit, he worked himself up to such a pitch of vehemence, that in a crowded court, who loudly applauded him, notwithstanding all the efforts of the lictor to maintain order, he broke out into a lamentation on the miserable state of Italy 924, then in danger of being again reduced, he said, into (530) the form of a province, and turning to the statue of Marcus Brutus, which stood in the Forum, he invoked him as "the founder and vindicator of the liberties of the people." For this he narrowly escaped a prosecution. Suffering, at an advanced period of life, from an ulcerated tumour, he returned to Novara, and calling the people together in a public assembly, addressed them in a set speech, of considerable length, explaining the reasons which induced him to put an end to existence: and this he did by abstaining from food.

END OF THE LIVES OF GRAMMARIANS AND RHETORICIANS.

# LIVES OF THE POETS.

(531)

## THE LIFE OF TERENCE.

Publius Terentius Afer, a native of Carthage, was a slave, at Rome, of the senator Terentius Lucanus, who, struck by his abilities and handsome person, gave him not only a liberal education in his youth, but his freedom when he arrived at years of maturity. Some say that he was a captive taken in war, but this, as Fenestella 925 informs us, could by no means have been the case, since both his birth and death took place in the interval between the termination of the second Punic war and the commencement of the third 926 ; nor, even supposing that he had been taken prisoner by the Numidian or Getulian tribes, could he have fallen into the hands of a Roman general, as there was no commercial intercourse between the Italians and Africans until after the fall of Carthage 927 . Terence lived in great familiarity with many persons of high station, and especially with Scipio Africanus, and Caius Delius, whose favour he is even supposed to have purchased by the foulest means. But Fenestella reverses the charge, contending that Terence was older than either of them. Cornelius Nepos, however, (532) informs us that they were all of nearly equal age; and Porcias intimates a suspicion of this criminal commerce in the following passage:—

"While Terence plays the wanton with the great, and recommends himself to them by the meretricious ornaments of his person; while, with greedy ears, he drinks in the divine melody of Africanus's voice; while he thinks of being a constant guest at the table of Furius, and the handsome Laelius; while he thinks that he is fondly loved by them, and often invited to Albanum for his youthful beauty, he finds himself stripped of his property, and reduced to the lowest state of indigence. Then, withdrawing from the world, he betook himself to Greece, where he met his end, dying at Strymphalos, a town in Arcadia. What availed him the friendship of Scipio, of Laelius, or of Furius, three of the most affluent nobles of that age? They did not even minister to his necessities so much as to provide him a hired house, to which his slave might return with the intelligence of his master's death."

He wrote comedies, the earliest of which, The Andria, having to be performed at the public spectacles given by the aediles 928, he was commanded to read it first before Caecilius 929. Having been introduced while Caecilius was at supper, and being meanly dressed, he is reported to have read the beginning of the play seated on a low stool near the great man's couch. But after reciting a few verses, he was invited to take his place at table, and, having supped with his host, went through the rest to his great delight. This play and five others were received by the public with similar applause, although Volcatius, in his enumeration of them, says that "The Hecyra 930 must not be reckoned among these."

The Eunuch was even acted twice the same day 931, and earned more money than any comedy, whoever was the writer, had ever done before, namely, eight thousand sesterces 932; besides which, a certain sum accrued to the author for the title. But Varro prefers the opening of The Adelphi 933 to that of Menander. It is very commonly reported that Terence was assisted in his works by Laelius and Scipio 934, with whom he lived in such great intimacy. He gave some currency to this report himself, nor did he ever attempt to defend himself against it, except in a light way; as in the prologue to The Adelphi:

> *Nam quod isti dicunt malevoli, homines nobiles*
> *Hunc adjutare, assidueque una scribere;*
> *Quod illi maledictun vehemens existimant,*
> *Eam laudem hic ducit maximam: cum illis placet,*
> *Qui vobis universis et populo placent;*
> *Quorum opera in bello, in otio, in negotio,*
> *Suo quisque tempore usus est sine superbia.*
> — — — — *For this,*
> *Which malice tells that certain noble persons*

> Assist the bard, and write in concert with him,
> That which they deem a heavy slander, he
> Esteems his greatest praise: that he can please
> Those who in war, in peace, as counsellors,
> Have rendered you the dearest services,
> And ever borne their faculties so meekly.
>
> Colman.

He appears to have protested against this imputation with less earnestness, because the notion was far from being disagreeable to Laelius and Scipio. It therefore gained ground, and prevailed in after-times.

Quintus Memmius, in his speech in his own defence, says "Publius Africanus, who borrowed from Terence a character which he had acted in private, brought it on the stage in his name." Nepos tells us he found in some book that C. Laelius, when he was on some occasion at Puteoli, on the calends [the first] of March, 935 being requested by his wife to rise early, (534) begged her not to suffer him to be disturbed, as he had gone to bed late, having been engaged in writing with more than usual success. On her asking him to tell her what he had been writing, he repeated the verses which are found in the Heautontimoroumenos:

> Satis pol proterve me Syri promessa – *Heauton*. IV. iv. 1.
>
> I'faith! the rogue Syrus's impudent pretences –

Santra 936 is of opinion that if Terence required any assistance in his compositions 937, he would not have had recourse to Scipio and Laelius, who were then very young men, but rather to Sulpicius Gallus 938, an accomplished scholar, who had been the first to introduce his plays at the games given by the consuls; or to Q. Fabius Labeo, or Marcus Popilius 939, both men of consular rank, as well as poets. It was for this reason that, in alluding to the assistance he had received, he did not speak of his coadjutors as very young men, but as persons of whose services the people had full experience in peace, in war, and in the administration of affairs.

After he had given his comedies to the world, at a time when he had not passed his thirty-fifth year, in order to avoid suspicion, as he found others publishing their works under his name, or else to make himself acquainted with the modes of life and habits of the Greeks, for the purpose of exhibiting them in his plays, he withdrew from home, to which he never returned. Volcatius gives this account of his death:

> Sed ut Afer sei populo dedit comoedias,
> Iter hic in Asiam fecit. Navem cum semel
> Conscendit, visus nunquam est. Sic vita vacat.
> (535) When Afer had produced six plays for the entertainment of the people,
> He embarked for Asia; but from the time he went on board ship
> He was never seen again. Thus he ended his life.

Q. Consentius reports that he perished at sea on his voyage back from Greece, and that one hundred and eight plays, of which he had made a version from Menander 940, were lost with him. Others say that he died at Stymphalos, in Arcadia, or in Leucadia, during the consulship of Cn. Cornelius Dolabella and Marcus Fulvius Nobilior 941, worn out with a severe illness, and with grief and regret for the loss of his baggage, which he had sent forward in a ship that was wrecked, and contained the last new plays he had written.

In person, Terence is reported to have been rather short and slender, with a dark complexion. He had an only daughter, who was afterwards married to a Roman knight; and he left also twenty acres of garden ground 942, on the Appian Way, at the Villa of Mars. I, therefore, wonder the more how Porcius could have written the verses,

> – – – – nihil Publius
> Scipio profuit, nihil et Laelius, nihil Furius,
> Tres per idem tempus qui agitabant nobiles facillime.
> Eorum ille opera ne domum quidem habuit conductitiam
> Saltem ut esset, quo referret obitum domini servulus. 943

Afranius places him at the head of all the comic writers, declaring, in his Compitalia,

> Terentio non similem dices quempiam,
> Terence's equal cannot soon be found.

On the other hand, Volcatius reckons him inferior not only (536) to Naevius, Plautus, and Caecilius, but also to Licinius. Cicero pays him this high compliment, in his Limo—

*Tu quoque, qui solus lecto sermone, Terenti,*
*Conversum expressumque Latina voce Menandrum*
*In medio populi sedatis vocibus offers,*
*Quidquid come loquens, ac omnia dulcia dicens.*

"You, only, Terence, translated into Latin, and clothed in choice language the plays of Menander, and brought them before the public, who, in crowded audiences, hung upon hushed applause—

*Grace marked each line, and every period charmed."*

So also Caius Caesar:

*Tu quoque tu in summis, O dimidiate Menander,*
*Poneris, et merito, puri sermonis amator,*
*Lenibus atque utinam scriptis adjuncta foret vis*
*Comica, ut aequato virtus polleret honore*
*Cum Graecis, neque in hoc despectus parte jaceres!*
*Unum hoc maceror, et doleo tibi deesse, Terenti.*

"You, too, who divide your honours with Menander, will take your place among poets of the highest order, and justly too, such is the purity of your style. Would only that to your graceful diction was added more comic force, that your works might equal in merit the Greek masterpieces, and your inferiority in this particular should not expose you to censure. This is my only regret; in this, Terence, I grieve to say you are wanting."

# THE LIFE OF JUVENAL.

D. JUNIUS JUVENALIS, who was either the son 944 of a wealthy freedman, or brought up by him, it is not known which, declaimed till the middle of life 945, more from the bent of his inclination, than from any desire to prepare himself either for the schools or the forum. But having composed a short satire 946, which was clever enough, on Paris 947, the actor of pantomimes, (537) and also on the poet of Claudius Nero, who was puffed up by having held some inferior military rank for six months only; he afterwards devoted himself with much zeal to that style of writing. For a while indeed, he had not the courage to read them even to a small circle of auditors, but it was not long before he recited his satires to crowded audiences, and with entire success; and this he did twice or thrice, inserting new lines among those which he had originally composed.

> *Quod non dant proceres, dabit histrio, tu Camerinos,*
> *Et Bareas, tu nobilium magna atria curas.*
> *Praefectos Pelopea facit, Philomela tribunos.*
> Behold an actor's patronage affords
> A surer means of rising than a lord's!
> And wilt thou still the Camerino's 948 court,
> Or to the halls of Bareas resort,
> When tribunes Pelopea can create
> And Philomela praefects, who shall rule the state? 949

At that time the player was in high favour at court, and many of those who fawned upon him were daily raised to posts of honour. Juvenal therefore incurred the suspicion of having covertly satirized occurrences which were then passing, and, although eighty years old at that time 950 , he was immediately removed from the city, being sent into honourable banishment as praefect of a cohort, which was under orders to proceed to a station at the extreme frontier of Egypt 951 . That (538) sort of punishment was selected, as it appeared severe enough for an offence which was venial, and a mere piece of drollery. However, he died very soon afterwards, worn down by grief, and weary of his life.

# THE LIFE OF PERSIUS.

AULUS PERSIUS FLACCUS was born the day before the Nones of December [4th Dec.] [952], in the consulship of Fabius Persicus and L. Vitellius. He died on the eighth of the calends of December [24th Nov.] 953 in the consulship of Rubrius Marius and Asinius Gallus. Though born at Volterra, in Etruria, he was a Roman knight, allied both by blood and marriage to persons of the highest rank 954 . He ended his days at an estate he had at the eighth milestone on the Appian Way. His father, Flaccus, who died when he was barely six years old, left him under the care of guardians, and his mother, Fulvia Silenna, who afterwards married Fusius, a Roman knight, buried him also in a very few years. Persius Flaccus pursued his studies at Volterra till he was twelve years old, and then continued them at Rome, under Remmius Palaemon, the grammarian, and Verginius Flaccus, the rhetorician. Arriving at the age of twenty-one, he formed a friendship with Annaeus Cornutus 955 , which lasted through life; and from him he learned the rudiments of philosophy. Among his earliest friends were Caesius Bassus 956 , and Calpurnius Statura; the latter of whom died while Persius himself was yet in his youth. Servilius (539) Numanus 957 , he reverenced as a father. Through Cornutus he was introduced to Annaeus, as well as to Lucan, who was of his own age, and also a disciple of Cornutus. At that time Cornutus was a tragic writer; he belonged to the sect of the Stoics, and left behind him some philosophical works. Lucan was so delighted with the writings of Persius Flaccus, that he could scarcely refrain from giving loud tokens of applause while the author was reciting them, and declared that they had the true spirit of poetry. It was late before Persius made the acquaintance of Seneca, and then he was not much struck with his natural endowments. At the house of Cornutus he enjoyed the society of two very learned and excellent men, who were then zealously devoting themselves to philosophical enquiries, namely, Claudius Agaternus, a physician from Lacedaemon, and Petronius Aristocrates, of Magnesia, men whom he held in the highest esteem, and with whom he vied in their studies, as they were of his own age, being younger than Cornutus. During nearly the last ten years of his life he was much beloved by Thraseas, so that he sometimes travelled abroad in his company; and his cousin Arria was married to him.

Persius was remarkable for gentle manners, for a modesty amounting to bashfulness, a handsome form, and an attachment to his mother, sister, and aunt, which was most exemplary. He was frugal and chaste. He left his mother and sister twenty thousand sesterces, requesting his mother, in a written codicil, to present to Cornutus, as some say, one hundred sesterces, or as others, twenty pounds of wrought silver 958, besides about seven hundred books, which, indeed, included his whole library. Cornutus, however, would only take the books, and gave up the legacy to the sisters, whom his brother had constituted his heirs.

He wrote 959 seldom, and not very fast; even the work we possess he left incomplete. Some verses are wanting at the end of the book 960, but Cornutus thoughtlessly recited it, as if (540) it was finished; and on Caesius Bassus requesting to be allowed to publish it, he delivered it to him for that purpose., In his younger days, Persius had written a play, as well as an Itinerary, with several copies of verses on Thraseas' father-in-law, and Arria's 961 mother, who had made away with herself before her husband. But Cornutus used his whole influence with the mother of Persius to prevail upon her to destroy these compositions. As soon as his book of Satires was published, all the world began to admire it, and were eager to buy it up. He died of a disease in the stomach, in the thirtieth year of his age 962. But no sooner had he left school and his masters, than he set to work with great vehemence to compose satires, from having read the tenth book of Lucilius; and made the beginning of that book his model; presently launching his invectives all around with so little scruple, that he did not spare cotemporary poets and orators, and even lashed Nero himself, who was then the reigning prince. The verse ran as follows:

*Auriculas asini Mida rex habet;*

King Midas has an ass's ears;

but Cornutus altered it thus;

*Auriculas asini quis non habet?*

Who has not an ass's ears?

in order that it might not be supposed that it was meant to apply to Nero.

# THE LIFE OF HORACE.

HORATIUS FLACCUS was a native of Venusium 963, his father having been, by his own account, a freedman and collector of taxes, but, as it is generally believed, a dealer in salted (541) provisions; for some one with whom Horace had a quarrel, jeered him, by saying; "How often have I seen your father wiping his nose with his fist?" In the battle of Philippi, he served as a military tribune 965, which post he filled at the instance of Marcus Brutus 966, the general; and having obtained a pardon, on the overthrow of his party, he purchased the office of scribe to a quaestor. Afterwards insinuating himself first, into the good graces of Mecaenas, and then of Augustus, he secured no small share in the regard of both. And first, how much Mecaenas loved him may be seen by the epigram in which he says:

Ni te visceribus meis, Horati,
Plus jam diligo, Titium sodalem,
Ginno tu videas strigosiorem. 967_

But it was more strongly exhibited by Augustus, in a short sentence uttered in his last moments: "Be as mindful of Horatius Flaccus as you are of me!" Augustus offered to appoint him his secretary, signifying his wishes to Mecaenas in a letter to the following effect: "Hitherto I have been able to write my own epistles to friends; but now I am too much occupied, and in an infirm state of health. I wish, therefore, to deprive you of our Horace: let him leave, therefore, your luxurious table and come to the palace, and he shall assist me in writing my letters." And upon his refusing to accept the office, he neither exhibited the smallest displeasure, nor ceased to heap upon him tokens of his regard. Letters of his are extant, from which I will make some short extracts to establish this: "Use your influence over me with the same freedom as you would do if we were living together as friends. In so doing you will be perfectly right, and guilty of no impropriety; for

I could wish that our intercourse should be on that footing, if your health admitted of it." And again: "How I hold you in memory you may learn (542) from our friend Septimius 968 , for I happened to mention you when he was present. And if you are so proud as to scorn my friendship, that is no reason why I should lightly esteem yours, in return." Besides this, among other drolleries, he often called him, "his most immaculate penis," and "his charming little man," and loaded him from time to time with proofs of his munificence. He admired his works so much, and was so convinced of their enduring fame, that he directed him to compose the Secular Poem, as well as that on the victory of his stepsons Tiberius and Drusus over the Vindelici 969 ; and for this purpose urged him to add, after a long interval, a fourth book of Odes to the former three. After reading his "Sermones," in which he found no mention of himself, he complained in these terms: "You must know that I am very angry with you, because in most of your works of this description you do not choose to address yourself to me. Are you afraid that, in times to come, your reputation will suffer; in case it should appear that you lived on terms of intimate friendship with me?" And he wrung from him the eulogy which begins with,

*Cum tot sustineas, et tanta negotia solus:*
*Res Italas armis tuteris, moribus ornes,*
*Legibus emendes: in publica commoda peccem,*
*Si longo sermone morer tua tempora, Caesar.* — Epist. ii. i.
*While you alone sustain the important weight*
*Of Rome's affairs, so various and so great;*
*While you the public weal with arms defend,*
*Adorn with morals, and with laws amend;*
*Shall not the tedious letter prove a crime,*
*That steals one moment of our Caesar's time.* — Francis.

In person, Horace was short and fat, as he is described by himself in his Satires 970 , and by Augustus in the following letter: "Dionysius has brought me your small volume, which, little as it is, not to blame you for that, I shall judge favourably. You seem to me, however, to be afraid lest your volumes should be bigger than yourself. But if you are short in stature, you are corpulent enough. You may, therefore, (543) if you will, write in a quart, when the size of your volume is as large round as your paunch."

It is reported that he was immoderately addicted to venery. [For he is said to have had obscene pictures so disposed in a bedchamber lined with mirrors, that, whichever way he looked, lascivious images might present themselves to his view.] [971] He lived for the most part in the retirement of his farm 972, on the confines of the Sabine and Tiburtine territories, and his house is shewn in the neighbourhood of a little wood not far from Tibur. Some Elegies ascribed to him, and a prose Epistle apparently written to commend himself to Mecaenas, have been handed down to us; but I believe that neither of them are genuine works of his; for the Elegies are commonplace, and the Epistle is wanting in perspicuity, a fault which cannot be imputed to his style. He was born on the sixth of the ides of December [27th December], in the consulship of Lucius Cotta 973 and Lucius Torquatus; and died on the fifth of the calends of December [27th November], in the consulship of Caius Marcius Censorinus and Caius Asinius Gallus 974; having completed his fifty-ninth year. He made a nuncupatory will, declaring Augustus his heir, not being able, from the violence of his disorder, to sign one in due form. He was interred and lies buried on the skirts of the Esquiline Hill, near the tomb of Mecaenas. 975

(544) M. ANNAEUS LUCANUS, a native of Corduba 976, first tried the powers of his genius in an encomium on Nero, at the Quinquennial games. He afterwards recited his poem on the Civil War carried on between Pompey and Caesar. His vanity was so immense, and he gave such liberty to his tongue, that in some preface, comparing his age and his first efforts with those of Virgil, he had the assurance to say: "And what now remains for me is to deal with a gnat." In his early youth, after being long informed of the sort of life his father led in the country, in consequence of an unhappy marriage 977, he was recalled from Athens by Nero, who admitted him into the circle of his friends, and even gave him the honour of the quaestorship; but he did not long remain in favour. Smarting at this, and having publicly stated that Nero had withdrawn, all of a sudden, without communicating with the senate, and without any other motive than his own recreation, after this he did not cease to assail the emperor both with foul words and with acts which are still notorious. So that on one occasion, when easing his bowels in the common privy, there being a louder explosion than usual, he gave vent to the nemistych of Nero: "One would suppose it was thundering under ground," in

the hearing of those who were sitting there for the same purpose, and who took to their heels in much consternation 978 . In a poem also, which was in every one's hands, he severely lashed both the emperor and his most powerful adherents.

At length, he became nearly the most active leader in Piso's conspiracy 979 ; and while he dwelt without reserve in many quarters on the glory of those who dipped their hands in the (545) blood of tyrants, he launched out into open threats of violence, and carried them so far as to boast that he would cast the emperor's head at the feet of his neighbours. When, however, the plot was discovered, he did not exhibit any firmness of mind. A confession was wrung from him without much difficulty; and, humbling himself to the most abject entreaties, he even named his innocent mother as one of the conspirators 980 ; hoping that his want of natural affection would give him favour in the eyes of a parricidal prince. Having obtained permission to choose his mode of death 981 , he wrote notes to his father, containing corrections of some of his verses, and, having made a full meal, allowed a physician to open the veins in his arm 982 . I have also heard it said that his poems were offered for sale, and commented upon, not only with care and diligence, but also in a trifling way. 983

# THE LIFE OF PLINY.

**984**

PLINIUS SECUNDUS, a native of New Como 985, having served in (546) the wars with strict attention to his duties, in the rank of a knight, distinguished himself, also, by the great integrity with which he administered the high functions of procurator for a long period in the several provinces intrusted to his charge. But still he devoted so much attention to literary pursuits, that it would not have been an easy matter for a person who enjoyed entire leisure to have written more than he did. He comprised, in twenty volumes, an account of all the various wars carried on in successive periods with the German tribes. Besides this, he wrote a Natural History, which extended to seven books. He fell a victim to the calamitous event which occurred in Campania. For, having the command of the fleet at Misenum, when Vesuvius was throwing up a fiery eruption, he put to sea with his gallies for the purpose of exploring the causes of the phenomenon close on the spot 986. But being prevented by contrary winds from sailing back, he was suffocated in the dense cloud of dust and ashes. Some, however, think that he was killed by his slave, having implored him to put an end to his sufferings, when he was reduced to the last extremity by the fervent heat. 987

THE END OF LIVES OF THE POETS.

# FOOTNOTES

1 ( return )

[ Plin. Epist. i. 18, 24, iii. 8, v. 11, ix. 34, x. 95.]

2 ( return )

[ Lycee, part I. liv. III. c. i.]

3 ( return )

[ Julius Caesar Divus. Romulus, the founder of Rome, had the honour of an apotheosis conferred on him by the senate, under the title of Quirinus, to obviate the people's suspicion of his having been taken off by a conspiracy of the patrician order. Political circumstances again concurred with popular superstition to revive this posthumous adulation in favour of Julius Caesar, the founder of the empire, who also fell by the hands of conspirators. It is remarkable in the history of a nation so jealous of public liberty, that, in both instances, they bestowed the highest mark of human homage upon men who owed their fate to the introduction of arbitrary power.]

4 ( return )

[ Pliny informs us that Caius Julius, the father of Julius Caesar, a man of pretorian rank, died suddenly at Pisa.]

5 ( return )

[ A.U.C. (in the year from the foundation of Rome) 670; A.C. (before Christ) about 92.]

6 ( return )

[ Flamen Dialis. This was an office of great dignity, but subjected the holder to many restrictions. He was not allowed to ride on horseback, nor to absent himself from the city for a single night. His wife was also under particular restraints, and could not be divorced. If she died, the flamen resigned his office, because there were certain sacred rites which he could not perform without her assistance. Besides other marks of distinction, he wore a purple robe called laena, and a conical mitre called apex.]

7 ( return )

[ Two powerful parties were contending at Rome for the supremacy; Sylla being at the head of the faction of the nobles, while Marius espoused the cause of the people. Sylla suspected Julius Caesar of belonging to the Marian party, because Marius had married his aunt Julia.]

8 ( return )

[ He wandered about for some time in the Sabine territory.]

9 ( return )

[ Bithynia, in Asia Minor, was bounded on the south by Phrygia, on the west by the Bosphorus and Propontis; and on the north by the Euxine sea. Its boundaries towards the east are not clearly ascertained, Strabo, Pliny, and Ptolemy differing from each other on the subject.]

10 ( return )

[ Mitylene was a city in the island of Lesbos, famous for the study of philosophy and eloquence. According to Pliny, it remained a free city and in power one thousand five hundred years. It suffered much in the Peloponnesian war from the Athenians, and in the Mithridatic from the Romans, by whom it was taken and destroyed. But it soon rose again, having recovered its ancient liberty by the favour of Pomnpey; and was afterwards much embellished by Trajan, who added to it the splendour of his own name. This was the country of Pittacus, one of the seven wise men of Greece, as well as of Alcaeus and Sappho. The natives showed a particular taste for poetry, and had, as Plutarch informs us, stated times for the celebration of poetical contests.]

11 ( return )

[ The civic crown was made of oak-leaves, and given to him who had saved the life of a citizen. The person thus decorated, wore it at public spectacles, and sat next the senators. When he entered, the audience rose up, as a mark of respect.]

12 ( return )

[ A very extensive country of Hither Asia; lying between Pamphylia to the west, Mount Taurus and Amanus to the north,

Syria to the east, and the Mediterranean to the south. It was anciently famous for saffron; and hair-cloth, called by the Romans ciliciun, was the manufacture of this country.]

13 ( return )

[ A city and an island, near the coast of Caria famous for the huge statue of the Sun, called the Colossus. The Rhodians were celebrated not only for skill in naval affairs, but for learning, philosophy, and eloquence. During the latter periods of the Roman republic, and under some of the emperors, numbers resorted there to prosecute their studies; and it also became a place of retreat to discontented Romans.]

14 ( return )

[ Pharmacusa, an island lying off the coast of Asia, near Miletus. It is now called Parmosa.]

15 ( return )

[ The ransom, too large for Caesar's private means, was raised by the voluntary contributions of the cities in the Asiatic province, who were equally liberal from their public funds in the case of other Romans who fell into the hands of pirates at that period.]

16 ( return )

[ From Miletus, as we are informed by Plutarch.]

17 ( return )

[ Who commanded in Spain.]

18 ( return )

[ Rex, it will be easily understood, was not a title of dignity in a Roman family, but the surname of the Marcii.]

19 ( return )

[ The rites of the Bona Dea, called also Fauna, which were performed in the night, and by women only.]

20 ( return )

[ Hispania Boetica; the Hither province being called Hispania Tarraconensis.]

21 ( return )

[ Alexander the Great was only thirty-three years at the time of his death.]

22 ( return )

[ The proper office of the master of the horse was to command the knights, and execute the orders of the dictator. He was usually nominated from amongst persons of consular and praetorian dignity; and had the use of a horse, which the dictator had not, without the order of the people.]

23 ( return )

[ Seneca compares the annals of Tanusius to the life of a fool, which, though it may be long, is worthless; while that of a wise man, like a good book, is valuable, however short.—Epist. 94.]

24 ( return )

[ Bibulus was Caesar's colleague, both as edile and consul. Cicero calls his edicts "Archilochian," that is, as full of spite as the verses of Archilochus.—Ad. Attic. b. 7. ep. 24.]

25 ( return )

[ A.U.C. 689. Cicero holds both the Curio's, father and son, very cheap.—Brut. c. 60.]

26 ( return )

[ Regnum, the kingly power, which the Roman people considered an insupportable tyranny.]

27 ( return )

[ An honourable banishment.]

28 ( return )

[ The assemblies of the people were at first held in the open Forum. Afterwards, a covered building, called the Comitium, was erected for that purpose. There are no remains of it, but Lumisden thinks that it probably stood on the south side of the Forum, on the site of the present church of The Consolation.—Antiq. of Rome, p. 357.]

29 ( return )

[ Basilicas, from Basileus; a king. They were, indeed, the palaces of the sovereign people; stately and spacious buildings, with halls, which served the purpose of exchanges, council chambers, and courts of justice. Some of the Basilicas were afterwards converted into

Christian churches. "The form was oblong; the middle was an open space to walk in, called Testudo, and which we now call the nave. On each side of this were rows of pillars, which formed what we should call the side-aisles, and which the ancients called Porticus. The end of the Testudo was curved, like the apse of some of our churches, and was called Tribunal, from causes being heard there. Hence the term Tribune is applied to that part of the Roman churches which is behind the high altar."—Burton's Antiq. of Rome, p. 204.]

30 ( return )

[ Such as statues and pictures, the works of Greek artists.]

31 ( return )

[ It appears to have stood at the foot of the Capitoline hill. Piranesi thinks that the two beautiful columns of white marble, which are commonly described as belonging to the portico of the temple of Jupiter Stator, are the remains of the temple of Castor and Pollux.]

32 ( return )

[ Ptolemy Auletes, the son of Cleopatra.]

33 ( return )

[ Lentulus, Cethegus, and others.]

34 ( return )

[ The temple of Jupiter Capitolinus was commenced and completed by the Tarquins, kings of Rome, but not dedicated till the year after their expulsion, when that honour devolved on M. Horatius Fulvillus, the first of the consuls. Having been burnt down during the civil wars, A.U.C. 670, Sylla restored it on the same foundations, but did not live to consecrate it.]

35 ( return )

[ Meaning Pompey; not so much for the sake of the office, as having his name inserted in the inscription recording the repairs of the Capitol, instead of Catulus. The latter, however, secured the honour, and his name is still seen inscribed in an apartment at the Capitol, as its restorer.]

36 ( return )

[ It being the calends of January, the first day of the year, on which the magistrates solemnly entered on their offices, surrounded by their friends.]

37 ( return )

[ Among others, one for recalling Pompey from Asia, under the pretext that the commonwealth was in danger. Cato was one of the colleagues who saw through the design and opposed the decree.]

38 ( return )

[ See before, p. 5. This was in A.U.C. 693.]

39 ( return )

[ Plutarch informs us, that Caesar, before he came into office, owed his creditors 1300 talents, somewhat more than 565,000 pounds of our money. But his debts increased so much after this period, if we may believe Appian, that upon his departure for Spain, at the expiration of his praetorship, he is reported to have said, Bis millies et quingenties centena minis sibi adesse oportere, ut nihil haberet: i. e. That he was 2,000,000 and nearly 20,000 sesterces worse than penniless. Crassus became his security for 830 talents, about 871,500 pounds.]

40 ( return )

[ For his victories in Gallicia and Lusitania, having led his army to the shores of the ocean, which had not before been reduced to submission.]

41 ( return )

[ Caesar was placed in this dilemma, that if he aspired to a triumph, he must remain outside the walls until it took place, while as a candidate for the consulship, he must be resident in the city.]

42 ( return )

[ Even the severe censor was biassed by political expediency to sanction a system, under which what little remained of public virtue, and the love of liberty at Rome, were fast decaying. The strict laws against bribery at elections were disregarded, and it was practised openly, and accepted without a blush. Sallust says that everything was venal, and that Rome itself might be bought, if any one was rich enough to purchase it. Jugurth, viii. 20, 3.]

43 ( return )

[ A.U.C. 695.]

44 ( return )

[ The proceedings of the senate were reported in short notes taken by one of their own order, "strangers" not being admitted at their sittings. These notes included speeches as well as acts. These and the proceedings of the assemblies of the people, were daily published in journals [Footnote diurna: which contained also accounts of the trials at law, with miscellaneous intelligence of births and deaths, marriages and divorces. The practice of publishing the proceedings of the senate, introduced by Julius Caesar, was discontinued by Augustus.]

45 ( return )

[ Within the city, the lictors walked before only one of the consuls, and that commonly for a month alternately. A public officer, called Accensus, preceded the other consul, and the lictors followed. This custom had long been disused, but was now restored by Caesar.]

46 ( return )

[ In order that he might be a candidate for the tribuneship of the people; it was done late in the evening, at an unusual hour for public business.]

47 ( return )

[ Gaul was divided into two provinces, Transalpine, or Gallia Ulterior, and Cisalpina, or Citerior. The Citerior, having nearly the same limits as Lombardy in after times, was properly a part of Italy, occupied by colonists from Gaul, and, having the Rubicon, the ancient boundary of Italy, on the south. It was also called Gallia Togata, from the use of the Roman toga; the inhabitants being, after the social war, admitted to the right of citizens. The Gallia Transalpina, or Ulterior, was called Comata, from the people wearing their hair long, while the Romans wore it short; and the southern part, afterwards called Narbonensis, came to have the epithet Braccata, from the use of the braccae, which were no part of the Roman dress. Some writers suppose the braccae to have been breeches, but Aldus, in a short disquisition on the subject, affirms that they were a kind of upper dress. And this opinion seems to be countenanced by the name braccan being applied by the modern Celtic nations, the descendants of the Gallic Celts, to signify their upper garment, or plaid.]

48 ( return )

[ Alluding, probably, to certain scandals of a gross character which were rife against Caesar. See before, c. ii. (p. 2) and see also c. xlix.]

49 ( return )

[ So called from the feathers on their helmets, resembling the crest of a lark; Alauda, Fr. Alouette.]

50 ( return )

[ Days appointed by the senate for public thanksgiving in the temples in the name of a victorious general, who had in the decrees the title of emperor, by which they were saluted by the legions.]

51 ( return )

[ A.U.C. 702.]

52 ( return )

[ Aurelia.]

53 ( return )

[ Julia, the wife of Pompey, who died in childbirth.]

54 ( return )

[ Conquest had so multiplied business at Rome, that the Roman Forum became too little for transacting it, and could not be enlarged without clearing away the buildings with which it was surrounded. Hence the enormous sum which its site is said to have cost, amounting, it is calculated, to 809,291 pounds of our money. It stood near the old forum, behind the temple of Romulus and Remus, but not a vestige of it remains.]

55 ( return )

[ Comum was a town of the Orobii, of ancient standing, and formerly powerful. Julius Caesar added to it five thousand new colonists; whence it was generally called Novocomum. But in time it recovered its ancient name, Comum; Pliny the younger, who was a native of this place, calling it by no other name.]

56 ( return )

[ A.U.C. 705.]

57 ( return )

[ Eiper gar adikein chrae, tyrannidos peri Kalliston adikein talla de eusebein chreon. —Eurip. Phoeniss. Act II, where Eteocles aspires to become the tyrant of Thebes.]

58

[ Now the Pisatello; near Rimini. There was a very ancient law of the republic, forbidding any general, returning from the wars, to cross the Rubicon with his troops under arms.]

59

[ The ring was worn on the finger next to the little finger of the left hand.]

60 ( return )

[ Suetonius here accounts for the mistake of the soldiers with great probability. The class to which they imagined they were to be promoted, was that of the equites, or knights, who wore a gold ring, and were possessed of property to the amount stated in the text. Great as was the liberality of Caesar to his legions, the performance of this imaginary promise was beyond all reasonable expectation.]

61 ( return )

[ A.U.C. 706.]

62 ( return )

[ Elephants were first introduced at Rome by Pompey the Great, in his African triumph.]

63 ( return )

[ VENI, VIDI, VICI.]

64 ( return )

[ A.U.C. 708.]

65 ( return )

[ Gladiators were first publicly exhibited at Rome by two brothers called Bruti, at the funeral of their father, A.U.C. 490; and for some time they were exhibited only on such occasions. But afterwards they were also employed by the magistrates, to entertain the people, particularly at the Saturnalia, and feasts of Minerva. These cruel spectacles were prohibited by Constantine, but not entirely suppressed until the time of Honorius.]

66 ( return )

[ The Circensian games were shews exhibited in the Circus Maximus, and consisted of various kinds: first, chariot and horse-races, of which the Romans were extravagantly fond. The charioteers were distributed into four parties, distinguished by the colour of their dress. The spectators, without regarding the speed of the horses, or the skill of the men, were attracted merely by one or the other of the colours, as caprice inclined them. In the time of Justinian, no less than thirty thousand men lost their lives at Constantinople, in a tumult raised by a contention amongst the partizans of the several colours. Secondly, contests of agility and strength; of which there were five kinds, hence called Pentathlum. These were, running, leaping, boxing, wrestling, and throwing the discus or quoit. Thirdly, Ludus Trojae, a mock-fight, performed by young noblemen on horseback, revived by Julius Caesar, and frequently celebrated by the succeeding emperors. We meet with a description of it in the fifth book of the Aeneid, beginning with the following lines: Incedunt pueri, pariterque ante ora parentum Fraenatis lucent in equis: quos omnis euntes Trinacriae mirata fremit Trojaeque juventus. Fourthly, Venatio, which was the fighting of wild beasts with one another, or with men called Bestiarii, who were either forced to the combat by way of punishment, as the primitive Christians were, or fought voluntarily, either from a natural ferocity of disposition, or induced by hire. An incredible number of animals of various kinds were brought from all quarters, at a prodigious expense, for the entertainment of the people. Pompey, in his second consulship, exhibited at once five hundred lions, which were all dispatched in five days; also eighteen elephants. Fifthly the representation of a horse and foot battle, with that of an encampment or a siege. Sixthly, the representation of a sea-fight (Naumachia), which was at first made in the Circus Maximus, but afterwards elsewhere. The combatants were usually captives or condemned malefactors, who fought to death, unless saved by the clemency of the emperor. If any thing unlucky happened at the games, they were renewed, and often more than once.]

67 ( return )

[ A meadow beyond the Tiber, in which an excavation was made, supplied with water from the river.]

68 ( return )

[ Julius Caesar was assisted by Sosigenes, an Egyptian philosopher, in correcting the calendar. For this purpose he introduced an additional day every fourth year, making February to consist of twenty-nine days instead of twenty-eight, and, of course, the whole year to consist of three hundred and sixty-six days. The fourth year was denominated Bissextile, or leap year, because the sixth day before the calends, or first of March, was reckoned twice. The Julian year was introduced throughout the Roman empire, and continued in general use till the year 1582. But the true correction was not six hours, but five hours, forty-nine minutes; hence the addition was too great by eleven minutes. This small fraction would amount in one hundred years to three-fourths of a day, and in a thousand years to more than seven days. It had, in fact, amounted, since the Julian correction, in 1582, to more than seven days. Pope Gregory XIII., therefore, again reformed the calendar, first bringing forward the year ten days, by reckoning the 5th of October the 15th, and then prescribing the rule which has gradually been adopted throughout Christendom, except in Russia, and the Greek church generally.]

69 ( return )

[ Principally Carthage and Corinth.]

70 ( return )

[ The Latus Clavus was a broad stripe of purple, on the front of the toga. Its width distinguished it from that of the knights, who wore it narrow.]

71 ( return )

[ The Suburra lay between the Celian and Esquiline hills. It was one of the most frequented quarters of Rome.]

72 ( return )

[ Bede, quoting Solinus, we believe, says that excellent pearls were found in the British seas, and that they were of all colours, but principally white. Eccl. Hist. b. i. c. 1.]

73 ( return )

[ ————Bithynia quicquid Et predicator Caesaris unquam habuit.]

74 ( return )

[ Gallias Caesar subegit, Nicomedes Caesarem; Ecce Caesar nunc triumphat, qui subegit Gallias: Nicomedes non triumphat, qui subegit Caesarem.]

75 ( return )

[ Aegisthus, who, like Caesar, was a pontiff, debauched Clytemnestra while Agamemnon was engaged in the Trojan war, as Caesar did Mucia, the wife of Pompey, while absent in the war against Mithridates.]

76 ( return )

[ A double entendre; Tertia signifying the third of the value of the farm, as well as being the name of the girl, for whose favours the deduction was made.]

77 ( return )

[ Urbani, servate uxores; moechum calvum adducimus: Aurum in Gallia effutuisti, hic sumpsisti mutuum.]

78 ( return )

[ Plutarch tells us that the oil was used in a dish of asparagus. Every traveller knows that in those climates oil takes the place of butter as an ingredient in cookery, and it needs no experience to fancy what it is when rancid.]

79 ( return )

[ Meritoria rheda; a light four-wheeled carriage, apparently hired either for the journey or from town to town. They were tolerably commodious, for Cicero writes to Atticus, (v. 17.) Hanc epistolam dictavi sedens in rheda, cum in castra proficiscerer.]

80 ( return )

[ Plutarch informs us that Caesar travelled with such expedition, that he reached the Rhone on the eighth day after he left Rome.]

81 ( return )

[ Caesar tells us himself that he employed C. Volusenus to reconnoitre the coast of Britain, sending him forward in a long ship, with orders to return and make his report before the expedition sailed.]

82 ( return )

[ Religione; that is, the omens being unfavourable.]

83 ( return )

[ The standard of the Roman legions was an eagle fixed on the head of a spear. It was silver, small in size, with expanded wings, and clutching a golden thunderbolt in its claw.]

84 ( return )

[ To save them from the torture of a lingering death.]

85 ( return )

[ Now Lerida, in Catalonia.]

86 ( return )

[ The title of emperor was not new in Roman history; 1. It was sometimes given by the acclamations of the soldiers to those who commanded them. 2. It was synonymous with conqueror, and the troops hailed him by that title after a victory. In both these cases it was merely titular, and not permanent, and was generally written after the proper name, as Cicero imperator, Lentulo imperatore. 3. It assumed a permanent and royal character first in the person of Julius Caesar, and was then generally prefixed to the emperor's name in inscriptions, as IMP. CAESAR. DIVI. etc.]

87 ( return )

[ Cicero was the first who received the honour of being called "Pater patriae."]

88 ( return )

[ Statues were placed in the Capitol of each of the seven kings of Rome, to which an eighth was added in honour of Brutus, who expelled the last. The statue of Julius Caesar was afterwards raised near them.]

89 ( return )

[ The white fillet was one of the insignia of royalty. Plutarch, on this occasion, uses the expression, diadaemati basiliko, a royal diadem.]

90 ( return )

[ The Lupercalia was a festival, celebrated in a place called the Lupercal, in the month of February, in honour of Pan. During the solemnity, the Luperci, or priests of that god, ran up and down the city naked, with only a girdle of goat's skin round their waist, and thongs of the same in their hands; with which they struck those they met, particularly married women, who were thence supposed to be rendered prolific.]

91 ( return )

[ Persons appointed to inspect and expound the Sibylline books.]

92 ( return )

[ A.U.C. 709.]

93 ( return )

[ See before, c. xxii.]

94 ( return )

[ This senate-house stood in that part of the Campus Martius which is now the Campo di Fiore, and was attached by Pompey, "spoliis Orientis Onustus," to the magnificent theatre, which he built A.U.C. 698, in his second consulship. His statue, at the foot of which Caesar fell, as Plutarch tells us, was placed in it. We shall find that Augustus caused it to be removed.]

95 ( return )

[ The stylus, or graphium, was an iron pen, broad at one end, with a sharp point at the other, used for writing upon waxen tables, the leaves or bark of trees, plates of brass, or lead, etc. For writing upon paper or parchment, the Romans employed a reed, sharpened and split in the point like our pens, called calamus, arundo, or canna. This they dipped in the black liquor emitted by the cuttle fish, which served for ink.]

96 ( return )

[ It was customary among the ancients, in great extremities to shroud the face, in order to conceal any symptoms of horror or alarm which the countenance might express. The skirt of the toga was drawn round the lower extremities, that there might be no exposure in falling, as the Romans, at this period, wore no covering for the thighs and legs.]

97 ( return

[ Caesar's dying apostrophe to Brutus is represented in all the editions of Suetonius as uttered in Greek, but with some variations. The words, as here translated, are Kai su ei ekeinon; kai su teknon. The Salmasian manuscript omits the latter clause. Some commentators suppose that the words "my son," were not merely expressive of the difference of age, or former familiarity between them, but an avowal that Brutus was the fruit of the connection between Julius and Servilia, mentioned before (see p. 33). But it appears very improbable that Caesar, who had never before acknowledged Brutus to be his son, should make so unnecessary an avowal, at the moment of his death. Exclusively of this objection, the apostrophe seems too verbose, both for the suddenness and urgency of the occasion. But this is not all. Can we suppose that Caesar, though a perfect master of Greek, would at such a time have expressed himself in that language, rather than in Latin, his familiar tongue, and in which he spoke with peculiar elegance? Upon the whole, the probability is, that the words uttered by Caesar were, Et tu Brute! which, while equally expressive of astonishment with the other version, and even of tenderness, are both more natural, and more emphatic.]

98 ( return )

[ Men' me servasse, ut essent qui me perderent?]

99 ( return )

[ The Bulla, generally made of gold, was a hollow globe, which boys wore upon their breast, pendant from a string or ribbon put round the neck. The sons of freedmen and poor citizens used globes of leather.]

100 ( return )

[ Josephus frequently mentions the benefits conferred on his countrymen by Julius Caesar. Antiq. Jud. xiv. 14, 15, 16.]

101 ( return )

[ Appian informs us that it was burnt by the people in their fury, B. c. xi. p. 521.]

102 ( return )

[ Suetonius particularly refers to the conspirators, who perished at the battle of Philippi, or in the three years which intervened. The survivors were included in the reconciliation of Augustus, Antony, and Pompey, A.U.C. 715.]

103 ( return )

[ Suetonius alludes to Brutus and Cassius, of whom this is related by Plutarch and Dio.]

104 ( return )

[ For observations on Dr. Thomson's Essays appended to Suetonius's History of Julius Caesar, and the succeeding Emperors, see the Preface to this volume.]

105 ( return )

[ He who has a devoted admiration of Cicero, may be sure that he has made no slight proficiency himself.]

106 ( return )

[ A town in the ancient Volscian territory, now called Veletra. It stands on the verge of the Pontine Marshes, on the road to Naples.]

107 ( return )

[ Thurium was a territory in Magna Graecia, on the coast, near Tarentum.]

108 ( return )

[ Argentarius; a banker, one who dealt in exchanging money, as well as lent his own funds at interest to borrowers. As a class, they possessed great wealth, and were persons of consideration in Rome at this period.]

109 ( return )

[ Now Laricia, or Riccia, a town of the Campagna di Roma, on the Appian Way, about ten miles from Rome.]

110 ( return )

[ A.U.C. 691. A.C. (before Christ) 61.]

111 ( return )

[ The Palatine hill was not only the first seat of the colony of Romulus, but gave its name to the first and principal of the four regions into which the city was divided, from the time of Servius Tullius, the sixth king of Rome, to that of Augustus; the others being the Suburra, Esquilina, and Collina.]

112 ( return )

[ There were seven streets or quarters in the Palatine region, one of which was called "Ad Capita Bubula," either from the butchers' stalls at which ox-heads are hung up for sale, or from their being sculptured on some edifice. Thus the remains of a fortification near the tomb of

Cecilia Metella are now called Capo di Bove, from the arms of the Gaetani family over the gate.]

113 ( return )

[ Adrian, to whom Suetonius was secretary.]

114 ( return )

[ Augusto augurio postquam inclyta condita Roma est.]

115 ( return )

[ A.U.C. 711.]

116 ( return )

[ A.U.C. 712.]

117 ( return )

[ After being defeated in the second engagement, Brutus retired to a hill, and slew himself in the night.]

118 ( return )

[ The triumvir. There were three distinguished brothers of the name of Antony; Mark, the consul; Caius, who was praetor; and Lucius, a tribune of the people.]

119 ( return )

[ Virgil was one of the fugitives, having narrowly escaped being killed by the centurion Ario; and being ejected from his farm. Eclog. i.]

120 ( return )

[ A.U.C. 714.]

121 (return)

[ The anniversary of Julius Caesar's death.]

122 (return)

[ A.U.C. 712-718-]

123 (return)

[ The Romans employed slaves in their wars only in cases of great emergency, and with much reluctance. After the great slaughter at the battle of Cannae, eight thousand were bought and armed by the republic. Augustus was the first who manumitted them, and employed them as rowers in his gallies.]

124 (return)

[ In the triumvirate, consisting of Augustus, Mark Antony, and Lepidus.]

125

[ A.U.C. 723.]

126 (return)

[ There is no other authority for Augustus having viewed Antony's corpse. Plutarch informs us, that on hearing his death, Augustus retired into the interior of his tent, and wept over the fate of his colleague and friend, his associate in so many former struggles, both in war and the administration of affairs.]

127 (return)

[ The poison proved fatal, as every one knows, see Velleius, ii. 27; Florus, iv. 11. The Psylli were a people of Africa, celebrated for sucking the poison from wounds inflicted by serpents, with which that country anciently abounded. They pretended to be endowed with an antidote, which rendered their bodies insensible to the virulence of that species of poison; and the ignorance of those times gave credit to the physical immunity which they arrogated. But Celsus, who flourished about fifty years after the period we speak of, has exploded the vulgar prejudice which prevailed in their favour. He justly observes, that the venom of serpents, like some other kinds of poison, proves noxious only when applied to the naked fibre; and that, provided there is no ulcer in the gums or palate, the poison may be received into the mouth with perfect safety.]

128 (return)

[ Strabo informs us that Ptolemy caused it to be deposited in a golden sarcophagus, which was afterwards exchanged for one of glass, in which probably Augustus saw the remains.]

129 (return)

[ A custom of all ages and of people the most remote from each other.]

130 (return)

[ Meaning the degenerate race of the Ptolomean kings.]

131 (return)

[ The naval trophies were formed of the prows of ships.]

132 (return)

[ A.U.C. 721.]

133 (return)

[ Because his father was a Roman and his mother of the race of the Parthini, an Illyrian tribe.]

134 (return)

[ It was usual at Rome, before the elections, for the candidates to endeavour to gain popularity by the usual arts. They would therefore go to the houses of the citizens, shake hands with those they met, and address them in a kindly manner. It being of great consequence, upon those occasions, to know the names of persons, they were commonly attended by a nomenclator, who whispered into their ears that information, wherever it was wanted. Though this kind of officer was generally an attendant on men, we meet with instances of their having been likewise employed in the service of ladies; either with the view of serving candidates to whom they were allied, or of gaining the affections of the people.]

135 (return)

[ Not a bridge over a river, but a military engine used for gaining admittance into a fortress.]

136 (return)

[ Cantabria, in the north of Spain, now the Basque province.]

137 (return)

[ The ancient Pannonia includes Hungary and part of Austria, Styria and Carniola.]

138 (return)

[ The Rhaetian Alps are that part of the chain bordering on the Tyrol.]

139 (return)

[ The Vindelici principally occupied the country which is now the kingdom of Bavaria; and the Salassii, that part of Piedmont which includes the valley of Aost.]

140 (return)

[ The temple of Mars Ultor was erected by Augustus in fulfilment of a vow made by him at the battle of Philippi. It stood in the Forum which he built, mentioned in chap. xxxix. There are no remains of either.]

141 (return)

[ "The Ovatio was an inferior kind of Triumph, granted in cases where the victory was not of great importance, or had been obtained without difficulty. The general entered the city on foot or on horseback, crowned with myrtle, not with laurel; and instead of bullocks, the sacrifice was performed with a sheep, whence this procession acquired its name."—Thomson.]

142 (return)

[ "The greater Triumph, in which the victorious general and his army advanced in solemn procession through the city to the Capitol, was the highest military honour which could be obtained in the Roman state. Foremost in the procession went musicians of various kinds, singing and playing triumphal songs. Next were led the oxen to be sacrificed, having their horns gilt, and their heads adorned with fillets and garlands. Then in carriages were brought the spoils taken from the enemy, statues, pictures, plate, armour, gold and silver, and brass; with golden crowns, and other gifts, sent by the allied and tributary states. The captive princes and generals followed in chains, with their children and attendants. After them came the lictors, having their fasces wreathed with laurel, followed by a great company of musicians and dancers dressed like Satyrs, and wearing crowns of gold; in the midst of whom was one in a female dress, whose business it was, with his looks and gestures, to insult the vanquished. Next followed a long train of persons carrying perfumes. Then came the victorious general, dressed in purple embroidered with gold, with a crown of laurel on his head, a branch of laurel in his right hand, and in his left an ivory sceptre, with an eagle on the top; having his face painted with vermilion,' in the same manner as the statue of Jupiter on festival days, and a golden Bulla hanging on his breast, and containing some amulet, or magical preservative against envy. He stood in a gilded chariot, adorned with ivory, and drawn by four white horses, sometimes by elephants, attended by his relations, and a great crowd of citizens, all in white. His children used to ride in the chariot with him; and that he might not be too much elated, a slave, carrying a golden crown sparkling with gems, stood behind him, and frequently whispered in his ear, 'Remember that thou art a man!' After the general, followed the consuls and senators on foot, at least according to the appointment of Augustus; for they formerly used to go before him. His Legati and military Tribunes commonly rode by his side. The victorious army, horse and foot, came last, crowned with laurel, and decorated with the gifts which they had received for their valour, singing their own and their general's praises, but sometimes throwing out railleries against him; and often exclaiming, 'Io Triumphe!' in which they were joined by all the citizens, as they passed along. The oxen having been sacrificed, the general gave a magnificent entertainment in the Capitol to his friends and the chief men of the city; after which he was conducted home by the people, with music and a great number of lamps and torches."—Thomson.]

143 (return)

[ "The Sella Curulis was a chair on which the principal magistrates sat in the tribunal upon solemn occasions. It had no back, but stood on four crooked feet, fixed to the extremities of cross pieces of wood, joined by a common axis, somewhat in the form of the letter X; was covered with leather, and inlaid with ivory. From its construction, it might be occasionally folded together for the convenience of carriage, and set down where the magistrate chose to use it."—Thomson.]

144 (return)

[ Now Saragossa.]

145 (return)

[ A great and wise man, if he is the same person to whom Cicero's letters on the calamities of the times were addressed. Fam. Epist. c. vi, 20, 21.]

146 (return)

[ A.U.C. 731.]

147 (return)

[ The Lustrum was a period of five years, at the end of which the census of the people was taken. It was first made by the Roman kings, then by the consuls, but after the year 310 from the building of the city, by the censors, who were magistrates created for that purpose. It appears, however, that the census was not always held at stated periods, and sometimes long intervals intervened.]

148 (return)

[ Augustus appears to have been in earnest on these occasions, at least, in his desire to retire into private life and release himself from the cares of government, if we may believe Seneca. De Brev. Vit. c. 5. Of his two intimate advisers, Agrippa gave this counsel, while Mecaenas was for continuing his career of ambition.—Eutrop. 1. 53.]

149 (return)

[ The Tiber has been always remarkable for the frequency of its inundations and the ravages they occasioned, as remarked by Pliny, iii. 5. Livy mentions several such occurrences, as well as one extensive fire, which destroyed great part of the city.]

150 (return)

[ The well-known saying of Augustus, recorded by Suetonius, that he found a city of bricks, but left it of marble, has another version given it by Dio, who applies it to his consolidation of the government, to the following effect: "That Rome, which I found built of mud, I shall leave you firm as a rock."—Dio. lvi. p. 589.]

151 (return)

[ The same motive which engaged Julius Caesar to build a new forum, induced Augustus to erect another. See his life c. xx. It stood behind the present churches of St. Adrian and St. Luke, and was almost parallel with the public forum, but there are no traces of it remaining. The temple of Mars Ultor, adjoining, has been mentioned before, p. 84.]

152 (return)

[ The temple of the Palatine Apollo stood, according to Bianchini, a little beyond the triumphal arch of Titus. It appears, from the reverse of a medal of Augustus, to have been a rotondo, with an open portico, something like the temple of Vesta. The statues of the fifty daughters of Danae surrounded the portico; and opposite to them were their husbands on horseback. In this temple were preserved some of the finest works of the Greek artists, both in sculpture and painting. Here, in the presence of Augustus, Horace's Carmen Seculare was sung by twenty-seven noble youths and as many virgins. And here, as our author informs us, Augustus, towards the end of his reign, often assembled the senate.]

153 (return)

[ The library adjoined the temple, and was under the protection of Apollo. Caius Julius Hegenus, a freedman of Augustus, and an eminent grammarian, was the librarian.]

154 (return)

[ The three fluted Corinthian columns of white marble, which stand on the declivity of the Capitoline hill, are commonly supposed to be the remains of the temple of Jupiter Tonans, erected by Augustus. Part of the frieze and cornice are attached to them, which with the capitals of the columns are finely wrought. Suetonius tells us on what occasion this temple was erected. Of all the epithets given to Jupiter, none conveyed more terror to superstitious minds than that of the Thunderer—

Coelo tonantem credidimus Jovem Regnare.—Hor. 1. iii. Ode 5.

We shall find this temple mentioned again in c. xci. of the life of Augustus.]

155 (return)

[ The Portico of Octavia stood between the Flaminian circus and the theatre of Marcellus, enclosing the temples of Jupiter and Juno, said to have been built in the time of the republic. Several remains of them exist, in the Pescheria or fish-market; they were of the Corinthian order, and have been traced and engraved by Piranesi.]

156 (return)

[ The magnificent theatre of Marcellus was built on the site where Suetonius has before informed us that Julius Caesar intended to erect one (p. 30). It stood between the portico of Octavia and the hill of the Capitol. Augustus gave it the name of his nephew Marcellus, though he was then dead. Its ruins are still to be seen in the Piazza Montanara, where the Orsini family have a palace erected on the site.]

157 (return)

[ The theatre of Balbus was the third of the three permanent theatres of Rome. Those of Pompey and Marcellus have been already mentioned.]

158 (return)

[ Among these were, at least, the noble portico, if not the whole, of the Pantheon, still the pride of Rome, under the name of the Rotondo, on the frieze of which may be seen the inscription,

M. AGRIPPA. L. F. COS: TERTIUM. FECIT.

Agrippa also built the temple of Neptune, and the portico of the Argonauts.]

159 (return)

[ To whatever extent Augustus may have cleared out the bed of the Tiber, the process of its being encumbered with an alluvium of ruins and mud has been constantly going on. Not many years ago, a scheme was set on foot for clearing it by private enterprise, principally for the sake of the valuable remains of art which it is supposed to contain.]

160 (return)

[ The Via Flaminia was probably undertaken by the censor Caius Flaminius, and finished by his son of the same name, who was consul A.U.C. 566, and employed his soldiers in forming it after subduing the Ligurians. It led from the Flumentan gate, now the Porta del Popolo, through Etruria and Umbria into the Cisalpine Gaul, ending at Ariminum, the frontier town of the territories of the republic, now Rimini, on the Adriatic; and is travelled by every tourist who takes the route, north of the Appenines, through the States of the Church, to Rome. Every one knows that the great highways, not only in Italy but in the provinces, were among the most magnificent and enduring works of the Roman people.]

161 (return)

[ It had formed a sort of honourable retirement in which Lepidus was shelved, to use a familiar expression, when Augustus got rid of him quietly from the Triumvirate. Augustus assumed it A.U.C. 740, thus centring the last of all the great offices of the state in his own person; that of Pontifex Maximus, being of high importance, from the sanctity attached to it, and the influence it gave him over the whole system of religion.]

162 (return)

[ In the thirty-six years since the calendar was corrected by Julius Caesar, the priests had erroneously intercalated eleven days instead of nine. See JULIUS, c. xl.]

163 (return)

[ Sextilis, the sixth month, reckoning from March, in which the year of Romulus commenced.]

164 (return)

[ So Cicero called the day on which he returned from exile, the day of his "nativity" and his "new birth," paligennesian, a word which had afterwards a theological sense, from its use in the New Testament.]

165 (return)

[ Capi. There is a peculiar force in the word here adopted by Suetonius; the form used by the Pontifex Maximus, when he took the novice from the hand of her father, being Te capio amata, "I have you, my dear," implying the forcible breach of former ties, as in the case of a captive taken in war.]

166 (return)

[ At times when the temple of Janus was shut, and then only, certain divinations were made, preparatory to solemn supplication for the public health, "as if," says Dio, "even that could not be implored from the gods, unless the signs were propitious." It would be an inquiry of some interest, now that the care of the public health is becoming a department of the state, with what sanatory measures these becoming solemnities were attended.]

167 (return)

[ Theophrastus mentions the spring and summer flowers most suited for these chaplets. Among the former, were hyacinths, roses, and white violets; among the latter, lychinis, amaryllis, iris, and some species of lilies.]

168 (return)

[ Ergastulis. These were subterranean strong rooms, with narrow windows, like dungeons, in the country houses, where incorrigible slaves were confined in fetters, in the intervals of the severe tasks in grinding at the hand-mills, quarrying stones, drawing water, and other hard agricultural labour in which they were employed.]

169 (return)

[ These months were not only "the Long Vacation" of the lawyers, but during them there was a general cessation of business at Rome; the calendar exhibiting a constant succession of festivals. The month of December, in particular, was devoted to pleasure and relaxation.]

170 (return)

[ Causes are mentioned, the hearing of which was so protracted that lights were required in the court; and sometimes they lasted, we are told, as long as eleven or twelve days.]

171 (return)

[ Orcini. They were also called Charonites, the point of the sarcasm being, that they owed their elevation to a dead man, one who was gone to Orcus, namely Julius Caesar, after whose death Mark Antony introduced into the senate many persons of low rank who were designated for that honour in a document left by the deceased emperor.]

172 (return)

[ Cordus Cremutius wrote a History of the Civil Wars, and the Times of Augustus, as we are informed by Dio, 6, 52.]

173 (return)

[ In front of the orchestra.]

174 (return)

[ The senate usually assembled in one of the temples, and there was an altar consecrated to some god in the curia, where they otherwise met, as that to Victory in the Julian Curia.]

175 (return)

[ To allow of their absence during the vintage, always an important season in rural affairs in wine-growing countries. In the middle and south of Italy, it begins in September, and, in the worst aspects, the grapes are generally cleared before the end of October. In elevated districts they hung on the trees, as we have witnessed, till the month of November.]

176 (return)

[ Julius Caesar had introduced the contrary practice. See JULIUS, c. xx.]

177 (return)

[ A.U.C. 312, two magistrates were created, under the name of Censors, whose office, at first, was to take an account of the number of the people, and the value of their estates. Power was afterwards granted them to inspect the morals of the people; and from this period the office became of great importance. After Sylla, the election of censors was intermitted for about seventeen years. Under the emperors, the office of censor was abolished; but the chief functions of it were exercised by the emperors themselves, and frequently both with caprice and severity.]

178 (return)

[ Young men until they were seventeen years of age, and young women until they were married, wore a white robe bordered with purple, called Toga Praetexta. The former, when they had completed this period, laid aside the dress of minority, and assumed the Toga Virilis, or manly habit. The ceremony of changing the Toga was performed with great solemnity before the images of the Lares, to whom the Bulla was consecrated. On this occasion, they went either to the Capitol, or to some temple, to pay their devotions to the Gods.]

179 (return)

[ Transvectio: a procession of the equestrian order, which they made with great splendour through the city, every year, on the fifteenth of July. They rode on horseback from the temple of Honour, or of Mars, without the city, to the Capitol, with wreaths of olive on their heads, dressed in robes of scarlet, and bearing in their hands the military ornaments which they had received from their general, as a reward of their valour. The knights rode up to the censor, seated on his curule chair in front of the Capitol, and dismounting, led their horses in review before him. If any of the knights was corrupt in his morals, had diminished his fortune below the legal standard, or even had not taken proper care of his horse, the censor ordered him to sell his horse, by which he was considered as degraded from the equestrian order.]

180 (return)

[ Pugillaria were a kind of pocket book, so called, because memorandums were written or impinged by the styli, on their waxed surface. They appear to have been of very ancient origin, for we read of them in Homer under the name of pinokes.—II. z. 169.

Graphas en pinaki ptukto thyrophthora polla.

Writing dire things upon his tablet's roll.]

181 (return)

[ Pullatorum; dusky, either from their dark colour, or their being soiled. The toga was white, and was the distinguishing costume of the sovereign people of Rome, without which, they were not to appear in public; as members of an university are forbidden to do so, without the academical dress, or officers in garrisons out of their regimentals.]

182 (return)

[ Aen. i. 186.]

183 (return)

[ It is hardly necessary to direct the careful reader's attention to views of political economy so worthy of an enlightened prince. But it was easier to make the Roman people wear the toga, than to forego the cry of "Panem et Circenses."]

184 (return)

[ Septa were enclosures made with boards, commonly for the purpose of distributing the people into distinct classes, and erected occasionally like our hustings.]

185 (return)

[ The Thensa was a splendid carriage with four wheels, and four horses, adorned with ivory and silver, in which, at the Circensian games, the images of the gods were drawn in solemn procession from their shrines, to a place in the circus, called the Pulvinar, where couches were prepared for their reception. It received its name from thongs (lora tensa) stretched before it; and was attended in the procession by persons of the first rank, in their most magnificent apparel. The attendants took delight in putting their hands to the traces: and if a boy happened to let go the thong which he held, it was an indispensable rule that the procession should be renewed.]

186 (return)

[ The Cavea was the name of the whole of that part of the theatre where the spectators sat. The foremost rows were called cavea prima, of cavea; the last, cavea ultima, or summa; and the middle, cavea media.]

187 (return)

[ A.U.C. 726.]

188 (return)

[ As in the case of Herod, Joseph. Antiq. Jud. xv. 10.]

189 (return)

[ The Adriatic and the Tuscan.]

190 (return)

[ It was first established by Tiberius. See c. xxxvii.]

191 (return)

[ Tertullian, in his Apology, c. 34, makes the same remark. The word seems to have conveyed then, as it does in its theological sense now, the idea of Divinity, for it is coupled with Deus, God; nunquum se dominum vel deum appellare voluerit.]

192 (return)

[ An inclosure in the middle of the Forum, marking the spot where Curtius leapt into the lake, which had been long since filled up.]

193 (return)

[ Sandalarium, Tragoedum; names of streets, in which temples of tame gouts stood, as we now say St. Peter, Cornhill, etc.]

194 (return)

[ A coin, in value about 8 3/4 d. of our money.]

195 (return)

[ The senate, as instituted by Romulus, consisted of one hundred members, who were called Patres, i. e. Fathers, either upon account of their age, or their paternal care of the state. The number received some augmentation under Tullus Hostilius; and Tarquinius Priscus, the fifth king of Rome, added a hundred more, who were called Patres minorum gentium; those created by Romulus being distinguished by the name of Patres majorum gentium. Those who were chosen into the senate by Brutus, after the expulsion of Tarquin the Proud, to supply the place of those whom that king had slain, were called Conscripti, i. e. persons written or enrolled among the old senators, who alone were properly styled Patres. Hence arose the custom of summoning to the senate those who were Patres, and those who were Conscripti; and hence also was applied to the senators in general the designation of Patres Conscripti, the particle et, and, being understood to connect the two classes of senators. In the time of Julius Caesar, the number of senators was increased to nine hundred, and after his death to a thousand; many worthless persons having been admitted into the senate during the civil wars. Augustus afterwards reduced the number to six hundred.]

196 (return)

[ Antonius Musa was a freedman, and had acquired his knowledge of medicine while a domestic slave; a very common occurrence.]

197 (return)

[ A.U.C. 711.]

198 (return)

[ See cc. x. xi. xii. and xiii.}

199 (return)

[ One of them was Scipio, the father of Cornelia, whose death is lamented by Propertius, iv. 12. The other is unknown.]

200 (return)

[ A.U.C. 715.]

201 (return)

[ He is mentioned by Horace:

Occidit Daci Cotisonis agimen. Ode 8, b. iii.]

Most probably Antony knew the imputation to be unfounded, and made it for the purpose of excusing his own marriage with Cleopatra.]

202 (return)

[ This form of adoption consisted in a fictitious sale. See Cicero, Topic. iii.]

203 (return)

[ Curiae. Romulus divided the people of Rome into three tribes; and each tribe into ten Curiae. The number of tribes was afterwards increased by degrees to thirty-five; but that of the Curiae always remained the same.]

204 (return)

[ She was removed to Reggio in Calabria.]

205 (return)

[ Agrippa was first banished to the little desolate island of Planasia, now Pianosa. It is one of the group in the Tuscan sea, between Elba and Corsica.]

206 (return)

[ A quotation from the Iliad, 40, iii.; where Hector is venting his rage on Paris. The inflexion is slightly changed, the line in the original commencing, "Aith' opheles, etc., would thou wert, etc."]

207 (return)

[ Women called ustriculae, the barbers, were employed in thin delicate operation. It is alluded to by Juvenal, ix. 4, and Martial, v. 61.]

208 (return)

[ Cybele.—Gallus was either the name of a river in Phrygia, supposed to cause a certain frenzy in those who drank of its waters, or the proper name of the first priest of Cybele.]

209 (return)

[ A small drum, beat by the finger or thumb, was used by the priests of Cybele in their lascivious rites and in other orgies of a similar description, These drums were made of inflated skin, circular in shape, so that they had some resemblance to the orb which, in the statues of the emperor, he is represented as holding in his hand. The populace, with the coarse humour which was permitted to vent itself freely at the spectacles, did not hesitate to apply what was said in the play of the lewd priest of Cybele, to Augustus, in reference to the scandals attached to his private character. The word cinaedus, translated "wanton," might have been rendered by a word in vulgar use, the coarsest in the English language, and there is probably still more in the allusion too indelicate to be dwelt upon.]

210 (return)

[ Mark Antony makes use of fondling diminutives of the names of Tertia, Terentia, and Rufa, some of Augustus's favourites.]

211 (return)

[ Dodekatheos; the twelve Dii Majores; they are enumerated in two verses by Ennius:—

Juno, Vesta, Minerva, Ceres, Diana, Venus, Mars;

Mercurius, Jovis, Neptunus, Vulcanus, Apollo.]

212 (return)

[ Probably in the Suburra, where Martial informs us that torturing scourges were sold:

Tonatrix Suburrae faucibus sed et primis,

Cruenta pendent qua flagella tortorum. Mart. xi. 15, 1.]

213 (return)

[ Like the gold and silver-smiths of the middle ages, the Roman money-lenders united both trades. See afterwards, NERO, c. 5. It is hardly necessary to remark that vases or vessels of the compound metal which went by the name of Corinthian brass, or bronze, were esteemed even more valuable than silver plate.]

214 (return)

[ See c. xxxii. and note.]

215 (return)

[ The Romans, at their feasts, during the intervals of drinking, often played at dice, of which there were two kinds, the tesserae and tali. The former had six sides, like the modern dice; the latter, four oblong sides, for the two ends were not regarded. In playing, they used three tesserae and four tali, which were all put into a box wider below than above, and being shaken, were thrown out upon the gaming-board or table.]

216 (return)

[ The highest cast was so called.]

217 (return)

[ Enlarged by Tiberius and succeeding emperors. The ruins of the palace of the Caesars are still seen on the Palatine.]

218 (return)

[ Probably travertine, a soft limestone, from the Alban Mount, which was, therefore, cheaply procured and easily worked.]

219 (return)

[ It was usual among the Romans to have separate sets of apartments for summer and winter use, according to their exposure to the sun.]

220 (return)

[ This word may be interpreted the Cabinet of Arts. It was common, in the houses of the great, among the Romans, to have an apartment called the Study, or Museum. Pliny says, beautifully, "O mare! O littus! verum secretumque mouseion, quam multa invenitis, quam multa dictatis?" O sea! O shore! Thou real and secluded museum; what treasures of science do you not discover to us, how much do you teach us!—Epist. i. 9.]

221 (return)

[ Mecaenas had a house and gardens on the Esquiline Hill, celebrated for their salubrity—] Nunc licet Esquiliis habitore salubribus.—Hor. Sat. i. 3, 14.]

222 (return)

[ Such as Baiae, and the islands of Ischia, Procida, Capri, and others; the resorts of the opulent nobles, where they had magnificent marine villas.]

223 (return)

[ Now Tivoli, a delicious spot, where Horace had a villa, in which he hoped to spend his declining years.

Ver ubi longum, tepidasque praebet

Jupiter brumas: . . . . . . . . . .

. . . . . . . . ibi, tu calentem

Debita sparges lachryma favillam

Vatis amici. Odes, B. ii. 5.

Adrian also had a magnificent villa near Tibur.]

224 (return)

[ The Toga was a loose woollen robe, which covered the whole body, close at the bottom, but open at the top down to the girdle, and without sleeves. The right arm was thus at liberty, and the left supported a flap of the toga, which was drawn up, and thrown back over the left shoulder; forming what is called the Sinus, a fold or cavity upon the breast, in which things might be carried, and with which the face or head might be occasionally covered. When a person did any work, he tucked up his toga, and girt it round him. The toga of the rich and noble was finer and larger than that of others; and a new toga was called Pexa. None but Roman citizens were permitted to wear the toga; and banished persons were prohibited the use of it. The colour of the toga was white. The clavus was a purple border, by which the senators, and other orders, with the magistrates, were distinguished; the breadth of the stripe corresponding with their rank.]

225 (return)

[ In which the whole humour of the thing consisted either in the uses to which these articles were applied, or in their names having in Latin a double signification; matters which cannot be explained with any decency.]

226 (return)

[ Casum bubulum manu pressum; probably soft cheese, not reduced to solid consistence in the cheese-press.]

227 (return)

[ A species of fig tree, known in some places as Adam's fig. We have gathered them, in those climates, of the latter crop, as late as the month of November.]

228 (return)

[ Sabbatis Jejunium. Augustus might have been better informed of the Jewish rites, from his familiarity with Herod and others; for it is certain that their sabbath was not a day of fasting. Justin, however, fell into the same error: he says, that Moses appointed the sabbath-day to be kept for ever by the Jews as a fast, in memory of their fasting for seven days in the deserts of Arabia, xxxvi. 2. 14. But we find that there was a weekly fast among the Jews, which is perhaps what is here meant; the Sabbatis Jejunium being equivalent to the Naesteuo dis tou sabbatou, 'I fast twice in the week' of the Pharisee, in St. Luke xviii. 12.]

229 (return)

[ The Rhaetian wines had a great reputation; Virgil says,

— — —Ex quo te carmine dicam,

Rhaetica.

Georg. ii. 96.]

The vineyards lay at the foot of the Rhaetian Alps; their produce, we have reason to believe, was not a very generous liquor.]

230 (return)

[ A custom in all warm countries; the siesta of the Italians in later times.]

231 (return)

[ The strigil was used in the baths for scraping the body when in a state of perspiration. It was sometimes made of gold or silver, and not unlike in form the instrument used by grooms about horses when profusely sweating or splashed with mud.]

232 (return)

[ His physician, mentioned c. lix.]

233 (return)

[ Sept. 21st, a sickly season at Rome.]

234 (return)

[ Feminalibus et tibialibus: Neither the ancient Romans or the Greeks wore breeches, trews, or trowsers, which they despised as barbarian articles of dress. The coverings here mentioned were swathings for the legs and thighs, used mostly in cases of sickness or infirmity, and when otherwise worn, reckoned effeminate. But soon after the Romans became acquainted with the German and Celtic nations, the habit of covering the lower extremities, barbarous as it had been held, was generally adopted.]

235 (return)

[ Albula. On the left of the road to Tivoli, near the ruins of Adrian's villa. The waters are sulphureous, and the deposit from them causes incrustations on twigs and other matters plunged in the springs. See a curious account of this stream in Gell's Topography, published by Bohn, p 40.]

236 (return)

[ In spongam incubuisse, literally has fallen upon a sponge, as Ajax is said to have perished by falling on his own sword.]

237 (return)

[ Myrobrecheis. Suetonius often preserves expressive Greek phrases which Augustus was in the habit of using. This compound word meant literally, myrrh-scented, perfumed.]

238 (return)

[ These are variations of language of small importance, which can only be understood in the original language.]

239 (return)

[ It may create a smile to hear that, to prevent danger to the public, Augustus decreed that no new buildings erected in a public thoroughfare should exceed in height seventy feet. Trajan reduced it to sixty.]

240 (return)

[ Virgil is said to have recited before him the whole of the second, fourth, and sixth books of the Aeneid; and Octavia, being present, when the poet came to the passage referring to her son, commencing, "Tu Marcellus eris," was so much affected that she was carried out fainting.]

241 (return)

[ Chap. xix.]

242 (return)

[ Perhaps the point of the reply lay in the temple of Jupiter Tonans being placed at the approach to the Capitol from the Forum? See c. xxix. and c. xv., with the note.]

243 (return)

[ If these trees flourished at Rome in the time of Augustus, the winters there must have been much milder than they now are. There was one solitary palm standing in the garden of a convent some years ago, but it was of very stunted growth.]

244 (return)

[ The Republican forms were preserved in some of the larger towns.]

245 (return)

[ "The Nundinae occurred every ninth day, when a market was held at Rome, and the people came to it from the country. The practice was not then introduced amongst the Romans, of dividing their time into weeks, as we do, in imitation of the Jews. Dio, who flourished under Severus, says that it first took place a little before his time, and was derived from the Egyptians."—Thomson. A fact, if well founded, of some importance.]

246 (return)

[ "The Romans divided their months into calends, nones, and ides. The first day of the month was the calends of that month; whence they reckoned backwards, distinguishing the time by the day before the calends, the second day before the calends, and so on, to the ides of the preceding month. In eight months of the year, the nones were the fifth day, and the ides the thirteenth: but in March, May, July, and October, the nones fell on the seventh, and the ides on the fifteenth. From the nones they reckoned backwards to the calends, as they also did from the ides to the nones."—Ib.]

247 (return)

[ The early Christians shared with the Jews the aversion of the Romans to their religion, more than that of others, arising probably from its monotheistic and exclusive character. But we find from Josephus and Philo that Augustus was in other respects favourable to the Jews.]

248 (return)

[ Strabo tells us that Mendes was a city of Egypt near Lycopolis. Asclepias wrote a book in Greek with the idea of theologoumenon, in defence of some very strange religious rites, of which the example in the text is a specimen.]

249 (return)

[ Velletri stands on very high ground, commanding extensive views of the Pontine marshes and the sea.]

250 (return)

[ Munda was a city in the Hispania Boetica, where Julius Caesar fought a battle. See c. lvi.]

251 (return)

[ The good omen, in this instance, was founded upon the etymology of the names of the ass and its driver; the former of which, in Greek, signifies fortunate, and the latter, victorious.]

252 (return)

[ Aesar is a Greek word with an Etruscan termination; aisa signifying fate.]

253 (return)

[ Astura stood not far from Terracina, on the road to Naples. Augustus embarked there for the islands lying off that coast.]

254 (return)

[ "Puteoli" — "A ship of Alexandria." Words which bring to our recollection a passage in the voyage of St. Paul, Acts xxviii. 11-13. Alexandria was at that time the seat of an extensive commerce, and not only exported to Rome and other cities of Italy, vast quantities of corn and other products of Egypt, but was the mart for spices and other commodities, the fruits of the traffic with the east.]

255 (return)

[ The Toga has been already described in a note to c. lxxiii. The Pallium was a cloak, generally worn by the Greeks, both men and women, freemen and slaves, but particularly by philosophers.]

256 (return)

[ Masgabas seems, by his name, to have been of African origin.]

257 (return)

[ A courtly answer from the Professor of Science, in which character he attended Tiberius. We shall hear more of him in the reign of that emperor.]

258 (return)

[ Augustus was born A.U.C. 691, and died A.U.C. 766.]

259 (return)

[ Municipia were towns which had obtained the rights of Roman citizens. Some of them had all which could be enjoyed without residing at Rome. Others had the right of serving in the Roman legions, but not that of voting, nor of holding civil offices. The municipia retained their own laws and customs; nor were they obliged to receive the Roman laws unless they chose it.]

260 (return)

[ Bovillae, a small place on the Appian Way, about nineteen miles from Rome, now called Frattochio.]

261 (return)

[ Dio tells us that the devoted Livia joined with the knights in this pious office, which occupied them during five days.]

262 (return)

[ For the Flaminian Way, see before, p. 94, note. The superb monument erected by Augustus over the sepulchre of the imperial family was of white marble, rising in stages to a great height, and crowned by a dome, on which stood a statue of Augustus. Marcellus was the first who was buried in the sepulchre beneath. It stood near the present Porta del Popolo; and the Bustum, where the bodies of the emperor and his family were burnt, is supposed to have stood on the site of the church of the Madonna of that name.]

263 (return)

[ The distinction between the Roman people and the tribes, is also observed by Tacitus, who substitutes the word plebs, meaning, the lowest class of the populace.]

264 (return)

[ Those of his father Octavius, and his father by adoption, Julius Caesar.]

265 (return)

[ See before, c. 65. But he bequeathed a legacy to his daughter, Livia.]

266 (return)

[ Virgil.]

267 (return)

[ Ibid.]

268 (return)

[ Ibid.]

269 (return)

[ Geor. ii.]

270 (return)

[ I am prevented from entering into greater details, both by the size of my volume, and my anxiety to complete the undertaking.]

271 (return)

[ After performing these immortal achievements, while he was holding an assembly of the people for reviewing his army in the plain near the lake of Capra, a storm suddenly rose, attended with great thunder and lightning, and enveloped the king in so dense a mist, that it took all sight of him from the assembly. Nor was Romulus after this seen on earth. The consternation being at length over, and fine clear weather succeeding so turbulent a day, when the Roman youth saw the royal seat empty, though they readily believed the Fathers who had stood nearest him, that he was carried aloft by the storm, yet struck with the dread as it were of orphanage, they preserved a sorrowful silence for a considerable time. Then a commencement having been made by a few, the whole multitude salute Romulus a god, son of a god, the king and parent of the Roman city; they implore his favour with prayers, that he would be pleased always propitiously to preserve his own offspring. I believe that even then there were some who silently surmised that the king had been torn in pieces by the hands of the Fathers; for this rumour also spread, but was not credited; their admiration of the man and the consternation felt at the moment, attached importance to the other report. By the contrivance also of one individual, additional credit is said to have been gained to the matter. For Proculus Julius, whilst the state was still troubled with regret for the king, and felt incensed against the senators, a person of weight, as we are told, in any matter, however important, comes forward to the assembly. "Romans," he said, "Romulus, the father of this city, suddenly descending from heaven, appeared to me this day at day-break. While I stood covered with awe, and filled with a religious dread, beseeching him to allow me to see him face to face, he said; 'Go tell the Romans, that the gods do will, that my Rome should become the capital of the world. Therefore let them cultivate the art of war, and let them know and hand down to posterity, that no human power shall be able to withstand the Roman arms.' Having said this, he ascended up to heaven." It is surprising what credit was given to the man on his making this announcement, and how much the regret of the common people and army for the loss of Romulus, was assuaged upon the assurance of his immortality.]

272 (return)

[ Padua.]

273 (return)

[ Commentators seem to have given an erroneous and unbecoming sense to Cicero's exclamation, when they suppose that the object understood, as connected with altera, related to himself. Hope is never applied in this signification, but to a young person, of whom something good or great is expected; and accordingly, Virgil, who adopted the expression, has very properly applied it to Ascanius:

Et juxta Ascanius, magmae spes altera

Romae. Aeneid, xii.]

And by his side Ascanius took his place,

The second hope of Rome's immortal race.]

Cicero, at the time when he could have heard a specimen of Virgil's Eclogues, must have been near his grand climacteric; besides that, his virtues and talents had long been conspicuous, and were past the state of hope. It is probable, therefore, that altera referred to some third person, spoken of immediately before, as one who promised to do honour to his country. It might refer to Octavius, of whom Cicero at this time, entertained a high opinion; or it may have been spoken in an absolute manner, without reference to any person.]

274 (return)

[ I was born at Mantua, died in Calabria, and my tomb is at Parthenope: pastures, rural affairs, and heroes are the themes of my poems.]

275 (return)

[ The last members of these two lines, from the commas to the end are said to have been supplied by Erotes, Virgil's librarian.]

276 (return)

[ Carm. i. 17.]

277 (return)

[ "The Medea of Ovid proves, in my opinion, how surpassing would have been his success, if he had allowed his genius free scope, instead of setting bounds to it."]

278 (return)

[ Two faults have ruined me; my verse, and my mistake.]

279 (return)

[ These lines are thus rendered in the quaint version of Zachary Catlin.

I suffer 'cause I chanced a fault to spy,

So that my crime doth in my eyesight lie.

Alas! why wait my luckless hap to see

A fault at unawares to ruin me?]

280 (return)

[ "I myself employed you as ready agents in love, when my early youth sported in numbers adapted to it."—Riley's Ovid.]

281 (return)

[ "I long since erred by one composition; a fault that is not recent endures a punishment inflicted thus late. I had already published my poems, when, according to my privilege, I passed in review so many times unmolested as one of the equestrian order, before you the enquirer into criminal charges. Is it then possible that the writings which, in my want of confidence, I supposed would not have injured me when young, have now been my ruin in my old age?"—Riley's Ovid.]

282 (return)

[ This place, now called Temisvar, or Tomisvar, stands on one of the mouths of the Danube, about sixty-five miles E.N.E. from Silistria. The neighbouring bay of the Black Sea is still called the Gulf of Baba.]

283 (return)

[ "It appears to me, therefore, more reasonable to pursue glory by means of the intellect, than of bodily strength; and, since the life we enjoy is short to make the remembrance of it as lasting as possible."]

284 (return)

[ Intramural interments were prohibited at Rome by the laws of the Twelve Tables, notwithstanding the practice of reducing to ashes the bodies of the dead. It was only by special privilege that individuals who had deserved well of the state, and certain distinguished families were permitted to have tombs within the city.]

285 (return)

[ Among the Romans, all the descendants from one common stock were called Gentiles, being of the same race or kindred, however remote. The Gens, as they termed this general relation or clanship, was subdivided into families, in Familias vel Stirpes; and those of the same family were called Agnati. Relations by the father's side were also called Agnati, to distinguish them from Cognati, relations only by the mother's side. An Agnatus might also be called Cognatus, but not the contrary.] To mark the different gentes and familiae, and to distinguish the individuals of the same family, the Romans had commonly three names, the Praenomen, Nomen, and Cognomen. The praenomen was put first, and marked the individual. It was usually written with one letter; as A. for Aulus; C. Caius; D. Decimus: sometimes with two letters; as Ap. for Appius; Cn. Cneius; and sometimes with three; as Mam. for Mamercus.] The Nomen was put after the Praenomen, and marked the gens. It commonly ended in ius; as Julius, Tullius, Cornelius. The Cognomen was put last, and marked the familia; as Cicero, Caesar, etc.] Some gentes appear to have had no surname, as the Marian; and gens and familia seem sometimes to be put one for the other; as the Fabia gens, or Fabia familia.] Sometimes there was a fourth name, properly called the Agnomen, but sometimes likewise Cognomen, which was added on account of some illustrious action or remarkable event. Thus Scipio was named Publius Cornelius Scipio Africanus, from the conquest of Carthage. In the same manner, his brother was called Lucius Cornelius Scipio Asiaticus. Thus also, Quintus Fabius Maximus received the Agnomen of Cunctator, from his checking the victorious career of Hannibal by avoiding a battle.]

286 (return)

[ A.U.C. 474.]

287 (return)

[ A.U.C. 490.]

288 (return)

[ A.U.C. 547.]

289 (return)

[ A.U.C. 304.]

290 (return)

[ An ancient Latin town on the Via Appia, the present road to Naples, mentioned by St. Paul, Acts xxviii. 15, and Horace, Sat. i. 5, 3, in giving an account of their travels.]

291 (return)

[ A.U.C. 505.]

292 (return)

[ Cybele; first worshipped in Phrygia, about Mount Ida, from whence a sacred stone, the symbol of her divinity, probably an aerolite, was transported to Rome, in consequence of the panic occasioned by Hannibal's invasion, A.U.C. 508.]

293 (return)

[ A.U.C. 695.]

294 (return)

[ A.U.C. 611.]

295 (return)

[ A.U.C. 550.]

296 (return)

[ A.U.C. 663.]

297 (return)

[ A.U.C. 707.]

298 (return)

[ These, and other towns in the south of France, became, and long continued, the chief seats of Roman civilization among the Gauls; which is marked by the magnificent remains of ancient art still to be seen. Arles, in particular, is a place of great interest.]

299 (return)

[ A.U.C. 710.]

300 (return)

[ A.U.C. 713.]

301 (return)

[ A.U.C. 712. Before Christ about 39.]

302 (return)

[ A.U.C. 744.]

303 (return)

[ A.U.C. 735.]

304 (return)

[ See before, in the reign of AUGUSTUS, c. xxxii.]

305 (return)

[ A.U.C. 728.]

306 (return)

[ A.U.C. 734.]

307 (return)

[ A.U.C. 737.]

308 (return)

[ A.U.C. 741.]

309 (return)

[ A.U.C. 747.]

310 (return)

[ A.U.C. 748.]

311 (return)

[ Ostia, at the mouth of the Tiber, about thirteen miles from the city, was founded by Ancus Martius. Being the port of a city like Rome, it could not fail to become opulent; and it was a place of much resort, ornamented with fine edifices, and the environs "never failing of pasture in the summer time, and in the winter covered with roses and other flowers." The port having been filled up with the depositions of the Tiber, it became deserted, and is now abandoned to misery and malaria. The bishopric of Ostia being the oldest in the Roman church, its bishop has always retained some peculiar privileges.]

312 (return)

[ The Gymnasia were places of exercise, and received their name from the Greek word signifying naked, because the contending parties wore nothing but drawers.]

313 (return)

[ A.U.C. 752.]

314 (return)

[ The cloak and slippers, as distinguished from the Roman toga and shoes.]

315 (return)

[ A.U.C. 755.]

316 (return)

[ This fountain, in the Euganian hills, near Padua, famous for its mineral waters, is celebrated by Claudian in one of his elegies.]

317 (return)

[ The street called Carinae, at Rome, has been mentioned before; AUGUSTUS, c. v.; and also Mecaenas' house on the Esquiline, ib. c. lxxii. The gardens were formed on ground without the walls, and before used as a cemetery for malefactors, and the lower classes. Horace says—

Nunc licet Esquiliis habitare salubribus, atque

Aggere in aprico spatiari.—Sat. 1. i. viii. 13.]

318 (return)

[ A.U.C. 757.]

319 (return)

[ A.U.C. 760.]

320 (return)

[ A.U.C. 762.]

321 (return)

[ Reviving the simple habits of the times of the republic; "nec fortuitum cernere cespitem," as Horace describes it.—Ode 15.]

322 (return)

[ A.U.C. 765.]

323 (return)

[ The portico of the temple of Concord is still standing on the side of the Forum nearest the Capitol. It consists of six Ionic columns, each of one piece, and of a light-coloured granite, with bases and capitals of white marble, and two columns at the angles. The temple of Castor and Pollux has been mentioned before: JUL. c. x.]

324 (return)

[ A.U.C. 766.]

325 (return)

[ A.U.C. 767.]

326 (return)

[ Augustus interlards this epistle, and that subsequently quoted, with Greek sentences and phrases, of which this is one. It is so obscure, that commentators suppose that it is a mis-reading, but are not agreed on its drift.]

327 (return)

[ A verse in which the word in italics is substituted for cunctando, quoted from Ennius, who applied it to Fabius Maximus.]

328 (return)

[ Iliad, B. x. Diomede is speaking of Ulysses, where he asks that he may accompany him as a spy into the Trojan camp.]

329 (return)

[ Tiberius had adopted Germanicus. See before, c. xv. See also CALIGULA, c. i.]

330 (return)

[ In this he imitated Augustus. See c. liii. of his life.]

331 (return)

[ Si hanc fenestram aperueritis,' if you open that window, equivalent to our phrase, "if you open the door."]

332 (return)

[ Princeps, principatus, are the terms generally used by Suetonius to describe the supreme authority vested in the Caesars, as before at the beginning of chap. xxiv., distinguished from any terms which conveyed of kingly power, the forms of the republic, as we have lately seen, still subsisting.]

333 (return)

[ Strenas; the French etrennes.]

334 (return)

[ "Tiberius pulled down the temple of Isis, caused her image to be thrown into the Tiber, and crucified her priests." —Joseph. Ant. Jud. xviii. 4.]

335 (return)

[ Similia sectantes. We are strongly inclined to think that the words might be rendered "similar sects," conveying an allusion to the small and obscure body of Christians, who were at this period generally confounded with the Jews, and supposed only to differ from them in some peculiarities of their institutions, which Roman historians and magistrates did not trouble themselves to distinguish. How little even the well-informed Suetonius knew of the real facts, we shall find in the only direct notice of the Christians contained in his works (CLAUDIUS c. xxv., NERO, c. xvi.); but that little confirms our conjecture. All the commentators, however, give the passage the turn retained in the text. Josephus informs us of the particular occurrence which led to the expulsion of the Jews from Rome by Tiberius.—Ant. xviii. 5.]

336 (return)

[ Varro tells us that the Roman people "were more actively employed (manus movere) in the theatre and circus, than in the corn-fields and vineyards."—De Re Rustic. ii. And Juvenal, in his satires, frequently alludes to their passion for public spectacles, particularly in the well-known lines—

————Atque duas tantum res serrius optat,

Panem et Circenses. Sat. x. 80.]

337 (return)

[ The Cottian Alps derived their name from this king. They include that part of the chain which divides Dauphiny from Piedmont, and are crossed by the pass of the Mont Cenis.]

338 (return)

[ Antium, mentioned before, (AUG. c. lviii.) once a flourishing city of the Volscians, standing on the sea-coast, about thirty-eight miles from Rome, was a favourite resort of the emperors and persons of wealth. The Apollo Belvidere was found among the ruins of its temples and other edifices.]

339 (return)

[ A.U.C. 779.]

340 (return)

[ Terracina, standing at the southern extremity of the Pontine Marshes, on the shore of the Mediterranean. It is surrounded by high calcareous cliffs, in which there are caverns, affording, as Strabo informs us, cool retreats, attached to the Roman villas built round.]

341 (return)

[ Augustus died at Nola, a city in Campania. See c. lviii. of his life.]

342 (return)

[ Fidenae stood in a bend of the Tiber, near its junction with the Anio. There are few traces of it remaining.]

343 (return)

[ That any man could drink an amphora of wine at a draught, is beyond all credibility; for the amphora was nearly equal to nine gallons, English measure. The probability is, that the man had emptied a large vessel, which was shaped like an amphora.]

344 (return)

[ Capri, the luxurious retreat and scene of the debaucheries of the Roman emperors, is an island off the southern point of the bay of Naples, about twelve miles in circumference.]

345 (return)

[ Pan, the god of the shepherds, and inventor of the flute, was said to be the son of Mercury and Penelope. He was worshipped chiefly in Arcadia, and represented with the horns and feet of a goat. The Nymphs, as well as the Graces, were represented naked.]

346 (return)

[ The name of the island having a double meaning, and signifying also a goat.]

347 (return)

[ "Quasi pueros primae teneritudinis, quos 'pisciculos' vocabat, institueret, ut natanti sibi inter femina versarentur, ac luderent: lingua morsuque sensim appetentes; atque etiam quasi infantes firmiores, necdum tamen lacte depulsos, inguini ceu papillae admoveret: pronior sane ad id genus libidinis, et natura et aetate."]

348 (return)

[ "Foeminarum capitibus solitus illudere."]

349 (return)

[ "Obscoenitate oris hirsuto atque olido."]

350 (return)

[ "Hircum vetulum capreis naturam ligurire"]

351 (return)

[ The Temple of Vesta, like that dedicated to the same goddess at Tivoli, is round. There was probably one on the same site, and in the same circular form, erected by Numa Pompilius; the present edifice is far too elegant for that age, but there is no record of its erection, but it is known to have been repaired by Vespasian or Domitian after being injured by Nero's fire. Its situation, near the Tiber, exposed it to floods, from which we find it suffered, from Horace's lines—

"Vidimus flavum Tiberim, retortis

Littore Etrusco violenter undis,

Ire dejectum monumenta Regis,

Templaque Vestae."—Ode, lib. i. 2. 15.

This beautiful temple is still in good preservation. It is surrounded by twenty columns of white marble, and the wall of the cell, or interior (which is very small, its diameter being only the length of one of the columns), is also built of blocks of the same material, so nicely joined, that it seems to be formed of one solid mass.]

352 (return)

[ Antlia; a machine for drawing up water in a series of connected buckets, which was worked by the feet, nisu pedum.]

353 (return)

[ The elder Livia was banished to this island by Augustus. See c. lxv. of his life.]

354 (return)

[ An island in the Archipelago.]

355 (return)

[ This Theodore is noticed by Quintilian, Instit. iii. 1. Gadara was in Syria.]

356 (return)

[ It mattered not that the head substituted was Tiberius's own.]

357 (return)

[ The verses were probably anonymous.]

358 (return)

[ Oderint dum probent: Caligula used a similar expression; Oderint dum metuant.]

359 (return)

[ A.U.C. 778. Tacit. Annal. iv. The historian's name was A. Cremutius Cordo. Dio has preserved the passage, xlvii. p. 619. Brutus had already called Cassius "The last of the Romans," in his lamentation over his dead body.]

360 (return)

[ She was the sister of Germanicus, and Tacitus calls her Livia; but Suetonius is in the habit of giving a fondling or diminutive term to the names of women, as Claudilla, for Claudia, Plautilla, etc.]

361 (return)

[ Priam is said to have had no less than fifty sons and daughters; some of the latter, however, survived him, as Hecuba, Helena, Polyxena, and others.]

362 (return)

[ There were oracles at Antium and Tibur. The "Praenestine Lots" are described by Cicero, De Divin. xi. 41.]

363 (return)

[ Agrippina, and Nero and Drusus.]

364 (return)

[ He is mentioned before in the Life of AUGUSTUS, c. xc.; and also by Horace, Cicero, and Tacitus.]

365 (return)

[ Obscure Greek poets, whose writings were either full of fabulous stories, or of an amatory kind.]

366 (return)

[ It is suggested that the text should be amended, so that the sentence should read—"A Greek soldier;" for of what use could it have been to examine a man in Greek, and not allow him to give his replies in the same language?]

367 (return)

[ So called from Appius Claudius, the Censor, one of Tiberius's ancestors, who constructed it. It took a direction southward of Rome, through Campania to Brundusium, starting from what is the present Porta di San Sebastiano, from which the road to Naples takes its departure.]

368 (return)

[ A small town on the coast of Latium, not far from Antium, and the present Nettuno. It was here that Cicero was slain by the satellites of Antony.]

369 (return)

[ A town on a promontory of the same dreary coast, between Antium and Terracina, built on a promontory surrounded by the sea and the marsh, still called Circello.]

370 (return)

[ Misenum, a promontory to which Aeneas is said to have given its name from one of his followers. (Aen. ii. 234.) It is now called Capo di Miseno, and shelters the harbour of Mola di Gaieta, belonging to Naples. This was one of the stations of the Roman fleet.]

371 (return)

[ Tacitus agrees with Suetonius as to the age of Tiberius at the time of his death. Dio states it more precisely, as being seventy-seven years, four months, and nine days.]

372 (return)

[ Caius Caligula, who became his successor.]

373 (return)

[ Tacitus and Dio add that he was smothered under a heap of heavy clothes.]

374 (return)

[ In the temple of the Palatine Apollo. See AUGUSTUS, c. xxix.]

375 (return)

[ Atella, a town between Capua and Naples, now called San Arpino, where there was an amphitheatre. The people seemed to have raised the shout in derision, referring, perhaps, to the Atellan fables, mentioned in c. xiv.; and in their fury they proposed that his body should only be grilled, as those of malefactors were, instead of being reduced to ashes.]

376 (return)

[ Tacit. Annal. lib. ii.]

377 (return)

[ A.U.C. 757.]

378 (return)

[ A.U.C. 765.]

379 (return)

[ A.U.C. 770.]

380 (return)

[ A.U.C. 767.]

381 (return)

[ A.U.C. 771.]

382 (return)

[ This opinion, like some others which occur in Suetonius, may justly be considered as a vulgar error; and if the heart was found entire, it must have been owing to the weakness of the fire, rather than to any quality communicated to the organ, of resisting the power of that element.]

383 (return)

[ The magnificent title of King of Kings has been assumed, at different times, by various potentates. The person to whom it is here applied, is the king of Parthia. Under the kings of Persia, and even under the Syro-Macedonian kings, this country was of no consideration, and reckoned a part of Hyrcania. But upon the revolt of the East from the Syro-Macedonians, at the instigation of Arsaces, the Parthians are said to have conquered eighteen kingdoms.]

384 (return)

[ A.U.C. 765.]

385 (return)

[ It does not appear that Gaetulicus wrote any historical work, but Martial, Pliny, and others, describe him as a respectable poet.]

386 (return)

[ Supra Confluentes. The German tribe here mentioned occupied the country between the Rhine and the Meuse, and gave their name to Treves (Treviri), its chief town. Coblentz had its ancient name of Confluentes, from its standing at the junction of the two rivers. The exact site of the village in which Caligula was born is not known. Cluverius conjectures that it may be Capelle.]

387 (return)

[ Chap. vii.]

388 (return)

[ The name was derived from Caliga, a kind of boot, studded with nails, used by the common soldiers in the Roman army.]

389 (return)

[ According to Tacitus, who gives an interesting account of these occurrences, Treves was the place of refuge to which the young Caius was conveyed.—Annal. i.]

390 (return)

[ In c. liv. of TIBERIUS, we have seen that his brothers Drusus and Nero fell a sacrifice to these artifices.]

391 (return)

[ Tiberius, who was the adopted father of Germanicus.]

392 (return)

[ Natriceus, a water-snake, so called from nato, to swim. The allusion is probably to Caligula's being reared in the island of Capri.]

393 (return)

[ As Phaeton is said to have set the world on fire.]

394 (return)

[ See the Life of TIBERIUS, c. lxxiii.]

395 (return)

[ His name also was Tiberius. See before, TIBERIUS, c. lxxvi.]

396 (return)

[ Procida, Ischia, Capri, etc.]

397 (return)

[ The eagle was the standard of the legion, each cohort of which had its own ensign, with different devices; and there were also little images of the emperors, to which divine honours were paid.]

398 (return)

[ See before, cc. liii. liv.]

399 (return)

[ See TIBERIUS, c. x.; and note.]

400 (return)

[ The mausoleum built by Augustus, mentioned before in his Life, c. C.]

401 (return)

[ The Carpentum was a carriage, commonly with two wheels, and an arched covering, but sometimes without a covering; used chiefly by matrons, and named, according to Ovid, from Carmenta, the mother of Evander. Women were prohibited the use of it in the second Punic war, by the Oppian law, which, however, was soon after repealed. This chariot was also used to convey the images of the illustrious women to whom divine honours were paid, in solemn processions after their death, as in the present instance. It is represented on some of the sestertii.]

402 (return)

[ See cc. xiv. and xxiii. of the present History.]

403 (return)

[ Ib. cc. vii. and xxiv.]

404 (return)

[ Life of TIBERIUS, c. xliii.]

405 (return)

[ See the Life of AUGUSTUS, cc. xxviii. and ci.]

406 (return)

[ Julius Caesar had shared it with them (c. xli.). Augustus had only kept up the form (c. xl.). Tiberius deprived the Roman people of the last remains of the freedom of suffrage.]

407 (return)

[ The city of Rome was founded on the twenty-first day of April, which was called Palilia, from Pales, the goddess of shepherds, and ever afterwards kept as a festival.]

408 (return)

[ A.U.C. 790.]

409 (return)

[ A.U.C. 791.]

410 (return)

[ A.U.C. 793.]

411

[ A.U.C. 794.]

412 (return)

[ The Saturnalia, held in honour of Saturn, was, amongst the Romans, the most celebrated festival of the whole year, and held in the month of December. All orders of the people then devoted themselves to mirth and feasting; friends sent presents to one another; and masters treated their slaves upon a footing of equality. At first it was held only for one day, afterwards for three days, and was now prolonged by Caligula's orders.]

413 (return)

[ See AUGUSTUS, cc. xxix and xliii. The amphitheatre of Statilius Taurus is supposed to have stood in the Campus Martius, and the elevation now called the Monte Citorio, to have been formed by its ruins.]

414 (return)

[ Supposed to be a house, so called, adjoining the Circus, in which some of the emperor's attendants resided.]

415 (return)

[ Now Puzzuoli, on the shore of the bay of Naples. Every one knows what wealth was lavished here and at Baiae, on public works and the marine villas of the luxurious Romans, in the times of the emperors.]

416 (return)

[ The original terminus of the Appian Way was at Brundusium. This mole formed what we should call a nearer station to Rome, on the same road, the ruins of which are still to be seen. St. Paul landed there.]

417 (return)

[ Essedis: they were light cars, on two wheels, constructed to carry only one person; invented, it is supposed, by the Belgians, and by them introduced into Britain, where they were used in war. The Romans, after their expeditions in Gaul and Britain, adopted this useful vehicle instead of their more cumbrous RHEDA, not only for journeys where dispatch was required, but in solemn processions, and for ordinary purposes. They seem to have become the fashion, for Ovid tells us that these little carriages were driven by young ladies, themselves holding the reins, Amor. xi. 16. 49.]

418 (return)

[ Suetonius flourished about seventy years after this, in the reign of Adrian, and derived many of the anecdotes which give interest to his history from cotemporary persons. See CLAUDIUS, c. xv. etc.]

419 (return)

[ See TIBERIUS, c. xlvii. and AUGUSTUS, c. xxxi.]

420 (return)

[ This aqueduct, commenced by Caligula and completed by Claudian, a truly imperial work, conveyed the waters of two streams to Rome, following the valley of the Anio from above Tivoli. The course of one of these rivulets was forty miles, and it was carried on arches, immediately after quitting its source, for a distance of three miles. The other, the Anio Novus, also began on arches, which continued for upwards of twelve miles. After this, both were conveyed under ground; but at the distance of six miles from the city, they were united, and carried upon arches all the rest of the way. This is the most perfect of all the ancient aqueducts; and it has been repaired, so as to convey the Acqua Felice, one of the three streams which now supply Rome. See CLAUDIUS, c. xx.]

421 (return)

[ By Septa, Suetonius here means the huts or barracks of the pretorian camp, which was a permanent and fortified station. It stood to the east of the Viminal and Quirinal hills, between the present Porta Pia and S. Lorenzo, where there is a quadrangular projection in the city walls marking the site. The remains of the Amphitheatrum Castrense stand between the Porta Maggiore and S. Giovanni, formerly without the ancient walls, but now included in the line. It is all of brick, even the Corinthian pillars, and seems to have been but a rude structure, suited to the purpose for which it was built, the amusement of the soldiers, and gymnastic exercises. For this purpose they were used to construct temporary amphitheatres near the stations in the distant provinces, which were not built of stone or brick, but hollow circular spots dug in the ground, round which the spectators sat on the declivity, on ranges of seats cut in the sod. Many vestiges of this kind have been traced in Britain.]

422 (return)

[ The Isthmus of Corinth; an enterprize which had formerly been attempted by Demetrius, and which was also projected by Julius Caesar, c. xliv., and Nero, c. xix.; but they all failed of accomplishing it.]

423 (return)

[ On the authority of Dio Cassius and the Salmatian manuscript, this verse from Homer is substituted for the common reading, which is,

Eis gaian Danaon perao se.

Into the land of Greece I will transport thee.]

424 (return)

[ Alluding, in the case of Romulus, to the rape of the Sabines; and in that of Augustus to his having taken Livia from her husband.— AUGUSTUS, c. lxii.]

425 (return)

[ Selene was the daughter of Mark Antony by Cleopatra.]

426 (return)

[ See c. xii.]

427 (return)

[ The vast area of the Roman amphitheatres had no roof, but the audience were protected against the sun and bad weather by temporary hangings stretched over it.]

428 (return)

[ A proverbial expression, meaning, without distinction.]

429 (return)

[ The islands off the coast of Italy, in the Tuscan sea and in the Archipelago, were the usual places of banishment. See before, c. xv.; and in TIBERIUS, c. liv., etc.]

430 (return)

[ Anticyra, an island in the Archipelago, was famous for the growth of hellebore. This plant being considered a remedy for insanity, the proverb arose—Naviga in Anticyram, as much as to say, "You are mad."]

431 (return)

[ Meaning the province in Asia, called Galatia, from the Gauls who conquered it, and occupied it jointly with the Greek colonists.]

432 (return)

[ A quotation from the tragedy of Atreus, by L. Attius, mentioned by Cicero. Off. i. 28.]

433 (return)

[ See before, AUGUSTUS, c. lxxi.]

434 (return)

[ These celebrated words are generally attributed to Nero; but Dio and Seneca agree with Suetonius in ascribing them to Caligula.]

435 (return)

[ Gladiators were distinguished by their armour and manner of fighting. Some were called Secutores, whose arms were a helmet, a shield, a sword, or a leaden ball. Others, the usual antagonists of the former, were named Retiarii. A combatant of this class was dressed in a short tunic, but wore nothing on his head. He carried in his left hand a three-pointed lance, called Tridens or Fuscina, and in his right, a net, with which he attempted to entangle his adversary, by casting it over his head, and suddenly drawing it together; when with his trident he usually slew him. But if he missed his aim, by throwing the net either too short or too far, he instantly betook himself to flight, and endeavoured to prepare his net for a second cast. His antagonist, in the mean time, pursued, to prevent his design, by dispatching him.]

436 (return)

[ AUGUSTUS, c. xxiii.]

437 (return)

[ TIBERIUS, c. xl.]

438 (return)

[ See before, c. xix.]

439 (return)

[ Popae were persons who, at public sacrifices, led the victim to the altar. They had their clothes tucked up, and were naked to the waist. The victim was led with a slack rope, that it might not seem to be brought by force, which was reckoned a bad omen. For the same reason, it was allowed to stand loose before the altar, and it was thought a very unfavourable sign if it got away.]

440 (return)

[ Plato de Repub. xi.; and Cicero and Tull. xlviii.]

441 (return)

[ The collar of gold, taken from the gigantic Gaul who was killed in single combat by Titus Manlius, called afterwards Torquatus, was worn by the lineal male descendants of the Manlian family. But that illustrious race becoming extinct, the badge of honour, as well as the cognomen of Torquatus, was revived by Augustus, in the person of Caius Nonius Asprenas, who perhaps claimed descent by the female line from the family of Manlius.]

442 (return)

[ Cincinnatus signifies one who has curled or crisped hair, from which Livy informs us that Lucius Quintus derived his cognomen. But of what badge of distinction Caligula deprived the family of the Cincinnati, unless the natural feature was hereditary, and he had them all shaved—a practice we find mentioned just below—history does not inform us, nor are we able to conjecture.]

443 (return)

[ The priest of Diana Nemorensis obtained and held his office by his prowess in arms, having to slay his competitors, and offer human sacrifices, and was called Rex from his reigning paramount in the adjacent forest. The temple of this goddess of the chase stood among the deep woods which clothe the declivities of the Alban Mount, at a short distance from Rome—nemus signifying a grove. Julius Caesar had a residence there. See his Life, c. lxxi. The venerable woods are still standing, and among them chestnut-trees, which, from their enormous girth and vast apparent age, we may suppose to have survived from the era of the Caesars. The melancholy and sequestered lake of Nemi, deep set in a hollow of the surrounding woods, with the village on its brink, still preserve the name of Nemi.]

444 (return)

[ An Essedarian was one who fought from an Esseda, the light carriage described in a former note, p. 264.]

445 (return)

[ See before, JULIUS, c. x., and note.]

446 (return)

[ Particularly at Baiae, see before, c. xix. The practice of encroaching on the sea on this coast, commenced before,—

Jactis in altum molibus.—Hor. Od. B. iii. 1. 34.]

447 (return)

[ Most of the gladiators were slaves.]

448 (return)

[ The part of the Palatium built or occupied by Augustus and Tiberius.]

449 (return)

[ Mevania, a town of Umbria. Its present name is Bevagna. The Clitumnus is a river in the same country, celebrated for the breed of white cattle, which feed in the neighbouring pastures.]

450 (return)

[ Caligula appears to have meditated an expedition to Britain at the time of his pompous ovation at Puteoli, mentioned in c. xiii.; but if Julius Caesar could gain no permanent footing in this island, it was very improbable that a prince of Caligula's character would ever seriously attempt it, and we shall presently see that the whole affair turned out a farce.]

451 (return)

[ It seems generally agreed, that the point of the coast which was signalized by the ridiculous bravado of Caligula, somewhat redeemed by the erection of a lighthouse, was Itium, afterwards called Gessoriacum, and Bononia (Boulogne), a town belonging to the Gaulish tribe of the Morini; where Julius Caesar embarked on his expedition, and which became the usual place of departure for the transit to Britain.]

452 (return)

[ The denarius was worth at this time about seven pence or eight pence of our money.]

453 (return)

[ Probably to Anticyra. See before, c. xxix. note]

454 (return)

[ The Cimbri were German tribes on the Elbe, who invaded Italy A.U.C. 640, and were defeated by Metellus.]

455 (return)

[ The Senones were a tribe of Cis-Alpine Gauls, settled in Umbria, who sacked and pillaged Rome A.U.C. 363.]

456 (return)

[ By the transmarine provinces, Asia, Egypt, etc., are meant; so that we find Caligula entertaining visions of an eastern empire, and removing the seat of government, which were long afterwards realized in the time of Constantine.]

457 (return)

[ See AUGUSTUS, c. xviii.]

458 (return)

[ About midnight, the watches being divided into four.]

459 (return)

[ Scabella: commentators are undecided as to the nature of this instrument. Some of them suppose it to have been either a sort of cymbal or castanet, but Pitiscus in his note gives a figure of an ancient statue preserved at Florence, in which a dancer is represented with cymbals in his hands, and a kind of wind instrument attached to the toe of his left foot, by which it is worked by pressure, something in the way of an accordion.]

460 (return)

[ The port of Rome.]

461 (return)

[ The Romans, in their passionate devotion to the amusements of the circus and the theatre, were divided into factions, who had their favourites among the racers and actors, the former being distinguished by the colour of the party to which they belonged. See before, c. xviii., and TIBERIUS, c. xxxvii.]

462 (return)

[ In the slang of the turf, the name of Caligula's celebrated horse might, perhaps, be translated "Go a-head."]

463 (return)

[Josephus, who supplies us with minute details of the assassination of Caligula, says that he made no outcry, either disdaining it, or because an alarm would have been useless; but that he attempted to make his escape through a corridor which led to some baths behind the palace. Among the ruins on the Palatine hill, these baths still attract attention, some of the frescos being in good preservation. See the account in Josephus, xix. 1, 2.]

464 (return)

[ The Lamian was an ancient family, the founders of Formiae. They had gardens on the Esquiline mount.]

465 (return)

[ A.U.C. 714.]

466 (return)

[ Pliny describes Drusus as having in this voyage circumnavigated Germany, and reached the Cimbrian Chersonese, and the Scythian shores, reeking with constant fogs.]

467 (return)

[ Tacitus, Annal. xi. 8, 1, mentions this fosse, and says that Drusus sailed up the Meuse and the Waal. Cluverius places it between the village of Iselvort and the town of Doesborg.]

468 (return)

[ The Spolia Opima were the spoils taken from the enemy's king, or chief, when slain in single combat by a Roman general. They were always hung up in the Temple of Jupiter Feretrius. Those spoils had been obtained only thrice since the foundation of Rome; the first by Romulus, who slew Acron, king of the Caeninenses; the next by A. Cornelius Cossus, who slew Tolumnius, king of the Veientes, A.U. 318; and the third by M. Claudius Marcellus, who slew Viridomarus, king of the Gauls, A.U. 330.]

469 (return)

[ A.U.C. 744.]

470 (return)

[ This epistle, as it was the habit of Augustus, is interspersed with Greek phrases.]

471 (return)

[ The Alban Mount is the most interesting feature of the scenery of the Campagna about Rome, Monti Cavo, the summit, rising above an amphitheatre of magnificent woods, to an elevation of 2965 French feet. The view is very extensive: below is the lake of Albano, the finest of the volcanic lakes in Italy, and the modern town of the same name. Few traces remain of Alba Longa, the ancient capital of Latium.]

472

[ On the summit of the Alban Mount, on the site of the present convent, stood the temple of Jupiter Latialis, where the Latin tribes assembled annually, and renewed their league, during the Feriae Latinae, instituted by Tarquinus Superbus. It was here, also, that Roman generals, who were refused the honours of a full triumph, performed the ovation, and sacrificed to Jupiter Latialis. Part of the triumphal way by which the mountain was ascended, formed of vast blocks of lava, is still in good preservation, leading through groves of chestnut trees of vast size and age. Spanning them with extended arms—none of the shortest—the operation was repeated five times in compassing their girth.]

473 (return)

[ CALIGULA. See c. v. of his life.]

474 (return)

[ A.U.C. 793. Life of CALIGULA, cc. xliv., xlv., etc.]

475 (return)

[ A.U.C. 794.]

476 (return)

[ The chamber of Mercury; the names of deities being given to different apartments, as those "of Isis," "of the Muses," etc.]

477 (return)

[ See the note, p. 265.]

478 (return)

[ The attentive reader will have marked the gradual growth of the power of the pretorian guard, who now, and on so many future occasions, ruled the destinies of the empire.]

479 (return)

[ See AUGUSTUS, cc. xliii., xlv.]

480 (return)

[ Ib. c. ci.]

481 (return)

[ Germanicus.]

482 (return)

[ Naples and other cities on that coast were Greek colonies.]

483 (return)

[ This arch was erected in memory of the standards (the eagles) lost by Varus, in Germany, having been recovered by Germanicus under the auspices of Tiberius. See his Life, c. xlvii.; and Tacit. Annal. ii. 41. It seems to have stood at the foot of the Capitol, on the side of the Forum, near the temple of Concord; but there are no remains of it.]

484 (return)

[ Tacitus informs us that the same application had been made by Tiberius. Annal. iii. The prefect of the pretorian guards, high and important as his office had now become, was not allowed to enter the senate-house, unless he belonged to the equestrian order.]

485 (return)

[ The procurators had the administration of some of the less important provinces, with rank and authority inferior to that of the pro-consuls and prefects, Frequent mention of these officers is made by Josephus; and Pontius Pilate, who sentenced our Lord to crucifixion, held that office in Judaea, under Tiberius.]

486 (return)

[ Pollio and Messala were distinguished orators, who flourished under the Caesars Julius and Augustus.]

487 (return)

[ A.U.C. 795, 796.]

488 (return)

[ A.U.C. 800, 804.]

489 (return)

[ "Ad bestias" had become a new and frequent sentence for malefactors. It will be recollected, that it was the most usual form of martyrdom for the primitive Christians. Polycarp was brought all the way from Smyrna to be exposed to it in the amphitheatre at Rome.]

490 (return)

[ This reminds us of the decision of Solomon in the case of the two mothers, who each claimed a child as their own, 1 Kings iii. 22-27.]

491 (return)

[ A most absurd judicial conclusion, the business of the judge or court being to decide, on weighing the evidence, on which side the truth preponderated.]

492 (return)

[ See the note in CALIGULA, c. xix., as to Suetonius's sources of information from persons cotemporary with the occurrences he relates.]

493 (return)

[ The insult was conveyed in Greek, which seems, from Suetonius, to have been in very common use at Rome: kai su geron ei, kai moros.]

494 (return)

[ A.U.C. 798, or 800.]

495 (return)

[ There was a proverb to the same effect: "Si non caste, saltem caute."]

496 (return)

[ Ptolemy appointed him to an office which led him to assume a foreign dress. Rabirius was defended by Cicero in one of his orations, which is extant.]

497 (return)

[ The Sigillaria was a street in Rome, where a fair was held after the Saturnalia, which lasted seven days; and toys, consisting of little images and dolls, which gave their name to the street and festival, were sold. It appears from the text, that other articles were exposed for sale in this street. Among these were included elegant vases of silver and bronze. There appears also to have been a bookseller's shop, for an ancient writer tells us that a friend of his showed him a copy of the Second Book of the Aeneid, which he had purchased there.]

498 (return)

[ Opposed to this statement there is a passage in Servius Georgius, iii. 37, asserting that he had heard (accipimus) that Augustus, besides his victories in the east, triumphed over the Britons in the west; and Horace says:—

Augustus adjectis Britannis

Imperio gravibusque Persis.—Ode iii. 5, 1.

Strabo likewise informs us, that in his time, the petty British kings sent embassies to cultivate the alliance of Augustus, and make offerings in the Capitol: and that nearly the whole island was on terms of amity with the Romans, and, as well as the Gauls, paid a light tribute.—Strabo, B. iv. p. 138. That Augustus contemplated a descent on the island, but was prevented from attempting it by his being recalled from Gaul by the disturbances in Dalmatia, is very probable. Horace offers his vows for its success:

Serves iturum, Caesarem in ultimos Orbis Britannos.—Ode i. 35.

But the word iturus shews that the scheme was only projected, and the lines previously quoted are mere poetical flattery. Strabo's statement of the communications kept up with the petty kings of Britain, who were perhaps divided by intestine wars, are, to a certain extent, probably correct, as such a policy would be a prelude to the intended expedition.]

499 (return)

[ Circius. Aulus Gellius, Seneca, and Pliny, mention under this name the strong southerly gales which prevail in the gulf of Genoa and the neighbouring seas.]

500 (return)

[ The Stoechades were the islands now called Hieres, off Toulon.]

501 (return)

[ Claudius must have expended more time in his march from Marseilles to Gessoriacum, as Boulogne was then called, than in his vaunted conquest of Britain.]

502 (return)

[ In point of fact, he was only sixteen days in the island, receiving the submission of some tribes in the south-eastern districts. But the way had been prepared for him by his able general, Aulus Plautius, who defeated Cunobeline, and made himself master of his capital, Camulodunum, or Colchester. These successes were followed up by Ostorius, who conquered Caractacus and sent him to Rome. It is singular that Suetonius has supplied us with no particulars of these events. Some account of them is given in the disquisition appended to this life of CLAUDIUS. The expedition of Plautius took place A.U.C. 796., A.D. 44.]

503 (return)

[ Carpentum: see note in CALIGULA, c. xv.]

504 (return)

[ The Aemiliana, so called because it contained the monuments of the family of that name, was a suburb of Rome, on the Via Lata, outside the gate.]

505 (return)

[ The Diribitorium was a house in the Flaminian Circus, begun by Agrippa, and finished by Augustus, in which soldiers were mustered and their pay distributed; from whence it derived its name. When the Romans went to give their votes at the election of magistrates, they were conducted by officers named Diribitores. It is possible that one and the same building may have been used for both purposes.] The Flaminian Circus was without the city walls, in the Campus Martius. The Roman college now stands on its site.]

506 (return)

[ A law brought in by the consuls Papius Mutilus and Quintus Poppaeus; respecting which, see AUGUSTUS, c. xxxiv.]

507 (return)

[ The Fucine Lake is now called Lago di Celano, in the Farther Abruzzi. It is very extensive, but shallow, so that the difficulty of constructing the Claudian emissary, can scarcely be compared to that encountered in a similar work for lowering the level of the waters in the Alban lake, completed A.U.C. 359.]

508 (return)

[ Respecting the Claudian aqueduct, see CALIGULA, c. xxi.]

509 (return)

[ Ostia is referred to in a note, TIBERIUS, c. xi.]

510 (return)

[ Suetonius calls this "the great obelisk" in comparison with those which Augustus had placed in the Circus Maximus and Campus Martius. The one here mentioned was erected by Caligula in his Circus, afterwards called the Circus of Nero. It stood at Heliopolis, having been dedicated to the sun, as Herodotus informs us, by Phero, son of Sesostris, in acknowledgment of his recovery from blindness. It was removed by Pope Sixtus V. in 1586, under the celebrated architect, Fontana, to the centre of the area before St. Peter's, in the Vatican, not far from its former position. This obelisk is a solid piece of red granite, without hieroglyphics, and, with the pedestal and ornaments at the top, is 182 feet high. The height of the obelisk itself is 113 palms, or 84 feet.]

511 (return)

[ Pliny relates some curious particulars of this ship: "A fir tree of prodigious size was used in the vessel which, by the command of Caligula, brought the obelisk from Egypt, which stands in the Vatican Circus, and four blocks of the same sort of stone to support it. Nothing certainly ever appeared on the sea more astonishing than this vessel; 120,000 bushels of lentiles served for its ballast; the length of it nearly equalled all the left side of the port of Ostia; for it was sent there by the emperor Claudius. The thickness of the tree was as much as four men could embrace with their arms." —B. xvi. c. 76.]

512 (return)

[ See AUGUSTUS, c. xxxi. It appears to have been often a prey to the flames, TIBERIUS, c. xli.; CALIGULA, c. xx.]

513 (return)

[ Contrary to the usual custom of rising and saluting the emperor without acclamations.]

514 (return)

[ A.U.C. 800.]

515 (return)

[ The Secular Games had been celebrated by Augustus, A.U.C. 736. See c. xxxi. of his life, and the Epode of Horace written on the occasion.]

516 (return)

[ In the circus which he had himself built.]

517 (return)

[ Tophina; Tuffo, a porous stone of volcanic origin, which abounds in the neighbourhood of Rome, and, with the Travertino, is employed in all common buildings.]

518 (return)

[ In compliment to the troops to whom he owed his elevation: see before, c. xi.]

519 (return)

[ Palumbus was a gladiator: and Claudius condescended to pun upon his name, which signifies a wood-pigeon.]

520 (return)

[ See before, c. xvii. Described is c. xx and note.]

521 (return)

[ See before, AUGUSTUS, c. xxxiv.]

522 (return)

[ To reward his able services as commander of the army in Britain. See before, c. xvii.]

523 (return)

[ German tribes between the Elbe and the Weser, whose chief seat was at Bremen, and others about Ems or Lueneburg.]

524 (return)

[ This island in the Tiber, opposite the Campus Martius, is said to have been formed by the corn sown by Tarquin the Proud on that consecrated field, and cut down and thrown by order of the consuls into the river. The water being low, it lodged in the bed of the stream, and gradual deposits of mud raising it above the level of the water, it was in course of time covered with buildings. Among these was the temple of Aesculapius, erected A.U.C. 462, to receive the serpent, the emblem of that deity which was brought to Rome in the time of a plague. There is a coin of Antoninus Pius recording this event, and Lumisdus has preserved copies of some curious votive inscriptions in acknowledgment of cures which were found in its ruins, Antiquities of Rome, p. 379. It was common for the patient after having been exposed some nights in the temple, without being cured, to depart and put an end to his life. Suetonius here informs us that slaves so exposed, at least obtained their freedom.]

525 (return)

[ Which were carried on the shoulders of slaves. This prohibition had for its object either to save the wear and tear in the narrow streets, or to pay respect to the liberties of the town.]

526 (return)

[ See the note in c. i. of this life of CLAUDIUS.]

527 (return)

[ Seleucus Philopater, son of Antiochus the Great, who being conquered by the Romans, the succeeding kings of Syria acknowledged the supremacy of Rome.]

528 (return)

[ Suetonius has already, in TIBERIUS, c. xxxvi., mentioned the expulsion of the Jews from Rome, and this passage confirms the conjecture, offered in the note, that the Christians were obscurely alluded to in the former notice. The antagonism between Christianity and Judaism appears to have given rise to the tumults which first led the authorities to interfere. Thus much we seem to learn from both passages: but the most enlightened men of that age were singularly ill-informed on the stupendous events which had recently occurred in Judaea, and we find Suetonius, although he lived at the commencement of the first century of the Christian aera, when the memory of these occurrences was still fresh, and it might be supposed, by that time, widely diffused, transplanting Christ from Jerusalem to Rome, and placing him in the time of Claudius, although the crucifixion took place during the reign of Tiberius. St. Luke, Acts xviii. 2, mentions the expulsion of the Jews from Rome by the emperor Claudius: Dio, however, says that he did not expel them, but only forbad their religious assemblies. It was very natural for Suetonius to write Chrestus instead of Christus, as the former was a name in use among the Greeks and Romans. Among others, Cicero mentions a person of that name in his Fam. Ep. 11. 8.]

529 (return)

[ Pliny tells us that Druidism had its origin in Gaul, and was transplanted into Britain, xxi. 1. Julius Caesar asserts just the contrary, Bell. Gall. vi. 13, 11. The edict of Claudius was not carried into effect; at least, we find vestiges of Druidism in Gaul, during the reigns of Nero and Alexander Severus.]

530 (return)

[ The Eleusinian mysteries were never transferred from Athens to Rome, notwithstanding this attempt of Claudius, and although Aurelius Victor says that Adrian effected it.]

531 (return)

[ A.U.C. 801.]

532 (return)

[ A.U.C. 773.]

533 (return)

[ It would seem from this passage, that the cognomen of "the Great," had now been restored to the descendants of Cneius Pompey, on whom it was first conferred.]

534 (return)

[ A.U.C. 806.]

535 (return)

[ A.U.C. 803.]

536 (return)

[ This is the Felix mentioned in the Acts, cc. xxiii. and xxiv., before whom St. Paul pleaded. He is mentioned by Josephus; and Tacitus, who calls him Felix Antonius, gives his character: Annal. v, 9. 6.]

537 (return)

[ It appears that two of these wives of Felix were named Drusilla. One, mentioned Acts xxiv. 24, and there called a Jewess, was the sister of king Agrippa, and had married before, Azizus, king of the Emessenes. The other Drusilla, though not a queen, was of royal birth, being the granddaughter of Cleopatra by Mark Antony. Who the third wife of Felix was, is unknown.]

538 (return)

[ Tacitus and Josephus mention that Pallas was the brother of Felix, and the younger Pliny ridicules the pompous inscription on his tomb.]

539 (return)

[ A.U.C. 802.]

540 (return)

[ The Salii, the priests of Mars, twelve in number, were instituted by Numa. Their dress was an embroidered tunic, bound with a girdle ornamented with brass. They wore on their head a conical cap, of a considerable height; carried a sword by their side; in their right hand a spear or rod, and in their left, one of the Ancilia, or shields of Mars. On solemn occasions, they used to go to the Capitol, through the Forum and other public parts of the city, dancing and singing sacred songs, said to have been composed by Numa; which, in the time of Horace, could hardly be understood by any one, even the priests themselves. The most solemn procession of the Salii was on the first of March, in commemoration of the time when the sacred shield was believed to have fallen from heaven, in the reign of Numa. After their procession, they had a splendid entertainment, the luxury of which was proverbial.]

541 (return)

[ Scaliger and Casauhon give Teleggenius as the reading of the best manuscripts. Whoever he was, his name seems to have been a bye-word for a notorious fool.]

542 (return)

[ Titus Livius, the prince of Roman historians, died in the fourth year of the reign of Tiberius, A.U.C. 771; at which time Claudius was about twenty-seven years old, having been born A.U.C. 744.]

543 (return)

[ Asinius Gallus was the son of Asinius Pollio, the famous orator, and had written a hook comparing his father with Cicero, and giving the former the preference.]

544 (return)

[ Quintilian informs us, that one of the three new letters the emperor Claudius attempted to introduce, was the Aeolic digamma, which had the same force as v consonant. Priscian calls another anti-signs, and says that the character proposed was two Greek sigmas, back to back, and that it was substituted for the Greek ps. The other letter is not known, and all three soon fell into disuse.]

545 (return)

[ Caesar by birth, not by adoption, as the preceding emperors had been, and as Nero would be, if he succeeded.]

546 (return)

[ Tacitus informs us, that the poison was prepared by Locusta, of whom we shall hear, NERO, c. xxxiii. etc.]

547 (return)

[ A.U.C. 806; A.D. 54.]

548 (return)

[ A.U.C. 593, 632, 658, 660, 700, 722, 785.]

549 (return)

[ A.U.C. 632.]

550 (return)

[ A.U.C. 639, 663.]

551 (return)

[ For the distinction between the praenomen and cognomen, see note, p. 192.]

552 (return)

[ A.U.C. 632.]

553 (return)

[ The Allobroges were a tribe of Gauls, inhabiting Dauphiny and Savoy; the Arverni have left their name in Auvergne.]

554 (return)

[ A.U.C. 695.]

555 (return)

[ A.U.C. 700.]

556 (return)

[ A.U.C. 711.]

557 (return)

[ A.U.C. 723.]

558 (return)

[ Nais seems to have been a freedwoman, who had been allowed to adopt the family name of her master.]

559 (return)

[ By one of those fictions of law, which have abounded in all systems of jurisprudence, a nominal alienation of his property was made in the testator's life-time.]

560 (return)

[ The suggestion offered (note, p. 123), that the Argentarii, like the goldsmiths of the middle ages, combined the business of bankers, or money-changers, with dealings in gold and silver plate, is confirmed by this passage. It does not, however, appear that they were artificers of the precious metals, though they dealt in old and current coins, sculptured vessels, gems, and precious stones.]

561 (return)

[ Pyrgi was a town of the ancient Etruria, near Antium, on the sea-coast, but it has long been destroyed.]

562 (return)

[ A.U.C. 791; A.D. 39.]

563 (return)

[ The purification, and giving the name, took place, among the Romans, in the case of boys, on the ninth, and of girls, on the tenth day. The customs of the Judaical law were similar. See Matt. i. 59-63; Luke iii. 21. 22.]

564 (return)

[ A.U.C. 806.]

565 (return)

[ Seneca, the celebrated philosophical writer, had been released from exile in Corsica, shortly before the death of Tiberius. He afterwards fell a sacrifice to the jealousy and cruelty of his former pupil, Nero.]

566 (return)

[ Caligula.]

567 (return)

[ A.U.C. 809—A.D. 57.]

568 (return)

[ Antium, the birth-place of Nero, an ancient city of the Volscians, stood on a rocky promontory of the coast, now called Capo d' Anzo, about thirty-eight miles from Rome. Though always a place of some naval importance, it was indebted to Nero for its noble harbour. The ruins of the moles yet remain; and there are vestiges of the temples and villas of the town, which was the resort of the wealthy Romans, it being a most delightful winter residence. The Apollo Belvidere was discovered among these ruins.]

569 (return)

[ A.U.C. 810.]

570 (return)

[ The Podium was part of the amphitheatre, near the orchestra, allotted to the senators, and the ambassadors of foreign nations; and where also was the seat of the emperor, of the person who exhibited the games, and of the Vestal Virgins. It projected over the wall which surrounded the area of the amphitheatre, and was raised between twelve and fifteen feet above it; secured with a breast-work or parapet against the irruption of wild beasts.]

571 (return)

[ A.U.C. 813.]

572 (return)

[ The baths of Nero stood to the west of the Pantheon. They were, probably, incorporated with those afterwards constructed by Alexander Severus; but no vestige of them remains. That the former were magnificent, we may infer from the verses of Martial:

— — — —Quid Nerone pejus?

Quid thermis melius Neronianis.—B. vii. ch. 34.

What worse than Nero?

What better than his baths?]

573 (return)

[ Among the Romans, the time at which young men first shaved the beard was marked with particular ceremony. It was usually in their twenty-first year, but the period varied. Caligula (c. x.) first shaved at twenty; Augustus at twenty-five.]

574 (return)

[ A.U.C. 819. See afterwards, c. xxx.]

575 (return)

[ A.U.C. 808, 810, 811, 813.]

576 (return)

[ The Sportulae were small wicker baskets, in which victuals or money were carried. The word was in consequence applied to the public entertainments at which food was distributed, or money given in lieu of it.]

577 (return)

[ "Superstitionis novae et maleficae," are the words of Suetonius; the latter conveying the idea of witchcraft or enchantment. Suidas relates that a certain martyr cried out from his dungeon—"Ye have loaded me with fetters as a sorcerer and profane person." Tacitus calls the Christian religion "a foreign and deadly [Footnote exitiabilis: superstition," Annal. xiii. 32; Pliny, in his celebrated letter to Trajan, "a depraved, wicked (or prava), and outrageous superstition." Epist. x. 97.] Tacitus also describes the excruciating torments inflicted on the Roman Christians by Nero. He says that they were subjected to the derision of the people; dressed in the skins of wild beasts, and exposed to be torn to pieces by dogs in the public games, that they were crucified, or condemned to be burnt; and at night-fall served in place of lamps to lighten the darkness, Nero's own gardens being used for the spectacle. Annal. xv. 44. Traditions of the church place the martyrdoms of SS. Peter and Paul at Rome, under the reign of Nero. The legends are given by Ordericus Vitalis. See vol. i. of the edition in the Antiq. Lib. pp. 206, etc., with the notes and reference to the apocryphal works on which they are founded.]

578 (return)

[ Claudius had received the submission of some of the British tribes. See c. xvii. of his Life. In the reign of Nero, his general, Suetonius Paulinus, attacked Mona or Anglesey, the chief seat of the Druids, and extirpated them with great cruelty. The successes of Boadicea, queen of the Iceni, who inhabited Derbyshire, were probably the cause of Nero's wishing to withdraw the legions; she having reduced London, Colchester, and Verulam, and put to death seventy thousand of the Romans and their British allies. She was, however, at length defeated by Suetonius Paulinus, who was recalled for his severities. See Tacit. Agric. xv. 1, xvi. 1; and Annal. xiv. 29.]

579 (return)

[ The dominions of Cottius embraced the vallies in the chain of the Alps extending between Piedmont and Dauphiny, called by the Romans the Cottian Alps. See TIBERIUS, c. xxxvii.]

580 (return)

[ It was a favourite project of the Caesars to make a navigable canal through the Isthmus of Corinth, to avoid the circumnavigation of the southern extremity of the Morea, now Cape Matapan, which, even in our days, has its perils. See JULIUS CAESAR, c. xliv. and CALIGULA, c. xxi.]

581 (return)

[ Caspiae Portae; so called from the difficulties opposed by the narrow and rocky defile to the passage of the Caucasus from the country washed by the Euxine, now called Georgia, to that lying between the Caspian and the sea of Azof. It commences a few miles north of Teflis, and is frequently the scene of contests between the Russians and the Circassian tribes.]

582 (return)

[ Citharoedus: the word signifies a vocalist, who with his singing gave an accompaniment on the harp.]

583 (return)

[ It has been already observed that Naples was a Greek colony, and consequently Greek appears to have continued the vernacular tongue.]

584 (return)

[ See AUGUSTUS, c. xcviii.]

585 (return)

[ Of the strange names given to the different modes of applauding in the theatre, the first was derived from the humming of bees; the second from the rattling of rain or hail on the roofs; and the third from the tinkling of porcelain vessels when clashed together.]

586 (return)

[ Canace was the daughter of an Etrurian king, whose incestuous intercourse with her brother having been detected, in consequence of the cries of the infant of which she was delivered, she killed herself. It was a joke at Rome, that some one asking, when Nero was performing in Canace, what the emperor was doing; a wag replied. "He is labouring in child-birth."]

587 (return)

[ A town in Corcyra, now Corfu. There was a sea-port of the same name in Epirus.]

588 (return)

[ The Circus Maximus, frequently mentioned by Suetonius, was so called because it was the largest of all the circuses in and about Rome. Rudely constructed of timber by Tarquinius Drusus, and enlarged and improved with the growing fortunes of the republic, under the emperors it became a most superb building. Julius Caesar (c. xxxix) extended it, and surrounded it with a canal, ten feet deep and as many broad, to protect the spectators against danger from the chariots during the races. Claudius (c. xxi.) rebuilt the carceres with marble, and gilded the metae. This vast centre of attraction to the Roman people, in the games of which religion, politics, and amusement, were combined, was, according to Pliny, three stadia (of 625 feet) long, and one broad, and held 260,000 spectators; so that Juvenal says,

"Totam hodie Romam circus capit."—Sat. xi. 195.

This poetical exaggeration is applied by Addison to the Colosseum.

"That on its public shews unpeopled Rome."—Letter to Lord Halifax.

The area of the Circus Maximus occupied the hollow between the Palatine and Aventine hills, so that it was overlooked by the imperial palace, from which the emperors had so full a view of it, that they could from that height give the signals for commencing the races. Few fragments of it remain; but from the circus of Caracalla, which is better preserved, a tolerably good idea of the ancient circus may be formed. For details of its parts, and the mode in which the sports were conducted, see Burton's Antiquities, p. 309, etc.]

589 (return)

[ The Velabrum was a street in Rome. See JULIUS CAESAR, c. xxxvii.]

590 (return)

[ Acte was a slave who had been bought in Asia, whose beauty so captivated Nero that he redeemed her, and became greatly attached to her. She is supposed to be the concubine of Nero mentioned by St. Chrysostom, as having been converted by St. Paul during his residence at Rome. The Apostle speaks of the "Saints in Caesar's household."—Phil. iv. 22.]

591 (return)

[ See Tacitus, Annal. xv. 37.]

592 (return)

[ A much-frequented street in Rome. See CLAUDIUS, c. xvi.]

593 (return)

[ It is said that the advances were made by Agrippina, with flagrant indecency, to secure her power over him. See Tacitus, Annal. xiv. 2, 3.]

594 (return)

[ Olim etiam, quoties lectica cum matre veheretur, libidinatum inceste, ac maculis vestis proditum, affirmant.]

595 (return)

[ Tacitus calls him Pythagoras, which was probably the freedman's proper name; Doryphorus being a name of office somewhat equivalent to almoner. See Annal. B. xv.]

596 (return)

[ The emperor Caligula, who was the brother of Nero's mother, Agrippina.]

597 (return)

[ See before, c. xiii. Tiridates was nine months in Rome or the neighbourhood, and was entertained the whole time at the emperor's expense.]

598 (return)

[ Canusium, now Canosa, was a town in Apulia, near the mouth of the river Aufidus, celebrated for its fine wool. It is mentioned by Pliny, and retained its reputation for the manufacture in the middle ages, as we find in Ordericus Vitalis.]

599 (return)

[ The Mazacans were an African tribe from the deserts in the interior, famous for their spirited barbs, their powers of endurance, and their skill in throwing the dart.]

600 (return)

[ The Palace of the Caesars, on the Palatine hill, was enlarged by Augustus from the dimensions of a private house (see AUGUSTUS, cc. xxix., lvii.). Tiberius made some additions to it, and Caligula extended it to the Forum (CALIGULA, c. xxxi.). Tacitus gives a similar account with that of our author of the extent and splendour of the works of

Nero. Annal. xv. c. xlii. Reaching from the Palatine to the Esquiline hill, it covered all the intermediate space, where the Colosseum now stands. We shall find that it was still further enlarged by Domitian, c. xv. of his life is the present work.]

601 (return)

[ The penates were worshipped in the innermost part of the house, which was called penetralia. There were likewise publici penates, worshipped in the Capitol, and supposed to be the guardians of the city and temples. Some have thought that the lares and penates were the same; and they appear to be sometimes confounded. They were, however, different. The penates were reputed to be of divine origin; the lares, of human. Certain persons were admitted to the worship of the lares, who were not to that of the penates. The latter, as has been already said, were worshipped only in the innermost part of the house, but the former also in the public roads, in the camp, and on sea.]

602 (return)

[ A play upon the Greek word moros, signifying a fool, while the Latin morari, from moror, means "to dwell," or "continue."]

603 (return)

[ A small port between the gulf of Baiae and cape Misenum.]

604 (return)

[ From whence the "Procul, O procul este profani!" of the poet; a warning which was transferred to the Christian mysteries.]

605 (return)

[ See before, c. xii.]

606 (return)

[ Statilius Taurus; who lived in the time of Augustus, and built the amphitheatre called after his name. AUGUSTUS, c. xxiv. He is mentioned by Horace, Epist. i. v. 4.]

607 (return)

[ Octavia was first sent away to Campania, under a guard of soldiers, and after being recalled, in consequence of the remonstrances of the people, by whom she was beloved, Nero banished her to the island of Pandataria.]

608 (return)

[ A.U.C. 813.]

609 (return)

[ Seneca was accused of complicity in the conspiracy of Caius Piso. Tacitus furnishes some interesting details of the circumstances under which the philosopher calmly submitted to his fate, which was announced to him when at supper with his friends, at his villa, near Rome.—Tacitus, b. xiv. xv.]

610 (return)

[ This comet, as well as one which appeared the year in which Claudius died, is described by Seneca, Natural. Quaest. VII. c. xvii. and xix. and by Pliny, II. c. xxv.]

611 (return)

[ See Tacitus, Annal. xv. 49-55.]

612 (return)

[ The sixteenth book of Tacitus, which would probably have given an account of the Vinician conspiracy, is lost. It is shortly noticed by Plutarch.]

613 (return)

[ See before, c. xix.]

614 (return)

[ This destructive fire occurred in the end of July, or the beginning of August, A.U.C. 816, A.D. 64. It was imputed to the Christians, and drew on them the persecutions mentioned in c. xvi., and the note.]

615 (return)

[ The revolt in Britain broke out A.U.C. 813. Xiphilinus (lxii. p. 701) attributes it to the severity of the confiscations with which the repayment of large sums of money advanced to the Britons by the emperor Claudius, and also by Seneca, was exacted. Tacitus adds another cause, the insupportable tyranny and avarice of the centurions and soldiers. Prasutagus, king of the Iceni, had named the emperor his heir. His widow Boadicea and her daughters were shamefully used, his kinsmen reduced to slavery, and his whole territory ravaged; upon which the Britons flew to arms. See c. xviii., and the note.]

616 (return)

[ Neonymphon; alluding to Nero's unnatural nuptials with Sporus or Pythagoras. See cc. xxviii. xxix. It should be neonymphos.]

617 (return)

[ "Sustulit" has a double meaning, signifying both, to bear away, and put out of the way.]

618 (return)

[ The epithet applied to Apollo, as the god of music, was Paean; as the god of war, Ekataebaletaes.]

619 (return)

[ Pliny remarks, that the Golden House of Nero was swallowing up all Rome. Veii, an ancient Etruscan city, about twelve miles from Rome, was originally little inferior to it, being, as Dionysius informs us, (lib. ii. p. 16), equal in extent to Athens. See a very accurate survey of the ruins of Veii, in Gell's admirable TOPOGRAPHY OF ROME AND ITS VICINITY, p. 436, of Bohn's Edition.]

620 (return)

[ Suetonius calls them organa hydralica, and they seem to have been a musical instrument on the same principle as our present organs, only that water was the inflating power. Vitruvius (iv. ix.) mentions the instrument as the invention of Ctesibus of Alexandria. It is also well described by Tertullian, De Anima, c. xiv. The pneumatic organ appears to have been a later improvement. We have before us a contorniate medallion, of Caracalla, from the collection of Mr. W. S. Bohn, upon which one or other of these instruments figures. On the obverse is the bust of the emperor in armour, laureated, with the inscription as AURELIUS ANTONINUS PIUS AUG. BRIT. (his latest title). On the reverse is the organ; an oblong chest with the pipes above, and a draped figure on each side.]

621 (return)

[ A fine sand from the Nile, similar to puzzuclano, which was strewed on the stadium; the wrestlers also rolled in it, when their bodies were slippery with oil or perspiration.]

622 (return)

[ The words on the ticket about the emperor's neck, are supposed, by a prosopopea, to be spoken by him. The reply is Agrippina's, or the people's. It alludes to the punishment due to him for his parricide.

By the Roman law, a person who had murdered a parent or any near relation, after being severely scourged, was sewed up in a sack, with a dog, a cock, a viper, and an ape, and then thrown into the sea, or a deep river.]

623 (return)

[ Gallos, which signifies both cocks and Gauls.]

624 (return)

[ Vindex, it need hardly be observed, was the name of the propraetor who had set up the standard of rebellion in Gaul. The word also signifies an avenger of wrongs, redresser of grievances; hence vindicate, vindictive, etc.]

625 (return)

[ Aen. xii. 646.]

626 (return)

[ The Via Salaria was so called from the Sabines using it to fetch salt from the coast. It led from Rome to the northward, near the gardens of Sallust, by a gate of the same name, called also Quirinalis, Agonalis, and Collina. It was here that Alaric entered.]

627 (return)

[ The Via Nomentana, so named because it led to the Sabine town of Nomentum, joined the Via Salara at Heretum on the Tiber. It was also called Ficulnensis. It entered Rome by the Porta Viminalis, now called Porta Pia. It was by this road that Hannibal approached the walls of Rome. The country-house of Nero's freedman, where he ended his days, stood near the Anio, beyond the present church of St. Agnese, where there was a villa of the Spada family, belonging now, we believe, to Torlonia.]

628 (return)

[ This description is no less exact than vivid. It was easy for Nero to gain the nearest gate, the Nomentan, from the Esquiline quarter of the palace, without much observation; and on issuing from it (after midnight, it appears), the fugitives would have the pretorian camp so close on their right hand, that they might well hear the shouts of the soldiers.]

629 (return)

[ Decocta. Pliny informs us that Nero had the water he drank, boiled, to clear it from impurities, and then cooled with ice.]

630 (return)

[ Wood, to warm the water for washing the corpse, and for the funeral pile,]

631 (return)

[ This burst of passion was uttered in Greek, the rest was spoken in Latin. Both were in familiar use. The mixture, perhaps, betrays the disturbed state of Nero's mind.]

632 (return)

[ II. x. 535.]

633 (return)

[ Collis Hortulorum; which was afterwards called the Pincian Hill, from a family of that name, who flourished under the lower empire. In the time of the Caesars it was occupied by the gardens and villas of the wealthy and luxurious; among which those of Sallust are celebrated. Some of the finest statues have been found in the ruins; among others, that of the "Dying Gladiator." The situation was airy and healthful, commanding fine views, and it is still the most agreeable neighbourhood in Rome.]

634 (return)

[ Antiquarians suppose that some relics of the sepulchre of the Domitian family, in which the ashes of Nero were deposited, are preserved in the city wall which Aurelian, when he extended its circuit, carried across the "Collis Hortulorum." Those ancient remains, declining from the perpendicular, are called the Muro Torto.—The Lunan marble was brought from quarries near a town of that name, in Etruria. It no longer exists, but stood on the coast of what is now called the gulf of Spezzia.—Thasos, an island in the Archipelago, was one of the Cyclades. It produced a grey marble, much veined, but not in great repute.]

635 (return)

[ See c. xli.]

636 (return)

[ The Syrian Goddess is supposed to have been Semiramis deified. Her rites are mentioned by Florus, Apuleius, and Lucian.]

637 (return)

[ A.U.C. 821 — A.D. 69.]

638 (return)

[ We have here one of the incidental notices which are so valuable in an historian, as connecting him with the times of which he writes. See also just before, c. lii.]

639 (return)

[ Veii; see the note, NERO, c. xxxix.]

640 (return)

[ The conventional term for what is most commonly known as,

"The Laurel, meed of mighty conquerors,

And poets sage,"—Spenser's Faerie Queen.

is retained throughout the translation. But the tree or shrub which had this distinction among the ancients, the Laurus nobilis of botany, the Daphne of the Greeks, is the bay-tree, indigenous in Italy, Greece, and the East, and introduced into England about 1562. Our laurel is a plant of a very different tribe, the Prunes lauro-cerasus, a native of the Levant and the Crimea, acclimated in England at a later period than the bay.]

641 (return)

[ The Temple of the Caesars is generally supposed to be that dedicated by Julius Caesar to Venus genitrix, from whom the Julian family pretended to derive their descent. See JULIUS, c. lxi.; AUGUSTUS, c. ci.]

642 (return)

[ A.U.C. 821.]

643 (return)

[ The Atrium, or Aula, was the court or hall of a house, the entrance to which was by the principal door. It appears to have been a large oblong square, surrounded with covered or arched galleries. Three sides of the Atrium were supported by pillars, which, in later times, were marble. The side opposite to the gate was called Tablinum; and the other two sides, Alae. The Tablinum contained books, and the records of what each member of the family had done in his magistracy. In the Atrium the nuptial couch was erected; and here the mistress of the family, with her maid-servants, wrought at spinning and weaving, which, in the time of the ancient Romans, was their principal employment.]

644 (return)

[ He was consul with L. Aurelius Cotta, A.U.C. 610.]

645 (return)

[ A.U.C. 604.]

646 (return)

[ A.U.C. 710.]

647 (return)

[ A.U.C 775.]

648 (return)

[ A.U.C. 608.]

649 (return)

[ Caius Sulpicius Galba, the emperor's brother, had been consul A.U.C. 774.]

650

[ A.U.C. 751.]

651 (return)

[ Now Fondi, which, with Terracina, still bearing its original name, lie on the road to Naples. See TIBERIUS, cc. v. and xxxix.]

652 (return)

[ Livia Ocellina, mentioned just before.]

653 (return)

[ A.U.C. 751.]

654 (return)

[ The widow of the emperor Augustus.]

655 (return)

[ Suetonius seems to have forgotten, that, according to his own testimony, this legacy, as well as those left by Tiberius, was paid by Caligula. "Legata ex testamento Tiberii; quamquam abolito, sed et Juliae Augustae, quod Tiberius suppresserat, cum fide, ac sine calumnia repraesentate persolvit." CALIG. c. xvi.]

656 (return)

[ A.U.C. 786.]

657

[ Caius Caesar Caligula. He gave the command of the legions in Germany to Galba.]

658 (return)

[ "Scuto moderatus;" another reading in the parallel passage of Tacitus is scuto immodice oneratus, burdened with the heavy weight of a shield.]

659 (return)

[ It would appear that Galba was to have accompanied Claudius in his expedition to Britain; which is related before, CLAUDIUS, c. xvii.]

660 (return)

[ It has been remarked before, that the Cantabria of the ancients is now the province of Biscay.]

661 (return)

[ Now Carthagena.]

662 (return)

[ A.U.C. 821.]

663 (return)

[ Now Corunna.]

664 (return)

[ Tortosa, on the Ebro.]

665 (return)

[ "Simus," literally, fiat-nosed, was a cant word, used for a clown; Galba being jeered for his rusticity, in consequence of his long retirement. See c. viii. Indeed, they called Spain his farm.]

666 (return)

[ The command of the pretorian guards.]

667 (return)

[ In the Forum. See AUGUSTUS, c. lvii.]

668 (return)

[ II. v. 254.]

669 (return)

[ A.U.C. 822.]

670 (return)

[ On the esplanade, where the standards, objects of religious reverence, were planted. See note to c. vi. Criminals were usually executed outside the Vallum, and in the presence of a centurion.]

671 (return)

[ Probably one of the two mentioned in CLAUDIUS, c. xiii.]

672 (return)

[ A.U.C. 784 or 785.]

673 (return)

[ "Distento sago impositum in sublime jactare."]

674 (return)

[ See NERO, c. xxxv.]

675 (return)

[ The Milliare Aureum was a pillar of stone set up at the top of the Forum, from which all the great military roads throughout Italy started, the distances to the principal towns being marked upon it. Dio (lib. liv.) says that it was erected by the emperor Augustus, when he was curator of the roads.]

676 (return)

[ Haruspex, Auspex, or Augur, denoted any person who foretold futurity, or interpreted omens. There was at Rome a body of priests, or college, under this title, whose office it was to foretell future events, chiefly from the flight, chirping, or feeding of birds, and from other appearances. They were of the greatest authority in the Roman state; for nothing of importance was done in public affairs, either at home or abroad, in peace or war, without consulting them. The Romans derived the practice of augury chiefly from the Tuscans; and anciently their youth used to be instructed as carefully in this art, as afterwards they were in the Greek literature. For this purpose, by a decree of the senate, a certain number of the sons of the leading men at Rome was sent to the twelve states of Etruria for instruction.]

677 (return)

[ See before, note, c. i. The Principia was a broad open space, which separated the lower part of the Roman camp from the upper, and extended the whole breadth of the camp. In this place was erected the tribunal of the general, when he either administered justice or harangued the army. Here likewise the tribunes held their courts, and punishments were inflicted. The principal standards of the army, as it has been already mentioned, were deposited in the Principia; and in it also stood the altars of the gods, and the images of the Emperors, by which the soldiers swore.]

678 (return)

[ See NERO, c. xxxi. The sum estimated as requisite for its completion amounted to 2,187,500 pounds of our money.]

679 (return)

[ The two last words, literally translated, mean "long trumpets;" such as were used at sacrifices. The sense is, therefore, "What have I to do, my hands stained with blood, with performing religious ceremonies!"]

680 (return)

[ The Ancile was a round shield, said to have fallen from heaven in the reign of Numa, and supposed to be the shield of Mars. It was kept with great care in the sanctuary of his temple, as a symbol of the perpetuity of the Roman empire; and that it might not be stolen, eleven others were made exactly similar to it.]

681 (return)

[ This ideal personage, who has been mentioned before, AUGUSTUS, c. lxviii., was the goddess Cybele, the wife of Saturn, called also Rhea, Ops, Vesta, Magna, Mater, etc. She was painted as a matron, crowned with towers, sitting in a chariot drawn by lions. A statue of her, brought from Pessinus in Phrygia to Rome, in the time of the second Punic war, was much honoured there. Her priests, called the Galli and Corybantes, were castrated; and worshipped her with the sound of drums, tabors, pipes, and cymbals. The rites of this goddess were disgraced by great indecencies.]

682 (return)

[ Otherwise called Orcus, Pluto, Jupiter Infernus, and Stygnis. He was the brother of Jupiter, and king of the infernal regions. His wife was Proserpine, the daughter of Ceres, whom he carried off as she was gathering flowers in the plains of Enna, in Sicily. The victims offered to the infernal gods were black: they were killed with their faces bent downwards; the knife was applied from below, and the blood was poured into a ditch.]

683 (return)

[ A town between Mantua and Cremona.]

684 (return)

[ The temple of Castor. It stood about twelve miles from Cremona. Tacitus gives some details of this action. Hist. ii. 243.]

685 (return)

[ Both Greek and Latin authors differ in the mode of spelling the name of this place, the first syllable being written Beb, Bet, and Bret. It is now a small village called Labino, between Cremona and Verona.]

686 (return)

[ Lenis was a name of similar signification with that of Tranquillus, borne by his son, the author of the present work. We find from Tacitus, that there was, among Otho's generals, in this battle, another person of the name of Suetonius, whose cognomen was Paulinus; with whom our author's father must not be confounded. Lenis was only a tribune of the thirteenth legion, the position of which in the battle is mentioned by Tacitus, Hist. xi. 24, and was angusticlavius, wearing only the narrow stripe, as not being of the senatorial order; while Paulinus was a general, commanding a legion, at least, and a consular man; having filled that Office A.U.C. 818. There seems no doubt that Suetonius Paulinus was the same general who distinguished himself by his successes and cruelties in Britain. NERO, c. xviii., and note.] Not to extend the present note, we may shortly refer to our author's having already mentioned his grandfather (CALIGULA, c. xix.); besides other sources from which he drew his information. He tells us that he himself was then a boy. We have now arrived at the times in which his father bore a part. Such incidental notices, dropped by historical writers, have a certain value in enabling us to form a judgment on the genuineness of their narratives as to contemporaneous, or recent, events.]

687 (return)

[ A.U.C. 823.]

688 (return)

[ Jupiter, to prevent the discovery of his amour with Io, the daughter of the river Inachus, transformed her into a heifer, in which metamorphosis she was placed by Juno under the watchful inspection of Argus; but flying into Egypt, and her keeper being killed by Mercury, she recovered her human shape, and was married to Osiris. Her husband afterwards became a god of the Egyptians, and she a goddess, under the name of Isis. She was represented with a mural crown on her head, a cornucopia in one hand, and a sistrum (a musical instrument) in the other.]

689 (return)

[ Faunus was supposed to be the third king who reigned over the original inhabitants of the central parts of Italy, Saturn being the first. Virgil makes his wife's name Marica—

Hunc Fauna, et nympha genitum

Laurente Marica Accipimus.—Aen. vii. 47.

Her name may have been changed after her deification; but we have no other accounts than those preserved by Suetonius, of several of the traditions handed down from the fabulous ages respecting the Vitellian family.]

690 (return)

[ The Aequicolae were probably a tribe inhabiting the heights in the neighbourhood of Rome. Virgil describes them, Aen. vii. 746.]

691 (return)

[ Nuceria, now Nocera, is a town near Mantua; but Livy, in treating of the war with the Samnites, always speaks of Luceria, which Strabo calls a town in Apulia.]

692 (return)

[ Cassius Severus is mentioned before, in AUGUSTUS, c. lvi.; CALIGULA, c. xvi., etc.]

693 (return)

[ A.U.C. 785.]

694 (return)

[ A.U.C. 787.]

695 (return)

[ He is frequently commended by Josephus for his kindness to the Jews. See, particularly, Antiq. VI. xviii.]

696 (return)

[ A.U.C. 796, 800.]

697 (return)

[ A.U.C. 801.]

698 (return)

[ A.U.C. 797. See CLAUDIUS, c. xvii.]

699 (return)

[ A.U.C. 801.]

700 (return)

[ A.U.C. 767; being the year after the death of the emperor Augustus; from whence it appears that Vitellius was seventeen years older than Otho, both being at an advanced age when they were raised to the imperial dignity.]

701 (return)

[ He was sent to Germany by Galba.]

702 (return)

[ See TIBERIUS, c. xliii.]

703 (return)

[ Julius Caesar, also, was said to have exchanged brass for gold in the Capitol, Junius, c. liv. The tin which we here find in use at Rome, was probably brought from the Cassiterides, now the Scilly islands. whence it had been an article of commerce by the Phoenicians and Carthaginians from a very early period.]

704 (return)

[ A.U.C. 821.]

705 (return)

[ A.U.C. 822.]

706 (return)

[ Vienne was a very ancient city of the province of Narbonne, famous in ecclesiastical history as the early seat of a bishopric in Gaul.]

707 (return)

[ See OTHO, c. ix.]

708 (return)

[ See OTHO, c. ix.]

709 (return)

[ Agrippina, the wife of Nero and mother of Germanicus, founded a colony on the Rhine at the place of her birth. Tacit. Annal. b. xii. It became a flourishing city, and its origin may be traced in its modern name, Cologne.]

710 (return)

[ A dies non fastus, an unlucky day in the Roman calendar, being the anniversary of their great defeat by the Gauls on the river Allia, which joins the Tiber about five miles from Rome. This disaster happened on the 16th of the calends of August (17th July).

711 (return)

[ Posca was sour wine or vinegar mixed with water, which was used by the Roman soldiery as their common drink. It has been found beneficial in the cure of putrid diseases.]

712 (return)

[ Upwards of 4000 pounds sterling. See note, p. 487.]

713 (return)

[ In imitation of the form of the public edicts, which began with the words, BONUM FACTUM.]

714 (return)

[ Catta muliere: The Catti were a German tribe who inhabited the present countries of Hesse or Baden. Tacitus, De Mor. Germ., informs us that the Germans placed great confidence in the prophetical inspirations which they attributed to their women.]

715 (return)

[ Suetonius does not supply any account of the part added by Tiberius to the palace of the Caesars on the Palatine, although, as it will be recollected, he has mentioned or described the works of Augustus, Caligula, and Nero. The banquetting-room here mentioned would easily command a view of the Capitol, across the narrow intervening valley. Flavius Sabinus, Vespasian's brother, was prefect of the city.]

716 (return)

[ Caligula.]

717 (return)

[ Lucius and Germanicus, the brother and son of Vitellius, were slain near Terracina; the former was marching to his brother's relief.]

718 (return)

[ A.U.C. 822.]

719 (return)

[ c. ix.]

720 (return)

[ Becco, from whence the French bec, and English beak; with, probably, the family names of Bec or Bek. This distinguished provincial, under his Latin name of Antoninus Primus, commanded the seventh legion in Gaul. His character is well drawn by Tacitus, in his usual terse style, Hist. XI. 86. 2.]

721 (return)

[ Reate, the original seat of the Flavian family, was a city of the Sabines. Its present name is Rieti.]

722 (return)

[ It does not very clearly appear what rank in the Roman armies was held by the evocati. They are mentioned on three occasions by Suetonius, without affording us much assistance. Caesar, like our author, joins them with the centurions. See, in particular, De Bell. Civil. I. xvii. 4.]

723 (return)

[ The inscription was in Greek, kalos telothaesanti.]

724 (return)

[ In the ancient Umbria, afterwards the duchy of Spoleto; its modern name being Norcia.]

725 (return)

[ Gaul beyond, north of the Po, now Lombardy.]

726 (return)

[ We find the annual migration of labourers in husbandry a very common practice in ancient as well as in modern times. At present, several thousand industrious labourers cross over every summer from the duchies of Parma and Modena, bordering on the district mentioned by Suetonius, to the island of Corsica; returning to the continent when the harvest is got in.]

727 (return)

[ A.U.C. 762, A.D. 10.]

728 (return)

[ Cosa was a place in the Volscian territory; of which Anagni was probably the chief town. It lies about forty miles to the north-east of Rome.]

729 (return)

[ Caligula.]

730 (return)

[ These games were extraordinary, as being out of the usual course of those given by praetors.]

731 (return)

[ "Revocavit in contubernium." From the difference of our habits, there is no word in the English language which exactly conveys the meaning of contubernium; a word which, in a military sense, the Romans applied to the intimate fellowship between comrades in war who messed together, and lived in close fellowship in the same tent. Thence they transferred it to a union with one woman who was in a higher position than a concubine, but, for some reason, could not acquire the legal rights of a wife, as in the case of slaves of either sex. A man of rank, also, could not marry a slave or a freedwoman, however much he might be attached to her.]

732 (return)

[ Nearly the same phrases are applied by Suetonius to Drusilla, see CALIGULA, c. xxiv., and to Marcella, the concubine of Commodus, by Herodian, I. xvi. 9., where he says that she had all the honours of an empress, except that the incense was not offered to her. These connections resembled the left-hand marriages of the German princes.]

733 (return)

[ This expedition to Britain has been mentioned before, CLAUDIUS, c. xvii. and note; and see ib. xxiv.] Valerius Flaccus, i. 8, and Silius Italicus, iii. 598, celebrate the triumphs of Vespasian in Britain. In representing him, however, as carrying his arms among the Caledonian tribes, their flattery transferred to the emperor the glory of the victories gained by his lieutenant, Agricola. Vespasian's own conquests, while he served in Britain, were principally in the territories of the Brigantes, lying north of the Humber, and including the present counties of York and Durham.]

734 (return)

[ A.U.C. 804.]

735 (return)

[ Tacitus, Hist. V. xiii. 3., mentions this ancient prediction, and its currency through the East, in nearly the same terms as Suetonius. The coming power is in both instances described in the plural number, profecti; "those shall come forth;" and Tacitus applies it to Titus as well as Vespasian. The prophecy is commonly supposed to have reference to a passage in Micah, v. 2, "Out of thee (Bethlehem-Ephrata) shall He come forth, to be ruler in Israel." Earlier prophetic intimations of a similar character, and pointing to a more extended dominion, have been traced in the sacred records of the Jews; and there is reason to believe that these books were at this time not unknown in the heathen world, particularly at Alexandria, and through the Septuagint version. These predictions, in their literal sense, point to the establishment of a universal monarchy, which should take its rise in Judaea. The Jews looked for their accomplishment in the person of one of their own nation, the expected Messiah, to which character there were many pretenders in those times. The first disciples of Christ, during the whole period of his ministry, supposed that they were to be fulfilled in him. The Romans thought that the conditions were answered by Vespasian, and Titus having been called from Judaea to the seat of empire. The expectations entertained by the Jews, and naturally participated in and appropriated by the first converts to Christianity, having proved groundless, the prophecies were subsequently interpreted in a spiritual sense.]

736 (return)

[ Gessius Florus was at that time governor of Judaea, with the title and rank of prepositus, it not being a proconsular province, as the native princes still held some parts of it, under the protection and with the alliance of the Romans. Gessius succeeded Florus Albinus, the successor of Felix.]

737 (return)

[ Cestius Gallus was consular lieutenant in Syria.]

738 (return)

[ See note to c. vii.]

739 (return)

[ A right hand was the sign of sovereign power, and, as every one knows, borne upon a staff among the standards of the armies.]

740 (return)

[ Tacitus says, "Carmel is the name both of a god and a mountain; but there is neither image nor temple of the god; such are the ancient traditions; we find there only an altar and religious awe."—Hist. xi. 78, 4. It also appears, from his account, that Vespasian offered sacrifice on Mount Carmel, where Basilides, mentioned hereafter, c. vii., predicted his success from an inspection of the entrails.]

741 (return)

[ Josephus, the celebrated Jewish historian, who was engaged in these wars, having been taken prisoner, was confined in the dungeon at Jotapata, the castle referred to in the preceding chapter, before which Vespasian was wounded.—De Bell. cxi. 14.]

742 (return)

[ The prediction of Josephus was founded on the Jewish prophecies mentioned in the note to c. iv., which he, like others, applied to Vespasian.]

743 (return)

[ Julius Caesar is always called by our author after his apotheosis, Divus Julius.]

744 (return)

[ The battle at Bedriacum secured the Empire for Vitellius. See OTHO, c. ix; VITELLIUS, c. x.]

745 (return)

[ Alexandria may well be called the key, claustra, of Egypt, which was the granary of Rome. It was of the first importance that Vespasian should secure it at this juncture.]

746 (return)

[ Tacitus describes Basilides as a man of rank among the Egyptians, and he appears also to have been a priest, as we find him officiating at Mount Carmel, c. v. This is so incompatible with his being a Roman freedman, that commentators concur in supposing that the word "libertus." although found in all the copies now extant, has crept into the text by some inadvertence of an early transcriber. Basilides appears, like Philo Judaeus, who lived about the same period, to have been half-Greek, half-Jew, and to have belonged to the celebrated Platonic school of Alexandria.]

747 (return)

[ Tacitus informs us that Vespasian himself believed Basilides to have been at this time not only in an infirm state of health, but at the distance of several days' journey from Alexandria. But (for his greater satisfaction) he strictly examined the priests whether Basilides had entered the temple on that day: he made inquiries of all he met, whether he had been seen in the city; nay, further, he dispatched messengers on horseback, who ascertained that at the time specified, Basilides was more than eighty miles from Alexandria. Then Vespasian comprehended that the appearance of Basilides, and the answer to his prayers given through him, were by divine interposition. Tacit. Hist. iv. 82. 2.]

748 (return)

[ The account given by Tacitus of the miracles of Vespasian is fuller than that of Suetonius, but does not materially vary in the details, except that, in his version of the story, he describes the impotent man to be lame in the hand, instead of the leg or the knee, and adds an important circumstance in the case of the blind man, that he was "notus tabe occulorum," notorious for the disease in his eyes. He also winds up the narrative with the following statement: "They who were present, relate both these cures, even at this time, when there is nothing to be gained by lying." Both the historians lived within a few years of the occurrence, but their works were not published until advanced periods of their lives. The closing remark of Tacitus seems to indicate that, at least, he did not entirely discredit the account; and as for Suetonius, his pages are as full of prodigies of all descriptions, related apparently in all good faith, as a monkish chronicle of the Middle Ages. The story has the more interest, as it is one of the examples of successful imposture, selected by Hume in his Essay on Miracles; with the reply to which by Paley, in his Evidences of Christianity, most readers are familiar. The commentators on Suetonius agree with Paley in considering the whole affair as a juggle between the priests, the patients, and, probably, the emperor. But what will, perhaps, strike the reader as most remarkable, is the singular coincidence of the story with the accounts given of several of the miracles of Christ; whence it has been supposed, that the scene was planned in imitation of them. It did not fall within the scope of Dr. Paley's argument to advert to this; and our own brief illustration must be strictly confined within the limits of historical disquisition. Adhering to this principle, we may point out that if the idea of plagiarism be accepted, it receives some confirmation from the incident related by our author in a preceding paragraph, forming, it may be considered, another scene of the same drama, where we find Basilides appearing to Vespasian in the temple of Serapis, under circumstances which cannot fail to remind us of Christ's suddenly standing in the midst of his disciples, "when the doors were shut." This incident, also, has very much the appearance of a parody on the evangelical history. But if the striking similarity of the two narratives be thus accounted for, it is remarkable that while the priests of Alexandria, or, perhaps, Vespasian himself from his residence in Judaea, were in possession of such exact details of two of Christ's miracles—if not of a third striking incident in his history— we should find not the most distant allusion in the works of such cotemporary writers as Tacitus and Suetonius, to any one of the still more stupendous occurrences which had recently taken place in a part of the world with which the Romans had now very intimate relations. The character of these authors induces us to hesitate in adopting the notion, that either contempt or disbelief would have led them to pass over such events, as altogether unworthy of notice; and the only other inference from their silence is, that they had never heard of them. But as this can scarcely be reconciled with the plagiarism attributed to Vespasian or the Egyptian priests, it is safer to conclude that the coincidence, however singular, was merely fortuitous. It may be added that Spartianus, who wrote the lives of Adrian and succeeding emperors, gives an account of a similar miracle performed by that prince in healing a blind man.]

749 (return)

[ A.U.C. 823-833, excepting 826 and 831.]

750 (return)

[ The temple of Peace, erected A.D. 71, on the conclusion of the wars with the Germans and the Jews, was the largest temple in Rome. Vespasian and Titus deposited in it the sacred vessels and other spoils which were carried in their triumph after the conquest of Jerusalem. They were consumed, and the temple much damaged, if not destroyed, by fire, towards the end of the reign of Commodus, in the year 191. It stood in the Forum, where some ruins on a prodigious scale, still remaining, were traditionally considered to be those of the Temple of Peace, until Piranesi contended that they are part of Nero's Golden House. Others suppose that they are the remains of a Basilica. A beautiful fluted Corinthian column, forty-seven feet high, which was removed from this spot, and now stands before the church of S. Maria Maggiore, gives a great idea of the splendour of the original structure.]

751 (return)

[ This temple, converted into a Christian church by pope Simplicius, who flourished, A.D. 464-483, preserves much of its ancient character. It is now, called San Stefano in Rotondo, from its circular form; the thirty-four pillars, with arches springing from one to the other and intended to support the cupola, still remaining to prove its former magnificence.]

752 (return)

[ This amphitheatre is the famous Colosseum begun by Trajan, and finished by Titus. It is needless to go into details respecting a building the gigantic ruins of which are so well known.]

753 (return)

[ Hercules is said, after conquering Geryon in Spain, to have come into this part of Italy. One of his companions, the supposed founder of Reate, may have had the name of Flavus.]

754 (return)

[ Vespasian and his son Titus had a joint triumph for the conquest of Judaea, which is described at length by Josephus, De Bell. Jud. vii. 16. The coins of Vespasian exhibiting the captive Judaea (Judaea capta), are probably familiar to the reader. See Harphrey's Coin Collector's Manual, p. 328.]

755 (return)

[ Demetrius, who was born at Corinth, seems to have been a close imitator of Diogenes, the founder of the sect. Having come to Rome to study under Apollonius, he was banished to the islands, with other philosophers, by Vespasian.]

756 (return)

[ There being no such place as Morbonia, and the supposed name being derived from morbus, disease, some critics have supposed that Anticyra, the asylum of the incurables, (see CALIGULA, c. xxix.) is meant; but the probability is, that the expression used by the imperial chamberlain was only a courtly version of a phrase not very commonly adopted in the present day.]

757 (return)

[ Helvidius Priscus, a person of some celebrity as a philosopher and public man, is mentioned by Tacitus, Xiphilinus, and Arrian.]

758 (return)

[ Cicero speaks in strong terms of the sordidness of retail trade— Off. i. 24.]

759 (return)

[ The sesterce being worth about two-pence half-penny of English money, the salary of a Roman senator was, in round numbers, five thousand pounds a year; and that of a professor, as stated in the succeeding chapter, one thousand pounds. From this scale, similar calculations may easily be made of the sums occurring in Suetonius's statements from time to time. There appears to be some mistake in the sum stated in c. xvi. just before, as the amount seems fabulous, whether it represented the floating debt, or the annual revenue, of the empire.]

760 (return)

[ See AUGUSTUS, c. xliii. The proscenium of the ancient theatres was a solid erection of an architectural design, not shifted and varied as our stage-scenes.]

761 (return)

[ Many eminent writers among the Romans were originally slaves, such as Terence and Phaedrus; and, still more, artists, physicians and artificers. Their talents procuring their manumission, they became the freedmen of their former masters. Vespasian, it appears from Suetonius, purchased the freedom of some persons of ability belonging to these classes.]

762 (return)

[ The Coan Venus was the chef-d'oeuvre of Apelles, a native of the island of Cos, in the Archipelago, who flourished in the time of Alexander the Great. If it was the original painting which was now restored, it must have been well preserved.]

763 (return)

[ Probably the colossal statue of Nero (see his Life, c. xxxi.), afterwards placed in Vespasian's amphitheatre, which derived its name from it.]

764 (return)

[ The usual argument in all times against the introduction of machinery.]

765 (return)

[ See AUGUSTUS, c. xxix.]

766 (return)

[ At the men's Saturnalia, a feast held in December attended with much revelling, the masters waited upon their slaves; and at the women's Saturnalia, held on the first of March, the women served their female attendants, by whom also they sent presents to their friends.]

767 (return)

[ Notwithstanding the splendour, and even, in many respects, the refinement of the imperial court, the language as well as the habits of the highest classes in Rome seem to have been but too commonly of the grossest description, and every scholar knows that many of their writers are not very delicate in their allusions. Apropos of the ludicrous account given in the text, Martial, on one occasion, uses still plainer language.

Utere lactucis, et mollibus utere malvis:
Nam faciem durum Phoebe, cacantis habes.—iii. 89.]

768 (return)

[ See c. iii. and note.]

769 (return)

[ Probably the emperor had not entirely worn off, or might even affect the rustic dialect of his Sabine countrymen; for among the peasantry the au was still pronounced o, as in plostrum for plaustrum, a waggon; and in orum for aurum, gold, etc. The emperor's retort was very happy, Flaurus being derived from a Greek word, which signifies worthless, while the consular critic's proper name, Florus, was connected with much more agreeable associations.]

770 (return)

[ Some of the German critics think that the passage bears the sense of the gratuity having beer given by the lady, and that so parsimonious a prince as Vespasian was not likely to have paid such a sum as is here stated for a lady's proffered favours.]

771 (return)

[ The Flavian family had their own tomb. See DOMITIAN, c. v. The prodigy, therefore, did not concern Vespasian. As to the tomb of the Julian family, see AUGUSTUS, c. ci.]

772 (return)

[ Alluding to the apotheosis of the emperors.]

773 (return)

[ Cutiliae was a small lake, about three-quarters of a mile from Reate, now called Lago di Contigliano. It was very deep, and being fed from springs in the neighbouring hills, the water was exceedingly clear and cold, so that it was frequented by invalids, who required invigorating. Vespasian's paternal estates lay in the neighbourhood of Reate. See chap i.]

774 (return)

[ A.U.C. 832.]

775 (return)

[ Each dynasty lasted twenty-eight years. Claudius and Nero both reigning fourteen; and, of the Flavius family, Vespasian reigned ten, Titus three, and Domitian fifteen.]

776

[ Caligula. Titus was born A.U.C. 794; about A.D. 49.]

777 (return)

[ The Septizonium was a circular building of seven stories. The remains of that of Septimus Severus, which stood on the side of the Palatine Hill, remained till the time of Pope Sixtus V., who removed it, and employed thirty-eight of its columns in ornamenting the church of St. Peter. It does not appear whether the Septizonium here mentioned as existing in the time of Titus, stood on the same spot.]

778 (return)

[ Britannicus, the son of Claudius and Messalina.]

779 (return)

[ A.U.C. 820.]

780 (return)

[ Jerusalem was taken, sacked, and burnt, by Titus, after a two years' siege, on the 8th September, A.U.C. 821, A.D. 69; it being the Sabbath. It was in the second year of the reign of Vespasian, when the emperor was sixty years old, and Titus himself, as he informs us, thirty. For particulars of the siege, see Josephus, De Bell. Jud. vi. and vii.; Hegesippus, Excid. Hierosol. v.; Dio, lxvi.; Tacitus, Hist. v.; Orosius, vii. 9.]

781 (return)

[ For the sense in which Titus was saluted with the title of Emperor by the troops, see JULIUS CAESAR, c. lxxvi.]

782 (return)

[ The joint triumph of Vespasian and Titus, which was celebrated A.U.C. 824, is fully described by Josephus, De Bell. Jud. vii. 24. It is commemorated by the triumphal monument called the Arch of Titus, erected by the senate and people of Rome after his death, and still standing at the foot of the Palatine Hill, on the road leading from the Colosseum to the Forum, and is one of the most beautiful as well as the most interesting models of Roman art. It consists of four stories of the three orders of architecture, the Corinthian being repeated in the two highest. Some of the bas-reliefs, still in good preservation, represent the table of the shew-bread, the seven-branched golden candlestick, the vessel of incense, and the silver trumpets, which were taken by Titus from the Temple at Jerusalem, and, with the book of the law, the veil of the temple, and other spoils, were carried in the triumph. The fate of these sacred relics is rather interesting. Josephus says, that the veil and books of the law were deposited in the Palatium, and the rest of the spoils in the Temple of Peace. When that was burnt, in the reign of Commodus, these treasures were saved, and they were afterwards carried off by Genseric to Africa. Belisarius recovered them, and brought them to Constantinople, A.D. 520. Procopius informs us, that a Jew, who saw them, told an acquaintance of the emperor that it would not be advisable to carry them to the palace at Constantinople, as they could not remain anywhere else but where Solomon had placed them. This, he said, was the reason why Genseric had taken the Palace at Rome, and the Roman army had in turn taken that of the Vandal kings. Upon this, the emperor was so alarmed, that he sent the whole of them to the Christian churches at Jerusalem.]

783 (return)

[ A.U.C. 825.]

784 (return)

[ A.U.C. 824.]

785 (return)

[ A.U.C. 823, 825, 827-830, 832.]

786 (return)

[ Berenice, whose name is written by our author and others Beronice, was daughter of Agrippa the Great, who was by Aristobulus, grandson of Herod the Great. Having been contracted to Mark, son of Alexander Lysimachus, he died before their union, and Agrippa married her to Herod, Mark's brother, for whom he had obtained from the emperor Claudius the kingdom of Chalcis. Herod also dying, Berenice, then a widow, lived with her brother, Agrippa, and was suspected of an incestuous intercourse with him. It was at this time that, on their way to the imperial court at Rome, they paid a visit to Festus, at Caesarea, and were present when St. Paul answered his accusers so eloquently before the tribunal of the governor. Her fascinations were so great, that, to shield herself from the charge of incest, she prevailed on Polemon, king of Cilicia, to submit to be circumcised, become a Jew, and marry her. That union also proving unfortunate, she appears to have returned to Jerusalem, and having attracted Vespasian by magnificent gifts, and the young Titus by her extraordinary beauty, she followed them to Rome, after the termination of the Jewish war, and had apartments in the palace, where she lived with Titus, "to all appearance, as his wife," as Xiphilinus informs us; and there seems no doubt that he would have married her, but for the strong prejudices of the Romans against foreign alliances. Suetonius tells us with what pain they separated.]

787 (return)

[ The Colosseum: it had been four years in building. See VESPAS. c. ix.]

788 (return)

[ The Baths of Titus stood on the Esquiline Hill, on part of the ground which had been the gardens of Mecaenas. Considerable remains of them are still found among the vineyards; vaulted chambers of vast dimensions, some of which were decorated with arabesque paintings, still in good preservation. Titus appears to have erected a palace for himself adjoining; for the Laocoon, which is mentioned by Pliny as standing in this palace, was found in the neighbouring ruins.]

789 (return)

[ If the statements were not well attested, we might be incredulous as to the number of wild beasts collected for the spectacles to which the people of Rome were so passionately devoted. The earliest account we have of such an exhibition, was A.U.C. 502, when one hundred and forty-two elephants, taken in Sicily, were produced. Pliny, who gives this information, states that lions first appeared in any number, A.U.C. 652; but these were probably not turned loose. In 661, Sylla, when he was praetor, brought forward one hundred. In 696, besides lions, elephants, and bears, one hundred and fifty panthers were shown for the first time. At the dedication of Pompey's Theatre, there was the greatest exhibition of beasts ever then known; including seventeen elephants, six hundred lions, which were killed in the course of five days, four hundred and ten panthers, etc. A rhinoceros also appeared for the first time. This was A.U.C. 701. The art of taming these beasts was carried to such perfection, that Mark Antony actually yoked them to his carriage. Julius Caesar, in his third dictatorship, A.U.C. 708, showed a vast number of wild beasts, among which were four hundred lions and a cameleopard. A tiger was exhibited for the first time at the dedication of the Theatre of Marcellus, A.U.C. 743. It was kept in a cage. Claudius afterwards exhibited four together. The exhibition of Titus, at the dedication of the Colosseum, here mentioned by Suetonius, seems to have been the largest ever made; Xiphilinus even adds to the number, and says, that including wild-boars, cranes, and other animals, no less than nine thousand were killed. In the reigns of succeeding emperors, a new feature was given to these spectacles, the Circus being converted into a temporary forest, by planting large trees, in which wild animals were turned loose, and the people were allowed to enter the wood and take what they pleased. In this instance, the game consisted principally of beasts of chase; and, on one occasion, one thousand stags, as many of the ibex, wild sheep (mouflions from Sardinia?), and other grazing animals, besides one thousand wild boars, and as many ostriches, were turned loose by the emperor Gordian.]

790 (return)

[ "Diem perdidi." This memorable speech is recorded by several other historians, and praised by Eusebius in his Chronicles.]

791 (return)

[ A.U.C. 832, A.D. 79. It is hardly necessary to refer to the well-known Epistles of Pliny the younger, vi. 16 and 20, giving an account of the first eruption of Vesuvius, in which Pliny, the historian, perished. And see hereafter, p. 475.]

792 (return)

[ The great fire at Rome happened in the second year of the reign of Titus. It consumed a large portion of the city, and among the public buildings destroyed were the temples of Serapis and Isis, that of Neptune, the baths of Agrippa, the Septa, the theatres of Balbus and Pompey, the buildings and library of Augustus on the Palatine, and the temple of Jupiter in the Capitol.]

793 (return)

[ See VESPASIAN, cc. i. and xxiv. The love of this emperor and his son Titus for the rural retirement of their paternal acres in the Sabine country, forms a striking contrast to the vicious attachment of such tyrants as Tiberius and Caligula for the luxurious scenes of Baiae, or the libidinous orgies of Capri.]

794 (return)

[ A.U.C. 834, A.D. 82.]

795

[ A.U.C. 804.]

796 (return)

[ A street, in the sixth region of Rome, so called, probably, from a remarkable specimen of this beautiful shrub which had made free growth on the spot.]

797 (return)

[ VITELLIUS, c. xv.]

798 (return)

[ Tacitus (Hist. iii.) differs from Suetonius, saying that Domitian took refuge with a client of his father's near the Velabrum. Perhaps he found it more safe afterwards to cross the Tiber.]

799 (return)

[ One of Domitian's coins bears on the reverse a captive female and soldier, with GERMANIA DEVICTA.]

800 (return)

[ VESPASIAN, c. xii; TITUS, c. vi.]

801 (return)

[ Such excavations had been made by Julius and by Augustus (AUG. xliii.), and the seats for the spectators fitted up with timber in a rude way. That was on the other side of the Tiber. The Naumachia of Domitian occupies the site of the present Piazza d'Espagna, and was larger and more ornamented.]

802 (return)

[ A.U.C. 841. See AUGUSTUS, c. xxxi.]

803 (return)

[ This feast was held in December. Plutarch informs us that it was instituted in commemoration of the seventh hill being included in the city bounds.]

804 (return)

[ The Capitol had been burnt, for the third time, in the great fire mentioned TITUS, c. viii. The first fire happened in the Marian war, after which it was rebuilt by Pompey, the second in the reign of Vitellius.]

805 (return)

[ This forum, commenced by Domitian and completed by Nerva, adjoined the Roman Forum and that of Augustus, mentioned in c. xxix. of his life. From its communicating with the two others, it was called Transitorium. Part of the wall which bounded it still remains, of a great height, and 144 paces long. It is composed of square masses of freestone, very large, and without any cement; and it is not carried in a straight line, but makes three or four angles, as if some buildings had interfered with its direction.]

806 (return)

[ The residence of the Flavian family was converted into a temple. See c. i. of the present book.]

807 (return)

[ The Stadium was in the shape of a circus, and used for races both of men and horses.]

808 (return)

[ The Odeum was a building intended for musical performances. There were four of them at Rome.]

809 (return)

[ See before, c. iv.]

810 (return)

[ See VESPASIAN, c. xiv.]

811 (return)

[ See NERD, c. xvi.]

812 (return)

[ This absurd edict was speedily revoked. See afterwards c. xiv.]

813 (return)

[ This was an ancient law levelled against adultery and other pollutions, named from its author Caius Scatinius, a tribune of the people. There was a Julian law, with the same object. See AUGUSTUS, c. xxxiv.]

814 (return)

[ Geor. xi. 537.]

815 (return)

[ See Livy, xxi. 63, and Cicero against Verres, v. 18.]

816 (return)

[ See VESPASIAN, c. iii.]

817 (return)

[ Cant names for gladiators.]

818 (return)

[ The faction which favoured the "Thrax" party.]

819 (return)

[ DOMITIAN, c. i.]

820 (return)

[ See VESPASIAN, c. xiv.]

821 (return)

[ This cruel punishment is described in NERO, c. xlix.]

822 (return)

[ Gentiles who were proselytes to the Jewish religion; or, perhaps, members of the Christian sect, who were confounded with them. See the note to TIBERIUS, c. xxxvi. The tax levied on the Jews was two drachmas per head. It was general throughout the empire.]

823 (return)

[ We have had Suetonius's reminiscences, derived through his grandfather and father successively, CALIGULA, c. xix.; OTHO, c. x. We now come to his own, commencing from an early age.]

824 (return)

[ This is what Martial calls, "Mentula tributis damnata."]

825 (return)

[ The imperial liveries were white and gold.]

826 (return)

[ See CALIGULA, c. xxi., where the rest of the line is quoted; eis koiranos esto.]

827 (return)

[ An assumption of divinity, as the pulvinar was the consecrated bed, on which the images of the gods reposed.]

828 (return)

[ The pun turns on the similar sound of the Greek word for "enough," and the Latin word for "an arch."]

829 (return)

[ Domitia, who had been repudiated for an intrigue with Paris, the actor, and afterwards taken back.]

830 (return)

[ The lines, with a slight accommodation, are borrowed from the poet Evenus, Anthol. i. vi. i., who applies them to a goat, the great enemy of vineyards. Ovid, Fasti, i. 357, thus paraphrases them:

Rode caper vitem, tamen hinc, cum staris ad aram,

In tua quod spargi cornua possit erit.]

831 (return)

[ Pliny describes this stone as being brought from Cappadocia, and says that it was as hard as marble, white and translucent, cxxiv. c. 22.]

832 (return)

[ See note to c. xvii.]

833 (return)

[ The guilt imputed to them was atheism and Jewish (Christian?) manners. Dion, lxvii. 1112.]

834 (return)

[ See VESPASIAN, c. v.]

835 (return)

[ Columella (R. R. xi. 2.) enumerates dates among the foreign fruits cultivated in Italy, cherries, dates, apricots, and almonds; and Pliny, xv. 14, informs us that Sextus Papinius was the first who introduced the date tree, having brought it from Africa, in the latter days of Augustus.]

836 (return)

[ Some suppose that Domitilla was the wife of Flavius Clemens (c. xv.), both of whom were condemned by Domitian for their "impiety," by which it is probably meant that they were suspected of favouring Christianity. Eusebius makes Flavia Domitilla the niece of Flavius Clemens, and says that she was banished to Ponza, for having become a Christian. Clemens Romanus, the second bishop of Rome, is said to have been of this family.]

837 (return)

[ A.U.C. 849.]

838 (return)

[ See c. v.]

839 (return)

[ The famous library of Alexandria collected by Ptolemy Philadelphus had been burnt by accident in the wars. But we find from this passage in Suetonius that part of it was saved, or fresh collections had been made. Seneca (de Tranquill. c. ix. 7) informs us that forty thousand volumes were burnt; and Gellius states that in his time the number of volumes amounted to nearly seventy thousand.]

840 ( return )

[ This favourite apple, mentioned by Columella and Pliny, took its name from C. Matius, a Roman knight, and friend of Augustus, who first introduced it. Pliny tells us that Matius was also the first who brought into vogue the practice of clipping groves.]

841 ( return )

[ Julia, the daughter of Titus.]

842 ( return )

[ It will be understood that the terms Grammar and Grammarian have here a more extended sense than that which they convey in modern use. See the beginning of c. iv.]

843 ( return )

[ Suetonius's account of the rude and unlettered state of society in the early times of Rome, is consistent with what we might infer, and with the accounts which have come down to us, of a community composed of the most daring and adventurous spirits thrown off by the neighbouring tribes, and whose sole occupations were rapine and war. But Cicero discovers the germs of mental cultivation among the Romans long before the period assigned to it by Suetonius, tracing them to the teaching of Pythagoras, who visited the Greek cities on the coast of Italy in the reign of Tarquinius Superbus.—Tusc. Quaest. iv. 1.]

844 ( return )

[ Livius, whose cognomen Andronicus, intimates his extraction, was born of Greek parents. He began to teach at Rome in the consulship of Claudius Cento, the son of Appius Caecus, and Sempronius Tuditanus, A.U.C. 514. He must not be confounded with Titus Livius, the historian, who flourished in the Augustan age.]

845 ( return )

[ Ennius was a native of Calabria. He was born the year after the consulship mentioned in the preceding note, and lived to see at least his seventy-sixth year, for Gellius informs us that at that age he wrote the twelfth book of his Annals.]

846 ( return )

[ Porcius Cato found Ennius in Sardinia, when he conquered that island during his praetorship. He learnt Greek from Ennius there, and brought him to Rome on his return. Ennius taught Greek at Rome for a long course of years, having M. Cato among his pupils.]

847 ( return )

[ Mallos was near Tarsus, in Cilicia. Crates was the son of Timocrates, a Stoic philosopher, who for his critical skill had the surname of Homericus.]

848 ( return )

[ Aristarchus flourished at Alexandria, in the reign of Ptolemy Philometer, whose son he educated.]

849 ( return )

[ A.U.C. 535-602 or 605.]

850 ( return )

[ Cicero (De Clar. Orat. c. xx., De Senect. c. v. 1) places the death of Ennius A.U.C. 584, for which there are other authorities; but this differs from the account given in a former note.]

851 ( return )

[ The History of the first Punic War by Naevius is mentioned by Cicero, De Senect, c. 14.]

852 ( return )

[ Lucilius, the poet, was born about A.U.C. 605.]

853 ( return )

[ Q. Metellus obtained the surname of Numidicus, on his triumph over Jugurtha, A.U.C. 644. Aelius, who was Varro's tutor, accompanied him to Rhodes or Smyrna, when he was unjustly banished, A.U.C. 653.]

854 ( return )

[ Servius Claudius (also called Clodius) is commended by Cicero, Fam. Epist. ix. 16, and his singular death mentioned by Pliny, xxv. 4.]

855 ( return )

[ Daphnis, a shepherd, the son of Mercury, was said to have been brought up by Pan. The humorous turn given by Lenaeus to Lutatius's cognomen is not very clear. Daphnides is the plural of Daphnis; therefore the herd or company, agaema; and Pan was the god of rustics, and the inventor of the rude music of the reed.]

856 ( return )

[ Oppius Cares is said by Macrobius to have written a book on Forest Trees.]

857 ( return )

[ Quintilian enumerates Bibaculus among the Roman poets in the same line with Catullus and Horace, Institut. x. 1. Of Sigida we know nothing; even the name is supposed to be incorrectly given. Apuleius mentions a Ticida, who is also noticed by Suetonius hereafter in c. xi., where likewise he gives an account of Valerius Cato.]

858 ( return )

[ Probably Suevius, of whom Macrobius informs us that he was the learned author of an Idyll, which had the title of the Mulberry

Grove; observing, that "the peach which Suevius reckons as a species of the nuts, rather belongs to the tribe of apples."]

859 ( return )

[ Aurelius Opilius is mentioned by Symmachus and Gellius. His cotemporary and friend, Rutilius Rufus, having been a military tribune under Scipio in the Numantine war, wrote a history of it. He was consul A.U.C. 648, and unjustly banished, to the general grief of the people, A.U.C. 659.]

860 ( return )

[ Quintilian mentions Gnipho, Instit. i. 6. We find that Cicero was among his pupils. The date of his praetorship, given below, fixes the time when Gnipho flourished.]

861 ( return )

[ This strange cognomen is supposed to have been derived from a cork arm, which supplied the place of one Dionysius had lost. He was a poet of Mitylene.]

862 ( return )

[ See before, JULIUS, c. xlvi.]

863 ( return )

[ A.U.C. 687.]

864 ( return )

[ Suetonius gives his life in c. x.]

865 ( return )

[ A grade of inferior officers in the Roman armies, of which we have no very exact idea.]

866 ( return )

[ Horace speaks feelingly on the subject:
*Memini quae plagosum mihi parvo*
*Orbilium tractare. Epist. xi. i. 70.*
*I remember well when I was young,*
*How old Orbilius thwacked me at my tasks.]*

867 ( return )

[ Domitius Marsus wrote epigrams. He is mentioned by Ovid and Martial.]

868 ( return )

[ This is not the only instance mentioned by Suetonius of statues erected to learned men in the place of their birth or celebrity. Orbilius, as a schoolmaster, was represented in a sitting posture, and with the gown of the Greek philosophers.]

869 ( return )

[ Tacitus (Annal. cxi. 75) gives the character of Atteius Capito. He was consul A.U.C. 758.]

870 ( return )

[ Asinius Pollio; see JULIUS, c. xxx.]

871 ( return )

[ Whether Hermas was the son or scholar of Gnipho, does not appear,]

872 ( return )

[ Eratosthenes, an Athenian philosopher, flourished in Egypt, under three of the Ptolemies successively. Strabo often mentions him. See xvii. p. 576.]

873 ( return )

[ Cornelius Helvius Cinna was an epigrammatic poet, of the same age as Catullus. Ovid mentions him, Tristia, xi. 435.]

874 ( return )

[ Priapus was worshipped as the protector of gardens.]

875 ( return )

[ Zenodotus, the grammarian, was librarian to the first Ptolemy at Alexandria, and tutor to his sons.]

876 ( return )

[ For Crates, see before, p. 507.]

877 ( return )

[ We find from Plutarch that Sylla was employed two days before his death, in completing the twenty-second book of his Commentaries; and, foreseeing his fate, entrusted them to the care of Lucullus, who, with the assistance of Epicadius, corrected and arranged them. Epicadius also wrote on Heroic verse, and Cognomina.]

878 ( return )

[ Plutarch, in his Life of Caesar, speaks of the loose conduct of Mucia, Pompey's wife, during her husband's absence.]

879 ( return )

[ Fam. Epist. 9.]

880 ( return )

[ Cicero ad Att. xii. 36.]

881 ( return )

[ See before, AUGUSTUS, c. v.]

882 ( return )

[ Lenaeus was not singular in his censure of Sallust. Lactantius, 11. 12, gives him an infamous character; and Horace says of him,

*Libertinarum dico;*

*Sallustius in quas*

*Non minus insanit; quam qui moechatur.* – *Sat. i. 2. 48.]*

883 ( return )

[ The name of the well known Roman knight, to whom Cicero addressed his Epistles, was Titus Pomponius Atticus. Although Satrius was the name of a family at Rome, no connection between it and Atticus can be found, so that the text is supposed to be corrupt. Quintus Caecilius was an uncle of Atticus, and adopted him. The freedman mentioned in this chapter probably assumed his name, he having been the property of Caecilius; as it was the custom for freedmen to adopt the names of their patrons.]

884 ( return )

[ Suetonius, TIBERIUS, c. viii. Her name was Pomponia.]

885 ( return )

[ See AUGUSTUS, c. lxvi.]

886 ( return )

[ He is mentioned before, c. ix.]

887 ( return )

[ Verrius Flaccus is mentioned by St. Jerome, in conjunction with Athenodorus of Tarsus, a Stoic philosopher, to have flourished

A.M.C. 2024, which is A.U.C. 759; A.D. 9. He is also praised by Gellius, Macrobius, Pliny, and Priscian.]

888 ( return )

[ Cinna wrote a poem, which he called "Smyrna," and was nine years in composing, as Catullus informs us, 93. 1.]

889 ( return )

[ See AUGUSTUS, cc. lxii. lxix.]

890 ( return )

[ Cornelius Alexander, who had also the name of Polyhistor, was born at Miletus, and being taken prisoner, and bought by Cornelius, was brought to Rome, and becoming his teacher, had his freedom given him, with the name of his patron. He flourished in the time of Sylla, and composed a great number of works; amongst which were five books on Rome. Suetonius has already told us (AUGUSTUS, xxix.) that he had the care of the Palatine Library.]

891 ( return )

[ No such consul as Caius Licinius appears in the Fasti; and it is supposed to be a mistake for C. Atinius, who was the colleague of Cn. Domitius Calvinus, A.U.C. 713, and wrote a book on the Civil War.]

892 ( return )

[ Julius Modestus, in whom the name of the Julian family was still preserved, is mentioned with approbation by Gellius, Martial, Quintilian, and others.]

893 ( return )

[ Melissus is mentioned by Ovid, De Pontif. iv 16-30.]

894 ( return )

[ See AUGUSTUS, c. xxix. p. 93, and note.]

895 ( return )

[ The trabea was a white robe, with a purple border, of a different fashion from the toga.]

896 ( return )

[ See before, c. x.]

897 ( return )

[ See CLAUDIUS, c. x1i. and note.]

898 ( return )

[ Remmius Palaemon appears to have been cotemporary with Pliny and Quintilian, who speak highly of him.]

899 ( return )

[ Now Vicenza.]

900 ( return )

[ "Audiat haec tantum vel qui venit, ecce, Palaemon."—Eccl. iii. 50.]

901 ( return )

[ All the editions have the word vitem; but we might conjecture, from the large produce, that it is a mistake for vineam, a vineyard: in which case the word vasa might be rendered, not bottles, but casks. The amphora held about nine gallons. Pliny mentions that Remmius bought a farm near the turning on the Nomentan road, at the tenth mile-stone from Rome.]

902 ( return )

[ "Usque ad infamiam oris."—See TIBERIUS, p. 220, and the notes.]

903 ( return )

[ Now Beyrout, on the coast of Syria. It was one of the colonies founded by Julius Caesar when he transported 80,000 Roman citizens to foreign parts.—JULIUS, xlii.]

904 ( return )

[ This senatus consultum was made A.U.C. 592.]

905 ( return )

[ Hirtius and Pansa were consuls A.U.C. 710.]

906 ( return )

[ See NERO, c. x.]

907 ( return )

[ As to the Bullum, see before, JULIUS, c. lxxxiv.]

908 ( return )

[ This extract given by Suetonius is all we know of any epistle addressed by Cicero to Marcus Titinnius.]

909 ( return )

[ See Cicero's Oration, pro Caelio, where Atracinus is frequently mentioned, especially cc. i. and iii.]

910 ( return )

[ "Hordearium rhetorem."]

911 ( return )

[ From the manner in which Suetonius speaks of the old custom of chaining one of the lowest slaves to the outer gate, to supply the place of a watch-dog, it would appear to have been disused in his time.]

912 ( return )

[ The work in which Cornelius Nepos made this statement is lost.]

913 ( return )

[ Pliny mentions with approbation C. Epidius, who wrote some treatises in which trees are represented as speaking; and the period in which he flourished, agrees with that assigned to the rhetorician here named by Suetonius. Plin. xvii. 25.]

914 ( return )

[ Isauricus was consul with Julius Caesar II., A.U.C. 705, and again with L. Antony, A.U.C. 712.]

915 ( return )

[ A river in the ancient Campania, now called the Sarno, which discharges itself into the bay of Naples.]

916 ( return )

[ Epidius attributes the injury received by his eyes to the corrupt habits he contracted in the society of M. Antony.]

917 ( return )

[ The direct allusion is to the "style" or probe used by surgeons in opening tumours.]

918 ( return )

[ Mark Antony was consul with Julius Caesar, A.U.C. 709. See before, JULIUS, c. lxxix.]

919 ( return )

[ Philipp. xi. 17.]

920 ( return )

[ Leontium, now called Lentini, was a town in Sicily, the foundation of which is related by Thucydides, vi. p. 412. Polybius describes the Leontine fields as the most fertile part of Sicily. Polyb. vii. 1. And see Cicero, contra Verrem, iii. 46, 47.]

921 ( return )

[ Novara, a town of the Milanese.]

922 ( return )

[ St. Jerom in Chron. Euseb. describes Lucius Munatius Plancus as the disciple of Cicero, and a celebrated orator. He founded Lyons during the time he governed that part of the Roman provinces in Gaul.]

923 ( return )

[ See AUGUSTUS, c. xxxvi.]

924 ( return )

[ He meant to speak of Cisalpine Gaul, which, though geographically a part of Italy, did not till a late period enjoy the privileges of the other territories united to Rome, and was administered by a praetor under the forms of a dependent province. It was admitted to equal rights by the triumvirs, after the death of Julius Caesar. Albutius intimated that those rights were now in danger.]

925 ( return )

[ Lucius Fenestella, an historical writer, is mentioned by Lactantius, Seneca, and Pliny, who says, that he died towards the close of the reign of Tiberius.]

926 ( return )

[ The second Punic war ended A.U.C. 552, and the third began A.U.C. 605. Terence was probably born about 560.]

927 ( return )

[ Carthage was laid in ruins A.U.C. 606 or 607, six hundred and sixty seven years after its foundation.]

928 ( return )

[ These entertainments were given by the aediles M. Fulvius Nobilior and M. Acilius Glabrio, A.U.C. 587.]

929 ( return )

[ St. Jerom also states that Terence read the "Andria" to Caecilius who was a comic poet at Rome; but it is clearly an anachronism, as he died two years before this period. It is proposed, therefore, to amend the text by substituting Acilius, the aedile; a correction recommended by all the circumstances, and approved by Pitiscus and Ernesti.]

930 ( return )

[ The "Hecyra," The Mother-in-law, is one of Terence's plays.]

931 ( return )

[ The "Eunuch" was not brought out till five years after the Andria, A.U.C. 592.]

932 ( return )

[ About 80 pounds sterling; the price paid for the two performances. What further right of authorship is meant by the words following, is not very clear.]

933 ( return )

[ The "Adelphi" was first acted A.U.C. 593.]

934 ( return )

[ This report is mentioned by Cicero (Ad Attic, vii. 3), who applies it to the younger Laelius. The Scipio here mentioned is Scipio Africanus, who was at this time about twenty-one years of age.]

935 ( return )

[ The calends of March was the festival of married women. See before, VESPASIAN, c. xix.]

936 ( return )

[ Santra, who wrote biographies of celebrated characters, is mentioned as "a man of learning," by St. Jerom, in his preface to the book on the Ecclesiastical Writers.]

937 ( return )

[ The idea seems to have prevailed that Terence, originally an African slave, could not have attained that purity of style in Latin composition which is found in his plays, without some assistance. The style of Phaedrus, however; who was a slave from Thrace, and lived in the reign of Tiberius, is equally pure, although no such suspicion attaches to his work.]

938 ( return )

[ Cicero (de Clar. Orat. c. 207) gives Sulpicius Gallus a high character as a finished orator and elegant scholar. He was consul when the Andria was first produced.]

939 ( return )

[ Labeo and Popilius are also spoken of by Cicero in high terms, Ib. cc. 21 and 24. Q. Fabius Labeo was consul with M. Claudius Marcellus, A.U.C. 570 and Popilius with L. Postumius Albinus, A.U.C. 580.]

940 ( return )

[ The story of Terence's having converted into Latin plays this large number of Menander's Greek comedies, is beyond all probability, considering the age at which he died, and other circumstances. Indeed, Menander never wrote so many as are here stated.]

941 ( return )

[ They were consuls A.U.C. 594. Terence was, therefore, thirty-four years old at the time of his death.]

942 ( return )

[ Hortulorum, in the plural number. This term, often found in Roman authors, not inaptly describes the vast number of little inclosures, consisting of vineyards, orchards of fig-trees, peaches, etc., with patches of tillage, in which maize, legumes, melons, pumpkins, and other vegetables are cultivated for sale, still found on small properties, in the south of Europe, particularly in the neighbourhood of towns.]

943 ( return )

[ Suetonius has quoted these lines in the earlier part of his Life of Terence. See before p. 532, where they are translated.]

944 ( return )

[ Juvenal was born at Aquinum, a town of the Volscians, as appears by an ancient MS., and is intimated by himself. Sat. iii. 319.]

945 ( return )

[ He must have been therefore nearly forty years old at this time, as he lived to be eighty.]

946 ( return )

[ The seventh of Juvenal's Satires.]

947 ( return )

[ This Paris does not appear to have been the favourite of Nero, who was put to death by that prince (see NERO, c. liv.) but another person of the same name, who was patronised by the emperor Domitian. The name of the poet joined with him is not known. Salmatius thinks it was Statius Pompilius, who sold to Paris, the actor, the play of Agave;

*Esurit, intactam*
*Paridi nisi vendat Agaven.*
— *Juv. Sat. vii. 87.]*

948 ( return )

[ Sulpicius Camerinus had been proconsul in Africa; Bareas Soranus in Asia. Tacit. Annal. xiii. 52; xvi. 23. Both of them are said to have been corrupt in their administration; and the satirist introduces their names as examples of the rich and noble, whose influence was less than that of favourite actors, or whose avarice prevented them from becoming the patrons of poets.]

949 ( return )

[ The "Pelopea," was a tragedy founded on the story of the daughter of Thyestes; the "Philomela," a tragedy on the fate of Itys, whose remains were served to his father at a banquet by Philomela and her sister Progne.]

950 ( return )

[ This was in the time of Adrian. Juvenal, who wrote first in the reigns of Domitian and Trajan, composed his last Satire but one in the third year of Adrian, A.U.C. 872.]

951 ( return )

[ Syene is meant, the frontier station of the imperial troops in that quarter of the world.]

952

[ A.U.C. 786, A.D. 34.]

953 ( return )

[ A.U.C. 814, A.D. 62.]

954 ( return )

[ Persius was one of the few men of rank and affluence among the Romans, who acquired distinction as writers; the greater part of them having been freedmen, as appears not only from these lives of the poets, but from our author's notices of the grammarians and rhetoricians. A Caius Persius is mentioned with distinction by Livy in the second Punic war, Hist. xxvi. 39; and another of the same name by Cicero, de Orat. ii. 6, and by Pliny; but whether the poet was descended from either of them, we have no means of ascertaining.]

955 ( return )

[ Persius addressed his fifth satire to Annaeus Cornutus. He was a native of Leptis, in Africa, and lived at Rome in the time of Nero, by whom he was banished.]

956 ( return )

[ Caesius Bassus, a lyric poet, flourished during the reigns of Nero and Galba. Persius dedicated his sixth Satire to him.]

957 ( return )

[ "Numanus." It should be Servilius Nonianus, who is mentioned by Pliny, xxviii. 2, and xxxvii. 6.]

958 ( return )

[ Commentators are not agreed about these sums, the text varying both in the manuscripts and editions.]

959 ( return )

[ See Dr. Thomson's remarks on Persius, before, p. 398.]

960 ( return )

[ There is no appearance of any want of finish in the sixth Satire of Persius, as it has come down to us; but it has been conjectured that it was followed by another, which was left imperfect.]

961 ( return )

[ There were two Arrias, mother and daughter, Tacit. Annal. xvi. 34. 3.]

962 ( return )

[ Persius died about nine days before he completed his twenty-ninth year.]

963 ( return )

[ Venusium stood on the confines of the Apulian, Lucanian, and Samnite territories.

*Sequor hunc, Lucanus an Appulus anceps;*
*Nam Venusinus arat finem sub utrumque colonus.*
Hor Sat. xi. 1. 34. ( Sat. i. 6. 45.)]

965 ( return )

[ Horace mentions his being in this battle, and does not scruple to admit that he made rather a precipitate retreat, "relicta non bene parmula."—Ode xi. 7-9.]

966 ( return )

[ See Ode xi. 7. 1.]

967 ( return )

[ The editors of Suetonius give different versions of this epigram. It seems to allude to some passing occurrence, and in its present form the sense is to this effect: "If I love you not, Horace, to my very heart's core, may you see the priest of the college of Titus leaner than his mule."]

968 ( return )

[ Probably the Septimius to whom Horace addressed the ode beginning

*Septimi, Gades aditure mecum.* — Ode xl. b. i.]

969 ( return )

[ See AUGUSTUS, c. xxi.; and Horace, Ode iv, 4.]

970 ( return )

[ See Epist. i. iv. xv.

*Me pinguem et nitidum bene curata cute vises.]*

971

[ It is satisfactory to find that the best commentators consider the words between brackets as an interpolation in the work of Suetonius. Some, including Bentley, reject the preceding sentence also.]

972 ( return )

[ The works of Horace abound with references to his Sabine farm which must be familiar to many readers. Some remains are still shewn, consisting of a ruined wall and a tesselated pavement in a vineyard, about eight miles from Tivoli, which are supposed, with reason, to mark its site. At least, the features of the neighbouring country, as often sketched by the poet—and they are very beautiful—cannot be mistaken.]

973 ( return )

[ Aurelius Cotta and L. Manlius Torquatus were consuls A.U.C. 688. The genial Horace, in speaking of his old wine, agrees with Suetonius in fixing the date of his own birth:

O nata mecum consule Manlio Testa. — Ode iii. 21.

And again,

Tu vina, Torquato, move Consule pressa meo. — Epod. xiii. 8.]

974 ( return )

[ A.U.C. 745. So that Horace was in his fifty-seventh, not his fifty-ninth year, at the time of his death.]

975 ( return )

[ It may be concluded that Horace died at Rome, under the hospitable roof of his patron Mecaenas, whose villa and gardens stood on the Esquiline hill; which had formerly been the burial ground of the lower classes; but, as he tells us, Nunc licet Esquiliis habitare salubribus, atque Aggere in aprico spatiare.—Sat. i. 8.]

976 ( return )

[ Cordova. Lucan was the son of Annaeus Mella, Seneca's brother.]

977 ( return )

[ This sentence is very obscure, and Ernesti considers the text to be imperfect.]

978 ( return )

[ They had good reason to know that, ridiculous as the tyrant made himself, it was not safe to incur even the suspicion of being parties to a jest upon him.]

979 ( return )

[ See NERO, c. xxxvi.]

980 ( return )

[ St. Jerom (Chron. Euseb.) places Lucan's death in the tenth year of Nero's reign, corresponding with A.U.C. 817. This opportunity is taken of correcting an error in the press, p. 342, respecting the date of Nero's accession. It should be A.U.C. 807, A.D. 55.]

981 ( return )

[ These circumstances are not mentioned by some other writers. See Dr. Thomson's account of Lucan, before, p. 347, where it is said that he died with philosophical firmness.]

982 ( return )

[ We find it stated ib. p. 396, that Lucan expired while pronouncing some verses from his own Pharsalia: for which we have the authority of Tacitus, Annal. xv. 20. 1. Lucan, it appears, employed his last hours in revising his poems; on the contrary, Virgil, we are told, when his death was imminent, renewed his directions that the Aeneid should be committed to the flames.]

983 ( return )

[ The text of the concluding sentence of Lucan's life is corrupt, and neither of the modes proposed for correcting it make the sense intended very clear.]

984 ( return )

[ Although this brief memoir of Pliny is inserted in all the editions of Suetonius, it was unquestionably not written by him. The author, whoever he was, has confounded the two Plinys, the uncle and nephew, into which error Suetonius could not have fallen, as he lived on intimate terms with the younger Pliny; nor can it be supposed that he would have composed the memoir of his illustrious friend in so cursory a manner. Scaliger and other learned men consider that the life of Pliny, attributed to Suetonius, was composed more than four centuries after that historian's death.]

985 ( return )

[ See JULIUS, c. xxviii. Caius Plinius Caecilius Secundus (the younger Pliny) was born at Como, A.U.C. 814; A.D. 62. His father's name was Lucius Caecilius, also of Como, who married Plinia, the sister of Caius Plinius Secundus, supposed to have been a native of Verona, the author of the Natural History, and by this marriage the uncle of Pliny the Younger. It was the nephew who enjoyed the confidence of the emperors Nerva and Trajan, and was the author of the celebrated Letters.]

986 ( return )

[ The first eruption of Mount Vesuvius occurred A.U.C. 831, A.D. 79. See TITUS, c. viii. The younger Pliny was with his uncle at Misenum at the time, and has left an account of his disastrous enterprise in one of his letters, Epist. vi. xvi.]

987 ( return )

[ For further accounts of the elder Pliny, see the Epistles of his nephew, B. iii. 5; vi. 16. 20; and Dr. Thomson's remarks before, pp. 475-478.]

# INDEX.

Acilius, C., his heroic conduct in a sea-fight, 42.
Acte, a concubine of Nero, 357.
Actium, battle of, 81, 82.
Agrippa, M., his naval victory, 80; presented with a banner, 88; his buildings, 93; aqueducts, 104; grandson of Augustus, 118; his character, ib. 119; adopted, 203; banished, 204; murdered, 208.
Agrippina, daughter of M. Agrippa and Livia, 254; marries Germanicus, 118; banished by Tiberius, 225; birth of Caligula, 255; daughter of Germanicus, Claudius marries her, 320, 327; suspected of poisoning him, 331; her character, 335.
Alban Mount, 276, 298, and note; festival on, 482.
Albula, the warm springs at, 131.
Albutius, Silus, an orator, 528.
Alexander the Great, J. Caesar's model, 5; his sarcophagus opened for
Augustus, 82.
Alexandria, museum at, 330; library at, 496, note; the key of Egypt, 449;
Vespasian's miracles there, 450, and note.
Amphitheatres; of Statilius Taurus, 93; description of, 262, note; the Castrensis, 265 and note; the Colosseum, 453 and note.
Andronicus, M. P. a scholar, 515.
Antony, Mark, at Caesar's funeral, 53; triumvir with Octavius and Lepidus, 75; opposes Octavius, 76; defeated by him, 77; their new alliance, ib.; dissolved, 80; defeat at Actium, 81; flies to Cleopatra, ib.; kills himself, ib.
Anticyra, island of, 272 and note.

*Antium, the Apollo Belvidere found there*, 217 *note; preferred by Caligula*, 256; *colony settled at*, 343 *and note.*
*Antonius, Lucius, brother of Mark, war with*, 76; *forced to surrender*, 78.
— — —, *Musa, Augustus's physician*, 116.
*Antonia, grandmother of Caligula*, 267, 272.
*Apollonius of Rhodes*, 4.
*Apple, the Matian*, 496.
*Apomus, fountain of*, 203.
*Apotheosis, J. Caesar*, 1, *note; and* 55.
*Apicius, his works*, 249.
*Aqueduct of the Anio*, 265 *and note*, 314.
*Arch of Claudius*, 303; *of Titus*, 467 *note.*
*Aricia, grove of*, 81; *a town near Rome*, 73.
*Arles, a Roman colony*, 195.
*Asinius Pollio, the orator*, 304.
— — — *Gallius, his son, ib.;* 329.
*Atteius, the philologer*, 513.
— — — *Capito, jurisconsult*, 521.
*Atticus, the friend of Cicero*, 517 *and note.*
*August, name of the month Sextilis changed to*, 95.
AUGUSTUS CAESAR, *his descent*, 71; *birth*, 73; *infancy and youth*, 74;
*civil wars*, 76; *battle of Philippi*, 77; *takes Perugia*, 79; *naval war with Pompey*, 80; *battle of Actium*, 81; *forces Antony to kill himself, ib.; and Cleopatra, ib.; foreign wars*, 83; *triumphs*, 85; *conduct as a general*, 86; *in civil affairs*, 88-90; *in improving the city*, 90-94; *in religious matters*, 95; *in administering justice*, 96, 97; *purifies the senate*, 98; *scrutiny of the knights*, 102; *his munificence*, 104; *public spectacles*, 105-108; *colonies*, 109; *the provinces, ib.; distribution of the army*, 110; *his clemency*, 111; *moderation*, 112, 113; *honours paid him*, 114-116; *his wives and family,*
117-119; *friendships*, 120; *aspersions on his character*, 121-124; *his*

domestic life, 125-129; person and health, 129-131; literary pursuits, 132-135; regard for religion and omens, 136-142; his last illness and death, 143-145; his funeral and will, 146-147; remarks on his life and
times, 148-191.

Aulus Plautius commands in Britain, 309 and note, 444; his ovation, 316.

Baiae, Julian harbour formed at, 79; frequented by Augustus, 126.

Basilicas, the, 7 and note.

Basilides, an Egyptian priest, 447 note; appears to Vespasian, 450.

Baths of Nero, 345 and note; of Titus, 470 and note.

Beccus, a general in Gaul, 439 and note.

Bedriacum, battle of, 423, 433, 447.

Berenice, queen, attachment of Titus to her, 469 and note.

Berytus, now Beyrout, 522.

Bibaculus, a poet, 507 note.

Bibulus, M., edile, 6 and note; consul with J. Caesar, 12;
lampoon on, 13.

Bithynia, J. Caesar sent there, 2.

Britain, invaded by Julius Caesar, 17; reconnoitred first, 38; Caligula's intended expedition, 282 and note; that of Claudius, 308, 309; Nero proposes to abandon, 848; revolt there, 368 and note.

Britannicus, son of Claudius, 320; his regard for him, 330; educated with Titus, 405; poisoned, ib.; honours paid him by Titus, ib.

Brutus and Cassius conspire against Julius Caesar, 49; they assassinate
him, 51; his dying apostrophe to Brutus, 52 and note; their fate, 55 and 78.

Bulla, the, worn by youths, 54 and note.

Caenis, concubine of Vespasian, 443; Domitian's conduct to, 490.

Caesonia, Caligula's mistress and wife, 269; threatened by him, 275;
slain, 291.

Caesario, son of Cleopatra by Caesar, 82.

Caius and Lucius, grandsons of Augustus, 89; their death, 118.

Caius Caesar, 74. See CALIGULA.

Calendar, the, corrected by Julius Caesar, 27 and note; by Augustus, 95.

CALIGULA, his birth, 254; origin of his name, 256; in Germany and Syria, ib.; with Tiberius at Capri, 257; suspected of murdering him, 258; succeeds him, ib.; his popularity, 259; honours to Germanicus and his family, 260; his just administration, 261; consulships, 262; public spectacles, 263; public works, 264; affects royalty, 266; and divinity, ib.; treatment of his female relatives, 267, 268; of his wives and mistresses, 269; of his friends, ib.; of the magistrates, 270; his cruelties, 271-274; discourages learning, 275; disgraces men of rank, 276; his unnatural lusts, 277; exhausts the treasury, 278; his rapacity, 279; his new taxes, 280; expedition to Germany, 281; bravado against Britain, 283 and note; his triumph, 284; his person and constitution, 285; style of dress, 286; personal accomplishments, 287, 288; his favourite horse, 289; conspiracies against him, ib.; omens of his fate, 290; he is assassinated, 291.

Calpurnia, wife of J. Caesar, 14.

Capitol, the, burnt by Vitellius, 438; rebuilt by Vespasian, 452; rebuilt by Domitian, 483.

Capri, island of, exchanged for Ischia, 137; Augustus visits it, 143; Tiberius retires there, 217; his debaucheries there, 219-220.

Carinae, a street in Rome, 203.

Carmel, Mount, Vespasian sacrifices at, 447 and note.

Caractacus, 309 note; 334.

Cassius. See Brutus.

– – – Chaerea, the assassin of Caligula, 289-291.

Caspian Mountains, pass through, 349 and note.

Catiline's conspiracy, 9, 11.

Cato, M., infuses vigour into the senate, 9; yields to political expediency, 12 and note; dragged to prison from the senate, 14; threatens to impeach J. Caesar, 21.

Catullus, remarks on his works, 67-69.

Celsus, the physician, his works, 249.

Censor, office of, 100 and note.

Census taken, how, 102.

Chrestus said to make tumults at Rome, 318.

Christians, confounded with the Jews, 215 note; accused of sedition, 318 and note; cruelties of Nero to, 347; poll tax on, 489 note.

Cicero, M. T., his opinion of J. Caesar, 7 and 21; appealed to by him, 11; commends Caesar's oratory, 35; remarks on the works of, 60-65; dream of, 140.

Cinna, Cornelius Helvius, a poet, 517 and note.

Circensian games, description of, 26 and note, 27.

Circeii, near Antium, 236.

Circus, Flaminian, 310 note; Maximus, 355 and note.

Civic crown, description of, 3.

Claudii, family of the, 192-194.

CLAUDIUS, his birth, 296; childhood and education, 297; Augustus's opinion of him, 298; fills public offices, 300; held in contempt, 301; unexpected elevation, ib.; elected by the praetorian guard, 302; honours to the family of Augustus, 303; his moderation, ib.; conspiracies against him, 304; conduct as consul and judge, 305, 306; as censor, 307; expedition to Britain, 309; his triumph, 310; care of the city and people, ib.; his public works, 311; public spectacles, 312, 313; civil and religious administration, 314, 315; military, 316, 317; banishes the Jews and Christians, 318 and note; his marriages, 319; children, 320; his freedmen and favourites, 321; governed by them and his wives, ib.; his person, 322; his entertainments, 323; cruelty, 324; fear and distrust, 325, 326; affects literature, 328, 329; death by poison, 330; omens previously, 331.

Clemens. See Flavius.

Cleopatra has Egypt confirmed to her by J. Caesar, 24; intrigues with him, 34; has a son by him, ib.; flies with Mark Antony, 81; kills herself, 82; her children by Antony, ib. and 81.

Coins of Caligula, 37; of Vespasian, 467.

Cologne, founded by Agrippina, 434 and note.

Colonies at Como, 19; foreign, 29.

Colosseum, the, begun by Vespasian, 453; finished by Titus, 470 and note.

Commentaries, Caesar's, 36, 37.

Comet before Nero's death, 366.

Comitium, the, embellished, 7 and note.

Como, colony settled there, 19 and note.

Compitalian festival, flowers used at 96, and note.

Confluentes, Coblentz, 250.

Cordus Cremutius, a historian, 99.

Cornelia, Julius Caesar's wife, 2; her death, 5.

Corinth. See Isthmus of.

Cornelius Nepos, account of, 101.

Cotiso, king of the Getae, 117 and note.

Cottius, his dominions in the Alps, 216, 349.

Crassus, aspires to be dictator, 6; his conspiracies, 6 and 7; becomes security for Julius Caesar, 11 note; reconciled to Pompey, 12.

Crates, a grammarian, 504.

Cunobeline and his son, 282; defeated by Aulus Plautius, 309 and note.

Curtius Nicia, a scholar, 517.

Curule chair, 89; description of, note ib.

Cybele, rites of, 121 and note, 194.

Date-trees, introduction of, 493 and note.

Dolabella, P., loses a fleet, 24; inveighs against J. Caesar, 32; prosecuted by Caesar, 35.

Domitia, wife of Domitian, 480; intrigues with Paris, 481; denies intrigue with Titus, 473; plots Domitian's death, 491.

DOMITIAN, his birth, 479; his youth infamous, ib.; escapes from Vitellius, ib.; assumes power in Rome, 480; governs despotically, ib.;

under Vespasian amused himself with poetry, ib.; plots against Titus,

ib.; succeeds him, 481; his wife Domitia, 480, 481; gives costly spectacles, ib. 482; his public buildings, 483; expeditions, ib.; his administration, 484; of justice, 485; his cruelties, 487, 488; extortions, 489; poll-tax on the Jews, ib.; his arrogance, 490; conspiracy against him, 481; alarms and omens, 492, 493; his assassination, 494; his person and habits, 496; lewd conduct, 497; he is lamented only by the soldiers, 497.

Domitii, family of, 337-339.

Domitilla, wife of Flavius Clemens, 494 note.

Druids, religion of, suppressed by Claudius, 318.

Drusilla, sister of Caligula, 268.

– – –, wife of Felix, 321 and note.

Drusus, brother of Tiberius, 196; his death, 198.

– – –, Tiberius's son, 197, 203; his death, 217, 224, 230; son of Germanicus, starved, 226; father of Claudius, 295; died in Germany, ib.; his character, 296.

Dyracchium, Cn. Pompey blockaded there, 23, 40.

Eagles, the standards, of the legions, 39, 259 and note.

East, the, prophecy of a Ruler from, 445 and note.

Egypt confirmed to Cleopatra, 24; supplies Rome with corn, 82; made

a province, ib.

Emperor, the title of, 46 note.

Ennius, account of, 506, 507.

Epicadius completes Sylla's Commentaries, 516.

Epidius, C., teaches rhetoric, 527.

Equestrian order, scrutiny of, 98, 102: procession of, 101 and note;

review of, 261; purified by Vespasian, 453.

Eratosthenes, the philosopher, 514.

Esseda, a light British car, 264 and note.

Family names and cognomena, 192 note.

Felix, governor of Judaea, 321; his wives, ib.

Flaccus, C. Valerius, a poet, 463.

Flamen Dialis, high-priest of Jupiter, 1 note.

Flavian family, account of, 441; temple of, 495.

Flavia Domitilla, wife of Vespasian, 443.

Flavius Clemens, Domitian's cousin, 492; put to death, ib. and note, 494.

– – – Sabinus, Vespasian's brother, 437; retreats to the capitol, 438; buried there, ib.

Forum, the Roman, 7; of Julius Caesar, 18; of Augustus, 92, 113; of Nerva, 483.

Fruits, foreign, introduced at Rome, 493 note.

Fucine lake, drainage of, projected by J. Caesar, 30; emissary of, 311, 314.

GALBA, not allied to the Caesars, 400; his descent, 401; birth, 402; studies the law, 403; courted by Agrippina, ib.; a favourite of Livia, ib.; proctor and consul, 404; commands in Gaul, ib.; in Africa, 405; in Spain, 406; on Nero's death assumes the title of Caesar, 408; marches to Rome, 409; his severity, 410; becomes hateful to the people, 411; and the troops, ib.; omens against him, 412; the praetorian revolt, 413; he is slain, ib.; his person and habits, 414.

Callus, Cornelius, prefect of Egypt, 120; friend of Augustus, ib.; his eclogues, 188; patron of Caecilius, a man of letters, 518.

– – –, L. Plotius, a rhetorician, 526.

Gaul, J. Caesar goes there as proconsul, 15; division of the provinces, ib. note; he levies troops in, 16; his conquests in, 17.

Germanicus marries Agrippina, 118; adopted by Tiberius, 203, 251; his triumph, *ib.*; his death, 217, 224, 251; his sons, 225; his character, 252; grief for, 253.

German tribes, defeated by J. Caesar, 17; they defeat Varus, 86; Caligula's expedition against, 281, 282.

Gessoriacum, Boulogne, 283, 309.

Gladiators, combats of, exhibited by Julius, 8, 19, 25; first introduced at Rome, 25 note; shown by Caligula, 262; by Domitian, 481.

Gnipho, M. A., a grammarian, 511-513.

Golden House, the, of Nero, 359.

Grammar, science of, 506.

Grammarians, what, 509.

Guards, the Spanish, 100; the German, *ib.*; disbanded by Galba, 409. See Praetorian.

Helvidius Priscus, a philosopher, 455.

Hirtius and Pansa, consuls, 76; defeated and slain, 77.

Horace, his life and works, 173-177, 642-545.

Horse, Caligula's favourite, 289; proposes to make him consul, *ib.*

Hyginus, Palatine librarian, 520; his works, 249.

Illyricum, conquered, 204.

Intramural interments at Rome, forbidden, 192 note.

Isthmus of Corinth, canal through, 265, 349.

Jerusalem taken by Titus, 467 and note.

Jews, rites of suppressed by Tiberius, 215; expelled from Rome by Claudius, 318; revolt of, 445; Vespasian's triumph over, 449, 454; fate of their sacred vessels, 449 note; figured on the arch of Titus, 467 note; poll-tax on the, 489.

Josephus the historian, taken prisoner by Vespasian, 447; predicts his
elevation, *ib.*

Journals of the proceedings of the senate published by J. Caesar, 13; includes speeches, trials, births, deaths, etc., *ib.*; discontinued by Augustus, 261; revived by Caligula, *ib.*

Julia, daughter of Julius Caesar, 2; married to Ca. Pompey, 4; her death, 17.

— — —, daughter of Augustus, married to Marcellus, 117; to Agrippa, ib.;
to Tiberius, ib. and 197; their children, 118; banished, 119.
— — —, granddaughter of Augustus, married to Lucius Paulus, 118;
banished, ib.

JULIUS CAESAR, marries Cornelia, 1; serves in Asia, 2; fills public offices, 4; commands in Spain, 5; joins Sylla and Crassus, 6; his public buildings, 7; chosen consul, 12; marries Calpurnia, 14; alliance with Pompey, ib. 15; has the province of Gaul, 15; invades Britain, 17; affects popularity and is lavish of money, 18; resolves on war, 20; crosses the Rubicon, 22; marches to Rome, 23; defeats Pompey at Pharsalia, ib.; his triumphs, 24; his public spectacles, 25; corrects the calendar, 27; his civil administration, 28, 29; projected works, 30; person and dress, ib.; his character, scandals on, 32-34; his extortions, 35; as an orator, ib.; as a writer, 36, 37; as a general, 38-43; as an advocate and friend, 43-44; his good qualities, 45; his abuse of power, 46, 47; conspiracy against him, 48-50; his assassination, 51; his will, 52; funeral, 53; apotheosis, 55.

Juvenal, account of, and works, 499, 500; life of, 536.

Laberius Hiera, a grammarian, 516.

"Latus Clavus," what, 31.

Laurel grove of the Caesars, 400 and note.

Lenaeus, a school master, 507.

Lepidus, master of the horse to Julius Caesar, 52; one of the triumviri, 75; the confederacy renewed, 77; banished, 80; his death, 95.

Libraries, public, one projected by J. Caesar, 80; the Palatine, formed by Augustus, 92; of Alexandria, 496; of the portico of Octavia, 520.

Lictors, attend the consuls, 13 and note.

Liveries, colours of the imperial, 490, note.

Livia Drusilla, wife of Augustus, 117, 295; mother of Tiberius, 202; his
treatment of her, 222, 223; her death, 224; divine honours decreed to, 303.

— — — Ocellina, mother of Galba, 402.
Livius Andronicus, account of, 506.
— — — Titus, remarks on his History, 161-165.
Lollius, governor of Agrippa, 201, 202.
Lucan, remarks on, 396, 397; life of, 544.
Lucius Aevius, a grammarian, 508.
— — — Crassitius, schoolmaster and philosopher, 519.
— — — Vettius, an informer, 11, 14.
Lucretius, remarks on his works, 69.
Lupercalia, feast of, 48, and note; and 96.
Marcellus, M. Pomponius, a critic, 523.
Marius, C., his trophies restored, 8.
Martial, account and works of, 503-505.
Marmillo, a kind of gladiator, 288, 487.
Mausoleum of Augustus, 259.
Mecaenas, Augustus complains of, 120; his house and gardens on the
Esquiline, 125, 203; his character, 153; patronizes Horace, 173, 541.
Melissus, Caius, librarian and friend of Mecaenas, 520.
Messalina, wife of Claudius, 319; put to death, ib.; her character, 335.
Misenum, a naval station, 110; Tiberius sails there, 236.
Mithridates revolts, 4.
Mitylene taken by storm, 3.
Money-lenders, lampoon on Augustus for his father's being one, 123;
note on ib.; and 340.
Mount Aetna, 286.
— —- Vesuvius, eruption of, 471, 548.
Muraena, conspiracy of, 83, 114, 120.
Naevius, his Punic war, 509.
Naples, a Greek colony, 303, note.
Narbonne, a Roman-colony, 195.

Narcissus, *a freedman of Claudius*, 321, 326.
Naumachia, *of Julius*, 27; *of Augustus*, 105; *Nero*, 344; *Titus*, 470; *of Domitian*, 482; *erected by him*, 483.
Nemi, *lake of*, 276, *note*.
NERE, *his descent*, 337-339; *birth*, 340; *youth*, 341; *succeeds Claudius*, 342; *begins his reign well*, 343; *gives spectacles and largesses*, 344, 345; *receives king Tiridates*, 346; *administration of justice, ib.; his public buildings*, 347; *cruelties to the Christians, ib., and note; undertakes no foreign wars*, 348; *appears on the stage, as a singer, at Naples*, 350; *at Rome*, 351; *as a charioteer*, 352; *in Greece*, 353; *triumphal return*, 354; *his revels and vices*, 356; *foul debaucheries*, 357; *prodigality*, 358; *his Golden House*, 359; *other works*, 360; *extortions, ib.*, 361; *his murders: Britannicus*, 362; *his mother*, 363; *his remorse*, 364; *marries Poppaea Sabina, ib.; Messalina, ib.; his butcheries*, 365, 366; *sets fire to Rome*, 367; *sings whilst it is burning, ib.; disasters in Britain*, 368; *and in the East*, 369; *lampoons on him, ib.; revolt of Vindex, in Gaul*, 370; *appeals to the senate*, 371; *Galba declares against him in Spain*, 372; *proposes to march against Vindex*, 373; *his perplexities*, 375; *escapes from Rome*, 376; *kills himself*, 378; *his person*, 379; *accomplishments*, 380; *religious sentiments*, 381.
Nicomedes, *king of Bethynia, Julius Caesar at his court*, 2; *scandals respecting them, ib., and* 32, 33.
Nola, *Augustus dies there*, 145; *him temple there*, 217.
Obelisks, *Egyptian*, 312, *and note*.
Octacilius, L. Pilitus, *instructs Pompey the Great*, 627.
Octavii, *the family of*, 71.
Octavius, Caius, *father of Augustus*, 72.
Odeum, *erected by Domitian*, 483.
Oppius Cares *writes on forest trees*, 509, *note*.
Opilius, Aurelius, *a grammarian*, 510.
Orbilius Pupillus, *a schoolmaster*, 512.

Organ, the Hydraulic, 37, and note.

Ostia, at the mouth of the Tiber, 200, and note; harbour formed, 311.

OTHO, his ancestors, 416; his birth, 417; gets into Nero's favour, ib.;

marries Poppaea pro forma, 418; sent into Spain, ib.; joins Galba, ib.;

practises against him, 419; chosen emperor by the pretorians, 420; and

Vitellius, by the German army, 421; he marches against them, 422; his

troops defeated at Bedriacum, 423; makes no further resistance, 424; calmly puts an end to his life, 425; his person and habits, ib.;

devotion of his soldiers, 426.

Ovation, description of, 85, note.

Ovid, on his life and writings, 177-185.

Oxheads, a street in Rome, 73.

Palatine Hill, 73, and notes; Augustus's house there, 125; enlarged by Caligula, 266, 267; the Golden House added by Nero, 359, 369; Tiberius's house, 438.

Pansa. See Hirtius.

Pantheon, built by Agrippa, 93.

Paris, an actor, intrigues with Domitia, 481.

Pearls found in Britain, 31 and note.

Persius, remarks on, 397-399; life of, 538.

Petronia, wife of Vitellius, 431.

Petronius Arbiter, remarks on, 392-395.

Phaedrus, account of, 248.

Pharmacusa, island of, 4.

Pharsalia, battle of, 23; speech of J. Caesar after, 21; his call to the troops at, 45; Lucan's poem on, 396.

Philippi, battle of, 77, 78; Augustus's escape at, 136.

Philosophers, decrees against at Rome, 524.

Pincian hill, 379, and note.

Piso, Cneius, conspires with Crassus, 7.

— —, *prefect of Syria*, 251; *suspected of poisoning Germanicus*, 252; *his conspiracy*, 366.

Plancus, L. Munatius, *the orator*, 529, *and note*.

Pliny, the elder, *remarks on*, 475; *his works, ib.*-478; *his life*, 545.

— — -, *the younger*, 546, *note*.

Polyhistor, Alexander, *the historian*, 520, *and note*.

Pomegranate, *street so called*, 479, *and note*.

Pompeius Sextus, *wars of Augustus with*, 76.

Pompeia, *wife of Julius Caesar*, 5.

Pompey, Cn., *reconciled with Crassus*, 12; *marries Julia*, 14; *supports her father J. Caesar*, 15; *meets him at Lucca*, 16; *sole consul*, 17; *offered Octavia in marriage*, 18; *his opinion of Julius Caesar*, 20; *flies to Brundusium*, 23; *defeated at Pharsalia, ib.; his statues restored*, 45; *his senate-house*, 49, 50, *and note*.

Pontine Marshes, *drainage of*, 30.

Poppaea, Sabina, *Nero's mistress*, 360; *he kills her*, 365; *Otho marries her pro forma*, 417, 418.

Porticos; *of Lucius and Caius*, 93; *of Octavia, ib., and note; of the Argonauts*, 94.

Posts *established*, 110.

Pretorian guards *of Tiberius*, 221, 229; *elect Claudius*, 302; *attend him to the senate*, 303; *salute Nero*, 342; *mutiny against Galba*, 411; *dispatch him*, 413; *disbanded by Vitellius*, 432; *commanded by Vitus*, 468.

Pretorian camp, 265, 302; *its position*, 376.

Probus, M. Valerius, *his mode of teaching*, 525.

Procurators, *their office*, 304, *note*.

Propertius, *on his life and works*, 188.

Psylli, *the*, 81, *and note*.

Ptolemy Auletes *expelled*, 8.

Public health, *augury of, and note*, 95.

Publius Clodius debauches Pompeia, 5; is Cicero's enemy, 14; murdered, 17; his trial, 44.

Puteoli, Caligula's bridge at, 263; the landing-place from the East, 467.

Quintilian, remarks on, 498, 499.

Quintus Caecilius, a schoolmaster, 519.

— — — - Catulus, repairs the Capitol, 10, and note.

Rabirius Posthumus prosecuted, 9, 308.

Ravenna, J. Caesar halts there, 20; a naval station, 110.

Reate, a town of the Sabines, 441; Vespasian born there, 442, 469; his estates near, 461; he dies there, ib.; as does Titus, 478.

Remmius Palaemon, a grammarian, 523.

Republic, the, Augustus thinks of restoring, 91; the forms of, preserved, 212; maintained by Caligula, 261; proposal to restore it; 292.

Rhetoric forbidden at Rome, 526; its progress, 527.

Rhine, the, suddenly thaws, 484.

Rhodes, J. Caesar retires there, 3; and Tiberius, 200.

Roman people, their love of public spectacles, 216; largesses of corn to, 311, 312.

Rome, improvements of Augustus, 91; divided into districts, 94; a fire there, 221; Nero's fire, 367; restored by Vespasian, 452; great fire under Titus, 471, and note.

Roads. See Via.

Rubicon, the, crossed by Jul. Caesar, 22.

Rutifius Rufus, soldier and historian, 510; note, 511.

Sallust, remarks on, 159, 160.

Santra, a biographical writer, 533, and note.

Saturnalia, account of, 262, note.

Scaeva, a centurion, his heroic conduct, 42.

Scribonia, wife of Augustus, 117.

Scribonius, a disciple of Orbilius, 521.

*Secular games*, by Augustus, 96; by Claudius, 313.

*Selene*, daughter of Antony and Cleopatra, 264.

*Sejanus*, Tiberius's suspicions of, 229, 257; his conspiracy, 232; account of, 244, 245.

*Senate*, filled up by Julius, 28; affronted by him, 47; scrutiny of, 98; qualification for, 104, 315; constitution of, 115, note; scrutiny of, by Caligula, 260; purified by Vespasian, 453.

*Seneca, Annaeus*, made Nero's tutor, 341; forced to kill himself, 365; remarks on, 386-392.

*Septa*, what, 105, and note.

*Septizonium*, the, description of, 465, note.

*Sertorius* commands in Spain, 4.

*Servilia*, mother of M. Brutus, J. Caesar intrigues with her, 33.

*Sesterce*, the value of, 457, note.

*Sextus Clodius*, professor, and friend of Antony, 528.

*Sibylline books* preserved by Augustus, 95.

*Silanus* betrothed to Claudius's daughter, 316; — the elder, put to death, 322, 326.

*Silius*, a paramour of Messalina, 322, 325.

*Silversmiths.* See Money-lenders.

*Slaves*, workhouses of, 96; writers and artists originally such, 457 note; chained as watch-dogs, 527, and note.

*Spain*, province of, governed by Julius Caesar, 5, 11; Pompey's army in, 23; Galba commands there, 406.

*Sporus*, Nero's freedman, 367, 376, 378.

*Standards*, Roman, 259.

*Statues* of the kings of Rome, 46; of Pompey, 96; of learned men, 513, 519.

*Statius*, his works, 500-503.

*Suburra*, a street in Rome, 31.

*Suetonius Paulinus*, commands in Britain, 423, note.

— — —, *Lenis*, the author's father, serves under Otho, ib.

*Suevius Nicanor*, a grammarian, 510.

*Sumptuary laws* of Julius Caesar, 29.

Sylla pardons Julius Caesar, 2; conspires with Caesar and Crassus, 6;
his statues restored, 45; his Commentaries, 516.

Taurus, Statilius, 93, 364.

Temples of Castor and Pollux, 8, and note, 266; of Jupiter Capitolinus repaired, 10, and notes, etc.; of Venus Genetrix, 47; Mars Ultor, 84, 92; Palatine Apollo, ib. and note; Jupiter Tonans, 93, and note; Hercules and Muses, ib.; the Parthenon, ib. and note; of Concord, 206,
and note; of Vesta, 223, and note; of Augustus, 264; Jupiter Latialis, 298, and note; of Peace, 453, and note; of Claudius ib.; of Jupiter Custos, 483; of the Flavian Family, 483, 495.

Terence, life of, 531.

Terracina, on the road to Naples, 23; Tiberius's villa there, 217; and note.

Tertia, mistress of Julius Caesar, 33.

Theatres — of Pompey, 96; rebuilt, 312; of Marcellus, 93, and note; repaired, 458; of Balbus, ib.; Pompey's restored by Tiberius, 221; by Caligula, 265.

Theogenes, an astrologer of Apollonia, 141.

Thrax, a kind of gladiator, 487.

Thurinus, a surname of Augustus, 74.

TIBERIUS, descent of, 192-195; his childhood, 196; youth, 197; in the
forum, 198; in the wars, ib., and 199; withdraws from Rome, ib.; retirement at Rhodes, 200, 201; returns to Rome, 202; commands in Germany and Illyricum, 204, 205; triumphs, 206; made colleague with
Augustus, ib.; succeeds him, 207; governs with moderation, 210-213;
sumptuary laws, 214; represses the Jewish religion, 215; and Christian,
ib., and note; his rigorous justice, 216; retires to Capri, 217; his debaucheries there, 218-220; his parsimony, 221; exactions, 222;

treatment of Livia, 223; of Drusus and Germanicus, 224; of Agrippina,
225; his grandsons, ib.; his harsh temper, 227; various cruelties, 228-231; his remorse, 233; his person, 234; literary pursuits, 235; his last illness, 236; and death, 237; rejoicings at it, 238; his will, 239.

Tiber, inundations of the, 91, and note; bed of, cleaned, 94, and note; floods, 223; criminals thrown into, 230; island of Esculapius, in, 317,
and note.

Tibullus, his life and works, 185-187.

Tiridates, king, at Rome, 346.

Titinnius, letter of Cicero to, 528, and note.

TITUS, his birth and disposition, 465; educated with Britannicus, ib.; the honours he paid him, ib.; endowments, personal and mental, 466; serves in Germany and Britain, ib.; in Judaea, ib.; takes Jerusalem, 467; returns to Rome, ib.; is colleague with Vespasian, 468;
is harsh and unpopular, ib.; his attachment to Berenice, 469; his character brightens, ib.; his moderation and munificence, 470; public buildings and spectacles, ib., and note; his clemency, 471; relief of great disasters, 472; avoids shedding blood, ib.; taken suddenly ill, 473; dies on his paternal estate, 474.

Toga, Praetexta, 101, 103, and notes.

— — Virilis, 101, and note.

Tomb of Domitian, 379, and note.

Treviri (Treves), 254, 256, note.

Triumphs of Julius Caesar, 24, 25; Augustus, 85; description of a, ib.
note; Tiberius, 206; Germanicus, 251; of Vespasian and Titus, 454, 467;
of Domitian, 484.

Valerius Cato, a grammarian, 516.

— — — — Maximus, account of his works, 248.

Varro, remarks on his works, 65, 67.
Varus' defeat by the Germans, 86, 205.
Velabrum, a street in Rome, 25, 355.
Velleius Paterculus, his life and Epitome, 247.
Velitrae, town of, seat of the Octavian family, 71, 74.
Venus of Coos, statue of, by Apelles, 457.
VESPASIAN, his descent from the Flavian family, 441; his birth at Reate, 442; fondness for it, ib.; serves in Thrace, 443; has the province of Crete and Cyrene, ib.; marries Flavia Domitilla, ib.; his children, ib.; serves in Germany and Britain, 444; is proconsul in Africa, ib.; goes into retirement, ib.; the Jews, revolt, 445; he is sent to quell it, ib.; the prophecy of a ruler from the East applied to him. ib. and note; his campaign, in Judaea, 446; consults the oracle at Carmel, 447; the Moesian army declares him emperor, 448; also the legions in Egypt and Judaea, ib.; seizes Alexandria, 449; consults Serapis, ib.; performs miracles, 450, and note; returns to Rome, 451; his Jewish triumph, ib.; reforms the army, 452; his public buildings, 453; his just administration, 454; and clemency, 455; his love of money, 456; encourages learning and art, 457; his person, 459; mode of life, ib.; his wit, 460; is taken ill, 461; dies at Reate, ib.
Vestal Virgins, the, 52; mode of appointment, 95; and note; their lewdness punished, 485.
Via Appia, 236, and note.
– – Flaminia, 94, and note, 146.
– – Nomentana, 376, note.
– – Sacra, a street in Rome, 31.
– – Salaria, description of 376 note; tomb there, 454.
Vienne, in Narbonne, 433, and note.
Vines forbidden to be planted, 484; edict revoked, 491; remarkable produce of a, 524.
Vindex, Julius, revolts in Gaul, 370, 406; his death, 408.
Vintage, the, 99, note.

VITELLIUS, his origin, 427, 428; and birth, 429; his youth vicious, 430; in favour with Caligula, Claudius, and Nero, 430; his marriages, 431; sent to Germany, ib.; saluted emperor by the troops, 432; marches

to Rome, 433; governs despotically, 434; his gluttony, 435; and luxury,

ib.; his cruel executions, 436; the legions declare against him, 437; agrees to abdicate, ib.; secretes himself, 438; is dragged out and slain, 439.

Virgil, account of his life and works, 165-173.

Vologesus honours Nero's memory 381; offers reinforcements to Vespasian,

449; demands succours, 480.

Vorones, king of the Parthians, 222.

Wild beasts shown in the public spectacles by Julius, 8; by Augustus, 105, 106; criminals thrown to, 305, and note; numbers exhibited, 470,

note; exhibited by Domitian, 481.

note; exhibited by Domitian, 481.